Tasting Coffee

The author cupping with T. N. Ramashesha of Allana Coffee Works in Hassan, India.

Tasting Coffee
AN INQUIRY INTO OBJECTIVITY

KENNETH LIBERMAN

Published by State University of New York Press, Albany

© 2022 State University of New York

All rights reserved

Printed in the United States of America

No part of this book may be used or reproduced in any manner whatsoever without written permission. No part of this book may be stored in a retrieval system or transmitted in any form or by any means including electronic, electrostatic, magnetic tape, mechanical, photocopying, recording, or otherwise without the prior permission in writing of the publisher.

For information, contact State University of New York Press, Albany, NY
www.sunypress.edu

Library of Congress Cataloging-in-Publication Data

Name: Liberman, Kenneth, author.
Title: Tasting coffee : an inquiry into objectivity / Kenneth Liberman.
Description: Albany : State University of New York Press, [2022] | Includes bibliographical references and index.
Identifiers: ISBN 9781438488974 (hardcover : alk. paper) | ISBN 9781438488981 (ebook) | ISBN 9781438488967 (pbk. : alk. paper)
Further information is available at the Library of Congress.

10 9 8 7 6 5 4 3 2 1

Contents

Acknowledgments   vii

Introduction   1

I. The Story of Coffee Purveying

1. A Brief History of Coffee   19

2. Coffee's Chain of Production   47

II. Objectivity and Its Labors

3. Historical and Epistemological Bases of Objectivity   65

4. Making Contact with the Object   93

5. The Dynamic Nature of Coffee   129

III. Tasting and Its Labors

6. Common Practices of Tasting   143

7. Down on the *Fincas* and with the Exporters: Harvesting, Processing, Blending   163

8. A Palette for the Palate: Using Taste Descriptors to Find Flavor   197

9. Professional Tasting   241

10. Tasting for Excellence   305

11. Importers, Roasters, Myths, and Marketers   343

12. Some Discovered Practices of Lay Coffee Drinkers
    (with Giolo Fele)   371

IV. Science and Its Labors

13. Science and Objective Practices   401

14. A Scientific Critique of Scientific Practices   439

Appendix: Sample Tasting Schedules   477

Bibliography   483

Authors Index   495

Subject Index   499

Acknowledgments

I hope to repay part of the debt I owe the many coffee people who shared with me their coffee wisdom by portraying their work and perspectives in this monograph. The majority of these splendid purveyors of coffee deserve to be placed at the very top of this list. Chief among these *cafeteros* are Rodrigo Alarcón, Arnold Baskerville, Willem Boot, Dr. Manuel Diaz, Benoit Gravel, Marcio Hazan, Dr. Pradeep Kenjige, Sunalini Menon, Dr. Enrico Meschini, Sunil Pinto, T.N. Ramashesha, Caspar Rasmussen, Ric Rhinehart, Franco Schillani, Angelo Segoni, Susie Spindler, and John Wolthers. In the interest of full disclosure, I must report that in kindness, generosity, and dedication, these people—every one of them—are among the finest people I have known in my life. How great it is for me that I love them all, and that their spirit made my field research a celebration of both coffee and life.

I would also like to thank my friend and colleague Prof. Giolo Fele of the Università di Trento, who was a collaborator during much of the Italian research for this monograph and is the co-author of chapter 12. His suggestions, encouragement, and sense of humor contributed greatly to these studies. Special thanks are also due to the Università di Trento and its Facoltà di Sociologia for their financial support in the form of a University Research Fellowship that funded much of the Italian research during the years 2013–15. Finally, it is important not to forget in this list of acknowledgements the deep debt I owe to the prolific and monomaniacal studies of Edmund Husserl and Georg Simmel, whose philosophical and social investigations instigated and guided many of these inquiries and to whose lineage (and monomania) I belong.

An earlier version of chapter 12 was published in the journal *Symbolic Interaction*, vol. 44, no. 1 (2021), in their special issue on "The Senses in Social Interaction."

Introduction

> Give me my coffee so that I can make phenomenology out of it.
>
> —Edmund Husserl (Bakewell 2016, 40)

In my travels to many countries, I am fond of asking people, "Who is in favor of objectivity?" Invariably, all hands will be raised, and this is so regardless of the continent, culture, ages, or professions. But if I should follow up the question with a second query, "Who can tell me what objectivity is?" no hands remain in the air. This is the situation of humanity in the 21st century. Objectivity has become an epistemic virtue even while people are not entirely sure what it is.

What is objectivity, really? I have spent much of the last decade pursuing an answer to this question. This extended monograph is an attempt to identify, describe, and specify just what objectivity is within the ordinary work practices of professional coffee tasters. Here the question of objectivity is pursued not as a theoretical problem or as a philosophical quandary (that has been done) but as a question for sociological inquiry. Like a modern-day Diogenes, I and my video camera have been on the hunt for the ordinary practices of people who with much diligence strive to be objective in their worldly work. I discovered many practices that serve objective knowledge. Here I investigate how these practices function, how they assist the discovery of the truth of affairs, and also how they occasionally occlude the truth of those affairs. Being human is no simple matter, and we have more evolving to do before we will possess a sapience that is worthy of our name, *Homo sapiens*. My studies led me to conclude that we are not quite human yet, but it remains a good idea.

These investigations are carried out with an ambition similar to that which motivated the contributions to the sociology of culture of Georg Simmel in *The Philosophy of Money*, Walter Benjamin in *The Arcades Project*, Theodor Adorno's inquiries into art and astrology in popular culture, and Harold Garfinkel's studies of social order in queues, games with rules, etc. These projects involved a search for a totality of meaning based upon painstaking description of the local details of mundane social forms. Because worldly practices normally exceed our theoretical idealizations, insight can be gained from studying the details of actual worldly practices. The painstaking discipline that each of these social scientists employed was an obsession, and a problem that they confronted was that they supplied too many details for the patience of many readers; however, locating and interrogating the local details of social practices, no matter how many details there are, remains the burden of rigorous sociological research. Fortunately for us, most readers seem ready to learn details about coffee.

The Study of Objectivity

The focus of this study is to discover what are the vital questions regarding objective and scientific inquiry as matters that are naturally part of the course of affairs for specialists who work actively in the worldwide coffee industry. This is basic research in the sociology of science: how is reliable knowledge organized, how can humans organize knowledge better, and how can the ways that they organize knowledge help them to deepen their understanding of matters? In the case of coffee tasting, we have a crucible that is suitable for investigating what objectivity really is.

Why coffee tasting? For the excellent reason that as a practical matter, the coffee industry requires objectivity and so pursues it painstakingly. A firm in Trieste, for instance, may have thousands of clients who have come to expect a unique flavor from the coffee that the firm provides them regularly. The flavor of this coffee depends on finding, processing, grading, purchasing, roasting, blending, and preparing coffee whose beans bear that identifying taste or blend of tastes, and the parties who staff all of these activities need to understand the flavors that are being sought; they also need to share among themselves their understandings of those flavors. Accordingly, the need to know flavors in an objective way is pertinent to the success of the coffee industry, and this makes coffee tasting a perspicuous case of objectivity in the world. Because hundreds of thousands of dollars are at stake whenever a firm's representatives in Brazil seek to purchase particular flavors, they must have already identified and described those tastes in a way that will allow the firm and the firm's associates in Brazil to succeed in locating those very same flavors. The firm's financial stake in reliably providing to their clients that same flavor of coffee compels the firm to employ objectivity in their work, work that consists of methods for identifying and describing the tastes of coffees in objective ways, even though everyone knows that gustatory experience is something that is abidingly subjective.

This situation compelled me to travel abroad in search of answers and discoveries. From Trieste, I went to Brazil with references in hand, and I spent two months in Santos, the first city of coffee, where I lived with a number of Brazil's most renowned coffee tasters and where I was able to videotape their work, participate in tasting, and observe the labors of storied coffee exporters. In search of the practices of tasters who concentrate upon specialty coffee, I went to Panama to explore the worlds of Gesha coffee and to participate in a Best of Panama tasting in Boquete, and I flew to Columbia in search of the flavor of the newly popular Huila single-origin, where I was hosted by the Federación Nacional de Cafeteros on a tour of Huila coffee farms (*fincas*) and coffee tasters. Needing to focus more closely upon the finer details of the work of professional coffee tasters, I attended Cup of Excellence competitions in El Salvador and Nicaragua, visited *fincas* in Costa Rica and India, tasted alongside coffee processors and exporters (governmental and private; tasters who examine for defects and tasters who taste for specialty grades), and met with many local coffee processors, *cafeteros*, and expert tasters. I took formal courses in Q-grading Arabica coffee and R-grading Robusta coffee from two of the world's most knowledgeable coffee tasters (Willem Boot and Manuel Diaz, respectively), who also became my friends. After discovering how very dissimilar coffee the beverage was across the world, I spent time touring the world's cafés; in addition to the roasters and cafés of Italy and the USA, I toured the cafés of Argentina, Canada, China, France, and Sweden. I tasted coffee alongside coffee quality examiners working at Italy's ports as well as alongside leading importers in Denmark and the USA. After an entire decade of field research, and with no diminishment in enthusiasm, this project in the sociology of objectivity had involved research in more than a dozen countries.

A question that many doctoral students taking my graduate seminars on field research methods often pose to me is "How do I know when I have completed enough field study and can begin to write?" Every social researcher must decide when they have learned enough to start writing the monograph. My answer has always been the same: when the data becomes repetitive and predictable, and one is beginning to grow bored with the repetition, then one has completed enough field research. The present project has had to confront a problem that is unique during the many field studies I have pursued in the course of my career: coffee tasting has not yet become boring, and somehow, I am unable to reach the end of my inquiries. But I face an additional problem: long ago, before I began this study, I committed myself to other important research projects in philosophical anthropology, which is why it was my original intention to devote only two or three years to this project. After much travel and field study, I discovered there was *always* much more to explore about coffee. Accordingly, this research persisted past the five-year mark, past the seven-year mark, and finally past a decade of study and inquiries. Therefore, I face a practical problem: I have become too old. At the time of this writing I am 73, and I have grown fearful that if I continue the present study until the data finally becomes repetitive (if it ever does), I will run out of years, and the other research projects to which I am committed will suffer; consequently, I decided to cut off this study of objectivity in the world of coffee. Despite this premature cessation, I still have a great many discoveries to report.

The coffee industry is suited perfectly for the problem of what it is to know objectively. For an illustration, let us consider Nespresso, the MOMA boutique of coffee capsules, which purveys a capsule of Mysore coffee that it calls "Indriya" (the Sanskrit word for "senses"). As one who has lived in Mysore District for four years, I can verify the authenticity of their capsule as a faithful representative of the typical peanut-husk flavor of Mysore coffees. Just how are they able to reproduce capsules that bear this identical flavor from one year to the next, even five years later? I will never know for certain what social practices Nestlé's tasters use to produce that kind of objective result, for the reason that when my colleague Prof. Giole Fele and I arrived at the gates of the Nespresso factory in Fribourg, Switzerland, with a recommendation from my cousin, who was one of the Geneva-based Walter Matter, Inc., coffee brokers that Nespresso relied upon regularly, we were refused entry. This was not the first time that a coffee firm has refused to allow sociologists on their premises; fortunately, most of the coffee industry was more welcoming than Nespresso was, and so this study is rich with many details of the tasting practices professional tasters use. For coffee purveyors, objectivity is nothing theoretical—they need to provide their clients with the flavors that their clients expect. As one European importer explained to me, "We usually buy in a certain flavor spectrum." While the qualifier "spectrum" offers some scope for error, most coffee purveyors know what they are purchasing and know what they are selling. The question I have been pursuing is a simple one: how do they know what they know?

The aim of a coffee purveyor is not only to offer coffee that tastes good; the tastes they provide need to be reproducible—otherwise, a faithful clientele cannot be cultivated. There are consumers who may explain their favorite coffee this way: "I like Folgers because it always has the right taste." But what are the practices by which Folgers provides that same taste? Folgers uses as many as 44 different beans to produce its blend of coffee, and each of those beans has a flavor that contributes to the taste profile of the blend. Beans bearing those flavors must be identified and repurchased from one harvest to the next. A diligent professional taster will want the tastes that are identified to be known objectively, so that they will be available to every drinker—there, in the cup. A maxim that coffee tasters use frequently is "Let the coffee speak for itself," but even the most committed positivist must acknowledge that coffee doesn't speak—people do. Nevertheless, more than one professional taster has suggested, "Our job as tasters is to be as objective as possible in defining the attributes that characterize the coffee we're tasting." But this begs the question, what is objectivity?

What makes the study of coffee especially interesting is that coffee purveyors cannot always be supplied with or use the same quantities of geographically specified beans each year, because coffee is a living plant whose "beans" (actually, the seeds of cherries) can vary in flavor from one year to the next, depending upon sunshine, rainfall, fertilization, diseases, humidity, fermentations, etc. Not only will the flavors vary, it is common for a few of Folger's 44 beans to be unavailable altogether due to crop failure. The coffee purveyor must continually seek alternative ways to reproduce that "same flavor," often improvising. One of the reasons Folger's uses 44 beans is that if some of them are unavailable, substitutions will be less noticeable to a consumer. As one importer told me, "You can't use the same strategy every year" in achieving that same flavor. So how do coffee tasters identify and achieve that flavor? The question is even more rich: how do growers, processors, graders, exporters, purchasers, roasters, blenders, and baristas identify that "same" flavor and communicate it along the chain of coffee production? The question is a sociological one—how does subjective knowledge become universal, serviceable across the global scope of coffee production?

The sociologist Alfred Schutz addressed what he calls the riddle of subjective objectivity. Just what is this relation of the subjective to the objective? Is objectivity that from which all subjectivity is removed? Does such an objectivity even exist? And if it did, would there be anyone to acknowledge it? This riddle has propelled social phenomenologists to study the work of persons who collaborate in producing the mundane objectivities that are essential for organizing our lives. Following in their footsteps, sociologists who specialize in "ethnomethodological" inquiry have taken up the task of studying the real work of parties who are engaged in one or another routine production of objective knowledge, and these ethnomethodologists have submitted the mundane details of this local work to close scrutiny. The present monograph examines the real work of measuring scientifically the many features of the taste of coffee, of manipulating taste descriptors and scoring, and the hermeneutic challenges involved in bringing the tasters' tongues to confront directly, discover, and explore the tastes of what is "in the cup."

The Occasioned Character of Coffee Drinking

With my attention focused closely on taste in this way, and scrupulously following the empirical demands of each occasion, I was surprised to discover during the course of my research that most ordinary drinkers of coffee are less focused on taste than I had assumed. And this was true in every country. To my surprise, coffee is more than a taste, it is a social reality. This is a discovery with important consequences. Coffee drinking is always situated, and the occasioned contingencies of drinking can affect what is tasted or not tasted. Take for instance this comment by a lay drinker of coffee, collected during one of the consumer studies undertaken by my colleague Giolo Fele in Rovereto, Italy. Attempting to describe the flavor of some coffee, the lay drinker said (the translation is mine), "That is a coffee that will eventually make you say 'Yes, that's good, that's fine.' It is, and then one can go to class." How does a taste that is situated inside a person's daily life in a way like this relate with the ideal taste that exists under a professional taster's microscopic analysis—and how do professional tastes relate to the tastes of our mundane lives? Once we become strictly empirical, the problems that surround taste multiply rapidly, and one of these other problems is that sometimes consumers of coffee have better things to do than to pay attention to the flavors of the coffee they are drinking.

The philosopher of tasting practices and Vice-Chancellor of the Slow Food Movement's University of Gastronomical Sciences in Bra, Italy, Nicola Perullo, makes a distinction between "naked taste" and "dressed taste" (2016, 79), that is, taste directly experienced by a drinker with an open mind who seeks only *il piacere nudo* (immanent, naked pleasure) (Perullo 2016, 67) and the taste of a person, lay or expert, who addresses wine (or coffee) with many preconceptions about its *cru*, origin, notoriety, rating, description, etc. The distinction is suggestive for our inquiries, except we need to acknowledge the fact that all taste is dressed. In seeking naked taste, Perullo (who was a student of Derrida) has identified an aspiration that is as elusive and indispensable as democracy or justice. A coffee firm's taster, a casual drinker, and a sensory scientist all have cultivated some orientation that they inevitably project upon whatever liquid is making contact with their tongues. But Perullo's distinction is useful for reminding us that one of the goals of human sapience regarding coffee is to establish direct contact with the coffee's naked taste, to learn about that taste without being closed-minded. As I discovered, this effort requires a good deal of work, work that includes not only knowing more but sometimes, as Socrates suggested, knowing less. Taste is so many things. As was written on the wall of a specialty café in San Salvador, "Una taza de café está llena de ideas" (A cup of coffee is full of ideas). Taste is endless.

Ethnomethodology's rigor involves respecting things the way they occur *in situ*, and ethnomethodologists remain attuned to the way occurrences are lived through in, and as, the occasions in which they are found, in the very way they are found there. Defined simply, ethnomethodology is the study of the local organization of naturally occurring ordinary activities, and its scientific obligation is to respect the occasioned character of each situation, without idealizing the occasion or subsuming it under the auspices of predefined academic categories before it is adequately understood. Ethnomethodology begins with the looks of the world and gives priority to the world in the way it is lived, a methodological commitment that has drawn the accusation that ethnomethodology is a variety of empiricism. Ethnomethodological investigators study how people *really* do the things that they do in their mundane lives. They have studied the astronomical discovery of an optical pulsar not as it was presented in the formal report published in a scientific journal but as it was actually lived through (and audio recorded) in real time, with none of the messiness swept under the rug (Garfinkel, et al. 1981; Hoeppe 2012). They have studied how chemists undertake their experiments, with all of the necessary bricolage exposed (Lynch 1985; Livingston 2008, 153–156). And they have studied how the ways that designers of photocopying machines intended their machines to work differ from how people who photocopy actually use them (Suchman 1987). Here we examine the work of professional tasters in determining the actual flavors of cups of coffee. Just how do they reach a scoring of "92.27," the highest rated coffee (100-point scale) of the El Salvador Cup of Excellence competition that I observed, and what does this rating mean across the world of specialty coffee? Just how did they identify its flavor characteristics to be "florals, apricot, peach, honey, mango, Bourdeaux wine, complex, structured, transparent, and savory," and how does each of those taste descriptors achieve its sense, and what efficacy do such descriptors offer? Science always depends upon local details.

In the course of pursuing details, I came across many "curious incongruities" (Garfinkel 2002, 122) between the requirements of the formal methods of professional tasting and their actual, situated deployment. Edmund Husserl (1970a, 131) has discussed the "troublesome difficulties" that modern science must face continually, and he suggested that "the paradoxical interrelations of the 'objectively true world' and the 'life-world' make enigmatic the manner of being of both." This enigmatic being is basic to our naturally occurring lives, every day and all day long. A sober examination of the work of sensory scientists will bring us face-to-face with this unavoidable enigmatic being. As Husserl (1970a, 131–32) sagely suggests, "In our attempts to attain clarity we shall suddenly become aware, in the fact of emerging paradoxes."

Here are a few of the paradoxes I discovered:

1. Part of the identity of sensory science is to be objective, but its data concerns one of the most subjective things in the world, taste experience. While the coffee industry has developed diverse methods and protocols for tasting coffee objectively, all gustatory experience remains subjective. Nevertheless, subjective tasting must *be made* objective in order for that knowledge to be useful and accurate, and for it to be communicated to other people. It can be said that here objectivity is a necessary impossibility. This is perhaps the principal irony, the underlying tension that inhabits the world's coffee industry. The reason that objectivity is necessary is that the flavors that coffee purveyors sell to their consumers must be provided in a reliably consistent way from one year to the next. They must procure the correct green coffee beans with the right flavors, and also roast them in the right way, and for this objective science is needed. Professional tasters must maintain the objective sense of the taste descriptors that they use, so that these descriptors can serve as tools for assessment and exploration of the taste of a coffee. If they do not work

at maintaining the objective character of these descriptors, there will be no objective knowledge. *Making tastes objective* is local work, and this entails that objectivity depend upon a variety of subjective practices that this local work comprises. This leads to the question, how is it that something objective is composed of subjective practices?

2. Many tasters stress the importance of tasting alone and silently, in order to limit the influence of others. Sensory scientists often taste in sterile booths that are painted white, with partitions that separate the tasters. Some tasters believe that this increases the objectivity of the assessment. At other times tasters have explained to me that really learning and discovering tastes is necessarily a collaborative activity, since frequently there is more to taste than one person is able to identify. The renowned coffee taster Franco Schillani of Trieste told me, "You always need some help from the other tasters," and it is an established practice in the labs of every coffee firm I studied in a dozen countries to use two or three tasters at a time, principally to maximize the tongues present for detecting defects and errors. Coffee tasters are always eager to learn from each other what more there is to taste in a cup of coffee, and their curiosity in this regard has no bounds. Collaborative tasting can be useful for discovering this "what more," and also for rigorous identification of positive taste attributes. If coffee is to be judged fairly, one must judge it alone; but if it is to be judged comprehensively and if one really wants to know its taste, the tasting must be done in a collaborative way.

3. Strategies of numeration are helpful, and it is important to understand just how they are helpful. Numeration supports both personal and institutional memory. However, merely converting experience into numbers and then comparing numbers is insufficient for determining flavor objectively. A respected taster from Italy advised, "All the people need to know perfectly what the numbers mean," which implies that there is an intersubjective component that is necessarily present. How does this intersubjective situation contribute to and/or detract from the accomplishment of objectivity? Moreover, the word "perfectly" employed by our Italian taster, like similar

words used in most formal accounts of numeration methods in the coffee industry, is both a commendation of formal rigor and a prayer. A corollary irony here is that those who use numeration strategies simultaneously employ more intuitive and qualitative measures as they do so, which is necessary for rendering the numeration strategies pertinent, while those who refuse to rely on numeration protocols almost always employ some quantitative methods in their work.

4. A final irony (this list could be extended) involves how taste descriptors are used to locate the taste in a cup even as these same descriptors keep getting in the way of the tasting. This is a phenomenological question. How can one tame the semiotics of these taste descriptors so that they can be employed in a reliable manner while simultaneously affording the taster some capacity for being flexible in assessing one's self-experience, which requires the degree of openness that is necessary for keeping one's mind clear for the next cup? The work of professional tasters very much depends on keeping one's mind clear, and yet the many tools of professional tasting and sensory science keep cluttering up the tasters' minds. The acute difficulty here, the one that pervades human enterprise, is that those habits of thinking that one must continuously transcend in order to learn what one needs to discover are the very same habits of thinking that constitute professional knowledge and give experts their expertise. It seems that the tools of objective science also require some hermeneutic skills if experts are to ascertain trustworthy knowledge about taste.

Professional tasters are familiar with these ironies, which inhabit every occasion of tasting coffee. In fact, they are what makes coffee tasting interesting, and they contribute to the humility acquired by most of the coffee tasters I have met. These ironies keep causing professional methods to fall short of being completely adequate, and this in turn makes it necessary for professional tasters to keep reexamining and continually revising their methods, without relief. This is not a bad thing; however, each tool—the rating schedules, the ways of numerating, the organization of taste descriptors, etc.—should be reexamined in the context of their being applied. This is a necessary part of science, since in this life there is zero possibility that perfection has been secured. Moreover, the purpose of these identifications, descriptions, ratings, etc. is for communicating across the chain of coffee production, from grower to consumer, and so these tools must be continually reassessed for how adequate the communication that they make possible really is.

There are a few tasters who are in denial regarding these paradoxes, and among them are those committed to marketing one or another solution for them. One competent coffee tasting methodologist, Luigi Odello of Brescia, Italy, explained to an audience of his clients (translation mine), "We must use rigorous 'procedure' [in English], fully elaborated and precisely respectful of a qualitative 'standard' [in English] that is certain and demonstrable." Odello relies on carefully designed quantitative protocols, full of clever devices to enhance reliability, but he recognizes that his victories must also be qualitative, and he would deny that the above stated paradoxes create any paralysis for sensory analysis. Instead, in the face of the unavoidable indeterminacies of tasting, he commends certainty; certainty is the default state of many who aspire to be scientific. Italians are not the only non-English speakers who use English terms when they wish to enhance the authority of their knowledge ("procedure," "standard"); I have observed that it is habit of coffee professionals throughout the world (India, El Salvador, Brazil, etc.), especially those who identify themselves as scientists. In her doctoral dissertation, "Tasting in Mundane Practices," Anna Mann (2015, 131–132) undertook ethnographic investigations of mundane "sensory engagements of food and drinks" among Germans, Swiss, Dutch, and other Western Europeans in a variety of ordinary settings, but "sensory science laboratories turned out to be the only site" where the English word "taste" was used consistently, as if the idea carried a more objective sense in English than its equivalents do in German, French or Dutch. As Erving Goffman (1959) proposed, ordinary life involves a certain amount of theater, and around the world English is used to signal that one is aiming to be scientific; nevertheless, the ironies I listed are not so easily evaded.

The Best of Both Worlds

Illy Coffee, perhaps Italy's most respected purveyor of coffee, inscribes its motto on its packaging: "Arte e scienza dell'espresso" (Art and science of espresso). It seems that Illy wants the best of both worlds. Can the coffee industry possess both art *and* science? Similarly, Franco Schillani of Trieste declared to me, "I only do objective tasting. I am seeking the maximum objective expression of subjectivity." Luigi Odello explained the identical aim to his Italian students: "We utilize these 'instruments' [in English] for the purpose of objectifying as much as possible what is producing pleasure. Our mission will always be to give an objective assessment of the sensory characteristics." Professional tasters want it both ways because they require it both ways, and this is the problem that motivates these inquiries.

It is interesting that coffee tasters simultaneously sustain some objectivist ideology—"I always let the scores speak"—while they continue to value the contributions of subjective intelligence—"There is a necessity for the scale, but personally I place more trust in the qualitative description that tasters write in the 'Notes' section" and "Our way of tasting in India is not with numbers." Odello posed our question by asking, "What is the center of the objectivity of sensorial analysis?" This center is elusive. In the context of this research, it is not an abstract philosophical question; it is a practical problem for the coffee industry, a daily problem, even though it concerns epistemological phenomena that comprise a central conundrum for humanity.

A team of scientists working on coffee tasting in Copenhagen came to a similar conclusion, albeit without the irony. Giaccalone et al. (2016) write, "Food quality is a multi-dimensional concept comprising both objective and subjective components." Are these components really separate? The phenomenologist William Earle (1955, 68) has observed that objectivity is a situation where one's personal feelings are held in abeyance: "The more a mind is filled with feelings, the less it apprehends any other object. . . . The objective world, or the world which must appear in order to be known, vanishes in proportion to the intensity of the feeling." How does Odello assess the pleasure of coffee, or make contact with the "naked pleasure" of which Perullo speaks, and still retain his objectivity? Here the embarrassing irony of professional coffee tasting raises its head once more: a professional taster needs to assess the pleasure of what is being tasted, but making contact with pleasure is a feeling, which can place the objectivity of the sensory assessment at risk.

During an early stage of this research, Giolo Fele of Trento and I submitted a bi-national application to the US National Endowment for the Humanities (NEH) that would have financed the field studies for this research. Although we received mostly positive reviews, one reviewer disapproved strongly, and so our application was not rated highly enough to receive funding in a "Great Recession" year in which only five projects were funded. The reviewer strongly objected to my assertion that objectivity was "a necessary impossibility" for the coffee industry, suggesting that such a statement was not logical. It seems that some of those who dispense research funds do not appreciate irony, even when it is a ubiquitous aspect of the human condition. But I did not invent the irony nor the situation that necessitates it, I only wish to study it. As Heidegger (1991, 18) discerned, "Contradiction is the inner life of the reality of the real." Still, reflection attempts to conceal from itself its own self-contradictions (Hegel 1969, 94), not recognizing that each contradiction possesses extraordinary capacity to elucidate our situation. Coffee tasting is an ideal site for investigating the reality of how subjectivity and objectivity are related.

Most people in the coffee industry immediately recognized the pertinence of our research topic. During our first field trip to Trieste, Giolo Fele and I visited Sandalj Coffee for the purpose of videotaping the work of their chief tasters. Our first task was to secure permission from the owner, Vincenzo Sandalj, to carry out research in his firm's tasting lab. When we explained how we were sociologists attempting to study how the world practices being objective, he recognized the problem to be an important one. But he quizzed us: "Your problem exists almost everywhere in society, you don't need to study coffee to investigate it." I replied by agreeing with him, "Yes, that is true, and previously I have completed other studies." "Which studies are those?" Mr. Sandalj asked me. I replied, "I completed a detailed study of how Tibetan philosopher-monks rely on formal logic in their public debates. These problems of formal logic are especially interesting in the context of coffee tasting." Mr. Sandalj, who happened to have an interest in Tibetan Buddhism, smiled and replied, "Yes, I can see that. Tibetan Buddhism is almost as interesting as coffee tasting." And so our study of the necessary impossibility of objectivity in tasting coffee began in Sandalj's tasting lab.

A Few Misconceptions

The NEH panel member who disapproved of our research design argued that if we wanted to develop a critique of objectivity we were loading the dice in our favor by selecting the most subjective of all experiences—taste and smell—to demonstrate the impossibility of being objective. The reviewer wrote, "The focal case here, coffee tastes, is inherently subjective, so undertaking a study of a subjectively based assessment to determine if objectivity exists seems a bit pointless." Unfortunately for us, the reviewer misjudged the target of our research. The aim, quite the opposite, is to identify and describe how—just how, and with what methods—subjectivity can be made objective, that is, how objectivity can be achieved successfully, even in the context of one of the most subjective situations one can imagine. Moreover, the situation of the taste of coffee does not differ all that greatly from any other human enterprise, since understanding, language, consciousness, social cooperation—in short, human subjectivity—will always be involved.

It is a widespread commonsense notion that there is a difference between facts and interpretations; however, there exist only interpreted facts. There is no duality here, or as Nietzsche said (Figal 2010, 51), "There are simply not facts, only interpretations." If there is a difference, it is only because social procedures have been organized to establish and maintain a difference. The paradoxes of human understanding and inquiry I am describing are inescapable. Harold Garfinkel used to say that despite the endless remedies people develop, the paradoxes are "without remedy." Apart from submitting our thinking and experience to one or another mythical version of experience, we must live with these ironies. And so we do.

The reviewer's misunderstanding can be instructive for the reader here. Our interest is not to debunk objective protocols, but to learn wherein lies their utility. How do we use these methods and protocols to get on with our worldly projects? We are interested in truth, but truth is not simply the mechanistic result of a method, as Hans-Georg Gadamer (1975) has established. Truth cannot be reduced to truth-habits. Lorraine Daston and Peter Galison (2010, 58) contend that "Truth comes before and remains distinct from objectivity." It requires insight into *the inherent problems with knowing anything*, including how the object that is grasped is necessarily formulated by the fore-structure of one's understanding (Heidegger 1982, 139–148). For this reason, along with "straightforward" inquiry, scientific investigation must include "radical self-understanding" (Husserl 1969a, 153). If our strategies for achieving objective understanding bear flaws, then we must depend on dialectics to ensure that our understanding, including the knowledge developed by science, improves. Dialectics entails continuous criticism, negation of received doctrines and established truth-habits, cooperation and contestation. Dialectics is the means by which understanding evolves. Science is not a pure land where we are finally able to rest secure, confident of our truths. The intention of this monograph is to advance science by understanding some details about how objective understanding works. Its aim is a positive one, but here we come upon another paradox: this positive advance ascends on the shoulders of many negations.

The reputation of sociology in the world is that of a discipline of thought that is quick to debunk accepted beliefs and received notions. But this is only how it appears from the outside, usually to those who have fully committed themselves in advance to their local interests. Social science has no investment in debunking anything; however, it does subject accepted beliefs and notions to rigorous scrutiny, in order to describe objectively just how those beliefs came to be. As Peter Berger and Thomas Luckmann (1966, 12) wrote, "The task of the sociology of knowledge is not to be the debunking or uncovering of socially produced distortions, but the systematic study of the social conditions of knowledge as such." Further, the phenomenological method I employ here is especially effective for locating and setting aside bias. One of its fundamental principles is to store within "parentheses" every presupposition and "put them out of action" (Husserl 1982, 59), in order to witness the world "just as it shows itself from itself" (Heidegger 1996, 30). Since phenomenology has been investigating objectivity for more than a century, it is sufficiently well developed to assist us in the present study.

Another confusion surrounds the word "taste." Originally, it was used to refer to the flavors one can experience, recognize, and appreciate; however, along with this taste-as-sense, since the 17th century (Perullo 2016, 40) there has also been a "taste" that is an indicator of status or aesthetic sensitivity; since Pierre Bourdieu, "taste" has been associated with its use by members of society as a marker of social class. Since Bourdieu's inquiries, sociologists have had a difficult time reading the word "taste" and thinking of anything except social class markers. That is not the topic here. I am interested in taste-as-sense, what is experienced by the nose, tongue, and mouth, and how one's understanding influences that immanent experience. Macrosocial definitions of coffees and coffee tastes do impinge on how taste-as-sense is experienced, but I am not concerned to follow up any of Bourdieu's topics; instead, I am interested in how people taste their coffee and in how what they know about flavors influences what they taste. My curiosities are seriously microsocial.

The principal topic of this study is to gain better understanding of how the knowledge of taste is established in an objective way as the day's work of professional coffee tasters, as the developing result of actual local processes and real procedures, through which tasters establish objective knowledge about the flavors of what they are drinking. By investigating these processes and procedures in a rigorous and ethnomethodological way, my ambition is to make a substantive contribution to basic research into the nature of objectivity in ordinary human life. Occasionally, there are subsidiary issues that will naturally engage my sociological interest. An advantage of participating in tastings as an observer and not as a participant is that one can retain a perspective broad enough to be able to notice certain dilemmas and problems, and so one may more readily reflect upon these than if one was tasting for a commercial firm. It is possible that some of my insights may be of assistance to the work of professional coffee tasters and even improve the science that is being marshaled within the worldwide coffee industry. Although improving ordinary coffee drinkers' experience with coffee is not a motive here, it too may be an inevitable result of these inquiries. Praising coffee is not a motive either, albeit I'm always happy to do so. The central interest of these investigations is to describe in their local details the ways that people who drink coffee and undertake painstaking sensory assessment of the tastes of coffee discover, describe, and organize their understanding of the features of those tastes. My intention is to locate and describe *just what* is going on when we drink our coffee. By making a survey of these goings-on, I am concerned to learn about what is objective knowledge. Anyone who is interested in exploring the experience of understanding coffee is welcome to join.

Part I

The Story of Coffee Purveying

"A cup of coffee is filled with ideas."
—written on the wall of a San Salvadoran café

Chapter 1

A Brief History of Coffee

> The US market, concentrated in the hands of a few suppliers, was saturated with poor quality, cheap coffee.
>
> —Jon Thorn (2006, 74)

Except in Ethiopia, coffee is not an ancient beverage. Outside traditional uses in Ethiopia and Yemen, which did not commence with consuming an infusion made from roasted beans, the history of coffee is surprisingly brief, no more than a few centuries. Today, coffee is ubiquitous and has become humanity's drug of choice. After oil, it is the second largest cash-traded commodity in the world, and some 125 million people depend on the coffee industry for their livelihood (Tucker 2001, 15). There are billions more who depend on coffee to make their day more fruitful.

Coffee Species

The genus *Coffea* originated in tropical Africa, and it has some 76 species, only two of which (*Coffea canephora* var. *robusta* and *Coffea arabica*) play a major role in brewing the world's coffees. *Coffea canephora* var. *robusta* ("Robusta") is genetically older than *Coffea arabica* and, unlike Arabica, it is cross-pollinating, which has given it much greater variety and has made it a hardier species. Robusta can also contain more caffeine than Arabica. Both offer considerable variation of flavors, but the flavor range of Robustas is wider than that of Arabicas. Although Arabicas usually offer more delicate flavors, Manuel Diaz explains, "The genetic complexity of Robusta is far superior to Arabica. It is our ignorance that has kept Robusta so far behind

Arabica." Another variety of *Coffea canephora* is *Coffea canephora* var. *nganda*. *Coffea liberica*, a spicy and astringent species, was established in Liberia in 1864 and provides only 1% of the world's commercial coffee, with most of it being grown in the Philippines. *Coffea lancifolia* grows in Madagascar, *Coffea stenophylla* grows in Sierra Leone, and *Coffea excelso* grows in West Africa. In 1983, *Coffea charrieriana* was discovered in Cameroon (Wechselberger and Hierl 2009, 7), and no doubt more species remain to be discovered.

While only two of *Coffea*'s 76 species are used for 98% of the world's brewed coffee, *Coffea arabica* is the one that most drinkers seek. Just two heirloom cultivars of *Coffea arabica*, Bourbon and Typica, provide (along with their many hybrids) most people's morning Joe (Weissman 2008, 40), a situation that Stephanie Alcala (2019) describes as a genetic bottleneck: "Arabica's historical domestication has resulted in a severe genetic bottleneck, with the majority of Arabica varieties cultivated today for global consumption deriving their genetic composition from Bourbon and/or Typica." *Coffea arabica* was first identified by Linnaeus in 1753 (Thorn 2006, 15) and was the result of a single hybridization event between two coffee species, *Coffea canephora* and *Coffea eugenioides*, that took place in the highlands of central Africa (Alcala 2019); however, most of *Coffea arabica* spread worldwide from Yemen rather than from its origin Ethiopia (Scalabrin et al. 2020), and because most of the coffee introduced to the world was procured from Yemen on the Arabian Peninsula, Linnaeus named the species "*arabica*." Genetically, *Coffea arabica* is the youngest of the coffee species (a hundred million years), and it is a self-pollinating coffee tree, which limits the genetic resources it can bring to bear to resist the leaf rusts and insect infestations that are increasing with climate change. As a result, agronomists are actively engaged in experimentation with grafts that combine Arabica and Robusta.

The caffeine that *Coffea* developed to attract pollinators also attracted humans, and the human conveyance of *Coffea* around the world and back has transformed the face of the earth, even as viewed from space. Bourbon was brought from Yemen to the island of Bourbon (La Réunion) by the French, and French missionaries carried it to many other African and Asian countries and eventually to Brazil in 1860. Bourbon developed out of the cultivar *Coffea arabica* var. *typica* that was grown on the island of Réunion. Typica was another cultivar derived from Réunion's *Coffea arabica* var. *typica*.

The story of coffee is astonishing, although some of the historical details are contested, originally by competing lore and later by genetic science. The basics of this incredible story are that some coffee seeds were smuggled to India from Yemen about 1620 by a Muslim pilgrim, Baba Budan, who avoided the Yemeni ban against exporting seeds (already the commercial value of coffee had been recognized) by taping some seeds to his chest. A coffee plant, possibly related to the coffee that Baba Budan brought to Mysore (or possibly another brought by boat, perhaps by the Portuguese) was taken from Malabar, India, to Java by the Dutch in 1699. In 1706, the Dutch brought a single plant to an arboretum in Amsterdam. In 1714, the Dutch gifted a plant to Louis XIV, and this tree was transferred to the Jardin des Plantes in Paris and then to the island of Martinique. It is the ancestor of many of the first coffee plants that grew in the French colonies in the Caribbean (Thorn 2006, 9) and in the Americas. There was much drama associated with the transportation of these seedlings by de Clieu and the theft of seeds by others to and about the Americas, but there is no need to repeat these stories here, since other commentators have recounted them at length (e.g., Pendergrast 2010, 15–16).

The Dutch sent their strain of *Coffea* from Amsterdam to Dutch Guyana in 1719, and to French Guiana in 1722, from where it was taken to Brazil in 1727. Halevy (2011, 65) reports, "The coffee brought to Dutch Guyana was recently discovered to be of a different varietal than the beans brought by de Clieu, establishing two independent sources to what is now the largest coffee growing region in the world." Today Typica is too susceptible to disease to be planted widely, though most hybrids descend from it. A Typica brought to Haiti/San Domingo from Martinique allowed that island to become where half the world's commercial coffee was grown in 1788, and this was probably the source of most of the USA's coffee during its early years. The extraordinary story of the journey of coffee, the ancestor of most of the coffee that the world drinks today, can be communicated by means of this diagram: Yemen → India → Java → Amsterdam → Paris → Martinique → Guyana → Brazil. That is a lot of traveling.

As a live species, coffee displays a dynamic existence, and its varieties have been mixed and matched by nature, by the accidental effects of replanting, and by scientific experimentation. Even the two most commonly used species, Arabica and Robusta, have given rise to a dizzying array of varietals. The well-known Timor Hybrid from East Timor developed as a natural hybrid of Arabica and Robusta. Another of the best-known cultivars, Caturra, is a natural mutation of Bourbon that was discovered in Brazil during the second decade of the 20th century. Catimore was developed in a Brazilian research lab from a hybrid of Caturra and Timorese Arabicas and is presently cultivated widely in Africa and Colombia. Further confusing the situation, the label

Catimore refers to a range of hybrids from Caturra, rather than to a distinct varietal, which is to say that coffee agronomists have partly abandoned the coffee taxonomy (science meets industry). Maragogype is a natural mutation of Typica that occurred in 1870 near the city of Maragogipe (Bahia) in Brazil, and it in turn (along with a mutation of Bourbon named after Señor Paca, the El Salvadoran farmer who grew it) contributed to the Salvadoran hybrid of Pacamara, a handsome, large-beaned coffee grown mostly in El Salvador. A popular coffee, "the Pacamara comes in two flavor profiles, one that is more floral and the other more herbal with a hint of green onion" (Halevy 2011, 122). This difference of flavor can confuse consumers. More recently, a Catimor-like hybrid (trademarked by Cenife in Colombia) has been developed to resist leaf rust (*la roya*) in the Americas.

In addition to these deliberate cultivars, the situation is made ambiguous by other cultivars that develop their own characteristics due to the terroirs where they are cultivated. These include Blue Mountain coffee in Jamaica, Kona coffee in Hawaii, Sumatra coffee in Indonesia, and many others. Here coffee identity and taxonomy are further confused. Sometimes it can be difficult to locate a line that can divide commercially cultivated strains and proper varietals, and further, the situation is always changing.

Complicating matters are identification systems developed around the world for selecting, selling, and purchasing coffees. Based upon the harvested and processed green bean (what is sold) rather than the plant, these systems of coffee identification are idiosyncratic by nature, since—like language itself—each geographic zone develops its own coherency largely independently of the others. The coffee industry requires systematic classification of commercial coffees for clarifying the bases of negotiations, and these classification conventions vary from country to country. To provide an idea of their complexity, here are some of them: Brazil uses Strictly Soft, Soft, Softish, Hard, Rioy, and Rio (Azienda Riunite Caffè 2013, 34). Somehow, in this system "Hard" (*duro*) came to mean soft, for the reason that the classification refers to the physical property of the bean, which results from the elevation where it was grown, not the flavor, a situation that can create confusion for drinkers and buyers. Santos exporter and taster Marcio Hazan explained to me, "What we call 'Hard' is soft in most places. Abroad 'Hard' is bad, but here it is somewhat sweet. 'Hard' has a nice aftertaste and is not really hard." This prompted the question, if "Hard" is soft, then what is "Soft"? Hazan explained further, " 'Soft' is a round coffee that involves one's tongue. You know, agreeable, you don't feel anything hard." Hundreds of coffees are receiving such classifications, which are tailored to the specific properties and geography of each country, and if one is a buyer, one will need to learn them all.

Colombia uses Supremo, Excelso, Caracol, Maragogype, and Usual Good Quality for classifying its coffees. Given the idiosyncrasies of local usage, it is necessary to learn what this "usual" can refer to. Costa Rica uses Strictly Hard Bean, Hard Bean, High Grown Atlantic, and Low Grown Atlantic. India uses Plantation A, Plantation B, Plantation C, PB (peaberry), Arabica Cherry (natural) PB, Arabica Cherry (natural) AB, and Arabica Cherry (natural) C. And the Ivory Coast uses Excellent, Extra Prima, Prima, Superior, and Courant (Azienda Riunite Caffè 2013, 49, 65, 61, 97). While it is reasonable that each producer has designed a system that best serves its own production of coffee, it runs against the grain of the standardization that has been the goal of the coffee industry in recent decades.

Given that the meaning of any word is indexical, in that it is always tied to the occasion of its use, some study of these local systems of usage is required, which makes professional coffee people part-time sociologists. In fact, this is one of the pleasures of being a modern coffee purveyor. Learning local systems is most successful when coffee purveyors are able to work alongside each other, importer next to exporter, with the coffees in hand. Only then can the importers seeking to purchase coffees learn the specific references of the terms and the contexts of their application. A set of descriptors will gain objective status by virtue of an intersubjective ratification of their use, side-by-side, in-house. Short of that, the learning curve can become lengthy, using these classifications to purchase coffees and then using what arrives to make one's comprehension of them more specific. Learning this way can take years.

Some specialty coffee purchasers will mostly ignore these systems in favor of cupping scores, which they better understand and place more faith in. The roaster/taster Enrico Meschini, of Livorno, Italy, argues, "A 'good cup,' 'fine cup,' 'NY 2, 3' means nothing. A '74' means more than that. . . . When you are trying to describe coffee, the more that you are using words, the less you are objective. A detailed numeration also requires an accompanying better analysis. But a perfect analysis is an impossibility." Numerical classification systems are necessarily practical objectivities. Methods of classifying coffees that depend less upon the physical properties of the bean or indications of growing locations or elevation, and instead rely upon a precise tasting that is able to produce reliable numerations, will require the extensive resocialization of the growers and exporters from whom importers and first-world roasters order their coffee.

"Normal Coffee"

The preparation of coffee around the world varies widely also, and the customary ways that each country has adapted coffee to its own culinary tradition can make what is a "normal" coffee in one country unrecognizable to another country's drinkers. According the Trieste taster Franco Schillani, clients are only accustomed to a certain taste, "which they call 'coffee.'" During travels to some 50 countries, I have frequently asked ordinary drinkers, "What kind of coffee do you like?" The replies that I receive often include the words "normal coffee" or "I just like regular coffee." While the answer employs identical wording, the referent changes considerably. One reply goes, "I like 'coffee coffee,'" so thoroughly do people accept the way that they customarily drink their coffee to be the way that coffee always is, when the essence of "normal coffee" depends upon local, contingent features of national custom.

Normal Coffee in Ethiopia

Not only did coffee originate in Ethiopia, hominins originated there. Between 2,500 and 3,500 varieties of coffee grow wild in Ethiopia (Weissman 2008, 85), which presents a complexity entirely distinct from that of most coffee-producing countries that grow some half-dozen designed cultivars in forests that are monocultures. For most of time that Ethiopians used coffee, they did not drink it, they ate it. The situation parallels that of the cacao cultures of Mayan Central America, who consumed their cacao in sauces, often along with corn, and for millennia did not consume it as a beverage.

The Ethiopians crushed and mixed their coffee with butter or fat and rolled the paste into hard balls (Roden 1994, 58). "According to early European travelers, the Oromo ground the coffee cherry and bean together with animal fat to create long-lasting, calorically dense food balls" (Tucker 2011, 37). Wechselberger and Hierl (2009, 8) tell us that "the pulp and the seeds were crushed. Fat, flour and water were added to make balls that were then fried." The first people not from Ethiopia or Yemen to use coffee regularly were the Sufis, and it was they who introduced coffee to the Arab world. Wechselberger and Hierl also tell us, "For the Sufis these balls were an effective means of making it through their long dances." As Arabic people had been used to making tea, which developed in China before the era of drinking coffee, it was probably they who popularized the idea of a beverage made from an infusion of the leaves of the coffee plant. Halevy (2011, 41) describes, "In the early 15th century Arabs crossed the narrow passage over the Red

Sea in their search for a leaf that could replace the tea to which they had grown accustomed," and it was likely the Sufis who first came up with the idea of pouring water over crushed beans (Wechselberger and Hierl 2009, 8).

The extent to which Ethiopians used the coffee leaves for an infusion is unknown, but for centuries now the Ethiopians have been consuming a drink prepared from the pulverized beans, although their beverage bears little resemblance to any coffee consumed in an Italian coffee bar or an American diner. Commentators differ regarding when the practice of roasting the beans first started. Roden (1994, 13) says that the practice was started "around the thirteenth century," and Pendergrast (2010, 5) writes, "It probably wasn't until sometime in the fifteenth century that someone roasted the beans." But the Ethiopian roasting of beans is nothing like the way beans are roasted in commercially organized Western countries, in that the roasting is done as part of a household ceremony with chants by women who have the primary responsibility for the daily roasting and preparing the beverage in a *jibana* clay pot, along with lots of cardamom and sometimes cloves, cinnamon, and sugar. Some of the time they only partially roast the beans, which creates a light yellowish, very hard bean that will break many grinders that are not a mortar and pestle. The result is a tasty drink that no Italian, Brazilian, or American would recognize as coffee. Even today most Ethiopians would not think of roasting their beans anywhere but at home. I have the habit of asking the Ethiopians of the diaspora that I meet (at a cash register, in a university, driving a taxi) whether they roast their own coffee at home in their kitchen, and the answer they give me is "Yes, of course."

NORMAL COFFEE IN TURKEY

One must be careful when speaking of the national culture of Turkey, since the cultural reach of the Turks stretches a quarter of the way around the globe, having controlled the Silk Route for a millennium and having at one time controlled most lands between Hungary and Mongolia and from the Caucasus to the tip of the Saudi peninsula. Their influence regarding coffee in particular was significant; in fact, it may be said that the Turks were the people who made coffee the commodity it is, just as they accomplished for sugar.

Under Salim the Resolute, the Ottoman Empire conquered Syria and Egypt (Thorn 2006, 12) and brought coffee back to Constantinople in 1517, and then to Damascus and Aleppo in the 1530s. While Oromo warriors from southwestern Ethiopia were fighting in western Ethiopia in 1537 and interfering with coffee production, Yemen became the world's center for coffee (Thorn 2006, 149), and for several centuries its port of Mocha was ground zero for coffee (today Yemen produces less than 30,000 bags). When Salim's son and successor, Suleiman the Magnificent, occupied Yemen, capturing Aden in 1538, the Turks took control of the coffee trade before the advent of the seafaring capitalism of the Western European colonizing powers. Constantinople's first coffeehouse opened in 1554, and by 1570 it had 600 coffeehouses (Thorn 2006, 54). "Coffee became the iconic drink of the Ottoman Empire" (Koehler 2017, 101). Keen to protect their monopoly over coffee, the Turks carefully guarded their coffee production in Yemen (Pendergrast 2010, 7) and prohibited the export of seeds that had not been boiled in order to prevent germination.

The Turks were also responsible for the introduction of coffee to Vienna. After defeating the king of Hungary in 1526, Suleiman the Magnificent took his forces to Vienna, where he laid siege to the city. He was unsuccessful, but his defeat was due more to rainfall and snowfall than to the ability of the Viennese soldiers. Taking Vienna remained a goal of the Turks, and a century and half later, in 1683, the Turks laid siege to Vienna for a second time, surrounding it with their camels. This time it looked to be successful; however, the Viennese sent urgent messages for assistance to their fellow Catholics in Poland and France, and the Poles arrived just in time to defeat the Turks, rescuing the Viennese from starvation. Among the Poles was George Kolschitzky, who had lived in Constantinople and acted as translator between the Turks and the Viennese. When the Turks departed with their camels, they left behind 500 sacks of green coffee (Pendergrast 2010, 11). As soon as the Viennese began to burn them, Kolschitzky intervened. We can do no better than imagine what Kolschitzky explained to the Viennese (e.g., "I would be happy to take the camel food off your hands") that convinced them to hand over to him the sacks of green coffee. The first coffeehouse in Vienna opened in 1685. Turkey traded the coffee across the Middle East, along the Silk Route, and probably to the southeastern coast of Italy (Puglia), as well as to Oxford and London. Even the founder of Jamestown brought coffee from Constantinople to America, in 1607.

Turkish coffee is strong and easy to make, since they boil the grounds with the water. One has to cultivate a liking for grounds of coffee in one's teeth, a definite pleasure for Turks (and for this author). "To this day in the Middle East, pounding in a mortar, preferably wooden, and with a stone pestle, is the method used to pulverize coffee" (Roden 1994, 72). This way to prepare coffee, one of the earliest, prevails today throughout the Middle

East and as far as North Africa and Greece, although the Greeks use a lighter roast than the Turks do (Halevy 2011, 148). "The Bosnians first boil the water, then add the coffee grounds and bring the mixture back to a boil" (Halevy 2011, 69). The Israelis make their "Turkish coffee" by placing the grounds in a cup, pouring water that has already boiled directly into the cup, and drinking without first straining the grains (the grains sink to the bottom of the cup), so it too features those desirable coffee grounds in one's teeth. In Turkish restaurants, much coffee is roasted and brewed directly in front of one, and one sometimes drinks one's coffee in refillable half-egg-shaped Turkish cups (Roden 1994, 38). It is not a brew that many drinkers in Europe, Asia, or the Americas would select, since the dark roast, the saturated infusion, and possibly even the green bean selection produces a bitter cup. Several exporters from India count on Turkish buyers to purchase their lower-rated coffees, and some Brazilian exporters will send *rio*-tasting coffees to the Turks (see chapter 4). As Roden (1994, 47) observes, even "rioy taste does, however, have a following." It is a cultural taste, and the Turks are acquainted with it.

NORMAL COFFEE IN ITALY

The Adriatic Coast was the first region of Italy to be exposed to coffee, around the mid-1500s. Puglia was probably the initial place, but the habit did not endure there. The earliest recorded evidence of coffee use in Italy was 1575, when a Turkish merchant entered Italy with a *finian* pot (Halevy 2011, 59). An Italian, writing from Constantinople in 1615, vowed to "impart the knowledge to the Italians" (Roden 1994, 16), and it was known in Venice by 1624, although the first coffeehouse there did not open until 1683 (Pendergrast 2010, 8). The most famous of Venice's coffeehouses, the Café Florian, opened in 1720 (Roden 1994, 23).

Italian inventions in the field of coffee preparation transformed the way that Europeans drank coffee. The Neapolitan pot (the "Napolitana") was an early and simple method of boiling and filtering coffee at home and is still in use today. The Moka pot is the most widely used system of preparing coffee in Italy and produces an espresso-like beverage on one's stovetop. Both the Napolitana and the Moka provide an ounce of dense coffee, an amount small enough to make most Americans shake their heads and cast their eyes about for where the rest of the coffee might have gone. These small, intense cups of *caffè* are "normal" coffee for Italians, and they dismiss with a hint of ridicule the overly large cups (you know, "*grande*," "extra *grande*," and "*enorme*") that are normal in most American cafés and homes, a brew that

Italians describe as colored hot water. My cousins from Italy treated me to a cappuccino in Naples one morning and introduced me to the barista, a friend of theirs. The barista asked me how I liked his cappuccino. After I replied positively, he asked me how good cappuccino was in the USA. I explained that there it was a different drink altogether and raised my open hand four inches above the cup and told him, "Our cappuccino is this tall." His eyes widened, and he expressed incredulity that anyone could drink that much coffee. I explained, "No, the amount of coffee is the same, they just add hot water and milk until it reaches the top." People's normal differs.

A Neapolitan invented the French press, although it is not used widely in Italy; it is not even used in France. When I requested a French press preparation in half a dozen Parisian cafés, both in English and in my passable French, no one knew what I was talking about. Confusion of this sort is commonplace in the history of coffee consumption. The earliest espresso machine was invented in 1884 in the northwestern Italian city of Torino. An improved design was patented in 1903, and displayed at the 1906 Milan Fair. Another machine was patented in 1938 by Achille Gaggia and first displayed at the 1939 Milan Fair. It was further improved in 1946 (Roden 1994, 30). The Italian espresso is the default coffee of Italy, and it features an ounce of coffee that possesses an intensely concentrated flavor that always captures one's attention. An Italian, Luigi Gogli, also invented the one-way valve bag, in 1970, which has been universally adopted by the international coffee industry (Pendergrast 2010, 308).

Even inside Italy what is a normal *caffè* changes a good deal from one region to another. While they are all made from blends of three to nine different beans, the percentage of Robusta and the degree of roasting varies. Blends are prepared not only for producing enough *crema* in the coffee—Italian drinkers seek mouthfeel more than they seek flavors—but also for developing creative ways to sell inexpensive coffees expensively. Italian roasters are ingenious at mixing average Brazilian coffees and African Robustas in ways that are highly palatable. A normal dark roast in northern Italy, say Milano or Verona, is equivalent to a dark roast in the USA, and the level of roast becomes darker the further one travels south. By Rome, an American drinker may begin to search for a McCafé (sometimes the only medium roast one can find in Italy, and it contains more than one ounce); but by the time one reaches Naples the dark roasting has turned all the coffees bitter. As Pendergrast concluded (2010, 193), "The farther south, the darker the roast tended to be, so that southern Italians nearly turned their beans to charcoal."

Desperate for an excellent cup in Palermo, Sicily, I and my Italian colleague Giolo Fele once made a tour of the old city looking for specialty coffee, but we were unsuccessful. Palermo is decades behind the times (which is its charm) and remains proud of its "normal" dark roasts. We finally discovered a traditional roaster at Caffè Stagnitta (founded in 1928) who was roasting quality Central American coffees at a "medium" roast level. His medium was equivalent to a dark roast in the USA; however, it was not roasted to the point of charcoal. He was proud of it and considered it to be the cutting edge. He himself was was the fourth generation of his family to be a blender-roaster.

Italy's own folklore awards to themselves credit for possessing not only the world's best food but the world's best coffee. They are right about their food, but the self-esteem that Italians display regarding their coffee is mostly mythopoetics. Citizens of Naples (where my family live in our original twelfth-century home) especially are confident that no better coffee can be found, even though it compares with a cup filtered through ground charcoal. Coffee exporters have commented that coffee tasters in the USA and northern Europe are more sophisticated than those from Italy. Young coffee professionals in several Italian cities have expressed to me the opinion that Italy has taken its espresso for granted, so it has not until recently explored deeply how to improve the taste of coffee. It is difficult to surmount any habit of drinking coffee, including what is brewed in our own kitchen, especially when it derives from a long and storied experience like the Italians have with their normal coffee. Halevy's (2011, 61) observation can be applied to most countries: "Some of the coffee taste preferences that have emerged over the years for historical and supply reasons persist today even if the original reasons are no longer relevant."

Normal Coffee in the Netherlands

We have mentioned the role that Holland played in the history of coffee. In 1616, a coffee plant was taken from Mocha to the Netherlands (Pendergrast 2010, 7), and the first coffee was sold in Holland in 1640. Coffee was already growing in Ceylon when the Dutch arrived there; however, the coffee grown there prior to the arrival of the Portuguese was grown for its leaves, which were used in curries (Boyle 2014). "The Dutch transplanted seedlings grown in Amsterdam to Ceylon (Sri Lanka) in 1658, and by the end of the seventeenth century, they had planted coffee successfully in Java. The first plantings on Java failed due to earthquakes and flooding, and new plants were brought from Malabar, India" (Tucker 2011, 38). The coffee brought from Malabar may have descended from the original coffee taken to India by Baba Budan. There was another planting in Java from Yemen in 1696, when Dutch traders sailed to Mocha before arriving in the East Indies (Thorn 2006, 136), and another in 1706 (Thorn 2006, 8). The first Java beans arrived in Amsterdam in 1706 (Koehler 2017, 103), and the Dutch planted coffee in Surinam in 1718. By 1736, the Dutch were producing six million pounds of coffee annually (Koehler 2017, 104).

The Dutch innovated the "normal" coffee that incorporates milk, adapted from the way they habitually drank tea: "Inspired by the drinking of tea with milk, Nieuhoff, the Dutch Ambassador to China, was officially the first person to try coffee with milk, around 1660" (Roden 1994, 95). The English copied them, and the habit was picked up by many Americans.

Normal Coffee in England

Few people realize that England was a coffee-drinking country before it was a tea-drinking country. In fact, in parts of northern Europe, coffee was closely associated with the English, even to the point that Germans named their coffeehouses "English Coffee House," just as one of the early coffee houses in Boston was named "London Coffee House." The first café in England was opened in 1650 at Oxford University, by Jacobs, a Lebanese Jew (Pendergrast 2010, 12), and the first coffee shop in London opened in 1652. In Hamburg and other port towns with whom the English traded, the "English Coffee House" restaurants served English sailors and merchants during the late 1600s and also introduced coffee to the Germans and others. By 1715, there were over 2,000 coffeehouses in London (Jaffe 2014, 39).

In part, the English had adopted coffee from the Dutch, who were the first to grow it. "Coffee was already a beloved part of Dutch life and commerce by the mid-to-late 1600s, when ships carrying settlers started beaching on New World shores. . . . while the English colonists hadn't had long exposure to coffee in the old country, they quickly picked up the custom after assuming control of what would be Manhattan, in 1664" (Meister 2017, 91).

When war between Britain and Spain (1745–46) interrupted coffee shipments, England's import duty on tea was reduced, and at home and abroad the British began drinking more tea. Britain took Ceylon from the Dutch in 1796 (Tucker 2011, 410), and the height of the English coffee-growing in Ceylon was in 1857, when Ceylon was producing more coffee than anywhere else in the world and 36 million kilos were shipped, mostly supplying London's cafés. By this time, capitalist purveying of coffee was well developed, as was an agronomy based on monocultures. Leaf rust began to devastate more than 90% of the Ceylonese trees in 1876 (Tucker 2011, 115; McKenna 2020, 4), and after a couple of decades of battling the disease, the English became primarily a tea-drinking country, especially during the heyday of its empire, with fine teas coming from Ceylon, Darjeeling, and the Nilgiris. Purchasing coffee from their Dutch rivals was not an option for the English, and it became "normal" for English to prefer tea.

Normal Coffee in France

While coffee was spreading through London's coffee shops in the 1660s, France's first café opened in Marseilles in 1671. Blaise Pascal opened the first café in Paris in the 1680s (Koehler 2017, 102), and Honoré de Balzac praised coffee, declaring that it makes one's "ideas come rushing like the battalions of a great army." The Sicilian Procopia Cutò opened the Café Procope in Paris in 1689 (Roden 1994, 24).

The French used an infusion method of preparation: "In 1710, rather than boiling coffee, the French first made it by the infusion method, with powdered coffee suspended in a cloth bag" (Pendergrast 2010, 9). In 1715, coffee plants were taken to Bourbon (La Réunion), so that the French could grow their own coffee, and French colonists brought coffee to Martinique in 1719 (Jaffe 2014, 39). Coffee consumption in France climbed from 50 to 250 million pounds between 1853 and 1900, though their coffee has never been considered excellent, largely because much of it was made from Robusta beans from their African colonies, and sometimes mixed with chicory.

Normal Coffee in India

We have mentioned that the Sufi saint Baba Budan smuggled coffee beans out of Yemen and took them to India, where he planted them in Chikkamagaluru about 1610, in the principality of Mysore. The first plantation was established in 1820, and the coffee-growing culture that developed in the Western Ghats among affluent plantation owners from Chikkamagaluru, Mysuru, and Kodagu (Coorg) Districts persists to the present. They produce the daily beverage of most residents of India's southern Indian states of Karnataka, Tamil Nadu, and Kerala.

The coffee they drink in South India is unique. Despite the severely hot climate, which can produce a terrific thirst, they drink their coffee in one-ounce stainless steel cups. These tiny cups stand inside a one-inch-high stainless steel canister, and both the cup and canister have metallic lips that allow one to hold a steaming hot metal container of coffee without burning one's fingers. If the coffee is too hot, the drinker can cool it down by pouring the ounce of coffee back and forth between the two metal containers. Each morning the Indians create a syrup of coffee concentrate, which they later add to boiled water. From the English, they adopted the custom of adding rich milk (Indian milk is very fresh, often unpasteurized) and they mix the coffee syrup, boiled milk, copious amounts of sugar (sometimes cardamom), and boiled water, sometimes with an acrobatic flourish as they pour the mix back and forth between two 12-ounce stainless steel glasses separated by a foot or more.

Like some French, Indians prefer coffee brewed with chicory. Several coffee experts have suggested to me that if you set the best Indian 100% Arabica gourmet coffee next to a coffee that had 40% chicory (the norm in South India, probably initiated during wartime shortages), and next to a cup of 100% chicory, the average Indian will prefer the 100% chicory cup, considering it to be "real" coffee. The second choice would be the one prepared with 40% chicory, and the 100% Arabica would be the least favored.

Outside of South India, most Indians drink tea. When northern Indians do drink coffee it is often Nescafé, which they serve with pride. Even in South India, a great deal of soluble coffee is consumed. In many first-class hotels in the coffee-growing regions, Nescafé is the only coffee one is able to order. When I visited a large coffee processing facility in Hassan, Karnataka State, the city's principal hotel had a coffee tree growing in its garden but still the only coffee they served me was Nescafé.

In Nepal, until recently, coffee made fresh from coffee beans was difficult to find. With an ideal (high and moist) geography for growing coffee, the situation is destined to change; however, its citizens express little interest in coffee, and in most restaurants only Nescafé is available. It is interesting to contemplate whether, as a coffee culture commences in Nepal for the first time, they will follow the lead of the one-ounce sweetened cups of South India or copy the coffee drinking fashions of Nepal's European visitors.

Normal Coffee in Vietnam

Although Vietnam has been growing coffee since missionaries brought coffee from La Réunion, the wars the Vietnamese fought against France restricted development, and only since the end of the Vietnam War with the USA did Vietnam begin large-scale coffee production. The army planted much of the coffee, and Vietnam went from 7,000 hectares in 1977 to 574,314 in 2012. Today 10% of the world's coffee originates from Vietnam. From 1991 to 2001 Vietnam rose from tenth place to second place in coffee production (14 million bags; Jaffe 2014, 44), after Brazil. Most of their coffee is Robusta, and much is grown on relatively flat, easily mechanized plantations. Some high-quality Arabicas can be found in in Dak Lek, Lam Dong, Dak Nang, and Gia Lai, but they use many chemicals, so Vietnam will soon face soil depletion problems.

The Vietnamese drink much coffee that they filter through aluminum or stainless steel pots that resemble the Napolitana pot, but the holes through which the brewed coffee is filtered are so tiny that it takes 10 minutes for an 8-ounce cup to drain. Vietnam's weather is hot and humid, so one does not mind drinking one's coffee lukewarm; however, this method does not extend very far into China, despite the two countries sharing a border.

NORMAL COFFEE IN BRAZIL

There is still a lot of coffee in Brazil, so much that it is difficult to define which brew in Brazil is the normal one. The best of their coffee is exported, leaving their nationals to drink mostly average or inferior coffee, and the quality ranges widely, from extremely good to extremely bad. "Because 95 percent of the country rests below 3,000 feet, Brazilian beans have always tended to lack acidity and body" (Pendergrast 2010, 25), but they are able to produce the world's least expensive coffee, upon which the profits of the world's coffee largest purveyors depend heavily.

Coffee was introduced to Brazil via French Guiana in 1727, although other coffee strains kept arriving from Java, Goa, and Africa. After San Domingo's predominance during the mid-1700s, Haiti became the world's top producer for a short time, until the defeat of Napoleon's troops in 1803 (Pendergrast 2010, 18). After French coffee production was interrupted, the Dutch filled most of the world's requirements from its plantations in Java. From the middle of the 19th century, a combination of slavery, the exploitation of workers after the end of slavery in 1888, and a flat landscape that easily lent itself to mass production all joined to make Brazil the powerhouse that inaugurated coffee as the global commodity that it is today.

From 1890 to 1901, Brazil's production increased from 5.5 million bags to 16.3 million bags. In 1901, over half of the world's production was brought by rail lines from São Paulo and Minas Gerais states, most of it processed through the port of Santos (Pendergrast 2010, 74), which was truly the world's coffee capital. During the early part of the 20th century, Brazil produced nearly 80% of the world's coffee. Even in 2010, Brazil was still the world's largest producer, supplying 30% of the world's coffee (50 million bags). The success of Brazil's production is based largely on how its terrain permits it to mechanize and standardize its coffees. Consider that whereas Ethiopia has 60,000 or more kinds of coffee, Brazil grows only 60 varieties. Many Latin American countries that have to pick all of their coffee cherries by hand because of the steep terrain have not been able to afford their labor costs during the low-price regimes of the early part of the 21st century, and among the Latin American coffee farms that do not grow specialty coffees, only Brazil's *fazendas* have been able to make regular profits at growing coffee, because of the large scale of the Brazil's production. Today they ensure their continued success by maintaining one of the strongest commitments to agronomic research, and the result is that Brazil's productivity is still rising.

Brazil's cities feature some of the world's best coffeehouses, but for the vast majority of Brazilians their coffee is made from beans that Brazil's exporters have rejected. After brewing, the coffee is made to sit much of the day in 3-gallon stainless steel vats and is very bitter, so it must be consumed with sugar; however, milk is not as common in Brazil as it is in English-speaking countries. What even the Brazilians will not drink is exported to Argentina or to airlines at very low cost, but the quality is also low, so many Argentinian coffee purveyors roast the beans with sugar *before* they grind and package roasted coffee. Their coffee would surprise drinkers in Italy, who rely heavily on Brazilian beans. As Pendergrast (2010, 244fn) has summarized, "Latin American countries exported their best beans and consumed cheap instant coffee"; this holds true for India as well. If one wants good coffee, a good strategy is to remain in New York or Stockholm.

The important lesson here is that when anyone thinks of "coffee," what they have in mind may not be shared by others who think the notion "coffee." Coffee may be a global commodity, but it has varying incarnations.

The Commodification of Coffee

Archaeological sites reveal evidence that even the earliest humans traded goods, including foods. In Africa and the Americas tools made from bones and stones traveled long distances. Australia's Aboriginal peoples highly prized pearl shells for 60,000 years, and North American Indians traded beads throughout their 13,000-year residence there. In Mesoamerica, hallucinogenic plants (peyote and mushrooms) have been found well outside the areas where they naturally grow. Phoenician boats left olive trees everywhere they traveled, and camel caravans across Arabia and along the Silk Route transported seeds, goods, religions, philosophies, and food innovations. It can be said without exaggeration that there were commodities before coffee; however, coffee was the first globally traded commodity.

Coffee beans at least 1,800 years old were discovered among primitive flints in a rock shelter south of Bonga, the capital of Kafa, Ethiopia (Koehler 2017, 49). Coffee was first exported to Yemen, where from the 6th to 9th centuries the Yemeni dominated coffee production. The first written record of coffee was that of the Persian physician Rhazes (865–925 CE), who mentions that the coffee trees had been deliberately cultivated for hundreds of years (Pendergrast 2010, 4). Ethiopians developed coffee cropping in Harare, and Arabs brought it to Yemen some time during the 14th to 17th centuries. The key moments in the history of coffee's spread in the world occurred during this period and include the Sufis' discovery and usage of the psychotropic properties of *qahwa* (coffee) during their ceremonies and its subsequent introduction to the Muslim world, as well as a series of coffee thefts: (1) the theft of coffee from Yemen by the Dutch (taken to Amsterdam, Ceylon, and Java), (2) the theft of seeds from Yemen by the Muslim pilgrim Baba Budan (taken to India), and (3) the theft of seeds in the early 18th century in French Guiana by the Portuguese diplomat and lover Francisco de Melo Palheta (taken to Brazil).

Coffee made its first commercial appearance outside of its region of origin when Constantinople's first coffeehouse opened in 1554, but the establishment of coffee as a global commodity was cemented during the latter part of the 17th century, when the first cafés opened in London (1652), Marseilles (1671), Venice (1683), and Vienna (1685). It can be said that coffee's time had arrived, and also that its end is nowhere in sight. Accordingly, coffee has been a global commodity for 350 years. Today, coffee production is close to 200 million bags annually. Just as cows (nearly one billion), pigs (almost as many), and chickens (uncountable) have overwhelmed the earth's surface, to the extent that their methane production is a significant contributor to global warming, so has humanity's global production of coffee transformed the planet's tropical biosphere, literally changing the face of earth.

The Standardization of Coffee: Normal Coffee in the USA

Placing the blame for much of the poor-tasting coffee in the world at the feet of American capitalism, especially in its Fordist incarnation, is not a popular position, and it can surely be argued that most every nation has pioneered its own route to poor coffee; nevertheless, it is not unfair to say that stale, inferior, pre-packaged, mass-marketed coffee is the end product of an identifiably American capitalist genius. Some coffee purveyors may become angered by this contention, although mostly they lack sufficient political training and interest to contest it, having given their priorities generously to a combination of a love for coffee and a preference for profits. Catherine Tucker (2011, 8) summarizes the situation concisely: "Nestlé, General Foods, and Philip Morris sought to increase their profits and decided to produce successively cheaper (and therefore less flavorful) coffee." It should be kept in mind that by 2000, only four companies accounted for half of the global purchases of raw coffee (Wechselberger and Hierl 2009, 44). However, it should also be noted that without capitalism (and without slavery, it should be added) coffee would not have become the ubiquitous drink that it is today.

For about a century, with steely determination transnational corporations have sought to procure and provide the cheapest coffee possible: price has driven their pursuit far more than flavor. Many buyers who work for these corporations hardly taste the coffees they purchase, and they do most of their purchasing on the basis of low prices that suddenly appear on their computer screens. They put more effort into managing their coffee supplies (including some purchasing of coffee on speculation) and developing skillful marketing strategies than they devote to appreciating the taste of coffee. Enjoying the taste is largely beside the point, and after a century of this, the result is that the people who plant and harvest the coffee have lost considerable income and the people who drink coffee have lost considerable quality, although the transnational corporations have been successful at keeping the prices of coffee low. Decades before the Big Mac became omnipresent, the coffee industry had accomplished its McDonaldization (Ritzer 1993) of the globe. The sad state of affairs to which this has led is that most consumers have no experience of what they are missing, and they are content with most low-cost morning coffees that are warm and look dark.

What happened to coffee may be accepted as a prototype for the stultifying alienation that can be produced by what the philosopher and turn-of-the-last-century sociologist Georg Simmel (Goodstein 2017, 154) has called "objective culture," which emerged along with the establishment of the money economy in the 19th century, especially at the end of that century. This alienation results from, and in fact requires, increasing distance from the lived experiences that produce coffee and to which this monograph is dedicated to describing. In the case of coffee, the experience of good-tasting coffee itself was lost amidst these mercantile policies, and, what is worse, it was forgotten.

In the USA, coffee drinking has been an enduring pastime that has completed four centuries. As Roden (1994, 8) observes, "America is . . . a country where once coffee was drunk at all times of the day, including before and during lunch, but where it was impossible ever to get a drinkable cup." For most of this period, the USA has been the world's largest consumer of coffee. Today, America drinks more than 300 million cups of coffee daily (Thorn 2006, 75), which, according to Tucker (2011, 18), represents 20% of the world's total coffee intake; historically, the USA was an even bigger player.

As mentioned, coffee drinking began with the Jamestown settlement in 1607. Because much of the water supply in early America was unhealthy, most people (including children) drank beer, even in the mornings; once coffee became widely available, it was recognized to be a superior substitute. The first coffee sales in Manhattan were in 1668, and coffee was served at Boston's "London Coffee House" in 1689, Boston's Gutteridge Coffee House in 1691, and New York's King's Arms in 1696 (Koehler 2017, 102). In the middle of the 18th century, England made a strategic shift to tea caused by (1) the war with Spain (1745–46), when coffee supplies were interrupted and the tea taxes were lowered, and (2) the British having a better monopoly with tea than with coffee, for which the Dutch competed successfully. America began drinking tea as well, but after England instituted a series of tax raises on tea, Bostonians responded by protesting tea, staging the Boston Tea Party in 1773, and it quickly became Americans' patriotic duty to return to the habit of drinking coffee. Americans did retain for their coffee the Dutch and English tea-drinking habit of adding milk and sugar, which is how this habit became so widespread in the USA, although it is not a widespread practice in most coffee-drinking countries. In 1825, seeds from Rio de Janeiro were taken to Hawaii, and coffee cultivation was begun there (Thorn 2006, 11).

For anyone interested in tasting coffee, what is important is that the early Americans always drank coffee that was *freshly* roasted. What coffee they did not roast themselves at home, those who lived in cities could buy freshly roasted from a corner grocery. Although Hollywood films never show the cowboys or wagon train migrants roasting their coffee, it is for certain that the coffee they carried across the plains was not pre-roasted in St. Louis. The plains of North America were too broad for that. There was usually green coffee in the saddlebags alongside the gold dust, and there is no doubt that that coffee always tasted fresh. Even John Wayne needed to grind his beans into coffee powder.

It was America's wars that made coffee drinking the national pastime it became. During the Revolutionary War, coffee was a symbol of resistance. During the Civil War, the North was able to import coffee while the South was not, and at the time some attributed the success of the Northern soldiers to the fact that they always drank coffee before their battles. Pendergrast (2010, 46–47) writes, "The Civil War gave soldiers a permanent taste for the drink. . . . Soldiers preferred to carry whole beans and grind them as needed. Each company carried a portable grinder." During World War II, the soldiers who were stuck in the trenches of France and Belgium became accustomed to drinking much coffee, a habit they brought home with them. And during World War II the use of instant coffee, developed in 1938, became commonplace; the returning soldiers socialized the rest of American coffee drinkers to accepting soluble coffee.

In 1864, John Arbuckle created the first branded coffee and sold it in paper bags in Pittsburgh, which was the beginning of standardized coffee. Grocers liked that it always tasted the same, since there were fewer complaints. From the very start of commercial coffee, sales relied on advertising and promotional skills more than on taste. Arbuckle's ads ridiculed the failed attempts of housewives who try to roast their own beans (Halevy 2011, 93). Roasting coffee is difficult, because one must convert the carbohydrates from the interior of the bean to sugars without burning the exterior of the bean; nevertheless, coffee today continues to be roasted at home in dozens of countries, but almost never in America's suburbia.

In 1865, Jim Folger began a coffee company in San Francisco, and mass production of coffee on the US west coast began. The post–Civil War period brought a boom to coffee drinking, as Northern soldiers brought home the habit to their families. "By 1876 the US was importing 240 million pounds of coffee annually, accounting for nearly a third of all coffee exported from producing countries" (Pendergrast 2010, 59); and "by the end of the nineteenth century, the US was consuming almost half of the world's coffee" (Pendergrast 2010, 42). Yet by the early 1880s, the quality of America's coffee had not yet decreased, and Americans, most of whom were purchasing their coffee from the corner store freshly roasted, could still recognize what good coffee should taste like. The early coffee entrepreneurs Caleb Chase and James Sanborn roasted their coffees by hand, ground it fine, and "compared it in the cup to another coffee with a fine reputation" (Pendergrast 2010, 52).

The demise of flavor accelerated with the invention of the vacuum can, pioneered by Hills Bros. in 1900 (Pendergrast 2010, 308). This made possible the mass production and distribution of coffee that could be kept in storage and on shelves for many months before its sale. Most importantly, and with the increase in the scale of production that it made possible, the cost could be kept low, and low cost has always been the most important influence on coffee sales everywhere. Coffee consumption grew, leading to a symbiotic relationship between the USA and Brazil, which in 1906 produced 82% of the global coffee supply (Tucker 2011, 60). Like the commercial production of branded and canned coffee in the USA, Brazil's production of coffee was implemented on massive scale, since its relatively flat plantation lands are suited to mechanization. Coffee was grown as a monoculture, which later proved problematic for the survival of Brazil's plants. Although Brazil ended slavery in 1888 (the last American nation to do so), slavery-like practices persisted, and many poor Italian workers fleeing the malaria-infected regions of Calabria and Sicily often worked as indentured laborers. Brazil became the premier producer of the world's coffee, and the USA the world's premier consumer.

In the USA, advertising replaced good flavor as the preferred way to sell coffee. In 1912, the J. Walter Thompson Agency in Manhattan mostly dismissed the importance of flavor and described the characteristics of a successful brand (e.g., Ivory Soap, Crisco, Cream of Wheat): "(1) high quality, (2) absolute uniformity, (3) an easily remembered name and trademark, (4) wide distribution, and as a result, (5) the product's purchase becomes 'an unconscious act—a national habit'" (Pendergrast 2010, 127). The agency also recognized that the ads must appeal primarily to women: "Even before a woman tastes it, she will have made up her mind that it is unusually good and that it is the coffee she has been looking for," which rendered tasting coffee beside the point, as was made clear in 1921, when the agency's account manager James Young conducted surveys of San Francisco and Chicago housewives that "revealed that 87% of the housewives cited *flavor* as the important factor in their brand choice. Yet 'it is extremely difficult for the average person to make clear distinctions where flavor is concerned.' Young concluded that although women might *think* they were buying flavor, they really sought social status" (Pendergrast 2010, 157). Perhaps it is time to reconsider Bourdieu. The conclusion was that taste-as-sense could be removed from the equation, while price remained critical.

By 1935, locally roasted and locally sold coffee had disappeared, and packaged ground coffee amounted to 90% of the US coffee sold (Tucker 2011, 151). It was a mass-produced and mass-consumed product, and its flavor suffered badly, but by then only the most elderly were able to recall what decent coffee should taste like. As Pendergrast sums up the situation, it is a story of "the abandonment of quality in favor of price-cutting and commodification" (Pendergrast 2010, xviii). The vice-chancellor of Italy's Slow Food university, Nicola Perullo (2016, 85), has argued, "Taste is formed through conditioning and interests, as a result of which we risk being manipulated, and food is likely to be considered a mere commodity."

Jon Thorn (2006, 74) describes the US coffee industry similarly: "The US market, concentrated in the hands of a few suppliers, was saturated with poor quality, cheap coffee." The situation between the World Wars was given a fitting epigram in the title of one of Pendergrast's (2010, 165) chapters: "Burning Beans, Starving Campesinos." And he comments, "By the end of World War II, American coffee has become a standardized product, a roasted and ground blend, based largely on average Brazilian beans" (Pendergrast 2010, 215). Price coffees (coffees that are sold by quantity and not by quality) overtook the coffee trade. Tasteless coffee experienced a further boom during the post–World War II period as giant global corporations mass-marketed coffee that was roasted many months before its purchase and sat on home shelves for months more because it was mostly bought many bags at a time during special sales ("three for the price of two"). It is not unusual for an American household to consume coffee even a year after it was roasted—a roasting done "several hundred pounds at a time on automated machines that require little human intervention" (Weissman 2008, 175).

Pendergrast summarizes M. F. K. Fisher's reporting in 1945: "It comes in uniform jars, which we buy loyally according to which radio program hires the best writers, so that whether the label is green or scarlet the contents are safely alike, safely middling." Pendergrast (2010, 215) reports that American "coffee went from 'safely middling' to awful within the next two decades." But those decades also brought forth the genius of American advertising, mostly on television, with jingles sung by every householder ("Head for the Hills! Head for the Hills Brothers Coffee!"), Mrs. Olson (a family favorite who spoke on behalf of Folgers Coffee), and the mascot who pioneered the future for the Marlboro Man and Dos Equis's Most Interesting Man in the World: the mule-leading Juan Valdez, who portrayed authentic Colombian coffee. The real genius of commodity capitalism is its capacity to offer the illusion of possessing a discriminating selectivity. Tucker (2011, 15) argues,

"The appearance of consumer choice obscures the behind-the-scenes control by just a few companies."

Nothing had changed by the 1960s, when Dutch coffee trader Alfred Peet arrived in the Folgers family headquarters of San Francisco Bay. Peet assessed the situation with accuracy: "Folgers bought lots of Brazils, Central American standards, and Robustas. I couldn't understand why in the richest country in the world they were drinking such poor-quality coffee. . . . People drank ten cups of that stuff a day. You knew it had to be weak. If you drank ten cups of strong coffee, you'd be floating against the ceiling" (Pendergrast 2010, 266). Peet, who developed his gustatory purview in Holland and not the USA, helped to initiate a rebellion against America's sub-quality standardized coffees, a rebellion that has led to what is known as the "second wave" and the "third wave" of USA coffee consumption; however, even though "specialty coffee" now possesses half of the USA market, which of the three waves will be victorious remains to be determined. The world's two largest exporters are the only two countries that have fully mechanized their coffee production—Brazil and Vietnam. Both of them have relatively flat tropical areas where automated planting, fertilizing, and picking can be done; this flatness comes partly at the cost of altitude, which means they do not grow mostly *Coffea arabica*, which is the denser, milder, and more tasty species of coffee. Instead they grow *Coffea canephora* var. *robusta* coffees, which usually have harsher flavors (with exceptions, most of which are naturally wild indigenous African Robusta varieties). The repeated warning that the world may run out of coffee because of the damage that global climate change is having upon coffee trees is perhaps overstated, for the reason that there will always be low-grown, often inferior mass-produced Robusta coffees. What the world may run out of is *good* coffee, but it seems that by the mid-1960s the USA had already run out of that, so perhaps few will notice.

Then came the explosion of instant coffee preparations and the advertising battles of the multinational corporations that produce them. It requires a huge investment to build a facility that can dehydrate coffee in a satisfactory way, so it was a natural place to inhabit for multinational corporations seeking monopolies. Soluble coffees were invented just prior to World War II, and the war proved to be a boon for their gaining acceptance. Since these coffees are tasteless anyway, it was the ideal destination for inexpensively purchased and inexpensively sold Robusta coffees. By the end of 1952, soluble coffee accounted for 17% of all US coffee consumption (Pendergrast 2010, 219). Weissman (2008, 3) summarizes, "By the time instant became the next new thing, American consumers were so acclimatized to bad coffee that they failed to notice the introduction of lower-quality beans from the far less expensive species called Robusta."

Americans were not the only people eager to sacrifice quality for convenience. In the 1970s, Britain and West Germany consumed two-thirds of Europe's instant coffee (Pendergrast 2010, 277). Instant coffee is a global phenomenon and is often the first coffee that nations that do not have longstanding traditions of coffee drinking will adopt, and some may not even know that alternatives exist. In Australia, for example, before the 1980s in most restaurants one could not order any coffee that was not instant. While today Australia can boast of some of the world's best-prepared coffee, before 1980 soluble coffees were ubiquitous. Azerbaijan in the 2020s is where Australia was in 1980 (Euromonitor International 2019), and even in many coffee-producing countries today Nescafé remains the default coffee. It is odd that "soluble coffee has become the trendy drink, a curious phenomenon which has overtaken many of the countries where people have a coffee tree in their back garden" (Roden 1994, 77). As I have described, I have been obliged to drink Nescafé in India while gazing at coffee trees in the garden. Advertisers boast about the *consistency* and *reliability* (those two traits perennially sought by coffee purveyors) of the flavors of instant preparations, and it is true that trying to brew "real" coffee with insufficiently hot water, incorrect brew times, leaving the coffee sitting on the stove too long, or, especially, the way that automatic percolators for decades subjected coffee grounds to severe punishment, all could render a soluble coffee preferable to real coffee. Regrettably, by the time the American percolator disappeared, Americans had forgotten the taste of real coffee.

America Defends its "Rights"

Pendergrast (2010, 348) has argued, "US citizens consider inexpensive coffee a birthright," and he chronicles the typically self-righteous American manner with which America defended its "right" to drink cheap, terrible-tasting coffee at the expense of poor Latin American *campesinos*. Ironically, even the most hardened Marxist will grow indignant at the notion of paying more than the barest minimum for their proletarian cup of coffee, which is often a price level that is insufficient to sustain a coffee industry or its workers.

During World War II, the USA signed the Inter-American Coffee Agreement, which guaranteed Latin American growers fair price levels, which would insure a steady supply of coffee for the troops, but in 1948 the USA allowed the agreement to expire (Pendergrast 2010, 216), leaving the growers to suffer the whims of manipulative markets. When the sacred right of a five-cent coffee rose to seven cents in 1948, "angry patrons broke mugs, stole silverware, and dumped cream and sugar on countertops in protest." In 1949, a bad drought in Brazil forced the seven-cent cup to rise to a dime, and the American political establishment, Democrats as well as as Republicans, became accusatory. Sen. Guy Gillette, an Iowa Democrat, directed his agricultural subcommittee to investigate coffee prices, calling coffee purveyors "manipulators" and "speculators" (Pendergrast 2010, 217). The Gillette Committee's 1950 report recommended hesitation in granting US government loans to coffee-producing countries and argued that the Marshall Plan should cease its purchasing of coffee. A severe frost in Brazil's prime coffee-growing area of Paraná in July of 1953 killed most of the trees in the region, and so matters only grew worse. When Americans found it more difficult to make Latin American growers and pickers shoulder most of the cost burden, US government opinion was that it must have been the work of communists. "President Eisenhower ordered the Federal Trade Commission to investigate coffee prices. In February, the US House of Representatives commenced coffee hearings [and] Maine Senator Margaret Chase Smith submitted a resolution suggesting that Communists must be behind the coffee price hike" (Pendergrast 2010, 227). Matters would grow much worse.

When Jacobo Arbenz Guzmán became president of Guatemala, which along with El Salvador and Nicaragua had truly predatory European plantation owners dominating their coffee industry, he handed over some former German coffee plantations to peasant cooperatives. American coffee industry giants (like General Foods, Standard Brands, Folger's, Hills Brothers, and A&P) joined with Nicaraguan President Somoza and the *Tea & Coffee Trade Journal* to accuse communist agitators of encouraging peasants to revolt. After the CIA, guided in part by the US ambassador John Peurifoy, overthrew Arbenz in 1954, and installed General Carlos Castillo Armas, this very modest agrarian reform was canceled. Armas himself was assassinated in 1957, Guatemala descended into three decades of civil war, including the brutal period of *los desaparecidos,* and chaos prevailed (Pendergrast 2010, 229–231). America has blood on its hands, and those who worked in the US coffee industry at the time are not to be excepted. As we will see in chapter 2, the events that occurred in El Salvador were equally horrific.

The American coffee monopolies grew, and lobbyists held influence in Washington. Brazil was also monopolistic, and in 1964, 1.6% of Brazil's *fazendas* owned more than half the cultivated land. The price of US coffee was kept low by using deteriorating blends of cheap Brazilians and African Robustas. Sympathy for the economic hardships of coffee workers and smaller growers developed during the Kennedy Administration, and the Alliance for Progress promoted an International Coffee Agreement that offered some protection against price fluctuations and manipulations, but the US Congress was skeptical, and it took three years for it to be ratified. Democratic Sen. Paul Douglas, a liberal hero, objected to the ICA implementation, fearing a rise in the price of his constituents' cup of coffee. It is ironic that today many American consumers are willing to purchase without complaint the mediocre coffee provided by K-cups for a price that equates to $40 per pound (Thorn 2006, 68), a willingness I attribute to the sunny, upbeat packaging and advertising of which the Keurig Company are masters. Only a third of that price would guarantee a livelihood for most Latin American coffee workers, provided that the chain of coffee production could be reorganized in an equitable way that shared profits.

Flavor Makes a Comeback

Perhaps it was inevitable, since coffee sometimes can speak for itself, but during the 1970s the natural flavor of good-tasting coffee somehow filtered through this morass of commodified coffee to a few coffee purveyors, who became amazed upon rediscovering the flavor of freshly roasted, good quality coffees. Alfred Peet was a pioneer, but other purveyors—many of them aging juvenile delinquents—figured out that they could make a good living providing tasty coffee to consumers, who were astonished by how coffee can be made to taste. Since both pride and profit could be served, decent coffee began to make a comeback. As Tucker (2011, 144) remarks, "The latest craze in coffee focuses on finding the most flavorful coffee beans."

Standardized, mass-produced coffee is sometimes referred to as "the first wave" of American coffee (as we have described, there were two centuries of coffee drinking before it). The wave inaugurated by Peets and Starbucks, which is based upon using high-quality but over-roasted Arabica coffee, is called "the second wave," and it changed the face of American coffee drinking. The chairman of Starbucks, Howard Schultz, discovered in Italy that coffee consumers sought not only good-tasting coffee but also some warm sociality, and so he provided his customers a pseudo-community experience. In a mainstream American fashion, the community was mass-produced as well. A "third wave" of coffee drinking rejected the McDonaldization disseminated by Starbucks and preferred quality coffee that was roasted lightly enough to allow delicate flavors untreated by flavorings to reach the drinker. A talented coffee purveyor, Nick Cho, writes (Halevy 2011, 19), "The first wave is all about consumption. The second wave is about enjoyment. . . . The third wave . . . is all about appreciating each coffee for what it truly is and takes whatever necessary steps to highlight the amazing unique character in every coffee." This conforms with Perullo's (2018b, 15–16) solution: "Decolonizing means . . . inconspicuously ridding oneself of the shell of 'good taste' as an invading colonization, in order to arrive, disarmed, at the less cultivated uplands where taste and goodness happen at the moment." Albeit belated, American coffee is finally giving some priority to taste. Of course, the three-wave metaphor is not applicable universally and reflects only the recent history of coffee in the USA; as we have seen, each nation has cultivated its own cultural relationship with coffee. But in the short run, the quality of America's coffees is improving: "The best coffees are in demand. Even commercial brand roasters have upgraded their coffees" (Roden 1994, 9).

Chapter 2

Coffee's Chain of Production

> An investigation of communication along the coffee chain requires not *an* ethnography but an ethnography of *each* position on the chain.

The coffee chain of production, a.k.a. "the supply chain," "the value chain," or (in Italian) *la filiera*, is a key notion in the coffee industry that attempts to make more comprehensible the complex relations of producing, purveying, roasting, marketing, etc. coffee around the world. The coffee chain represents a filament of social and commercial relations by which raw coffee travels from the laborers who plant the seedlings to the final consumer, even though the people who occupy many of the intermediate positions in the chain are invisible to each other. The coffee chain is partly an imaginary gloss that necessarily simplifies its representation of social and commercial relations, yet the importance to the coffee industry of this metaphor is made evident by the focused energy and respect with which coffee purveyors always speak its name, whether that name is "the chain of production," *la filiera*, *la cadena* (Spanish), or the often-repeated reference, "from seed to cup." The Specialty Coffee Association (in a mass email dated October 19, 2020) has developed an initiative to replace the metaphor of "chain" with that of "map" in order to recognize "that the interaction of the parts is not static, but dynamic and fluid" and that there are too many individual actors to be represented within the limited space of a "chain." Either metaphor works adequately for providing an initial point of reference for the many things taking place in the production of this global commodity.

There are 25 million smallholder coffee-producing households in 60 or more developing countries, who grow more than 90% of the world's coffee (McKenna 2020, 7), and another 100 million people who depend upon coffee for their livelihood (Tucker 2011, 15). No matter how one composes a

48 | Tasting Coffee

model for the chain, some of these people will be left out. As Peter Giuliano, Chief Research Officer of the Specialty Coffee Association, warns, "The coffee chain is complex." Other researchers have identified missing links and absent constituencies in these representations. The chain I have drawn is not necessarily the best one, but it will assist us while we navigate through the maze of coffee production:

The Coffee Chain

Planters and Pickers
|
Farm Managers
|
Farm Owners
|
Tasting Consultants (or Employees)
|
Wholesale Brokers
|
Exporters
|
Importers
|
Roasters (incl. Blenders and Tasters)
|
Cafés (Bars)
|
Baristas
|
Consumers

Studying the Chain

Sociologists sometimes point out that unlike rocks and stars, the object of study for social scientists—society—exists only in the imagination of the people who live together (Collins and Makowsky 1972). The notion "society" is an invention like other notions such as "history" and "evolution," developed during the 18th and 19th centuries. While it is a useful explanatory concept, it is an imaginary one. In the same way, the "chain of production" in the coffee industry is not a substantive thing but only a way to think about the relations in the coffee trade; no matter how one designs it, some things will be missing. As an icon for the industry, it represents some of the remarkable collaborations that support humanity's favorite beverage.

The Specialty Coffee Association sponsors an extensive series of courses in coffee production, including courses on tasting. Their "GE 103 Introduction to Cupping" course has a handbook that offers guidance to the course instructor and emphasizes the importance of the coffee chain, explaining it by relating it to "traceability." Traceability, another key notion, has itself achieved mythical status in the industry; in particular, it helps to organize and motivate those who work with specialty coffees. The GE 103 course handbook cites traceability as the first of four purposes of cupping, and it advises the instructor to discuss "how communication of objective coffee analysis flows in the seed-to-cup chain. State how objective taste evaluation of coffee is communicated in each link of the seed-to-cup chain." That is a tall order. While the other three purposes of "cupping" coffee—price discovery, creating blends, and purchasing decisions—are important, the meme "the seed-to-cup chain" stands out as a central theme.

Memes are fundamental for organizing any community. "Traceability" functions to motivate coffee purveyors and drinkers, even while it falls short of fact. A sacrosanct status in the culture of coffee purveying causes it to function as a mytheme; nevertheless, it plays an important role in organizing the modern coffee industry, and it offers direction for dedicated coffee professionals seeking to reform the industry. What is being traced? The coffee beans are being traced, from the cup back to their source. This is sometimes not easy to do, even with the development of blockchain technology, because for economic reasons the activities and decisions at some of the stages of the coffee chain are kept concealed. Most bags of coffee one purchases do not bear an indication of where they come from, and when one asks the people who serve coffee in the cafés where their coffee comes from, most of them do not know, perhaps because the coffee that is placed in sealed bags is collected from different places and the blend under any given label keeps changing in order to keep up with the available supplies of coffees.

In their guidance for cupping coffee, the GE 103 course handbook also advises, "Having a consistent protocol is the first step to analyze coffee as objectively as possible." The protocol is an instrument of objectification. Why is objectivity important? For clear communication. The SCA emphasizes that communication along the chain of production is important and recognizes that objectivity is connected with communication. At some nodes of the chain the communication is limited, which has important consequences for the goal of objectivity in the global industry.

For objectivity and for communication, a common language and a common perspective are required. Of course, "objectivity" is nearly as indeterminate a notion as "society"; it is used in many ways and plays different roles in many language games. As well as being a policy recommendation for reliable thinking and analysis, its iconic status in modern culture has made it a cultural myth, one that is an important component of the definition of modernity itself. The GE 103 handbook's inclusion of the phrase "as objectively as possible" amounts to an acknowledgment that objectivity is a guiding aim rather than an easily achieved and immobile end-state, following which everyone can finally take some rest. Objectivity is essential for attaining secure, dependable knowledge, and it provides a foundation for clear communication. But we need to be clear with ourselves about just what we mean when we employ the term. Among the varieties of objectivity and strategies for attaining it is a policy for using objectivity that awards value to self-understanding as our thinking is developing, and also to continuous criticism of just how the selected methodology and protocol we are employing is biasing our vision and our conclusions. Absent continuous self-criticism and peer review, any methodology we have developed for implementing our aim to be "as objective as possible" can suffocate both the phenomenon and ourselves; we can afford no time-out from self-reflective scrutiny.

When this research began, I realized I needed to pay attention to communication about taste that takes place at each node between each pair of positions on the chain of production (e.g., between owners and tasting consultants, between importers and exporters, between baristas and consumers, etc.). Each node featured some communication about taste, but the nature of that communication and the objectivity that adjacent coffee purveyors produced to facilitate it varied across the nodes of the chain. I quickly discovered that a sociological investigation of communication along the coffee chain required not *an* ethnography but an ethnography of *each* position on the chain. Many ethnographies were required, so I attempted this, which is what extended the project beyond a few years to more than a decade. As with everything else in the world, the situation proved to be more complicated than expected, just as Giuliano warned.

Inequalities in the Chain

It is not a main objective of this book to carefully investigate the inequalities that exist along the coffee chain. But I would not be a responsible sociologist if I did not offer an acknowledgment of some astonishing inequities that exist with various positions in the chain. The industry sometimes refers to this chain as "the value chain" because every group at each stage necessarily adds a fee to cover their costs and to provide a livelihood. Industry members have devised various charts that describe the costs that purveyors at each position face, costs that place tangible limitations upon how "reasonable" or "fair" any pricing can be. Growers must pay for wages, fertilization, transport, etc.; café owners must pay for their mortgage, swizzle sticks and napkins, dishwashers, utility bills; everyone must pay taxes, and so on. The result is that in 2016 the export value for producing countries was about 10% of the profits in the coffee retail market (Quiñones-Ruiz 2020, 2).

Given the history of exploitation in the production of coffee, it is natural for each occupant of these positions to develop some mistrust of the other ones, and also for farmers to be astonished when they learn how small a percentage of the price that a consumer pays for a cup coffee finds its way to them. When a coffee-producing country introduces a minimum wage law to guarantee coffee laborers a decent living, that does not relieve the owner of the need to calculate those expenses, and if the costs exceed the income than can be derived from sales, they must sell the farm, quite literally. With the growth of leaf rust (*roya*), "Farmers in Latin America must now also bear the cost of spraying their trees with fungicide five or six times a year to have any hope of keeping ahead of the leaf rust" (Dunn 2019), but this may not make it into the price determination in New York or London. Similarly, most coffee growers may not be thinking of swizzle sticks, but the café owners need to provide them just the same. Each person sometimes thinks they are the sole focal point of the chain. Given this situation, some coffee purveyors became angry with me when I asked them questions about the essential fairness of the distribution of profits along the coffee chain. I once asked the owner of an upscale café if he thought that coffee would be able to survive the end of slavery and slavery-like practices, and he nearly threw me out of his building. But that does not change the reality that the dollars that are in play during negotiations at the consuming end of the chain turn into pennies at the growers' end, and all too frequently the losers have been the farm laborers. Maria Hill (2014) comments about this:

> The only person in this process that is truly subjected to the whims of the market is the farmer. If a roaster suddenly increases their price on wholesale coffee, the retailer has the option to raise menu prices. If a roaster is told by their importer to expect a cost increase, the roaster has the option to raise prices for their wholesale customers. If the cost of production suddenly goes up for a coffee farmer, they have few to no options, because the selling price for coffee is determined by an average market price.

It would be delusory to think that the situation is improving in any significant way. Tucker (2011, 33) has reported, "The proportion of profits retained by producing nations has fallen substantially in the past 20 years." At the vast majority of coffee *fincas*, *fazendas*, and plantations I have visited, owners proudly show me the housing they have built for their workers, the installation of satellite dishes for them, internet, schoolhouses for the children, etc., and so one cannot use broad brushes to characterize this history, but the story of coffee renders absurd any outrage displayed by first-world coffee purveyors regarding the notion that there could exist anything like a slavery-like practice in the world of coffee.

Thorn (2006, 123) describes a situation that is worsening: "Through the 1970s and 1980s, producing countries had retained around 20 percent of the total income. . . . By 1995, the proportion obtained by producing countries fell to 13 percent. . . . By 2002 coffee farmers received about 2 percent of the cost of a cup of coffee sold in a coffee shop." Globalization has brought few benefits to cherry pickers and small producers. A small farmer in Mexico confessed his low expectations to Jaffe (2014, 241), who recounts, "All that they dare to hope for is a market that would return them 4% of what the consumer pays, rather than the 2% they now receive." The situation is somewhat better with "fair trade" coffee, but not by a great deal (the individual farmer usually receives between 5% and 10% of the retail price; Jaffe 2014, 25). Given the fact that throughout its history coffee has traveled "hand in hand with colonialism" (Tucker 2011, 40), it is ridiculous for an occupant of any position on the coffee chain to deny the existence of inequalities. Especially, it is important to recognize, as Tucker (2011, xv) does, that there is "a history of agony hidden in each cup."

The number of slaves who went to Brazil was much greater than the 500,000 slaves who came to the USA. In what is one of the major tragedies in the history of humanity, "Over the span of 200 years, three million slaves were brought to work on Brazil's coffee plantations, and another five million for sugarcane" (Halevy 2011, 127). Coffee earned its ubiquitous status as the global beverage on the backs of these slaves. Coffee production was also a tragedy for the social and cultural life of countries that never had slavery. El Salvador began growing coffee after slavery was outlawed. Coffee production in that country increased in part due to the colonialist efforts of James Hill of Manchester, England, who went to El Salvador in 1871, where he established 18 plantations. He lobbied the government to privatize the natural species of food that the nearby Indians depended on, making the Indians subject to arrest and imprisonment (worse was to come) for trespass when they persisted in eating foods for which they had been foraging for centuries (Sedgewick 2020, 158–174). Hill systematically removed all trees and plants that provided the Indians nutrition naturally (fruit trees, avocados, tomatoes, etc.) and punished any Indians who ate food from plants he had not removed. When hunger drove the Indians to become indentured or low-paid laborers in Hill's coffee fields, Hill obtained the low-cost labor he required. Having spent four months in El Salvador, I can report that if you mention to anyone in El Salvador that there was no slavery in that country, most Salvadorans will laugh wryly or look at you as if you are demented, for there is no doubt that the brutality that Salvadorans have suffered at the hands of the coffee barons equaled the suffering of any nation that had slavery.

In recent years, there is more concern about the situation of workers. Coffee purveyors, large and small, have sometimes been more effective than governments at teaching growers how to increase their profits and improve the quality of their crop. Even under the Sandinistas, ENCAFE, the official Nicaraguan coffee agency, paid producers only 10% of the international market price, which was not sufficient to permit the growers to pay their workers decent wages (Pendergrast 2010, 317–318). International organizations like World Coffee Research have allied with agronomists to construct grassroots programs of experimental plots to find coffee plants that are more resistant to disease, more prolific, or better tasting, and this has provided tangible benefits to many farms. Some third-world nations have instituted minimum wage regimes, but sometimes this has led to reduced hiring, since these increased labor costs have not been factored into the commodity pricing regimes in New York and London. Around the world, these low price levels have made it impossible for some small producers to keep growing coffee, and some larger landholders are selling their plantations to land developers. In 1992, small producers in Mexico experienced a 70% drop in income, and many abandoned their coffee plots, except for growing enough coffee for family consumption (Jaffe 2014, 43).

In many countries, cooperatives have been organized to assist smaller farmers with improving growing practices, better marketing, and higher price levels, but cooperatives can have their troubled relations with coffee laborers as well, yet they do present a qualitatively different situation from that of large landholders and, in some cases, they are quicker to experiment with social policies and economic relations that have been developed to remedy inequalities. The problem is that most of the remedies have fallen short of the ideals that motivated those who developed them. It seems that attempts to restructure economic relations in a way that allows more money to flow to poorer workers will face strong headwinds if they are partly at the expense of the more affluent occupants of the value chain.

Remedies for Inequities

Sections of the coffee industry have responded to the needs of farm workers and small farmers with some sympathy, and this even includes larger coffee purveyors like Illy Coffee and Starbucks; however, some of the largest multinationals have given the inequities of the coffee value chain little more than lip-service. Coffee industry initiatives for remedying problems have addressed fair trade, environmental sustainability, organic farming, and direct trade, but the results have not yet been remarkable. The largest of these efforts, fair trade, had perhaps the most promise, but as Geoff Watts (2013) sums up the situation concisely, the fair-trade movement was "hijacked by multinationals." Tucker (2011, 146) offers a more academic version of this assessment: "The history of the fair-trade movement shows that even a committed and dynamic social-justice movement can be distorted by the structural arrangements and neoliberal rationality of the modern world economic system that prioritizes market efficiencies and profit maximization."

No matter what pricing system or fair-trade policy is at work, multinational corporations like Procter & Gamble, Kraft (Maxwell House), Starbucks, and others will find ways to subvert it to their advantage. Multinational corporations even argue that they have a legal responsibility to do so, since they have fiduciary responsibilities to their investors. It has become evident that the larger a coffee plantation is, the easier it is to gain certification that one is operating in compliance with fair-trade standards. The process of certification necessarily requires a bureaucracy to ensure to the buyer (ultimately, the consumer who chooses to purchase a Fair Trade–labeled product) that there has been compliance with the aims of the initiative, and small farmers and cooperatives find it more difficult to navigate that bureaucracy than do larger landholders and multinational corporations. Most of the foreign inspectors required for making the necessary on-site certification (for fair-trade, sustainable, organic, bird-friendly, etc.) charge rates commensurate with the salaries they must be paid in Europe and the USA, which exceed the capabilities (and sometimes the imagination) of smaller farmers, and so the farmers who need support the most are often unable to avail themselves of the system. As Tucker (2011, 142) explains, "Unexpectedly, fair trade itself has exacerbated inequity by excluding the most disadvantaged farmers."

Some multinational coffee purveyors have employed a strategy of purchasing a small percentage of their green coffee via the fair-trade system, while keeping the majority of their purchases outside the system. This allows them to advertise their cooperation and brag about their support for fair trade without having to participate in a way that would be truly transformative. Governing bodies of international initiatives are cognizant of the importance of getting multinational corporations on board with the program, so they permit this tokenism, thinking that it is a door that will lead to expanded participation by multinationals. The alternative would be to operate a program that affected such a tiny percentage of the world's green coffee purchases that it would be tantamount to not having an effective program. In this way, large companies making minimal fair-trade purchases can receive as much credit as do movement-oriented businesses who deal exclusively in fair-trade products (Jaffe 2014, 31); moreover, these tokenist fair-trade purchases of large companies do not undermine these companies' ability to offer their coffee at price levels that undercut the prices that companies must receive when they purchase 100% of their coffee from the fair-trade system.

The fair-trade systems make little distinction made between movement-oriented companies and profit-oriented companies, and this works to undermine the enthusiasm of smaller companies who are more committed to remedying inequities. Moreover, when a distinction is made, it can be to the disadvantage of movement-oriented companies. For example, Fairtrade Labelling Organizations International insists that producer organizations open their books for scrutiny; however, they "at the same time allow Procter &

Gamble to keep its books closed and obscure the actual percentage of its purchases that occur on fair-trade terms, on the grounds that such information constitutes a trade secret, a blatant double standard that misleads consumers and makes a mockery of the system's values" (Jaffe 2014, 254).

Another strategy that multinational corporations employ is to bypass the Fairtrade Labelling Organizations process altogether and erect their own alternative system that can provide them with a pseudo-certification. In a process that is too complicated for the average coffee consumer to follow, "Walmart created 'The Sustainability Consortium' and its badge 'Made by Sustainable Leaders.' Its members include Nestlé, JM Smuckers, Monsanto, Dow Chemical, and Dupont. To place the badge on their products, companies pay a membership fee, but Walmart requires no verification that products meet any sustainability criteria" (Tucker 2011, 135). Tucker jests, "While it is unclear whether fair trade is transforming transnational corporations it certainly appears that transnational corporations are transforming fair trade."

Other more legitimate labeling and certification regimes have been set up by Rainforest Alliance and consortiums concerned about organic farming and other environmental matters (e.g., bird-friendly), but they come with complicated bureaucracies, which favor farmers large enough to hire an accountant or lawyer. As Pendergrast (2010, 365) points out, much organic coffee comes from poverty-stricken smallholders whose coffee is organic by default, since they cannot afford fertilizers or pesticides. Since they probably cannot afford proper pruning and processing either, their coffees are not always the best ones; moreover, most of them are not certified as organic. It is possible, on the other hand, for organic certification to be given to large landholders who devote only a portion of their plantations to organic methods. In this way, growers who are less organic are able to gain some certification while farmers who grow exclusively organic are not, which distorts the situation. It should be noted that while organic growing is healthy for relieving problems of soil depletion, I have been tasting organic coffees for decades and can report that it has little relationship with the taste quality of the beans. Organic growing is only one of many factors that go into producing a coffee's flavor (as we will learn in chapter 5), and while with every food crop the quality of the soil is the origin of good taste and good nutrition, organic management is only one of many assets that contribute to a given soil's character. The term "organic" has become a meme itself, and while coffee consumers sometimes drink their memes with enthusiasm, it is a cultural value that may not be understood in the same way by the small communities who live on tropical hillsides. One Mexican agent working on certification called international organic certification "a class of ecological neo-colonialism" (Jaffe 2014, 152).

Well-motivated and progressive industry purveyors may set themselves up to sell coffee that is grown organically, or by cooperatives, but there are small producers who consider this to be "interference" (Tucker 2011, 140) in that it is a paternalistic imposition of values that have originated from the global North. Further, first-world coffee purveyors have long idealized or romanticized the experience of third-world producers: "Another problem arises in the images used to market fair trade goods—often showing happy, exotic people whose dress indicates clear contrasts with Western culture, suggesting a naiveté. Such images reinforce stereotypes, misrepresent people's diversity and struggles, and implicitly reproduce the systemic inequities that create poverty" (Tucker 2011, 141). Here is where better communication is really needed.

To an extent, this better communication is occurring in the increasing face-to-face contacts that are taking place in the emerging world of specialty coffees. Effective initiatives have been undertaken by purveyors of higher-priced coffee; again, Illy and Starbucks are included, but more importantly there are many new commercial relations being established by a wide range of smaller specialty roasters from nearly every city of the USA, whose staff make what are cultural as well as commercial pilgrimages to farms and *fincas* around the world. They are developing an extensive network of direct trade relationships with coffee producers. Also called "relationship coffees" (Quiñones-Ruiz 2020, 2) or "value added markets," these first-world purveyors guarantee premium prices to growers who can learn and apply the best processing practices in order to produce coffees that are able to qualify as specialty-grade. What is more, by eliminating two or three levels of coffee brokers, a larger percentage of these higher prices can be retained by the growers. Illy has sent its staff to Colombia and to India to teach better processing techniques to their producers and to dissuade farmers from simply mixing their coffees in piles; Illy even started running competitions, offering higher prices for small lots of excellent coffees. Starbucks has taught better processing techniques to their producers in El Salvador, maintaining long-term relations with most of their growers, to whom they pay a premium for superior processed coffees. Some independent specialty coffee purveyors, like Willem Boot of California, have set up their own programs that operate independently of the standard coffee marketers. Boot has gone to Ethiopia to run classes for growers and laborers who live in small villages in northwestern Ethiopia, teaching them how to cup their coffees so that they themselves can identify the tastes that the specialty coffee industry is seeking; and he also runs the annual Gesha Village Auction, which obtains for the farmers the highest prices possible. This is the direction in which a genuine solution to the prevailing inequities is located.

The specialty coffee movement has a unique role to play because instead of using the nearly century-old Fordist (i.e., mass-produced and mass-marketed) model of selling tasteless coffee at the lowest possible prices, they are using a model of selling coffee that features extraordinary flavors at higher price levels. While specialty coffee costs more to produce and the yields are smaller, higher price levels can cover the additional costs. Roasters also face higher risks when they purvey more expensive coffee, for the reason that when the roasting of a micro-lot of expensive specialty coffee goes wrong, which can happen when roasting the first batches of a new season or origin, "a lot of very expensive coffee goes up in smoke" (Weissman 2008, 176), so the roasters need to raise their prices as well in order to cover these losses. The idea of higher coffee prices has met with market resistance, especially when facing the widespread American sentiment that inexpensive coffee is a basic right: even coffee drinkers who are politically conservative are champions of proletarian coffee. However, it is the idea of the Specialty Coffee Association that one solution to the inequities in coffee's value chain is to charge coffee drinkers higher prices. Despite market resistance, the market share held by specialty coffee has been rising steadily. Thorn (2006, 74) summarizes the situation comprehensively: "Although in general the United States is not a nation of quality coffee drinkers, there is a large and growing market for specialty coffees," which now make up some 27% of the global supply for washed Arabica (Quiñones-Ruiz 2020, 2).

As we will learn, there are all kinds of ways to classify coffee. In the roughest terms, there are two kinds of coffee that are sold on the world market: commodity coffee and specialty coffee. Sometimes coffee purveyors refer to the former as price coffees and the latter as quality coffees. This division excludes substandard coffees that are sold in the domestic markets of producing countries or made into soluble (instant) and decaffeinated coffees. Typically, the best specialty coffees are high-grown, where the colder climate produces beans that have dense cellular structures. Not only do they contain more cells per bean, there is less open space between each cell. These require much care when roasting because one must convert all of the carbohydrates in the interior of the bean into sugars without burning the bean's surface. Lower-grown coffee that has fewer cells per bean and more spacing is chosen for processing with flavorings (vanilla, hazelnut, etc.) because there is space for the flavoring to enter and saturate the bean. While many consumers favor these flavored coffees, doing so guarantees that they will be drinking poorer-quality coffees. A better strategy would be to purchase high-quality beans and then add to one's cup a quality flavoring of one's choice (think Starbucks). Again, pricing levels will deter consumers who prioritize low prices.

Another way to divide coffees that are marketed internationally is to classify the coffees that have high acidity (often with notes of citrus) separately from the softer or rounder coffees that often feature chocolate-like notes. Specialty coffees frequently have higher acidity, although not always. The acidity comes from the bean and from the roasting—a lighter level of roast will preserve the flavors of a specialty coffee and along with them the acidity (it also better preserves the caffeine). Drinkers who dislike acidity will seek medium-dark roasts that in the better coffees tend toward natural chocolate-like, nutty, or vanilla-like flavors. Over-roasted coffee tends to taste bitter, but opinion differs about what is over-roasting.

Coffees are also divided according to how the cherry that covers the bean was de-pulped. "Washed coffees" receive a processing that completely removes the sugary fruit pulp from the beans. They present bright, clean flavors and are more "reliable" in that they are less likely to be transformed by fermentation or have defects, and it is easier to reproduce the same flavor profile from one harvest to the next. "Natural coffees" are sun-dried on the ground or on raised beds, and then the dried cherries are removed mechanically. They feature deeper-toned flavors, sometimes earthy and sometimes fruity or flower-like (floral flavors derive from the maturation of the enzymes in the coffee), much of which is the result of fortuitous fermentations. While all coffees gain some of their flavor from the fermentation, natural coffees and "honey-processed" coffees (a process that is midway between washed and natural, in that the cherry is removed but the super-sweet mucilage that surrounds the green bean is left) acquire additional flavors from the more extensive fermentation they experience. Washed coffees are safer coffees because the fermentation process is less likely to go awry (another source of expense), and while there are natural coffees that even the most conservative coffee buyer will appreciate, some natural coffees can become so funky that only an enthusiast will prefer them. On the other hand, lovers of naturally processed coffees sometimes express the opinion that while many washed coffees are indeed "clean," that is all they are, since the washing can bleach out much of the taste. Some lack complexity and possess little flavor that can become evident after the taints are cleaned away.

The important consideration for farmers is that specialty coffees that are directly traded can produce decent incomes. One grower in Guatemala who worked closely with Intelligentsia Coffee was given a base price that was 25% higher than what even Fair Trade certification was offering, plus a series of bonuses for coffees that could receive cupping scores higher than 85 (Weissman 2008, 73). Before that can happen, the coffee must actually possess tastes that are excellent enough for consumers to be willing to pay more for them. Intelligentsia and similar "third-wave" coffee purveyors, and some "second-wave" purveyors, discovered that they needed to train the producers on the farms how to "cup" their coffees. Pendergrast (2010, 353) reports, "Starbucks' Farmer Support Centers first opened in San Jose, Costa Rica, in 2004. The company realized that it needed to teach farmers to cup their own roasted beans." During the century-long regime of producing "price" coffees, few growers devoted much effort to learning the tastes of the coffees they grew. Old habits die hard, so the growers who are learning the proper way to cup coffees are often younger members of a coffee-growing family. Not only are these younger members eager to learn how to cup, they are proud to be able to contribute to the financial well-being of their family, and the family is pleased that their next generation is willing to carry on the family's tradition rather than run off to the city. This "win-win-win-win" situation (younger producers, older producers, first-world purveyors, and third-world consumers) has made training producers how to cup into a transformative event in the history of consuming coffee. It may surprise the reader, but a grower's tasting all of the coffees that one grows and sells is one of the most significant developments in the history of commercial coffee.

All of this comes with a warning. As soon as the multinational corporations saw that there were profits to be made in this way, they were attracted to the specialty coffee industry. Rather than develop their own programs of teaching growers to process and taste their coffees, multinational corporations have simply tried to buy up the specialty coffee start-ups. Unlike software start-ups, most of these coffee entrepreneurs did not develop their businesses with the intention of selling it to a high bidder; nevertheless, the financial rewards of selling their business to one or another multinational corporation have proven irresistible, and many of the best specialty purveyors are now subdivisions of globalized companies. These multinational companies are more successful at packaging and marketing than they are at purveying quality coffee: sometimes one will find "Rwanda!" in two-inch red type, "Single-Origin" posted across the cover of the bag, and a blue-ribbon of some sort of certification on the rear of the package, etc., all of which offer suggestions of authenticity without possessing any. Global companies are even using the term "direct-trade" on their packages, undermining conscientious consumers' faith in the reliability of the term. Everything can become a marketing tool.

While such labeling attracts purchases, disappointment is frequently the result. Just as the "counter-culture" of the late 1960s was quickly purchased by clothiers and record companies, the high aims of the third-wave coffee entrepreneurs risk suffering a similar destiny, and it is uncertain whether the newly found good flavors of specialty coffees will survive or whether global coffee capitalism will for a second time kill the taste of coffee.

The Pricing Solution

The controls that global centers for the exchange of coffee have been able to exercise over pricing mechanisms in the coffee trade have been too successful. They have managed to keep price levels so low that many farmers, large and small, are unable to operate in the black. While it is second nature for capitalist markets to squeeze suppliers, what has not been factored into the present system are the effects of climate change, which has led to coffee diseases like the leaf rust that have increased fertilization expenses, insect infestations that require pesticides, more challenging conditions for the *Coffea arabica* that requires cool growing habitats, and increased labor costs. During 2020, coffee traded at New York spot prices in the range of $1 per pound, and often coffee was selling below a dollar. Betty Adams, the proprietor of a 412-acre farm in western Guatemala, explains that coffee would have to fetch about $8 more per pound to enable farmers to pay their workers the current US minimum wage of $7.25 an hour (Pendergrast 2010, 348). The dire situation presented to small farmers is well represented by this testimony of a 38-year-old Mexican cooperative coffee farmer: "I kept track of all my expenses, and I lost half of what I invested! Next year I won't harvest it all . . . only a little bit, honestly" (Jaffe 2014, 101). That "little bit" will be for providing her family and a few friends with their coffee needs, and little more than that.

A longer-term problem is becoming more likely: price levels may be kept so low that so many farms will go out of business that there will be insufficient coffee to meet world demand. It prompts one to be reminded of Marx's observation in *Capital* that it will be capitalism's success that will lead to its failure. If that happens, the likely solution will be to depend upon the old standby of mass-produced, poor-tasting coffee, in this case mostly Robusta coffees, since they are better able to tolerate the warmer climates that will come. Geoff Watts believes that any price under $2 per pound for green specialty coffee is not sustainable, and that level has surely risen since he made his observation in 2013. The more that the price of coffee falls, the more deforestation there will be, because the plantations that are sold will be converted to tourism developments (in the case of larger coffee growers) or be clear-cut to allow a small farmer to grow corn (Jaffe 2014, 141). Weissman (2008, 174) quotes Shari Bagwell of Stumptown Coffee: "Many farmers in Guatemala are planting sugar for ethanol because it is easier to grow and sugar prices are increasing. If we can't increase what the farmers earn, there won't be any coffee farms left in Central America."

Plantations that are sold to land developers often become vacation homes for the wealthy who live in nearby cities, or they become mountain resort centers that serve tourists. The newly deforested hillsides that result will contribute further to global warming. In a further irony, many of the tourist industry firms who purchase coffee plantations end up marketing their resorts as "ecotourism," taking advantage of the romance of coffee after its growing has been abandoned. I have witnessed such resorts in the mountains outside of San Salvador and in the Kodagu mountains adjacent to Mysore District in India. It should be noted that growing coffee is hard work. Not only must the plants be husbanded continuously, one's labor force requires daily consideration, world markets must be monitored regularly, and there is always a fear of crop failure or environmental calamity. There is no point in committing that much energy when the chance of making a profit, or even breaking even, is remote. Rachel Peterson of Finca La Esmeralda offers a justifiable lament: "When buyers fight us for pennies, they never think that they're taking money from our pickers. But they are. There's just not enough to go around. If producers don't cover costs, you know social programs go first" (Weissman 2008, 154). And Wilford Lamastus of a neighboring Panamanian *finca* reported to me in 2019 that no coffee farmer besides those who are growing high-end specialty coffees can make a profit during the reigning pricing regime, except for the Brazilian plantations that are so highly mechanized they can make a few pennies profit on each pound of the vast quantities of cherries they harvest.

The pricing dilemma has left these choices: sustain the profits of the multinational corporations, divert more of those profits to coffee growers, or charge more for each cup of coffee. The coffee industry likes the last possibility best, but that leaves open the question of who will benefit most from any increase. History tells us that it is not unlikely that those who need the benefit the most, the small coffee producers, will be the last ones to benefit. By the time each occupant of the coffee chain has taken their cut of any increased income, it is possible that not much will be left for the coffee workers who inhabit the earliest stages of the chain.

PART II

Objectivity and Its Labors

There is some coffee stuck in the grinder, always.

—Dr. Manuel Diaz

Chapter 3

Historical and Epistemological Bases of Objectivity

Interpretation, understanding, and objectivity belong together.
—Günter Figal (2010, 121)

A Historical Account of Objectivity

In their 500-page-long treatise on the historical foundations of objectivity, Lorraine Daston and Peter Galison (2007, 375) observe, "There was epistemology before (and after) the advent of objectivity, there were selves before and after the emergence of subjectivity." As any social scientist will tell you, "objectivity" and "subjectivity" are sociohistorical achievements. How did this talented pair come to be, when did they arrive, and why are they almost always found in tandem? There was a long history of "knowers and knowing" (Daston and Galison 2007, 376) before the emergence of objectivity in the 19th century, but this dualism of the knower and what-is-known has dominated the court of European reason since Kant. Early in the 20th century, some proposed that a solution to establishing objectivity might lie in *excluding* the knower, while retaining the known. Of course, not a few philosophers objected to the idea that this could be science. From its beginning, the notion of objectivity has been a revolving mixture of morality, metaphysics, and methodology.

Daston and Galison (2007, 380) identify several of the abiding features of objectivity. First, it is always opposed to subjectivity. It is significant to note that being opposed is really another form of coupling, and so subjectivity will remain present even when it is exiled. As the contemporary German philosopher Günter Figal (2010, 237) has noted, "Every position belongs together with other positions . . . [and] the one who is excluded belongs no less than the one who we take to be 'one of us.'" Without subjectivity, it is likely that no one could develop a clear idea of what objectivity is; objectivity gains its status mostly at the expense of subjectivity, and so it is not independent of it. Objectivity sometimes "checks willful self-assertion by enforced passivity and rigid procedures" (Daston and Galison 2007, 380). This is a property that, like capitalism (Weber 1958), can be traced to the Protestant ethic, if not to Puritanism. Objectivity can have an accompanying social temperament, which can be witnessed in the prosodic contours and bodily bearing of scientists' speech and gesture. In his literary ethnography of the culture of the scientists who were working at NASA Space Center, *Of a Fire on the Moon*, originally serialized in *Life Magazine*, Mailer (1970) described how every scientist he met at the Houston Center spoke their English as if they were machines, without employing any inflection of tone or pitch, providing perfectly level prosodic contours as if these embodied the cold neutrality of their thinking. It was a social form and an advocacy of a way of being. This variety of objectivity is not simply a method of research but a sociohistorical *spirit* (in Hegel's sense of spirit: the form of life of an era or of a culture). Surely the objective spirit is something that we want to retain, at least if we want to land on Mars, but it can always benefit from a heavy dose of self-criticism.

We should avoid ethnocentrism and take a historical perspective here as we inquire, from where does objectivity come? Or as Nicola Perullo (2016, 18) has asked, "For what reason have we created objectivity?" Edmund Husserl devoted his final book, *The Crisis of the European Sciences* (1970a, 347), to investigating "the radical problem of the historical possibility of 'objective' science." Humanity is still quite early on this voyage of rigorous scientific explorations it began a few centuries ago, and we will serve ourselves well by taking as little for granted as possible. Daston and Galison (2007, 17) write, "Objectivity has not always defined science. Nor is objectivity the same as truth or certainty, and it is younger than both," They emphasize that objectivity has a history of its own. "How can objectivity have a history?" they ask (2007, 27), and they answer that objectivity is a cultural accomplishment, and every cultural achievement has a history. More to the point for us here, "The history of scientific objectivity is surprisingly short. It first emerged in the mid-nineteenth century, and in a matter of decades became established not only as a scientific norm but also as a set of practices." Let us briefly trace this emergence, as depicted by Daston and Galison.

"Objectivity," which is derived from the Latin adverb *obiectivus*, was introduced by 14th-century scholastic philosophers such as Duns Scotus and

William of Ockham, when it meant nothing like it does today. The term "objectivity" as a substantive form that we would recognize today "does not emerge until much later, around the turn of the nineteenth century" (Daston and Galison 2007, 29). For most of its history, "objectivity" has been paired with "subjectivity," but according to Daston and Galison (2007, 29), the original sense of these two terms was almost the opposite of what they are today:

> "Objective" referred to things as they are presented to consciousness, whereas "subjective" referred to things in themselves. One can still find traces of this scholastic usage in those passages of the *Meditations on First Philosophy* (1641) where René Descartes contrasts the "formal reality" of our ideas (that is, whether they correspond to anything in the external world) with their "objective reality" (that is, the degree of reality they enjoy by virtue of their clarity and distinctness, regardless of whether they exist in material form).

Both "objectivity" and "subjectivity" fell into disuse during the 17th and 18th centuries, but they were revived by Kant (Daston and Galison 2007, 30); however, objectivity still retained its interior relation with actual sensible experience, something that had not yet fallen under the suspicion that it carries today.

The virtue of being *clear and distinct* came to be widely associated with "objectivity" by northern European and Anglo-American societies. The Nobel Prize–winning Mexican poet Octavio Paz (1956, 87) has observed,

> Our world has been the world of the clear and trenchant distinction between what is and what is not. Being is not nonbeing. This first extirpation—because it was an uprooting of being from the primordial chaos—constitutes the basis of our thinking. On this conception was built the edifice of "clear and distinct ideas," which, if it has made Western history possible, has also condemned to a kind of illegality every attempt to lay hold upon being by any means other than those of these principles.

Anyone who has spent time with a traditionally oriented people anywhere in the world does not doubt that an insistence upon presumed exactitude and clarity is a European cultural preference, a precipitate of history that was in no way inevitable. Heidegger (1991, 80) discerned, "What is new is that this coming-to-light manifests a decisiveness with which being is determined within the realm of the subjectivity of Reason, and only there," which is to admit that amidst this activity of objective inquiry, subjectivity is actively producing it.

Being clear and distinct is one of objective science's most prized attributes, and "clarity and distinctness for its own sake" were identified by Harold Garfinkel (1967, 267) as one of the assets of rational thinking that distinguishes science from common sense. While making things clear and distinct is part of the scientific project, nevertheless it can be an artificial imposition from the outside, and this way of conceiving matters may require some selective reduction, or even distortion, of our local affairs in order to preserve that clear and distinct edifice. This situation is tolerable, so long as we make only modest claims for what we are proposing. Alfred Schutz (1971, 5) wrote, "This does not mean that in daily life or in science, we are unable to grasp the reality of the world. It just means that we grasp merely certain aspects of it, namely those which are relevant to us . . . from the point of view of a body of accepted rules of procedure of thinking called the method of science."

Daston and Galison (2007, 31) continue, "Sometime *circa* 1850 the modern sense of 'objectivity' had arrived in the major European languages, still paired with its ancestral opposite 'subjectivity.' Both had turned 180 degrees in meaning." There were accompanying changes in the operative notions of what it was to be objective. Through the 19th century, scientific atlases that presented plants, animals, and insects followed a "truth-to-nature" concept, which tried to depict the ideal plant or insect, an ideal that was faithful to a generalized notion of the reality of what was being represented, even if these representations had a perfection and symmetry that no individual plant or insect possessed. By the late 1920s, as objectivity had become a regulative ideal (Daston and Galison 2007, 171), a status it retains to the present day, these rigidly symmetrical insects ceded way to a view of their objective being that depicted messier plants and insects (Daston and Galison 2007, 368). "What had once been a *scientific* virtue, the ability to synthesize a composite from many individuals was now relegated, pejoratively, to the 'artistic' " (Daston and Galison 2007, 169). If an insect had flaws, the new objective view retained those flaws just as they were found; one finds something similar happening in literature and in the *cinéma vérité* and *film noir* genres of film (the television series "Dragnet" was a pertinent illustration). This spirit took hold of 20th-century culture and became part of the spirit of modernity, which involved the surrender of perfection and a capitulation

Historical and Epistemological Bases of Objectivity | 69

to "just the facts." Fidelity to the imperfections of reality was carried proudly as a badge of scientific maturity.

One of my early professors, Michael Novak (1970, 37), summarized the situation:

> Objectivity is a highly selective, highly developed, subjective state. It is the selection of one set of values in preference to others, the shaping of perception and other mental operations along specified lines, and the establishment of social matters of verification. . . . Objectivity, in short, has the logical status of a myth: it builds up one sense of reality rather than others. It is a myth whose attainment and maintenance demands of subjects a rigorous and continual asceticism.

We need to acknowledge that the lack of sentiment is also a sentiment, being the personal as well as historical choice of scientists and technicians.

Daston and Galison describe an illuminating case of the metaphysical aspect of being exact and orderly. Arthur Worthington was a noteworthy scientist who worked on fluid flows. During the period 1875–94, he had composed meticulous drawings of how various liquid substances splashed in ways that differed from each other. Excited by the fresh objectivity that the new technology of photometry could bring to his portrayals of how these fluids splashed when hitting a hard surface, he enthusiastically made a series of photographs of the same phenomena he had already drawn. He imagined that these photographs would be even more exact and perfect than his drawings were; instead, "Those droplet photographs left Worthington stunned to find that the perfect symmetry of his splash drawings had been a chimera" (Daston and Galison 2007, 163). The photos of Worthington on fluid flows revealed *more* irregularity, leading him to the discovery that nature was imperfect, at least compared with his models and his drawings of fluid flows; all of the photographs displayed unpredictable variations, much like life itself. "But after his 1894 shock, Worthington instead began to ask himself . . . how he and others for so long could have only had eyes for a perfection that wasn't there" (Daston and Galison 2007, 15) and "that had never been present" (156).

During the same period, the biomedical scientist Richard Neuhauss felt a similar disappointment when observing photographs of snow crystals: "At first, Neuhauss conceded, the new photographs might seem hardly an advance over drawings: 'One misses in them the absolute regularity and the perfect symmetry that is so characteristic of the [drawn] snow crystals of Scoresby and Glaisher'" (Daston and Galison 2007, 150; my insertion). We will later discuss the discovery of Götz Hoeppe (2012, 2014) that until astronomers have made a judgment regarding which parts of the visual field of their photometry are artifacts of their instrumentation and which represent actual stars, their data will not be intelligible. "Precision measurements often enlist trained judgment to separate signal from noise" (Daston and Galison 2007, 381). Daston and Galison (2007, 21) call this sort of subjectively trained judgment the "subjective smoothing of the data."

Daston and Galison's conclusion is that objectivity is a cultural position, one that is sustained by language and ideology. Sociologists of science have noted that a strict empiricism, though desirable, will be abandoned when it impinges too heavily on the edifice of what is clear and distinct that operates in most typical scientific narratives (Garfinkel et al. 1981). It can happen that scientists are forced to "choose between truth and objectivity" (Daston and Galison 2007, 28); "the naturalism of the individual object" (Daston and Galison 2007, 42) may be suppressed when it renders a picture that is too messy for the realistic expectations of scientists, or even for the elementary requirements of a clear narrative. It might be said, without irony, that objectivity is not objective. We can conclude, therefore, that objectivity should be submitted to reason before any final judgment is reached. This is another way of saying that the scope of reason is larger than that of objectivity.

This situation continually introduces tensions into scientific work, and so the perspectives, methods, and routines of scientific practices are continually evolving. There is no unmediated knowledge, and pure perception is a naïve illusion. Perception itself is selective, and selection always occurs within the perspective of what interests are being projected. William James (1890, 488) described raw perception as a "great blooming, buzzing confusion." This will not do for science, since scientific inquiry requires organized perception. Any organization is a collaborative social project, and it will reflect the current state of scientific evolution.

Georg Simmel (Goodstein 2017, 309) viewed objectivity as a relative rather than an absolute phenomenon, since its dependence upon intersubjective activities is not able to support anything absolute. Nicola Perullo (2016, 18) asks, "When did we start to need objectivity? Objectivity comforts us and puts us at a safe distance, but its invention is not an inevitable fact of human history." Instead of our commencing with formal definitions and operating from the top down, let us use a typical ethnographic strategy and work from the bottom up by making a brief survey of how "objective" inquiry functions in the everyday world. Daston and Galison (2007, 51) suggest, "Before it can be decided whether objectivity exists, and whether it is a good thing or bad thing, we must first know *what objectivity is*—how it functions in the practices of science." Orienting ourselves by observing actual worldly practices, we can assess the scope of what we need to investigate. "If actions are substituted for concepts, and practices for meaning, the focus on the nebulous notion of objectivity sharpens" (Daston and Galison 2007, 52).

An Inventory of Objectivities

While searching empirically for objectivity in this way, I discovered many objectivities. What is it to be "objective"? Objectivity is not just one thing, and it always arrives situated or occasioned. Whether it is situated in a chemist's laboratory, in a plotted archaeological dig, or on a cupping table, objectivity employs many strategies that are derived from and applied to the needs, circumstances, and social demands of different situations. Let us commence our inquiry by employing a Wittgensteinian strategy and briefly review some exemplary formulations and situations in which the term/notion "objective" is used by persons who act in naturally occurring social contexts; by doing so, we can bring the expression "objectivity" into the actual world. We ourselves can be more objective by being reluctant to supply its meaning by definition, ahead of our investigation, or by placing a principled version of the notion ahead of a "corpus"-derived delineation of it: let us find it in the world.

We will start with the political scientist Nate Silver, who offers a version of "objective" that is common in everyday life when he speaks of "objective in a scientific sense of the term." What does he mean by that? Obviously, there is no notion of objectivity in a non-scientific sense of the term, and both terms Silver mentions ("objective" and "scientific") are tropes. If one were to ask Silver what he means, it is possible that he would not be able to say. Is this "objective" an epistemological notion? Is it a cultural notion? A hope? A mythology? Further, what does it mean to say that something is "scientific"? Analyzed objectively, Silver's statement is an invocation of being objective, which is something that can range from being conscientious to being an actual scientific practice. Silver's reference surely has something to do with being unbiased, that is, carrying out one's investigation without interference derived from having a stake in what the results the inquiries might bring, and perhaps he meant nothing more than that.

Measurement is an effective method for keeping track of things and for controlling them, but it is not without its limitations. It is a strategy that is sometimes successful and sometimes not. The problem is that commonly very many things are taking place at once, some of which cannot be measured. Even among matters that can be measured, one must select a subset of them, which introduces a subjective element into the process. Principal among these is the problem that it is restricted to attending to only phenomena that can receive numerical representation, and this leaves out many matters of consequence. It is like filtering grain through a sieve—the grains that do not fit through the holes of the sieve will be ignored. Left like this, one's representation will be incomplete, so it will not do, unless "objective" is going to be permitted to have a scope narrower than truth. Measurements have many ways to assist us, but they are only a single component of a comprehensive methodology, and we use it intelligently only so long as we keep recalling that the perspective it provides will always be a partial one.

There are other occasions where an invocation of "objectivity" is for silencing opponents. It is possible that as a strategy of governance objectivity will be genuine and contribute to good government, but in the hands of the sophistries of politicians, the notion "objectivity" can be twisted to disguise one's motives or avoid frank political dialogue. For example, the introduction of genetically modified crops is a strongly contested matter in India, and the Government of India introduced the trope of "objectivity" to justify its seeking a professional solution that would not be influenced by special interests: "The Indian Parliamentary Standing Committee on Agriculture decided to take on the mammoth task of an objective assessment of the pros and cons of introducing GM crops" (Chaturved 2012). Farmers and environmentalists at once recognized that they had to remain vigilant to observe whether the government was being candid and to learn which objectivity this one would turn out to be. Not all objectivities are the same.

As we will see, objectivity is usually related with a need to communicate clearly, and the coffee sensory scientist Dr. Maya Zuniga (2017, 7:00) emphasized this benefit of being objective: "You want to make sure that you can share that experience and be objective in how you are communicating with your colleagues." Surely, communicating with others is where being objective is born and develops, and it makes possible invaluable cooperation among researchers. Zuniga offered a second aspect of objectivity that is ubiquitous in the coffee industry: "Consistency is how you get objectivity into your program." In any complicated investigation or industrial exercise, being consistent allows one to compare, evaluate, and keep track of strategies. To some degree, "consistency" is simply a gloss for good thinking practices: analysis that knows what it is doing, is able to accurately reproduce those methods that were successful, and can recollect accurately what was accomplished on previous occasions. Throughout the coffee industry, being consistent is a hallmark of objectivity.

During my research in a dozen countries, I observed that one of the important aspects of coffee purveyors being objective was for them to keep notes. One of the first steps used by green coffee processors in India who seek to be more objective about how they process their coffee is to teach the farmers, who bring them their green beans in burlap sacks, to separate their green coffee according to which plants they came from (by genotype, elevation, the sections of the farm where they grew, soil condition, etc.), which makes it necessary to identify, separate, and label them. Only by being organized and consistent will farmers and coffee purveyors be able to track those coffees that might obtain a higher value in the marketplace. Simply mixing all the coffees together, a common practice of farmers who fail to pay attention to the taste of coffee, is too sloppy and makes it impossible to learn more about the flavor attributes of the individual coffees. In Colombia too, owners of *fincas* named this practice of sorting and labeling "scientific." We can conclude that being organized and being consistent are properties of being objective.

Philosophers vary widely in their versions of objectivity. One of the better-known accounts, that of Karl Popper (1972, 154), contends that "ideas in the objective sense are ideas that are independent of consciousness." But there can be no such thing, and this is not much more than a commonsense notion of objectivity. Popper further suggests that something is objective if it has objective logical content, but what is it that grounds logic? Even when one has identified what grounds one's logic, one will need to find grounds for that too, which leads to a problem of infinite regress.

Popper (1972, 66) explains in some detail that knowledge "in the objective sense" is related to "linguistically formulated expectations submitted to critical discussion," and he offers as examples (1972, 74) "theories published in journals and books and stored in libraries; discussions of such theories; difficulties or problems pointed out in connection with such theories, and so on." Each of these is a reference to an *intersubjective* phenomenon, that is, to deliberations that take place among a cohort of analysts. It is inconsistent for him to conclude that such knowledge can be "autonomous." Autonomy is a part of a mythology of objectivity, a mythology that may think that humans are so fallible it is necessary to place one's trust only in an extra-human realm that possesses sufficient autonomy to ensure that it will not be contaminated by the foolishness to which humans are generally disposed. Popper (1972, 109) tells us, "Knowledge in this objective sense is knowledge without a knower: it is knowledge without a knowing subject." Knowledge without a knower is nonsensical. No doubt, knowing subjects will always complicate a mythology of objectivity; but they cannot be dispensed with, since without a knowing subject, the knowledge cannot be known, a fate worse than the tree that fell in the forest unseen. While Popper (1972, 118) argues that objective knowledge should be autonomous, occasionally he hedges his assertion by adding qualifiers like "to a large extent." With that qualification, his arguments may be more acceptable.

The account proposed by Edmund Husserl (1970b, 314) offers more promise: "We shall call an expression *objective* if it pins down (or can pin down) its meaning merely by its manifest, auditory pattern, and can be understood without necessarily directing one's attention to the person uttering it, or to the circumstances of the utterance." This is a more empirical and less ideological version of affairs, and it provides us both independent and dependent aspects of objectivity, which reveals why objectivity is a paradox. Interestingly, Husserl too provides a qualification ("or can pin down"), which leads one to wonder why it is that discussing objectivity forces us to employ qualifications.

Have Husserl and Popper exhausted the meaning of objectivity? Objectivities do not occur on their own, they involve focused, practical work by parties who collaborate in the task of understanding something. Tasting is subjective, but it must be *made* objective if it is going to be useful and if there is going to be adequate communication about it. Communication aids the growth of knowledge in many ways. In articulating our ideas, we clarify them and better understand them ourselves; it also makes it possible for people to teach and learn with each other. Objectivity serves the interest of communication, and this may be the principal motive for its existence. Here our main aim is to identify the practical work by which tastes are made objective. The function of categorical objectivities, such as bean types, roasting profiles, or flavor categories, is to "present" phenomena to our understanding, to hold and preserve our discoveries, and especially to present them in ways that will make our (always) provisional understandings available for the criticism of our collaborators, criticism that Popper acknowledges is essential for objectivity.

Günter Figal (2010, 121) trains his philosophical observations upon the practical scope of the work of being objective: "Interpretation, understanding, and objectivity belong together. Only what is objective has to be interpreted; it is disclosed as what it is through interpretation alone, because only presentative recognizing preserves the exteriority of its matter." Preserving the exteriority proves to be key for the practice of being genuinely objective, whereupon we discover one more paradox: the practices of interpretation, understanding, and objectivity that give us our access to something can also obscure it when we become too fully absorbed with those practices. We always seem to get in our own way.

Direct Evidence (*Evidenz*)

Edmund Husserl developed his doctrine of *Evidenz* for the purpose of explaining how understanding begins with the self-givenness of direct evidence. To an extent, Husserl's account replaces the Cartesian "I" as the starting point for reflection. Because Husserl starts with the object, he is not really an idealist, although he did not transcend every idealist orientation. Simply stated, in real knowledge we have an immediate experience of something and know it to be so; and as scientists, we have a primary obligation to be honest with the authority of that original experience. As William Earle (1955, 26) clarified while commenting upon Husserl, "If there were not an immediate conviction of truth and essential validity of apprehension, no further grounds could ever provide it." The *vide* in *Evidenz* means "to see."

The point of Husserl's doctrine of *Evidenz* is that the original experience of *the object itself*, in the immanence of that experience, and as that immanence, is the proper foundation for knowledge. This is where all phenomenological analyses commence, and this is reflected in what Husserl (1982, 44) called "the principle of all principles: that every originary presentative intuition is a legitimizing source of cognition, that everything originarily (so to speak in its 'personal' actuality) offered to us in 'intuition' is to be accepted simply as what it is presented as being, but also only within the limits in which it is presented there." With this coda, phenomenology actualizes the scientific spirit. This idea of objectivity holds that truth rests in the character of the things themselves and not in our assertions about things, assertions that must be adjusted continuously in light of direct evidence.

Martin Heidegger (1982, 208) concurred with his teacher Husserl's method and contended that *Evidenz* and not principled assertions is the origin of understanding, because "in order for something to be a possible about-which for an assertion, it must *already* be somehow given for the assertion *as unveiled* and accessible. Assertion does not as such primarily unveil; instead, it is always, in its sense, already related to something antecedently given as unveiled." What Heidegger says about assertions may be said as well for methodologies. For Maurice Merleau-Ponty (1964, 25), the immediate perception of what is given "is a nascent *logos*; it teaches us, outside all dogmatism, the true conditions of objectivity itself." Heidegger (1984, 126) further specified, "The point of departure for every genuine clarification of a phenomenon lies in first grasping and holding onto what presents itself. . . . It is important to maintain the primary givenness and from these inquire into the full structure of the phenomenon in question." The obligation of phenomenologists is to be faithful to primary givenness, and formal assessment has validity only on the basis of the immanent *Evidenz* of what is given in experience.

According to Leibniz (Heidegger 1984, 67–68), "to be true is equivalent to being adequately perceived by intuition," which "is not the same as to be perceived clearly and distinctly." What can be the sense of "adequate" here? It is the coherent connection of a thing's mutually compatible determinations, and this *coherence* is a project of both subjectivity and intersubjectivity. Adequate understanding involves a good deal of effort sustaining the many aspects of an ongoing inquiry, aspects that must be synthesized into a coherent unity. Sustaining the determinations and synthesizing them into a unity is part of the work of making objectivities. The idea that there can exist autonomous "facts" that float around somewhere separate from this work has no basis in reality, and operates under "the assumption that one could separate the pure facts, the givens, which can produce real effects on the material organism, from the significant patterns which would be imposed on the givens by the sensibility of the organism—meanings put on them by mental operations. The practice of this separation is as old as metaphysics—indeed it is metaphysics" (Lingis 1985, 41). Husserl always sustained his focus upon the fundamental situation of the transcendental relations between thinking and objects, for the reason that this is how the world emerges.

The work of making objectivities is both subjective and intersubjective, and indeed these two cannot be separated. Husserl held that "objectivity . . . could not be constituted on a solitary egological basis" (Zahavi 2001, 16), and "I experience objectivity by way of the other" (Zahavi 2001, 162). Objectivity requires corroboration by others' experience and perception, which makes objectivities social objects. A student of Husserl who was once nominated for the Nobel Prize, Karl Löwith, said that the consensus view among philosophers is that it is not possible to "attain true objectivity for oneself about anything purely by oneself" (cited in Zahavi 2001, 228). Consensus is the ground and guarantor of the objectivity and truth of knowledge (Zahavi 2001, 174). Another of Husserl's followers, Alfred Schutz, took the lead in exploring the intersubjective foundations of objectivity, and he adhered to Husserl's description of objectivity when he described it as something that has its life as anyone's knowledge "objective and anonymous, i.e., detached from and independent of me and my fellow-human's definition of the situation, our unique biographic circumstances as the actual and potential purposes at hand" (Schutz 1971, 12). Yet these "intersubjective thought objects" originate in the structural socialization of knowledge (Schutz 1971, 13). Objectivity is produced when everyone agrees upon a matter, and this agreement too is usually an "anonymous achievement" (Zahavi 2001, 9).

It is important to take cognizance of the fact that this objectivity makes no ontological claims; rather, it consists of ideas, notions, models, accounts, etc. that one proposes and then are confirmed by consociates, and so they are in part a social production. It is common that the process of social confirmation frequently concludes with the parties who participated in confirming the truth of a matter forgetting the role of their participation, and treating the produced objectivity as though it has a status, Popper-like, that is independent of its production (Liberman 2018). Once produced, objectivity becomes a social obligation, and it draws a good deal of its heft from this. Our world is experienced as an objective world by virtue of "the categorial form, 'once for all truly existing,' not only for me but for everyone" (Husserl 1969a, 236). While the categorial form is extraneous to the object, being my subjective or our intersubjective production, just when, where, and *how* does my subjective object become public property? And when they become public property, can my ideas, notions, models, and accounts still be free? This is a genuine worry because if they cannot be free, how can the objectivity of my thought be preserved and not simply become an ideology? It is also possible that some of these models, accounts, etc. *began* their life as public property. Can it be that objectivity and freedom of thought are sometimes antagonists?

George Herbert Mead (1934, 90) maintained, "Our so-called laws of thought are abstractions of social intercourse. Our whole process of abstract thought, technique and method is essentially social." When professional tasters evaluate a coffee or a blend of coffees, they do stare at the cup (the subjective part), but they also look at each other (the intersubjective part), with looks that are long and penetrating. The taster is soliciting with his or her gaze a dense but precise response from a consociate. These mutual gazes are uniquely collaborative, and I suggest that they gain some of their force from an appreciation of the fact that objectivity has intersubjective origins. With taste, so much is uncertain and indeterminate that some collaboration is desirable. As one of Brazil's foremost tasters, Arnold Baskerville, told me, "I always prefer to have somebody else to discuss the flavors with." His exporting firm uses three tasters in order to address the coffees with a wider palate. Baskerville cautioned, "Any taster can make a mistake at any sip," so tasting alongside other tasters can offer some protection.

No one really thinks alone: "No one can recognize something *as* something without using linguistically mediated conceptual determinations" (Zahavi 2001, 171). Heidegger (1971a, 190) has questioned the epistemological notion that assumes that we transfer private thinking into language, and he argued that mostly language speaks us. That is, the public language directs our thinking. The structure of our thinking necessarily is driven by pre-structures of understanding (cultural, linguistic, religious, theoretical, etc.), all of which introduce some bias, yet this is the context in which we are obliged to develop our objective knowledge.

Another part of the mythology of the European lifeworld holds that first there are individually constituted objects and that these then are shared with others, debated, confirmed, etc. In fact, objects can *first* gain their objectivity by intersubjective collaboration; consequently, the intersubjective constitution of the object can be prior to the individually constituted object: "Transcendental intersubjective sociality is the basis in which all truth and all true being have their intentional source" (Zahavi 2001, 16). Meanings must be shared in order to be fully known or confirmed as reasonable. This is precisely why most professional coffee tasting sessions commence with a day of "calibration," so that before they begin to create objectivities the tasters come to share an intersubjective orientation to knowing and describing the tastes of the coffees. These calibration sessions are vital tools for establishing intersubjective sociality. Rationality is a process, often methodical, of converting subjective awareness into objective understanding, and this process is intersubjective.

During a presentation of the theories of Thomas Kuhn, Harold Garfinkel suggested that when, in 1897, J. J. Thompson first discovered particles that were smaller than an atom, given that there were many possible interpretations of the laboratory work that Thompson and his fellow scientists were engaged in, it became "a matter of an election, or a community agreement, as to what made the experiment into the demonstration that it was, that there was an elementary particle" (personal class notes, undated). Thompson and his colleagues had to collaborate in deciding what was reasonable and true, and therefore to determine what was "objective." Being intersubjective does not disqualify the possibility that something can be made objective; on the contrary, it is the means by which things are made objective.

"Objects offer the unremitting wellspring of intelligibility" (Figal 2010, xi), and the success of any scientific grasping of that wellspring depends upon *making contact* with that object. To that end, methods and protocols provide vital service, but they can also get in the way. Much depends upon remaining open to the object, which includes an ability to observe and consider not only what we expect but what we do not expect. Heidegger (1967, 26) specified that "*objectum* means something thrown against you." To make contact with a transcendent object, an object that is up against us in some way, requires more than a domineering method, it calls for a receptivity and attunement to what shows itself. That an object is transcendent does not mean we play no part in its constitution, but it is what guides our investigation and understanding: "Active experiencing subjects do not remain unaffected by the objectivity they help to constitute, but are rather reciprocally affected and constituted by it" (Thompson 2007, 83).

According to Theodor Adorno, there are two objectivities. One is the objectivity of *Evidenz*, or what Adorno refers to as "*the real objectivity*," like the coffee in the cup. It is the objectivity that keeps evading and transcending any system of descriptors or other socially produced objectivities, including the ones produced by the methodological routines of professionals and scientists. This real objectivity differs from *methodologically provided objectivities*. Methodologically provided objectivities possess a different heritage in that they result from professionally accepted and agreed-upon practices for managing the public demonstration of objective expressions. These forms of objectivity are artifacts even when they are efficacious, and it is the nature of these kinds of objectivities to be intersubjective. These are what Husserl (1970a, 356) called "an ideal objectivity," under which most analytic conclusions are assumed. At its base, they are intersubjective productions, and like other scientific constructions, their origins are in the lifeworld of the historical era that produces them. The contrast between real and methodologically provided objectivities can be compared with the contrast Husserl (2001, 333–337) offers between a state-of-affairs and judicative propositions: there is the object that is presented in experience and there is also an object that is being judged and made available to analytic cognition.

Real objectivity is the flavor in the cup, a flavor that will always exceed any identification professional tasters can supply for it. In Adorno's (1973, 170) words, the real objectivity is "the objectivity heteronomous to the subject, the objectivity *behind* that, which the subject can experience." It is this objectivity that confronts any formal practice of understanding and that can disturb a practice of understanding: "The structure of a mode of thought is no longer imposed on it by the authority and sovereignty that creates and generates its objects from within itself, but by the shape of whatever confronts it" (Adorno 2008, 39). When an object of understanding disrupts the monologue of a formal analytic understanding or a routine method, it may be inconvenient; but for anyone seeking objective knowledge it is where science begins.

Objectivity and Intersubjectivity

How, just how, are objectivity and intersubjectivity related? Richard Rorty (1987, 41–42) has asserted, "Objectivity is intersubjectivity," and Georg Simmel (1978, 85) stipulated similarly when he wrote, "objectivity = validity for subjects." An observation by Friedrich Nietzsche (1994, 87) explicated this equation in practical terms at a time when the notion "objectivity" was just coming into vogue among scientists and philosophers: "the *more* eyes, various eyes we are able to use for the same thing, the more complete will be our 'concept' of the thing, our 'objectivity.'" Nietzsche placed "objectivity" in quotation marks because the notion was still relatively new and its idea unsettled. There is something in each of us that seeks confirmation from others before we consider the objectivity of a matter to be settled, and this is probably the most observable, if mundane, practice of being objective. In one of his last lectures, "The Origin of Geometry," Husserl (1970a, 360) emphasized the importance of how concepts are made objective by and in the social world: "In the unity of communication among several persons, the repeatedly produced structure becomes an object of consciousness, not as a likeness, but as the one structure common to all." A contemporary Husserlian commentator (Hopkins 2010, 151) interpreted this: "According to Husserl, to the very meaning of 'objectivity' and therefore to the world's 'objectivity' there belongs the experience and knowledge of something that is experienced and known to be identical by a plurality of subjects."

In his *Phenomenological Psychology* (cited in Zahavi 2001, 191), Husserl states more comprehensively, "Transcendental intersubjectivity is the absolute and only self-sufficient ontological foundation, out of which everything objective draws its sense and its validity." In our everyday life, we naturally appeal to the transcendental acceptance by others (Zahavi 2001, 26). Just how does this work? Here is a perspicuous illustration taken from one of those many occasions when, upon learning that I am studying coffee tasting, a person volunteers an account of how they prefer their coffee. One such volunteer told me, "I like to put maple syrup in my coffee!" After some initial recoiling, I wondered to myself, is that reasonable? Being familiar with the many times I have been wrong about matters, my first tendency generally is to check the other people around me for what they think about it. Accordingly, on this occasion instead of settling quickly upon a negative conclusion regarding having maple syrup in coffee, I sought for confirmation or disconfirmation of this being reasonable from the others who heard the statement. This instant solicitation of the judgment of others, a leap really, demonstrates how one is guided spontaneously and continuously by the views of one's consociates. How is it that confirmation is so vital to the validity of my own experience? Why cannot one drink one's favorite coffee without needing to convince others of its worth? How do I know, in an objective way, that putting maple syrup in coffee is not a good practice? I know by consulting others who are nearby, the congress of my peers, and I wait for a consensus to emerge. In our everyday life we do much waiting like this. Intersubjective agreement can provide the authority for accepting or rejecting the suggestion to put maple syrup in one's coffee.

At this point one may wonder whether there exists an objectivity that is not merely intersubjective but is truly transcendent. As Shapin (2012, 175) has pointed out, "Taste responses have got to do with objects, not just subjects." When one goes mining for gold, one better be digging up gold. And gold is gold, is it not? Of course, the preciousness of gold is not something that exists in the metal inherently, and still less does the greed that causes it to be highly esteemed; the value is objective only in a conventional sense; nevertheless, it is the contingent result of an intersubjective consensus. And we can confirm the truth of such an objectivity, so long as we do not reify it, or treat it as an "essence" inherent in the gold itself.

Rigorous investigations of the intersubjective constitution of objectivities have only been proceeding for a couple of generations, since the discovery of objectivity itself by Western civilization, and these studies have been hindered by a nearly exclusive focus upon how *concepts* are shared. It is not only that some pre-existing personal experience can be made intersubjective, communicated to each other and objectified with others; it can also happen that the original delineation of an object *commences* within our intersubjective life, before our settling any individual determination that would originate independently of the social world. An object's definitiveness, its sense and reference, develops during these intersubjective experiences, and so does its objectivity. As one works with one's fellows to build an *account* that adequately describes the local situation, these accounts can receive *confirmation* and gain credence. People may be aware that they are collaborating in making sense and order, and most anyone is free to extend, amend, or reject an account as it is being built up by the participants; however, these accounts can also occur serendipitously, driven by the momentum and tendencies of the local contingencies of a discussion, which involve social dynamics that precede and exceed conceptualization (Liberman 2018). At some point, a confirmed account gets reified, and intimations arise that these understandings are true independently of the cohort of social actors who just created them. Both the natural flow of interaction and deliberate efforts lead toward an *objectivation* of confirmed accounts, stabilizing them in ways that render them nearly unassailable. This objectivation confers authority upon what is established as true, and another social fact is born. As Berger and Luckmann (1966, 34) explained, "The process by which the externalized products of human activity attain the character of objectivity is objectivation."

Shortly following objectivation, parties tend to forget, or even deny, that they had a hand in producing the objectivated accounts that, as objects shared during the sociality of the occasion, come to acquire moral force. A *disengagement* with the activities of production ensues, and parties stick to the task of following the local system of order and obligations as they have just instituted them. That is, a form of social amnesia takes hold, and it may be here where objectivity finds its most celebrated existence. Garfinkel has called for more sociological investigation of this neglected objectivity of social facts.

The conceptual aspects of experience are not the only foci of our interpersonal collaborations; our mundane activities consist of, and proceed from, some live experiencing of something alongside and *along with* other people. It is a discovering together, and on occasion it can happen that no single person effects a solution before all have done so. Heidegger (1996, 145) described this situation with precision: "Letting someone see with us shares with the others the beings pointed out in their definiteness. What is 'shared' is the *being toward* what is pointed out which has a way of seeing common to all." Similarly, Maurice Merleau-Ponty (1962, 405) described a situation wherein others are not simply monads who operate externally to my experience: "I do not think of a flow of private sensations indirectly related to mine through the medium of interposed signs, but of someone who has a living experience of the same world as mine." To capture these activities in a rigorously phenomenological way may require that we abandon some individualistic idealizations regarding how people construct knowledge.

Alfred Schutz (1970a, 17) elaborated, "The intersubjective world as the correlate of intersubjective experiences, mediated through empathy, plays a constitutive part in 'objective' experience." This discovery of the role of empathy in producing objectivities is highly significant (see Zahavi 2014). No "intersubjectively identical thing" (Schutz 1970a, 16) can be objectivated by parties without the parties having some affiliation with each other, an affiliation that includes responsibility, obligation, learning and teaching, sympathy, and even a moral compass. The workings of intersubjectivity are more intricate and multifarious than even phenomenological research has described (Zahavi 2001, xvii), and it may be that the term "intersubjective" itself is a relic of classical metaphysics in that it suggests and prioritizes a separateness of subjective life that is not always evident. As Garfinkel often remarked, thinking is a public activity.

Husserl proposed (cited in Zahavi 2001, 33) that "the objective world *rests* on the transcendence of foreign subjectivity." Not only does the object, in its transcendence, continually disrupt what I have understood, the object is not *my* sole possession. "The object is no longer exhausted in its being-for-me, but is torn away from me. Through the other, the object is constituted as reaching beyond me" (Zahavi 2001, 38). Schutz (1970a, 26) concluded, "Only by intersubjectivity is the objective world fully constituted." Intersubjectivity can strip my meaning and my world right out of my hands, which is something that every person has experienced.

Here we are undertaking an inquiry into a world-creating intersubjectivity, but the term "constituting intersubjectivity" may be too general, and for those wanting to gain a deeper understanding of this constituting intersubjectivity it may be better to rely upon the specifications that can be provided by our examination of tasting coffee. We will witness how specific qualities of flavor, being strong, persistent, or unexpected, can disrupt our categorial objectivities, and we will observe how regaining our equilibrium after any disruption is something accomplished by and with the assistance of fellow tasters. A sociologist who studied baristas (Ott 2018, 1) discovered that sense-work, the work of identifying and describing sense experience, is collaborative: "sense-work . . . crafts shared meaning from individual sensory experience"; in fact, this "shared" meaning may be the *origin* of the meaning that arises in a given situation (such as a head roaster and his assistants who are assessing the results of their roast), and once proposed and confirmed, it may guide any individual's sensory experience. Another sociologist of sense-work, Steven Shapin (2012, 177), has expressed the need for more detailed studies of the intersubjective production of taste judgments: "What would be good to have are ethnographies—contemporary and historical—of how taste judgments come to be formed, discussed, and sometimes shared." And the more details we can observe, the more we will learn.

Making tastes objective is local work. This means that objectivity is dependent upon intersubjective practices. Because the tastes are tied to those practices, Hennion and Teil (2004b, 524) contend that "there is no such thing as an 'object' of taste," at least in an independent sense. Rather, for taste to become an object some social work is required. The difficulty here is that sometimes when that work has finished, the "object" that a taste has become is something that it is not. Husserl is clear about the fact that the unity that the sense of an object possesses is *our* accomplishment, being a synthetic unity that emerges from our intersubjective activity. This unity is essential to the identity of a phenomenon, and (rightly or wrongly) it is our initial appropriation and understanding of the object. It gives us our access to the thing, but this unity sometimes wears out its welcome. These earliest reckonings involve not only our active and deliberate choices and fixations regarding what is most salient about an object or a taste but also what arrives passively and prior to deliberation about it. In Husserl's view these objects "emerge for us"; that is, they develop passively, "taking place prior to the occurrences of the higher lying activity of cognitively fixing the common element" (Husserl 2001, 177). Formal science, of course, excels in scrutinizing the active constructions, but there is always a risk that they will overlook the contributions of passive understanding.

Elizabeth Ströker (1997, 203) argues that objectivity is not an inherent property of things, or of an experience; rather, things "must be brought to that objectivity," based upon original evidence. Garfinkel examined the work of measuring things, or the "metrological" practices that introduce a regime that reckons everything as something that is calculable. This "situated metrological work" (Garfinkel 2002, 270) wants to measure anything that can be measured, but the practical benefits of this strategy occur only when parties at the work site find uses for what is measured. The arithmetic properties such a methodology generates provide knowledge that is clear and distinct, i.e., that very definiteness that characterizes the culture of science. As Simmel (1959, 337) described it, "Sense impressions become objects as they are transformed thereby into fixed regularities and into a consistent pattern." These objects constitute the victories of science.

According to Garfinkel (2002, 270), situated metrological work has two components. First are "the arithmetic properties of measurement's things," and, second, "the actual work of measurement's things" with which those numbers are *made revelatory* by and for experts who seek to establish objective information about tastes. Formal measurement practices can produce numbers that represent bean density, bean humidity, the color of the roast, and ultimately acidity, sweetness, and other features. These numbers are measurement's things, and it is "the situated metrological work of their production" that will locate and establish useful connections for the collected measurements. Every newly discovered connection (between a measure and a taste) is heralded, for not only is a flavor feature identified (usually with the intention of making it controllable), it is produced as an objective finding, and so there is celebration. In this way, the interactional organization of the experience of coffee professionals aims at accomplishing durable and intersubjectively valid accounts of flavors, which can become uncontested objective accounts. In the coffee business, the intention then is to sell these; and only flavors that can be tamed (made objective) will receive financial investment sufficient for making it to market.

These activities are part of the active constitution of objectivities. What about features that are less determinate than "facts" but that still influence taste, i.e., those "passively" apperceived features that are also a component of experience? If they cannot be assigned definitively to one of the numerical representations, will they be ignored? As tasters work through the contexture of the flavor profile of a coffee, there is an equally durable thematic field of determined indetermination (Gurwitsch 2009 and Schutz 1970a, 93–94) that can play an important part in the experience of drinking a coffee. This field of flavors is the soil from which a comprehensive appreciation of a coffee will emerge. An objective investigator should honor all of the evidence, of immanent experience as well as measurements, and not be too quick to idealize features of the taste in ways that are constantly biased toward the metrological structures of an inquiry. The Italian sensory scientist Luigi Odello once told me, "We use sensorial analysis to understand, or even better, to define the taste." Understanding incorporates both active and passive aspects of experience, but *defining* suggests that the methodology should dominate the field of flavors, that is, create from the subjective side of methods what should more properly originate from the object or from inside our experience of it. While taking the deliberate role of "defining" has advantages and can lead to discoveries, it may not really be "better" if it has ceased being receptive to important qualities of the flavor that have been left unidentified. Perhaps constant movement between these two strategies is more desirable (Bakewell 2016, 241).

Zahavi (2001, 96) suggests, "The separating of idealities from their subjective origin—a separation that is itself, of course, a subjective achievement—easily leads to an abstraction from their subjective sources, so that these sources themselves are forgotten." This is difficult terrain. Part of the work of purveyors of coffee, work necessary for success, is that they render tastes stable and objective so that they can commercialize them. Since this work involves intersubjective and even intercultural communication, there is a continuing need for coordinating the strategies they use for stabilizing tastes, a coordination that will benefit from a simple system of objectification. In working this way, they produce objective knowledge, but they also will benefit from remaining attentive to what they may be excluding. The solution to achieving objective knowledge of tastes is not simply to minimize the subjective faculties, "which has been treated more as a trouble for objectivity than as a knowledge-making mode open to systematic study" (Shapin 2012, 170), but to employ one's rigorous subjectivity to the task of refining and enhancing an ability to notice the full scope of what is happening in the cup. Most professional tasters understand well that the rigor of their work requires many proficiencies. Objectivity is nothing so straightforward as we imagine. One professional taster summarized for me his solution to this intricate situation: "I'm still doing the math, but I don't let the math take over."

Phenomenological Considerations about Objectivity

One understands an object by applying a notion to it, but a concept can never exhaust the truth of an object. As a course of formal analysis formulates the concepts that define an object clearly and distinctly, it must also provide for ways to *let that object keep revealing itself*. When conceptualization seizes upon an object, it circumscribes it within the confines of its formal organization, and it can fail to leave sufficient opening for that object to reveal itself "from itself" (Heidegger 1996, 30). It is all too common that the knowing that results is a precipitate of projecting preconceptions so thoroughly that the analysis, formal or occasional, will be too "subjective" to be reliable. When thinking is prepossessed with settling the identity of an object, or is too strongly fixated on an understanding that has been settled, the object's identifying particularities are vulnerable to being subsumed under the logical identity of that concept, or what Levinas (1979, 203) has called "the tranquil identity of the same." This insures the unavailability of further learning. Even on those occasions when such logical subsumption is considered to be objective, having received its authority from one or another generally accepted method of analysis, it will remain a case of thinking that is *subjective*. In other words, advocates of objective analysis can be as blind as any to the subjective influences of their own high standards and rigorous procedures, and consequently be working in too subjective a manner. Prejudice is usually blind to its own biases.

Unfortunately, one strategy for being "strictly objective" is to remain oblivious to the prejudices that are built-in to the ontological, methodological, and metaphysical assumptions of one's approach to the world. To a degree all knowledge is biased; and a better way to inquire objectively is to remain aware of the assumptions one is adopting and to topicalize each of the received notions that one is employing. Husserl (1969a, 153) has called this "radical self-understanding." The more practical question here, especially for the advancement of science—"science" is viewed here as a uniquely human capacity to marshal the resources of formal analysis for understanding phenomena better—is to investigate what kinds of methods, protocols, and routine procedures are efficacious. Equally important is developing an enduring vigilance (Liberman 2007, 85–118) regarding the prejudices that are produced by the ways that one has structured one's knowing. A paramount task here is to learn how one can sustain this vigilance throughout one's mundane labors. Remaining vigilant about the prejudice of others is easy; remaining vigilant about one's own prejudices is difficult.

Formal analysis makes the world comprehensible, as well as shareable, by imposing axiomatic definitions; unfortunately, the benefits for the clarity that such definitions and concepts provide are matched by equally significant constraints being placed on the availability of what remains to be witnessed. Theodor Adorno (1973, 12) has issued a general caution against "the compulsive identification which the concept brings." Phenomenologists have extensively interrogated the constraints of formal reasoning, and they have concluded that when an objective analysis does not give ample opportunity for the object to reveal itself from itself, that reasoning will be extraneous to the object and therefore subjective, in the sense that the framework for understanding they provide may not be grounded sufficiently in the object. The preservation of *the authority of what is given* is what defines real scientific rigor, a lay translation for which might be "keep it real."

What is subjective and what is objective is not as straightforward as some methodological rhetoric suggests it is, and it can be difficult to separate knowledge that results from the routinized understandings of our formal analysis and knowledge derived from our "direct experience," especially when that "direct experience" itself is being directed by what is conceptualized. Adorno (1982, 129) observed, "Epistemological analysis of the immediate cannot explain away the fact that the immediate is also mediated." Just as Merleau-Ponty claimed that humans are condemned to meaning, we are equally condemned to seeking objective knowledge. How do we identify and describe what is objective in the world? What might genuine objectivity be, and which objective methods have efficacy in contemporary life? The scope of Adorno's inquiries includes also identifying and describing how subjectivity can be employed more effectively.

Adorno opposed both idealism and positivism, and sought a middle path. Husserl's own focus was similar to some degree. Husserl was not a classical idealist since he was always directed to knowing the thing itself, and considered it to be the real source of objectivity; accordingly, Husserl paid attention both to the object and to consciousness, emphasizing an "objective transcendence," which is not my own essence and is not a constituent part of my essence, although it acquires its sense by my activities. According to Husserl (1970a, 639–640), an "objectifying act" is an act in which a collective object is constituted by a conjunctive synthesis and "becomes the simply presented object of a new 'single-rayed' act, and so is made objective in the pregnant sense of the word." Once an objectifying act contributes this *unity* to a sense, experience will find itself already entwined within the categorial objectivities that such a unity entails; in that event, pure sensory experience will have ceded, at least in part, to the organizing motives of consciousness. A unity of sense is not always the result of some formal and deliberate constitution, but, as Husserl progressively recognized, this constitution can be more passive than idealist accounts would allow. Sometimes we find our way to our prejudices without knowing how we arrived there.

How does one gain access, and preserve that access, to the object in a way that does not contaminate one's understanding and that will result in delivering "objective" knowledge? Adorno devoted much of his research to this question. He was an objectivist, although his empirical inclinations caused him to track closely all active subjective processes of developing knowledge, and he emphasized the importance of keeping one's attention focused on "the real objectivity" of what one is studying. The rigor of reason is essential for any inquiry, but Adorno held that reason cannot be rigorous unless it recognizes its own inherent limitations. "The thing itself," Adorno (1973, 189) tells us, "is nonidentity through identity." That is, a thing necessarily *exceeds* whatever identity or unity of sense our rigorous conceptualizing has provided for it, even as that identification is what affords us our access to it. Moreover, the objective schemata that constitute part of reason's rigor assist us to understand the thing and to organize our knowledge about it;

however, the real objectivity of the thing cannot be made a captive of the formal analytics one employs during an inquiry.

Adorno turned to a *dialectical* method of inquiry and reflection. "Dialectics" is a term that is often applied vaguely, but Adorno intended something precise. He recognized that formalities guide all knowing, and so they are essential: all inquiry necessarily involves some formalization of one's analysis. Along with the benefits that formal rigor brings, formal analysis will introduce limitations. *The historical task of human reason is to learn how to limit those limitations*, and dialectics, the legacy and the promise of that historical task, arises from an acknowledgment of the limitations of theoretical totalizations.

According to Adorno (1973, 5), "Dialectics says no more, to begin with, than that objects do not go into their concepts without leaving a remainder." In other words, dialectics is the recognition of the natural shortcomings of knowledge, shortcomings whose only solution is continual negation and self-scrutiny: "Thought as such, before all particular contents, is an act of negation, of resistance to that which is forced upon it" (Adorno 1973, 19). "Nonidentity" is not a reference to any mystical notion, but a scientific attempt to undo the mystification erected by impossibly hopeful positivist commitments to the conceptual identifications one has made and committed oneself to. "To change this direction of conceptuality, to give it a turn toward nonidentity, is the hinge of negative dialectics" (Adorno 1973, 12). An objective methodology that never addresses what may exceed its boundaries could never be more than a caricature of objectivity, and no objective method fails to pay a price for its conciseness. Dialectics is addressed to the failures that will necessarily accompany every praxis of formal analysis.

What is the best way to investigate these matters? Here we intend to elucidate these reflections about objectivity by examining the perspicuous case of coffee tasting as it transpires in the world. This will enable us to pursue many of the intricacies of formal thinking, objective and subjective, in perspicuous circumstances. Wittgenstein (1978, 9) once observed, "There is no such thing as phenomenology, but there are indeed phenomenological problems." Accordingly, here we take up the case of the industry-wide effort of purveyors of coffee to determine the taste of the world's coffees in an objective manner, which affords us a classical "phenomenological problem." Most coffee tasters sustain and even benefit from objectivist ideology while they continue to value the contributions of subjective intelligence.

Methodologically provided objectivities include professionally accepted and agreed-upon practices for managing the presentation of objective expressions. These forms of objectivity are *artifacts* even when they are efficacious, and so it is the essence of these kinds of objectivities to be subjective. Not a few coffee purveyors seek formulaic methods for overcoming the difficulties of identifying tastes objectively, and they are ready to pay good money to any consultant who can provide them reliable methods, although the purveyors themselves may be unfit to judge the reliability of what they have purchased. A pervasive problem is that there can be so much preoccupation with fulfilling the requirements of correct methods and formal protocols that the real objectivity gets ignored. Adorno (1973, 300–301) anticipated this paradox: "That activity breaks men of the habit of experiencing the real objectivity to which they are subjected." Practitioners of received methodologies can miss the fact that their scrutiny is limited to a reduced version of the object. For example, while numerated methods employed along with a tasting schedule that rates aspects of flavor are among the effective ways to probe the taste of a cup of coffee, they can also occlude the authority of the sensory experience itself. Bureaucracies serve humans by helping them keep their knowledge organized, but we should take care not to eviscerate the experience of tasting, replacing its authority with something extraneous, or subsume it underneath what is ideology, even when that ideology is canonized as science.

Many tasters have acknowledged this to me: "I strongly believe in having a very set form that actually works for you, but the ideal does not exist," and "Everyone is gaming the chart." Just what is it to "game" the chart? How do the hermeneutic strategies employed to retain control affect the objectivity of what is understood? Further, what is bad about losing control? Could there be something good about it? The employment of objective methods seems to always be accompanied by a flotilla of contingencies. Methodologically provided objectivities are essential for keeping our inquiries organized, but they require extensive local work to be made dependable. Tasters as well as phenomenologists are interested in what ways the objective methods that are employed are helpful, and wherein their probativeness lies, and they should also be interested in what inherent limitations they may introduce.

It seems inevitable that real objectivity has subjectivity associated with it. According to Adorno (1974, 69–70), the way that modern culture applies objective practices conflates subjectivity and objectivity, resulting in imprudent methodologies that are practiced blindly and that possess little chance of becoming truly scientific:

> The notions of subjective and objective have been completely reversed. Objective means the non-controversial aspect of things, their unquestioned impression, the façade made up of classified

data, that is, the subjective; and they call subjective anything which breaches that façade, engages in the specific experience of a matter, casts off all ready-made judgments and substitutes for relatedness to the object the majority consensus of those who do not even look at it, let alone think about it—in other words, the 'objective' itself. Just how vacuous the formal objection to subjective relativity is, can be seen.

In this stunningly lucid observation, we learn that what is accepted as objective can actually be subjective, and what is really objective (in our case, the taste of the coffee) is relegated to the status of "subjective," a demotion required by the demands of a formal procedure. The "objectivity" Adorno is negating here is one that has demoted the status of objects to only what can be provided for by the person who is inquiring, which itself is a form of being subjective, whereas what we really require for furthering our knowing is "*object*-ivity," an investigation that takes its lead from the object more than from ourselves. As the experienced taster Dr. Manuel Diaz summarized in an epiphany expressed midway during a week-long Robusta-grader course he taught in Thailand, "Either you forget about your science, and you focus on the flavor; or you apply the standard repeatedly and pay less attention to the flavors."

Another way to appreciate the situation that Adorno is describing is to acknowledge that there is no such thing as an objective objectivity; rather, there is only a subjective objectivity. If one finds this situation unacceptable, one needs to cultivate more maturity and overcome one's delusions. Adorno's conclusion is that real objectivity requires an active subjectivity that engages it. Contrary to the feeble commonsense assumptions that operate across much of the coffee industry, subjectivity and objectivity are not mutually exclusive. An active subjectivity is what is responsible for freeing understanding from an overly mechanical compliance with routines. There is safety in routines, but they also foster narrow-mindedness. The aim of an objective method should be "to give the object its due instead of being content with the false copy," a false copy produced by one's method. To accomplish this, "the subject would have to resist the average value of such objectivity and to free itself as a subject" (Adorno 1973, 170–171). As Socrates taught us, true knowledge is knowledge that remains free. Surely routines are necessary, since no progressive understanding can advance without some routinization, but the objectivity of the method *also* depends upon empowering our subjectivity to be vigilant so that it will prevent the surrender of the truth to those methodological routines upon which we rely. In short, a methodology should operate in the service of knowledge and not the other way around! An interpreter of Adorno has commented, "The subject is not merely passive in relation to the object, and the object is not exhausted by the categories of the subject" (O'Connor 2004, 48). As Adorno (1973, 139) has summarized our problem, subject and object "reciprocally permeate each other," and each without the other lacks full intelligibility. Professional coffee tasters do attempt to address both the subjective and objective aspects of taste, since as a practical matter they must do so; however, because their protocols assume they can keep the two separated, they occasionally lose sight of the basic nature of objectivity and subjectivity, which is to be interconnected and interdependent.

Adorno was keen to *not* restrict his analyses to the conceptual, a flaw he spotted in many phenomenological analyses. O'Connor (2004, 71–72) has observed that "the subject is not simply a concept manipulator," and true understanding must penetrate beneath the concepts that one employs for rendering the nonidentical visible. Accordingly, we should be interested not only in how tasters stabilize the meanings of the taste descriptors they use but also how, once these unities of sense are stabilized, these descriptors may introduce an element of alienation into the system of understanding they are using (an element that is an inevitable part of the Hegelian dialectic). We are especially interested in identifying how professional tasters resist that alienation. Objectivity, in the sense of preserving and scrutinizing the real objectivity of an object, consists of sterner stuff than what most methodologically provided objectivities have put forward. Rigor in analyzing the taste of coffee must involve more than simply excluding what is "subjective." Rigor, in a phenomenological sense, includes sustaining the contributions of subjectivity to the vital tasks of locating, identifying, and learning what is really there.

Chapter 4

Making Contact with the Object

"Analytic procedures need to offer an intensification of our relation to things."

—Aron Gurwitsch (1964, 182)

People make many claims about what is real. We have repeated with approval Adorno's category of "the real objective" and illustrated it by referencing "what is in the cup," as though that is a matter unhampered by complications. We will learn that it is not exactly this way, and it is best to tread carefully when making such a claim. Hegel (1969, 36) has warned, "These very things which are supposed to stand beyond us and, at the other extreme, beyond the thoughts referring to them, are themselves figments of subjective thought." Coffee tasters are familiar with the experience of having what they know with confidence about the taste of some single-origin coffee begin to slip away from them as soon as they start cupping. Slippage like this must be followed up by them, even if they are uncertain where it is heading: it is especially this that is being objective, proof that being objective cannot be the same thing as being clear and distinct.

The philosopher of food tasting Nicola Perullo contests the notion that the "real taste" resides "in the cup." He writes (2018a, 19–20, my translation), "That phrase 'only what is in the glass counts'—people still say it, and with arrogance, as if it revealed a profound truth—it does not mean anything. There is nothing only inside the glass, because what is inside is always outside as well." Perullo is correct that the taste resides both inside and outside the cup and that "the cup is never alone." Nevertheless, there is some wisdom in the suggestion to consider only what is in the cup, in that such a policy can prevent one from overthinking the experience. Thinking can interfere with one's openness to what is unexpected or to what has not yet been provided already by the encyclopedia of one's biases. The most common advice given to me by professional tasters, often expressed to me in the midst of an international cupping competition, has been, "The less you think, the more accurate your sensory evaluations will be—just taste the coffee and fill out the form." What is vital about honoring "what is in the cup" is to make *direct contact* with the coffee. We should be able to claim at least that the coffee in the cup offers us, in Figal's words (above), an "unremitting wellspring of intelligibility" or, as Adorno described, an "objectivity heteronomous to the subject." We come up against something we are not able to control, even as we necessarily fashion our access to it.

What Perullo is objecting to is the idea that the taste in the glass is straightforward; rather, the textures of the dark liquid in the glass offer us a disorienting labyrinth. There is little about taste that is unproblematic, and part of the danger of the catchphrase "what is in the cup" is that its simplicity encourages overlooking complications that lie beneath the surface. It is a slogan for the mind, not for the tongue, so it is self-delusion. Coffee works outside of concepts; it influences the limbic brain, and so influences our emotions, which are hardly available for scientific circumscription. If the taste is decent, it will resist being pinned down, especially if we retain our contact with it, follow up its suggestions, and do not cede our experience to schemes for knowing. Perullo's annoyance springs from his response to the arrogance in the tone that tasters commonly use when they utter the advice to consider only what is inside the cup. As a received notion, even if it has practical utility, it can be a glib maxim that we need to move past if we are going to appreciate how it is we experience tastes.

What Is Phenomenology?

A phenomenology of tasting coffee can play an important role in this inquiry. What does "phenomenology" mean in this context? At first hearing, it sounds less empirical and more subjective than "science." In fact, phenomenology is more empirical than science. The objectivity of science depends heavily on adopted methodologies and protocols that reduce the actual experience of things to measureable accounts and procedures that risk losing contact with the object and that operate extraneously to the horizon of actual experience. As Zahavi (2001, 161) describes it, "No appearing object is thinkable in principle without the horizon of what is co-meant." If you reduce one's access to this horizon, you will reduce the experience. Losing the horizon is to lose the phenomenon, and it is one of phenomenology's tasks to retain this horizon, even if it may grow less clear at the edges. The actual experience of things is the only experience there is, whether it is distinct or indeterminate. When it comes to taste, an important phenomenological principal is not to surrender this actuality.

Ronald Bruzina (1970, 170) emphasizes the importance of this horizon of experience when he writes, "The meaning of the concept . . . can never be thought of as extricable from its matrix." There is more to an object than its concept or what can be abstracted from the scene by an analytic practice and then awarded independent status, separated from the network of relations in which it has its natural life. Phenomenology seeks to respect and describe the looks of the world for the people who live in that world. Its project is description, and it never takes sides. It operates with "radical presuppositionless neutrality" (Bruzina 1970, 172), a situation causing phenomenology to be rejected by everyone who retains a vested interest in their research.

A phenomenological analysis of the structure of thinking and experience describes phenomena that pass unnoticed by methods that restrict themselves to counting things. Thinking and experience are interwoven and have a reciprocal relation; phenomenology aims at appreciating just how an understanding emerges from a real situation. In its concern to be objective, phenomenology keeps close track of how thinking influences our commerce with objects. Here our aim is not simply to get access to the judgments tasters make, but to take a step back and gain access to the thinking about coffee they use for arriving at those judgments—that is, how they have organized their understandings about coffee and how that organization of their practical knowledge affects their decisions about what coffees they will purchase.

Phenomenological analysis addresses what is given just in the way it is given, and it is an equal opportunity inquirer, in that both objectivity and subjectivity are its targets. In fact, Simmel, Husserl, and Garfinkel were all more suspicious of subjectivity than of objectivity, but they recognized that both were essential and inseparable. Simmel (cited in Goodstein 2017, 5) wrote, "When will the genius come along who frees us from the spell of the subject as Kant freed us from that of the object?" Like Dorothy's dog Toto, phenomenology pulls open the curtains that conceal our pre-understandings, including the "methodological convictions masquerading as objectivity" (Goodstein 2017, 132); this is not because it opposes objectivity but because it has accepted a responsibility to expose false objectivity. That is, phenomenology does not simply receive the object exactly as meant but investigates the genesis of its meaning, the "how" by which the dynamic work of sense-making produces it, and phenomenology seeks to unearth the moment of "the original bestowal of meaning" (Husserl 1970a, 47).

Husserl (1970a, 56) expands upon this task:

> The developed method, the progressive fulfillment of the task, is, as method, an art which is handed down; but its true meaning is not necessarily handed down with it. And it is precisely for this reason that a theoretical task and achievement like that of a natural science (or any science of the world)—which can master the infinity of its subject matter only through infinities of method and can master the latter infinities only by means of a technical thought and activity which are empty of meaning—can only be and remain meaningful in a true and original sense *if* the scientist has developed the ability to *inquire back* into the *original meaning* of all his meaning-structures and methods.

This is what Heidegger has called "digging" (Bakewell 2016, 57), working one's way to the roots of things. Phenomenology's method is to dig down to the roots of our understanding, and in that way it is "radical" reflection.

Rather than naively and unquestioningly adopting received notions—a taste descriptor, for example—phenomenologists inquire into its essential nature, the local history of its development, and the horizon of its use, including the lived details and orientations of the taste it is disclosing. Many positivist sensory scientists prefer to proceed by first defining each descriptor clearly, ignoring what is still indeterminate about a taste or what might be working at, alongside, or beyond the boundary of a descriptor; further, the *independence* of the existence of a descriptor is sometimes presumed before it is defined. In a similar spirit, the respected coffee entrepreneur Geoff Watts (2013) has insisted, "You need to start by defining what you are trying to do." As Watts no doubt appreciates, this may not always work out well. One can start out with a clearly defined perspective only on the condition that one remains open to transforming it as soon as the shortcomings of one's account are revealed, which will surely happen.

Phenomenology holds that confining a taste to what is predefined is like standing in the middle of a stream and trying to prevent the stream from flowing. Ferdinand de Saussure taught us that terms, words, and labels—both the words themselves in their relations with other words *and* the words' relations with their meanings—are in continual flux. Aron Gurwitsch (2009,

487) insisted on describing things "as they offer and disclose themselves in direct perceptual experience, with all their vagueness, indeterminateness, incompleteness, and openness." Language and concepts can be used to provide things more determinacy so that we can better communicate about them, but any true science is obligated to delve beneath these glosses and idealizations, and rediscover the opaque world out of which sense emerges. This is the aim of phenomenological research.

Objectivity in the World of Coffee Purveyors

Once again, we will commence by locating our phenomenon in the lived world. The first internationally renowned coffee taster I met for this research was an Italian taster who was pleased to learn that a sociologist was studying his discipline, and he was quick to explain, "I only do objective tasting." I did not bother to quote Heidegger (1991, 80) to him: "The objectivity of objects is completely based in subjectivity." He probably knew this already. As I have been discussing, tasters are fond of insisting, "The coffee has to speak for itself," even though coffee doesn't speak; people do. When a taster says, "I always let the scores speak," what they mean is that they have taught themselves to disregard their personal opinions and give preference to the numerical result produced by a formal protocol. Another taster took an even stronger position: "People say coffee cupping is subjective. It is not. Coffee is very objective. There is floral or not. Acidity or not. Sweetness or not. Coffee has body or it doesn't."

Most professional coffee tasters are not heavily invested in their opinions about coffees. Franco Schillani of Trieste explained, "In the coffee business, personal taste doesn't exist." And Marcio Hazan, who comes from three generations of coffee tasters who have worked on the Rua do Comércio in Santos, summed up a lifetime of tasting experience this way: "There is no such thing as a good coffee. There is only what the client likes." These tasters are trying to be objective; however, there is not a singular objectivity, but many objectivities. Because these objectivities must be tailored to the needs of the purchasers, there is an objectivity for each client, and these are all practical objectivities. Here "objective" entails that what a sensory assessment means for one taster is more or less what it means for another taster. For example, the precision and effectiveness of a blend that an exporter has designed for an importer of coffee is oriented to the taste that the importer's buyers, roasters, and tasters are expecting. This is a standard that results from a history of purchases more than an articulation of specific taste descriptors, and its adequacy requires the serious work of sensory evaluation by both the importers and exporters, who are concerned not only to evaluate the coffees but to communicate clearly with each other about them. Since these standards and expectations keep undergoing modifications—there are shifts dictated by the market as well as shifts resulting from the readjustment of interpretations—there is an occasioned character to these objectivities. The world does not conform to a single standard, and what is present for a Japanese buyer may not be what is present for a German buyer. There is small scope for absolutism.

It is sometimes said that the better characteristics of coffee may differ from taster to taster but that all tasters will agree about the defects. This is mostly, though not always, true. Most tasters do claim it is easier to "be objective" about defects than about the positive features of the taste of coffees, and this places a special burden on those tasters who wish to operate objectively about the better coffees. Having spent a week observing the work of Italian tasters who certify espressos for specialty grading, I can attest to the strictness of their work, in which consistency is key and each coffee is given equal consideration. The daily workbench activities of these tasters reminded me of herding cats, and, like herders, the tasters needed to carry sticks to whip the exploding flavors into objective assessments. The wildness of some of these coffees' positive features makes it essential for the tasters to remain organized, and the unwieldiness of these flavors is what propels assessors to emphasize the necessity of achieving a secure standard. Objective tasting is challenging work, but it is not impossible, so long as we recognize that the result will be a practical and not an absolutist objectivity.

Professional coffee tasters have advised, "You need a system." One requires a system for keeping track of the tastes one has identified, begun to identify, and is still stalking as the coffee cools. There are many features of interest, and in following up one feature, other ones get neglected. At one international competition, I was told, "You need a way to stay organized." Without a schedule to follow and fill in, many features of taste will be overlooked; which system one uses for staying organized is not as important as having a system. Applying the identical methodology to each coffee one samples, as well as using the same criteria for one's numerical evaluations, is more important than the particular merits of a given methodology or any personal tendency to provide scores that are high or low. Consistency is what matters, and by making one's sensory assessments in a standardized and consistent way, one becomes more objective. This raises the question, are standardization and objectivity the same thing?

Casper Rasmussen, head taster for Denmark's largest coffee purveyor, BKI Coffee, explained to me, "Our main target is to be consistent. But can we measure it? Or use a computer that will tell you which beans to buy to make this consistency? I'm not so sure." It was his judgment that remaining attentive to flavors would produce better results than ceding authority to formulaic measurements, although he maintained that being consistent remains a necessity. He added, "You can measure things, and you can give numbers to the acidity level [either by chemical measurement or by quantified tasting protocols], but it's still very much a subjective evaluation of what we're doing, and what coffees we're buying." However, Rasmussen was not at all absolutist about his way of working, explaining, "I'm not to judge the reasons why others do it," but he questioned, "How do you really measure what is the heart of it?" Another taster followed a similar policy and argued that the fundamental practice was to locate and experience the flavors: "We have trust in our own ability to perceive the flavors that we're seeking." If we are able to do that, he suggested, "why would we want to take measurements?"

Debates about this issue rage across the coffee industry, with most of the tasters I met in Brazil and India highly skeptical of the notion of removing all subjectivity from the process and most tasters from Italy and the US insisting upon doing so, at least in their rhetoric. The accomplished Indian sensory scientist Dr. Pradeep Kenjige, of Coffee Day (Karnataka), suggested that there is not a communication "gap" between European/American and Indian tasters as much as there is "a huge wall." The elevated respect for subjectivity sustained by most Indian tasters may result from millennia-long cultural differences; it certainly does not stem from a lack of scientific training. This returns us to the question of what is science. If we do not exclude its original sense of possessing knowledge that is comprehensive, we must acknowledge that there is a genuine need for both rigorous procedure *and* the insight of judgment.

No matter where they may be located, most tasters welcome some formalization of sensory assessment that can make their task more manageable, but it is interesting to witness how cannily suspicious many coffee tasters are about the protocols they use regularly. One skilled Italian taster, Lorenzo Martinelli of Arco Coffee (Lake Garda), insisted, "Non sono regole" (There are no rules). His meaning is that there is no way to appreciate coffee strictly by the governance of rules. "Rules" can and should be involved, but they are to be used as resources and not as *diktat*. In coffee tasting, formal protocols have considerable utility, but their real objectivity derives from how the tasters use them to make *direct contact* with the taste of a coffee.

In other words, what is real is not easily tamable by rules (if it is easy, then it is likely that the protocol is poor); however, neither is taste easily tamable without any rules. Of course, I am speaking of professionals who buy and sell coffee and have a need to render tastes more docile, not a consumer whose sole responsibility is to please him- or herself. One needs rules, a society needs rules, but one also needs something more. The solution was best articulated by a San Francisco Bay coffee roaster who declared, "I want to know all the information and the numbers, but I don't feel under any obligation to be directed by them."

The broader sense of science requires something more than simply providing data that is clear and distinct; in order to be more than simply naive, science must be capable of recognizing both the active and passive synthetic operations of understanding that contributed to establishing the data. Consider the reflexive way that taste descriptors work. It is not as straightforward a matter as simply that a coffee generates a descriptive representation, such as

$$\text{coffee} \rightarrow \text{taste descriptor}$$

Nor am I endorsing any nominalism that would hold that the descriptor produces the flavor:

$$\text{taste descriptor} \rightarrow \text{coffee}$$

The fundamental reflexive nature of what is taking place is better depicted this way:

$$\text{taste descriptor} \leftrightarrow \text{coffee}$$

Taste descriptors find their life in the tastes to which they direct the tasters' tongues and in the work of tasting that they help to accomplish, and not by what they convey in the abstract. A descriptor can direct us to a flavor that is actually experienced, but it is only that real flavor that, once located, provides the specificity tasters require. Taste descriptors not only describe the taste that they find, they find the taste that they describe (Liberman 2013, 220–221). We will examine this situation in more detail in part III.

Having committed several decades to the profession of coffee tasting, the highly regarded American taster Ted Lingle, author of *The Coffee Cupper's Handbook*, recognizes the complexity of sensory analysis when he claims (Lingle 2001, 2) that it is the aim of the *Handbook* to "combine the traditions of the cupping table with the science of flavor chemistry to help teach the art and science of sensory evaluation." Here again a coffee purveyor wants the best of both worlds because both are needed. Lingle (2001, 3) writes, "A coffee flavor language must reflect both the trade and lay terminology used by non-chemists—for example, green coffee growers, importers, brokers, buyers, and roasters—as well as the precise scientific terminology of chemists, chemical engineers, food technologists, and flavorists." The instability of sensory assessment makes the continual revision of tasting schedules, lexicons, and protocols necessary. Such changes should not be considered a failure to be objective; rather, they are what objectivity consists of, and are motivated by continually renewed insights into how objectivity is to be obtained. Any operative ideology that believes that the way to achieve objective knowledge is simply to remove all subjectivity, or to keep objectivity and subjectivity strictly separate, fails to appreciate just how, in any empirical situation, objective knowledge is actually produced. As Maurice Merleau-Ponty (1973, 9) observed, "We must, therefore, be subjective, since there is subjectivity in the situation." There is nothing objective about denying the existence of something that, empirically speaking, is operative.

Why Is Subjectivity Inescapable?

Let us consider real situations of professional coffee tasters at work and identify a few illustrative workbench activities where subjectivity was essential to the mission of the tasters' sensory assessments, and where there was little or no scope for removing those subjective aptitudes. Take for instance the taster in Boquete, Panama, who attempted to explain to the other professional tasters the reason for his high score for a coffee: "For me, there is a better roast point for this coffee, so I was reluctant to penalize it too much." At a Cup of Excellence tasting, a taster remarked, "I would have roasted it differently, and I would have given it a higher score if I had roasted it the way I think it should have been roasted." Presumably, a strictly empirical tasting praxis that attended only to the taste that was "in the cup" would involve sipping the coffee, finding it good, adequate, or unsatisfactory, and then recording the score. Here something more complicated was involved, something that had to do with the taster's expertise. While tasting, these tasters found something that had promise but had not managed to fully reveal itself. Comments like these are frequent at cuppings. It can even happen that when many tasters agree with such an assessment, the organizers will have the coffee re-roasted (lighter or darker) in the way that the tasters specify. I have witnessed situations where re-roasting has enhanced the flavor and an equal number of occasions where the flavor did not display any noticeable improvement; however, in the absence of any re-roasting, occasionally a coffee will receive an assist by including consideration of something that is not strictly present. Does this practice belong in objective sensory evaluation?

Another dilemma regarding objective practices involves the policy of some international competitions to give each of the coffees the same degree of roast. This reduces the likelihood that the roasting level will influence the judges' scoring more than the taste that is inherent in the bean. There are two problems with this policy. First, a bean is best assessed at the roast level that is optimal for what is in the bean. If the bean is to express its best qualities, it requires an appropriate level of roast, and by giving the bean a sub-optimal roast, one disadvantages that bean. Rarely is this done to favor a competing coffee deliberately, but it subjects the coffees to the instabilities of providence. Practically speaking, there are too many coffees at a competition to make it convenient to pre-cup each entry (in fact, one could run out of green samples or use up the supply one hopes to auction). A second problem is that one purpose of competitions is to probe harvests for beans that importers may wish to purchase. It is for certain that any firm that purchases green beans will undertake some research in their tasting labs to learn what is the optimal roast level (optimal for the firm's purposes) for that lot of coffee. The firm is usually not going to roast it at the level stipulated by the competition's protocol; therefore, the coffees being tasted at the cupping for the competition do not accurately reflect what the actual coffee will be for the importers who are the target audience of the competition. If one of objectivity's purposes is to foster clear communication, then this is a flaw. For this reason, tasters instinctively project, as part of their common work practice, how the bean is likely to perform at what they think is its optimum roast level (again, optimum for the coffee purveyors who sent them to the international competition). Objectivity is necessarily situated, but which situation is a matter that needs to be decided. Some assessments are achieved by tasting and others by reasoning, which runs counter to the ubiquitous advice, "Don't think too much, just taste and score."

Coffees are also rated for their fragrance, and this score is based on smelling some grounds of roasted coffee that are placed at the bottom of a small glass or ceramic cup. A slight sweet smell that might merit a higher score than a coffee with a fragrance less sweet may not receive that higher score because it may be concluded that the sweetness was due to its having received a lighter roast. Moreover, one may be hesitant to rate it every bit as good as it smells when a taster recognizes that it will ultimately be given a darker roast by the firm for which it is being purchased. While compensating for this is a subjective act, it serves the interests of objective assessment. Tasters who are buyers are more likely than tasters on a competition panel to give credence to what they think is likely to happen when they roast it at their home facility, although many tasters perform both roles. Commercial requirements may provide more scope for subjective adjustments than pure sensory science prefers to tolerate. Which strategy is the more objective? Knowing well the roast that their firm is likely to give it, tasters sometimes score a coffee for its promise as much as its reality. Since tasters on a competition's panels are frequently traders and their day jobs involve purchasing coffees, they may be of two minds. It is useful to recollect that most tasters are not tasting simply to appreciate flavors—they are always and without relief looking for ways to make a profit. Accordingly, they may be especially happy to discover a coffee that presented badly at a light level of roast, knowing that it will have some value when they roast it at a darker level and hoping that the other tasters did not notice, which might make it possible for them to purchase a superior, non-award-winning coffee at a low price.

Factors that influence ratings but are not there in the cup are ubiquitous, and when they are derived from professional expertise, consideration of them is well tolerated by the industry. Espresso tasters in Italy indicated to me during their cupping that they are not reducing a score for the *crema* of an espresso that is presenting a *crema* that is too light in color to properly receive a good score, for the reason that they roasted it several days previously, and so it would be unfair to judge it too strictly. This is an illustration of when empirical data is submitted to judgment before finalizing a decision. On many occasions, I have been impressed with professional tasters who are able to detect a particular defect that is the result of poor brewing rather than due to the coffee itself. Here again, they are not judging the cup in a strictly empirical sense but submitting their sense perception to a course of reasoning. Is this being subjective? A coffee can be given a "good" or an "adequate" rating (they are usually using numerical scales) that is not directly evident at the time of the tasting. Of course, one aspires to be empirical, but being reasonable, or using what goes by the name of rationality, is equally important. It should be noted that being rational involves more than calculus.

Here is another curious objective practice. As mentioned, when professional tasters cup coffees, they strive to be consistent in how they assess each coffee they sample. If there are eight samples on a table, each of them presenting five cups for tasting, the taster will take care to taste from each one of the five cups for every coffee. In Nicaragua, I observed that one highly respected taster from Japan took only one sip from a single cup of a sample. When I inquired about it, it happened that he found the coffee too astringent, so astringent that he feared it would ruin his palate for tasting the other coffees. He gave priority to keeping his mouth fresh for the other seven coffees on the table. While being objective is usually correlated with being consistent, on this occasion reasoned reflection warranted a change in procedure. Always, local contingencies complicate straightforward rules for any practice of being objective. In this way, objectivity is always occasioned.

Dr. Enrico Meschini, the head taster of the laboratory in Italy that is responsible for certifying Italian espressos as specialty grade, once explained his assessing practice as he executed it: "This is sweet, but there is just a little astringency. Very little, which is probably more due to the machine than to the coffee. I won't penalize the coffee, but I will write in brackets, 'Not penalized.'" An important part of being objective is to take good notes, which makes it possible to reexamine matters should that become necessary. While keeping careful records is not the most glamorous part of the scientific method, it can make significant contributions. By retaining notes about empirical sensory details in the record, one enhances one's capacity to have crucial information at hand when one needs it.

In Panama, a taster reported that he lowered his rating for a coffee from 87 to 83 (on a nominally 100-point scale) because he detected that the pleasant flavor was due to some fortuitous bacterial transformation of the bean that would be difficult to repeat, making the flavor feature a "risky" proposition for any buyer. Most coffee purveyors place a higher priority upon tastes that can be reproduced than tastes that are simply excellent. No market can be developed for a coffee that will have a particular taste for one year only (unless one has built a specialty business that has trained clients to drink one-off, idiosyncratic coffees, a business model that is rare). A taster bears some responsibility to spare a client from purchasing coffees that will be inconsistent, and more importantly, tasters fear being blamed for recommending the purchase of a coffee whose identifying features may disappear. The issue here is, was the taster justified in lowering the score? It might be said that objectively one should register the flavor that is "in the cup," and if that was really an 87, so be it. If one is being strictly objective, one simply assesses the liquid in the cup, and considering something that is not there in the cup introduces a subjective element into the evaluation. But in practice professional tasters continually make distinctions between what is thought to be inherent in the bean and what is thought to be due to some fortunate or unhappy effect created during the washing, de-pulping, or fermentation, molds that developed during the drying and storage, or over-roasting that overwhelmed flavors that were thought to be inherent in the bean. How is a distinction between a taste inherent in the bean and tastes that are the result of some effect of the processing or handling made? Does this distinction rest "in the cup," or is it the activity of a subjectivity operating in the service of rationality? There are many objectivities, and this judge's rating was a subjectively informed objectivity that was accepted as valid by the fellow tasters. Hence, being objective includes scoring things that are not there.

On another occasion, in another Central American country, the advice from the head judge to the tasters was that when they were testing naturally processed coffees, they needed to be careful not to be too severe in punishing the coffees for lack of uniformity. A "natural" process is one that involves de-pulping the coffee cherry without the use of water, a method that can introduce a variety of fermentations to the bean, resulting in beans that are less uniform than coffees whose cherries were de-pulped using a "washed" process. The scoring categories "Uniformity" and "Clean Cup" refer not to flavor attributes but to differences in uniformity from cup to cup or to the occasional presence of flaws that mar the cleanliness of the coffee. The head judge was concerned that coffees not be penalized by how they were processed; but is it being objective to alter one's use of the form in this way? Here again, when one is judging only what is present in the cup, applying a category that is derived from what is not present seems to be an intelligent application of a subjective process that is working in the interest of an objective assessment of the coffee. As Perullo (2018b, 265) has observed, "Taste perception is always situated," and here is another situated objectivity. Tasting for a "clean cup" is directed more to deficiencies than to positive features of flavor, especially deficiencies that mask the virtues that a coffee possesses. When I asked one head taster to explain to me more precisely what is intended by the category, she replied, "You want to ask yourself, 'Are any of the flavors in the coffee from outside the coffee, rather than inside?'" But if one is being strictly empirical, isn't everything "inside"? Evidently not.

The founder of the field of the sociology of knowledge, Karl Mannheim, observed a comparable phenomenon that occurs commonly during historical analysis whereby "the historian is able gradually to make himself at home in the 'mental climate' of the work whose expressive intent the historian is seeking to understand" (Mannheim 1952, 55). Until the historian is able to recognize the historical and cultural "background" of a sculpture or sample of architecture or a document, etc., the historian will not be able to understand it in an objective way. According to Mannheim, this background is necessary for obtaining a clearer understanding of the document. But this process of interpretation is not "objective" in a standard sense, since it is invoking what is "outside" something for the purpose of understanding the phenomenon. Mannheim (1952, 55) explains, "Whereas objective interpretation is concerned with grasping a completely self-contained complex of meaning," the "documentary meaning" necessarily "points beyond the work," and here something remarkable occurs: in looking *beyond* what is there, one identifies an "ethos" that renders meaningful what is given immediately. Note the circularity at work here: it is the document that causes us to look beyond it to what is not there, but it is that very same domain that is not there that directs us to the truest sense of the document. Hans-Georg Gadamer (1975, 261) called this circularity "the circle of understanding," and argued (Gadamer 1975, 236), "In the circle is hidden a positive possibility of the most primordial kind of knowing." By reckoning a "natural" processing or a method of brewing or the effect of a dated roast (or a roast that is "too dark," or "too light"), etc., the coffee taster is giving credence to what is not there and allowing that to influence the objective evaluation. As William Earle (1955, 98) observed, "We *never* confine our attention to what is strictly given to us through perception."

During his own investigations into this primordial level of knowing, and following Mannheim's lead, Harold Garfinkel called this hermeneutic circle "the documentary method of interpretation," and he suggested that it was ubiquitous in human understanding. Garfinkel (1967, 78) summarizes Mannheim:

> The method consists of treating an actual appearance as "the document of," as "pointing to," as "standing on behalf of" a pre-supposed underlying pattern. Not only is the underlying pattern derived from its individual documentary evidences, but the individual documentary evidences, in their turn, are interpreted on the basis of "what is known" about the underlying pattern. Each is used to elaborate the other.

All that is present is the thing, or the document, but it gains its definite sense and its reference from an underlying pattern, a pattern that is indicated by the document itself but occurs outside it. This is the origin of Garfinkel's conception of the reflexive nature of understanding. The idea that "Each is used to elaborate the other" offers a view of rationality that treats rationality as always occasioned, and it stipulates a mode of analysis that resists any obligation to defer to "a supra-temporal Reason" (Dahl 1994, 118), the legacy of European metaphysics.

Much professional sensory analysis rehearses this metaphysical position, which, in spite of its claim to objectivity, puts into doubt the idea that it is unbiased. It is so deeply entrenched in our particular culture of rational praxis that the method is used as the default routine for every situation, without the practitioners even being aware they are doing so. However, Garfinkel submitted that it is little more than a "Just-So" story, tidy in the telling, and he commended investigating affairs more deeply, in order to catch the work of "'fact production' in flight" (Garfinkel 1967, 79), i.e., as it is happening. Further, perhaps this recent expanded investigation into the deeper hermeneutic issues that accompany rational activities constitutes part of the historical destiny of the European sciences, a transition through which we are presently living.

Mannheim recommended that the work of disclosing this "documentary meaning" should include seeking further evidence in order to make one's characterization of the historical context complete, and he suggested that this task will benefit from ranging over "several pieces of evidence" and examining many comparable documents (sculptures, architectural works, etc.). However, in his investigations Mannheim (1952, 57) came to an astonishing discovery: "The peculiar thing is, in fact, that in a certain sense one single item of documentary evidence gives a complete characterization of the subject." In other words, the *one* thing that we have in our hands is able to generate, by itself, the entire frame of reference that contextualizes it and provides it with its objective sense. As Zahavi (2001, 40) has written, "No perception *of the object* would be possible if we were only conscious of what was actually given." That one thing is not alone but is accompanied by what Husserl calls the "inner horizon" of our experience, which we bring to it and is part of any object's reality as much as the outer horizon is.

There are other subjectivities that arise naturally in coffee tasting that result more from national and cultural orientations than from the hermeneutics of taste judgments, which offer further evidence that subjectivity is inescapable. Opinions regarding tastes resulting from the fermentation of naturally processed coffees are subject to national differences. For a long period, a "good" coffee was considered to be a coffee that is free of unwashed flavors, but that has changed. The specialty coffee industry especially has had to adapt its objective standards to the growing acceptability of "naturally processed" and "honeyed processed" coffees. This has not been easy for the Specialty Coffee Association (SCA), and their graders are still reluctant to assess naturals along with washed coffees. Even today the Q-Grader examinees cup the naturals in a separate tasting session, so that they are not evaluated alongside washed coffees. In many international competitions, when a natural coffee competes with a washed one, especially during the semifinal and final rounds of a competition, some tasters will lower their score for the natural coffee by several points. While these tasters insist they are scoring objectively, they will rate fabulous, flowery coffees lower because these coffees do not conform to their preconception of the ideal coffee. Is that a form of subjective assessment? It is well tolerated.

Colombia has been successful in exporting its coffees and is known for producing mild, sweet coffees that possess few defects. When it comes to tastes in coffees, they are a conservative country. They have a strong preference for washed processing, so strong a preference that in Colombia naturally processed coffees may be given lower scores simply because the wildness of flavors produced by the fermentations of natural coffees is considered to be a deficiency of processing, especially when the tasters expect to be cupping clean, mild, smooth flavors. While Colombians dislike naturals, many Chinese like them. My own preference is more for the wilder, high-citrus, flower-basket flavors of naturals, and during one cupping I rated a predictable, good-quality ("sweet," "smooth") washed Tolima coffee lower than the 93 scoring average it achieved. Since the judges were tasting silently and also reluctant to expose themselves during the post-cupping debriefing, it was impossible to know just what the panel of tasters were using as a base for their professional standards; it is possible that the 93 rating was a celebration of the Tolima coffee having met their expectations of a typical Colombian flavor profile. Meeting expectations can influence scoring, and it too is subjective; however, the judges' decision here seems like a fair way to proceed if one is Colombian. Such a situation introduces a bit of caution into the notion that the ratings of professional coffee tasting panels are globally applicable, and it reveals possible difficulties with some routine uses of the term "objective."

Take for instance the naturally processed coffee that earned sixth place in an El Salvador Cup of Excellence. The grower was deeply disappointed, and he expressed to me his opinion that it was the prejudice against naturally processed coffees of several Korean judges that had lowered his rating. While he agreed that Korean tasters are entitled to their preferences, he considered it incorrect to insist upon conformity with a personal standard. Being objective and conforming to predetermined, standardized notions can get conflated, since tasters might argue that conforming with widely confirmed standardized notions is being objective. This has some sense, but one can point out that other objectivities exist.

Comments like "It betrayed me" and "It didn't hold up" are ubiquitous. The complaint "It never got to where it needed to be" may be true, except how did the taster know where it "needed" to be if that place never existed? What are the limits of what can be real? Heidegger (1996, 141) has noted, "What is initially 'there' is nothing else than the self-evident, undisputed prejudice of the interpreter." Merleau-Ponty (1968, 38) said much the same: "We put into things what we pretend to find in them." However, if one banishes from sensory analysis every element of taste that has an association with something subjective, there will be nothing left to taste.

There is another region of subjectivity that exercises extensive influence over how tasters make their assessments, and despite always being present it is mostly unnoticed. A primary motive for how tasters undertake their work is an abiding tendency to satisfy local social expectations that occur serendipitously inside the immediate context in which the tasting is being carried out. Almost always, people find it desirable to harmonize with the orientations of their fellows; in fact, the calibration sessions are designed as a vehicle for supporting this process. If being objective means analyzing by means of using methods, language, and results that can be understood generally, and accepted, as Popper and Husserl have both argued, then objectivity can run into a double bind when one finds one's way of working and thinking being influenced at the outset by the general social milieu and specific expectations of the fellow tasters *in situ*. Yes, professional tasters taste silently, but that is after a local social orientation to the activity has already been settled. Even the more austere tasting that happens in the white booths of tasting labs occurs after considerable socialization of the tasters has taken hold. The contingencies of each local social interaction exercise their influence.

Cultural biases can be tenacious, and they can be invisible. For example, since what is considered a "bitter" coffee varies considerably by region, how is an objective score in this category possible? Americans tolerate coffees that are more bitter than Scandinavians do. Even in the USA, while West Coast drinkers expect their coffee to be a bitter dark roast (it should be noted that they often drink their coffee with cream and sugar), most East Coast drinkers expect "coffee" that has a medium roast. When Italians drink the coffee of either US coast, they will say it is not coffee but only hot colored water. For its part, the tongue of an American hardly knows what to do when it meets with an Italian espresso, so how can it grade anything? A Dane once suggested to me that drinking an espresso from southern Italy was like drinking an infusion of powdered charcoal (he has visited Napoli!); and an accomplished Italian taster once referred to Scandinavian coffees as "undeveloped coffees." Where is the scope for objectivity? The taste descriptor "lemon," often associated with Kenyan coffees, has become popular in the specialty coffee industry, so it is interesting that in the tasting courses offered in Cosenza (Calabria) by Caffèitalia, "lemon" cannot be found anywhere in their schema of possible flavors. How can one apply a descriptor in an unbiased manner when it is not recognized? I have been told that in Italy they roast coffee dark because their colonies, Somalia and Eritrea, mostly sent them Robusta coffees, which require darker roasts than does Arabica. For whatever reason, they love their coffees dark and with much body.

On many occasions, I have attempted to get one Italian colleague or another to appreciate a highly prized lemon-scented African coffee, but I have always failed. One reason for their disliking citrus-tasting coffees is that Italians are fond of making cappuccinos in the morning, which requires blending a good deal of milk into the beverage; because milk does not go very well with citric and floral flavors, most Italians avoid purchasing those coffees and so they are largely unknown, whereas coffees with a "chocolate" taste, which are highly suitable for cappuccinos, are ubiquitous. This predilection for "chocolate-tasting" coffees has caused this taste descriptor to proliferate to the point where it has become practically unreliable as a taste descriptor. This discussion of flavors in the coffees that Italians drink is all the more interesting when one considers that when an Italian is drinking "un caffè," he or she is preoccupied with the coffee's body, and thinking to experience flavor is almost an afterthought. Italian coffees are all about mouthfeel and about the texture of what is occurring between the tongue and the cheek, something that barely registers for an American drinker. In such a situation, what kind of universal system for grading coffee can develop?

Especially interesting is the Italian vigilance for disliked coffees that possess a "rioy" taste, which originates from phenolic sources, like molds. Pendergrast (2010, 26) describes the *rio* flavor as "strong, iodine-like, malodorous, rank," yet Indian exporters have reported to me that coffees with this feature are desired by some Middle Eastern buyers, who will even give them a light roast! Exporters in Brazil have learned that Japanese buyers will never complain about a *rio* taint. Whether the Japanese do not notice the taste or whether they detect it but do not have a response to it is uncertain. If taste can be objective, and if detecting defects is more amenable to objective assessment than is tasting for positive features, how is it that a *rio* defect can pass undetected by any professional taster who is being objective? What is a defect, then? In South India, I met a coffee purveyor who actually searches for coffees that have a mild amount of rancidity, for selling to Turkish buyers. The manager of one medium-sized Indian coffee processing facility explained to me that Turks prefer those coffees. One cannot accuse the Turks of being unsophisticated about coffee, since they are the people who, centuries ago, made coffee the global commodity that it is. Pendergrast (2010, 345) reports that some consumers have become accustomed to the taste of *rio*, including Greeks: "Harsh, fermented Rioy Brazilian beans, despised by most connoisseurs, are prized by the Greeks." That these coffees can be bought and sold at low price levels could be another part of the motivation of those who purchase these coffees. Also, sometimes these coffees will be processed as dried solubles, and so any flavor that strongly recalls coffee, even coffee taints, may be welcome. But the national differences in responding to such a strong defect as *rio* puts into question the notion that universal objective standards for good taste can be established.

Japanese drinkers appreciate blueberry flavor more than South Americans do, and Japanese like fruity, winey coffees. Italians prefer malic acid, which helps coffee taste buttery. Chinese, Koreans, and Japanese are able to better differentiate salty flavors than Europeans are, and sometimes they assess acidity differently. Sensory scientists have argued that *the fact* of saltiness or acidity is objective and pre-subjective, and that subjectivity can be brought in later when "like" and "dislike" enter the situation. But this is only a happy narrative solution to the problem, and the differences in perceiving tastes I have been describing, differences that are due to national habits and cultural preferences, operate at more fundamental and intransigent levels.

The Living Reciprocity of Knowing

Three sociologists of sensory analysis (Vannini, Waskul, and Gottschalk 2012) treat the somatic work of sensing as a process, by which they mean that sense data are not docile objects but subject to their ongoing relations with whoever is doing the sensing. They write, "Sensing is an active and interpretive process, rather than a passive reaction to external stimuli endowed with pre-formed meaning" (Vannini et al. 2012, 11). This accords with the classical view of Hegel (1969, 172): "Truth is to be grasped and expressed only as a becoming, as a process . . . not as being, which in a proposition has the character of a stable unity." For the most part, sensory science has adopted the dualistic assumption that treats sensory characteristics as pre-formed and existing independently of the participation of the one who is sensing. We ourselves have been mostly retaining a dualistic perspective during our discussion of the inescapability of subjectivity. About this, Heidegger (1967, 27) issued a warning: "We cannot invoke the common answer which says that if determinations are not 'objective' they are 'subjective.' It could be that they are neither, that the distinction between subject and object, and with it the subject-object relationship itself, is a highly questionable, though generally favored, sphere of retreat for philosophy." Let us consider this radical proposal further.

Georg Simmel emphasized the fact that the being of any object, material or social, rests upon reciprocal relations it has with other beings, reciprocity that makes obsolete the notion that "object" and "subject" could exist independently. The one always entails the other. Simmel (1958, my translation) discovered, "The central notions of truth, value, objectivity, etc. were disclosed to me as precipitates of active and effective reciprocal relations [*Wechselwirkung*]." Things exist, but their identities are neither static nor absolute; rather, they arise in a situation and remain dependent upon the contingencies of the situations in which they have emerged. Simmel even considered *Wechselwirkung* to be "a comprehensive metaphysical principle," albeit a metaphysics not found frequently in European science. There is a "mutual dependence of subject and object," and we are advised to solicit "a simple perception of content" that "is not yet divided between them" (Simmel 2004, 67). Simmel (1958) insisted this was not simply some skeptical relativism that would weaken our ability to analyze matters, but the very means for an affirmation of their real objectivity and therefore able to serve as a bulwark against skepticism.

The Italian philosopher of tasting Perullo (2018b, 266) summarizes this perspective: "Things are not *in* relation; rather, they are relations." Moreover, they are only relations; there are nothing but relations (here is where this observation becomes metaphysics). The consequence of this is that to know tastes objectively, we are required to capture experience *in its course*. Not only *in* its course, but *as* its course. This entails identifying how things emerge during our analyses, even as they are conscripted immediately to serve as part of our analysis. We organize the intelligibility of the world by objectifying our knowledge, which brings us to the crucial matter of reducing being to knowing. What knowing can there be that does not pollute the well?

Truth must be located in what appears to us, but not everything that appears to us is true, so what methods do we develop for "objectifying what was vague, implicit, and entangled with the very subject knowing it" (Earle 1955, 34)? The situation is confounded by the fact that these entanglements are vital tools. Let us taste some coffee and see how we make out.

There is an exercise called triangulation that is used for training coffee tasters. This exercise requires tasters to identify the odd cup of coffee in a trio of cups. Not only are novice tasters trained using this technique, it becomes part of the examination that they will be given at the time they are tested for certification as professional tasters. They are presented with six sets of three cups, which are placed about a single table. In each set, one coffee is unique and two are identical. It sounds eminently easy, but that assessment does not take into consideration the capacity of the mind to spin tales about what one is tasting. It is an exercise in which the more one thinks about the coffees, the more confused one can become.

Of six sets of three coffees on a table, it is common that for two sets the odd cup will be obvious, and another two sets can be deciphered by means of some focused attention. There are several professional tricks that are recommended, which include remaining with one's initial decision, relying upon aroma more than flavor, and always assigning to each cup some specifically named flavor attribute (licorice, clove, lemon, caramel) or at least a category of flavor (spicy, fruity, etc.). The idea is that the more specificity one can apply to the coffee's taste, the less likely it is that it will slip from one's memory as one proceeds with the cupping. These tricks illustrate the contributions that can be made by formalizing one's knowledge. Settling a coffee this way helps to create stability; however, the synthetic work of defining/identifying (here these come to be the same thing) the taste always involves an object that is entwined with our subjective activity. This is not to disparage these identifications; on the contrary, it is to praise the contribution that thinking can make to tasting even as it impedes it.

Unfortunately for the taster who is being tested, one or two of the sets of coffees can be diabolical. As one tastes and re-tastes, the coffee that seems to be unlike the other two of the trio keeps shifting, and neither synthetic analysis nor direct intuition produces any solution. There are so many features of taste that one may locate a difference in the body that isolates a coffee that is different than the one that can be isolated by identifying the flavors detected. One keeps retesting one's assessment by re-cupping the coffees, and each time one does so one may project upon the cup a specific inquiry: if one projects a distinctive body, one confirms or disconfirms that; if one projects a unique flavor, one notices that. The problem is that too frequently the cup that seems to be different is not the same one. After several re-tastings in hope of clarifying the situation, one finds oneself gradually becoming lost in an aphasia of triangulation, and so one decides to move along to the other sets of coffee on the table (hopefully, to a more obvious set) in order to regain some equilibrium and self-confidence. As one circles the table and returns to the problematic set, having regained some confidence, the coffees have cooled, and so they present an altered flavor profile (perhaps some sweetness becomes prominent, or a formerly dominant aspect of taste has subsided). It can happen that one can nail the obviously different coffee at that time, but it is equally likely that any tentative conclusion one had come to previously is unseated by a thoroughgoing reevaluation. It can even happen that each one of the three cups can, for a time, be suspected of being the odd cup. Bravo. Just at this moment, the head taster may announce that only two minutes remain. The vertigo to which one is propelled by one's own thinking demonstrates how entangled with what one knows any perceived taste can be.

Garfinkel (2002, 199) has suggested that part of the work of ethnomethodology is to study how the intelligibility of something is produced: "the *coherence of the thing* is what we're up to." Any unity of sense that something comes to possess is a result of our entanglements with it, and there is no experience, of taste or of anything else, that does not include this sort of participation. The coherency of the object (let us say, an identified taste of a cup of coffee) stems from "the continual synthetic unity of a streaming present" (Husserl 2001, 174), and Husserl is clear about the fact that this unity is our accomplishment, based upon our "primordial syntheses" of our perceptions and experiences with an object. This unity is essential to the identity of a phenomenon and is our initial understanding and appropriation of the object. These earliest reckonings involve not only deliberate choices and fixations regarding what most identifies a taste but also what arrives passively and pre-deliberatively. In establishing some unity of sense so that we can proceed with our tasks, how can we prevent this unity from becoming so reified that it locks up the rest of our experience inside a prison of our imagination? Simply deferring to "what is in the cup" is insufficient, since we too are in the cup.

Nor is it reasonable to deny there is an object. Figal is critical of both Husserl and Heidegger for some unidirectionality in how they address this question of the subject and the object, and Figal expresses a desire to give more agency to the object, arguing that once we make genuine contact with the object, *it* will reveal its nature; and this, for Figal, is object-ivity. Note that objectivity here has more vitality than most accounts of objectivity propose. Figal would agree with Adorno that there is real objectivity. The problems are instituted when we begin to reify our relations with the coffee and try to remove ourselves artificially from the activity that is making contact with it. Hegel (1977, 32) argued that truth is the entire movement of thought. Taste is complicated and it must be captured on the fly, as it were, not as a docile representation. Fidelity to experience demands this. For some sensory scientists, objectivity includes an object's locally experienced details, and while there is a routine according to which their quantitative measures guide most of their decisions, they may feel it is necessary to allow scope for exceptions, provided the exception can successfully pass their attuned sensory assessment.

Taste as a process, taste as a task (Perullo 2018a), the objectivity that is a precipitate of knowing as movement, complicates any simple solution to objectivity. If this strikes one as unfortunate, consider that it is nevertheless required by the real complications of living in the world. There is a seminal passage at the conclusion of Martin Heidegger's *What Is a Thing?* (1967, 243) that can guide us to a deeper appreciation of the situation:

> Our attention is directed either toward what is said of the object itself or toward what is explained about the mode in which it is experienced. What is decisive, however, is neither to pay attention only to the one nor only to the other, nor to both together, but to recognize and to know: 1. That we must always move in the *between*, between man and thing; 2. That this *between* exists only while we move in it; 3. That this *between* is not like a rope stretching from thing to man, but that this *between* as an anticipation reaches beyond the thing and similarly back behind us.

Eugene Gendlin (1967, 258) comments, "This 'between' is not as though first we and things could have existed separately and then interacted. Rather, what a person is is always already a having things given, and a thing is already something that encounters." This suggests that this "between" is the origin of matters.

The situation implies that we should cultivate nondualist ways of investigating; however, according to Figal nondualism is not some obscure sense of unity but comes with specifications, in accord with the sort of interdependence that Simmel described. What is inside the cup and what is outside "do not sink into a diffuse commonality like figures formed by the current that always and again dissolve into the river as it flows on. Rather, each of the two 'sides' is only what it is based on the other" (Figal 2010, 324). Both exist, but in a reciprocal way.

Ethnomethodology

Ethnomethodology studies the naturally organized orderliness of ordinary activities. These orderlinesses are not always the order of legislators, theorists, or textbooks. Perhaps policemen have a better appreciation of these natural orders because they live closer to mundane situations. Since the present research has been carried out by means of ethnomethodological research, a few words about these are warranted.

The founder of ethnomethodology, Harold Garfinkel, insisted upon what he called "the unique adequacy requirement of methods" (Garfinkel 2002, 175), according to which the methods that are adequate for discovering the local orderliness of some people's daily affairs are "only available in the *lived in-courseness of the local production*" of those affairs. The notion "local" is key here, because all orders find their way about by means of local details that are contingent features of each situation, and this includes even those orders that have gone to law school and come back educated. The aim of ethnomethodologists is to view such ordering at work, as it is lived in a local setting, and to describe the ongoing organization of the orderliness that operates there. In order to gain access to the minute details of that local orderliness, and to witness the work of its organization, the social analyst must gain some competence with using, or at least recognizing, the methods that the parties themselves are using. Ethnomethodologists are quick to avoid theorizing their way through data; instead, they search for what people are doing and then describe those doings. The question for an ethnomethodological researcher is, just how do people accomplish what they are doing? Ethnomethodologists identify, and they describe, the methods that are "uniquely possessed" (Garfinkel 2002, 176) by the parties, and so the analyst must come to some familiarity with them. Moreover, it is unlikely that the social analyst could have known what they are in advance, unless they are restricting their research to only what the researchers provide themselves.

Because an ethno-method originates with the parties themselves, there is no scope for imposing some externally derived account upon people, or burying their lifeworld underneath a "news from nowhere" disciplinary framework. The methods of ethnomethodologists do not come from any place except the scene itself. They are the "methods" for accomplishing the world that are employed routinely by the people (the "ethno") under study. These are the ethno-methods that ethnomethodology studies. To this end, ethnomethodology complies with the demand of Adorno (2000, 72) in his *Introduction to Sociology* when he said, "The method cannot be posited as absolute in opposition to its subject matter; rather, the method of sociology must stand in a living relationship to this subject matter and must, as far as possible, be developed from it."

Further, these activities are captured in the course of their being lived, in real time, that is to say, in the time of those who are living them, and not in the time of those who manage the laboratory. For this reason, I try to avoid parroting the prejudices of either coffee purveyors or sensory scientists and address only what I witnessed directly. The adequacy of these "adequate" methods is adequate to the looks-of-the-world for the people who are under study; and for ethnomethodology, this includes the *horizon* of meaning and potential experience that always accompanies those "looks." This "in-courseness" respects the flow of lived experience, or the "flusso" (flow) that Perullo (2018a, 86) often speaks of, and which is essential to retain when one analyzes taste. Ethnomethodology concurs with Perullo's project when he says, "We are not interested in 'isolated' taste(s) or flavor(s), but rather in taste *in use*" (Perullo 2018a, 265).

A note to the reader: please do not misunderstand the aim of these inquiries. While it may sometimes seem that I am studying subjective experience, in fact I am motivated primarily to learn the transcendent life of what is objective, and this is what I am concerned to identify and describe. Ethnomethodology would be misinterpreted if it was understood as a form of subjectivism, and it broke from the idealist remnants of Husserl's methodology quite early. Nor is it a behaviorism or a structuralism. Its research objectives have nothing in common with the projects of neuro-cognitive science nor Bourdieu-motivated research into how "tastes" and fashions are shaped by social class. The French sociologists of sensory experience Hennion and Teil (2004a, 19) describe the situation well:

> When it comes to the status of products concerned with taste, the various disciplines are divided, unsatisfactorily, along the lines of a nature-culture approach: either food products are just things, and their properties are analyzed through laboratory tests and

measurements; or they are simply signs, the media for various rites and mechanisms of social identity, in which case their physical reality disappears in the analysis.

Neither of these approaches helps us very much. The investigations of Lévi-Strauss, Bourdieu, and some political economists are not only important, they are for the most part true, but this study, while it is about coffee, is addressed to a different phenomenon: the "taste" that happens on one's tongue. If one argues that addressed this way coffee becomes a trivial topic, I would only point out how ubiquitous are the flavors that occur in one's mouth and how much coffee drinking occurs every day in the world. The theories mentioned are globally disseminated social theories whose currency rests in how popular these recent traditions of analysis have become, but we need to re-embed them in real occasions, actual places where people *taste* coffee, along with the local relations that inevitably surround such tasting.

To my thinking, sociology's near-total ignoring of taste-as-sense, rather than taste-as-a-status-indicator, is a scandal and amounts to sociologism. Many of these sociologists claim to be studying "everyday life," and yet they are unable to find any real flavor happening in the mundane world, and instead only find food for the discourse of social class. Without rejecting the importance of that discourse, taste-as-sense too deserves attention, especially by those who claim to be interested in studying the mundane world. It may not be as important as class conflict, but the fact that there is so much tasting going on in the world each day suggests that it merits some attention. Hennion and Teil (2004a, 21) remark, "Research has therefore turned away from the question of perception and towards that of consumption." Ethnomethodologists seek to avoid materialist and sociological determinisms, and especially we do not want to reduce tasting to an analytic puppet *before* we have tasted anything at all. It is possible to undertake research without adopting a scientism or sociologism. In this regard, the strategy of sociology of sense-experience researcher Lorenza Mondada (2019, 51) is commendable: "Between these two opposite orientations, what is missing is an account focusing on activities in which people actually perceive, sense, and experience the world, make relevant the sensory features of these experiences for others, and share them intersubjectively, by collectively and jointly producing and coordinating them, and by publicly expressing, displaying, and witnessing them."

Our topic is the sense-making and legitimacy-making activities of objective practices in the coffee industry. An inquiry into tasting practices such as this is a legitimate topic for sociological research. As Vannini et al. (2012, 6) have argued, "The human senses and sensations are certainly the subject matter of cultural and social scientists, and not the sole domain of physiology and cognition." We are attempting phenomenological clarification of the ground and local organization of the efficacious objective practices of professional coffee tasters who work in the international coffee industry. Taste, the taste that has flavors, is our topic.

Still, one phenomenon of the taste of coffee is abstracted from the many and varied occasions where people drink coffee. Real coffee drinking is always occasioned, in one's kitchen, at a favorite bar or café, at a dinner party or card game, in a laboratory, etc., and these occasions are endlessly many, so if we are going to be faithful to the occasioned character of these occasions, we face a nearly infinite task. An unexpected consequence is that we must work with an idealized situation that sometimes makes more of taste than the people drinking the coffee may make of it themselves; here the unique adequacy principle of methods requires us to witness what the drinkers are really doing before we impose our own interests on the scene. Once the occasioned character of drinking coffee is lost, one is left with a narrowed analytic reduction of the real phenomenon. In this way, phenomenology and ethnomethodology have their unique notions of what it is to be rigorous, and ethnomethodologists do their best to relinquish their interests in favor of the priorities and detailed actual looks of things for the people they are studying.

Simmel, a pioneer of studying the micro-bases of macrosocial structures, was perhaps the first person in sociology to argue not by theorizing but by in-depth analyses of perspicuous mundane phenomena. His special interest, in addition to tangible topics like money (Simmel 1978), tourism (Simmel 2013), and the structure of the meal (Simmel 1997), was in how the matters that are developed within mundane social interaction gain objective status and come to seem independent of those intersubjective activities. Garfinkel (1967, 182) describes this topic this way: "Society hides from its members its activities of organization and thus leads them to see its features as determinate and independent objects." Simply because they are hidden does not mean that these activities cannot be exposed and studied. Although ethnomethodological research is not without controversy, we are quite adept at uncovering quotidian practices that, like the water that fish are swimming in, normally pass unnoticed and unremarked upon.

The principal research tool used by ethnomethodologists is observing naturally occurring activities, and participant observation can be a way to accomplish this. Ethnomethodologists do not usually ask people questions, unless this can happen in a way that is naturally occurring. The problem with questions is that most persons respond by offering the answer that they imagine the researcher wishes to hear. It is a peculiar thing, but most people will fail in guessing correctly what the researcher wants to hear (in part because a good researcher has no preferences). But the important point here is a different one: people's replies are unreliable, and in most instances they should not be made the basis of scientific social research; moreover, the very act of questioning causes the researcher's frame of reference to dominate the situation. Since the goal is to witness not one's own frame of reference but the frame of reference of those who are being studied, it is better for the researcher to remain silent. Surveys play no role in ethnomethodological research since they are mostly fictions, for many reasons that are beyond the scope of this monograph. If one asks a professional taster about how they taste, one will receive lectures, many of them lengthy, but nowhere in those lectures can one witness practices of tasting, in the course of tasting. When interviewing, logic plays a stronger role than it plays during tasting, since while tasting the practicalities of the flavors predominate. Among the research tasks for this study was learning to recognize what is happening on the tongue, and so a special sort of participant observation was required. In this case, it was a pleasant obligation. If one is interested in how tasters use taste descriptors, one could ask them about it, but that is not as informative as observing how coffee tasters use descriptors *in situ*. The *"in situ"* means in the world that the tasters inhabit, not the world that social scientists inhabit. Tasting alongside professional tasters became the best methodology. Long may it live.

In a pioneering study by Nicholas Cho (2011) for *The Specialty Coffee Chronicle*, lay consumers of coffee were interviewed. They were asked, "What is a great cup of coffee to you? What makes for a bad coffee experience? What makes for a great coffee experience?" Unfortunately, a methodology of questioning like this operates too remotely from the occasioned experience of tasting to capture much data that will be reliable. Accordingly, ethnomethodologists do not use interviews or distribute surveys. Where possible, they do try to video or audio record naturally occurring situations, for the reason that tape recordings capture some of the fine detail of local scenes that can later be examined repeatedly by the social analyst. When transcripts of the tapes are made, and the tapes are reviewed while reading a printed transcript for the tape, a plenum of pertinent data can be exposed.

Making Contact with the Transcendent Object

The abiding interest of nearly all of Husserl's investigations was the nature of "an object that transcends consciousness" and always accompanying that, "the problem of the purely immanent objectlike formation" performed by subjects' lived experience (Husserl 2001, 171). It is necessary to describe the relations of subjects and objects in a way that is shorn of dualism. For Husserl, these two are always conjoined, and for anyone cognizing the world, the immanent formation of the object is something "lying deeper and essentially preceding" the transcendent object. The situation is intricate: "something objective cannot be adequately given" by a presentive consciousness or cohort of actors; rather, "only the *idea* of that something objective can be given" (Husserl 1982, 343); yet Husserl's primary interest was in delineating just what *the object* itself is, in its objectivity. Husserl (1982, 348) references "the actual object," which is the object *simpliciter* that is prior to "the object in the how of its determinacies" (Figal 2010, 111). The "problem" is that while Husserl recognizes the unavoidable fact that the given object is always given by the synthetic activity of consciousness, Husserl admits (as Figal describes it) that one has some relation with the transcendent object "that cannot be imminently understood as a 'relation of consciousness to its intentional object.'" It sounds mysterious when one theorizes about it, but it is the most common thing in the world. Just what are the relations between subjects' lived experience and a transcendent object?

Garfinkel and Liberman (2007, 6) pose the question, "This vital issue is: making contact with a transcendent object. Just-how is such contact actually made?" Husserl (1999, 29) himself elaborated, "Knowing is something other than the known object; knowing is given, but the known object is not given; and yet knowing is supposed to relate to the object, to know it. How can I understand this possibility?" This is the essential question of how something comes to be known objectively. Garfinkel was especially interested in how scientists make contact with an object. Somehow contact is made with a transcendent object, with a real thing, even as this object of the scientists is disclosed by means of the "procedurally coherent details" of their formal analytic methods (Garfinkel 2007, 35). The thing is revealed as "an organizational thing," but it *is* revealed—contact is made—and it is made *with the aid* of their formal analytic methods.

Husserl (1999) suggested that there are times when something that lies in things seems to impose itself upon knowledge, that arrives almost as a requirement that any conscious attention must acknowledge and experience. Hennion (2004, 109) has spoken of the "inexpressible instantaneousness" of taste, and any coffee that is particularly striking is an excellent example—there are coffees that are so bitter, or so full of fruits and flowers, that no one fails to attend to them. A terrible smell is another example, or the sound of a bell (Figal 2010, 321). These are objects that possess a "drop-in" saliency that becomes, tangibly, a *thing* that is evident to all. Other transcendent objects have more subtle features, ones that may be overlooked, but by attending to them carefully one can acknowledge and experience them too. *The key question for us here is, how is it that "the fundamental relationship between us and things is intensified"* (Figal 2010, 303)? This is a clue that can guide us in examining how the formal analytic methods used by scientists, or by anyone, gives us or fails to give us access to the transcendent object: does the method *intensify* the contact we can maintain with the object?

Hennion and Teil (2004b, 521) observed that the object's "ability to interrupt, surprise or respond" to our engagement with it is where its objectivity is revealed. Much depends upon the objects' "power to make themselves more present": "They give themselves, they hide, they impose themselves on us." But it also depends on *our* capacity to intensify our engagement with the object. The distal model of awareness, frequently employed in sensory science, imagines there exists considerable distance between a docile subject an inert object, and the greater that distance is, the more objectivity is presumed. This is misguided; and further, damage is caused by the demand that objects be made fully submissive to our methods. As Hennion and Teil (2004b, 535) argue clearly, the question is not to give *less* power to the object but to let it have more influence. In the distal model, the object has little power of its own, its objectivity is thought to pre-exist the subject, and the objectivity of our knowledge is guaranteed only by a formal banishment of the subject. In this way the role of subjectivity, which is the goose that lays the golden eggs, is diminished. Making contact with the transcendent object, which is the sole source of real objectivity, *requires* an active subjectivity because only an enhanced subjectivity can make contact with a transcendent object. In this way, objectivity and subjectivity are not as opposed to each other as the distal model of sensory assessment supposes them to be.

The best way to be objective is to stick with the object, so here the coffee predominates. For example, when doubts about the objectivity of one's taste descriptors or scoring arise, most tasters do not reflect more deeply; instead, they return to the cup for another taste. Only the object itself can guarantee objectivity. Husserl (2001, 174) prioritizes "the purely immanent formation and the constitution" of an object, and he focuses upon the "synthetic strategies" with which *we* maintain the coherency of an object. "Immanent" here is the decisive term, since it directs us to the origin of our own mastery of what is transpiring in front of us, both with (i.e., the dualist perspective) and as (i.e., the nondualist perspective) our engagement with a thing, before we have had an opportunity to submerge that object and accompanying experience beneath ideological or disciplinary concerns. This immanent experience is *Evidenz*, the origin of any truth about the real that is in the cup, as opposed to the methodologically determined "real." The coherency of the object, here the identified taste of a cup of coffee, stems from "the continual synthetic unity of a streaming present." Husserl is clear about the fact that this unity is our accomplishment, often accomplished in concert with others, and is founded on "primordial syntheses" of our perceptions and experiences with an object.

This unity is essential to our initial appropriation and understanding of the object, and it is the basis of the identity of a phenomenon. These earliest reckonings involve not only salient sensory features along with our active and deliberate choices and fixations regarding what is most identifying about a taste attribute, but also what arrives passively and pre-deliberatively. In Husserl's words, these objects "emerge for us," i.e., they develop passively, "taking place prior to the occurrences of the higher lying activity of cognitively fixing the common element" (Husserl 2001, 177). Formal science specializes in studying active mental constructions, but if we overlook the role played by the passive syntheses of sense simply because they are less tangible and so more difficult to address, there is a risk that we will over-idealize matters and miss the world. That some matters are less tangible ("non-exact meanings, the meanings in play in actual experience" (Bruzina 1970, 149)) does not mean they do not exist. Speaking about the phenomenology of "specifically experiencing reason," Husserl (1982, 344) asks, "How can empirical thinking, grounded in experience, be of further help there? How is it possible scientifically to determine physical affairs as unities posited according to experience, yet which include infinitely many significations?" We need *both* to preserve our access to the infinities of our experience and to clarify an individually unique object by developing an identity for it that is capable of accumulating our observations and insights. A sort of dialectics operates between the "infinitely many significations" and the unity that collects them.

Consider, for example, the sensory experience and initial cognition of a cup of coffee that is sampled just prior to a taster's recording with a pencil his or her sensations on the tasting form. One can witness professional tasters who are stalled during the course of their work, apparently waiting for this initial coherency of the flavors to congeal in their minds before settling on any conclusive numerical assessments. They are cautious about allowing their labeling practices to dictate the terms of what they have experienced; rather, as we have been reviewing, they prefer that the taste itself speak. One may detect a taste and then go searching for a label, a descriptor—is the coffee's taste "plastic" or "limescale"? Is it fruity or floral, and if so which floral?

This activity of turning the flavor of a coffee into a "unity" is both passive and active. Husserl suggested that the passive operates first, and various sensory observations seem to find their way to a unitary synthesis almost on their own. The hesitation of tasters, which at times approaches aphasia, derives from their having to abandon the productive passive syntheses and enter the professional world of active verbal formulations and numerations. Determination is necessary here, but at the same time it demands a delimitation of what has been tasted. Once that latter world is entered, the descriptors that tasters develop for describing the unity that identifies a coffee's taste become subject to intersubjective confirmation, criticism, and a general semiosis, including unavoidable references to standard professional itineraries of descriptors and terminological fashions. At that point, which is a period of active synthesis, the more immanent field of passive synthesis is left behind. But the formal assessment only has validity in terms of the immanent *Evidenz* of the flavor as first experienced, and so on occasion the taster's solution, at least in my witnessing, is to put the pencil down, pick up the tasting spoon, and return to the more primordial world of tasting the coffee. But this time the tasting may be done with one eye kept on resolving any formal analytic problems that have emerged from the taster wrestling with the tasting schedule the taster is trying to complete in a competent manner; the result is that the taster tastes with divided attention, where commonly there is less immanence.

The saving grace here is that there is a transcendent object: there is a taste in the cup to which the taster can keep returning. It can happen that by that time the coffee has cooled, and it will present a flavor profile that has changed to some degree; these changes attract the taster's attention, thereby intruding freshly upon the formal analytic tasks, even as those tasks can propel the taster to inspect aspects of taste that previously may not have been fully examined. There can be a collision of inquiries. The very object, which is really there, is nevertheless dependent upon the concerted practices we have constructed to teach ourselves what we have in hand, including skillful applications of methods, and skillful manipulations of our smelling and looking. What is critical here is usually not which tasting protocol is used but *how* it is used. We are interested in how the taster makes contact with that transcendent object, and retains contact with it throughout the train of all the other practical and professional obligations, logging of notes, mathematics, and self-generated distractions that tasters confront during the course of their normal work.

With these methods a difficulty can be introduced, which is that contact with the transcendent object is not made, so Garfinkel and Liberman (2007, 6) also ask, "Just-how, on occasion and in any actual case, is actual contact with a transcendent object *not* made?" A scientific method does not guarantee making contact with the object. What else can there be that leads tasters to make real contact, and what are the lived details of those ways by which their methods can occlude the object? Both are topics for investigation. Ethnomethodology is concerned with how scientists make that contact, with how that contact is maintained, and with how that object can be lost. Their interest is feeding from that "unremitting wellspring of intelligibility" (Figal 2010, xi) that an object provides. This is object-centered objectivity.

Making contact with a transcendent object is not enhanced by presuming an *a priori* knowledgeability, and slogans about "objectivity" are not the best route to the transcendent object or to objectivity. What is that best route? According to Merleau-Ponty (1968, 139–140), the object we are seeking "is not a fact or a sum of facts." What makes the facts make sense? Drinking coffee, and especially actually tasting the coffee while one is drinking it, requires creativity, which operates on the ground of that openness wherein flavors express their features. Heidegger (1994, 83) has described our situation with precision: "The essence of something is not at all to be discovered simply like a fact; on the contrary, it must be *brought forth*, since it is not directly present in the sphere of immediate representing and intending. To bring forth is a kind of making, and so there resides in all grasping and positing of the essence something creative." This requires more than calculations. Calculation can assist our making contact, or it can obscure the object. Specifying this requires ethnographic investigation.

How is the transcendent object made into an enduring acquisition for conscious reflection and disciplined exploration? How is the continuity of an understanding developed and maintained in ways that do not close off our access to the wellspring? Our notions require unity, not only so we can communicate them to others and thereby solicit their assistance, but so that we can recall them ourselves when that is required. The aim of science is to develop a heightened relation to the object, not to remove the inquiry from that source of knowledge. Science requires that we provide a unity of knowing and build it up over time, but objectivity in scientific work also requires that we preserve the exteriority of the object. We should establish procedures that make contact with the phenomenon and not so completely dominate the object that its foreignness is lost; even worse, amidst a preoccupation with our methods, the fact that the object has been lost can itself be missed. Garfinkel, following Heidegger (1967), named this lost object "the missing What," and he argued that an object does not become lost in any which way, but is lost specifically because of the detailed ways that a given formal analytic method cultivates the object. Instead of the established procedures (e.g., a tasting protocol) losing the object, the analytic procedures need to offer an intensification of our relation to things, drawing us closer to them, so that we are always dealing with objects "as they really are" (Gurwitsch 1964, 182). That is, established procedures should facilitate the tasters' attunement to the tastes.

Our study departs from the unidirectionality of phenomenological research that investigates how consciousness constitutes the object. Although the relation between subjects' lived experience and the transcendent object is "not symmetrical, it is nevertheless a correlation" (Figal 2010, 301); that is to say, objects are not without agency, and they continually impinge on our being. Objects provide us with the clues we use to maintain the coherency of their identity, and the key to objectivity is to let objects show themselves from themselves. Alfred Schutz (1970a, 49–50) has summarized Husserl: "The object as it is meant has to be brought by the process of clarification to perfect self-givenness, to perfect lucidity and vividness." Bringing the object to perfect self-givenness is the task that any successful tasting protocol should achieve. Here "clarification" is a reference to one of Husserl's most consequential discoveries, the contribution made by bringing a radical self-understanding to the job of exposing and identifying every aspect of the object's identity that has its origin in the thinking, theorizing, methodic procedures, etc. that we ourselves have supplied it during our work of synthesizing the identity of the object. This does not mean that we reject these theoretical or methodological contributions, only that we recognize them for what they are and understand that they are *our* contribution to the objectification of the phenomenon in hand. Here our preoccupation with subjectivity operates in the service of being objective, and so it is not any subjectivism.

Finally, we must give proper consideration to the persistent role that collaboration with our consociates plays in scientific or professional inquiry. Every step that we have been describing is in part dependent on the guidance of others. For example, a taster may say to us, "Did you notice the tingle at the back of the tongue?" And suddenly there is a tingle. The contribution of others is basic to our coming to know what is really objective, because "If the world can also be experienced by another subject, it is not reducible to my acts. . . . In other words, the genuine transcendence of reality implies its experienceability for a stream of consciousness transcendent to me" (Zahavi 2001, 34). In this way part of the transcendence of objectivity has its origin in *the transcendence of others*. Being alongside others, we are able to share a being-toward the object, and this provides us not only with concepts but with a mutual energy, one that further provokes us to focus our attention more strongly upon the taste. The focus that we share with others can propel us to make closer contact with the object. It happens at every cupping.

Chapter 5

The Dynamic Nature of Coffee

> Cupping is an exercise in trying to be objective about a moving target.
> —Scott Conary, Chapel Hill (NC)

It is necessary to keep in mind that coffee is alive and that the ongoing transformations it has, by virtue of its interactions with everything that surrounds it, do not conclude with the harvest. Speaking generally, the phenomenologist William Earle (1955, 141) has stated, "A force cannot be a force in ontological isolation from a world of forces." A coffee bean's location is at the center of a vortex of forces that are continuously influencing its taste. Coffee is a living entity and never achieves stasis. Earle's succeeding comments are also apt: "Its very being is its interaction. Similarly, a living organic thing cannot *be* in the way it is by simple presence in the world; its very being is its life." It is a great mistake to reduce coffee to a simple presence, yet defining the taste of each harvest does require that manner of objectification. A coffee bean is not a static being (though it may appear that way when it sits as a commodity on supermarket shelves), since it has manifold material encounters with other phenomena (sunshine, mold, wind, fermentations, etc.) as well as spiritual encounters with the humans who drink it.

During these encounters there are hundreds of matters that influence the taste of coffee beans. Flavor can vary according to where the beans are stored, how they are shipped, the size of the grind, the temperature of the water, the method of extraction, the size of the cup, the material of the cup, and one's sensory acuity from one morning to the next. Coffee is hardly more tamable than a wild stallion is; however, being wild is a good thing, because if it were possible to fix its taste easily, coffee would be much less interesting and less compelling to trade, and to study. Michaele Weissman

(2008, 54) observes with acuity, "Part of coffee's beauty is its evanescence." The professional burden that coffee tasters must shoulder is that they need to tame the flavors' wildness without denying them that evanescence.

Lingle (2001, 22) suggests that coffee undergoes five phases in its journey from seed to cup: drying, storage, roasting, staling, and brewing. Each of these stages can influence the final flavor in positive or negative ways. In truth, there are more than five phases, and the road from seed to cup is a long one. Just as scientists who predict the weather may require a supercomputer for some predictions in order to handle all the contingent variables, predicting the flavor of a coffee based upon only one or two of its variables is a fool's errand. Too much is taking place for a designer to be confident about maintaining control. This is why Illy Coffee requires "art" as well as "science," and luck is a third partner. The brute truth that some purveyors are reluctant to admit is that coffee is only partially controllable. A designer must continuously honor the worth of a bean by drinking attentively and stepping into *the flow* of the taste, which does not stop evolving. Perullo (2016, 45, my translation) speaks with some humor about this effort to fix the taste of something that is uncontrollable: "Rather than declaring the impossibility of control and opening up to the virtues of the flow, they design complex systems—patterns, concepts, classifications, and categories—that implode into absolute autism," and it may be said without overstatement that every professional coffee taster has at times found him- or herself experiencing some of this autism. Nevertheless, for the most part, and in accord with how European civilization functions in the modern era, the aim of the coffee industry is to subject matters to as much control as possible, even to the point that the project of gaining control overwhelms them, in the end incapacitating them.

No matter how much we like to think of commodities as things, frozen in the identities we have crafted for them, coffee plants themselves are still evolving. The beans too are alive and undergo transformations before, during, and following the harvest. A 63-year-old Nicaraguan taster who spent 34 years in the coffee business once told me that during his lifetime the tastes of coffees have changed a great deal, and these changes are due both to genetics and to changes in farming and processing practices. The practices of the coffee trade itself are always changing, and what is common wisdom one decade can be forgotten or ignored in a succeeding decade. We would like to think that there exists at least some genetic stability, but despite our cultural predilection to reify every identification we make, coffee sometimes escapes our practices of categorization: coffee is alive and presents growers with surprises. The identical sub-species can change its flavor after being transplanted in a different climatic zone, soil regime, or terroir (with unique winds, humidity, solar radiation, alkalinity, etc.). A sub-species that is grown even on the same plantation can offer unanticipated taste characteristics.

When does a coffee plant that has adapted to a changed habitat become a formal genetic variety? Generally, three generations of a coffee tree are required to develop dependable acclimatization to a new micro-climate, and five generations are needed before it is considered to be a new variety. These identities, therefore, pass through to the reasoning practices of scientists and are subject to agreements among them about what constitutes a dependable difference, i.e., a thing in itself. This may be part of the reason why not every "variety" of coffee possesses the same capacity to adapt to a change in the local environmental conditions, and some varieties display more stability than others. As with everything else, there is what is happening in the world and there is also how we understand it and capture it inside the ways we have organized our understanding. Accordingly, any "fact" that results is a hybrid phenomenon.

Moreover, these changes never come to stop, and no identity is forever. Weissman (2008, 84) tells us, "*Coffea arabica* produces varieties of coffee as different from one another as concord grapes are from champagne grapes or Muscat grapes." The taste of coffee grown on a particular estate varies depending on the type of tree, soil, atmospheric conditions, and processing. The flavor potential of the many varieties of *Coffea canephora* var. *robusta* coffee have still not been fully explored, and new surprises are waiting for coffee professionals to notice them, such as some recently discovered Robusta varieties from Uganda, Tanzania, and elsewhere that have superior flavors, which I have tasted. *Coffea arabica* coffee varietals languishing in East African arboreta, planted by the English a century ago, have been rediscovered and replanted elsewhere and have dramatically transformed the flavor topography of coffee.

One of the first coffee scientists I met during this research was a geneticist from Trieste who, upon learning I was studying coffee tasting, professed, "The taste of coffee is determined strictly by the genes." But I was to learn that the story is more complex than simple genetics. A single plant can produce beans that offer different tastes, since the coffee cherries that mature at the top of a coffee tree, where there is much light, heat, and exposure to insects, may grow differently than what develops in the plant's interior or at its bottom, where it is shadier and cooler. The sizes and densities of the beans can vary, and the density of a coffee bean has an important effect upon the taste. The cooler the climate (which is partly a function of elevation), the denser the beans will be. Dense beans bear many taste-filled and nutritious oils inside their cellular walls, whereas less dense beans have more empty spaces in their interior, which can absorb external moisture, oxygen, and even odors that, over time, may destroy flavor. Beans with low density, however, are ideal for receiving added flavorings like amaretto or vanilla; consumers fond of coffees flavored this way practically guarantee that they will be brewing their coffee from inferior beans, since the better-tasting, denser beans are unable to absorb such flavorings as well and so are never used for this purpose. Roasting denser beans presents more of a challenge to the roaster, since it is possible to burn the surface of a batch of beans before the dense interior cells have fully caramelized. For this reason, beans are sorted by size, shape, and sometimes by density. Measuring the density quantitatively or sorting by weight along with size can result in a better roast, since beans of lesser density that might be burned alongside denser beans can be roasted separately, but this can be a costly and time-consuming process. Picking beans by maturity, which will involve more than one collection, can reduce the problem, but this too is costly. There is an extensive arsenal of tools for harvesting, sorting, processing, weighing, and roasting, all of which afford opportunities for making adjustments that influence the flavor, so long as one can keep track of which tool is influencing what.

Coffee growers are aware that there is perpetual variation in the flavor characteristics of their annual crops. Superior coffees that win a competition one year may not achieve a high rating the subsequent season. Crops can fail altogether (too little rain, too much rain, disease, etc.), and there can be unanticipated variation. The director of the Indian Coffee Board once explained to me, "The same mother plant will render different qualities each year. The mother is the same, the father is the same, but the offspring is different." That is, pollination naturally produces different genetic combinations, which are not predictable. Climate (rain, sunshine, heat, frost) varies considerably; and especially fermentations, whose bacterial action upon the coffee's natural sugars (when it ferments the sweet parenchyma), produces much flavor and has considerable impact on the final result. Many coffee growers tell me that they must change the way they classify their own coffees on an annual basis, crop by crop. Writing in *Roast Magazine*, Spencer Turner (2018, 56) offered this practical advice: "To appropriately judge a coffee's quality, the cupper must experience at least three harvests to properly understand it."

The taste of a bean can be affected by the bean remaining in the cherry too long, since the enzymes that naturally exist in coffee cherries that have not been harvested on time can begin to break down the components of the bean. Similarly, spending too long in the fermentation tank can change a bean's flavor in dramatic ways. Green coffees stored in high humidity can develop mold growths, and beans that have spent too much time drying (whether by machine or the sun) can lose some of their flavor. These effects can be positive or negative, and I have met farmers who had a successful crop that scored well at an international cupping but who were hard pressed to identify just which part of the processing of their cherries played the most critical role. Now that the world's coffee industry has broken the myth that only washed coffees are acceptable, there are more opportunities for naturally processed and honey-processed coffees, which are introducing a transformed flavor palate that has surprised many consumers. Our "morning Joe" is not the same. Some producers in search of new flavors are experimenting after de-pulping with the deliberate introduction of yeasts and bacteria. Chemical reactions occur in the coffee continuously from harvesting to brewing, and variations can be attempted during the stages of drying, storing, and roasting, and even after the brewing is completed. We are in a period of rapid innovation, and Robusta coffees too have attracted more attention than previously, in part because the future of Robusta coffee is assured by the direction of climate change. Many coffee professionals expect that the pace of changes in tastes and taste preferences will increase.

When coffees are dried on the ground, they can pick up taints from the earth and may even earn the sobriquet "earthy." Sunalini Menon, Mysore's most accomplished taster, recounted the story of a processor from Mysore District whose coffee began to have an unacceptable taint that made their coffees unmarketable, the source of which the producer could not identify. In this region, most coffee cherries are dried on the ground, where taints can be absorbed. When Sunalini visited the processing facility, the purveyor described how careful he was in keeping his coffee works clean, and he explained how he took the additional effort of applying insecticide to the ground to prevent insects from damaging the beans as they dried. Sunalini was able to identify the insecticide as the source of the problem with the processor's harvest.

Essentially, processing coffee is like having your own chemistry experiment. Lingle (2001, 5) writes, "Many of the natural components of coffee's flavor are unstable at room temperature, either rapidly evaporating or recombining with other elements to form new filter compounds." Purveyors of coffee try to store coffee in a manner that reduces these ongoing chemical reactions, and both the bulk storage (before, during, and after transport) and commercial packaging will influence the final flavor. "After the third and fourth year, the [Bourbon Santos] bean changes in character" (Roden 1994, 54). "Most coffees improve with aging between three and ten years" (Roden 1994, 47). In my own experience, green coffees do not really improve after ten years on the shelf, but they do not always get much worse; however, the flavor of some green coffees can improve during the first years of storage.

In part I, we discussed that the invention of the vacuum-packed can provided the opportunity for the mass marketing of standardized coffees; however, even in a vacuum can coffee is able to grow stale or be baked by warm temperatures. When some purveyors of coffee noticed that the coffee in their vacuum cans was not always fresh-smelling, they learned to add to the can some volatile gases of fresh coffee aerosols so that upon opening the can a pleasant and familiar odor would be released, but it was an odor that faded quickly and forever. Many people who purchase freshly roasted whole beans keep their beans in the refrigerator to reduce staling, but this only affords the beans an opportunity to absorb all of the odors that are circulating inside. Alterations in the coffee's flavor do not cease once one has purchased the coffee.

Coffees that taste grassy or herbal shortly after harvest evolve and undergo enzymatic changes that eventually reduce the grassiness. Some Brazilian coffees that are earthy or harsh "age well, losing their grassy flavor" (Roden 1994, 54), and occasionally Java coffees are aged deliberately to reduce their earthiness. In this way, a knowledgeable coffee professional does not operate with an image of coffee as a static, objectified thing-in-itself but as a breathing, ever-emerging form of life, whose course of continuous transformations needs to be tracked and tapped in flight. Additionally, how the coffee is stored is another influence, and must be anticipated.

Some coffees gain their identifying flavor during the sea voyage. The musty flavor of some Javanese coffees develops during shipment. The "Monsooned" coffee from Mangalore, India, is illustrative. No coffee grows in Mangalore itself; it is only the port (like Santos, Brazil, or Mocha, Yemen) where coffee is collected for shipment. Most coffee there arrives by train and truck from the uplands of Chikkamagaluru, Coorg, and Mysore Districts. The coffee is unloaded near the dock and sits for up to seven weeks on porches under metal roofs in the open seaside air of Mangalore's hot and humid monsoon climate, usually during July and August, awaiting shipment to Europe by boat, and as it waits, it experiences a favorable fermentation (Thorn 2006, 146).

Influences like this, which occur at each step of the chain of production, keep the coffee business interesting, and most coffee purveyors allocate some of their time to detective work. Whatever the problem may be, I have heard a similar boast from baristas, roasters, and the exporters who design blends: they say that by applying their knowledge and craft, they can repair nearly any difficulty. This reflects the fact that along the chain there are many "nodes" where key transformations of flavor can occur.

To a degree all coffee is bitter, but bitterness is like beauty in that its desirability is in the eye of the beholder. The practiced drinker learns there is a good bitter and a bad bitter, but coffee drinkers are a diverse lot, and what is good or bad is not identical for everyone. Humans are adaptable, and it does not take much to adapt to the bitterness of one's brew; shortly following some adaptation there is habit, then expectation, which eventually becomes preference. This process also takes place on a national and even cultural basis (Ethiopian coffee, Turkish coffee, Italian coffee, American coffee, Vietnamese coffee, etc.). Roasting at high temperatures can scorch beans, creating an additional bitterness, but it can also burn up the molds and rancid oils that create most bad bitternesses. Using filtered pour-overs can reduce some bitterness, in comparison with infusions. Not only do the expectations-cum-preferences of the consumer affect the success of the result, how the consumer treats the coffee—the temperature of the water when one prepares it, the temperature when one drinks it, the addition of milk or sugar—will change the perception of bitterness. As coffee cools, it becomes sweeter and a little bit saltier. There is also a bitterness that occurs when a coffee becomes stale. Drinkers who store their coffee above the stove (a widespread practice, however mistaken) can end up with a gourmet coffee that possessed an original bitterness from the bean, a bitterness acquired from the roast, and a third bitterness from staling or being baked while it sits in the cupboards; moreover, it is possible that the person who drinks such coffee drinks it black each morning, without sugar, and that it has become just the coffee they enjoy and look forward to daily.

Variables that result from the temperature, storage, grind, roast, etc. occur in addition to any "inherent" characteristics of the bean, and these complicate effective identification of characteristics. Angelo Segoni, a senior blender/taster/buyer for Quarta Caffè, the largest coffee purveyor in Puglia, Italy, described his difficulties trying to replicate the taste of the coffees they routinely cup in their lab. Some coffees would not sit still long enough to be identified:

> When we were selecting coffee for competitions or for purchasing for our roaster, we would have our first cupping and perhaps

love a few of them on the table. But following each re-roasting, the flavor profile would keep changing slightly. In my opinion, there were very few coffees for which we were able to replicate the brew. Sometimes we were able to reproduce only *one* of the many flavors we had in the first brew; and even that distinct one would present a different intensity, but at least we could taste it. If it is difficult for those of us who work in the coffee business to identify specific characteristics of a coffee in a reliable way, the task must be even harder for the final consumer.

This is a taster who speaks the truth about his work. At home, it is often impossible to replicate the tastes that are described on a package of coffee because home brewing is not always consistent. Like snowflakes, no two infusions are alike: even with the same coffee that is ground the same way, infusions differ each time one prepares one. Even on my Saico espresso machine, by sliding the lever against the spring slowly instead of rapidly, I produce a different brew. I have concluded that if I want to experience the body of my coffee and an intensity of flavor, the espresso is the best route. But if I wish to explore and understand the full variety of flavors a particular bean can present, a slower brewing, preferably infused, is better. Geoff Watts (2013) advises that if one wants to learn the variety of flavors a coffee can present, one can discover a lot of different traits through tasting various roasts and trying various extraction processes.

While one is tasting coffees on a cupping table, attempting to sort out just where the previously identified flavors have disappeared or second-guessing one's original judgments, the coffee will cool gradually and the flavors that one is tracking will change some more, while other characteristics become noticeable. One head taster, Scott Conary, once described to me the difficulty that professional coffee tasters face when attempting to be objective: "Cupping is an exercise in trying to be objective about a moving target." A similar sentiment was expressed by Jaime Duque, of Catación Publica in Bogotá, who proposed, "Each coffee contains its own particular expression. It has a thousand components that are all changing every moment. I don't believe you can plan for all these." Occasionally, a coffee will preserve the same flavor notes from hot to cold; and tasters, who are big fans of consistency, will approve (however, it is less than certain that consistency is essential to the pleasure of drinking coffee, and the flavor judgments of professional tasters are influenced by how they plan to market it). More commonly, the flavor notes that identify a coffee will undergo some kind of transformation.

Lingle (2001, 13) explains, "Taste discrimination depends somewhat on temperature." I once experimented in Rimini, Italy, with drinking two cups of coffee—one cup prepared with water heated to 194°F and the second cup with the same dry grounds prepared with water heated to 200°F—and it was impossible to believe, let alone recognize, that they were the identical coffee. In a similar way, in São Paulo, Brazil, I experimented with drinking a drip-filtered coffee using two cups of different sizes—one cup was served in a latte cup and the other in an espresso cup—and similarly, I could not believe it was the identical coffee. The barista explained the difference to me as being the effect that the cup size has upon the nasal absorption of the flavors, but to me it was magic. These experiments demonstrate how dynamic coffee is, and genetics is never the sole variable: the temperature, the cellular density of the bean, the grind size, and the extraction time all have their influence. If we had used a coarse grind at 200°F, it might not have had the same effect as the medium grind that we used. This is the meaning of "dynamic."

A sociologist who spent two years of field research working as a barista in specialty cafés, Brian Ott (2018, 69), reported this astonishing discovery: "Individual coffees might require different brewing variables at different times, even within the same day." This demonstrates once more that because coffee is dynamic and is continually responding to its environment, it cannot be treated as a docile object. A coffee purveyor must step into the flow of the coffee's existence if the intention is to tap into the resources for taste that are available. The grind of a coffee (fine, medium, or coarse) has an important effect on the flavor and is one of the important tools that a barista uses. Grinds that are fine offer more surface to the hot water and produce stronger coffee; when one uses a drip method of extraction, the fine grinds can slow the passage of water, resulting in coffee that is over-brewed. Coffees that are naturally strong can benefit from a thicker grind. Change the grind, and one changes the brew. The popular and inexpensive blade grinder, used in many homes, has the problem of grinding coffee beans unevenly, so one will have both problems—some of the coffee will be under-extracted and another portion will be over-extracted, in the same cup. Nevertheless, any type of grind that is made within five minutes of brewing the coffee will exceed in quality the identical coffee that was ground days, weeks, or months previously. For the home consumer, grinding one's own coffee just prior to preparation is half the journey to achieving a satisfactory cup.

There is benefit from *remaining in proximity* with what the coffee is doing; this is the meaning of becoming a "participant." Ott (2018, 88) describes an exemplary situation: " 'Oh, this is a newer bag, same grind, same time. Let's get a little more water in it because it's a little sharp up front.' " Because coffee is always changing, adjustments like this are required if one is to derive the most from one's coffee, and paying attention is the initial step. One can be attentive to the taste of the coffee only when one drinks while having a reciprocal relationship with the coffee, instead of merely applying a few unidirectional assumptions by rote. Since coffee is unpredictable, one needs to keep noticing what it is becoming, but more than a few regular coffee drinkers do not care to bother about this and have explained to me that they need to have their coffee first, before they can even begin to consider such matters.

Acidity is highly variable, vulnerable to aging, and will express stunningly different aspects according to the temperature of the water, the length of the infusion, espresso vs. filter preparation vs. infusion, etc. On one occasion in Arco, Italy, Prof. Fele and I cupped two very different coffees. The first was a naturally processed Ethiopian Arabica, with fabulous-tasting citric notes when roasted light and made in an infusion, but extremely bitter when roasted dark and used in an Italian espresso preparation. Here I appear to speak of the coffee as something by itself, when in fact the critical factors must include the sensory orientations of the people who are doing the cupping. The second coffee was brought to us by the grower from the Galapagos, Chile, who was proud of his product. It too was an Arabica, but it tasted flat when roasted lightly and prepared in infusion (having a slight flavor of tobacco) but terrific when roasted medium dark and prepared in an espresso, presenting delightful chocolate notes. It was truly amazing to us how drastically different each coffee tasted in the two presentations (infusion and espresso). This difference from preparation rivaled any difference that was "inherent" in the two Arabica varieties themselves. Even more amazing, however, was how the nearly undrinkable, bitter cup of the darkly roasted Ethiopian beans changed its aspect 180 degrees after we added a tiny mini-spoonful of sugar to the espresso cup. A soon as the sweetness occluded the bitterness, the citric acid flavors reappeared, and it once again became an excellent cup. For me, this was a cautionary tale about not developing universal or doctrinaire prohibitions against the use of sugar.

Tasting the impacts of processing, selection, roasting, blending, etc. is difficult because so many factors are at work. The dynamic character of coffee contributes to making most coffee professionals humble. If the aforementioned advice to cup a coffee for three years before settling a coffee's nature is correct, then it is a mistake to fix the identity of a coffee firmly.

One's thoughts are ever vulnerable to the dialectics of how knowledge endlessly transforms itself, and identification can convert anything it discovers into formal significations and things said. In this way, our thoughts acquire expectations; however, coffee always "turns our expectations into derision" (Merleau-Ponty 1968, 93–94). "Being is not made up of idealizations or of things said" (Merleau-Ponty 1968, 94). We attune ourselves to the sensuality of the taste experience. We do not possess an obligation to exercise dominion over taste, and we often cannot succeed when we try, since complex tastes lead us into more directions than we are capable of controlling. As Hennion and Teil (2004b, 535; my translation) conclude, "the problematic and uncertain formation of links between measurable effects and perceived effects" can foil many of our attempts to control taste. Our duty is to accompany the taste and to participate in "the thinking of the sensible" (Carbone 2004, 45), which is more reflexive and participatory than it is deductive.

Echoing Hegel's observation (1977, 519) that "Fluidity, pure movement, is the essence of the living," Hennion and Teil (2004a, 35) insist, "Taste is an action, not a fact; it is an experience, not an object." Perullo (2018a, 53) reports comparably, "The same wine I drink, even if it was for the five hundredth time, is always different because I too am different"; the same holds for coffees. Any following morning one can use the same roast, the same grind, the same method of brewing, the same temperature of the water, the very same cup, and still the coffee may not be recognizable as that perfect coffee one enjoyed the morning previous. Lingle (2001, 7) has said, "The same coffee, served at the same time, will exhibit slightly different aromatic characteristics to different people. Similarly, the same coffees will show slightly different characteristics when served to the same person at the same time." This can be a disturbing phenomenon for a modern culture that is essentialist and objectivist and prefers that things be "pinned and wriggling on the wall" (Eliot 1963, 5); it is even more disturbing for the world of professional coffee purveyors, which has made considerable financial investments in maintaining what is mostly an essentialist and objectivist regime. Starbucks, for example, uses fine coffees, but their tasters are obsessed with maintaining their hyper-standardized taste. Like a fussy old aunt or uncle, they treat the ceaseless transformations of life as if they were the enemy.

These transformations can be disorienting. My mood, what I ate the previous evening, and my present expectations all influence my gustatory experience. Not infrequently I have wondered to myself, "This coffee was perfect yesterday, so why is it so uninteresting today?" The coffee or its preparation may not have changed, but I have, both physically and emotionally.

As scientists, we may like to think that if we are being strictly empirical, then there is only one taste; but the truth is there are many tastes. Fidelity to what is actually being tasted here and now, the only empirical there is, the taste before elaborate structuring by the intellect, proscribes our effort to pull the inside and outside apart (i.e., the coffee and ourselves) and then elevate the status of what is inside the bean, making it into something that is independent of the fellow who is outside. Perullo (2016, 39) emphasizes, "If knowledge is relationship, the relationship is movement" and "Wine is *not* its constituents; instead, it is its whole set of ongoing correspondences occurring in the midst of the various experiences" (Perullo 2018b, 267). The reflexivity of our understanding is always at work, and our understanding participates in the taste of our coffee, transforming the coffee as much as the humidity does.

Perullo (2918a, 15) contends, "Taste is not really some thing; before it is analyzed and fixed, the taste rather becomes and develops gradually." It is not only professional tasters who do this fixing; each drinker fixes one's understanding, perceptions, and expectations, and these can have a tremendous influence upon the taste. In this way also, the taste of coffee is not static like an essence but a temporary result of the nature and profiles of the ongoing correspondences it is having with us. Many coffees are not inherently good or inherently bad, and much depends upon each situation. A complex and intriguing coffee can be very good on the initial experience (say, the first cup) but not so good if one has to drink it regularly. An uninteresting coffee might be preferred if one is going to drink it all day long. "Taste is precisely about managing this creative uncertainty: it is not about liking something from what we already know, but about changing our ability to like from the contact with a new thing" (Hennion and Teil 2004a, 32). This is being attentive. That is why we should learn to improvise strategic techniques when we drink (Perullo 2018a, 64). For example, is this roast, at this grind, better for a pour-over, or should I brew it in a French press in order to make the flavors a bit wilder? And then I can go searching for which wilder flavors have resulted. In this way, our understanding is very much a part of the dynamic nature of coffee, and the Latin *sapere* ("to know") merges with the Latin *sapore* ("to taste"). The conclusion of Emma Sage (2016, 21), writing in *The Specialty Coffee Chronicle*, is the right one: "Great tasting specialty coffee can be produced using many/any/all/unknown production strategies." In fact, the one that is "unknown" may have been the one that did the trick.

PART III

Tasting and Its Labors

I want to work for my flavor. I want my mind to think and give me a flavor. I don't want a flavor that hits me in the face.

—A professional coffee taster

Chapter 6

Common Practices of Tasting

> Neither the pleasing nor the displeasing aspects of coffee's flavor are fully understood.
>
> —Ted Lingle (2001, 5)

How do you tell good coffee from bad coffee? What is this "good" and where does it come from? Does it rest inside the coffee or inside my mind—or in the accepted standards and preferences of a cohort of professionals and experts, or of society at large? Is this "good" something that is objective, or is it subjective? Is it objective when experts impart it? Do experts know what it means to be objective? Do we? Tasting is a site that is ideal for unearthing the natural relations between objectivity and subjectivity.

Are expert coffee tasters able to tell laypersons what is good coffee in the way that wine critics do? Can baristas teach customers what is good coffee? As any barista will tell you, doing this is not so easy, because drinkers are extraordinarily stubborn in adhering to their habitual relations with their coffee. Coffee is personal, and much of the time good is simply what we do. Experienced baristas know that they need to tread carefully when offering their customers advice about how to taste their coffee. What does it take to be able to say, "This coffee has both good body and good acidity"? What is it to know "good body"; what is it to know "good acidity"? How many lay drinkers would be able to locate these in their coffee, even after they have spent a lifetime drinking their favorite brew? There is much to learn.

"I like" does not mean "good." Surely, "good" is a consensually negotiated value, and therefore travels the same roads that objectivity travels. "Like" is the sentiment of an individual, while "good" is a feature achieved by a social system; however, this falls short of the "objective" that fills the dreams of sensory analysts. The stability of anything known is established by a process of social interaction, and parties always face the practical task of rendering their findings durable acquisitions, a social task in addition to determining the content of those findings.

The main aspects of tasting coffee involve taste, olfaction, and tactile sensory inputs (i.e., touch; here this is the texture sensed by the tongue and mouth). Lingle (2001) divides flavor into three components—aroma, taste, and mouthfeel—and his *Handbook* is divided along these lines. There is some confusion about the use of "taste" versus "flavor," a confusion that is not unnatural for ordinary language usage. A few people have described "flavor" as being broader than "taste" and something that can include aroma and body. However, some professional tasters have explained to me just the reverse: "Taste is the combination of aroma and flavor with the texture having some influence." If there is confusion among professional tasters, how can lay drinkers use these terms intelligently? Any solution will be by convention, involving the adoption of a language game that has won ratification by local usage and that then can be used to clarify communication; it will be adequate so long as all participants know and share the same conventions. Here I mostly use "taste" as being broader than "flavor," although for convenience and to interrupt the tedium of the prose, on occasion I will use them interchangeably when the distinction is not critical.

Like language games, particular tastes, as well as objectivity itself, are products of social construction and social confirmation. Zahavi (2001, 109) observes, "The constitutive process is characterized by a *reciprocity* and *mutuality*." Nothing objective will be established by a single person; or if it is, his or her very first inclination will be to rush out and seek confirmation. Further, objectivity's purpose is to facilitate clear and mutual understanding. "Reciprocal understanding is only possible through the constitution of transcendental objectivity" (Zahavi 2001, 111). Just as with settling the usage of the terms "taste" and "flavor," settling what is "good" involves the local production of some transcendental objectivity. We create objects to service our communication with each other. In fact, the structures of our communication are as important as their content; and in the very way that parties use the organizational features of their discourse and thinking to provide for a local orderliness, we can discover the birth of objectivity, along with the moral force it usually bears.

Constructing and confirming objects that are clear and distinct (the *de facto* European preference) serves well our interest in communicating effectively. Further, the sense of vision has been given priority over the other senses, even to the point of remaking *Homo sapiens* biologically. Perullo (2016, 23) suggests that Locke, Descartes, and Galileo defined smells and tastes as secondary qualities because they lack the solidity and stability to be included in the channel of any clear and distinct, neutral and perfect science. Whereas vision knows things at a distance, a distance that presumably facilitates rendering matters more objective, taste knows things only from the inside. Smell, taste, and touch are science's outlaws, less susceptible to the totalizing visions of positivist thinking. Whether that is something welcome or a problem depends upon one's politics. I have observed that most coffee professionals in the USA are happy to run with the outlaws; however, the Swiss and Italians prefer the control afforded by the distal, which minimizes indeterminacies. Moreover, it seems that everywhere the more money one earns in the coffee industry, the more inclined one will be to prioritize the visual and the distal. Smells and the tactile are more difficult to control, and the money lies in controlling.

Confounding this situation is that a wilderness resides in every cup of coffee. One can tame it with a heavy hand, the way the Georgia-Pacific Corporation tamed the forests of the Pacific Northwest, or one can learn to enjoy wildness. Just as we use methods to subdivide and better understand a natural wilderness, dividing the landscape into plant communities, ecological zones, etc., there are so many attributes for taste residing in each cup of coffee that in order to avoid vertigo, we choose to employ some system, standardized or developed spontaneously, for organizing our thoughts about what we are tasting, and for identifying flavors clearly enough to serve as a basis for shared communication with others. The demands of sharing life are a *primary* motive for the objectification of whatever we know. Truth itself may be a consideration subsidiary to that of organizing the orderliness of our communication. The relations between truth and the need to organize our social life offer scope for sociological inquiry.

What Tasters are Tasting

Coffee Quality Institute offers a course on "Cupping Skills" that is intended to teach lay tasters how to become professional tasters. They include intriguing exercises with many attributes of taste that professional tasters find useful in their sensory evaluation of coffees. The first assignment of evaluating coffee is to assess the gases that rise from the dry grounds, which is called *fragrance*; this is followed by an assessment of the *aroma* of the vapors that rise from the cup when the boiling water is added to the grounds and an infusion is produced. Since more flavor is registered by the nose than by the tongue, it is important to commence one's sensory analysis by smelling. For millennia, quotidian midday Chinese tea drinking commences with pouring a bit of the tea into a thimble-sized cuplet, pouring it out, and then smelling the fumes that remain in the cuplet. The typical Chinese tea drinker accomplishes this prior to having the first sip, and the practice awakens the olfactory senses, which causes one's tasting to be maximally attuned to flavors just as one's drinking begins. The *flavor* (the impression upon the taste buds) is assessed between one's initial and final sips, and in coffee tasting the *aftertaste* is carefully reckoned at the back of the palate, generally up to 30 seconds or so after the sipping. This differs from the professional tasting of fine Chinese teas, where the aftertaste will not receive a final judgment until 30 *minutes* after the drinking. Close inspection of aftertaste can introduce a casual drinker to a new dimension of tasting. Flavor here is considered to be a category that is evaluated separately from the coffee's *acidity* (bright or sour, lively or pale, sometimes with a fresh-fruit character), which is experienced immediately and so properly speaking is also a part of the flavor. Acids can increase the perception of sweetness, and sugars can reduce the sourness of acids. Salts also reduce the sourness of acids. All this can render the flavor a moving target. *Body* is the tactile feeling in the mouth, especially between tongue and roof and sides of the mouth, and it is the effect of sensing the undissolved oils that originated deep in the cell walls of the coffee bean. It is sometimes described as fullness. Lingle (2001, 20) offers the following advice about discerning body, a term that is often used too casually by lay drinkers and has been made thoroughly ambiguous by marketers: "Body should be differentiated from strength, which is an intensity measure of the amount and type of soluble material present. Strength gives coffee its taste characteristics, whereas body gives coffee its mouthfeel characteristics. It is possible to brew coffees that have a heavy body but not a strong taste."

Sweetness is a peculiar category, since nearly all coffee is bitter to some degree. Yet it is important. Intelligentsia Coffee's Geoff Watts (2013) has declared, "Without sweetness, all is lost," but it seems that coffee professionals can detect sweetness where lay persons cannot, and it is a particular sweetness that coffee possesses. Additionally, "sweet" can refer to coffees that lack bitterness; that is, "sweet" can mean "not-bitter," and it is sometimes used as a general reference for a pleasing cup. It is a popular taste descriptor and is used in many countries as if it were the principal feature of coffees, although its use is to a degree metaphorical, even hopeful. I was once handed a slightly under-roasted bean from Ethiopia that was described as "sweet," but it had no sweetness at all; however, it did not have the slightest bitterness. It is not strange to have a coffee exporter hand a cup of "sweet" coffee to a novice buyer and bewilder the buyer, but most professional tasters swear by the descriptor. Sweet would seem to be one of those things that should be strictly empirical, except that the capacity of one's palate to detect sweetness varies from person to person, from day to day, and even during a single day. Accordingly, a coffee that tastes sweet one day may not taste as sweet on a later occasion. One can wonder to oneself, "How did I miss the sweetness of this cup before?" And there is still another source of "subjectivity" that influences how we taste sweetness: our thoughts, those intruding reflections that keep assisting or impeding what we think we are tasting.

Balance involves how the flavor, aftertaste, acidity, and body all work together, like an orchestra, although this property can fade into indeterminacy more quickly than the others. This does not diminish its importance, although talk of balance can produce some wild semiosis. *Uniformity* refers to the consistency (and therefore reliability) among the sample cups, and *clean cup* refers to coffees that do not possess local taints that interfere with one's ability to read the flavors that are characteristic of the coffee. *Defects* is a category of tasting that is easier to grasp; they are taints or "off" flavors that are less than overwhelming. Their detection is sometimes akin to identifying the-animal-in-the-foliage, and tasters often find themselves uncertain about where to draw the line between what is part of the flavor and what is properly a taint. On the other hand, *faults* are persistent defects or off-flavors that are overwhelming, obvious, and can render a coffee undrinkable; they should already be perceptible in the fragrance and aroma, and endure to the taste and aftertaste. Finally, there is the *overall* impression, which is less a possession of the coffee and more the assessment of the drinker, but it too can possess its objectivity.

When one begins to taste, it can be exciting because one learns to notice and identify many new things, and one's coffee is transformed into a landscape that one had not suspected existed. Even drinkers who are perfectly content with their "morning coffee" will nevertheless benefit from moving beyond their conservative habits. Once these new features, which were present all along, are identified, they can be shared, and so a common sociality is fostered, which can contribute further to a coffee drinker's enthusiasm. Recently trained tasters become eager to adopt newly learned standards, the canonic lexicon-based schedule of descriptors, the techniques for enhancing sensory aptitude (such as how to employ the cupping spoon to smell the coffee before drinking, or how to slurp the coffee to the back of the mouth in order to enhance one's retronasal aptitude), and they become willing to accept all of it without incredulity, even with passion. If one is already working in the coffee profession, one can learn new skills that one can put to use in one's work and for organizing how one thinks and communicates with others about the tastes of the coffees one is trading. Willem Boot reported that his coffee grower students in Ethiopia who took the advanced tasting classes he taught there were not only delighted to acquire these cognitive and physical skills; they were pleased with how they afforded a collection of coffee workers an effective means for thinking in a common fashion, and for using a common language when inspecting and considering the tastes of their coffees. Boot reported, "The Ethiopian cuppers really liked the format of the course since they were also trained in the standardization of their cupping language." In this situation too, the social contributions to shared competence that objectivity makes possible are of great importance.

Perullo (2016, 78, my translation) is more skeptical about using a lexicon of taste descriptors: "One usually fancies some descriptors, pleased in an adolescent gesture of wanting to control and deluded enough to crystallize such transformative traces into referential syntagms." That is, the system provides a language that one can use to make more definite the traces of tastes one has intuited but not yet defined; the danger is that one may bestow positivity upon a flavor too soon. One can ignore the fact that the apparatus is made up of conventions and become so pleased with what the apparatus is capable of achieving, including the discoveries it will open up, that one accepts the language *too literally*, and a lexicon can come to foster a prejudice that the world exists on its own in the very way one has just conceived for it. More commonly, one follows up tastes that may suggest several directions at once; one both leads and is led. Some of the time one is confounded by being unable to nail down, in an objective manner, just what the flavor is. Some of the time what one has are only traces—they are not nothing, nor are they under one's control. It is the intention of most methods for tasting to bring matters under control, but it is uncertain whether this is the best route for making discoveries. The indeterminacy of these traces will sometimes subvert our belief that we are masters of our tasting, and so we wrestle with them, even as we continue to be transformed by them (especially as the coffee cools and its taste profile changes some more), until we are finally able to overcome the aporia and, using the tools of the apparatus, convert the traces into a concretized meaning, a meaning that will be pressed into service immediately by the coffee industry (after adjustments by the advertising office) for its purposes of management, marketing, and control. There is nothing wrong with marketing or profit, but it is possible that with one's competence with one's method those traces, which can bear the most delightful aspects of the taste, will be lost.

Perullo suggests that these crystallized "referential syntagms" are at their base metaphors, and nearly all taste descriptors—since they are to an extent the arbitrary concretizations of the traces—operate as metaphors and communicate their sense and reference in metaphoric ways. Consider, for instance, these three descriptors given justly to a cup of coffee by a specialty roaster in southern Oregon: "grapefruit, raspberry, and stone fruit." The coffee is none of these, and it is not even possible that these three fruits could occupy a common flavor. But they suggest a domain of taste (a harvest of traces) that renders them not at all contradictory, provided one's hold upon the descriptors is loose: the descriptors together point one toward a domain, and when one tastes the coffee under the direction of these descriptors one will be able to find what they can specify; and whatever one finds will define, reflexively, what these descriptors meant "all along." We can agree with Husserl (2001, 614) when he says, "Genetically, empty shapes precede all types of intuitions, all perceptual constitution of objectlike formations." In this way, subject and object are mutually determining, and neither empirically nor ontologically are the "subjective" and the "objective" separable; nevertheless, separating them appears to be a central mission of most undertakings of modern sensory science. Still, by using these procedures one does come to know better the coffees that one is purveying or drinking. The utility of the sensory identifications one makes rests in how well they are communicated to others across the chain of production, and especially in the utility these identities have for those who sell and purchase the coffee. For this reason, the objectivity here is a practical objectivity.

Vannini et al. (2012, 55) speak of "performing wine," and any truly attentive sensory assessment will *participate* in what the drink is doing. As Perullo remarks in his nondualist fashion, "I learn its language even as I create it." The point is to taste the coffee, not simply to dominate it. Everyday tasting differs from routinized protocols for tasting, but both of them depend on enhancing and intensifying one's attentiveness to tastes. If this can be achieved, then either kind of tasting will lead to a richer life. Our first objective should be to locate the distinct attributes that identify the most discernable characteristics of the coffee, but identifying what is most characteristic should not be allowed to obscure aspects of taste that have only begun to reveal themselves. Figal (2010, 106) praises the unintelligible and insists that it "is an integral moment of understanding itself. It is the openness in understanding, in which understanding sets in anew and is able to further be developed." Similarly, "The texture of possible determinacy . . . is always unlimited and is thus something that always keeps itself in reserve, never completely shows itself" (Figal 2010, 223). The drive to identify a coffee can place a straitjacket over one's openness to what is still unknown, an openness that is essential to discovery.

Earle (1955, 94) suggests that we give broad scope to what we do not yet understand: "The reality of the perceptual field itself has determinations to infinity, all of which do not appear as object to me; but some of these determinations do appear. . . . We have then partially determinate realities before us, or 'unclear objects.' . . . Investigation serves to render the unclear object clearer." Note that "clearer" is still not "clear," and we should hesitate to force clarity upon what is not clear, a hesitancy that is contrary to the aims of some tasters. When the clarity we impose is derived from our own categorical schema and not from the phenomenon, our investigation will be led astray. Hesitation like this is an important aspect of being objective.

Tasters are usually open to the suggestions of other tasters who are nearby, whether they are professional tasters or not. The indeterminacy that flavors possess has made many tasters humble, and so they are willing to listen to the perspective of nearly anyone who possesses a fresh tongue. Tasters are obsessed with discovering and identifying the flavors. Solving these mysteries makes them feel more alive, and it is rare that the story of any cup of coffee is ever fully told. Earle (1955, 94) comments, "I shall never completely determine [it]. . . . But I can render it determinate to whatever extent my purposes require, or my procedures can guarantee. The inquiry into an object, thus, must be partly empirical and partly rational." Whenever an absolute objectivity is impossible, a practical objectivity is made to suffice.

There is cupping for the soundness of a coffee, which is a tasting for defects, and there is cupping for the flavor profile; these are very different practices. The coffee industry uses what they call tasting "protocols," which can be divided into three general categories: hedonic, discriminative, and descriptive. Hedonic tasting is dichotomous—one either likes it or dislikes it, although the scale can be carried to nine degrees ("like extremely" to "dislike extremely"). Sometimes the coffee will be sampled both black and with added sugar, and sometimes the tasters for a firm will need to anticipate the likely response of their clients, so their tasting is on behalf of another drinker. A café will occasionally offer its clients hedonic tastings. The most common kind of tasting in the industry is discriminative (pass/no pass), which serves as a gatekeeper and may be an examination for taints and defects. This kind of cupping protocol is used for deciding whether to purchase a reasonably priced green coffee or for determining whether the coffee that has arrived by ship has acquired any taints *en route*, or is in fact the coffee that one ordered. Some of these tasters are located at the ports (such as a tasting lab I observed at the port of Savona), and a quick, discriminative tasting of a coffee sample will be made before the coffee is permitted to be unloaded on the dock. Exporting countries like India and Costa Rica use this kind of tasting before they issue to exporters the license or formal clearance that is required for shipment abroad, the idea being to protect the reputation of the nation's coffee by excluding defective beans from the international market (rejected beans are sold on the domestic market). Descriptive protocols of tasting are used for the better coffees, including specialty coffees, and their purpose is to identify taste attributes with the idea of matching sellers to buyers. Each coffee purveyor, and each trade association, will use their own standard form, which can vary from improbably simple to overly complicated, depending on the practical needs of the firm.

The purpose of these protocols is to formalize examination of coffees. The idea is that each coffee should receive the same or similar treatment, so that a comparative and objective decision can be made. Routinization of a praxis of tasting helps to prevent capricious judgments that could become costly. For the coffee industry objectivity is a matter not so much of truth as of profit. All of these protocols are oriented toward the real objectivity in the cup, but it is not an objectivity in the way that there is a coin in one's pocket. It is more like a figure in the foliage that needs to be extracted, with the aid of both sensory and cognitive skills.

Organizing Knowledge

A formal organization of knowledge (*Sinnbildung*) is required so that whatever is discovered can be recollected, made reliable, and readily communicated to others, where it can be evaluated for its comprehensiveness and continually extended as community knowledge. This is accomplished by the practical work of objectivating ideas so that, first, they have the same form to all, and following that they can acquire a sense and reference to which all of the actors can become calibrated. This entails a social praxis that is oriented to adequacy of understanding, which is antecedent to objectivity. The objectivation of insights and discoveries leads to social confirmation and ultimately to legitimation and objective knowledge. The aim is accuracy and truth, but there are many opportunities for sophistry and confusion along the way.

"Truth is . . . the identity of an appearing object with the object as it really is. But this gives us no single criterion or test; there will be as many tests and criteria as there are types of object, and ways of appearing. And so we must go on as before, trying to get as much light on each particular topic as we can, in the particular way appropriate to that object" (Earle 1955, 93). This implies that there will always exist a tension between the singularity of a coffee (and what that singularity demands) and the standardization of sensory information, generalized according to familiar categories that make it communicable and readily usable by a large group of interested parties. The unity of meaning for the coffee that is built up is directed "beyond its actual play in the stream of conscious life [to] the intersubjectivity of a common world" (Bruzina 1970, 134). The situation is complicated further by the fact that what we know may still be largely indeterminate. The practice of tasting can involve throwing a net of terms over a beverage in hopes of making an indeterminate flavor more determinate. Some of the flavor will slip through the net and be missed, and some of it will be caught. The task is to narrow the flavor to something that can be communicated effectively, while somehow managing to keep oneself open for tastes that are either not yet discovered or are perceived imprecisely.

There is a taste that rests in the cup, and there are those interests, expectations, and structure of understanding that one projects onto the coffee, which are based on what one already knows. Much like human sexual attraction, what gets projected has as much to do with the flavor that is discerned as does the coffee itself, and the dilemma is that they arrive on one's tongue as the same taste. Professional tasters work to diminish the influence of what is being projected, in a sort of lay bracketing of one's biases, but if one projects nothing, then no taste can be experienced, since understanding always involves some projection of meaning. Tasters are confronted with the task of somehow getting past themselves to discover what they do *not* yet know. I witnessed eight aspirants for professional Q-Grader certification immersed and buried inside the tangled web of their efforts to comprehend which cups contained a disqualifying phenol taste. They were searching for the transcendent object, which in the case of phenols is said to be obvious; nevertheless, five of the aspirants never found it. Projecting phenol into the wrong cups, they misidentified the offending cups, and so did not receive their certifications. All understanding works in a similar way, whether what is being projected is correct or not.

Sometimes we have a heavy hand, and becoming a competent taster involves learning how to taste while keeping a light hold upon one's impressions. Yet this light hold cannot always survive the social process of stabilizing the sensory knowledge, which is a process that requires definition and conformity. The systematic character of a coffee reveals itself slowly. As its attributes congeal in our consciousness, we verify them and refresh our intuition by taking more sips. As we become more familiar with its flavor and the surprises it offers gradually subside, we develop an identity for it; we synthesize the properties we notice into alleged continuities and "fluid meaning-unities" (Bruzina 1970, 79). From that point, the prejudice that is natural to every course of thinking takes hold, and we carry on routinely with less perceptive intuition and more self-fulfilling prophesy: "Once the intention to an object has been formed on a suitable intuitive basis, it can be revived and exactly reproduced without the help of a suitable act of perception or imagination" (Husserl, 1970b, 684). This economy of analysis both services and impedes our assessment. As Merleau-Ponty (1962) suggests, we are condemned to meaning.

The creative moment of sensory assessment can be brief: "Attentiveness to a phenomenon can be of the shortest duration. Something is phenomenon only for a moment, then it already becomes a 'fact of experience.' . . . Its phenomenality lasts only as long as the tension of showing is maintained" (Figal 2010, 201). The "tension" of taste exploration and discovery is what provides the gold, and tasting protocols should be evaluated not simply for how objective their results appear to be but also for how well they foster intensifying one's sensory attention; in other words, for how they empower subjectivity. The two, objectivity and subjectivity, are not always opposing forces, and so some sensory scientists may operate with a flawed epistemology.

Whatever we grasp by attention and intuition still must be transformed into thematic clarity. First an "indefinitely general thought" is aroused (Husserl 1970b, 686), and then the task of tasters is to turn this into more determinate knowledge; this can be something that tasters struggle with, in part because what we have begun to recognize in the taste is indeterminate. Sometimes it is a struggle because we fear we can do violence to the integrity of what is intuited, and also because we are unable to find words to describe our experience. Here are some attempts of lay tasters that are typical of attempts to describe the taste of the coffee one is drinking:

> —"I do not know, it seems raw to me. That is, I don't know how to explain it, but to me it seems, I don't know . . . it doesn't have that taste of, ummm. I don't know. I don't have a definition."

—"I liked the taste very much and I found it too . . . , that is, a good . . . I don't know how to say it. Creaminess? Can it be said? I don't know."

—"I really liked the scent, I tried to think of what I could remember but nothing came to mind, that is, I just thought it was very good."

—"What I'm sensing has a very suggestive flavor" [without specifying].

As Lingle (2001, 13) says, "A person is usually more limited by language and vocabulary than by the ability to discriminate between different coffee taste sensations."

Sometimes during one's sensory assessment of coffee, one's senses will become dulled. This happens quickly with sensing fragrances and aromas, but one's sense of taste can also run into a brick wall. At such times, it can help to drink some water or eat a saltless cracker. One must work to ensure that the mind stays attuned to what one is perceiving. There are tricks such as waiting for the coffee to cool, or adding sugar or milk to provide a different reading. Once, while I was tasting in India, one of the coffees bore a hint of spice with a bit of herbal or grassy aroma, but the spice defied definition. My colleague suggested, "It has some refinement." So then our task became comprehending that "refinement." When we added milk, the herbal aspects disappeared, but the subtle spice remained and turned a little sweet, and became more available for sensing: it was closer to cinnamon than to pepper. One is pleased when one is better able to understand the taste, yet here there was some lingering disappointment that the "refinement" was never fully defined. Far from confounding tasters, these ambiguous situations are sought after as part of the challenge that tasters find intriguing. As one taster told me, "I want to work for my flavor. I want my mind to think and give me a flavor. I don't want a flavor that hits me in the face."

Some sensory scientists think that until a flavor is fully determined, it is not real and cannot be relied upon. It is true that it cannot be used to purchase or sell a coffee, and this can put pressure on tasters to make what they are sensing determinate before it is time. They do this by constituting an identity, and here "constituting" refers to the building up of a unity of meaning, "a building up of the object in its objective identity" (Zahavi 2001, 105). This identity is then projected onto the taste, and it usually discovers what it is looking for. The problem with some tastes that one identifies is that "as soon as one believes that one has it and can hold it firmly, it disappears again" (Figal 2010, 7). To be objective one must respect the dynamic nature of the coffee and not insist too strongly upon one's own logocentric formulations.

The satisfaction a taster can experience when identifying clearly a taste that one has located can bias the taster toward the identity that the taster is projecting. For tasters and lay drinkers alike, satisfying one's expectations is agreeable and an intellectual pleasure in its own right, one that can compete with successfully locating objective qualities of the flavor. This satisfaction may be derived from the relief one feels upon having sorted out one's thinking in a manner that has some real correspondence with the world. One may think, "Oh, I've got that now." It even can happen that one may give a higher rating to a flavor that one has identified clearly after some serious sensory work than one would offer to a lingering flavor that one has yet identified. Thinking intervenes with our sensory assessments in this way. A corollary danger here is that once we have acquired competence with a given taste descriptor (for example, "cinnamon"), one becomes inclined to cast it everywhere. This happens on a national basis too, and flavors commonly adopted by one national tradition or another will be employed more frequently, although only inside the country. Surely, some allowance is made for the coffee, but these national predispositions have a heavy influence. Once the projecting of a particular sensory attribute has commenced, it is difficult to restrain the practice; however, here restraint emerges as another important component of the work of being objective. Since there always exists some pressure to communicate successfully, there is a natural tendency toward conformity.

The taste descriptors we project operate reflexively, in that they provide the organization of the meaning-unities of the coffee's taste that we claim exists independently of that constitutive organization. A roaster from Trento, Luca Torta, declared that one of his blends featured the classic "tostatura all'Italiana" (the typical Italian roast). A collection of seven clients cast each other quizzical looks and then re-sipped their espressos to identify just what was the meaning of "a typical Italian roast." What they found, whatever they found, with the aid of his label and some calibrating among themselves, became the meaning of the description. Without Torta's account, they might not have noticed anything special. We are always in our own way, though we do not always discern that we are. This is true for every descriptor. We cannot see what our projections are because they are the very ground on which our knowledge takes its shape (Bruzina 1970, 84). Fish do not notice the water they are swimming in.

Gadamer (1975, 237) asks a question that is pertinent here: "How can we break the spell of our own fore-meanings?" Being able to do so is another aspect of being objective. A tendency to define experiences clearly and distinctly often works in favor of our biases, and a capacity to tolerate instability operates to the benefit of objectivity. It is incorrect to assume that stability and that European pair "clear and distinct" always best serve the interests of objectivity. When one reads a poem for the first time, being too quick to understand it can interfere with a fuller appreciation, and indeterminacy can lead to an expansion of our understanding. The problem is that the global character of contemporary culture, the global scope of coffee production and consumption included, demands standardization, which in turn depends on stabilizing the sense of matters: Hegel has died at the feet of capitalism.

Keeping the Mind Clear

One of the important challenges for any taster is to keep the mind clear for each next cup. The advice sounds simple, but it is one of the most difficult tasting practices to exercise. Why is keeping the mind clear so difficult? It is because we are almost never not entangled inside our own thinking, and this is especially true when there is a complicated form that requires filling out. As I have observed, the universal advice of professional tasters is that one should not think too much. Perhaps they give this advice as solace for their frustration with having so much bookkeeping to do. Manuel Diaz offered this counsel to his students: "To cup well you need to use your senses, not your thinking." One's attention can be directed to one's tongue, or it can be connected to one's reflections, including one's ideology (which can be anything—a scheme for making profits, commitment to environmentally grown coffees, preference for particular processing systems, etc.—our ideologies have no limits). An enthusiastic coffee drinker once offered me coffee that was grown by a social cooperative that shared the profits; when I concluded that it had a bland taste, my friend was offended, although my comments were addressed to the flavor, not to social justice (which I admire). Even in the case of tasting only with one's tongue without ideology, there is always some structuring of one's inquiry, and whatever one knows about taste is what gives us our access to what is there (Perullo 2016, 92). The result is that one will find oneself entangled inside one's thoughts even when attempting to avoid doing so. At the least, we should try to not become addicted to our thinking.

Here we encounter once again that quandary of civilized humanity: the routines and ideology required for organized, collaborative thinking can prevent us from seeing clearly. The very tools we use for analysis and for increasing our appreciation are what conceal what we are investigating. As the Pulitzer Prize–winning American poet Gary Snyder (1980, 172) concluded, "Language, custom, ego, and personal advantage strategies all work against clear seeing." In this way, the language, protocols, tasting schedule, and wheel of flavors, which are the very tools that assist the taster's craft, can also suffocate it. As Perullo (2016, 28) maintains, "Wisdom in tasting involves having a flexible and elastic attitude." As with every other formal analytic tool of civilization, one can use them, but one should try to avoid becoming trapped by them.

Appreciating a coffee's taste requires opening up, and this is especially true for scents and aromas. The limbic brain, and not only the neocortex, has its work to do. The more confounding a taste is, the more one must open up and experience it attentively. Heidegger (1994, 19) gives us important advice: "Openness is the ground and the soil and the arena of all correctness." Routinization of knowledge requires less thinking, but this can come at the cost of not opening up, since routines are usually inattentive. Routines are peculiar things, in that they sometimes assist direct sensing and sometimes warp it. A mind that is too full of routines is prone to numbness and is rarely a fresh mind, and yet a mind without routines is often confused.

On occasion, we can feel some desperation in our efforts to understand an unclear taste, and we are driven to find some orientation that will help us overcome our confusion. At the same time, one needs to remain open to whatever the taste descriptors that we are presently using are not handling well. Accordingly, one not only uses routines, sometimes one must disrupt them! If during their efforts coffee tasters find something in the taste that resists being said, that perhaps even resists being organized into their discourse, that is where they should focus their attention. This temperament is an important part of what makes them professional tasters.

Willingness to disrupt the security of one's routines requires courage. The Santos master taster Arnold Baskerville once explained, "For cupping, you need an original personality. A weak person, a yes man, will always follow the others, without his own opinion." The dynamic and indeterminate character of the taste of coffees, especially the better ones, can make tasters uneasy, confound them, and drive them into the false security of what they can make clear and distinct. Employing the formal descriptors of a flavor wheel is a useful heuristic tool, but it can also be a prison; those who are brave can describe flavors without becoming imprisoned inside their own propaganda. Sometimes drinking more coffee can supply the courage.

A competent taster must be open to everything that is going on in the cup, even when all of it is too much for one to get one's head around. Nevertheless, that is where the real phenomenon lives; our formal proceedings are not the phenomenon. The epigraph on the wall of that San Salvadoran café, "A cup of coffee is filled with ideas," serves to remind the café's clients that when they drink their coffee they have work to do. As the subtitle to Perullo's book (2018a, my translation) goes, "Taste is not a sense, taste is a task." The Salvadoran café's clients are exhorted to remember that there will always be more taste in the cup than what can be said about it.

Our thought naturally forms into a routine system, which becomes the means by which we think further, and each new thought will be warped in the direction of the systematic concerns of what we organize. This is the price that the manifestation and clarification of our thoughts demands. The open and anarchical can betray itself by conforming to what we have organized, which is thought that is "absorbed by what it thinks" (Levinas 1998, 173) and that forgets itself. While such a betrayal is a byproduct of the reification of ideas executed by analytic practice, betrayals can and should be reduced. Undertaking this reduction is a component of the practice of tasting because it keeps providing us more immediate access to the taste.

Tasting is occasioned and serendipitous, and for it to become methodical and consistent some imposition of ideology is required, as well as some imposition of ideal categories. These categories and all of the tools of tasting and communicating about taste can facilitate the work, but along with them a successful taster needs to exercise enough vigilance about their use to ensure that that they will always operate in the service of the taster's genuine interests.

Real Tastes

We have been emphasizing that coffee has an organic life and is a living entity that expresses a character irreducible to every abstraction (Perullo 2016, 31). The people who drink coffee work with real tastes, and real tastes make their own categories. What Sweeney (2008, 27) describes for wines holds true for coffee: "There is no single tasting template to which all wines conform, and there is no single standard by which all wines should be judged. . . . Wines of different styles are ingested and experienced in different ways on one's palate." This presents to tasters the practical problem that tastes are more diverse than the supply of categories. If the tasters are working honestly and attentively, when they run out of categories they will formulate their own; however, if they persist in doing so, the formal system will quickly become unwieldy and fail at its fundamental purpose of organizing an orderliness for the purveying of coffees. How does one maintain the viability of a social system and at the same time remain faithful to the singularity of each coffee? Real tastes are difficult to keep tamed.

This can complicate when making numerical evaluations. Paul Reps, one of the writers who introduced Zen Buddhism to America after the Second World War, used to teach, "Each one is best." Perullo (2018a, 65) argues similarly, "Every encounter is an experience that is valid for itself." Matt Kramer (2008, 227) applies this policy to sommeliers' judgments about terroirs: "The French do not ask of one site that it replicate the qualities of another site." How does one allow for each coffee to present its own "best"? More baffling, how does one compare these "bests" and then rate them numerically? How does one respect what is unique about a coffee, which is the thing one wants most to convey to a client, while still conforming with the standards and categories of professional thematizations? The essential practice here involves using the standards, even when they do some violence to the coffee's real tastes, while refusing to permit their use to blind *oneself* to the tastes that are still swirling about in the cup, that "more" to the taste that will always be there after one has totaled up the points. This essential practice is demanding, but it operates at the heart of coffee tasting. If most of what constitutes the singularity of a coffee is removed, we will be left only with abstractions that lack flavor.

The singularity of each coffee directs tasters to what the pertinent priorities are, and so this singularity cannot be ignored. At the same time, one needs to find a way to communicate the singularity. Communication facilitates deeper and more collaborative exploration, and it supplies the consumer with helpful information; however, this latter benefit is complicated by the fact that many lay drinkers of coffee do not know what they want or what they are tasting. This introduces an additional handicap for communication, since getting the taste described perfectly will do little good if the description is not understood and so cannot be made serviceable. Communicating successfully places such a heavy burden upon taste descriptors that the adequate descriptions of a firm's professional tasters will frequently be dumbed down by the firm's advertisers, and the result can be that little is left of the coffee's singularity. Too many coffees have "good body" and are "well balanced."

The flavor descriptions on commercial packages are "a universe of abstract generalizations" (Perullo 2016, 24) and offer too much standardization.

Meaning can originate in the senses, and Vannini et al. (2012, 20) have called bringing this meaning to articulation "somatic work." Meanings can be "had" before they are "known," and Dewey (2002, 32) has told us that one comprehends the being of something prior to comprehending its whatness. How can we allow the whatness to be recorded without losing the site of that being? Not infrequently, there is something in the taste of the coffee that strikes us, but what it is that solicits us is not yet our own. This is why professional tasters and lay drinkers alike find it difficult to describe what they are tasting. A lay drinker of coffee told Prof. Fele, "Something, I don't know. I don't know, like a tea with herbs, we say, a thing of that sort." And even a head taster once declared, "This coffee has a lot of body, I don't really know how to define it." A taste can be clear and consistent, and still one can be unable to name it. Further, when the tastes in a cup lead us in many directions at once, which direction do we follow?

"One should not always feel compelled to reduce this experience to ontologically fixed and isolated elements" (Perullo 2018a, 27). Also, Vannini et al. (2012, 5) advise, "The taste, the smell, the tactile feel of coffee in the morning—no one sensation is distinct from the others—blend into a total sensual experience in which the whole is greater than the sum of its parts." Speaking generally, Earle (1955, 153) offers the instruction, "Knowledge is no property of logical calculi, linguistic structures, calculating machines, electric brains, or anything that is not related to the world in that distinctive way which Brentano called 'intentionality.'" This intentionality, which is the activity of our following up our intuitions, means that we participate in the taste. A good coffee is so lively one cannot always describe all its aspects, and sometimes it is better to leave it that way instead of forcing a category upon it. It is notable that at every international tasting I have attended, the head taster or the assistant has had to keep beseeching the professional tasters to come up with specific taste descriptors, and this beseeching occasionally develops into scolding. Part of the tasters' reluctance may proceed from fears that their judgments will face criticism by their peers, but it can also be attributed to their respect for an indeterminate taste that they are reluctant to subsume under a determination that is premature. They may turn to their scoring sheets and experience a bit of paralysis when they contemplate how to allocate a lively but still undefined flavor to "aftertaste" or to "mouthfeel," with both of these to be numerated. What sort of standards can one have for evaluating what is not yet definite? Interestingly, even when they do not assist the identification of a characteristic flavor, a retreat into the categories of the protocol can provide some cognitive relief to a taster, since in the midst of the taster's confusions the categories will supply some direction. Once again, bravery and a capacity to tolerate creative ambiguity have contributions to make.

Participation

Drinking coffee is participatory, and what a person brings to the task is as important as what the coffee affords. Most experienced baristas have come to this conclusion, even if they have done so with some regret. Coffee offers us paths we can pursue (Perullo 2018a, 75), but the choosing is largely up to us. Hennion and Teil (2004b, 536) declare that "the object does not go without its project." Without participation, one's appreciation of what one is eating or drinking will be greatly diminished, and one might as well cede priority to reading the newspaper. Recall the Ethiopian coffee that tasted like burnt tobacco when it was hot and fresh; it tasted better as it cooled, and even became good once a bit of sugar was added to neutralize its bitterness. What a coffee offers needs to be followed up in this way, and drinking coffee should be as active as it is passive. People who lack curiosity should drink milk. As the Dutch taster Willem Boot advises, "When you find a fruity coffee, follow it from hot to cold, so you can catch any dynamics."

The tools of a tasting protocol can assist one to notice things. For instance, one may never have paid serious attention to aftertaste or have given the slightest consideration to consistency, a favorite term of tasters. When being compelled to rate flavors, one may notice more carefully that some flavors are durable, while others are transitory. In professional assessments, one is sometimes faced with the problem of how one should rate a good taste that is durable against an outstanding taste that is transitory, but if one is simply drinking one's coffee one can just sit back and enjoy, one's enjoyment having been enhanced by having noticed the difference.

Heidegger (1971a, 181) has distinguished between two kinds of thinking, one that represents and one that responds, and the latter may be more honest with coffee. The former is what Perullo (2018b, 266) has called "an objectifying and referential sensory analysis," while the latter has "the power to give joy and provide conviviality" (Perullo 2018b, 268). Both have their place in tasting. But the most important contribution of any method is to make us participate more in the drinking, and thereby be more attentive to what is taking place. As Hennion and Teil conclude (2004b, 521), the thinking that responds can cause an increase in attention, contributing to the cultivation of "an attention that focuses and a stronger presence of the object tasted—each reinforcing the other. . . . It responds, it provokes a stronger contact and an increase in presence."

Chapter 7

Down on the *Fincas* and with the Exporters

Harvesting, Processing, Blending

> There is more to good coffee than the freshness of the beans and the talent of the barista.
>
> —Geoff Watts, Los Angeles

Coffee production and coffee exporting vary greatly from one country to another. There are 125,000 coffee producers in Guatemala, who exported 3.1 million bags of green coffee in marketing year 2020 (Tay 2019), while Brazil has only 2,000 producers who exported 35.9 million bags (*International Comunicaffe* 2020). The socioeconomic situations of these two coffee cultures are hardly comparable. Smallholder producers predominate in Colombia, Costa Rica, Ethiopia, Mexico, Papua New Guinea, and Puerto Rico, where cooperatives run by small farmers are common. In Mexico, for example, coffee has become a mostly peasant product; farmers who cultivate fewer than 5 hectares (12.3 acres) hold 64% of Mexico's coffee-growing lands, and two-thirds of these producers grow on less than two hectares (4.9 acres). About half of Mexican coffee farmers are indigenous people (Jaffe 2014, 40). Brazil, El Salvador, and India have a history of elite families who grow coffee, and large landholders still dominate the trade.

Colombia, Ethiopia, and Panama, which grow the coffees that have inspired the more discerning drinkers who pay attention to the taste of the coffee they drink, export much less coffee than Brazil does: 14 million, 6.5 million, and 40,000 bags respectively. As Dunn (2019) has commented, "[Non-Brazilian] Latin America produces a small share of the world's overall coffee volume, but when it comes to the coveted specialty beans sold by roasters like Intelligentsia, Blue Bottle, and others like them, it is arguably the world's most important growing region—and one dominated by smallholder farmers." In the emerging model of coffee economics, small landholders and the specialty coffee purveyors seem to be made for each other, especially as direct trade relations between them accelerate.

In an address to the Specialty Coffee Association (SCA) in 2010, Vince Fedele explained that there were 30 things that can happen along the way to ruin the coffee, and in this chapter we examine many, as well as the coffee-purveying decision-making required to cope with them. As Geoff Watts (see epigraph; Weissman 2008, 21) has it, "there is more to good coffee than the freshness of the beans and the talent of the barista." Naturally, planting and harvesting coffee is the producers' first task, but close behind that is the critical need to eliminate defective beans. Even after the lots of harvested coffee have been dried and edited, coffee is still undergoing transformations, due to enzymatic reactions, fermentations, oxidation, etc. While it is not apparent to those who purchase a bag of coffee, during their journey from seed to cup the beans that one takes for granted have been studied and supervised by a great many eyes and hands.

Professional coffee tasters taste for contaminations at several steps along the way. Some growers will taste their coffee at the *finca* (plantation). *Cafeteros* at the *beneficios* (coffee works) and brokers taste to assess how great a challenge a given lot will be for them to clean, process, edit, and market; exporters do the same; and export boards taste to eliminate poor coffees that could damage a nation's reputation. Before the coffee is let off the boat at the importer's country, a taster at the wharf's edge will sample each arriving shipment for defects, including those acquired during the voyage. The importing firm's tasters will evaluate the arriving coffee and compare it with the sample that was air-shipped prior to purchase. In addition, there are roasters and baristas, so that by the time the consumer has a cup at a café or at home, the coffee has been scrutinized many times. The result is that if there are defects, they have been incorporated into the price, and in the majority of instances, you get what you pay for.

Being a living entity, coffee has flaws, and these flaws must be repaired or minimized. This may require determining their sources, which is something that can become a focus of tasting. More coffee tasting is oriented to the detection of defects than is oriented to ascertaining and defining a coffee's positive characteristics. Defects can come from the bean or from how the beans were processed or stored. As Ted Lingle (2001, 24) explains, "Many of the flavor taints and faults associated with coffee are the result of contamination from outside sources and are not part of the natural chemical reactions within the beans before, during, or after the roasting process." This notion of "outside processes" raises a serious issue for tasting coffee. It can be difficult to distinguish between the flavor that is "inherent" in the coffee and what has come from other places, and yet professional tasters display much skill at attributing flaws in the flavors to problems with processing, shipping, roasting, etc. Which tastes can be attributed to something in the bean, or to the fermentation, or to the blending, roasting, or brewing? The quantity of factors that contribute to a successful outcome is what transforms the practices of coffee purveying from a science to an art. When one evaluates a coffee during sensory analysis, the intention is to be objective. That would seem to favor assessing only what is in one's mouth and not in one's mind: what are the principal features of a coffee, are they good or bad, how good and how bad, how does the flavor evolve during the drinking, as the cup cools, etc. Nevertheless, professional tasters will reward or punish beans that have flavors that they judge to be "external" and not intrinsic to the bean, which raises the question, are these concerns about "outside processes" subjective projections that might interfere with strictly empirical judging?

If one is evaluating what is in one's mouth, everything is "inside" the mouth. To raise a score due to a roast level that was judged to be imperfect, or (as we have seen) to some staling that damaged the durability of the *crema* thanks to a fault in the scheduling of the tasting lab and not the coffee, or to lower the score of a delicious coffee because a fortuitous fermentation is deemed "too dangerous" to purchase it, may not conform with a strict version of objective sensory assessment; however, it does conform with the financial risks that any potential purchaser considers, which is a practical objectivity that is given preference. The problem with tasting "only what is inside the bean" and not "outside processes" is that the division is not straightforward, and its discernment originates in skills that are associated with subjective judgment. Is there anything in the world that exists without being influenced by something external to it, and so is truly "independent"? If so, which one is that? Everything under the sun is influenced by external factors. In the case of coffee, is the mucilaginous mesocarp that surrounds each bean "external" to the bean? It is the sweetest part of the coffee fruit. Cherries are sweet, and there are natural sugars in the bean itself, but the mucilage is a gift from heaven: it possesses a durable sweetness that does not diminish even after the seed of a cherry has been in one's mouth for five minutes; this sweetness contributes to the luxurious fermentation activity that has the capacity to create a superior flavor. Shall we include this with what is "inside" the bean? Are processing techniques that take fuller advantage of this sweet mucilage an "outside source"?

A "clean" cup of coffee is one whose identifying flavor can be discerned clearly. Professional tasters prefer such coffees not only because their tastes may be better but because it makes the coffees more reliable. Further, clean coffees also make the tasters' work easier; however, they diminish complexities of flavor that can sometimes improve the quality of taste. Coffees are wild things, and it is not the case that everything wild improves by being tamed. While influences created by the methods of processing are considerably less tangible (and so more difficult to control) than are the variables introduced by blending or roasting, a courageous coffee producer will be willing to take on the challenge, explore various methods, and determine an ideal system for cleaning, fermenting, and drying beans. Since there is some safety in predictability, this drive to tame and standardize frequently curtails creative exploration. The managers of Gill Coffee Traders in Bylakuppe, India, explained to me that processing one's coffee in the same way each time contributed far more to a standardized taste than anything else they could do or that could happen, including seasonable variations in rainfall and sunshine. In their interest to stabilize and secure their production and make profits predictable, they have an interest in routinizing their insights, no matter what discoveries may remain to be found. They systematize their factory's production and do what they can to guarantee a foreseeable outcome. Routines serve to clarify social organization as well, but the downside is that routines sometimes breed stupidity. It is not easy to maintain originality when faced with the "30 things" that can ruin coffee and the hundreds of micro-decisions that are required to cope with them.

We learned in chapter 5 that the principal factors that affect coffee quality include genetics, altitude, processing, selection, and roasting. In the Coffee Museum in Santos, Brazil, on the street where coffee first became a truly global commodity, a sign explains, "Coffee has a wide variety of flavors and aromas depending on the region, manner of cultivation, harvest, and preparation." This leaves out specific reference to processing, which is a vital factor. In this chapter, we review growing, harvesting, processing, editing, blending, and storage.

Growing

Plant cultivation, experimentation, and hybridization could occupy a book by itself, but this is a study of tasting coffee, not agronomy. In addition to growing and planting seedlings, a farmer must be expert at fertilizing, irrigating, pruning, controlling for pests, developing systems for fungal control, and harvesting protocols, all before the delicate processing of the cherries begins.

Shade-grown coffees are popular coffees that are easily marketed under that moniker, no doubt because it is a more environmentally sustainable practice; however, because coffee trees that grow in full sun provide greater yields, some greedy farmers cut down their shade trees in order to obtain those higher yields. They quickly learn that those coffee trees have a shorter life and that without the shade they are more susceptible to insect infestation, such as the coffee berry borer that has ravaged many Indian plantations. Consequently, planting coffee trees in direct sun requires greater use of expensive pesticides and fertilizers, which also raises the labor costs.

Most growers fertilize their trees, since it makes them more resistant to fungal diseases like *roya* and can improve flavor. Some fertilizers are chemical and others are organic, and quite a few farmers will recycle their own cherries in fertilization mixes after de-pulping. The application of fertilizers can take place about every three months. Phosphoric acid fertilization can dramatically improve the acidity of Robustas, but they require microorganisms to ensure full absorption, so it is even more labor intensive. Generally speaking, good fertilization can improve bean density and can raise a coffee's cupping score as much as 10 points, so some cost/benefit analysis is required. Here, keeping careful records is more effective than relying exclusively upon intuition or habit. Not all intuition is reliable: two farmers in Karnataka, India, one a third-generation and the other a fourth-generation coffee farmer, grow cardamom, vanilla, citrus, coriander, and other spices alongside their coffee trees, not only for the additional income they bring but because they believe that they infuse their coffee plants with more interesting flavors. This seems unlikely, although during storage, adjacent spices can be absorbed by a dried green bean (even a roasted bean).

Growers are natural innovators, and they are always engaged in experiments with the microclimates on their properties (e.g., northern side vs. southern side), new hybrids suggested by a local agronomist or an international research agency, testing the effects of elevation upon their favorite varieties, etc. Some small coffee farmers treat many trees as pets, looking after them and tracking their progress regularly. Farmers know the trees better than they know the tastes of the coffee they produce, and the judgments they make are more related to the health of the leaves, their resistance to disease, and the quantity of fruit than they are to flavor. While they are experts about the taste of their cherries (in season, the farmers are always snacking), many are unfamiliar with the flavors that the seeds inside the cherries give to coffee, and few farmers are able to talk about or provide much detail about the flavors of the coffees they grow.

Harvesting

A Brazilian coffee expert claimed, "The process of harvesting is 99% of the quality." This can be compared with the coffee botanist in Trieste who declared, "It's 99% genetics." During my field research, I have encountered quite a few of these 99%-ers. Certainly, high among the things that people claim count for 99% of the quality is ripeness, and picking the cherry at the right time is essential. That is when the beans will have the most sugars and the fewest chlorogenic acids. Fruit that remains attached to the coffee tree too long can over-ferment, especially under humid conditions, so the cherries need to be picked in a timely fashion. During the three months of harvest, the better plantations will pick the cherries every 15 days. It is easy to select ripe cherries when one picks by hand, which is necessary on the steeper farms where tracks and machines are unable to operate. The more mechanized plantations necessarily collect the unripe (and over-ripe) along with the ripe cherries, so what they collect will need to be sorted carefully, for sale at different price levels.

Once picked, the cherries must be transported to the mill swiftly, usually within 12 hours of picking. In washed processing, they will be de-pulped right away, since "If the beans are left for too long before processing, the pulpy flesh becomes more difficult to separate from the beans, leading to imperfect separation" (Thorn 2006, 20). In natural processing, the cherries will dry as much as two weeks or more in the sunshine, preferably on raised beds, before de-pulping. The chemical processes that can occur during this time produce interesting flavors and not a few defects. The aim of most coffee growers is to produce the largest quantity of beans that lack any defects that might make sale difficult or even disqualify the crop for export. In many cases, positive taste characteristics are barely noted, and such matters are left to the middlemen, *beneficios*, coffee works, exporters, and the rest. As a green bean buyer for Sandalj Coffee in Trieste once told me, "Flavors are only for exporters." Only those farmers who are deliberately growing for quality will taste their crop. It is not so much like the blind leading the blind as it is experts with sight leading blind farmers, and the profits from sales are distributed accordingly.

A coffee importer expounded, "Farmers often do not know what coffees they have on their hands, but they are becoming more aware." This transformation is an important event in contemporary global coffee production, and it has barely begun. As Vince Fedele told an SCA audience, "The coffee industry is woefully inadequate in tasting their own coffee." When Paul Katzeff of Thanksgiving Coffee asked a group of Nicaraguan farmers, "How many of you have tasted your own coffee?" no one raised a hand (Pendergrast 2010, 358). At homes I visited in India, it was usual for a coffee owner to drink an inferior coffee (often adulterated with chicory) purchased from a village shop, rather than his or her own coffee, even when it has been judged to be of specialty quality. It is not simply that some farmers cannot afford to drink their best coffee, it is that—like most consumers of coffee everywhere—they are not so much interested in the taste. This could be the biggest surprise I discovered during a decade of field research.

One Indian coffee grower, proud when a Marriott Hotel in Bangalore featured his coffee in its hotel rooms, declared, "I feel like there's some identity to my coffee now." But he added, "Where the bulk of it goes once it's exported, I still have no idea" (Bengali 2014), and the same is true for many growers around the world. Admitting he was uncertain about the taste of his own coffee, the farmer defended himself by pointing out that the West African farmers who grow most of the world's cacao have never tasted chocolate. The farmer is correct; in a parallel (but still extraordinary) fashion, "Togo has been growing cocoa for more than 120 years, but we only export it. Cacao farmers don't even know the taste of chocolate," according to Komi Agbokou, a psychologist who promotes the Choco Togo brand of chocolate (AFP 2016. A South Indian born in Wisconsin who now works as a specialty coffee purveyor in Delhi reports, "A lot of farmers barely know they're growing coffee." Despite his having sold seven tons of specialty coffee in 2013, this broker's in-laws' beverage of choice each morning is Nescafé (Bengali 2014). A study of Salvadoran growers by a sociologist (Dougherty 2008, 73) concluded, "Farmers need to know how their coffee tastes, not just to them, but to potential buyers." By knowing the tastes, not only will they improve their coffee, they will improve their profits.

Processing

While there is a steady pace of innovation in all facets of coffee production, including finding more-resistant and better-tasting hybrids, locating new strains, and improving roasting machines, as well as many professional associations, conferences, and certification regimes for roasters, tasters, and baristas, no facet shows as much potential for the improvement of coffee as the innovations in processing methods that are being developed worldwide. By "processing" we include crop separation, pulp removal, fermentation, drying, silver-skin removal, defect editing, and the rest. My field research included observing coffees being processed and cupped for Illy, Starbucks, Lavazza, Dunkin' Donuts, Nespresso, BKI, and other major brands. Some of them involved shipments of coffee that had as much as a million dollars in value.

Crop Separation

The process of improving crop quality requires more than knowing about taste. Before anything else happens, it is important to separate the kinds of cherries one is harvesting before they are sent to the coffee works for processing. Keeping harvested coffees in separated lots can become extremely valuable for a farmer. It is important for improving quality and is one of the simplest processing improvements to implement. Even before the cherries are separated according to over-ripe, under-ripe, and just-right, they need to be kept segregated so that if the farmer or consultants discover that they have a taste that is especially marketable, they will know where to go to find more of it. Failure to keep one's crop differentiated will reduce the earning opportunities for producers, since anonymous coffees earn little and leave growers subject to the strategies of their brokers and exporters. Further, a quality coffee that is made traceable can receive a premium in the contemporary specialty market.

Sunil Pinto, the director of tasting for a large coffee works in India, explains, "Not everyone in India keeps their harvest separate. Most just mix it all up together, so you can no longer differentiate the coffees." It is not costly to separate one's lots, so this is something that every farmer can do, but there is a significant educational hurdle to be overcome. As one major Indian grower told me, "We're going for quantity here, not quality." Interestingly, this grower drinks only tea at home. This emphasis on quantity was reinforced by a nationalized system that for decades rewarded only quantity: the Indian government purchased and exported all the coffee in India, and no tasting for positive characteristics or marketing of them was performed. Since Indian farmers were obligated to sell their entire crop to the government, there was no possibility to earn a profit by growing quality coffee, and so until recently no one did. After decades of this practice, many growers find it difficult to understand the need for taking care in maintaining crop separation. Even today, many lots are mixed, so there is no point for the exporting board, which examines coffees for defects prior to issuing an export license, to undertake sensory analysis beyond disqualifying coffees that possess defects. That is, many of the coffees that arrive are a "one-off" collection that will be exported and will have no future no matter what their price of sale is. Coffees with a future are coffees that have positive taste characteristics and that growers and producers know the exact source of. This situation makes it necessary to communicate to farmers the purposes and benefits of separating their crop. Pinto reports that after investing much effort explaining this importance to farmers, it is typical for many farmers to return to their old habitual practices in the succeeding year. Pinto laments, "Their efforts are half-hearted and half-organized, controlled mostly by random activities." Converting random practices to a more organized harvest requires more than good advice; it requires resocialization.

Step one in this transformation is to educate all growers to separate the beans at harvest, which requires picking one type of coffee tree at a time. Step two is to keep track of the coffees until a thorough sensory assessment of their quality can be made. Step three requires keeping some documentation of what the lots are (which variety of coffee it is, where on the farm they were harvested, etc.). What is later discovered about the tastes can be added to the documented record so that the information can be retrieved when required. Spencer Turner (2010, 299) advises that all measurable variables should be documented. This third step Pinto calls "getting control," but he emphasizes that the challenges of even the first step are considerable:

> The first step to quality is to understand that keeping the coffee separated helps. So we are still in step one. We are trying to compete with all of the specialty coffees of the world, and we are still at step one. We need to be able to do it without having to go back every year and explain it all over again. After that, farmers can get control over what they pick. Efficiency comes from the grower putting some interest into keeping coffees separated and knowing why they are keeping them separate. Right now, I'm just giving them the steps, but they don't understand why they're doing it. That requires a change in the mindset of the growers. Now we're getting it done and realizing that we can do it, but we're not really teaching the growers why we are doing it.

Susie Spindler, who served for many years as the director of the Alliance for Coffee Excellence (ACE), puts much emphasis on the importance that processing has upon the quality of flavor of a coffee, and she too suggests that the most critical aspect is to keep the product of the harvest separate, and to *maintain the separation* throughout the processing (pulping, drying, storage, shipping). Importers who have attempted serious outreach to farmers have had some success, in part because they are respected as the people with the purchasing money, and their efforts have resulted in a win-win situation. In Brazil, Illy Coffee started running coffee competitions, offering high prices for small lots of excellent-tasting coffees. According to several farmers in Huila, Colombia, Illy taught people how to process their coffees properly, not to pile it in heaps or let it roll around on the ground. Prior to 2002, the coffees of Huila were of poor to average quality and included phenolic defects. A phenolic defect is believed to be caused by circumstances that influence a coffee tree's survival, such as the tree's efforts to fight an invasion by insects, and this self-protective hormone can produce a defective taste. Illy also began a project of teaching growers how to taste their coffees and to notice the differences in the taste as they improved production. This led to higher-quality coffees in the Huila growing area, as assessed by the farmers there, and also to a growth in the popularity of Huila coffees as a single origin. Geoff Watts of Intelligentsia (2013) describes what this process of education is like: "Ernesto submitted ten lots of coffee, and nine of them qualified at 85 or above and several cupped above 90. With him as a concrete example, we could then say to the other farmers, 'Look how Ernesto scored. What did he do that you didn't do?' Finally, we had a concrete way to talk to farmers about how they could earn the highest scores."

The coffees should be evaluated lot by lot as each one passes through the hands of brokers, middlemen, exporters, and even importers on their way to sale, so that an informed and mutually communicating army of purveyors can enhance everyone's attention to flavor and improve each person's sophistication about the tastes that the coffees can provide. This is step four; however, this step can only happen if the brokers are *willing* to communicate insights about taste to the grower. Some brokers see no profit in a farmer's sophistication—quite the contrary, and I have met brokers, exporters, and even farmers who do everything they can to conceal the flavor characteristics of even their better coffees. Central to this problem is that communicating about tastes can open up a hornet's nest of confusions, and in a situation where suspicions often accompany negotiations, these flavor descriptions are not fully trusted. Farmers are especially afraid of leaving out of their descriptions the very feature that an importer is searching for. Complicating matters further, the importer is often reluctant to reveal just what that is, for fear of hiking the price of coffees with those features. The result is that even when a farmer learns just what flavor resources he or she is producing, the communication about tastes can be kept quite limited, and without better communication the meme "from seed to cup" will lack substance.

FERMENTATION

The post-harvest work of eliminating defective beans is one of the critical tasks, and so is handling the fermentation. In fact, since some of the methods used for eliminating defective coffee involve immersing the cherries or beans in water, so that over-developed beans and detritus can sink and underdeveloped beans float and be skimmed off, the work of elimination and the work of fermentation have some overlap. Some fermentation is necessary for removing the sweet mucilaginous layer of the seed and for enhancing flavor.

In naturally processed coffees, after the most obviously defective cherries are removed, the cherries are spread out to dry in the sun and must be rotated continuously. If they are dried too slowly, the molds increase; and if they are dried too quickly, the drying will be uneven and the acidity may increase. There is considerable experimentation with extended drying times, and every climate will require its own procedure. Weissman (2008, 15) observes, "Virtually every coffee-growing region develops its own idiosyncratic processing techniques." Here the keeping of careful records of any experiments is important; in fact, keeping written records is a central feature of any science. All coffees were naturals until the 18th century, and the dry or "natural" method is more economical—and necessary wherever water is scarce. At times, there is at work a false presumption that what costs less means it is worse, but this is not necessarily the case, and naturals can be better or worse than washed coffees. Recently, an explosion of experimentation with fermentations has revealed how complicated it really is. Fermentation commences as soon as the cherry is picked, and continues as the cherries dry in the sunshine, preferably on raised beds, for one week in hot, humid climates and two weeks or more in cool highland locations. It is common for cherries picked at higher elevations to be brought to the outskirts of a town on some nearby plains that receives more sunshine and less rain, presenting fewer risks of molding. While the cherries require sunshine, they also need some covering at night so that the dew does not promote molding, and even condensation that can occur underneath the covering must be monitored. At the end of this phase of processing, the cherries will be removed mechanically, as will the now less tenacious mucilage.

The "wet" or "washed" method was invented in the West Indies and popularized in Sri Lanka and Costa Rica, and it has been much less common in Brazil (Pendergrast 2010, 34). The principal motivation was that some of the new coffee-growing areas that were lower in elevation and more humid than the Ethiopian highlands needed a method of fermenting the beans that would reduce the time and intensity of the process (Brando 2013). Hondurans believe that the bean gains some flavor from the cherry as it dries (Tucker 2011, 105), and the sweet, slippery mucilage (approximately 0.5–2 mm thick, made of sugar and pectin) that immediately surrounds the parchment contributes much to flavors produced during fermentation. While washed coffees are cleaner and their fermentations less wild, soaking all the cherries in the same soup risks having a few defective cherries distribute some damage across the remainder of the beans. As we have noted, and can now begin to keep count, there are "30 ways" to ruin coffee.

There are also "semi-washed," "honeyed," and other hybrid processing techniques. As Weismann observes, "There are myriad variations on fermentation, which is one of the factors that makes coffee from different locales taste so different." That serves to point out, again, that as much as the soil and climate of a "terroir" influences the taste of a bean, the bacterial bases of the fermentation that vary by local contingencies can have as much influence as genetics or density; hence, we can add fermentation to our list of things that contribute "99%" of what is important for the flavor. Fermentation is an art as much as it is a science, in that no protocol can be duplicated precisely, for the reason that changes in local conditions requires continuous readjustments (e.g., cold days vs. hot days), making duplicating previous results difficult. Fermentation is an embryogenic activity in which yeasts or bacteria convert sugars into different chemicals. When you pick the cherry, the embryo starts to react as it seeks the right time to germinate. Up to a point, a longer fermentation will create a sweeter coffee as the embryo converts sugars to fructose, but over-fermenting can quickly destroy the taste. Importantly, just because one does it just right one year and wins the prize does not mean that one can repeat the same fermentation the succeeding season.

Drying

After the cherry and mucilage are removed, drying is critical in order to keep the embryo alive. If the green bean is dried so much that it cracks, breaking its cellular structure, the coffee's essential oils will escape and oxidize, and the green beans might arrive at the importer already stale or aged. Interrupting the drying is important, since if one dries continuously there is a greater risk of damaging the cells' structure, and an improperly dried coffee will make optimum roasting impossible. On the other hand, beans that are not fully dried can arrive at the importing country full of molds, and the effects of continuing fermentation during voyage cannot be predicted. A moisture analyzer is usually used to achieve the optimum level of drying. The ideal is a moisture content of shipped beans between 10% and 12% humidity, although coffee purveyors argue over the differences within the 10–11.5% range used for most washed Arabica, and many purchasers prefer lower moisture content in order to play it safe.

Drying is critical in order to avoid molds that produce mycotoxins, which not only destroy flavor but can contain carcinogenic ochratoxins. Molds that develop during shipping can cause a shipment of coffee to be rejected at the port of arrival, leaving the exporters scratching their heads, requiring DHL sample shipments for re-tasting, and sometimes arbitration. While drying at first seems to be one of the simpler aspects of processing coffee, it can become the source of many problems and disputes. We must add it to our list of "30 ways."

Drying on site is a facet of processing that after some initial financial investment and education has the potential to increase profits. Instead of the farmer directly shipping the cherries off to processors, it is a stage the farmers can perform themselves. They must be able to afford some outlays, which many smaller farmers are unable to manage, but the less that farmers are vulnerable to the decisions of processors who operate as middlemen between the farmers and the exporters, the greater their profits will be and the more independence they will have.

Editing the Coffee

After the coffee cherries have been sorted according to where they were collected and sorted by their level of ripeness, the more obviously defective or immature cherries removed, the coffee beans (actually seeds) de-pulped, and the green beans dried, they will be sorted more. This editing of green coffee will first focus on detecting and removing defective beans, and then the tasters will explore what positive taste features the remaining beans may possess, keeping in mind likely clients for them as they taste. During the later stages of editing, they will consider the potential that each lot of green beans may have for becoming part of a blend that can be sold.

Before defective beans can be removed effectively, the beans are sorted by screen size. Green coffee is sold by screen size, largely because roasters will roast beans that have the same size (otherwise, the larger beans would be able to attain a full roasting at the cost of burning the smaller ones). When an exporter purchases local coffees, all sizes arrive mixed together, even if they have been kept separate according to location and type. Sorting by screen sizes is easily achieved. A large mechanical sifter progressively allows smaller sized beans to slip through sized holes at various levels of screens, precipitating out at the level appropriate for their size. Left behind at each level are beans of the same size. Samples of each size of beans are kept in sample boxes, which are then subjected to further inspection. After the beans are sorted, the entire lot must be "cleaned up," and the labor of removing defective beans commences in earnest. According to one common protocol for assessing the quality of a batch of coffee, the amount of 16 different defects (6 primary and 10 secondary) in a sample of 250 grams is counted. Arabicas and Robustas are evaluated according to slightly different standards, with more defective beans per 250 grams permitted for lots of Robustas, and the number of permissible defective beans is written into the contract and priced accordingly. Using the beans that reside inside the sample boxes, purveyors will identify and count what defects inhabit each lot of coffee, following which they will be returned to the boxes because the samples must be kept accurately representative of what exists in the batches of coffee in storage. The next task, which is a genuine challenge and a major part of the work of purveying coffee, is for the processor to remove the identified defective beans from the lots in storage.

Identification and removal of defective beans takes place both by machine and by hand, and there are a variety of machines: optical-selectors, wind machines, weighing/density scales, etc. This fosters an intimate relationship between professional processors and their machines. The coffee professionals do not so much search for every observed defect; rather, they adapt to their machinery by searching for defects the machines are capable of removing. While assessing a sample by hand, the processor tries to duplicate what the machine can accomplish, and it takes expertise to know what this will be. While an optical-selection machine can easily remove spoiled beans that are orange in color or dark green, lighter green beans with defects can be more difficult for it to select, and too many kinds of greens can make it tricky for the machine to operate effectively. For this reason, the lot may be divided by shades of green, and once the colors are more or less homogenous, they can better use the photographic separator to remove the defective beans: the color characteristics of a defective type of bean will be determined, the optical selection programmed, and the machine will remove them automatically. This may require several runs with each color shade, with the lot becoming cleaner after each run. There is an interesting reflexivity that occurs with this colorimetrics, and the examiner continuously alters the parameters of a defective bean's metric representation according to how successful the result of each run turns out to be. Much like surfing a wave, as soon as one learns what a particular decision accomplishes, one alters the decision according to this feedback, which is continuous. One-hundred-percent removal of defective beans is not the objective of most exporters (only micro-lots of specialty coffees receive this sort of treatment, which is why the defects they have will usually be removed by hand); rather, the goal is to render the number of defective beans below the quantity that is permissible according to the contract of sale. The beans that remain are usually the ones that were too difficult to remove, which is usually a number so small that their influence on the coffee's taste will be difficult to detect. Most under-ripe and otherwise flawed beans that are removed will be sold to the local market. Exported coffees are the best beans.

Before shipping an order of 2,280 bags of green beans to a large coffee firm in Switzerland, one Brazilian exporter divided their green coffees into three groups in order to make them serviceable for the optical-selection machines (such as the Bühler Sortex optical-electronic sorter) that are programmed to remove beans by color. After finding some shells, under-developed beans, and even some small bits of wood, they sent the lot to the wind machine, which blew most of these away after three runs though the machine. The work of editing is like the labor of a sculptor in that the final artifact takes form gradually. During the later stages more tasting is done, and if an offending flavor is detected, the green beans are reexamined (using the sample box) to locate the offending bean. Not all defective beans damage taste to the same degree. In such a large order, one needs to locate all defective beans that can be removed mechanically. If one cannot remove enough of them, the lot may have to be sold to a customer who is seeking a lower price level (with a higher number of defects written into the contract) or spread thinly across a number of orders. As the exporter and expert taster Arnold Baskerville summarized, "It starts to become complicated. You have to decide whether to buy the coffee or not, because you know it's going to be more difficult." In this way, the relative ease of the task of editing that an exporter will face comes to compete with the quality of the flavor itself when settling the price at which the exporter will purchase the green beans from the grower or a local broker. And not every year is the same. Another exporter once told me, "This year's crop is totally crazy" due to excessive rains; therefore, the standards vary from season to season.

When processing a green coffee for export and examining carefully for defects, they work with half-kilo samples of green beans that come from shipping containers (as much as 20,000 kilos) of that green coffee. After most defective beans have been removed, a 300-gram sample will be roasted, and the coffee will be cupped and approved or receive further examination for defects and further removal of defective beans by various machines, including the optical-selection machine. Professional tasters must simulate the work of their machines; otherwise, there will be a gap between the samples they process by hand in their lab and the results of the mechanical processing of thousands of kilos of coffee. There is no benefit in performing the removal of defects better than what the machines will accomplish, since that is the coffee they will be shipping to importers. Eliminating defective beans by hand for that large a batch is not practical, though a few firms pay a premium for hand removal of defects. It is estimated that the wind machine is capable of eliminating defective beans amounting to as much as 10% of a shipment of coffee and that an optical-electronic sorter is capable of removing another 15%. In both cases, the machines are guided by the hands-on expertise of professionals who have learned to perform like their machines: they are the machine's brains; and it is a sophisticated skill.

After they have removed all the defective beans their machines can, they roast another 300-gram sample and cup the result. If the result is satisfactory, the factory will process the shipment of coffee. When that is completed, they then cup the factory-processed coffee "to see if it reaches the same level" as what they accomplished by hand. If it does, the coffee can be exported as is or used in a blend; if it does not, they may run the thousands of kilos through the wind machine or the optical-selection machine again until a satisfactory result is achieved.

Processing of highest-quality coffees is a hands-on procedure, since human hands are able to remove defects better than a machine, which is why Illy Coffee insists that its main Indian processor use humans and not machines to remove defects (the results are quite good). They pay a premium for that labor, mostly accomplished by Indian women who appear to have a fine time chatting as they sit together calmly, cross-legged, in a circle. For lesser-quality, so-called "price" coffees, larger coffee purveyors will perform the processing by machines, and so no premium charge will accrue to the cost of the coffee. Such coffees gain clients more on the basis of price than on quality. In the coffee world these two aspects are always joined at the hip.

Willem Boot suggests that "Grading green beans is a meditative exercise," and grading quality by hand is unique multi-sensory work. The creator of Maxwell House Coffee famously relied on a British broker who was able to distinguish among Colombian, Mexican, and Brazilian coffees "simply by sniffing the unroasted beans" (Pendergrast 2010, 123), and much about the quality can be ascertained by sight, smell, and even feel. Marcio Hazan of Santos revealed to me, "When the coffee is too green, you can *feel* the difference." Over the three weeks that I observed Marcio, while he was engaged in examining coffees for several blends, he was continuously handling unrelated green beans, occasionally grabbing a fistful and raising them to his nose for a good sniff. As he worked on the main matters that were before him, he kept handling these unrelated beans with a kneading motion in the manner one might use for kneading bread. One day, having spent a few hours kneading and occasionally smelling the green beans absent-mindedly, and after completing the blends that were required for the shipments that needed to go out that day, he had an hour to spare. He decided to follow up a hunch, and he combined two of the beans he had been kneading with another green bean he had been working with several days previously: he had an intuition about a blend. He decided upon a ratio for the three beans, roasted a sample, and then we cupped the result, which presented a pleasant taste. It was as if the blend had organized itself, with Marcio's hands simply being the medium, facilitating an event that was more passive than a process of active deduction. If that was meditation, it was meditation without an analytic direction, almost a séance.

Blending is a major strategy in the exporter's editing toolkit. If an exporter has a coffee too difficult to clean, the exporter can spread them very thinly across a large number of already blended green beans. For example, an exporter had 1,700 bags of coffee that they determined was ideal for a client who ordered 2,000 bags. In their lab, exporters retain samples of the green coffees that they store in their warehouse. Some of the sample cans contain beans from previous shipments, and the task exporters face is to devise a way to optimize the use of any positive flavor characteristics they may have or distribute any negative aspects so thinly that they are no longer ascertainable. The boxes that hold the samples are marked in general ways, listing the coffee's basic worth, whether it has been through the photo-separation and the wind separation processes (and how many times), and its screen size; however, the labels do not bear detailed flavor indications. One archived sample container reading "17–18, fine cup, strictly soft" was selected for making up the 300-bag shortfall (out of 2,000). A sample blend that contained 15% of this remnant coffee was prepared, and then roasted and cupped. The head taster did not like what the remnant coffee did to the 1,700 bags that he had already approved, so he re-roasted and re-tasted a combination that used half as much (7.5%) of the archived sample, and he found that to be acceptable. After this, he needed to find another coffee for making up the difference of 150 bags in the total order, one that would work well with the blend already achieved for the 1,850 bags. After approving a solution using sample blends, the exporter then had the challenging task of evenly mixing the two lots of 150 bags throughout the 1,700 other bags.

Blending by Exporters

One reason that exporters develop a blend is to improve the taste of their coffee, and another purpose is to use blending as a medium that makes it possible to sell all of the lots of coffee one has for sale. In the first instance, the blend developed should be better tasting than any of its individual components. For example, a Brazilian exporter may design a blend of Mogiana, South Minas Gerais, and Cerrado coffees to take advantage of the benefits (acidity, sweetness, and body) that each one contributes. As Wechselberger and Hierl (2009, 64) suggest, "Some varieties become more harmonious and rounder when combined with others." Thorn (2006, 62) adds, "Some people would argue that the best coffee is achieved by blending the best characteristics from a range of different coffees—bright acidity from one, a floral aroma from a third—to make the best final product." In blending as a medium for selling inferior lots of coffee, a decent coffee can become the vehicle for an exporter to sell beans that cannot stand on their own or ones that are left over from an earlier blend. Coffee that is too bitter can be difficult to sell, but once the bitterness is diminished by blending it with a milder bean, it can provide just enough bitter flavor to make the coffee interesting. As Ted Lingle says (2001, 14), "Modulation of the bitter taste contributes greatly to the total flavor profile." Blending can permit a coffee purveyor to disguise poorer-quality beans in a way that they can still be sold at a good price, and every lab has its favorite techniques. Roasters have reasons of their own for the blends they prepare, and we will examine some of these roasters' blending practices in chapter 11.

Perhaps the original and most iconic blend of coffee was the "Mocha Java" sold by Dutch traders during the 18th and 19th centuries, which was a blend of beans from Java. Perhaps the practice of marketing coffee under origin identities had its inauspicious beginning at the end of the 19th century and beginning of the 20th in San Francisco, where any coffee that was a peaberry was marketed under the origin identity "Mocha," and any non-peaberry coffee was marketed as "Java." Most of each was grown in El Salvador. In 1886, the San Francisco *Chronicle* reported, "Not one coffee drinker in a hundred can tell the difference between Java, Costa Rica, Salvador, or East Indian brands of coffee" (Sedgewick 2020, 62–63), and the situation is much the same today. Also in the early part of the 20th century, a bean from Santos (which was collection of beans from several railroad lines that ran through the coffee-growing states of Paraná, São Paulo, and Minas Gerais) was blended either with Robustas from Africa to make a standard blend for espresso or with an Arabica from Colombia for a higher-grade blend. "A good Santos can serve as a reliable base for a blend, to which it gives body, sweetness and provides a structure for adding other components" (Azienda Riunite Caffè 2013, 227), although we should note that a "Santos" itself is a partly imaginary identity since it is composed of dozens of kinds of beans collected along the railway lines, and so it is already a blend.

What part of blending is logic and what part intuition? Today, everyone wants to turn coffee purveying into a science. They believe it is more rigorous that way, but some older coffee tasters dismiss this idea as a gilded form of laziness. Arnold Baskerville explained, "Perhaps the best blending is by recollection and imagination. A rational process cannot be that imaginative." It is possible that imagination is more important than science, but there are ways for the two to work together. Science can be highly imaginative, but it can also operate in a literal-minded way that lacks imagination. Although coffee purveyors are always eager to find an easy and secured solution, no serious coffee professional is prepared to surrender their judgment to an algorithm.

It is important to acknowledge that there is considerable serendipity to achieving a successful blend. For instance, after settling on a provisional blend, one taster did not like the smell of the least mature beans, so he went back through the many lots of beans that contributed to the blend, smelled them one by one, and removed two of them because they smelled too "green." A slightly green taste is not really a serious problem since as the coffee ages, this defect will be diminished. As he tasted, he had in mind the

Japanese client who would receive the blend. Then he re-roasted a sample without those two types of beans, tasted it, and concluded that it was still too green, not for him but for his client. Knowing what the client is thinking is something difficult to program into an algorithm; and not simply what the client *says* they want, but what they really do want, despite what they say. Perhaps that is beyond the scope of science.

When working a blend, more than one taster tastes at a time. On one occasion when the taster for a Brazilian exporter located one *rio* cup in a flight of 20 cups of a sample, he required some confirmation of his finding. He invited a number of tasters from the firm's lab into the cupping room in order to learn whether they too could (blindly) locate the offending cup. When they did confirm it, objectivity was accomplished, and they declined to send the blend to their client. If there are three or four tasters, frequently each one will make a few notes on a card. Interestingly, the more expertise a taster possessed, the less the taster wrote on the card. In one lab, I tasted along with them (tasters are eager to put an additional palate to work for them), and the coffee samples were decent, soft coffees, but a few of the cups had a green taste. The taster simply wrote, "duro, verde" (hard, green). When I asked an accomplished taster, "You write down so little?!" he replied, "I don't write. It doesn't matter so much." Instead, his ken was always stuck on a trail of tastes in the manner of a hunting dog. Not all of the tasters agreed about which cups were the offending ones, but it is not unusual to lack a consensus. Their ability to tolerate a lack of consensus about taste is part of the attractiveness of the work of tasting, and it serves to keep the tasters open to aspects of taste they have yet to notice.

Coffees that may be unsatisfactory by themselves can still contribute something positive to a blend, and such a coffee can be used to fill a blend inexpensively if it does not pollute it. One lab run by Coffee Day in India adds 56% Robusta to one of their blends just to increase the aftertaste. An inexpensive coffee that was described as "Good cup, but with a low profile, not very pronounced; slightly sweetish" might become just the right vehicle for adding some Robusta, thereby producing a satisfactory blend that could be produced at a low cost. Similarly, in Brazil we had a coffee from Paraná that offered no body, no sweetness, and no acidity, but it was ideal for providing a sort of canvas with which a blender can work. It provides volume to a blend without doing damage. Used as 50% of a blend, it will accommodate a highly acidic bean, like some coffees from Minas Gerais, which are too costly to compose 100% of a coffee. In this manner, the finer features of the Minas will not be overpowered, and its better features can be maximized, in the sense of distributing their benefits across the maximum possible lots of coffee.

One bean might offer a nice lemon-like taste that might not be capable of standing alone but could contribute something important to a blend that includes some soft, aromatic Robustas. Tasters very much enjoy this work of finding the right combination of flavors and profits; moreover, each year the tasters need to start over again, since changes in the weather create changes in the coffees. For example, as the Cerrado coffees became more acidic, purveyors had to reduce the amounts that they used in their blends, and they need to keep re-tasting it in order to determine just what amount to use each year. This way the blends are always evolving. Exporters keep records of the percentages used for the blends previously sold, but old percentages do not necessarily work for a succeeding season. A taster explained, "I know how it's changing crop by crop, so I discuss with my colleagues, and we change the blend." His colleague sells the coffee via the internet to overseas clients and so can inform the taster about the target selling price, which will allow the taster to decide how to compose the blend: the quality will be adjusted to the price. They may not always use numerical ratings, although some purveyors speak in general categories, such as line 1 (the highest), line 2, line 3, line 4, and line 5, but even without any numerated division the price itself will serve as a numeration, and it will dictate the selection of the positive flavor characteristics that will be introduced into the blend.

A taster explained, "This year the crop is very bad, so we need to try a lot of blends in order to discover a suitable taste quality for our clients: it gives us more work. This year we might need to do 10 blends to find one that is suitable for our clients. Not suitable for me, but suitable for our clients." Each of these blends will be air-shipped to clients in North America, Japan, Europe, etc. When they taste a prospective blend before shipping, they need to taste using the imagination of their clients—how does one numerate that? This situation exceeds what numerated assessments are able to capture. Frustrated with beans that were too earthy but cognizant that green beans possess a dynamic life, a taster may decide to wait six months "for the coffee to rest" so that aging will reduce its immature taste and more of it can be used.

In Santos I observed an interesting praxis of business: an exporter would not always immediately seek beans that conform to the priorities stipulated by the clients at the time they gave their orders; rather, they would taste all of the beans they had on hand, experimenting with some blends composed in the lab, and then draw on their knowledge of the taste preferences of their clients to decide how to best allocate to their clients the blends they had been tasting, which ones are exportable, to whom, and at what price levels. Instead of simply following the client requests and then locating coffees to match, they survey the full range of what is available and then choose samples for air delivery from the blends most likely to match the clients' needs. For example, Marcio Hazan's family has three generations of experience at coffee purveying, so many of his customers have come to rely upon him for just this expertise. When he rejects some beans for one client, he may notice that they might work perfectly for another one. According to Rodrigo Alarcón of Alma Café in Bogotá, "Scandinavians prefer high-acidity coffees, and the French and Italians prefer low-acidity coffees." Accordingly, a smart exporter sends each client the coffee that is suitable for them. Hazan holds fast to the rule, "There is no such thing as a good coffee—there is only the coffee that your client likes." This conforms with the view of Franco Schillani of Trieste, who told me, "In the coffee business personal taste doesn't exist." But not all exporters appreciate this to the same extent. Among coffee-exporting countries, some self-doubt can influence their work. For example, Indians may keep their numerical ratings of their own coffees low, thinking that the coffees are incapable of achieving higher ratings. Enrico Meschini describes a situation he discovered in El Salvador, whose coffee purveyors want so much to be like the Guatemalans, whose coffees frequently achieve higher ratings, that they seek to produce a Guatemalan type of acidity; however, being an Italian blender and roaster, Meschini prefers the pleasing but not too strong natural acidity of El Salvadoran beans, which have less acidity than Guatemalan coffees. He believes that the Salvadorans underappreciate their own coffee.

While firms that design blends for export sometimes engage in designing that has a deductive nature, mostly it is discovery that guides their preparations. Blends commence not so much from a deliberate, analytic rationality; rather, they commence with hunches or even blind experimentation: one tries, fails, tries again, and then succeeds. Only then is it that some analysis may be applied to determining the reasons for success. It is no wonder that blending can be the enjoyable business craft that it is, a continuing balancing act between quality and price. A successful blend becomes "the right blend" for the coffees that one has been facing, and it may even achieve an objective recognition as such, although the present blend is only a momentary bubble that floats upon the surface of a great ocean.

Working a Blend

Blending by exporters is accomplished for the purpose of selling all of the stocks of coffee that the exporter has purchased from growers. When one exporter commenced an assessment of 21 containers of green coffee, each container worth about $50,000 wholesale, they sampled each one to learn just what they had purchased. They had previously cupped samples of these coffees before purchasing them; however, some of the coffees were better than they had thought they were buying, while other coffees were worse. Although an exporter tries to acquire lots that will be easy to sell, not every lot will turn out to be easy. A Brazilian exporter once said to me, "This coffee is difficult to blend, so I'm trying it different ways." What can make a lot difficult to blend? First in line is the fact one is trying to please a client who lives halfway around the world, speaks a different language, and is oriented to purveying coffee to a coffee culture that one may not understand well. An Indian who drinks daily a stainless steel one-ounce cup of coffee with a sweetened milk-and-chicory concoction may have little idea of what a Scandinavian who drinks eight ounces of sugarless black coffee is anticipating. While sensory analysts invest much effort to establish "good"-in-itself for a coffee, in actuality there is only good for a client, whose interests and uses may not be fully known.

In seeking "the right blend" one also needs to index the results of one's experiments to the level of roast the beans will receive in the coffee culture of the client. That is, the taste of the blend, and hence its success, depends on the particular roast levels that their client is likely to use. If one knows what that is, one can roast the test samples in the same way, but when one does not know that roasting profile, which can be a trade secret (exporters try to guess by tasting a finished package), one cannot be certain about which positive features and which taints will survive the roasting. One can generalize about how each country performs its roasting, but since a good deal of money is at stake, any uncertainty will be troubling.

Exporters are uncertain which additional coffees will be blended by the importer with the one being exported. Indian exporters complain that it is difficult to ascertain the role their Indian coffee will play in a blend, which is important to know since the pricing of the coffee is related to the importance of that role. An exporter may have a contract to provide Nespresso with a component for its "Mysore Nuggets" capsule, but Nespresso is never going to reveal what coffees it uses to make that blend. The exporter will purchase a Nespresso system, taste the Mysore Nuggets capsule, and, knowing what their own coffee tastes like, attempt to subtract their flavor from the capsule's flavor and deduce the other coffees that compose that blend.

Each year, an exporter must assess all of the coffees that have arrived during a current season and ascertain their resources and shortcomings. This assessment is necessarily based on how these coffees taste in themselves; however, what the exporter's tasters must do, but cannot do, is to make some assessment of how they will taste alongside the other coffees that the importer will be purchasing during the current year. Especially, the exporters need to know "How will our coffee fit in?" How can they "peg" their coffee to the needs of the importers' blends when they cannot be certain what role their coffees will be playing in those blends? Most Indian exporters know that most of their coffees are being purchased not for making a major contribution to the flavor of the ultimate blend but for making a contribution to the profit margin. I asked Sunil Pinto, "You once said that the Indian coffees were mostly 'team players' rather than candidates for single origins. What characteristics do they contribute to the team? Do you know why your buyers purchase it, that is, what they use it for? Do they tell you how they will use it?" He replied, "Not entirely. If they were to let you know just how they think it is important, their fear is that this might increase its value. They don't say all that much about it."

Indian exporters look to sell coffees that will not interfere with the tastes of the coffees from Colombia, Rwanda, etc. with which their coffee will be blended. In particular, they do not want to be the cause for detracting from the more general characteristics of the body or "the sweetness" of a blend. They are able to sell their coffees because of their lower cost, so they do not need to contribute very much, but neither should they take much away. Often the best that their coffee can achieve is to "tone down" some of the characteristics of other coffees that might become tastier when made less pronounced. But exporters are never really sure just how the importers will use them. The importers may not be sure themselves at the time they purchase them, since their blenders and roasters will need to change their blends each year. India produces both Arabica and Robusta, and the larger farms grow about 50% of each. Because they wash nearly all of their Arabica (water is readily available in the region of India where coffee is grown), the equipment is already on hand, so some Robusta gets washed, sometimes accidentally. In this way, India has discovered for itself a small niche for washed Robustas, and Italy has become a big client for them since they are often clean Robustas that will easily disappear in a blend, and they are always cheap.

When a client was happy with a previous order, an exporter has the ideal place to begin. Having samples of orders shipped previously, the problem becomes how to achieve a similar taste with a new year's crop. As Roden (1994, 66) observes, "Customers expect the blends to remain the same. It is a challenge for the blender to maintain consistency with the changing factors involving the beans and to find replacements for those that become unavailable or too expensive." Their work begins by re-tasting the sample of the previous order; here the question of objectivity rears itself in a tangible form: one must identify its taste characteristics accurately if one is going to reproduce it. Even if the blend one shipped previously was the serendipitous outcome of a series of experiments with the coffees that one had on hand at that time, since this has become "the right blend" for that client, one must reconstruct just that with the new season's offerings. For instance, how does one reconstruct the nebulous contribution of those 150 bags of "filler" coffee that constituted the last 7.5% of that 2,000-bag shipment? The exporter's tasters will prepare a selection of candidate blends and begin tasting them, and during these cuppings I noticed that the tasters are never entirely certain when they have landed on the mark. Here is where there is a spontaneous urge to share one's understanding of a taste with fellow professionals, and the intersubjective origins of sensory assessment become fully evident. On occasion, even the exporter's accountant will be dragged into the tasting room, and this is where the participant part of my participant observation took place. Few exporters rely upon elaborate schedule-driven and numerated protocols that split the taste into categories for separate assessment, but all of them rely upon the collaborative judgment of a cohort of tasters who have over time have achieved some dependable intersubjective calibration.

One more observation must be mentioned: the objectivity they are pursuing is not the abstract objectivity of a detached scientist but the practical objectivity of people who are usually working against a deadline. More important to them than finding the correct taste is another matter: "We have only five hours to decide. The ship is sailing." Exporters do enjoy the work of experimenting with various ways to improve a blend, especially on occasions when they are able to recognize just where the asymmetry of its balance lies and have an idea how to repair it. A taster once said to me, "If the coffees are of the same value, and I might make the blend better by using a different coffee, why not experiment? But if the deadline has come, I'll try just one or two experiments and then ship it."

On one occasion an exporter was certain that one minor component of a blend was a small problem; however, since the deadline had arrived and there was insufficient time to replace the offending bean with another bean of the same type, he shipped the lot slightly flawed. A motto from the world of exporters took precedence: "The deadline is first." On another occasion an exporter received a rush order from an importer, and they tried a blend of 20 coffees, each contributing 5% to the blend. When they cupped the result, they identified some problems and removed two of the beans from the blend. Unfortunately, the deadline for air shipping the TNT Express sample to Europe had arrived, and there was no time to re-roast and re-cup the redesigned blend. Since part of the reputation of an exporter depends upon responding promptly to requests, they decided to ship the sample without re-cupping it. They explained to me that the coffee was already decent, and that the change they had made would only improve it; besides, the importer's lab would make the pivotal assessment after they received the 300-gram sample.

When exporters taste a coffee and discover some taints, their task will be to learn where any bad beans are coming from. Because they are not going to throw 3,000 kilos of green coffee into the dump, they will undertake serious investigation, which includes a close visual inspection of the beans, use of machinery like wind machines to remove quaker beans (beans that have not fully ripened, and so are lighter, and give a woody taste to a lot), and testing optical-selection choices to learn whether they can get their machinery to remove the offending type of beans *en masse*. They may have a really great coffee that has only a few overly fermented beans, so if those beans can be eliminated through editing, they can bring out the full potential of the lot. During one such problem an exporter said to me, "This problem is a good problem—you have lots of good coffee and only one small problem."

I have been told, "Sometimes a small difference can have a large effect upon the final blend." They may reduce one of the contributing coffees to 20% from 30%. If the 20% does not work out well, they may reduce it further or remove a second component of the blend and then re-taste to learn whether the blend changes positively or negatively. Sometimes they will taste the old blend and the new one side-by-side. Here again, anyone in the room who possesses a tongue can become a consultant. As they taste, working cooperatively, they come to know the coffee better. On one occasion when a reduction from 30% to 20% was successful, another problem revealed itself: "Today the blend is perfect. That blend yesterday contained 30% two-year aged coffee. Now I changed it to 20%, and it has lost its woody flavor. It's very nice, sweet. But it's uneven since out of 20 cups one of them tastes 'green' and a second cup has a bit of *riado*. But they all have nice body—this is a much better blend." If they cannot remove the *riado* taint, they will need to find another client who is less sensitive to or more tolerant of *riado*. *Riado* is a harsh taste that is a little bit metallic, and "It's one of the main things we have to be aware of in our Brazilian coffees." If one out of 10 cups has *riado*, they will reject it for a northern European order because in a light roast like they do in Scandinavia it is impossible to hide it." *Rio* is similar, only more intense, a very bad taste. Hiding it by blending it and giving it a dark roast can work with some countries, and if all else fails, they can sell the coffee to a buyer who is looking for an inexpensive shipment.

In another blend they tasted 30 cups, only one of which revealed a *rio* taste. A *rio* taint is more serious than a *riado* one, but only one cup that had it, so they needed to make a decision:

A Do you think they will be able to taste the one cup of *rio* in the blend?

B No, I don't think so.

C When the cup is like that earlier one, really open, they get it. But not this one.

At this point they checked the price that the purchaser had agreed to pay. If the importer has contracted for the highest price level, they will not ship such a coffee; however, if the agreement was for a lower price level, they may decide to ship it. It is a policy of many exporters to always ship coffees that are of slightly higher quality than what an importer has agreed to pay for, for the reason that disputes can become so awkward and time-consuming, with communication over the internet always difficult, that they prefer to avoid such disputes altogether.

On another occasion, a coffee rated "fine cup" was showing some *rio* faults, which they thought could be a problem. They surmised that this was due to some scraps that may have been left over in the micro-roaster from the previous roast. The micro-roaster they usually use for their premium blends had been sent for repair, and so they had to roast the "fine cup" coffee in the micro-roaster they use for their Brazilian national blends. They cleaned the micro-roaster by roasting a full load of neutral coffee and then re-roasted a batch of the "fine cup" coffee, and the *rio* taste disappeared. A single lingering bad bean can contaminate 15 cups of coffee.

While meticulous blending in the producing country is performed by exporting firms, the component coffees that they use for their blends may already have been blended. Growers frequently mix several types of their coffees together without much consideration. In Brazil, coffees identified by the railroad lines that picked up the sacks were named accordingly, and in this way a single moniker was applied to the harvest of many plantations. The result was that the flavors that corresponded to these monikers were allowed a wide and varying range. More deliberate pre-export blending occurs at the *beneficios* and processing facilities that clean up the coffee cherries arriving from the farmers before passing along the green beans to brokers. In these small semi-rural facilities, one can meet some of the keenest tasters in the world. Typically, they are eager young men who work under the tutelage of expert tasters, and these young professionals are obsessed with reading the flavor of every coffee that arrives. Their keenness reminded me of the keenness of the young Aboriginal hunters of kangaroos that I knew in Central Australia, to whom a remote Aboriginal community would entrust the bulk of their hunting responsibilities. After a small, three-acre farm sends its 60 one-hundred-pound bags to the *beneficio*, they are tasted in order to be paired with beans similar in flavor, so that the size of a lot of coffee will be large enough for an exporter to be interested in purchasing it. When the processor discovers batches of coffee that look and taste similar, they will be combined into the processor's own sub-types, and these blended sub-types are what exporters will use for their blending. While they will have some taste features in common derived from the method of processing the *beneficio* uses, they also have differences that stem from their different origins. By the time the beans reach the importer's shores they will already be a blend of blends, yet roasters in the importer's country will treat it as a single type (e.g., a "Santos") that they will use in various ways for the blends that they design. No wonder origins are not always labeled on the package. While the importer's or roaster's blends are composed of three to nine of these coffees, it is more probable that the actual number of different coffees is closer to twice that. At this point, attempting to correlate a coffee's taste with its origin can become pointless.

When the farmers ship off their raw cherries, most of the profits accrue to processors and middlemen: "The *beneficio* owners had a great deal of clout and could set artificially low prices, reaping most of the profits" (Pendergrast 2010, 39). Part of the solution to the economic survival of small farmers lies in these farmers learning how to do some of the processing themselves. Growers can increase their income substantially, and therefore increase the wages they are able to offer their workers, by doing the de-pulping, fermenting, and drying at their own facilities; however, many small farmers lack facilities. Some do not even have sufficient patio space for drying all coffee they grow. Here is where national investment (by governments, private groups, and NGOs) can contribute a great deal, and a number of importing nations' governments finance foreign aid programs that teach small farmers how to process their coffees at their home sites.

Communication Between Exporters and Importers

While the cohort of tasters in the exporter's lab are well calibrated, as are the tasters in the labs of the importers, communication between the two tasting labs can be problematic. Although all of these tasters are highly competent, they do not often speak the same language, literally and figuratively. Each country has its own tasting culture, way of roasting coffee, and different assessment protocol. Exporters must learn the sense and references of the industry terms that are customary in each of the importers' countries, and at times there can be a zoo of indexical expressions (for a discussion of indexical expressions see Garfinkel and Sacks 1970, 348–350). It is not enough to know that an Italian importer like Pellini, Lavazza, or Segofredo thinks that the shipment was "too earthy," nor is it important what the exporter's idea of "earthy" might be; rather, the exporter needs to know what is the importer's "earthy." How is the exporter able to know that when those tasters must work without the local historicity of the importer's lab that has stabilized that meaning? *Frutos rojos* ("red fruits") can index a key flavor for Central American exporters, but this taste descriptor loses clarity when it is transmitted to a Danish importer, since the Danes possess a more elaborate taxonomy for red fruits and berries than do Central Americans. Such descriptors require more specificity if they are to offer guidance.

In Colombia, I once asked a farmer who engages in direct trade why he was unwilling to offer a potential importer a more detailed description of the flavor of his coffee. This exporter explained, "When I describe the coffee to them, the importer wants to come and see it. Then when they taste my coffee, they find something else. Both perspectives may have validity, but they differ. The importers come with the intention of finding and evaluating what I have described; however, they do not find that, they find something else. It can be better, but it's not what I described to them. That kind of difference is slowing down the development." By "slowing down the development," the Colombian farmer meant that sorting out the problems with communication becomes cumbersome and can delay the negotiation of a sale. Moreover, he prefers that importers find right away the tastes they are interested in, tastes with which the farmer may not be as familiar as the importers themselves are.

Exporters who are preparing shipments that have already been sold are guided by an interest in avoiding sending any beans that might be rejected for taints, since it is too costly to ship refused beans back to the producing country and they will have to be sold from the port at a substantial discount, sometimes at a loss. When I asked an exporter why it is rare that tasters in Switzerland never complain about a taint called "green," the exporter replied, "Probably they taste it, they just don't care about it." The situation is that taste values vary across the world coffee industry, and these differences must be considered. As one large exporter described it, "I know my clients—this client I can send more green beans; others not." Once again, it is not which coffee is inherently the best, but what the coffee buyer prefers.

It is not unusual for a shipment rejection to come as a complete surprise to exporters, even as the importer is filled with a suspicion that the exporter has tricked them. An exporter could have deliberately, possibly proudly, sent above-grade beans (i.e., above the price level that was paid) to an importer, in the interest of avoiding just such a problem. When a problem occurs, exporters will re-taste their saved samples, and the importer will ship a sample of the beans that were rejected. These two samples will be tasted side-by-side in the exporter's lab in an effort to detect any difference between what the exporter sent and what has arrived from the importer. If they cannot taste a problem, the rejection of the order can seem like an occult phenomenon.

On one occasion, the tasters in the exporter's lab re-tasted the previous three shipments they had sent to the importer, shipments for which there were no problems, in an attempt to recover not only what the importers might be tasting but the background horizon with which the importer's tasters are working; however, on this occasion they did not find a major difference between these and the lot that was rejected. Then the exporter tried roasting the suspected sample at different temperatures, to see if some taint would become apparent at another roast level. If they are still unable to identify a problem, they can contest the rejection, and independent government-sponsored mediators in the exporter's country will taste them and arbitrate.

Many importers are paranoid about being sent bad shipments, especially during a year when the rainfall and humidity is higher than average and has been spoiling beans. Amid such fear and mistrust, importers can become so vigilant that they start to project problems that do not exist. As we have begun to appreciate, knowledge is partly what the object is presenting and partly what one's discernment is projecting onto the object. On the exporters' side, they may harbor a suspicion that an importer is finding problems just to play games, since many disputes are resolved by negotiating a lower price, so it can be to the importer's advantage to complain about defects; consequently, exporters also may project more suspicions than are warranted. Communication across continents and cultures is difficult, and emails are a flawed instrument for resolving these differences. Even when, upon reexamination, an exporter detects a problem, the problem they detect may be a different one, i.e., other than the one that the importers have been trying to describe. The exporter's tasters are usually better experts about their own coffees than are the importer's tasters, especially when they apply the sharply focused attention of a cohort of tasters to the task of identifying what an imagined problem of a shipment of coffee could be. At this point the exporter faces another conundrum: the tasters want to discover the source of the problem, but they do not want to suggest to the importer other problems they may discern that the importer is not yet aware of. In this situation, they need to peg their inquiry closely to the still indeterminate description of the problem that the importer has provided them.

The question "But just what do you mean?" may require exporters to fly to the home site of an importer to taste together in the importer's lab. An exporter from Santos may travel to Italy to cup alongside the importer's tasters. Oddly, even these visits and shared cupping may not resolve the root of the matter. At least biannually most importers will send tasters to visit the exporting country in order to become better calibrated with the people there who are selling them their coffee. During the visitations exporters make to the importers' countries, the exporters' tasters will note carefully the size of the cups the importers use when tasting the coffee, the roasting profiles they use, and anything else about the cupping protocol of their labs. This will inform them about how they need to cup that client's coffee back in their own tasting lab.

This conundrum of communicating successfully about tastes is something that is fascinating for a sociologist to study, because when one or the other party has traveled halfway across the globe in order to resolve a problematic communication and they fail to do so, it reveals and makes observable the prevalence that anarchy that has in our everyday lives. A fuller account of this anarchy is presented in chapter 12 ("Some Discovered Practices of Lay Coffee Drinkers"), but here we can mention that the inability to resolve the differences of the sensory assessments of the exporter and importer can be the result of what I call "the serendipity principle": every situation of social interaction proceeds according to exceedingly local needs of interacting, needs that are difficult to anticipate. These locally contingent demands include the consequences of treating other persons respectfully, exercising caution about any criticisms one might have (especially when one is interacting with long-standing business partners with whom one intends to maintain a business friendship), and unanticipated local contingencies and distractions that arise and obstruct clear communicating. One can never be certain what these local contingencies will demand, since most of them are serendipitous. In local interaction, people naturally drift toward common outlooks and gratuitous accords, i.e., agreements that lack clearly defined content, and my research has discovered that people will even agree to things they do not yet understand (Liberman 2018). Emmanuel Levinas (1979, 1981) has described the important effects of coming face-to-face with another person, an occasion that provokes in our thinking an immediate sense of responsibility for the other person. Levinas tells us that the gaze of another is the origin of ethical behavior, and we spontaneously take care to preserve the integrity and self-respect of others; however, this can cause us to fail to expose our own objective assessments and opinions, avoiding sharing insights that might directly contradict another's perspective, and so it can happen that common civility and courtesy will hinder face-to-face communication. In one case, I had the opportunity to visit both the tasting lab of an exporter and the lab of the importer, both of whom had highly competent tasters who were conscientious people, and the reason for the difference in their sensory assessments was never resolved in a clear manner that would have made it unlikely the problem would reoccur. Their meeting took place surrounded by a good deal of sociable activity (dining together, renewing old conversations, etc.), and by the time the meeting took place, other impending business interests had been added to the agenda. During the local situation, rather than forcing one side's reading of the taste "problems," the parties agreed to a minor adjustment in the price and never specified what the flaw could have been. *Absorbed in the local contingencies of their face-to-face interaction*, they decided simply to "move on." The same result could have been achieved without the international air travel. Frequently, we underrate the importance that serendipitous local contingencies of social interaction have for substantive matters of any occasion.

Storage and Shipment

Sometimes defects can be the result of a fermentation that occurred while the beans were on the boat. We have described how such a fermentation was fortuitous in the case of monsooned Malabar coffees traveling from Mangalore to Sweden; however, it is more usual for such fermentations to damage the taste. Occasionally exporters project the possible effects that port-sitting and transport might have on the beans. Spoilage during storage or shipment is another of the "30 ways" to ruin coffee. This was not the reason for the rejection described in our previous example, since such a transformation would have been detectable as soon as the sent sample of the arriving allotment of green coffee was tasted by the experts in the exporter's lab.

When shipping green coffee, some 37,500 pounds of coffee will be loaded into a 20-foot-long container, which will be referred to as one "lot" of green coffee. Micro-lots are smaller and can consist of 5 to 15 bags. Exporting such small amounts of coffee can be difficult and impede specialty exporters who wish to deal in direct trade relations with small roasters and wholesalers. Sometimes the burden of paperwork, transport, customs, etc. is not that much less for micro-lots than it is for a full lot, and this work can inhibit sales and raise costs.

Coffee is sensitive and can absorb any odor nearby. Storage affords opportunities for molds to grow, fermentation to occur, and toxins to be collected from the surroundings; insufficient drying before shipping can be disastrous. Contamination during storage or shipping can overcome a coffee's flavor. As Susie Spindler said at a cupping session, "Coffees do not always arrive at the port with the same flavor they had when they were first cupped in the producing country."

Chemical changes are among the post-production issues that occur naturally in all coffees. After they are sent, flavors can improve or fade, and taints also change. This makes proper storage an important concern. Some coffees can be stored for a long time. Beans from Indonesia and Papua New Guinea can barely survive a year in storage, but some from Brazil still taste decent after three years, although their taste does evolve. I have had good results home-roasting seven-year-old Brazilian beans of specialty quality (butterscotch at a light roast level), but a ten-year-old Hawaiian Kona that was originally of poor quality (circa a cupping score of 70) tasted of cardboard at a medium roast level. Much like finding the optimum roast for a bean, some roasters will seek the optimum aging for a lot of green beans they intend to roast. There may be some experimentation to discover a given green bean's sweet spot, especially if one has purchased a good deal of it. Here again, the dynamic character of coffee cannot be understated.

Chapter 8

A Palette for the Palate

Using Taste Descriptors to Find Flavor

> What are things, that they need words in order to be?
>
> —Heidegger (1971b, 141)

In chapter 6 we discussed the types of tasting common in the world of coffee: hedonist (or affective), discriminative, and descriptive. In this chapter, we take a closer look at descriptive analysis. Deliberately, and with deliberation, the coffee industry has devoted decades to developing a precise and communicable terminology for describing the flavors that can be found in coffees, and nearly every year there is another comprehensive effort to get things right. The problem is not that the many tasting schedules and flavor wheels are flawed: all of them make something available to tasters, and all of them fall short to some degree. They fall short because the taste of coffee will always exceed categories. That is what makes tasting coffee interesting. As we learned in chapter 5, coffees are dynamic and not static, as are the tastes and interests of the people who drink coffee; consequently, there is continual change in the tastes and in the understanding of the tastes. Therefore, it is inevitable that tasting forms will require revision, without end. Every language is evolving, and dictionaries are powerless to stop them; in fact, dictionaries are always one step behind and struggle to keep up if they are to retain their utility. What is alive will always exceed definitions.

Each tasting form makes some aspects of the coffee salient for the taster. Purveyors and roasters redesign forms for their own purposes, or they develop a local practice of using someone else's form to fit the needs of their firm. We are concerned to identify and describe just how taste descriptors help tasters organize their experience of tasting coffee. Beyond serving as a guide for exploring the flavors of coffee, tasting forms are only as good as the competencies of the people who use them, and one of those competencies is learning how to use the form without allowing it to limit one's sensory purview. Coffee professionals are an independent-minded lot (maybe it is the caffeine), and so they are very good at using the forms without being boxed in by them.

Describing an experience makes one more attentive to what is happening and therefore enhances the experience and one's understanding of it. At the same time, the task of describing can seize the show; that is, one's attention is channeled toward those aspects the form has selected for description. In tasting coffee, this involves a broad and convivial collection that includes mouthfeel, aroma, bitterness, astringency, sweetness, roundness, balance, body, aftertaste, and "flavor" (a fruit, a spice, etc.). But with every concentration of attention upon some aspects, other aspects risk being neglected, and spontaneity is among the first things to be sacrificed. A single schedule may be applied to coffees that are very different in their characteristics, and tasters sometimes struggle to allow original coffees to be revealed adequately on the tasting form; this struggle is another of the competencies required of professional tasters. A form should assist a taster to become aware of all the principal assets and liabilities of any coffee. While a form is useful for reminding one to examine a broad range of aspects, including ones that one might have otherwise overlooked, one cannot permit the form to lead one around by the nose. One must retain originality while also taming the form. Descriptions aid cognition at the expense of refocusing it; the two go hand-in-hand, and we are condemned to be imprisoned by what we know. Perhaps this is the true original sin of *Homo sapiens sapiens*.

How a Word Means

How are coffees best described, and what about a coffee is most important to communicate? Placing the meaning totally inside the linguistic sign is a flawed epistemology, as if meaning were some static thing. Dictionaries are helpful guides, but anyone who learns a language can tell you what my ninth-grade English teacher once taught me: "You determine the meaning of a word by looking it up in a dictionary and by the context." Our lives are *never* context-free. While this complicates our affairs without relief, one would not wish to live any life that was empty of these complications. In any event we have no choice in the matter, unless we want to participate in a fictional parade, which in fact is what we often choose to do.

"Context" is a term too vague to make up its mind, so it must be given specification. Here "context" is being contrasted with dictionary definition. Dictionary definitions are popular everywhere because they are clear, distinct, and present little ambiguity, whereas "context" raises a problem of indeterminacy; however, our lifeworld is filled with indeterminacies. Taste descriptors are always situated. As Silvia Gherardi (2009, 536) has described it, "Taste may therefore be conceived in terms of taste-making, i.e., a situated activity." Being situated, taste descriptors are always accompanied by local contingencies, and that is why dictionary meanings are not definitive, despite their appearance, for what counts is how one "makes use of the word" (Wittgenstein 1972, 17). Always, "one refers to a *point of time* and to *a way of using the word*" (Wittgenstein 1972, 175). Even more, any situation is capable of turning words on their heads (Liberman 1999, 2012). A local "context" is capable of taking a gloss that people are using and running away with it, leaving the parties to chase after it in an effort to learn what they have done. Garfinkel (1967, 33) sagely suggests, "The policy is recommended that any social setting be viewed as self-organizing with respect to the intelligible character of its own appearances." Accordingly, there is not one flavor lexicon, there are hundreds of them.

Ethnomethodology has adapted the notion of the philosopher Bar-Hillel, who was the first to offer a detailed description of the use of indexical expressions. As Garfinkel (2002, 203) summarizes, "An expression is going to have the definiteness of its sense and its reference according to where it occurred, or *just* where it occurred, or just when, in an ongoing *in vivo* in-courseness of a project." The *in vivo* is everything. "*In vivo*" means that "a phenomenal field of ordered details" (Garfinkel 1996, 4) is ongoingly and developingly revealed (passive) and built up (active) as part of practical on-site work. If one is going to deny the *in vivo*, then one will deny the world the way the world really is. And if one is going to deny that, then one will be condemned to engage in a fit of highly organized foolishness. But there is a lot of that.

Sensory scientists may explain that they are not referring to any "social" setting. Just where will they find a site for their work that is not social? They may claim they are speaking only about "the facts" as they are scientifically and not socially determined. This is mythological thinking. The *clarity* of "the facts" is something supplied by local parties who collaborate in the production of what Schutz (1970a, 23) calls "unifying formations." It is ethnomethodology's own science to identify and describe the "members' methods for making evident that setting's ways as clear, coherent, planful, consistent, chosen, knowable, uniform, reproducible connections—i.e., rational connections" (Garfinkel 1967, 34). The clarity of facts is a social production.

It should be obvious what the taste descriptor "cherry" means; however, in a cup of coffee the sense of this descriptor requires some local work, both by the drinker and by the tasters, who concert their efforts to provide the descriptor specificity. A descriptor like "snappy," which has sold plenty of coffee, requires more work. It can guide a drinker, but there remains some "taste-making" for the drinker to do. In the case of "dried mango and papaya, with a tamarind finish," the pride of a small specialty roaster in Oregon, the drinker will have much "taste-making" to perform. Accordingly, we need to recognize that descriptors are nothing more than *an index for the work that tasters do with them*, and that the descriptors are situated and collect their sense and reference from how and where they are used. If they have clarity, it is because the tasters who use them have made them clear, for themselves and for each other. This is necessary because real tastes are complex and fleeting, and it is impossible for a taste descriptor to capture inside it every nuance that can be referenced by it, even descriptors strong enough to strangle any tasting experience. As Henri Bergson (1910, 131) describes so well, "The word with well-defined outlines, the rough and ready word, which stores up the stable, common, and consequently impersonal element in the impressions of mankind, overwhelms or at least covers over the delicate and fugitive impressions of our individual consciousness."

Morana Alaç (2017, 160) observes about descriptions of perfumes, "Words are impotent when taken on their own"; to have pertinence, they need to be related to the fragrances they are describing. A literature scholar will tell you that dictionaries, while helpful as guides, rarely provide a final solution to the meaning of a word. There are complicating factors everywhere, and it is a mistake to think that taste descriptors carry their meanings on their backs, a notion that only reproduces "the prejudice of the world," which is that things exist in themselves just the way we think them, an assumption that does not deserve the name of science. Descriptors are porous, as is language. That is a good thing. Descriptors are unities "having a particular meaning-structure, which to be sure, is always changing and subject to modification" (Schutz 1970a, 28). "Always" subject to modification, Schutz tells us. Contrary to being clear and distinct from the outset, taste descriptors very much *require* porosity if they are to be sufficiently adaptable to be useful. It is the descriptors that must adapt to the coffee, and not the obligation of tastes to adapt to the descriptors. If the descriptors are reliable, that is because professional tasters have concerted their labors to make them reliable, which involves social work.

By using concrete examples, the *Sensory Lexicon*, composed by World Coffee Research (WCR 2016) for defining the tastes precisely in positive and inflexible terms, makes great effort to avoid indeterminacy or drift in the sense and applicability of their descriptors, but it also imprisons those terms within their illustrations. The strategy of the many competent sensory scientists who wrote the *Lexicon* is a return to what Daston and Galison have called the turn-of-the-last-century scientific model of "mechanical objectivity." Daston and Galison (2010, 115–190) describe in detail how the composers of scientific atlases turned to mechanical procedures so as to ward off the distortions produced by "true to nature" idealizations, used by some scientists, but at no point did this mechanistic model permeate all of science, although it was (and remains) among the options that scientific practitioners can choose. Daston and Galison (2010, 43) write, "Mechanical objectivity was needed to protect images against subjective projections, but it threatened to undermine the primary aim of all scientific atlases, to provide the working objects of a discipline." That is, the practice failed to provide tools that were responsive enough to the phenomena under study to be capable of offering maximum utility. Daston and Galison (2010, 346) suggest that the reason the mechanical objectivity model never became adopted universally by science was that it offered insufficient scope for judgment and reason, and because accuracy is as important as objectivity (Daston and Galison 2010, 321).

Why do some coffee professionals and scientists who study coffee adopt the mechanical objectivity model? Here I have nothing more to propose than an untested theory.[1] It is possible that taste and smell are such subjective senses that sensory analysts feel vulnerable to the criticism that they are not being objective enough, and so they have chosen to take refuge in a model of objectivity that is antiquated. Here a desire to guarantee certainty about what one knows is obstructing the route to knowing. The "blind sight" (Daston and Galison 2010, 342) of mechanical objectivity can place a straitjacket around tastes that are better left to their own resources for expressing themselves, without the benefit of predefined, pre-judged terminology. The task of the taster is to become attuned to those expressions of taste, not to control them.

---

1. If I was not in my eighth decade of life and had more years to devote to this study, I would work alongside these sensory scientists to better understand why they work in this way.

The clear definitions offered by flavor wheels, lexicons, and tasting schedules lend themselves to ready communication, and the certainty of understanding they provide gives them considerable utility and popularity; however, in most cases the world will eventually fail to conform to that precision, and so these tools can produce distortions. As Ronald Bruzina (1970, 170) concludes in his study, *Logos and Eidos*, "To concede meaningfulness to a signification—to a word or 'idea'—is to concede the effective presence 'underneath' that signification." Throughout these investigations, we operate in pursuit of that effective presence.

As Dr. Manuel Diaz has discerned, "Most of the sensory attributes are metaphors." For instance, Fara Coffee of Nicaragua purveys a coffee that they describe as having a "light roast with body and bright flavors." Here "bright" functions as a paramount descriptor for the coffee. Despite the fact that it acts as a metaphor, it functions well to indicate what its taste might be like, and the descriptor will direct the drinker to search for those flavors that will provide more specific determination of what it means. That is, as a descriptor it is effective: *it leads to discoveries*. Even taste descriptors that seem very specific function as metaphors. For example, one of my preferred coffees has a "cinnamon" taste. Well, of course it is not cinnamon; rather, it does something to the roof of my mouth that is like one of the many things cinnamon does. If simply one aspect of a taste descriptor is accurate, we can ignore other features of that taste that may be missing. Used as a metaphor in this way, the taste descriptor is efficacious for directing a drinker to a taste experience, and then the drinker's own experience can fill in the sense of the descriptor; it is accurate—it assists communication and aids the drinker's understanding. However, its accuracy is metaphoric rather than literal, and the drinker will collaborate with the coffee in making specific the sense and reference of the taste descriptor.

Flavor descriptors that tasters commonly use are not always inherently meaningful; rather, they require additional work by tasters, working together on local occasions, for the purpose of developing sufficient specificity for the descriptors to enable them to be employed with precision. Oddly, some sensory scientists denigrate professional tasters who use descriptors this way. But all taste descriptors operate as metaphors, even when they are well defined, and this includes the taste descriptors of sensory scientists. More study of linguistics would assist them in their work. A taster announces, "This has clear notes of vanilla," and puzzlement on the faces of the other tasters is visibly apparent. Here the "clear" probably means not so clear. To some lay drinkers it may seem strange that an unflavored coffee tastes like vanilla, and so they will try another sip, with the idea of "vanilla"—whatever this will turn out to be—riding on their tongues. Is there really one "vanilla" that applies equally and in the same way to all coffees, or does the "context" of a coffee and a tasting transform in some way the scope and sensibility of what is *this* "vanilla"? Never mind that there is a McCormick Pure Vanilla Extract (WCR 2016, 46) referenced. Is it more scientific to give priority to the McCormick Spices version over the one that the coffee before presents? The local historicity of descriptors—the reasonableness and efficaciousness of the descriptors as they are used to explore the coffee—is part of the context that will define the "vanilla." Descriptors are local and indexical. Here "indexical" means they are indexed to a real time and a real place. Moreover, the tasting schedule is a constituent detail of the work of tasting the very same tastes that the schedule itself is describing. What is serviceable at one moment may not be helpful at another, which is partly why professional tasters are occasionally left groping for words. Flavors escape from descriptors, it's the strangest thing, despite persistent effort to tame the meanings of the descriptors. The semantic scope of a taste descriptor is protean, broadening and then being reined in as a taster moves through a flight of coffees on the cupping table. When I was describing this phenomenon during a lecture about tasting coffee, Christian Heath once remarked, "That is just the way I grade papers."

For instance, what is "cherry"? Could any coffee ever taste just like cherry, objectively speaking? The answer depends on what one means by "objective." One can use quantitative measures, and also achieve some adequacy of intersubjective understanding by means of a robust calibration of usages, and it is possible to apply a standardized protocol intelligibly; in this way, it can satisfy the principal requirements of tasting "cherry-like." But this is a cherry-by-convention. Or perhaps a cherry-by-convention and an objective cherry are the identical phenomenon. The coffee may influence the same region of the mouth that a cherry would or may recall a recent experience of having cherries (cherry pie? cherry Coke? cherry liqueur?). It is for certain that one can use the term "cherry" to communicate successfully a region of flavor that could guide a potential drinker to an enhanced experience of the coffee that results by using the descriptor to explore the coffee's identifying flavor.

Using Taste Descriptors

We propose neither a nominalist nor an essentialist position: taste descriptors do not mean just anything, but they also cannot be closed up in a lockbox.

We seek to describe the competent use of descriptors and especially how they are used to elucidate and amplify the taste profile. What are the practices that make descriptors familiar and even customary, and that *make them sharable*, more reliable, and therefore more objective?

Real objectivity is the taste in the cup before it becomes an analyst's artifact. Accordingly, the practical work of using taste descriptors should not consist only of searching for ways to conform with standardized definitions—such a pursuit would carry one *away* from the taste that one is already smelling inside the cup. Rather, productive use of descriptors involves manipulating them to lead tasters to make direct contact with the real objectivity in the cup. It is this direct encounter, in its immediacy, that is the pay-off of an effective practice of tasting. The situation is not simply that a representative descriptor is deduced from the taste, it is nothing so straightforward as that; rather, it is finding a way for the representation to lead one to further experiencing and understanding, experience that then contributes to refining the representation. As the diagram from chapter 4 exhibited, the actual relation is like this:

$$\text{taste descriptor} \longleftrightarrow \text{coffee}$$

Skeptics who claim that taste descriptors are mostly nonsense are doing their thinking on the basis of an abstract understanding and are not themselves *using* descriptors in active exploration of flavor. They are nihilists who negate too much. Further, they are not sufficiently respectful of the social demands of practical objectivity.

This brings us to the most important part of our study: how do tasters use descriptors to locate real tastes and how do descriptors assist tasters in their work? Just how do descriptors help expand the sapience of the taster? Descriptors do not stand apart from this work with an isolated meaning that has already been made explicit, congealed, and "scientific." To be useful, they require some open-endedness. Descriptors exist alongside the tastes they collect. Descriptors are always situated; they inscribe themselves in the taste. The point of sensory assessment is not only to evaluate the coffee but to *explore* the coffee. Descriptors are useful for serving as containers that help keep that exploration organized. Alaç (2017, 148) writes that the work of perfume tasters is "to anchor smells into words." This work will always have a local history, one that has a location and a staff that supports it. Figal (2010, 144) concurs when he writes about "an understanding that still remains as yet unrevealed but that is nevertheless harbored in linguistic usage." Taste descriptors are harbors. Figal (2010, 221) specifies how these words work: "The word itself first announces the respective act of intending something and the possible enactment of this intending in an intuition; it 'pretends,' that is, it provides the pretense of determinate possibilities of intentions and their possible enactments." We cannot do this work without the words, but neither do the descriptors perform the work by themselves, without our participation.

At the level of the individual taster, what one is projecting upon what one is tasting can become self-fulfilling prophesy. For example, it is all too easy to convince myself that "pineapple" is the right descriptor for the Ethiopian Gesha that I roasted this week, especially since that is the descriptor supplied by the exporter, who probably derived it from the exporter's tasters. With this "pineapple," I can hold on to a direction of inquiry, even though I recognize that it is not yet adequate. At this point in my tasting, I need that descriptor "pineapple" to help me initiate my own inquiries, and it does not need to be defined perfectly. "Speech is a process in time whose purpose is to make something present to mind. In language, it is possible to retain something in presence that passes away in time and would be lost without language" (Figal 2010, 145). Speaking of pineapple, Shapin (2011, 27) notes, "At the very end of the seventeenth century, John Locke too tried to come to terms with the taste of pineapple, and he reckoned that then-current vocabularies for describing such a thing rendered description impossible." But I know what pineapple is well enough to use it to explore what this cup of Ethiopian Gesha is offering me. It might even bear enough accuracy to use for advertising the coffee. The fecundity of a taste descriptor does not require being defined in absolutist terms. While keeping open a descriptor's indeterminacy may risk distorting a descriptor, that is preferable to altogether forgetting the direction my inquiry was taking or forcing a premature conclusion.

Occasionally, descriptors are employed as if they were empty boxes or vacant containers. Told that the coffee she was drinking was "round," Marina, a lay drinker, carried the descriptor "round" into her drinking in order to learn what it could mean, and other drinkers nearby listened closely to her discussion about it in order to pick up what might be an appropriate usage of the term "round." In this manner, the ways that a descriptor is used and the understanding derived from those usages are part of an ongoing social collaboration.

A vague descriptor can be used as a placeholder for a taste that one has clearly isolated but cannot determine a name for. For example, I once roasted at home some green beans that a farmer in Huila, Colombia, had given me. I could taste its character at once, which subsisted through each subsequent sip, but I was unable to recollect just what that familiar flavor was. Even when a taste is distinct and recognizable one may not be able to think of the right descriptor for it. I wrote "butterscotch" in my notes, but I knew that was not quite right. It was some other kind of nutmeg cream, very sweet, and it kept eluding me. I added "sweet" in my notes, but "sweet" can mean so many things, and it did not contribute to my making progress. Progress at what? As a drinker of coffee, my primary purpose is not to define the coffee but to enjoy it. By interrogating the coffee from Huila, I was entering its ecology, its notes and nuances were beginning to take shape, and in my noticing these as part of my effort to describe the coffee, their qualities were enhanced, made more evident, richer, and hence more pleasurable. So "sweet" was good enough for the moment, while I was also oriented to a very round sort of sweetness. I left the "butterscotch" as a placeholder for that, with hopes that when I roast more of it later, I may be able to hone the flavor to a better descriptor. This kind of tasting is a hybrid between a descriptive and an affective sensory analysis, and it is not unreasonable to use a descriptive sensory analysis to increase one's enjoyment. Surely, this can be permitted; or will it detract from the objectivity of one's tasting? If we are forced to choose between enjoyment and objectivity, which one shall we choose? Fortunately, they are not mutually exclusive; and it may be our present historical task to finally learn how to employ the latter in the service of the former, rather than demoting enjoyment. Vannini et al. (2012, 55) are correct when they suggest that the point is "to become able to *make* a quality come to life through a lexicon of sensations."

The work of another placeholder was evident when a professional Italian taster declared, "I'm not telling you that it is 'lemon,' but that is the sort of sensation there." Using a descriptor under negation in this way allows one to sustain a presentation while remaining open and attentive to what it could become. At the same time, it allows one to be less of a target for the criticism of colleagues who are also tasting. Use of descriptors under negation is ubiquitous in coffee tasting. This way of speaking is employed freely by professional tasters as well as by lay tasters, and on my video and audio recordings, they occur as frequently as do positive assertions of taste descriptors. "It is not excessively bitter" is more common than "not bitter" or "sweet." Most professional coffee tasters are neither scientists nor philosophers, and they have a minimal interest in truth by itself. They are devoted to coffee, which can provoke considerable honesty on their part, but they are equally devoted to profits, and their requirements are more practical than truth concerns. They have practical interests in learning how to use the tasting form and protocol for discovering flavors that they can market successfully.

Descriptors work as guideposts. In his "Translators' Introduction" Theodore George (Figal 2010, xx) recognizes "a word's potential to determine and, so, lift something out of the texture to which it belongs." One taster says "almond," and the orientation of all the other tasters shifts to that region of flavor. After a sip, another taster says "fig," and both descriptors are included in the final description, which will be sent to potential buyers, for the reason that professional tasters know that these descriptors are not exact but work as guiding metaphors. By enhancing the semantic possibilities of the developing assessment, the two taste descriptors together increase the precision of what can never be precise.

There is also the case of "juicy orange juice." I never drink orange juice and coffee together, but this one Bhabudan coffee in India did taste like orange juice. Sunalini Menon commented, "Not all Bhababudan coffees are like a juicy orange juice, just this one is. This particular Bhababudan perhaps is more reflective of the plant strain grown at that higher level and not a reflection of the region per se. It's just that that particular strain that grows at an altitude of 4,200 feet and upwards has developed a bright tanginess and highlighted all the intrinsic fruit notes of those beans." Of course, its taste is not the taste of orange juice, but the descriptor points us to where the most pleasurable part of this coffee's flavor profile resides.

It is important to note that descriptors do not operate in identical ways. Their purpose is to enable discovery of the nature of a coffee, which is further evidence that they are not intended to function as definitions that are clear and distinct. Some descriptors may be more literal (e.g., "sweet") than others, and others more metaphoric ("woody"). Some are intended to provoke a reaction ("lively") in the taster that will propel the taster to renew his or her efforts at sensory assessment. While it is unnecessary to throw out a dozen or more descriptors, it will serve to suggest one or two main characteristics that can stimulate further exploration.

The Reflexivity of Taste Descriptors

Descriptors are used not only for the purpose of *describing* the taste, but also for *finding* the taste. There is a reflexive relationship between a descriptor and the flavor it describes. A descriptor directs the taster regarding what to look for, and what the taster finds under its auspices can serve to specify what the descriptor actually means, in each case. Even when coffee drinkers do not know what a descriptor means, they will use the taste to help define the descriptor. In this way, "each was used to elaborate the other" (Garfinkel 1967, 40). Taste descriptors not only describe the tastes they find, they find the tastes they describe. The Italian taster Odello's preference was that descriptors "define" the taste straightforwardly, but they can accomplish that only when a fence is erected that surrounds the tastes that a descriptor is permitted to handle, and any flavor notes that reside outside of those boundaries will be excluded. Taste descriptors can provide a useful initial orientation to a brew; they have the capacity to lead a taster to distinguish flavors that reside somewhere in the specific terrain of that tasting, discoveries that then can provide for a descriptor a fuller intelligibility.

Those who taste along with colleagues, sharing a descriptor and perhaps engaging in some coordination about it, can create a tool they are able to use reliably; however, this reliability, in that it has reference to a local specificity, is valid for that local cohort only—for instance, a head roaster, those who are assisting, and those clients they can educate—and is not universal. The coffee industry would prefer universal validities, so a good deal of standardization of descriptors occurs; but this carries descriptions away from the site where flavors reside and into abstractions, and by the time a packet that bears those descriptors arrives on a store shelf, the descriptors are practically meaningless. Sensory professionals can blame consumers for their ignorance or try to educate them, but they cannot avoid the fate of all languages: innovation, semantic drift, lability, and evolution. It will remain the task of every cohort that uses descriptors to recreate their precise sense and reference for the local coffees *on site*, and they will do this, reflexively and intersubjectively, each time as if it was the first time through. To the extent that they apply a descriptor by rote, to that same extent they risk missing news about flavor.

In order for "bright" in general to become an actual bright, what Husserl (2001, 106–109) calls "meaning fulfillment" is required. The local work of fulfilling the meaning of an indexical expression like "bright" works like this: [bright] ⟷ a bright coffee. What lives inside the brackets is a notional descriptor that will require meaning fulfillment by a customer, who will need to experience the self-giving of the flavor; the indexical expression in the brackets is useful, but it should not be given priority over the taste itself. The fetch of a descriptor can capture a good deal, and it reflexively collects the taste that the descriptor will come to represent in the discourse and deliberations among the tasters. After the descriptor is used during some tasting, the descriptor returns with an education.

By way of illustration, I relate a story. After three months of drinking nothing but home-roasted Gesha coffees from Panama and Ethiopia, at last I grew tired of even their splendid flavors, which recall fruits or flowers, or (in a lighter roast) limeade, and I sought out some other kind of coffee, something softer and more chocolate-like. I roasted the pound of green Nicaraguan coffee that a mostly female-run coffee cooperative (SOPEXCCA) had given me to sample. I gave it a medium roast, loaded a hefty dosage of fresh grounds into a chemex filter, and was delighted by its flavor, which was very different from the previous months' cups; however, I was unable to describe it. I kept tasting it, several cups over several days: it was clean, and while heavy, it possessed no bitterness. But it had an identifying flavor, only I could not identify what that was. It was not quite sweet or fruity, nor was it exactly "nutty" either, but that was closer. Sip after sip, I struggled with my cupping spoon. In spite of my frustration, I loved every sip. Enjoying coffee that one is unable to describe is a laudable skill to possess, and a useful one, since drinking coffees that one cannot describe adequately happens often enough.

What was its flavor? I consulted the SCA/WCR Flavor Wheel for guidance. The more finely detailed descriptors of the outer ring of the Flavor Wheel can be overwhelming, so I commenced by using the intermediate ring of flavor domains: cereal, brown spice, nutty, etc. I knew which domains of flavor to reject, but I was uncertain of which ones to explore—nutty, cereal, or brown spice. After a while, using the flavor descriptors on the Flavor Wheel came to resemble a game of pin-the-tail-on-the-donkey (blindfolded): that the flavors were there on the wheel in living color made it easier to choose one than to know its meaning. In some fashion, I settled upon "molasses" and "nutmeg." I wondered what flavor there could be that could be *either* molasses or nutmeg? One may be able to select a descriptor or two, but they are only rough indications of the direction in which a coffee drinker should keep looking, and it requires some poetic license to get most descriptors to index a real taste one has in one's mouth.

The Flavor Wheel offers a "taste" that is intended to convey a taste. As an indexical expression, a descriptor does not lead a drinker to a taste in the way that a positivist thinks of a taste, because how the indexical expressions get employed (their metaphorical suggestiveness, the reflexive waywardness with which they are comprehended, the way they assist one to make contact with the transcendent object, etc.) exceed the straitjacket of the positivist's dream. And yet, the Flavor Wheel served as a genuine aid to my inquiry: molasses was close to what I was experiencing in my mouth; and while nutmeg was less near, it seemed important for me to sustain the suggestion that there was still an undefinable spice that would not go away, so even nutmeg was of assistance. That descriptor will alert a drinker to be conscious of something spicy that is going on, despite being unable to pin it down. There and then, with the Flavor Wheel in hand, I was on the way to better understand the coffee I was roasting.

Beneficio El Borbollen (Santa Ana, El Salvador) offers a coffee that features "buttery mouthfeel and sweetness reminiscent of apple pie and ice cream." This description clearly communicates the mouthfeel, and their attempt to specify the catch-all phrase "sweetness" for a drink that tastes mostly bitter is commendable, but "apple pie" and "ice cream" are a bridge too far. Here I prefer the Flavor Wheel. What could "apple pie" or "ice cream" really be in a coffee, and will I be able to find it; or is it simply an effort to sell coffee?

Taste descriptors are used to locate the taste in a cup even as the descriptors keep getting in the way of the tasting. We are condemned to language. How does one cup with flexibility and keep the mind clear for the next cup? How can rigor and flexibility coexist? How can rigor and openness coexist? The tasting card offers a classic account of coffee tastes, but these schedules have peculiar reflexive properties in that their utility rests as much in their capacity for expanding the tasters' attention to tastes as in their use for objective measurements. When tasters *retain contact* with the taste while using a schedule, the sapience of their tasting increases. But this means that the usefulness of a tasting schedule does not rest in its mathematics but in its hermeneutics. A taste is not definitive in itself, nor is "there is a passive receiving of object data. Rather, an object comes to definiteness and unity by virtue of our approach" (Bruzina 1970, 64).

Types of Descriptors

Every flavor descriptor does not possess the same salience, nor is it necessary that it operate in the same language game. A "check-all-that-apply" list used in sensory research of consumer taste preferences at UC Davis mixed and matched a decent selection of descriptors: tea/floral, green/vegetative, cereal, caramel, roasted, sweet, fruit, paper/woody, nutty, bitter, sour, rubber, citrus, burnt, dark chocolate, astringent, and thick/viscous. These descriptors are derived from all three of the flavor rings (general category/taste domain/

specific flavor) of the SCA/WCR Flavor Wheel. The idea was probably not to overwhelm the lay tasters, but dark chocolate, sour, and rubber are very different orders of description. Descriptors like "graham cracker and oats" and "fully ripe passion fruit" are highly specific, while "well-rounded" and "rich" are very general.

The first task of a taster is to identify the taste. This is not something that is always achieved before choosing a descriptor, although a mythology of positivist inquiry maintains this idea. More commonly, a taste is identified *with*, and by means of, the descriptors one is applying. A flavor difficult to describe is interesting because neither direct intuition nor the application of a protocol may produce a satisfactory result, and an accurate description can elude a taster. One is then positioned at the frontier of knowing, the very place every phenomenologist wants to be.

How is it that a taste becomes salient? Skilled tasters are able to discriminate among tastes that come from different language games. While it is possible to derive a taste from the chemical components of a bean, there are too many chemicals, lipids (coffee can contain 80 different lipids), acids, minerals, carbohydrates, etc., and far too many synergetic effects to allow for the development of a predictive science, even though that remains the dream of the coffee industry and one of the motives for the industry turning to science. Much interesting flavor is created by the methods of processing, and considerable experimentation with this has been taking place in recent years, which may yet prove fruitful, although fermentations are even less easy to control. Storage can destroy flavors; roasting can remedy taints and draw out sugars; and the brewing system (filters, infusions, water temperature, etc.) influences the result. Most tasters try to sort out which tastes come from the green bean (e.g., floral, grassy, herby, peanut, sour, and sweet) and which result from processing, storage, roasting, or method of preparation.

The ways that people have described coffee have evolved during the centuries that coffee has been a world commodity, but according to Shapin (2011, 41), "The full efflorescence of the vocabulary of alimentary connoisseurship is a twentieth-century phenomenon." In the seventeenth century, a competent attempt to describe the tastes of wine employed only four descriptors (Shapin 2011, 15). The contemporary firm that manufactures Play-Doh describes its smell as "a sweet, slightly musky, vanilla fragrance, with slight overtones of cherry, combined with the smell of a salted, wheat-based dough" (Associated Press 2018). They nailed it. I am not sure who Play-Doh's audience is—some savvy preschoolers, no doubt—but their descriptors evolved within a process of signification that included a speaker or writer, a sign, and an auditor or reader. It is a process of communication, and at both ends (the person devising the descriptor and the one trying to understand it) people apply their imagination to signs that serve as the focus for intersubjective collaboration. A coffee purveyor has an audience in mind or their effort at description will fail. Paul Songer once suggested that descriptors need to be effective enough to identify and convey "what are the real differences between, let's say, a Guatemalan and a Costa Rican coffee." This is a practical objectivity. Two key factors are (1) that the descriptors must address something substantial that can be used to *identify* the coffee and (2) that they must be *communicated* successfully. This situation implies that at the basis of taste description exists a socio-semiotic state of affairs and that successful description is rooted in conversation.

The top five coffees of the final round of a Cup of Excellence competition received these descriptors: flowers, butterscotch, vanilla, smooth, and "decent, sound acidity." This, along with the numerical scoring, is probably sufficient information to allow a purchaser to make a decision; however, acidity can be a challenging descriptor. Lingle (2001, 46) tells us that "acidy" is "a taste that has sharpness, snap, and life, as compared to a sweet, heavy, mellow flavor." That is, there is a basic flavor contrast between a "lively" coffee and a "smooth" coffee. Most descriptions of a decent coffee will try to provide a clue about the category in which a coffee belongs. A Mysore "Extra-Bold" that is "well balanced, sweet, good body" probably works in the "smooth" category, despite its boldness, but this kind of description is too vague to settle matters—no one will advertise a weak body, and there are many ways for a coffee to be "bold." Occasionally one will be provided a specific and unambiguous flavor, such as "peach." During our research into lay coffee drinkers, Prof. Fele and I discovered that very few drinkers could identify a "peach" flavor when they were given some advertised peach-flavored coffees to sample. As with the case of "chocolate," sometimes a descriptor works with a specific kind of accuracy and sometimes it works more metaphorically, and unless one was in the tasting room with the tasting staff at the time they settled on the descriptor "peach," one may never be able to experience it for oneself. One Modo Mio (Lavazza capsules) Arabica coffee that we used was advertised as "sweet," but our lay tasters rated the coffee's sweetness as only 5 (out of 10). On the other hand, a 50% Robusta Modo Mio coffee that carried no reference to sweetness was rated by these same tasters as having a sweetness of 9. What the designers (or the firm's advertisers) meant by "sweet" had little relation with what lay tasters were conceiving as sweet.

Some of the best descriptions are discursive: "A great roasted nut undertone accompanied by a slight semi-sweet chocolate." This tells exactly what the coffee is. Some specific descriptors have national significances that possess idiosyncratic references that are broader than the terms taken explicitly. "*Caramelo*" (butterscotch) is a common descriptor in Colombia and is applied to many coffees. A coffee descriptors chart used by the Huila branch of Alma Café, a processing and coffee quality assurance firm in Colombia, includes more descriptors (nine) for "caramelized" tastes than for any other category, including "fruity." Another frequent descriptor throughout Central America is "red fruits" (*frutas rojas*), which has moved beyond being an empirical noticing to an objective pigeon-hole available for tasters to store a variety of flavors they are used to tasting. In Nicaragua, the use of "passion fruit" (*maracuya*) is widespread. The development of any of these descriptors is dependent upon having received some intersubjective confirmation that earns it a place within an objective system of sensory assessment. Their introduction and the development of its use proceeds as an instructed procedure. People are able to teach each other just what the semantic province of "green passionfruit" can be. The semantic scope of highly conventionalized descriptors can become broad. The head taster for an Indian exporting firm uses "orange" for nearly any flavor note that possesses a good deal of presence, and for him most coffees were either "ordinary" or "orange."

We have already discussed "sweetness." It is a general category for what should be an eminently straightforward and even empirical notion; however, it works as a metaphor that can signify a broad semantic range. To remedy the ambiguity, a professional coffee taster might try to define it—for example, "Sweetness should have at least five grams of sugar for a liter of water," which is the lowest level of sweetness that it is said one is able to taste; however, in my experience "sweet" is used for nearly any nice, clean, soft coffee that is free of harshness.

The highest rated coffee at a Nicaraguan Cup of Excellence (92.24) was described as having "florals, apricot, peach, honey, mango, Bordeaux wine, complex, structured, transparent, savory," which has the appearance of having just won the jackpot at a slot machine; however, having tasted it myself, I can attest to its accuracy. The description of an 89.17 coffee, "peach, cedar, jasmine, coconut, creamy body, and butter," was more problematic and probably required some further deliberation among the tasters to sort out which meanings are compatible and which are not; to a prospective client it could be perplexing. A Guji Gesha (Oromia, Ethiopia) has been described as "misty cannabis," but I was not able to locate it, despite experience with the flavor. One might nail a flavor with a descriptor, so idiosyncratic descriptors can be apt, but if it does not communicate well then it is not very useful. The purpose of communicating well is two-fold: to direct other tasters to explore that region of flavor so they can share knowledge and learn more about it, and to provide some indication of flavor to a prospective buyer.

One taste descriptor with a national origin and national provenance is "*rio*"—an acrid, medicinal, iodine-like flavor that results from a humidity-induced, bacterially promoted enzymatic activity that affects the coffee cherry before it is harvested, usually while it was left too long on the tree. Uker's Coffee Buyer's Guide describes the *rio* flavor as having "heavy and harsh taste characteristics of coffees grown in the Rio district of Brazil, and sometimes present even in fancy mild coffees" (Capella 2009, 400). *Rio* is strongly offensive, and its cousin *riado* is less aggressive but more subtle, possibly a taste acquired while the coffee was drying on the ground after being harvested and having endured some damp weather. It is said that they occur when trees are planted close to a river and that the construction of dams and hydroelectric plants in Brazil has changed some of the microclimates, ruining some formerly excellent coffee.

Stabilizing the Identity

How do coffee descriptors maintain their identities across usages? If their meanings are protean, what is the work that professional coffee tasters do to stabilize them? We have observed that descriptors are unities of sense and that this having a unity is an intersubjective achievement of tasters who work in concert with each other. To be useful, a taste descriptor must be capable of enframing the flavor it addresses within some limits, but as Sallis (2018, 1) observed astutely about a word, "Its sense will overreach such would-be limits, and slippage and mutation will set in." Since slippage is inevitable, we should not treat it as a mortal enemy. Slippage can even become a tool that helps understanding grow; any poet will tell you that. Further, most genuine tastes will resist a professional practice that attempts to exercise total control. Every salience that emerges is not the deliberate achievement of some professional mastery. The work of professional tasting cannot be limited to a language of judgments that has been bootstrapped, with objectivity being the yield.[2] Sometimes the coffee does speak for itself. Just as Sallis (2018, 2) suggested, the analysis cannot be exclusively active; rather, the object being assessed is the result of work undertaken "in the middle voice," midway between passive and active, and midway between constrained and without

---

2. Thanks are due Doug Macbeth for this observation.

limits. Those who like rules prefer that everything happens in the same way, but tastes do not work like that.

One of the more important labors of tasting is stabilizing the meaning of descriptors to the point that they can be used with some consistency. If significances come to be fixed, it is because people are fixing them, and not because they are fixed in themselves. Take, for example, the drift of the meaning of "balance" across the world of coffee description. Even excluding mentions of "balance" by clueless advertisers, genuine uses of the term by coffee tasters are spread across a broad semantic field: "a little citric acidity up front balanced with way cool herbal and spice notes"; "raspberry balanced with chocolate undertone"; "a deep-semi-sweet chocolate note blended with just a hint of floral aspect"; "citrus and floral balanced with a full-bodied dry toasted walnut tone." Shall we order? People deceive themselves by the conviction that there are always fixed significances. In fits of self-deception, and faced with what Nietzsche calls a fluid army of metaphors and metonyms (Figal 2010, 225), people try to turn what is flowing and contingent into something that is absolutely fixed and predictable. Derrida (1982, 227–271) considers this an aspect of "the white mythology," i.e., a cultural preference of northern Europeans and Americans. As an anthropologist who has spent seven congenial years living in pre-modern societies, I can attest to the fact that this preference is not universal, at least not yet.

Let us examine how a descriptor is made to possess a unified significance. Here is a transcript of a sensory assessment by lay coffee drinkers in Italy:

SILVIO: I'm still feeling it now that minutes have passed and even a vague hint of ferrous, I do not know why.

HOST: Ferrous?

SILVIO: Ferrous, yes . . .

ILARIA: Without sugar it is a bit too bitter, and I found the feeling of ferrous in fact, even now minutes later . . .

LUCA: Compared to the previous one, that aftertaste of iron or cardboard could be detected strongly.

The parties collaborate in firming and confirming the descriptor "ferrous." After rehearsing the term, they pull it apart from the local contingencies and make it into an independent, positive feature that can stand alone, as something objective. The descriptor "ferrous" is adopted by the drinkers as a tool for communication and is used in their subsequent tasting and describing. The key moment of the objectivation of the term "ferrous" occurs in the tiny demonstrative "that": "that aftertaste of iron," which indicates that this understanding is not the *private possession* of Luca but a publicly objectivated, *corporate* assessment, although it is a possession not yet fully defined: note that they are using it while they are still trying to determine just what it means. This independence, and the unity that a description can have, are social achievements of the local work that the three of them perform cooperatively. In short, the drinkers are engaged in the social work of building an account, which can be objectivated and thereby made a pillar of their interaction. If we were to follow it through to the end of the data, we would learn that the flavor "ferrous" came from the staleness of an open bag of coffee that over some days had absorbed whatever was in the room. At some point, *ferroso* (ferrous) is pulled *apart from* the local contingencies and made into an independent feature able to stand alone, as something "objective." "Ferrous" is provided its objective sense and reference by the intersubjective process of objectivation, and the subjectivities are left behind, and forgotten.

The local contingencies of making descriptors mean something can do strange things to the sense and reference of words. What is important about taste descriptors is that they be given some unity and reliability. Words themselves bear little intrinsic value; rather, *they are tied to the work that people perform with them.* In Brazil, somehow "hard" (*duro*) got to be "soft." Brazilian tasters use "*duro*" for coffees that do not have taints or off, *riado*-like flavors, coffees that are reliably good. The problem for Brazilian exporters is that when importers read the "*duro*" in an official taste description, uninformed importers may fear what it might taste like. For that reason, even though "*duro*" means "hard" in Portuguese, the Brazilian exporters translate it as "soft" to English-speaking buyers. And that is alright because that is what it mostly means. In the Brazilian world of coffee "good cup," "fine cup," "strictly hard bean," etc. all describe acceptable coffees, but Brazilian coffee purveyors must remember to describe a "hard" bean as "soft." This is another illustration for why a strictly literalist theory of language should be avoided. Zahavi (2001, 95) reminds us, "It is through linguistic embodiment that ideality attains its true ideal objectivity, receiving, in its documented form, an objective existence." The objectivity is derived from the work people do with terms, and not from the terms themselves.

There is a dialectic between any grammar and the usage of language in the world, and each of these can transform the other. In fact, such transformation never ceases, as new usages become repeated and standardized, and yet continually find their way to newer usages by parties who keep tweaking the words for everything they can be made to do. This is dialectics in an original sense of the term, and one does not want to inhibit the process; and yet—and this is the most remarkable thing about dialectics—one *still* relies on, counts on, grammar. But in the end, grammar succeeds by the work of bricolage that people do, and the meanings of terms must be stabilized, again and again. Wittgenstein's comment (1978, 18–19) about descriptions may be applied to any tasting schedule: it has an intelligibility that lives "on the borderline between logic and the empirical, so that their meaning shifts back and forth and they are now expressions of norms, now treated as expressions of experience." The resolution of inconsistencies, contradictions, indeterminacy, etc. rests in the hands of the tasters who use the descriptors. When a cohort of tasters has stabilized enough terms to use them in reliable ways, a grammar for tasting will be created. Even so, semiotic interplay of stabilized terms, especially when thrown off balance by unexpected flavors, can disrupt the system. That is why restabilizing the meanings of the descriptors will always be a task that tasters must perform, without any relief.

Stabilizing the meaning of descriptors is related to tasters' labors to maintain the objective sense of the descriptors, which is hardly spoken about except indirectly via broad references to calibration. If tasters do not work continuously at maintaining the objective character of their descriptors, so that whatever their terms come to mean is shared by the other tasters, there cannot be objectivity. In this way, at its root objectivity is dependent upon intersubjective practices. Calibration procedures, to which professional tasters are devoted, reveal some of the social activity that underlies the labors of tasting. There is no other route to objective knowledge, and there is no time-out for this work. The coffee industry emphasizes how important calibration is when it reminds tasters that calibration must be continually renewed, unofficially as well as officially. Even the expert baristas who participate in the World Barista Championship must undergo two days of calibration prior to the competition. The procedures of sensory science are derived from some carefully designed and intersubjectively adequate *social praxis*. The dream that we can produce flavor descriptors and then reify those cultural artifacts forever—so that they can come to stand on their own, apart from those social practices and independent of the local contingencies of their use ("Look Ma, no hands!")—is a false promise: the hands are always there. The brute truth, which any serious coffee taster will tell you, is that the local contingencies are the story. But that does not remove the real demand that purveyors of coffee need to communicate globally about flavors as best they can, which requires some standardization. In brief, the solution I am offering in these pages is to develop those standards without having the local contingencies disappear from sight.

During my research with lay coffee drinkers in the US, I came across many drinkers who paid little or no notice to mouthfeel. When asked to assess mouthfeel, many did not know what to do and asked me what it was. One coffee package they sampled stated that it featured a "big mouthfeel," and I was asked, "What does this mean?" We would re-taste the coffee and try to locate it. No doubt, many baristas have experience with this exercise. This category of descriptors, which is part of the palette of taste categories available for use by coffee professionals, has an effective capacity to communicate to coffee drinkers a domain of experience that possesses the potential to lastingly improve their acumen. The purpose of sensory description is to communicate something to others, not to satisfy philosophical or scientific truths. The activity of sensory description is social at its inception and social at its conclusion.

One cannot find a taste descriptor that does not possess some local historicity. The length, diction, style, and form of taste descriptions conform to local practices. Some coffee professionals use elaborate descriptions, such as "dried papaya and jasmine-infused caramel." Other professionals prefer more concise, tidy descriptions. The director of the Indian Coffee Board (Bangalore) told me, "We should not write unnecessary things, imagining things." And his view agrees with that of the Dutch coffee purveyor who revolutionized American coffee, Alfred Peet, who disliked pompous terms for describing coffee (Houtman 2016, 137). One wholesale broker in Brazil records only short descriptors, such as "hard, green" (*duro, verde*), terms that have a history in Brazil and at their firm. Because they have a local history, they can be used in objective ways to sort coffees. As mentioned, in India "orange" is found on many tasting forms. I lived in India for many years, drinking coffee daily, but I tasted few coffees that possessed an orange flavor. I eventually learned that "orange" was a gloss for *any* fruity note, not only for citrus fruits. At some facilities the descriptor is used not to describe the flavor but to indicate that the coffee was genuinely good and it carried an implication that it should be priced accordingly. In this way, it was an effective industrial practice, but one that is difficult to transmit abroad.

A description of a Colombian coffee operated in a middle ground: "High acidity, medium bodied, sweet notes, clean cup, and a pronounced aroma." This communicates quite a lot without pomposity, but the recipient will still need to know what is "body," what is "sweet," and what is "clean cup." Further, there is the interesting question of whether "sweet" in Colombia is what "sweet" is in India, or whether what "body" is in Italy is what "body" is Australia. One can standardize the terms by means of lexicons, socialization at international conferences, etc., but it would be wise to leave enough semantic flexibility for Italians to teach Australians what more there could be to body than what they have so far reckoned.

Coffee tasters search for the right descriptor with one eye on commercial potential. This searching can lead tasters in a number of directions, some of them serendipitous. When done in concert with other tasters, which is what happens at most firms, as soon as the tasters land somewhere with the aid of a descriptor, it is *that* location that then directs matters henceforward. Let us examine two short examples:

ALLEN: Fruit pie.

BARBARA: Maybe peach. I got a peach cobbler.

SHERRIE: Yes, or apricot.

ALLEN: Tobacco.

BARBARA: Sweet tobacco.

The thinking here is a public activity, and much of the flow is unplanned and serendipitous. But even serendipitous solutions need to be made objective if they are to be useful. Parties follow up each other's leads and build upon a developing account, which is a public possession more than a private one. The peach and apricot operate in the same domain of stone fruits, and the parties refine their description collaboratively as they confirm it for each other. "Tobacco" alone did not quite communicate the excellence of the taste, so it was amended. The objective description that is the precipitate of concerted examinations like these will leave behind its local contingencies and stand alone as "fact." Fact production too is a precipitate of public collaboration; that is, a fact is an occasioned production, social at its core, and what is transformed into an objective descriptor will need to be revivified by the recipient if it is to serve for guiding taste experience. The critical factor is not developing a formal definition but how the tasters collaborate in maintaining the objective sense of a descriptor *as they use it*, teaching each other what they are and how to apply them, there and then. These descriptors, produced in just that way, become tools available for tasters to use in assessing and exploring the taste of any coffee.

Words and glosses do not mean the same thing to everyone automatically. For instance, "earthy" in India presents a puzzle for Brazilian exporters, so a Brazilian exporter seeking to expand their understanding of earthy flavors will have the task of locating the Indians' "earthy." It makes no difference what "earthy" means in general or in Indonesia or in a dictionary, since this "earthy" is something specific for Indians. What is *this* "earthy," and how can *it* be made to communicate something? Some tasters use "earthy" as a synonym for "full-bodied," reserving "vegetative" for the less desirable flavor, but that obliging convention does little good if it is not shared, which requires social interaction; and in this way, social practices are not absent from the scene. A taster once explained to me that "earthy" smells come from carcasses of dead fungi on coffee beans, but there are other explanations. Numeration without communicating the taste has little utility, and it is foolish to talk like "I gave its flavor a 6" or "No, I gave it only a 3" without having coordinated an intersubjectively adequate understanding about what specifically it is they are numerating; however, many conversations occur just this way, by professional tasters as well as lay tasters. Many people, perhaps most, fill out surveys without specifying just what their numerations are assessing. Little expertise is required to fill in a bubble on a form. What a descriptor intends to convey is a locally occasioned event, and solutions to problems of communication can be serendipitous, despite every effort by a firm, the coffee industry, or a scientist to standardize the use of descriptors. Words do not exist apart from the local circumstances of their use. Some regret this fact, but that does not change the situation.

Similarly, "green" has a broad semantic field (Manuel Diaz: "What does 'green' mean? It means 'I don't know'"), even though it is a common descriptor. It will be given a local meaning, renewed each time a local cohort of tasters gets together. "Green," "earthy," and "vegetative" are sometimes used as synonyms, but during one session of cupping the tasters organized a handy local system, one that seemed to emerge autochthonously, by which "green" was tart and "earthy" was full-bodied and chocolatey. Ambiguity is reduced by a process of socialization to usages more than by any reliance upon preexisting definitions, and the solutions are local and not universal.

While this permits them to assess effectively a table of coffees and decide how to proceed with a blend, it may not communicate successfully on a package.

Tasters may invent an apt descriptor that exists in no one's lexicon. At the 2017 World Brewer's Cup, a Gesha coffee was described as "banana liqueur." If other tasters are able to employ the descriptor in a productive way, it might come into vogue. During a cupping, once a taster introduces a term that has not been used, like "green apple," it is not unusual that it will be used repeatedly, and so descriptors surface in clusters. Only after sufficient intersubjective coordination has taken place can anything surface like an objective descriptor (e.g., "smooth") that possesses sufficient reliability to offer assistance. Far from being independent of local circumstances and social practices, a descriptor will collect its specific sense and reference from just how and just where it is used, including the local semiotic structuring, adventitious neologisms and phrasings, and also the coffees' particularities (which provide the material things to which a label like "smooth" can be applied). Not all smooths are the same, nor should they be.

Instructed Actions

Simply because a descriptor is broad or indeterminate does not mean that it cannot be useful, and what tasters do with descriptors is more important than the semantic content the descriptors bear. A literal-minded approach to descriptors is not helpful. In fact, descriptors that are less determined sometimes offer tasters more scope for applying them in a way that allows tasters to probe flavors in a productive manner. However, eventually the tasters will need to specify the sense and reference of their descriptors as they teach each other how to use them. Instructed action like this is an ongoing component of the sociality of each and every occasion. This does not mean that the descriptions they will produce will not be objective; rather, it means that objective descriptions can be produced in this way.

All organized activity involves some instructed action. In order for parties to get on the same page, they need to display for each other the way to act in local situations; this is part of socialization. Sometimes the instruction is explicit ("Roundness is detected with the cheeks") and sometimes it operates implicitly by mimetic copying of correct behavior (e.g., how a cupping spoonful that is inhaled to the back of the palate should sound). As Adorno (1973) has suggested, mimesis is as vital to understanding as rationality is, and this holds true for how taste descriptors are used. As I have been emphasizing, a descriptor will collect its specific sense and reference from just how it is used, and so tasters spend a good deal of time observing the performances of others in order to learn the meaning of descriptors and how to do things with them, even when they are tasting silently and independently. Here I say "performances" because some of what local parties are doing is designed intentionally for how they will serve to instruct collaborators about effective practices at the worksite. People are purposefully cooperative in this way. A descriptor used like that, for just this coffee, and the interpretive work that it is capable of achieving are things that other tasters can witness, and then reproduce, in a manner that will conform to an emerging model. This process of display and reproduction is part of how the descriptors' sense and reference is stabilized: here is the origin of that *reproducibility* that any productive science strives to achieve. Its accomplishment is not simply inherent in a given protocol but is a result of active, intersubjective work by tasters.

A calibrated palate is a collective palate, and things do not come to be collective without concerted effort. Achieving a mutually intelligible object is an ongoing social project that tasters accomplish. They learn from each other continuously, both about the sense of the objects and about the local practices according to which objects are being made mutually intelligible. Each fresh tongue has eyes, but for its insights to be communicated to others, a taster will need to also learn the local praxis for expressing and communicating discoveries. These social aspects are unavoidable, and part of the job of tasters is to display and teach each other these social practices. Taste descriptors assist drinkers in discovering tastes and communicating about them, including tastes that are not yet settled. Tasters also use descriptors to explain to each other how a coffee is working, which is an aspect of taste that can exceed isolated, individuated descriptors and linear protocols. More intricate than this, the tasters use descriptors to teach each other the ways they can be used for discovering together the "what more" of any taste, so these instructed actions not only address particular content but are oriented to teaching a praxis for using them. Professional tasters are eager to explore how a coffee is working, and they have genuine respect for each other's discoveries for the reason that they are grateful to learn something new. Every descriptor can be employed as an occasion for instruction. When a taster makes a comment like "Notice the floral finish," a fellow drinker can learn there is such a thing as a floral flavor in coffee, that it can be found in this coffee, and that there can be such a thing as a "finish" to a taste, which instructs them about the dynamic quality of coffee flavor. At the same time, they learn how to use those words in public society, and they may recycle any descriptor when they describe a succeeding coffee, such as "Notice the bitter finish."

We teach each other how to talk and how to taste, and the two are related. It is unlikely one will discover the meaning of "round" or "sweet" for coffee by consulting a dictionary, yet tasters successfully instruct each other how to use these taste descriptors appropriately. A descriptor is a ladder to be climbed that exposes an aspect of taste and is not an end in itself. For consumers of coffee, descriptors can be helpful for making purchases and for exploring the flavors of a coffee, but tastes are the thing. The tastes will survive even when the descriptors are cast aside, and so the descriptors do not need to be fetishized or expressed for the purpose of enhancing social standing, although more than occasionally they are used that way, which may be why both Alfred Peet and the director of the Indian Coffee Board rejected use of pompous descriptions. What is important about using taste descriptors is that each person knows what he or she means by a term and uses the term consistently, and that what one person means approximates what the next person means, with what sociologists call intersubjective adequacy. This makes it necessary that people continuously coordinate their understandings of descriptors for the purpose of stabilizing the meanings. Coordination involves displaying and witnessing. Even the method cooperating tasters use for stabilizing an understanding of taste is an instructed action.

In one tasting course, we were studying astringency. This is an objective notion, and it is subject to consensual calibration, but I was having a problem distinguishing the acceptable boundaries of astringency. Was what I was projecting as "astringent" what it really is, and how could I be certain? How does that characteristic achieve its clear definition? In other words, how is something elusive made into a thing? By words. While I was tasting the coffees, sorting out which cups had astringency and which did not, I became lost in the camouflage, and I was no longer certain about the accuracy of what I was projecting into the notion of astringency. I suspected that for a couple of the cups I may have been adding some other off-flavor taste to my assessments. At that point, the instructor advised us to be careful, which only increased my uncertainty. He said, "Acidic tastes are frequently confused with astringency." So now there was another distinction I needed to locate: what part was the acidity and what part was the astringency—a question that can confound. Are those aspects separable? When I confessed my uncertainty to the teacher, I was advised that acid tastes occur immediately and disappear quickly, whereas astringency comes on more slowly and endures longer. I wondered to myself how I could be certain that my distinctions conform well with the standards that the others were using. In fact, my search for this distinction between acidity and astringency led me to become clearer about what my standards for astringency were, although I still needed to learn how my standards compared with the others' standards. My standards may not have been the appropriate ones, since when we were asked to taste five cups of coffee and decide the order of astringency from most to least, I selected only two of the five correctly.

On another occasion, some lay drinkers in Italy detected a spicy sort of flavor (*pizzicorìo*, or "tingling") in the coffee that was being served to them. Having publicly announced the finding, the lay drinkers collaborated in teaching each other about its limits and characteristics:

1	SILVIO:	Al contatto con la lingua sentivo un **pizzicorìo**,
2		*Upon touching it with the tongue, I felt a tingling,*
3		qualcosa che non mi aspettavo invece dall'odorato.
4		*something I was not expecting from smelling it.*
5	LUCA:	Poi sì, è meno cremoso e il retrogusto è minore,
6		*Then yes, it is less creamy and the aftertaste is less,*
7		solo che lascia una sensazione simile al **piccante**.
8		*it is just that it leaves a sensation similar to spicy.*
9		Almeno al primo sorso.
10		*At least at the first sip.*
11	HOST:	Ah. Ah. Ah.
12	LUCA:	Cioè nel senso, **pizzica** un po'.
13		*That is, it tingles a bit.*
14	SILVIO:	Sì sì sì, quel **pizzicorìo** che dicevo.
15		*Yes yes yes, that tingling that I was speaking about.*

This is the sort of instructed action that tasters continually engage in. Not only do they confirm each other's assessment, thus offering reassurance to themselves that they have made contact with a transcendent object (Garfinkel and Liberman 2007: 6), they are teaching each other how to delimit it, and ultimately how to appreciate it. This is the way people learn. Sometimes they proceed cautiously: it is not spicy but "similar to spicy" (lines 7/8), and by thinking publicly and together (lines 12–15) they finally manage to calibrate their understanding of their descriptor (lines 14/15). Similarly, while tasting a succeeding cup, a taster announced a peculiar sort of discovery, which also reveals that thinking can be public: "This is not aromatic, right?" After this, the parties collaborated to draw the boundaries of the assessment more clearly. Not only is their thinking public, they need to think publicly, and this is related to their need to produce objective knowledge.

If one does not know the meaning of a descriptor, say the *"riado"* that we discussed, one can ask and be instructed by a taster who does know, but most instructions occur coincidentally. They always require a community. A taster announces, "This is puckery stuff." What is "puckery"? Is it an acquired taste? If so, there has to be a community to join and find instruction from, and that is more than informational, by which I mean it is not something that sits alone by itself, a docile object without relations to the actions of parties. It is intimate and communitarian, and surely involves the cultivation of an attentiveness to a puckery-ness that they are teaching each other to appreciate. In other words, the labor of tasting is intersubjective. The common use of terms is coordinated, and a taste descriptor wins its definiteness of sense by regular usage.

In some roasting facilities, a usage becomes a local tradition. The accuracy and reliability of the terms do not reside inside the term as if there it bore a kernel of meaning, nor is a literal-minded employment of taste descriptors productive, because it introduces the myopia of positivism, something that no professional taster can afford. More making meaning takes place outside the term than inside it, but the making of meaning could not take place without the term. The accuracy of a descriptor resides in the commonality and instructability of its usage. At the microsocial level of working with other tasters in an intersubjective way, a way that one has used a descriptor is not accepted as correct until it is confirmed and then objectivated by a cohort of tasters. Its meaning is not fixed from the start; rather, it develops as parties learn and teach each other what they can do with it. Here the "can do" exceeds the "is" in importance. At the macrosocial level, there is a foundational question of what is being communicated across national boundaries and along the chain of production. Compromises made in the interest of clear communication inhabit the scene: is the descriptor that a cohort of tasters have settled upon capable of being communicated to the person who will read the description on a package? What good is "passion fruit" or "macadamia nut" for people who have no experience with these? There has been too little investigation of this problem. If it is ignored, the communication will be poor; if it is attended to, then the effectiveness of sensory description can be enhanced.

A taste that is captured by and with (this "with" is the "can" part) a taste descriptor should be "an intersubjectively identical thing" (Schutz 1970a, 16–17). This means that a taste, like any other object, is provided a *unity* of sense by the determinations of tasters who "stand in a relation of mutual understanding." This is calibration. Cooperatively, acting in concert with each other, the tasters settle a unity of meaning for a descriptor. This coherence of the taste is a practical achievement of the parties, and it is one of the elemental tasks of professional tasters, even though they are not philosophers or linguists; moreover, this task is never completed once and for all. Every speaker in the world is a part-time linguist. Once a cohort of tasters, for instance the managers of a specialty café, settles the unity of the meaning of the taste descriptors they are using, the process does not conclude—they also need to educate their clientele to their chosen flavor palette and use it for the purpose of enhancing their clients' appreciation and attentiveness to the tastes they are being offered. Descriptions are embodied in practices.

Once taste moves into the realm of language and discourse, it is inevitable that all manners of nonsense commence, including sophistries, top-down theories and ideologies, use of social status markers, etc., and customers can become confused or overwhelmed. The surfaces of a language introduce further semiotic opportunities and distractions, which inhabit discourse. With any language learning, one utters words without knowing precisely what they mean, and sometimes one utters them in order to learn this. One can pick this up by witnessing what they come to mean in the situation. The emerging semiotic relations of those terms with terms that are already in play can alter the sense of one's own words. One learns by tracking what happens to one's words and by observing what the descriptors one uses are capable of accomplishing.

Occasionally people use descriptors the way that a parrot would, but one can also use them while knowing really how to use them. Using descriptors is a skill that involves more than knowing descriptors; however, in order to provide them with an objective meaning, we must engage in intersubjective dialogue. The other person will listen to my usage, and I will observe the other's usage; we assess any differences, adjust our usages, and then settle upon a common solution. The more people who are involved in establishing the meaning of a descriptor, the more likely it is that one will develop an effective (if not ever universal) solution. The success of a description like "good body with medium acidity, providing a pleasing balance in a morning cappuccino" depends on having calibrated our understandings of body, acidity, and balance.

I have discovered that even terms we do not fully understand have the capacity to instruct us. Sunalini Menon tasted a very unique citric Chikkamagaluru coffee for the very first time and commented, "The coffee has very good structure. Very good body to it, and in that body is interwoven acidic nuances. Very nicely balanced. Very clean cup." I knew enough to appreciate the relationship that she described between the body and the acidic nuances, and I knew what a "clean cup" was, but here I had an opportunity to learn what "structure" could mean for a cup of coffee. I had heard the term used before, but I was uncertain about just what it meant, yet the term was still instructive—it described a stability in the relationship between the body and the acidity. I might have called that "balance." But the meanings are not as important as the tasting that the terms promote. Remember, the taste is the thing. A subsequent coffee we tried was described as "Very balanced. There is a little bit of structure to it. There is a little bit of acidity to it. Very clean finish," but this description left me confused: if the second coffee was "very" balanced how is it that its "structure" was only "little"? What is *little* structure anyway? It must be that structure is not like pregnancy. I wondered, did I need to revise my understanding of the relation between "structure" and "balance"? The terms remained in play for the remainder of our tasting, even as I used them to increase my understanding of and attentiveness to the tastes. While we worked to settle and fix the sense and reference of the terms, the task was complicated further by the fact that I did not want to reveal to the master taster Ms. Menon that I was unsure what "structure" meant. In everyday life a good deal of this sort of nondisclosure takes place, including during interaction among coffee tasters. Further, the semiotic play of the term with the other descriptors caused the semantic borders of all the terms to keep shifting while we continued to taste coffees. That is not necessarily a bad thing. It is nothing we need to fear, especially when those transformations are mostly provoked by the influences of flavors.

The Trained Tongue

Everyone has a tongue, but not all tongues are educated. One way that a palate is educated is by concerting one's tasting with others. When I discover something distinctive in a coffee, I may ask myself, "Am I sensing correctly what is in the cup, or am I making a mistake?" Then I will listen to others, and after that, cup again. As the Italian taster Luigi Odello emphasizes, "General group discussion sharpens the capacity of tasters." I have witnessed the most expert tasters turn toward rank novices tasting beside them for confirmation of a tentative assessment they have made. Most tasting is a social activity, even though many scientific models institute strict individuation in the interest of reducing the intrusion of others' opinions. Most competitive cuppings restrict social interaction, although such restriction is never total (see chapter 10). The restriction is imposed in the interest of fostering the objectivity of the assessments, but as we have learned, most establishment of objective knowledge requires some intersubjective authority. Professional tasters find *ad hoc* solutions to this double-bind of the objectivity that proceeds from independent tasting and the objectivity that proceeds from intersubjective validation.

How does this latter validation function? That is, how are meanings made objective? We have arrived at our principal question. Lingle (2001, 3) describes the process: "When several cuppers sense the aromatic and taste properties of the same brew at the same time, they can begin to agree on the vocabulary pertinent to the flavor being experienced, leading to effective communication of aroma, taste and body impressions." Drawing from my sociological expertise, I will expand Lingle's description. As one interacts with one's fellows to build an *account* that adequately describes the local ordering, these accounts can receive *confirmation* and gain credence. People may be aware that they are collaborating in making sense and in making order, and most anyone is free to extend, amend, or reject an account as it is being built up by the participants. At some point, a confirmed account gets reified, and intimations arise that these understandings are true independently of the cohort of social actors who just created them. Both the natural flow of interaction and deliberate efforts work toward the *objectivation* of confirmed accounts, stabilizing them in ways that render them nearly unassailable. Shortly following, parties may forget or deny that they had any hand in producing these objectivated accounts that, as objects shared in the sociality of the occasion, acquire a moral force. *Disengagement* with the production activities ensues, and parties stick to the task of following the local system of order and obligations, forgetting that they are mostly the authors of those same obligations.

This social process of intersubjective validation can be diagrammed like this:

Account → Confirmation → Objectivation → Disengagement

For objective knowledge to be produced in this way, tasters need to cup together, i.e., to teach each other these usages and applications, and coordinate and calibrate their understandings.

One of the weaknesses of individualized tasting is that tasters may end up evaluating different aspects of the categories or use different understandings of categories. When one collects from tasters only their category names and some associated numbers, the results appear to be highly compatible, but no one really knows for certain just what the categories, or the numeration practice, were for every taster. As Garfinkel (1996, 11) has described, the actual lived phenomenon as it is experienced is lost with the same technical methods that are used to represent it. Once a "signed" representation *replaces* a procedurally understood and lived-through phenomenon, the resulting "data" can be made to serve any analytic purpose, and it can be turned into sophistry. The people, along with their experiences, will have nothing to say because little of those experiences remain. "Signed objects are objects whose entire specifications are found and in various ways are demonstrated by treating the [document] as a collection of signs and symbols, and then assigning to any items an interpreted significance" (Garfinkel 1996). The world is lost, but the scientific analyst emerges victorious. Hidden underneath this tidy surface structure could be chaos, a situation similar to the ten blind men who are describing an elephant ("It is like a hose," "like a broom," "like a tree stump"), yet one will be satisfied with any averaged score, especially when that average is carried to two decimal points. The way that professional tasters are calibrated and even the professional certification of that calibration do not provide absolute guarantees (everyone acknowledges this). Still, there is a widespread but incorrect presumption that it is possible for each taste descriptor to bear its sense inside it, like a kernel. When the coffee is given minimal opportunity to influence the palette of descriptors, serious problems can occur. While tasters insist that "A coffee must speak for itself," under some tasting protocols a schedule of predefined descriptors does most of the speaking.

Something even more essential is lost. The efficacy of collective tasting rests in the way it can serve to intensify our attention to taste. As Figal (2010, 303) wisely counsels, the important question is how is it that "the fundamental relationship between us and things is intensified." The problem is not calculative so much as it is hermeneutic, although calculations can have hermeneutic benefits. The claim here is that objectivity's victories are not metaphysical, nor are they exclusively concerned with truth: the victories are practical. The purpose of cupping is to enhance our capacity to taste, which is the source of improving our understanding of the flavors that a coffee affords us. In fact, the efficacy of any protocol rests in this hidden *raison d'être* of objectivity. When I explained this to Doug Macbeth, he observed, "In this distinction between efficacy and objectivity; the former may be the measure of the latter."

Do the meanings of descriptors ever get settled once and for all? Many professional coffee tasters try to accomplish this, and some social scientists criticize the coffee industry for not doing so, but is a demand for determinacy a reasonable stipulation? The productive uses to which descriptors like "round" "bold," "bright," etc. can be put have not yet been exhausted, and strong-arming these terms into lockboxes is not helpful; more importantly, it would be a distortion of linguistic praxis to try to do so. These terms do require continual attention and taming in order to remain serviceable and objective, but to use a phrase of Garfinkel, the natural lability of descriptors is something that is "without remedy."

It is interesting that the degree of lability varies from one descriptor to another. Some descriptors (like "sour") have a narrower reference than others (such as "bold"), yet both kinds have efficacy. Descriptors gain their sense not from a meaning that they carry around in some pocket but from the sign-system that they contribute to establishing; however, a sign-system keeps transforming itself, and the necessary instability that results can complicate objectivity. A descriptor is a mark within a system of differences, and it wins its pertinence by virtue of the reciprocal delimitations of all of the terms. Earlier we saw how "earthy" and "vegetative" could be used to delimit each other's provinces. Similarly, "roundness" and "body" influence each other's scope and applicability. Only a myopic naiveté could lead to the suggestion that settling the meaning of a taste descriptor once and for all time would aid our understanding of flavors, since descriptors will continue to be affected each time they are partnered with new descriptors. If they are to function as tools for genuine discovery, they must remain open to the local contexts to which they are applied; otherwise, we condemn ourselves to an endless monologue of the same, and that is not the way I want my coffee.

As Sally Wiggins (2004, 30) has observed, "Our understandings about food and eating are bound up with our discursive practices," but we should try to avoid placing the discursive practices, or what Wright (2014, 168) calls "the infrastructure of taste descriptions," into a dominating position. The tastes need to be able to act upon the discourse, transforming it if necessary. And they do, only there is sometimes a professional pretension that they do not. In a dozen volumes Derrida has argued something even more radical: for any sign, what is signified is never separable from the signifier, and vice-versa since they reciprocally determine each other. Only an imposed metaphysics will try to keep them strictly separate.

The Natural Indeterminacy of Taste Descriptors

When observing that taste descriptors possess a natural indeterminacy, it is sometimes suggested that this is a problem that requires a remedy. This is not always the case. It is true there are many ambiguities, both in the taste descriptors themselves and in how they are used by tasters and by people who drink coffee. Let us investigate the situation and collect some information we can use in assessing whether the indeterminacy of taste descriptors is always a problem.

One conspicuous case of indeterminate taste descriptors is the widespread notion of "balance" in the taste of coffee. When Sunalini Menon tells me, "A very balanced coffee—good strength, good acidity," what does it mean to say, "a very balanced coffee"? A lay coffee drinker once spoke of balance, "I have no go-to favorite. I wouldn't be picking something from Panama or something. I actually do like what my people would call a 'boring' coffee, like a really good Colombian or something like that, as opposed to a spikey Kenyan. I really like a good, balanced cup!" Everyone wants a good, balanced cup, but not everyone can identify it, and at times "balance" is so vague, even when it is good, that it has problems making up its mind what it means. As a descriptor, "balance" is more labile than most, which is to say it is an adaptive descriptor, one that is able to find a useful orientation in diverse situations; nevertheless, it can possess a remarkable capacity for revealing and highlighting local circumstances of flavor.

Much of the time, when I ask coffee professionals, "What is balance?" their reply commences with a pause. They will say, "Well . . ." Ask your barista this question the next time you order coffee in a café. Even Luca Torta, roaster *straordinario* of Trento, with 25 years of loving experience, told me that balance is very hard to pin down. A roaster from Sicily agreed, explaining, "It's not easy to define the word 'balance.'" That it is not easy has not prevented it from being employed as one of the most frequently exercised descriptors in the coffee industry. This is because the taste of coffee is complicated, so the industry has need for a descriptor that addresses itself to the dynamic ways that the taste of a coffee works. "Balance" is an important but not simple concept. Part of the indeterminacy of the notion is that inherent in "balance" is the acknowledgment that there is more than one thing going on, that there is a relationship among multiple aspects of taste, yet which aspects are being related are not always stipulated. Package labels commonly refer to "good balance" without specifying which aspects are considered, which renders the information news from nowhere. "Perfectly balanced" is not any better. Possibly it is used to indicate that there is some complexity that would require balancing, but what is being conveyed by using the adjective may not be specified. A consumer might purchase a package because it is "perfectly balanced," attracted to the idea of perfection even without knowing what is being balanced.

What can "harmonious balance" possibly mean? Is there a "balance" that can feature disharmony? The coffee that was given the taste descriptor "harmonious balance" was rated 91.45, so with that additional qualification a potential buyer is likely to take it seriously, though it remains ambiguous. This is another example of how descriptors as signifiers influence each other (here I treat the numerical ratings as another signifier). Similarly, what sense can one make of "very balanced," given to a coffee rated 89.84? I have witnessed conversations like,

A   This is a very balanced coffee.

B   Yes, yah.

Of what does such agreement consist? I have written studies of what I call "gratuitous concurrence" (1980; 1985, 197–202; 2018), and it is little more than social grease that permits collaborators to continue talking, in hope that what was meant will eventually become apparent.

> COFFEE TASTER: Natural coffees are often rounder in flavor. Semi-washed coffees can be sweeter or sharper, sometimes with more chocolate.
>
> STUDENT: [Nods head in acknowledgment]
>
> COFFEE TASTER: Do you know what I mean by "round"?

Here the student was caught out. When "round" is part of a description on a package, how many understand what it is? Moreover, it can mean different things to different tasters.

When someone tells me, "This coffee is very balanced, which is the specialty of the Chikkamagaluru region," what am I going to find in the cup of coffee I am tasting that will conform with "balance" used in this way, for just this coffee? My discovery works like "the classic Italian roast" we reviewed in an earlier chapter, where the term "classic" commends its acceptance without our asking what it is. I can report one exception that occurred during our consumer testing in Italy. When asked to evaluate a coffee's "balance," one lay drinker responded with unqualified honesty: "Balance. I have no idea what to say here."

The head of quality control for Gita Coffee Traders of Coorg explained to me they are seeking a round cup that is balanced, so I asked him what the difference was between "round" and "balanced." He replied that they were similar. He said, "I use this 'round' terminology when the body is 3–4, good cups with no off notes, and good aroma . . . Balance is basically similar." This taster had a system as well as some consistency, and it is true that balance often involves body, but frequently usages of "balance" are too general.

In other parts of the world as well, "balanced" is sometimes accompanied by the descriptor "round," but these two terms are not equivalent. There is confusion about how these descriptors should be used and how they should be distinguished. An exporter in Santos communicated that "Brazil has an incredibly balanced and well-rounded flavor." So what is "balanced" and "well-rounded"? A Danish taster who buys Brazilian coffees told me, "Brazilian coffees offer some softness that can lower the acidity and make the coffee more round or balanced." When I asked him whether "round" and "balanced" were synonyms, he said they were not. Even so, professional purveyors of coffee sometimes use the terms interchangeably. The literature of the Italian firm Lavazza described one of their coffees as "dolce" (sweet), a term used frequently in Italy; however, in their brochure's English version it was translated as "well-rounded," possibly because the latter term is used more frequently by English-speaking coffee drinkers. The actual distinction between "round" and "balanced" has to do with texture or body. Roundness is more tactile, but balance can be more diverse in its referents; however, there is some overlap between the two descriptors: a "round" coffee is always a balanced coffee, since it will feature flavors no single one of which overwhelms the others; however, a balanced coffee is not always "round." In the case of roundness, the tongue and cheek are involved equally, while balance can have more to do with the effects of flavor on the tongue alone. Yet Luca Torta's explanation was divergent: "If it occupies all parts of the mouth, the coffee is balanced, but if it occupies some zones and not others, it does not have good balance." Coffee purveyors seem to take "balance" in many directions. What are we looking for under the guidance, "It gets rounder and rounder as the coffee cools"? In the face of such ambiguity, how many things will ordinary consumers be able to do with "round"? About as many as they can do with "balance."

There are many ways of defining or pinning down what "balance" is. A coffee that is balanced is one in which all the characteristics of a coffee participate in the gustatory experience without any one of them strongly dominating. But then how does one distinguish this from "round," which an Italian lexicon describes as "having taste features, none of which overwhelm the others" (Azienda Riunite Caffè 2013, 192)? Dr. Enrico Meschini explained, "Balance is like measuring how the coffee is an orchestra." And Ted Lingle (2001, 31) has written that balance is "the overall flavor impression that assesses the degree to which the various tastes and aromas fit together." If a single attribute, such as a sweet fruit or a winy tone, dominates the other attributes, the balance will be poor. The senior Korean taster San Choi offered me some practice advice: "For balance, I ask myself what is missing that would make it a better cup."

When using the term, it is helpful to specify *which* aspects it is that balance each other. There could be a balance between body and acidity, or between the sweetness and the bitterness, or between fruitiness and a flavor like vanilla (or chocolate or some nut), between acidity and the mouthfeel, or between strength and acidity. There are many ways a coffee can be balanced, yet it is rare that consumers are given sufficient information to inform themselves. At a minimum, "balanced" will signify that something complicated is going on, but it would be advantageous for the specifics to be included. If there are numerous ways to achieve balance, what does that do to its meaning when it appears as a single word, unqualified by anything other than a superlative, on a package? If this descriptor is going to be meaningful to a consumer who is considering a coffee purchase, the kind of balance it is should be indicated; otherwise, it is white noise.

During my research I discovered that most lay drinkers were less interested in balance than I am. Drinking coffee is an occasioned event, and a drinker may not feel compelled to settle the specification of balance: "It has a balance between, that is, between the bitterness of coffee and other notes, how could that latter be? And that is a coffee that will eventually make you say 'Yes, that's good, that's fine.' It is, and then one can go to class." Lifting her spirits before class was sufficient diversion, and she demanded no more from her coffee than that—specifying the taste was beside the point, especially if she was going to make it to class on time.

Professional tasters find the term "balance" too useful to discard, and there are many who define it carefully. Other tasters who have experience with the active engagement with tastes that this descriptor promotes are content to leave some scope for how the term is to be applied. Their work with "balance" requires tasters to enter the more dynamic qualities of tastes, and observe, identify, and describe any synergy that might be happening. Taste is a matter of harmonies and oppositions, which are sometimes given the name "balance." Use of the term can alert a drinker to be more attentive to the complexity of the "structure." Terms require engagement by the one who is tasting before they acquire their clarity. Without the term "balance," the canvas would be duller, and it is a descriptor that can add an extra dimension to sensory analysis. But when a professional taster numerates "balance," just what is it that is being numerated? Is the taster numerating its pleasantness, its strength, or its symmetry? The number itself does not tell you that. A taster once declared, "Balance is a value judgment—the harmonious combination of all flavor and texture nuances." How does one calibrate that?

"That Crazy Table"

Taste descriptors that bear a clear unity of sense one moment and that have found a place within a routine of concerted tasting can lose their coherence in the face of distinctive or unusual coffees. Sometimes flavors outstrip the capabilities of the methods they are using, both the capabilities of a lexicon and the system for applying them that a group of tasters has developed as a community of practice over the course of a week of cupping.

At the Best of Panama tastings in 2008, there was this discussion between two of the international tasters:

    A At first extraction, it was fine. But by the time I got through with that crazy table, and this cup was coming on and coming on, I decided it was really outstanding. It has a good, light, fine acidity. It's not a fantastically interesting coffee, but it's a very solid one.

    B It definitely stepped up.

The same day, another taster remarked aloud, "I'm still trying to recover from that crazy table." What is a "crazy table"? And how does a flight of coffees get to be that way? They are coffees that render inadequate the quiver of taste descriptors one is accustomed to using for exploring flavors. The "Gesha" coffee grown by the Petersons and now by others originated in Ethiopia and languished in arboreta for decades. It first appeared at the Best of Panama of 2004. It was grown not for its flavor, which no one anticipated, but for its properties that might resist disease. By the Best of

Panama of 2006, it had earned worldwide attention for what Ric Rhinehart of the SCA, characterized as "a basket of flowers." Its flavor begins over the top and keeps ascending from there. The flavors of a Gesha are difficult to assess because they are all over the place and defy being pinned down. Gesha has been called "the sex goddess of coffees" (Weissman 2008, 133) and "a Yirgacheffe on Central American acid" (Koehler 2017, 174); other tasters have described it as the psychedelic of coffees. A few sensory analysts first interpreted the crazy flavors as defects, but eventually even tasters who are skeptical of wild or naturally processed coffees found themselves unable to reject it. Weissman's (2008, 133) description is apt: "The fragrance is like papaya drenched in maple syrup, fresh-cut sugarcane and jasmine," which conforms perfectly with that of Willem Boot of the Boot Coffee Campus: "jasmine, papaya, lime, and honeysuckle." Another taster chose "mango, papaya and peach, aftertaste of bergamot." The Esmeralda Gesha was described by Duane Sorenson as being like Juicy Fruit gum (Weissman 2008, 32), but to my palate it tastes even better (and Juicy Fruit was my favorite gum). It is as if the enduring sweetness of the mucilage has managed to enter the bean itself. The Panamanian coffee grower Wilford Lamastus cut through all the descriptions when, with a twinkle in his eye, he advised me, "This is coffee that you never spit out. You swallow it."

Gesha was discovered in Ethiopia in 1931 (Weissman 2008, 146) when a British diplomat collected its seeds for planting in arboreta in Kenya (1932), in Lyamungu agricultural research station in Tanzania (first recorded 1936), and in Uganda. It was sent to Costa Rica in 1953 (Koehler 2017, 177) as a disease-resistant strain, proving once again that disease can drive innovation. "In the 1960s, Francisco Serracin, an employee of the Panamanian Ministry of Agriculture, was seeking coffee plants that might be resistant to leaf rust, and he obtained some Gesha trees from Costa Rica" (Weissman 2008, 39). When planted at medium elevations it had low yield and ordinary taste, and no one had any notion that it could possess an extraordinary flavor. The son of Price Peterson, the owner of La Esmeralda Finca, experimented with growing it at the highest elevations on their plantation and was surprised by its flavor. It is another illustration of the dynamic character of coffee. Peterson argues that the Esmeralda Gesha is not the same Gesha as the historical Gesha. This is quite possible, given how loose the names of coffee cultivars can be. Price says there are two Geshas, one with green leaves and another bronze colored (Weissman 2008, 146), and he theorizes that the British consul "probably collected them in bulk from different trees." This is an old story in the coffee business. In fact, there are three towns in Ethiopia with the names "Gesha," "Geisha," and "Gecha," and Peter Giuliano of SCA believes this Gesha is not from any one of the three!

That first Gesha auction had the cuppers—who are not supposed to speak—talking to themselves and exclaiming about the coffee in vain efforts to determine a description that would do its taste justice. The tasters recognized that they had a responsibility to describe it accurately for the world of coffee, but the flavors kept outstripping the usual categories, and the more they re-tasted the coffees, the more their confusion increased: "It got harder to distinguish differences after tasting them all on a revisit." During the 2008 Best of Panama tasting that I attended, tasters reported things like, "That was the toughest table for me in a long time." "That crazy table" came to reference a table of Gesha cups bearing unruly flavors that kept changing the meaning of the descriptors that the tasters were trying to apply to them for the purpose of defining the flavors. A taster who is faced with wild coffees can fail to keep track of everything going on, especially when there are several such coffees on a table. Even remembering which cup was doing which crazy thing can prove demanding. Some coffees have so many flavor features that some features can disguise others; not only can some features be novel, they can disappear and then reappear as the coffee cools. They set up so many possible avenues of inquiry for a taster that all of them cannot possibly be followed up adequately at the same time, and some of them are forgotten because a taster is unable to retain so many ideas at once.

If such a coffee is inconsistent across cups, sometimes presenting a sweet, fruity acidity and at other times an overripe, almost sour acidity, a taster may be challenged. It is especially problematic when a coffee displays enough promise to be truly outstanding but is inconsistent and presents some cups of lower quality. A professional taster is reluctant to dismiss or disqualify such a highly promising coffee, so they work especially hard to test the coffee's limits, even while it keeps changing the flavors it presents. Another reason for a table being crazy is when two very high scoring coffees sit next to each other on the table and present different reasons for being excellent. One cannot let the performance of one coffee cloud one's perception or opinion of the other. This task can become overwhelming for anyone.

Coffees that do not conform to usual expectations can sometimes suffer in the evaluation, but these Panamanian coffees were so clean no one could impugn them. Present were some of the world's best professional tasters, and so they were a collection of tasters who do not become disturbed easily by having their formal categories transgressed. Perullo (2012, 99) has noted that many tastes are characterized by "ungovernability" and that such tastes are not easily "dressed." Most decent tasters are capable of resisting strongly rationalized controls when those controls begin to interfere with tasting, although they acknowledge there is a necessity for them. For these tasters, the flavor will always be given precedence. Coffee people tolerate and find helpful information that is methodologically objective, but they do not easily tolerate dictates. In practice, this can be a fine line, and it is a line that is drawn differently in different parts of the world. Few tasters from the US West Coast, India, and Brazil will subordinate their free imagination to numerical routines. Some tasters are able to better tolerate what Garfinkel calls the necessary "specific vagueness" of indexical expressions, and they recognize that their purpose is to facilitate sensory evaluation and not to replace it with an analytic schema.

In Boquete, Panama, one taster told me, or rather he exclaimed to the ceiling, "I'm still trying to figure out what I tasted," and that was after an extraordinary amount of time had already been given to tasters for completing the filling out of their tasting forms. As Kierkegaard once said, "The instant of a decision is a madness" (Derrida 1992, 255). In tastings like these, the sensory analysts place more emphasis on their written "Notes" than they normally do, and the 100-point scale for numeration itself became problematic by becoming congested in the 95+ region, a part of the tasting schedule that is visited infrequently. One notation, from a US national barista competition a few years later, described a Panamanian Gesha as having "very forward flavors with intense florality," which describes it concisely.

At the present time, coffee growers are continually discovering and developing new coffee varieties for *Coffea arabica* and *Coffea canephora* in the jungles of their homelands in Ethiopia, Kenya, and Uganda, and in experimental plots around the world. The world's coffees are destined to keep changing in important ways, and some of these coffees will present novel tastes that the current palette of descriptors may not be well equipped to handle. World Coffee Research and other institutes of research have been experimenting vigorously with new hybrids that offer desirable flavors and resistance to disease. As these new strains of coffee make their way into the world's coffee plantations, new flavors will appear. One of the good things about coffee is that it is alive and still evolving, and so is able to keep surprising people.

As Perullo (2016, 157) points out, it can be helpful to have one's tasting schema interrupted and transgressed. This will disrupt the illusion that one has formulated the perfect system, a realization that will reduce the likelihood that one will become blinded by it or that the method one is using for formal assessment will obscure the coffee. Perullo (2016, 76) suggests, "Naked pleasure buzzes around awareness and sometimes puts what one knows into question." "That crazy table" is an opportunity for tasters to learn something new, which is one of their most important tasks. In the words of Hennion and Teil (2004b, 534), such a situation can even produce "the expert who has become a lover in spite of himself."

Chapter 9

Professional Tasting

> The first person who can be mistaken is me.
>
> —Franco Schillani, Trieste

Purveyors of coffee engage in two basic types of coffee tasting—tasting for defects, which comprises the preponderance of commercial tasting, and tasting for positive characteristics, which is carried out with the better coffees, including specialty coffees. Brazilian coffee professionals reported to me that in 1967 tasters had very little to do with their business—after all, the point of the coffee business for investors is to make money, not to provide good-tasting coffee. On every continent tasters find themselves at odds with their company's marketers, and few international corporations (who purvey the vast majority of the world's coffee) will permit tasters to stand in the way of maximizing profits. The result is that quantity and price levels have piloted their affairs. In recent years the coffee business has begun to pay more attention to quality, and tasters are playing an increasingly consequential role. As the importance of flavor in marketing coffee increases, exporters devote more of their time and resources to tasting; however, coffee purveyors still invest as much energy in labeling their packages as they invest in tasting for and identifying quality flavors. In lieu of purveying quality coffees, they develop packaging that simulates the presentation of quality, sometimes even featuring "single-origin" coffees. This is for a good reason: as Pendergrast (2010, 143–233) has described, marketing has always sold more coffee than flavor has. Even so, the current trend across the coffee world is for more consideration to be devoted to taste. As smaller specialty roasters establish direct-trade relations with growers of fine coffees and sales of "micro-lots" earn an increasing share of the world's exports, multinational corporations and the trade associations of exporting countries have had to investigate just what is taking place with flavor. The Colombian Federación Nacional de Café, for example, now regularly tastes samples of specialty micro-lots exported from Colombia in order to keep abreast of what flavors are finding success in the world market.

Another problem for "quality" being able to compete for attention with "quantity" is that quality is a more subjective phenomenon. In the past, purveyors have preferred to leave such decisions up to the consumers. In recent decades, professional tasters tried to develop reliable, repeatable, and discriminating methods for sensory analysis. Not only have they sought a system that is accurate, their goal is to establish a system that will produce results that are repeatable by other tasters in other locations, thereby reducing "the subjectivity" associated with discerning quality, and improving the communicability of specifications about quality. Communicability derived from a system that is shared increases the likelihood that the understanding of tastes will be elaborated and developed continuously. Well-organized coordination of investigations by a cohort of experts is an essential part of what identifies a scientific approach.

The objectivity professional coffee tasters seek is not an abstract objectivity but one that will assist them in their work of purveying coffee. They require a system that will probe flavors and allow them to retain in their minds what they have learned about the tastes of their coffees while they undertake their work of purchasing, roasting, and blending coffees. This objectivity will help them to put into effect a revised goal of trying to make profits without sacrificing the quality of the coffees' tastes. Compromises are still required, but such compromises are endogenous to creative reflection—thoughts *must* take some form, yet whatever structure results will become alienating for subsequent thinking; still, neither thinking nor its communication can proceed in the absence of some formal structure. This is a dilemma that has operated throughout human experience since the development of language.

According to Perullo (2016, 59), "Training taste means learning to perceive, recognize, and appreciate standard characteristics." In training taste this way, much is gained, and much is lost. It is the dream of the coffee industry to institute a form of objectivity in tasting that would be as stable and dependable as the platinum meter rule that sits in Paris, France, which serves as the worldwide model for measurements of length. But coffee is much more dynamic than the meter rule, and the best that the coffee industry has been able to produce are protocols, which vary by purveyor and by country. While the principal industry tasting schedules (see appendix) developed by the Specialty Coffee Association (SCA), the Cup of Excellence (COE), the

Sustainable Coffee Institute (SCI), etc. provide a basis for "objective" tasting, these forms are not always suitable for the practical bench-work of most roasters and purveyors. As Geoff Watts (2013) has explained, "The SCA, COE, and other forms . . . are not always ideal for daily quality control," because they are not sufficiently responsive to the local contingencies each firm faces. That the industry's protocols are continuously evolving, getting better over time, reveals that the objectivity of tasting protocols has been less perfect than that of the platinum rule of Paris.

The success of these protocols is related to social organization and standardization—in other words, to conformity. As Brian Ott (2018, 84) has noted, and as we have observed during our tour of the various taste preferences of nations (chapter 1), standards for quality are not identical and always "the concept of 'ideal' taste is a decision of the organization." One might have thought that consumers might rebel against standardization, but as the marketers of Starbucks in China and India predicted, they usually do not; mostly consumers will conform, possibly because they do not devote all that much attention to taste. While Starbucks's operations in each nation generally result in an improvement of the quality of coffee and they treat their exporters with respect, they have taken an inflexible and essentially imperialist stand by insisting that they know better than their Chinese and Indian partners what tastes the Chinese and Indian coffee drinkers prefer. While the Indians have been more compliant than the Chinese with the demands of Starbucks tasters located in Switzerland and Seattle, in the end the taste preferences of Starbucks's first-world marketers has prevailed over the taste recommendations of the third-world purveyors. Further, when it comes to quality in coffee, standardization and objectivity are frequently conflated, and most decisions are economic, not aesthetic.

This study of the work tasters and of professional protocols could not have been made without the instruction, assistance, patience, and self-revelations of hundreds of professional tasters I befriended in 14 countries. Much as Garfinkel (2002, 271) once noted with regard to the bench-work of physicists, to make the work of professional tasters visible and adequately articulate, to make them "examinable," requires the disciplinary expertise of *both* professional tasters and sociologists, as a collaborative project. The tasters may know what they are doing, but they do not necessarily know that they know, since much of their knowledge is tacit, unreflective experience; the ethnomethodologist is capable of identifying many of the key aspects of organizing bench-work interaction and the local work of producing shared knowledge. Together we are able to learn more than either would be able to learn separately. I am grateful that most coffee tasters were as eager as I was to explore the issues that motivate this research.

Protocols: Giving the Subject the Agency

A tasting protocol is a methodic procedure that helps one to break down the character of the bean. Such a procedure is an organized activity performed by a person, or persons who act in concert, and thus in its essence it is human subjectivity at work. A protocol relies on socially developed and socially approved practices for maintaining tight control over the worldly things that are being examined and that portend disorder at every turn. The reader will recall the Italian taster Luigi Odello's definition of a protocol: "a rigorous procedure developed primarily for the purpose of obtaining a demonstrable qualitative standard." It is the aim of a protocol to turn a qualitative experience (one could simply say "experience" since all experience is qualitative) into reliable, objective, and socially sharable knowledge, or what Earle (1955, 47) calls, "the explicit objectification of what is implicit." This does not happen without consequences, and as with the application of any system of rationality, there are significant losses and significant gains.

Taste and smell are wild and involve the more primitive "reptilian" part of the brain. If one's aim is to control tastes, then it is better that *visual* activity be given priority over gustatory and olfactory experience. Protocols and tasting schedules that require elaborate calculations allow the visual to reassert priority and permit conceptualization to eclipse the pre-conceptual realms of tasting and smelling. They provide an organization of experience and knowing practices. Calculative methods of knowing are preferred by scientists, and by this time most humans as well. This preference for visual knowing has resulted in a gradual biological diminution of the human sensory capacities for smell, which over the course of recent evolution has produced corresponding genetic transformations. And yet, as one especially capable and broad-minded professional taster in Boquete, Panama, advised me, tasting without having an effective means of keeping track of what one has found, especially which coffees were better and which ones worse, will result in wasted effort. "You need a system," he said. The objectivity of this taster was a practical objectivity: he needs to purvey coffee. Dr. Enrico Meschini expressed a similar sentiment: "I strongly believe in having a very set form that actually works for you, but the ideal does not exist." As we are saying, you have to have a system, and every system will be flawed. While these tasting protocols vary by tasting lab and by country, what is most essential is that each lab's system operates in a consistent manner so that the coffees they examine can be compared, both with each other and with themselves over more than a single season.

The Coherence of a Coffee's Taste: Giving the Object the Agency

The first mission of any protocol is to make contact with the taste, i.e., with the coherence of the transcendental object in one's mouth. A good protocol does not simply produce objective knowledge, it produces objective knowledge *about taste*, which requires that an investigation of a coffee never abandon the local *endogenous coherence* of what is being tasted. Because coffee is dynamic, this coherence does keep shifting, but that does not relieve a professional taster of this responsibility. COE head taster Scott Conary perhaps formulated the project best (see chapter 5): "Cupping is an exercise in trying to be objective about a moving target."

If one is tasting properly, the coffee speaks first; that is, the agency is given to the object and not to the investigator, whose primary task is only to respond to the coherence of the coffee's taste. The taste of the coffee possesses an integrity that should not be subjected to too many conceptual manipulations. This means that original coherence does not come from outside the experience, by rule or by principle. Harold Garfinkel (1993b) has written, "The coherence arose and was given in and as the stream of perception and was not needed in an exterior provision. It didn't then enter the stream of perceiving in order to provide for what the coherence was, but the coherence was already given." The "already given" attests to the agency that *the object* possesses, and this is part of what founds objectivity. This conforms with the written advisory instruction given to all Cup of Excellence tasters: "Be honest with the coffee."

It happens often that the coffee itself, in its singularity, directs the taster to the pertinent priorities. Standards are useful, but in the end each coffee must invent its own criteria. Tension between standardization and a coffee's singularity is fundamental to assessing coffee, and in fact is without remedy. A taste can draw the analysts' attention away from the form and the analyst's routines for applying abstract categories. The initial sensory experience of a sampled coffee takes place prior to a taster's recording the sensation on the tasting form with the pencil. One can witness professional tasters stalled at the outset of their work, apparently waiting for this initial coherency of the flavors to congeal in their minds before attempting to determine conclusive numerical assessment. There seems to be a gulf between the subcortical experience and the work of translating that experience into logical, formalized terms. Professional tasters enjoy this work—"This cupping form is one of my favorite things. I enjoy working with it"—perhaps because of the ways the different parts of the brain are set into correspondence with each other. Before this occurs, tasters can appear paralyzed, with their pencils suspended in the air, and the indecisiveness of the occasion is where much of the creativity of professional tasting takes place. Derrida (1992, 24–25) offers some insight about this situation: "The indecidable remains caught, lodged, as a ghost at least, but an essential ghost, in every decision, in every event of decision. Its ghostliness deconstructs from within all assurance of presence, all certainty or all alleged criteriology assuring us of the justice of a decision." Tasters use the categories and a criteriology, but justice will always exceed these.

The smell of a coffee serves as the initial guide for most tasters. Before sipping the coffee, tasters commence their assessment nose-first: they smell the powder (called "fragrance"), then they smell the brewing cups ("aroma"), and many smell the back side of the cupping spoon right after some stirring as if it held secrets more precious than tea leaves read by a Scottish Highlands tasseographer. By this time an expert taster will have appropriated an arsenal of intuitions, which the taster follows up while taking a highly aerated sip that is absorbed by the retronasal cavity at the back of the mouth, before spitting out the coffee into the spittoon. The better tasters prefer to be led instead of leading, which places them into conflict with the praxis of some sensory scientists; both an active and a passive synthesis are required, and the tension between the singularity of the coffee and the demand for standardization is always center stage. Most professional tasters do not want their labeling to dictate the terms of what they have experienced; rather, as I have been instructed many times, they prefer that the taste itself speak. One detects a taste, experiences its coherence on its own, and only then goes searching for a fitting descriptor—is there some "limescale"? Is it astringent or acidic?

While this activity of turning the flavor of a coffee into a notional unity is both passive and active, according to Husserl the passive operates first, and various sensory observations seem to find their way to a unitary synthesis mostly on their own, "endogenously" as Garfinkel has described it. The hesitation of tasters, which at times can approach aphasia, derives from having to abandon productive passive syntheses and enter the professional world of control. Many immediately intuit the distortions they may be introducing, which trouble them. Once that world is entered, the descriptors they may develop for describing the coherence become subject to further intersubjective confirmation, criticism, and general semiosis, including unavoidable references to the standard professional itineraries of descriptors and terminology of all sorts. It is here that *the subjectivity* that is a protocol waxes powerful, and from that point, which is an era of active synthesis, the more immanent field of passive synthesis is left behind.

The work of developing a value structure for each tasting category one assesses can result in postponing attending closely to the flavor's coherence. Generally, a professional taster experiences the flavor first, and does not directly run to numeration. Perullo's distinction between "naked taste" and "dressed taste" is apt here, and it is better that the dressed taste comes after the naked taste, although it is nearly impossible. This is comparable to Husserl's suspension of belief. Tasting without the professional grammars does not necessarily mean that one is tasting directly: it can be that one does not notice anything. To be sure, verbal formulations and knowledge lead us to notice flavors, and tasting directly is a difficult phenomenological project. Formal processes of sensory analysis can contribute their own hermeneutic benefits, especially when employed by adept tasters. Numerical knowledge also can lead to noticings and come to have hermeneutic import, but only if the integrity of the objectivity of the object, which is rooted in its agency, continues to be respected.

Rationality and Tasting

The rationalization of tasting relies on a methodical process of converting subjective awareness into objective understanding. As the Trieste taster Franco Schillani phrased it (see introduction), "I am seeking the maximum objective expression of subjectivity." To be professional is to be standardized and calibrated to a social system. One can be original, but that originality needs to be socialized. When asked to explain his method for assessing coffee, Lorenzo Martinelli, the second-generation owner of Omkafe (a coffee roasting factory in Arco, Italy), silently gestured to his tongue, then to his brain, and finally to his heart. It is highly significant that when describing how one organizes one's understanding of the taste of coffee, the activity is glossed by gestures to both the brain and the heart. There is rationality at work, but the rationality does not stand unaccompanied.

Professional tasters aim at taste, but what they do is "tasting," which is a highly structured, formal event. Tasting begins with a taste in the cup, but this taste is submitted to a highly organized meaning system, "a dressed taste" in Perullo's terminology, which is a social artifact. Using the pedagogy of Garfinkel, we can depict how taste is dressed by a protocol: taste → [taste]. The taste in the brackets is not the same taste as the taste before it is reduced in this way. Enrico Meschini of Livorno has developed the habit of calling what lies in the brackets "the form's taste" (*scheda assaggio*). This recalls Adorno's description (from chapter 3) of the two objectivities, the real objectivity and the methodologically derived objectivity. Both tastes are real things in the world, and taste requires this sort of treatment by a protocol in order for it to be communicated, but the naked taste and the dressed taste should not be conflated.

This is not the end of the itinerary of tastes, because the methodologically achieved, professionally dressed taste is then handed over to advertisers and marketers, is further idealized, iconized, and in the form of signs and rumors made to play a public role in the wider world of coffee purveying. The [taste] of the protocol gets twisted into idiosyncratic uses that carry the meaning even further away from the taste that was in the cup: taste → [taste] → "taste."

I should add a clarifying note for social scientists who are reading this that none of these three are Bourdieu's "taste." In the world of coffee, there is a great deal of talk about taste, and conflation of these semantic fields produces enough confusion that ordinary consumers who might be interested in thinking about taste become discouraged.

Luigi Odello of Brescia has explained, "Part of the task of the commercial purveying of coffee consists of taming and rendering stable an objective taste that can be marketed." Every taster, every brand, every café, and every coffee bar wants to give a taste an identity. Peet's Coffee, Dunkin' Donuts, Starbucks, etc. all offer coffees whose taste is faithful to their identity no matter which of their establishments one visits, and this is accomplished by employing the professional methods of their tasters. In Odello's terms, they have "tamed" their coffees by means of their tasting protocols. The objectivity of the flavor is the product of a method, something that is guaranteed in advance, and so it is the result of a subjective activity. In spite of an objectivist metaphysics that pretends that the objectivity of the flavor is what comes first, the flavors discovered in the transcendent object (the coffee in the cup) are mostly founded on the methodology of the sensory assessment, and these active subjective practices are responsible for producing those objective and reproducible results. By this fact, any dualist ideology is discredited. Heidegger

(1967, 102) has commented keenly, "Method is not one piece of equipment of science among others but the primary component out of which is first determined what can become object and how it becomes an object."

A protocol is knowledge-instigated tasting of a particular sort. It is not uncommon for a disciplined taster who is engaging in some formal analysis to lose contact with the first of the three tastes of our diagram. Perullo (2018a, 84) says, "Sensory assessments *are something made*, as elaborations that never place us in direct contact with reality but rather with the presumption that we can objectify it from the outside, from above, with a neutral and detached gaze."

The work of professional coffee tasters includes developing categories of flavor using precise descriptive adjectives for taste that are standardized, and this precision is a strange thing. The sociologist Steven Shapin (2011, 7–8) reports that the professional taster relies on a specialized vocabulary as well as concepts for orienting to taste, and he suggests that whatever is in people's heads (even lay tasters) as they put things in their mouths influences what is being tasted. We have already observed that without categories, no data can be intelligible, and categories developed by cognitive intuition are always subjective things. As the philosopher William Earle (1955, 91) writes, "The precise characterization of sense data involves using all sorts of categories which could not themselves be the data of any sense." In this way, there is a mixing of "top-down" and "bottom-up" work using categories to clarify, organize, and communicate particulars, even as those particulars continuously influence the categories.

The processes by which a system of classification is made authoritative are social and political and involve a confirmation that operates largely outside of the realm of direct tasting. While the guarantor of truth is the tasters' tasting, this original empirical moment is transported swiftly to approved semiotic spheres of professional sensory assessment, where it can lose itself. Odello (2009, 5, my translation) describes this process well: "A mental grammar leads tasters to ask continuously how the sensory characteristics can be made determinate." This kind of professional practice has led Perullo (2012, 43) to develop the term "the grammarian taster" for those who reproduce the perspectives of "the books that teach syntactical correctness," and in this way, "tasting would become an activity of control: measuring the adherence of tastes to this grammar" (Perullo 2012, 31). As Steven Wright (2014, 68) tells us, "The decision on *'Which beer is best?'* is based less on the personal whim of the judges and more on how well the entered beer matches world class commercial examples of the style."

The Priority of the Rational

Drinking coffee is not primarily about reason, although whenever humans are involved, organized knowledge will usually take over the scene. Pleasure and knowledge cohabit experience, and according to Perullo (2016, 126) neither should try to operate alone. Not everything in the world requires being controlled, although this has not been the predilection of politicians and scientists since the start of the Enlightenment. While it can be appropriate to surrender control sometimes, especially if one is a drinker, no Cup of Excellence winner has ever been produced exclusive of some rational controls, and those are some pretty fine coffees.

It is a contradiction for professional tasters to rationalize their work even while offering the universal advice to not think while tasting. As we cited in part I, Manuel Diaz advises, "To cup well you need to use your senses, not your thinking." And Odello warns his students, "If you think too much your nose will get tricked." Why then does so much rationality surround professional tasting? It is because if one kept the mind entirely in check, one would never learn anything. Unfortunately, philosophy and sophistry always arrive at the dance as partners, much as justice and law do. In truth, a tasting schedule, which is the product of rationality, must find its accuracy and precision somewhere beyond reason, in how professional tasters use them. Effective use of the form is informed by "contact with that pre-reflexive ingenuity that characterizes an infant's gaze" (Perullo 2016, 76). A group of elderly Brazilian tasting experts once declared to me that their preferred form was a blank piece of paper.

One of the main purposes of rationality is to service communication. A slide presented at a course offered by San Salvador's Escuela de Café (cited in Dougherty 2008, 78) read, "A certain *standard* must exist so that expert cuppers and producers can communicate their preferences to one another." The president of the British beer association BJCP, Gordon Strong, has written similarly, "Beer styles are part of a structured method for categorizing and describing beer. They are intended to be a convenient shorthand for discussing beer, and to allow all who taste the beer to be able to describe it using a common framework and language . . . providing a frame of reference" (Wright 2014, 17). The depth of this observation—that providing a common frame of reference competes with truth as a motive for using formal analysis—needs to be fully appreciated. Normally we think that logic and rationality are employed in order to determine the truth; however, competing with this function is the contribution that formal analytic schemata offer to parties who are seeking to communicate and to think collaboratively. I have described the minute ethnomethodological details of logic in my monograph on Tibetan logicians at work (Liberman 2004, 176–194 and 230), where I describe how the Tibetan scholar-monks formulate their epistemological insights in logical terms so that their collaborative thinking can be kept organized, so that these ideas can be shared and discussed in their formal public debates on philosophical topics, a customary practice that is more than 800 years old. Throughout their debates, logic serves as *an organizational device* as much as it is a method for determining truth.

Another example of rationalizing thinking is musical notation. Musical notation is more than simply a representation, it is a translation of musical ideas. The formal notation can offer assistance to musicians and provide a place for them to begin their consideration of a composition. It adds value but only so long as it does not replace the motivating musical insights; otherwise, it will kill the goose that lays the golden eggs. Some commentators on music assert that the tonal elasticity and rhythmic vitality of the blues cannot be translated into the language of musical notation. Of course it can, but the notation will always fall short, just as it will with classical composition. The truth of music is located over its course, in and as its flow, which is something that is lived through. Music can be fragmented and denoted, but following our diagram, that would be an instance of music → [music]. Aron Gurwitsch (1964, 256) offers the illustrative case of the final note of a melody, which can be an isolated, individual note at the moment that it strikes the ear. To be strictly empirical, at that moment it is the only note. Shall we give the note a numerical rating (perhaps on an 8-point scale)? Gurwitsch observes that what is important about that isolated note is that it is vivified by the entire melody, which provides that note its sense and reference. How helpful would it be to separate out each note of a musical score and give each one its own numerated assessment, and then add them together in order to determine a defining total score? How closely would that unity conform with the naturally occurring unity of the melody? Neither music nor life works in that way, so why should the taste of coffee? It would require more than the single rating category of "Overall" (also limited to 8 points) to remedy the damage done to the integrity of the experience.

Reason, logic, and the standardization of judgments influence experience, sometimes positively, but they should not exceed experience nor be divorced from it. Language can be used to teach and to learn tastes, and by oneself the growth of one's tasting acumen is condemned to remain limited. Accordingly, standardization is unavoidable and even beneficial. Professional tasters do listen to each other and do learn from each other. Some of the time "an assertive approach" (Perullo 2016, 131) that in the interest of "objectivity" seeks an immediate consensus can make an important contribution, but it is reluctant to ever *let loose* its firm grasp of things or to remain open to experiencing what it does not know. As Robert Barker (2017, 298) has suggested, "Approach each coffee with an open mind," which may require the taster to tone down the assertiveness. Further, one must be willing to acknowledge that the produced objectivity is the product of a social system and not some magical artifact that can be made to stand alone. This is not any fault with the methodology for producing objectivity, it is simply the way things are. It is nothing that can be remedied, although one attempts remedies, without relief; but in the end, they will not change matters. More important than these remedies is to remain clear-minded about the actual ontology of the objectivities one has produced.

A Starbucks taster once told me, "When the form is complex, it is more objective." It is true that when a form is not complicated, one usually needs to be an insider to understand what is being recorded. On the other hand, while a complicated methodology can produce a momentary unity of knowledge, the communicability of the "objective" results it produces may suffer, and this will defeat one of the purposes of objectivity. We always need to ask ourselves, what does "objective" mean each occurrence we speak of it; here it means that the meaning is available to anyone and has been made less vulnerable to local interpretations. But local interpretations will never disappear altogether. The Seattle and Lausanne labs of Starbucks sometimes disagree about the assessment of a coffee, and their disagreements can be plagued not only by differing opinions but by poor communication, since communicating the findings of tasting can get lost inside of a methodology that is too complicated, which will take a toll on the resulting product. Hence, the shortcomings of the simpler forms, which operate in ways that are indexed to local circumstances, will not be evaded entirely. The momentary comprehensive unity of knowledge that the protocols produce is available to a cohort of sensory scientists who work together at the same time and at the same place. As Franco Schillani insisted, "All the people need to know perfectly what the numbers mean," and such perfection happens best when the collaboration is face-to-face. The coherency of the taste is something that gets organized locally by persons who collaborate in producing that coherency. Halfway around the world there may be a second cohort of sensory scientists who have slightly different local solutions, even when they are working with the same basic protocol. In both cases there is an identified flavor of the coffee, but the two descriptions may not necessarily be identical. Oddly, variation like this often leads professional tasters to make new discoveries about the coffee.

Objectivity and Routines

Surrounding these inquiries has been the question of what kind of tasting is subjective and what kind is objective, and our investigations have led us to conclude that a dualistic ontology is insupportable, for the reason that there is never subjectivity without objectivity nor objectivity without subjectivity. Some coffee purveyors have proposed to me that tasting is subjective while taste is objective, but that is nothing more than rhetoric. We need to move past this dualism if we are to discover just how taste is known. Objective knowledge can be produced, but wherever objective knowledge is produced, it is subjectivity that put it there.

Protocols make their most important contribution to developing objective knowledge when they *heighten our relationships with objects*, instead of making the coffee more remote. In fact, most professional tasters are quite good at accomplishing this, and they pursue tastes with more determination than the cookie monster exhibits in his pursuit of cookies. In every tasting lab in the world I have visited, tasters will regularly acquire higher-scoring coffees that they have never before tasted and are not like any of the coffees they handle regularly, in order to examine and learn new characteristics and qualities. They keep abreast of the times this way. If they can, they will cup them using the same form that the international judges used, in order to try to better reproduce the perspective of the judges that led them to their evaluation; however, the taste of the coffee will necessarily exceed the taste of the form. An unfamiliar, winning coffee is like a wilderness to such tasters, and the cupping of one becomes an occasion for collaborative instruction about tastes. Coffees can be assessed by rules or protocols, but their actual value, their real objectivity, is to be discovered by tasting them freshly. The protocols influence the thinking and experience of the tasters, but the coffee has agency too.

Some expert tasters are more fixated on forms than others, and a few hold on to the form out of "the fear of losing the objective knowledge" (Perullo 2012, 39). Tasters routinize their thoughts in order to use them, especially in factory production. But routines can breed stupidity. Taking refuge in routines can numb one's subjectivity, and a deadened subjectivity will lead to superficial sensory analysis. Here we discover the paradox that a mechanical style of working and thinking can sometimes be used to assess a coffee effectively. While describing how in early 20th-century science a mechanical objectivity supplanted for scientists the "truth-to-nature" objectivity, Daston and Galison (2010, 370) explain that only mechanical procedures were thought to be capable of evading bias. Some professional tasting can transform a mundane drinker seeking a pleasurable experience into a passively registering machine that is accustomed to applying this mechanistic objectivity. "By *mechanical objectivity* we mean the insistent drive to repress the willful intervention of the artist-author, and to put in its stead a set of procedures that would, as it were, move nature to the page through a strict protocol, if not automatically" (Daston and Galison 2010, 121). This works for removing the influence of unwanted subjectivity, but it may also remove desirable subjectivity by confining the purview of the tasting. Eventually most scientists abandoned the blind sight of mechanical objectivity in favor of trained judgment (Daston and Galison 2010, 342).

On many occasions, there are too many coffees and too little time for being very refined, and so one must be methodical if one is to be comprehensive about more than a dozen aspects of flavor to be attended to faithfully for 40 sample cups of coffee; nevertheless, a "purely mechanical" practice that might seem less subjective may occlude a more thorough sensory evaluation. Garfinkel (1956, 186) speaks of "routine as a necessary condition of rational actions": what is central about routines is that *they make it easier for people to concert their actions.* "The stability of social routines is a condition which enables persons to recognize each other's actions, beliefs, aspirations, feelings and the like as reasonable, normal, legitimate, understandable, and realistic" (Garfinkel 1956, 187). Fortunately, there is something in the temperament of coffee tasters that resists excessive routinization. One senior taster reported to me, "After nearly 20 years of cupping coffee on an almost daily basis, it still never becomes automatic." The tensions of professional tasting, which are never resolved fully by either artisans or scientists, are analogous to the tensions that are present in all social life.

There is tasting willfully, as Husserl might have described it, which is tasting during which "the active, strivingly active ego appropriates to itself an acquisition" (Husserl 2001, 95), and there is tasting that is performed without much thinking. These are two different kinds of tasting. It is the task of professional tasters to convert what is automatic into what is educated. The Argentinian journalist Nicolás Artusi (2014, 342, my translation) describes it well: "The automatic ritual, unconsciously and unreflectingly drinking some coffee, transforms it into a unique sort of *expertise* from which emerge a variety of spices, origins, countries, plantations, cultivars, washed and unwashed varieties, and toasts." In fact, real competence cannot be made automatic; it is something hard-earned *and requires continual self-criticism* as well as being open for what one does not yet know. The goal of routines is to assist one to assess coffee quality consistently and accurately, i.e., to rate coffee flavor attributes in a consistent manner. But the skilled taster understands that, in Emerson's words (1907, 89), "A foolish consistency is the hobgoblin of little minds." Here, as always, the tastes must reign supreme.

Judgment is a routinized, repeated and repeatable, confirmed and confirmable, scrutiny that often reaches accurate accounts by rote, but may exclude insight; or rather, it is better to ask, how can we keep ourselves open for insights while we are judging? Judgment is essentially a subjectively objective act, and tasting protocols are subjective procedures that have become reified. This is why tasters sometimes complain about being "coerced" by the form. Judgment is made useful because people know how to *use* rules, how to think with them while not becoming trapped by them. William Earle (1955, 133) advises, "No propositional calculus . . . can supply any guarantee whatsoever of the truth. Truth must be *seen*." Derrida concurs: "Justice can always be reappropriated by the most perverse calculation, [but] incalculable justice *commands* calculation. . . . Not only *must* one calculate, negotiate the relation between the calculable and the incalculable, and negotiate without a rule . . . one *must* do so beyond the already identifiable zones" (Derrida 1992, 257). It is not like there is an objective machine that simply produces facts by itself without human hands, although this sort of mythology is not absent among coffee tasters. Routine calculations and what is "beyond the already identifiable zones" coexist.

What is it to be "professional"? Professionalization has something to do with having made one's peace with uniform, standardized, and commercialized systems that are organized in formally structured ways that render it more difficult to tune in to local particulars. Professional routines are oriented toward making matters safe and predictable. Regrettably, professionalism often has to do with cultivating a disposition to conform to the policies and wills of those who hold positions of power (a.k.a. pandering to authority). As Wright (2014, 232) has observed about the exam for certification as a professional beer taster, "The taste exam assesses much *other* than tasting and discrimination ability, rather it tests knowledge of the language of the style guide." Professionalism also has something to do with science, but one cannot ignore its relation to the economic and political hierarchies that exist everywhere. Sometimes professionalism bears an identifying personality: confidence and being "self-assured" (Daston and Galison 2010, 370). But it also is characterized by an inclination to suspend self-interest in the search for truth.

Open Intersubjectivity

Science is ultimately rooted in a "community of scientific activity" (Husserl 1970a, 130). For example, Ott (2018, 69) reports, "The barista's sensory capacity is bound in a way of tasting that is standardized across employees," and it is from this community that it derives insights, learns to become objective, and engages in a dialectical development that conducts the parties to important discoveries. It is not that the scores in themselves provide so much, but that when scores differ, they call for more careful attention and prompt one to make further inquiries. It is like shining a headlight on an aspect of taste. In this way, a tasting schedule can play a crucial role in assessment. Its contribution, however, is not the result of an inherent objectivity; rather, it consists of the practical consequences of how the form is being used to facilitate and promote communication and discussion in ways that are beneficial for understanding a coffee.

When a taste is stuck fast in some original indeterminacy, tasters turn to intersubjective discussion, as demonstrated by a group of Italian tasters who relied on cooperative inspection to confirm for themselves the objectivity of their fresh insights and for sustaining the momentum of a developing taste descriptor. After sampling some fresh coffee, one taster announced tentatively, "Could it be a bit grainy? I'm not sure, I found something like that." After a second taster declared "Yes, I found it too," the taste descriptor "grainy" won an ongoing life in the collaboration. After the coffee grew cold, minutes later the first taster elaborated, "At first I didn't really know what I originally meant when I said 'grainy' or something like that." The second taster confirmed again, "Me too," which still sustained the credence of the emerging account. The first taster continued, "And in fact now I seem to sense something inside that is sort of powdery, I don't know." The descriptive account has *a developing objectivity* that gains status over the course of the discussion. In fact, all descriptors and all numerical scales possess a developing objectivity that are subject to continual revision. In another case, an Italian taster had awarded the first coffee on the table with the highest rating that "aftertaste" could achieve. When she found that the third sample on the table possessed an even better aftertaste, she erased the first score, lowered it one point, and then handed the maximum score over to the third coffee. In this way, "objective" ratings are reciprocally determining and remain in evolution, which is why they are developingly objective. This bolsters the conclusion that the objectivity of tasting is not something that appears magically but is a practical achievement of the parties.

Numerations operate similarly, and they derive much of their efficacy by how they offer occasions for noticings and how they can promote closer examination and collaboration. The score itself may not be where the value of numeration lies; rather, its vital contribution can rest in how it *creates saliencies* that attract the parties' attention. Some tasting pedagogies lean heavily on numerals, but parties are thinking and communicating as they use numbers, so the sense and reference of the numbers is not independent of their intersubjective relations; however, the numbers may lose their reference after they sit in the firm's file of records for a period of time.

Intersubjectivity is an engine of sensory assessment, especially when the intersubjectivity is open to what is emerging in the situation, which Husserl (cited in Zahavi 2001, 51) named "open intersubjectivity": "Every appearance that I have is from the very beginning a member of an open, endless range of possible experiences of the same, and the subjectivity of these appearances is the *open intersubjectivity*." It is this open intersubjectivity that conducts parties to important discoveries. The process of producing objectivities is never completed.

Tasters are always teaching each other, and so discussion plays a vital role in the developing objectivity of a sensory assessment. When tasters employ cautious self-protection, instruction that otherwise might take place is stifled. Few tasters make an assertion without downgrading it with qualifying terms like "maybe," "it seems," and especially "for me," as in "It is highly bitter, for me." This is designed to mute any criticism, since it is acknowledged that a person is the best authority of what that person is experiencing, but this can preclude criticism that could be productive for the work of tasting. Instruction that might have taken place is moderated by this gambit that tasters use to protect themselves. However, even when downgrading one's assessment, these discursive devices can promote productive discussion, as in "Kind of like papaya, I get, a little bit" or "For a millisecond it tasted a little lemony to me." Padding one's account with qualifiers like "millisecond," "a little," and "to me" is a safe way to position a perspective in the ken of other tasters; without exposing oneself by making a firm public commitment, one can still initiate some open collaboration by parties.

The Tasting Protocol

A tasting protocol is a strategy for investigating flavor, a strategy for *probing* the reality of a coffee. Hence, a protocol is not only about judgment: it is a hermeneutic probe. It is on this basis that tasting protocols are embraced enthusiastically by most professional tasters. The quotidian tasks of a professional taster are directed toward clearly experiencing immanently perceived flavors, and the taster needs to locate not only the dominant flavors but also secondary taste characteristics. Although sommeliers are sometimes accepted as a model for professional coffee tasting, in fact coffee is more complex than either wine or beer (Watts 2013). In addition, the taste of wine endures on the palate longer than the taste of coffee does, making it more obvious than the taste of coffee. Tasting forms can help professional tasters to keep track of a coffee's complexity, especially that of the secondary characteristics.

The usefulness of these forms rests primarily in helping tasters concentrate their attention upon the tasting. A good protocol fosters intimacy with the flavors. Odello (2008, 5) has called coffee tasters "superior explorers." Analytic thinking can provide an assist, but the task is fundamentally exploratory and hermeneutic, and a taster must be careful to use formal analysis without allowing it to distract the exploring. Protocols are oriented to identifying the characteristics of a coffee and enhancing the taster's focus, but there is a danger that they will take over. Protocols can be made to work successfully, but the crux of that success lies in *how they are made to work* by professional tasters who know how to use them. Tasters have advised me with enthusiasm, "A format really helps you break down the character of the bean," explaining that tasting is "all about being organized." However, being organized does not guarantee that we fully appreciate the flavors. This work of "being organized" will be impotent if the tasting is subordinated: instead of being a taster, one can be transformed into an accountant.

A form and the protocol that accompanies it are critical for exploring a coffee, and it is exploration that matters most. Their success is not because the tasting schedules produce numbers or that numeration is superior to other forms of evaluation; rather, the numerating directs the tasters' attention deeply inside the coffee, permitting the tasters to inspect what is happening there. As *an organizational object*, i.e., a tool that helps tasters to keep their explorations organized, a good protocol will lead to an enhancement of subjectivity, not to subjectivity's removal. The tasting forms work, but the question here is just *how* they work.

One can have a good result with using numbers, and one can have a good result without using numbers; consequently, something more than numeration alone must be involved in successful tasting. Both qualitative and quantitative evaluations can contribute to understanding a coffee. They can call attention to certain salient features of taste and provoke discussion about them. It is not the rating by itself but the social interaction that the ratings prompt that makes them valuable. While numerated evaluations provide an indication to roasters and purveyors about a place where they can begin their explorations, the written notes and lexical descriptors that also appear on a tasting form can suggest just how the coffee in question might be usable in their blends or in their café. For instance, the descriptor "hazelnut" might offer a coffee retailer more specificity than a score will. "Above all, written comments are most valuable for cup-to-cup comparisons, ratings, and rankings" (Barker 2017, 285), although both comments and numeration together can convey more than either can separately. Manuel Diaz comments about this situation: "You cannot do descriptive analysis without using qualitative descriptors as well as quantitative ones." One limitation of exclusively quantitative tasting is that it tends to reduce one's tasting to liking and not liking. Diaz once scolded his students, who were seeking certification as Robusta graders: "You are not consumers, you are tasters. When you are a good taster, you are capable of describing all the good flavor in the cup." Purveyors use a numerical score to help them decide whether it is worth their time to taste a coffee. Especially when they are seeking a particular feature for a blend (e.g., sweetness, body, crema, appearance, acidity), a numerical value for these categories can lead them to select particular coffees for further investigation. Qualitative descriptors provide them a clue about which features to search for.

An important skill in tasting coffee is to be able to detect complex and excellent tastes that reside underneath a veil of defects that may come from beans that can be edited, defects such as quakers (underdeveloped beans) or flaws produced by the roasting, etc. Some flaws due to processing can be remedied, and a professional taster should be able to distinguish these and also determine how much work a shipment of coffee will require to make it serviceable. A green coffee having minor flaws might be available at a lower price level, and it is the skill of the professional taster that discerns such an opportunity. It should be observed that tasters not only assess the coffee that is in front of them but also consider what the coffee can become after it has received proper editing. Similar judgments need to be made about what the roasting and blending can do for each coffee being tasted. Most tasting protocols call for tasting coffees that have been given a light roast ("to first crack or a little after," Schillani 1999, 14) because it permits the taster to understand all the characteristics, even though many coffees, especially in Italy, will be given a darker roast. Judging the potential of a sampled coffee under circumstances that are not present demands that subjectivity not be separated from objectivity.

Some of the world's tasters have peculiar ways of making assessments. As we described in chapter 7, the smell and even the feel of green beans provide important clues. On occasion, instead of scores, buyers and tasters employ such tangible techniques for selecting the coffees they choose to purchase. Buyers from Turkey sometimes taste the dry instant powder with their index finger and the tip of their tongue and make their purchase without cupping, and Saudi Arabian buyers will make large purchases based on chewing some roasted beans. Specialty coffees and trade coffees receive vastly different treatment, and some commercial quality coffees are purchased without any contact with the bean at all (the only contact is with the price board that appears on one's computer screen)—these are sometimes called "price coffees."

Humility

One of the first characteristics of professional tasters that caught my attention was that the complexity of the tastes of coffees renders most tasters humble about the sensory assessments they put forward. One of the first things Franco Schillani of Trieste told me was "The first person who is mistaken is me." For this reason, most professional tasters respect the viewpoints of other tasters, including novice tasters. Tasters are all about the coffee, and few of them have large egos that require constant protection. I cannot think of another profession that sustains humility to this same degree. Marcio Hazan of Santos, a senior taster who grew up tasting coffee in the firm of his father, told me, "Am I feeling correctly what is in the cup, or am I making a mistake? Then I listen to the others, and often cup it again. I can learn from you as much as you can learn from me." This sentiment was echoed by Vince Fedele in a 2010 talk to the Specialty Coffee Association: "A team approach to tasting is best: I don't believe in the golden tongue."

Another taster offered the advice, "The first step in becoming a great cupper is to have a profound recognition that we are all flawed." Prof. Nicola Perullo (2012, 87) agrees: "We are all naked and equal in power." Nearly every tasting lab of every importer, exporter, or roaster that I have visited—and there have been hundreds of them—operate with a camaraderie that exceeds the social solidarity that is necessary for running a business. There has always been a deep commitment, a sense of mutual responsibility, and genuine respect for fellow tasters. Tasters are sometimes competitive in their enthusiasm for their ideas about the coffees they are tasting, but above all they perform their work with respect for each other and a willingness to learn because the coffee always offers more than they have understood, and they especially respect the head taster, the taster who really knows and is willing to share what he or she knows. This respect for elders sometimes recalls the respect for lamas and gurus that I witnessed in Tibetan monasteries. On the wall of the tasting lab of one exporter in Santos, Brazil, was the photograph of the former head taster of the lab, not yet deceased, encircled by a garland, much in the way that portraits of Catholic saints are hung on living room walls. The devotion the tasters felt for this figure that adorned their labors was almost spiritual, and respect like this can serve to diminish egoism.

One of the early field research attempts I made was at the main roasting facility of a chain of gourmet coffee shops in Oregon, Allann Bros Coffee. After explaining my research into tasting to the founder and owner, I requested permission to observe his tasting lab. While friendly (and supportive through the years of this research), he replied, "I can't do that." I asked him, "Why not?" He explained, "That's a sacred space in there. It's fine to have a research interest, but that is not sufficient respect for entry." His notion was that there was something transcendent taking place in his coffee tasting lab, something that should not be subjected to trivialization. I think now I understand that coffee is so multifaceted, so subtly complicated, that it will confound mundane inspection. The head scientist at Colombia's Federación Nacional de Café, Rodrigo Alarcón, once explained to me, "Coffees are like human beings. If you try to rank human beings, you will understand well that you cannot easily compare one with another. They are each the best at their own particular style. But they are all different. And it is the same with coffee. Each coffee smells and tastes different, just as everyone of us is different." Without having already cultivated this sort of respect, the owner of Allann Bros did not want me inside his cupping room. He suggested that I return after I learned more.

More Details of Tasting Practices

MUNDANE SKILLS

Throughout these inquiries, our approach—ethnomethodology—is more than a form of participant observation with salt on its tail. It undertakes phenomenologically shrewd inquiries that derive and maintain their orientation from "the looks of the world" (as Garfinkel often termed it) for the people they are studying. This is consonant with the dictum of phenomenology to describe affairs in the very way that they show themselves from themselves (Heidegger 1996, 30). Accordingly, we are less interested in what professional tasters and sensory analysts say that they do than in what they do. A study of praxis like this examines doings, i.e., matters lived through in their course, as much as it considers concepts and theories.

In chapter 4 we described the task of probing the endogenous coherence of the taste of a coffee as being a search for the transcendental object. Sometimes the taste is readily apparent, and at other times it is a figure in the foliage, and a dynamic figure at that. Professional tasters not only work to locate this transcendental object, they are constantly teaching it to each other. Sometimes they can do no more than make poorly specified stabs at an aspect of it, but if they are doing their job well what they indicate directs their colleagues not to a semiotics of taste descriptors but to discerning the outlines of an object that survives and transcends those descriptors and that transcends their protocol and their talk. For sensory analysis, this is the truest source of objectivity in tasting, and what is most important about taste descriptors is that they help tasters to direct each other to this object. An initial gloss can provide grounds that will propel tasters to make further specifications, although these specifications never really conclude. The efforts of professional tasters are local practices for discovering the transcendental object.

While they are tasting, tasters participate in a social system. Ott (2018, 84) tells us, "Cupping involves a negotiation of what tasting notes are present in coffees," and these "negotiations" take place according to the standards of the *locally occasioned* interests of the firm, export board, café, or sensory lab that is sponsoring the tasting. For example, the Indian Coffee Board will taste three to five cups of each sample coffee, and they will taste it at both hot and cold temperatures, looking mostly for taints. They taste only within a specified range of roasting, measured by color, and their examination is more discriminative than it is descriptive. All of their exploration is confined by these interests. As Ott informs us, each coffee bar has its preferred sensory scheme, and the cuppers who know the scheme best will have some epistemic priority over tasters whose investigations are more general. Scientific sensory labs operate similarly, according to their own socially produced standards, which guide their probing and their analysis, although much like Catholics in heaven they sometimes think they are the only ones who are fully authorized. It should be noticed that in all of these cases the subjective *is* the objective, and necessarily so in that the subjective approaches of the developed methodology become what is widely accepted to be the standard.

One of the first professional tasters I met explained to me while we were staring at the cupping table, "Everyone has their own routine," and he suggested that one routine was not necessarily superior to another because each routine was derived from specific needs and interests; however, he cautioned that it was important to always be consistent with one's own methodology. An ecumenical perspective like this is a fellow traveler with the humility we just discussed. Perullo (2012, 113, my translation) offers us advice that could become an anthem for tasting: "Methodologically employed analytic systems should not prevail over attuning 'directly' nor make it impossible to taste without prejudice, and with equanimity and openness."

Ethnomethodologists (Garfinkel 2002, 263–285; Lynch 1985) have learned that the pedigree of scientific work rests upon a foundation of mundane skills that are situated in the local contingencies of a laboratory's work. In coffee tasting these practices may be no more sophisticated than remembering to keep the eraser handy and being able to recall clearly what one was tasting for before sampling other coffees on the cupping table. Geoff Watts (2013) advises, "You need to bring a very disciplined and focused natural state every time you do it. . . . If your mind isn't clear, your ability to accurately decipher what is actually going on in the coffee is diminished." Similarly, George Howell (Weissman 2008, 55) observes, "Cupping is about paying attention. It's like trying to remember the numbers on the license plate of a passing car."

With 40 or more cups on every table, one must stay organized. And one must do so within severe time constraints, set in place by the time that the organizers of a cupping session have allotted for the tasting or, in the case of a private firm, by the need to make critical assessments while the coffees are still hot. This keeps one scurrying about the cupping table trying to catch other coffees before they cool, even though one has not yet settled upon one's assessments or descriptors for the cups one has already sipped. The worst error is to confuse coffees, and one learns to use tricks for remembering which coffee presented which features. One of these tricks is to identify and recollect the coffee by the intensity of its fragrance or by the aroma of its crust, so that even before sipping one has created a mnemonic device for identifying each coffee. A taster's professional capacity is judged in part by the competence and the speed with which he or she is able to cup and use the schedule. Odello has advised, "The faster you are, the less likely it is that you will make a mistake. . . . Don't reason too much about the numbers. Above all, don't engage in reasoned reflection. Look quickly at the semantic charts, and then go straight to your instincts, without reasoning." The coffee taster who tries to reason is left behind.

It is no mean feat to work quickly amidst performing the many varied tasks one must accomplish while grading coffees, but they compose the day's work for a taster. There are generally some four to five tasting assessments to make for each coffee (flavor, acidity, body, sweetness, and aftertaste). In addition, there are two sorts of olfactory assessments to be made, which never quite disappear from one's evaluation. One must taste for and note any non-uniform cups, detect any taints or defects, and there are several general assessments to be made ("balance," "overall"). There is also settling (finding, understanding, taming) some descriptive notes for each of the coffees. For tasters who use formal schedules, as they are tasting they must quantify their tasting, which involves constant addition, subtraction, and a bit of multiplication. It is imperative that if there are six coffees numbered at random (3750, 7941, etc.) one records one's assessments alongside the correct number, without inadvertently applying a scoring to the wrong coffee; if there are three coffees being evaluated on each of two pages of the tasting schedule, one must take care not to mix up the pages by recording one's assessments on the incorrect page, a mistake that will require one to erase entire lines of scores and rewrite what one has already recorded, by the end of which the time for tasting may have expired.

While one is trying to remain organized, further mundane skills are involved. These include insuring that one's eyeballs do not get obstructed by the line of one's bifocals just as the hot water that one is pouring reaches the brim of the cup, causing one to spill the coffee over the lip of the cup and onto the table, leading one's fellow tasters to lose faith in one's abilities; or making certain that one's spoon does not contaminate the other cups ("Did I wash it already?"); not dropping one's pencil on the floor as one is juggling the spoon and the clipboard (but don't drop the spoon); and remembering to mark the line levels that indicate the direction of the quality of one of the coffee's features as the coffee cools. One must do all of this while people are constantly bumping into one, asking "Are you finished with that coffee yet?" complaining that one is taking too much time, or making accusations that one forgot to clean one's spoon, etc. Toward the later stages of evaluation there is often increasing erasure action; and at any moment one's concentration can be distracted by the need to attend closely to any announcements the head taster makes about anomalies in the coffees (announcements that may affect one's assignment), so that one will not have to ask one's fellow taster, "What did she say?"

As with most professions, the solution is practice. Some coffee professionals say that no one can become competent at professional tasting in less than five years. Weissman (2008, 35) writes, "These guys train their senses the way pianists train their hands—they practice, practice, practice." Professional tasters carry their cupping spoons around the way Sherlock Holmes carries his magnifying glass, and they often move through the world cupping spoon first.

Free Description

We have observed that the descriptive comments and notes that are written on tasting forms are as useful to coffee purveyors as the numerical scoring. Willem Boot kept pressing his students trying to qualify for the Quality Grader certification (for Arabica coffees) at the Boot Coffee Campus to describe the details of the flavor, constantly reminding them, "When you rate a coffee high, you must find a reason for that among the flavor descriptors." During debriefing sessions that are held at international competitions following each flight of tasting, during which the tasters teach each other about the coffees they have been cupping, most head judges usually press the other judges hard to compose specific taste descriptors. What distinguishes lay tasters from professional tasters is that professional tasters have as a priority the clear detection of sensory properties. The Alliance for Coffee Excellence (ACE) advises that tasters should rely on "clearly defined sensory properties," and many of the professional tasters I have encountered give this effort priority over numerical assessment. During the triangulation portion of the exam at one of the ACE Q-Graders (Quality Graders, for Arabica coffees) courses, when student tasters-in-training are required to select the cup of coffee that is different from the two remaining cups that are identical, the instructor advised the students to suspend any hedonic scoring and focus upon clearly identifying the distinctive sensory properties of each cup being tasted—"You really want to zero in on the specific nuances of each cup." The problem is that there are many sensory properties, and assessing them all together (especially when they work synergetically, and their aspects are continually changing over the dynamic evolution of the cup as it cools) is not easily amenable to the causality that is part of most scientific models. There are enough flavors at work, always transforming slightly, to give pause to any verbal description.

Taste descriptors are an essential part of professional tasting, but how do descriptors help tasters locate and understand tastes? It seems that the calibration of free description is more difficult to attain than the calibration of numerated assessment. The polysemy that is natural to language use continually undoes the periodic stabilization of the sense and references of taste descriptors. However, it may be that calibration of numerated assessments is equally difficult, but the numerations are better at presenting an appearance of being well calibrated because one does not need to specify the content that fills the numeration. While free description is more difficult to tame, what calibration is attained may be more meaningful. The attempt to find flavors that were used to describe a coffee can be challenging. Sometimes matters proceed straightforwardly: the "sweet caramel tones mixing with a little floral acidity" was clear enough (neither too complicated nor too simplified) for me to locate those flavors in the Kona I drank last week. And the "lemon" that was offered for my recent cup of Kenyan coffee was also straightforward, though somewhat metaphorical. While this "lemon" filled the fore-structure of my probing the coffee and successfully led me to discover what I was looking for, it rendered me less capable of taking note of other flavor features, such as spices; however, whether it was the work of my projection or not, I was satisfied that the Kenyan was lemony.

There are other occasions when I have a difficult time coming up with taste descriptors. I was led to near aphasia by a batch of Limmu green beans from southwestern Ethiopia that I had home-roasted to a perfect medium roast. It was full-bodied and possessed a roundness that influenced my entire mouth (the tip of the tongue, rear of the tongue, palate, etc.). It was so "full" that I wanted to say that it had a lot of flavor, except that I was not able to give any definition to the flavor. It had one of those "coffee coffee" or "normal coffee" kind of flavors that my research subjects keep mentioning to me, coffees that are all about body and little about flavor. The classic Limmu is said to be a coffee having "citrus acidity, soft berry undertones, chocolate and floral notes," but the coffee that I roasted had no citrus or floral tastes that I was able to locate. If one extended the notion of "chocolate" very broadly (and we often do so with the descriptor "chocolate," but this can leave it with so little specificity that its utility is diminished), then "chocolate" could be used, yet I thought that this taste descriptor contributed little to defining this coffee's character, which rested in its strength—it came on fully frontal and without any bitterness, which is a trait that some tasters might call "sweet"; I am more reluctant to use that description. In the end, I was unable to find my way to a taste descriptor, not even to one that could temporarily hold in place some of my early intuitions. This elusiveness, however, did not deter me from enjoying every mouthful.

As with any language, descriptors are rooted in local dialects and idiomatic usages, and the use of taste descriptors is always locally occasioned. They are indexical expressions, and one must be familiar with the meaning they are given in the context of each situation if one is going to acquire a clear understanding of just what the descriptors are intended to communicate. Note that I am speaking of *using* taste descriptors and not about any dictionary definition of the descriptor. This investigation of the use, which is directed to the "how" rather than the "what," is the empirical commitment of ethnomethodological research. Wittgenstein (1972, 82) has observed, "Language is a labyrinth of paths. You approach from *one* side and know your way about; you approach the same place from another side and no longer know your way about." Taste descriptors work best among personnel who work together at a single roasting facility whose tasters are well calibrated. In such a situation, the flavor notes the tasters identify and express are understood well; however, further along the chain of production and across oceans and cultures, the adequacy of understanding can be sufficiently problematic that many importers do not place much stock in what they read before they proceed to taste for themselves.

In addition to tasting for defects and tasting for positive characteristics, there is a third kind of tasting that occurs: tasting an undistinguished coffee. This can be the most challenging tasting of all, since it is not always easy to find a suitable descriptor to allocate to an undistinguished coffee. Sometimes tastes are nothing more than traces, yet part of the task of a professional taster is to transform those traces into something definite. On occasion a taste descriptor begins its life as nothing more than a mnemonic device for holding onto a trace that was detected, and one can carry that descriptor as a gloss while one proceeds to taste further, and refine it as one goes along. There are many tasks in sensory assessment, and one is continually multitasking, so retaining intuited notions by means of a gloss is helpful. The "enframing" of ideas by language both assists and conceals. It helps by giving us some initial access to a coffee (e.g., "lemon"), but it simultaneously conceals by aggressively imposing a "challenging claim" (Heidegger 1977, 19) upon it that *substitutes* its agency for the agency of the transcendental object itself (the taste, without any brackets); the taster's own agency or the agency of a methodology is given priority. It is peculiar that the latter agency is given the name "objective" while the agency of the object is often labeled "subjective." Only after the transcendental object is fully subdued by our method and by our objectifying representations, by our "setting upon" (Heidegger 1977, 24) the coffee, does the objectivity of what we find get endorsed, while "a more original and revealing" experience (Heidegger 1977, 28) with the coffee is eclipsed.

One can assess the effectiveness of taste descriptors by applying some objectivist criteria, reifying their sense and reference, establishing criteria for correctness, finding some way to mathematize the analysis, etc.; or one can assess the utility of taste descriptors by considering the hermeneutic contribution they are capable of making within an actual situation, i.e., the ways that they may enhance our probing of the tastes. The routes to the success of taste descriptors can vary, and the deepened experience they can lead to will always be a chiasm of subjectivity and objectivity; taste descriptors are a professional tool that tasters possess.

When composing descriptors, one needs to keep in mind the people for whom the descriptors are written—are they one's fellow tasters, tasters from a distant firm, or lay consumers? It is not enough to be correct; the point of taste descriptors is to use them for communicating. The weakness of dictionary definitions for descriptors is that they do not provide for consideration of the abilities or frames of reference of the target audience (and there is always a target audience; otherwise, one would not bother to describe). Many descriptors that are adequate for coffee professionals may confound lay consumers and do more harm than good. Like the linguists who study only speakers and fail to give equal consideration to the interpretive tasks of listeners, some coffee purveyors think only about getting a descriptor that will be "right" for themselves or their fellow tasters, or the boss. One's detailed description can be perfectly accurate, but any myopia in describing can cause one to communicate nearly nothing to a customer. In most instances, one should be cautious when proceeding beyond three adjectives. Generally, accuracy is preferable to poetics, and being clear is more important than winning the approval of the head taster. The advertisers will add their poetics later anyway.

A description given to a Mogiana from Brazil—"dark-toned, edgy, and full of malt, chocolate and nuttiness"—offers practical information to a consumer in a way that is understood easily, and nothing about this description for a Kenyan coffee is obscure: "strong, crisp, lemony floral brightness." Even if one is unsure how a coffee flavor can be "bright," the "lemon" and "floral" offer constructive clues. Burman Coffee, a wholesaler from Madison, Wisconsin, that sells small lots of green beans to home roasters, did a good job with a difficult-to-describe Ethiopian Sidamo: "a wonderful gingerbread spice with a light fruit tone, almost grapefruity in flavor and reminiscent of a spiced lemon cookie." While this description is intricate, its appropriateness for the coffee being described affords it some license for pertinent elaboration.

"Full bodied, strong and darker toned" is simple, and if one knows Timorese coffees, perfectly apt. "A rich cup with just a hint of acidity and some darker fruit notes mixed with some baker's chocolate underneath," given to a coffee from Papua New Guinea, offers a lot of detail, perhaps too much, but it is well communicated. Its merit rests in how it can provoke some deeper probing of the coffee. "Smooth, sweet, complex notes of vanilla and fruit" captures perfectly the genuine Jamaican Blue Mountain it was describing. Real Blue Mountain coffee (and most coffee sold as Blue Mountain is not genuine) offers a potent aroma of chocolate, but the actual flavor is closer to vanilla. Why chocolate and vanilla (one crop originates in Central America and the other in Madagascar) are frequently associated with each other is curious, and the reason could be more cultural than gastronomic. Burman Coffee deserves more praise for providing a full description of an Ethiopian Harare: "This is not a super-clean coffee; it has complexities and a bit of roughness, many layers of lemongrass, berries, smokiness, and lemon peel." Because this description is realistic, operating under the genuine discipline of keeping to only what the tongue has sensed, it is alright for the description to be drawn out a bit more than is usually advisable.

A Nicaraguan coffee received a highly detailed description: "The mixture of smokiness, sweetness, a hint of caramel and floral tones in the aroma lures you in. There are a lot of great flavors going on in this cup and when you have your first sip you're going to want a moment to take it all in. The cup starts with some smoke, nuts, and sweetness like caramel. The middle has just enough grapefruit tones to wake up your taste buds and then finishes with dark chocolate that lingers on your tongue." It is almost a course in coffee tasting. Effective descriptions are more concise: "citrus and soft fruit" (a Pacamara from El Salvador) can be sufficient. "There is dark fruit, oak, licorice, and some vanilla spice, like a good dry red wine with just hints of lemon zest" for a coffee from India is probably too much information. "Blackberry and plum" (from Bali) is better for getting a coffee drinker started on his or her own inquiries.

Many descriptions refer to balance, but when the taste descriptor "balanced" is used by itself, a favorite of advertisers, it is news from nowhere because it fails to specify just what the balance consists of. "Sweet citrus notes balanced with cocoa underneath" explains the situation. This description conveys the dynamic quality of the coffee in a marvelous way: "There is a sweet edge to this cup, but it doesn't linger, and a dryer nuttiness is what remains on the tongue."

Uses of "sweet" and "bitter" can be as problematic as "balance" sometimes is. Either can acquire an iconic usage (i.e., a standardized usage that reflects a settled praxis of professional tasting that has become routine and during which the meanings have become generalized), and one that is not identical in every country. There are many sweets and many bitters, and tasters are tasked with numerating them, which can be like comparing apples with oranges. The SCA tasting schedule affords the category "Sweet" a discriminative and not a numerical assessment, while the SCI form affords a category that must be numerated. The form used in Europe for certifying SCA espressos offers separate numerable categories for both sweetness and bitterness, but the SCA form for Robusta coffees combines "sweetness" and "bitterness" together in a single category, placing them at the opposing ends of a single scale. When assessing an espresso's bitterness, how does one numerate a bitterness that is pleasant tasting but weak in presence? And does one give a coffee with a strong but unpleasant bitterness a low score or a high score? There are answers to these questions, but not every taster is cognizant of them. Ted Lingle (2001, 12) tells us, "Using bitter as a solely negative attribute of coffee's taste is technically incorrect. Bitterness is often a positive taste contributor." And complicating any assessment of bitterness is its ubiquity: Lingle (2001, 14) says, "Bitterness is the basic taste character of caffeine." Offering "bitter" as a descriptor can communicate more clearly than a numeral can, since one is able to qualify the bitterness, as in this description that was written on an Indian Coffee Board's tasting card: "Very bitter, musty, unpleasant taste." The worst bitter is the one that is so influential that it conceals subtle positive flavor characteristics that the coffee may also possess but can go undiscovered by an undiscriminating taster.

Despite efforts by the coffee industry to fix in place the meanings of taste descriptors, it is the basic nature of meanings to be labile, capable of adapting to situations. A meaning depends upon a word to convey its sense, but this turn to language commits one to an unanticipated network of ongoing semiotic relations that will keep transforming the meaning of the term one has chosen, in a process of semantic drift that can end up obscuring the sense that one first intended. Derrida (1978, 25) describes this as "the indefinite referral of signifier to signifier." Any fixed sensory lexicon is powerless to halt such naturally occurring semiosis.

In recent years, the importance of free taste descriptors has been increasing in the coffee world. First, many new consumers are taking an increasing interest in taste. Second, during the Covid isolations more consumers began to purchase their coffee online, so they are paying more attention to written descriptions. In addition, the increasing importance of fermentation for some coffees has created a demand for describing the variety of fermentation in some detail, as evidenced in the SCI form that includes a non-numerated evaluation of the fermentation. Eventually, this sort of description may require its own lexicon, yet to be developed. Language is like a river: new conventions are created as a matter of course, and it is as pointless to try to stop them as to try to stop a river from flowing; instead, we need to learn from these linguistic flows.

The increasing importance of free description has led the Sustainable Coffee Institute (SCI) to develop a "Descriptive Cupping Form" that places more focus on descriptors. It provides a cell for notes for each category being assessed, instead of only a single space at the bottom of the tasting form. As professional tasters focus more attention upon taste descriptors, it can be expected that discursive assessments will play an increasing role, become more refined in their details, and perhaps become more standardized. SCI advises (in a mass email dated March 23, 2020, emphasis theirs), "A numeric value has a role, but let us not forget that *description* is the goal." Like everything else in tasting, free description will evolve as a collaborative effort.

Consistency

Professional tasters do not only assess the flavor, aroma, body, and aftertaste for quality; they taste these features with an eye to how consistently they can be reproduced (Azienda Riunite Caffè 2013, 224). Much tasting, by both purchasers and roasters, is a matter of looking for consistency. We discussed the importance of consistency in chapter 7, where we described how exporters will taste the blend they are currently making for a client alongside samples of the blends sent to the client previously, with the aim of maintaining consistency.

Coffee purveyors are not necessarily looking for the best coffee; rather, they are searching for the best coffee that they can provide consistently. Professional tasters fear inconsistent, unpredictable, and nonstandard coffees; this may lead tasters to reject a good coffee because its variability can become costly, and sometimes this assessment of consistency is worked into the scoring for each category. Sample lots of Brazilian coffees used by Dunkin' Donuts will be examined by their graders in Santos who are searching for above-average coffees, or what the firm numerates as 3.5 (on a 5-point scale). One 4.5 Magiano coffee that was the best cup on the table when I was tasting with them was rejected by these tasters as being "too good." They are concerned to select coffees that will provide the same standardized taste experience so that a customer at a Dunkin' Donuts store in Maine will drink the same coffee that is served in Florida. Excellent-tasting coffees (4.0+) are difficult to acquire in the quantities needed to be able to provide them regularly to their 9,500 shops.

The Q-Grader program of SCA and Coffee Quality Institute (CQI) emphasizes consistency and communicative efficacy (Croijmans 2020). The goal is that any coffee will achieve similar and understandable scores and descriptors at any tasting lab in the world. But these scores depend not only on the coffee but also on how the tasting schedule is used, and there is a variety of strategies for using a schedule. Most professional forms key the scoring to a 100-point scale, but this "100" is an artifact of the chosen methodology. During evenings following a day of tasting coffees, there is some debate among the tasters (sometimes at the bar) about the proper ways to use a schedule, especially how to apply the schedule to the particular coffees that were sampled that day. Fortunately, coffee people are a tolerant breed and most of them come to the conclusion that what is important is not that every taster uses the schedule in an identical way but that each taster remains consistent regarding how he or she uses it with each one of the coffees. As a Brazilian salesperson once told me, "Consistency is better than being accurate." Similarly, consistency is a market strategy for most of the larger coffee firms. Caspar Rasmussen, the head taster for BKI Coffee in Denmark, explained to me, "Our main target is to be consistent."

This word "consistency" has a key role in the argot of professional tasters. There are many kinds of consistency: (1) from cup to cup among the five samples of a coffee on the tasting table (do they taste the same?); (2) in the flavor profile of the coffee as it progresses from hot to cold (is the profile stable; does each cup change in a similar way?); (3) across the harvest from a single season; and (4) among crops of the same coffee from different seasons. There is consistency among the cuppers, consistency in the calibration, and consistencies across temperatures, and a taster must keep track of the tastes of all five cups for each of six to eight samples of coffee on the sampling table. Interestingly, it can happen that a coffee with an average taste that is stable can receive the same score as a coffee with an excellent taste that is unstable. Further, consistency in flavor makes a coffee easier to assess, and judges can be so relieved by how easy the taste is to discern that they may reward the coffee with a slightly higher score. This happens with aromas too; some aromas are difficult to discern clearly, whether because the aroma is subtle or because the taster has been doing too much sniffing for the olfactory sense to register anything. This can result in the aroma for a coffee being downgraded a point or two. Aromas that can be detected clearly have an advantage.

Pedagogies

All professional tasters are learners; they are very good learners because they must be learning all the time. Lingle (2001, 29) tells us, "Good cuppers will take every opportunity to learn from each other." Tasters are continuously formulating the practices for each other, and a pedagogy for sharing and developing the practices is always in play. Ott (2018, 84) has described the ways that baristas negotiate tasting notes, and Gherardi (2009, 536) extends the topic of these negotiations to their practices of tasting, to "the constant negotiation of what is thought to be a correct or incorrect way of practicing within the community of its practitioners." Similarly, Alaç (2017, 172) reports that the texts of perfumistas "function as instructions for use."

The languages of professional sampling are structured as pedagogies. "This has a woody taste" can be heard as a call for collaborative assessment, and tasters may even compete to find just the feature that makes "woody" ring true. "That one seems like it's got a little floral in it" will direct tasters to another aspect of flavor. Descriptors are used in ways that prompt tasters to better define what they themselves mean. One can declare to fellow tasters that a coffee has "a good bitterness," and then the other tasters will go searching for it, and once they locate a candidate, they will try to teach it to each other and solicit confirmation or disconfirmation. Some tasters may be confused and have little idea about what they are searching for, yet they will cast these words over the coffee and try to see if they can run into anything that will correspond. A descriptor and its taste mutually elaborate each other.

The situation is further complicated by the fact that descriptors are subject to being distorted by idiosyncratic understandings of them. Tasters try to avoid such trouble by closely monitoring the emerging specification of the sense and use of each descriptor. Even an idiosyncratic understanding can be made into an objective understanding, common to everyone, by its being shared intersubjectively, by using it repeatedly in a specific way, and by observing that way and then adopting that way. Part of this process includes a full complement of strange things that can happen in any mundane social interaction: there will always be incongruities of understanding; there are agreements and disagreements; there are sometimes disagreements when in fact there is no disagreement (only linguistic confusion); and there are agreements when the parties are thinking entirely different things but don't realize it.

Here taster B was prepared to learn about a defect, but learned something even more important: what is not a defect.

A No, it isn't a defect. It's just the flavor.

B [Re-tastes] Right, it's not a defect.

Taster D tries to teach fellow taster C what they are tasting:

C It's got a back flavor.

D I would consider that to be "woody."

Once in Brazil I was told that a blend we tasted included a two-year-aged coffee that made the coffee taste "woody," and so I tried to find it. When I could not, Marcio Hazan brought in a cup of some five-year-aged coffee that was "woody" (most five-year-aged coffee will lose its acidity and body and gain a "woody" or "cardboard" taste), roasted it for me, and I tasted that. Yes, the characteristic flavor was more distinctive, and I could make it out, but I could not determine why it was called "woody." It was not that I could not locate a taste and a smell that *could* be "woody," but I had no way of knowing for certain that what I had located was what Marcio himself meant by "woody." Marcio then explained that it tastes much like the woodiness in wines that are aged in barrels. This work of getting fellow tasters to locate a taste that has been found is an important skill of professional tasters, and a hermeneutic one. "Is it good?" I asked him. "Not 'good,'" Marcio replied. "Some guys like it, and other guys don't like it."

Here taster F directs E to where to look for the transcendental taste of "bergamot":

E Is that bergamot flavor at the end or the beginning?

F Right off the bat, right in the beginning, and then it's just gone.

Learning how to locate these tastes, i.e., learning "the observability of those things" (Garfinkel 1993a, 8), is part of the curriculum of learning to taste coffee. Taste features are made salient, visible, and witnessable. Above all, tasters are addressed to the work of teaching each other about the "more" to the taste that exists in the coffee than they have identified. This "more" operates center stage of the pedagogy: "The coherence of these witnessable or revealed details of the figure was tied entirely to the way of coming upon the more there is to it" (Garfinkel 1993a, 10–11). Tasting skills are active, and they emerge from practices and not from docile knowledge.

These tasters are attempting to teach each other the intelligibility of "oily":

MARGRIT: The first? Yeah, I described the first one as compact and oily.

MOHAMMED: Do you mean the smoothness?

MARGRIT: Not smooth, it's more like a kind of film that it leaves . . .

MOHAMMED: OK.

HELENA: With the first one?

MARGRIT: With the first, right exactly.

HELENA: Yeah, yeah.

Many taste descriptors start out having a specific vagueness are employed in a tentative manner that will direct other tasters to look for it, find it, and then participate in its specification.

A   It has a structure.

B   Search for a light structure.

C   A structure.

How will they find their way? They are trying to use the term in order to learn not what it means but how it can be used. On other occasions, a descriptor can be definite for an expert but vague for a novice. When a taster who knows what she is doing points out the "structure," one goes to look for it even when one is uncertain what "structure" means. Two experts can have a definite idea of what a taste descriptor entails for a particular coffee (e.g., "round"), but their two ideas are not identical, and any novice listening to them must somehow learn from both of them, in which case some indeterminacy is sustained and even necessary. In such ways, tasters collaborate in learning the meaning of descriptors. This process is continuous and never really concludes. If it does conclude, one should place one's practice of tasting under suspicion. This situation contributes further to the humility that is natural to most professional coffee tasters.

Tasters also teach each other how to make their local work more orderly and how to coordinate their explorations, including their use of descriptors. In this way, a descriptor is not merely a definition but an instruction about in-the-course, worldly ways of using it. Language helps me learn the flavors at the same time I am learning how to use the language. This means that there is a twofold purpose for using descriptors: using them for finding tastes and using them for organizing the orderliness of the local discussion of flavors. Calibration itself is a component of instructed action, and one adjusts one's scoring to an observed practice. As the sociologists of sensory assessment Vannini, Waskul, and Gotschalk (2012, 15) have made clear, tasters "must *make sense* of somatic experience. In this way, sensing and sense-making are necessarily conjoined, codetermined, and mutually emergent." Garfinkel (2007, 36) summarizes how this topic can be researched: "The issue is making adequate and evident provisions for making researchable the congregationally produced and concertedly accountable structures of mutually instructable actions of ordinary society. Just how are structures of social action as witnessable properties of endogenous populations actually and accountably produced?"

These concerted productions should not be mistaken for some deliberately designed orderings that proceed strictly by means of clearly understood and clearly shared concepts. In fact, it is more common that a serendipitously emerging local structure of interaction leads the parties than that the parties design structures deliberately (see chapter 12). If they do design them, their most important effects will be unanticipated. There is always at work a socially motivated tendency toward conformity and acting in uniform with others, even when one does not understand the basis of that uniformity (Horkheimer and Adorno, 1972, call this "mimesis"). This drives people to fill out their forms before they have fully understood them and learned what the form can be made to do; they will use features of the form in order to discover what they mean. This may sound odd to anyone accustomed to imposing a hyperrationalism upon their mundane experience of the world, but a basic truth of instructed actions (and most of our living in society is instructed action) is that people do not always know what they are doing, and they do things in order to learn what that is. Doug Macbeth calls this "the work of the world." Since most things they do are done in concert with others, learning takes place in an intersubjective context, and building and clarifying sense and reference mostly remains outside of the hands of any single individual.

Instructed action is a naturally occurring aspect of everyday intersubjective life. Tasters keep teaching each other about what they are tasting; and as they teach each other, they teach researchers like me as well. Since teaching involves the continual exhibiting of candidate devices for making knowledge orderly, this can be witnessed by anyone in the room. And when tasters discover their local orderliness by means of these witnessed exhibitions, ethnomethodological researchers can discover it too, and at the same time that the parties themselves do.

Tasting Schedules

Let us make a closer examination of the tasting schedules used in professional tasting. Though widespread, these forms are not ubiquitous; and their design varies, despite worldwide efforts toward standardization. Nevertheless, a good deal of the claim for objectivity in tasting is based on these forms. The purposes of these forms are three: (1) to help the tasters probe the flavors, (2) to organize the orderliness of the tasters' activities, and (3) to produce objective evaluations. CQI tells us that the purpose of the tasting schedule is "to fully explore what a coffee has to offer." That is, the real value of a tasting form is its capacity to assist the *probing* of the many aspects of flavor, and they direct the taster's attention to certain gustatory features that otherwise may be overlooked. A well-functioning formal schedule that is used for sensory assessment will carry the taster into all of the more important aspects of flavor.

We have already mentioned a few of the commendations by professional tasters regarding the second purpose of the form, to keep the tasting organized, and this refers to the organization of both individual and group activities. Parties always use whatever is at hand to organize some local orderliness for any situated occasion. Coffee tasters, even those tasters who place little trust in schedules and are suspicious of them (the majority of tasters in Brazil, India, and Colombia), will use a schedule for helping to organize the social interaction. Having a physical thing in hand and something to do allows parties to collaborate in establishing a local system of order that makes the routines evident and predictable, routines that serve to set them on their way (even if the routines are not in every case useful and even when participants are unsure about just what they are doing). Much of the intricate work that use of the form performs on behalf of coordinating intersubjective relations is hidden. Forms provide tasters with a common language, shared dilemmas, and a structure for thinking through problems together. Wright (2014, 230) has observed, "Standardized vocabularies and numeric descriptions . . . act to craft fixed points of reference from incoherent local accounts." They facilitate communication, but tasters must make them flexible enough to capture the pertinent tastes each time. In addition, the ubiquity of the clipboard, the pencil, the spoon, and the brown cupping apron offer tasters a shared identity and a presentation of self, which help to cement the social solidarity of the tasters.

Regarding the third purpose of tasting schedules, professional tasters have explained that using schedules debunks the notion that the quality of coffee is purely subjective. When tasters speak of the quantitative representation of qualitative experience, in addition to recognizing the authority of both, in practice they mean that they "translate the sensory experience into the language of the categories and relatively standardized referential vocabulary to describe the individual experience and provide a judgement as a number" (Wright 2014, 231). A senior taster once said to me, "The majority of this form is objective," which is a very good way to phrase it, since perfection of a form's "objectivity" is a goal always deferred (like democracy or the messianic era), at once admirable and unattainable. One early piece of advice several SCA international cuppers offered me was "Everyone is gaming the chart." What is to "game" the chart? This was explained by head taster Manuel Diaz: "So what you do is work backwards—you decide that the coffee is an '85' and then you will work the categories to achieve that." Another senior taster explained, "Your calculations take you to a '79' score, but you have a gut feeling that it is a '76,' so you rethink the scoring for the individual categories." This is a practical objectivity, which is to confirm that it is an objectivity capable of rendering service to the coffee industry: the numeration assists thinking, focusing it; but it cannot replace thinking. As one barista in the USA reported, "We go by a lot of numbers and parameters, but in the end the palate is king" (Ott 2018, 87). The conundrum of transmitting an aesthetic experience into numbers is ultimately a philosophical problem. As a mechanism for social order and for facilitating communication, it is justifiable, so long as one does not entirely lose sight of the experiences that generated the numerating. An extensive notation of flavor descriptors and other contextual features in the spaces provided on the cupping form can contribute to retaining some characterization of the experiences; however, once one's scores are aggregated with others' scores, the numbers can carry the assessment far from the site of anyone's experience.

The "work" of the tasting sheet itself can be so overwhelming that it renders the taster less able to focus upon tasting. Manuel Diaz explained, "You can either evaluate well or taste well." One might be inclined then to dismiss the "evaluating" and concentrate only on tasting, but that is an impossible choice: its impossibility is due to the fact that simply discovering a taste that is enjoyable is helpful to no one but oneself. If we need to purvey coffees around the globe and along the chain of production (and we do; otherwise, coffee would not be available), and purvey them in a manner that elevates the importance of flavor, then the tastes one is sensing must be made communicable in a manner that makes them available and comprehensible to all the stakeholders. The sociality of the situation demands some standardization; hence, standardized sensory assessment, qualitative and quantitative, is necessary. Yes, these formal assessments will always be distorted by the compromises that must be made in the interest of communicating clearly; that is why alongside this we will need some means for alleviating "the betrayal which philosophy is called upon to reduce" (Levinas 1981, 151–152).

Rodrigo Alarcón of the Federación Nacional de Café de Colombia once posed to me the dilemma of how one might express the beauty of the Mona Lisa in a numerical form. No doubt we could, but something will be lost. Nicola Perullo (2016, 80–81, my translation and emphasis) is stronger in his criticism: "Taste . . . is handed over to codes that are already known [so that] *the otherness* of the matter paradoxically almost disappears." Otherness is vital since what we are not yet familiar with can become a source for new knowledge. Respect for the other and for what is new or foreign joins with humility and openness, and ultimately with scientific discovery. When pre-structured terms and codes are given the final say, the uniqueness or singularity of the experience risks being ignored. This raises the enduring question of how these dual needs of standardization and respect for the singularity of the coffee coexist, which they inevitably will, something I am trying to understand in more detail. Pure lands are hard to find, and once again we must acknowledge frankly that we need some standardization: "Without this process of assimilation we would be hopelessly lost in a confusion of absolute novelty" (Earle 1955, 45). Novelty is fine if we are only an individual coffee drinker, but for a worldwide industry standardization is needed. This is a classical sociological topic (inaugurated largely by Simmel) of the alienation that is entailed when we live in complex social arrangements.

There is a critical tension between the justifiable need of the coffee industry to standardize assessments and proper respect for the singularity of a coffee. Satisfying both claims, when one is able to do so, is a cause for some of the satisfaction expressed by professional tasters who work with tasting forms. Part of what must be going on is that the coffee itself, in its singularity, is directing the taster to pertinent priorities of the coffee's taste, which are explored and described. That is, in addition to the assessment sheet, the taster is making an *open* inquiry into the coffee; and what the coffee is presenting directs the taster to appropriate priorities that need to be communicated effectively, somehow using the form to do so.

Tasting schedules can assist sensory assessment, but precisely *how* are they helpful? It has little to do with the scoring; rather, the efficacy of schedules has to do with the way they are used to broaden and focus the tasting inquiry. One reason that a tasting form is successful is that every professional taster understands well the form's shortcomings and so is doing things to make it work, both with and without the form. At the least, one cannot permit the influence of the scoring sheet to be so overwhelming that one misses the way a coffee invents itself, which is the coffee's singularity. It is the professional commitment of tasters to remain attentive to the coffee, and so tasters work continuously to cope with this problem. The scoring sheets have efficacy because tasters *have learned how to work with them.*

While it is the intention of the form to provide for objective, even universally valid evaluations, the tasting forms exercise a subjective influence of their own upon the tasting. They outline in advance what sort of objects can be discovered. While the form itself remains the same, presenting the appearance of perfect standardization, each occasion of its use is uniquely informed by a locally constructed method for using it. While the "reasoned" tasting form is accepted as formally identical for a cohort of tasters, the "procedural" specifics that *each* taster develops, as his or her way of working with the form, can differ. As one senior taster once explained to me, "You come up with your own little shtick in order not to lose control." Further, it seems that a schedule can be better suited to describing some coffees than other coffees, and it even happens that a coffee can teach the taster new ways of using the form and change how the form is used in ways that may be carried forward to subsequent coffees, such as the way that Gesha coffees, after exposing a few inadequacies of the forms, caused the tasters in Panama to figure out ways to apply the form to the coffee. Tasting schedules are used to render assessments more objective, but this objectivity is not an automatic result, nor does it reside inside the form; instead, any objectivity the schedule achieves is the practical accomplishment of each taster who uses the form. Is that accomplishment subjective or objective? It is both.

Professional tasters have more fidelity to the taste of coffee than they have to any methodology. Yet part of the responsibility and competence of professional tasters is fragmenting the unity of the coherence of the taste that they experience. Aron Gurwitsch (1964, 121) notes that the coherence is what is actual, and that "the part is what it is only as a constituent of the Gestalt-contexture and as it is integrated into its unity." A Gestalt-like contexture is something that is always experienced as a whole. Gurwitsch (1964, 138) explains, "A Gestalt-contexture does not consist of parts, if 'parts' are meant to be independent and self-contained elements, each entirely determined in and by itself, irrespective of the contexture into which it is integrated." The taste features work together, as a synergy. They are reciprocally integrated; that is, each aspect of taste is interconnectedly dependent upon the other aspects:

> In thoroughgoing reciprocity, the constituents assign to, and derive from, one another the functional significance which gives each one its qualification in a concrete case. . . . If a part is extracted from its contexture and transformed into an element, the part may undergo most radical modifications. Since its functional significance is no longer determined by references to other constituents, the extracted part may *cease* to be what it phenomenally was. (Gurwitsch 1964, 134–135, emphasis mine)

Once the phenomenal experience of the extracted part is removed from its original unity, *its reality is distorted*. This presents professional tasters with the sometimes mind-numbing task of being faithful to the pre-fragmented quality by making use of the fragmented data of the tasting form. They can do this successfully—this is part of what makes them professionals—but in this way *the tasting schedule becomes a constituent detail of the flavors* being described. There is no way this could be anything other than subjectivity at work.

A tasting form requires that each of the aspects be separated from each other, whereas in real life (which is where one finds objectivity) they are interconnected and influenced by each other, or rather by the whole that they help to compose. The fragmentation of this unity into the several categories of a form occurs in part in response to demands to conform to the local requirements and may not always be prompted by the singularity of the coffee. Sometimes when tasters perform this fragmentation, they do so with less than full sincerity.

The rationality of the analytic tasting form is assured by tasters' locally engaged practices. The procedurally situated form involves a series of unexplicated practices, or what that senior taster referred to as "shticks." Shticks are the things that the tasters do to make the form work, or in Garfinkel's words (1966), "The rationality of descriptors in use is guaranteed by the way in which the member makes use of unexplicated features of those practices." These shticks are the keys to the success of a tasting form's objectivity.

While the schedule consists of a single sheet, in practice there are really two tasting schedules: the formal analytic tasting form and the procedurally situated tasting form. The formal analytic tasting form is disengaged, which makes it available for whatever formal analysts want to make of it. The procedurally situated tasting form is always engaged with the coffee and offers opportunities for the coffee's singularity to inform this engagement. Singularity can confound or constrain the work of the formal analysts, whereas the disengaged character of the analytically reasoned tasting form provides formal analysts with considerable currency across the industry.

Garfinkel (2002, 187–190), with an assist from Eric Livingston (1986), has described these paired phenomena (the formal analytic account and the lived work of using it *in situ*) as "*Lebenswelt* pairs." Garfinkel observes that the formal analytic account ignores the reflexive and embodied work of making the account clear (i.e., "accountable"), while the lived work of using it preserves the looks of the world for the users and is oriented to the "developingly objective and developingly accountable" results. Because many of these reflexive practices are hidden inside a tasting form, which always presents an outward, documentary appearance of near-perfect conformity, this conformity is largely illusory; however, there may be no way to know this since the procedural sense is usually not recoverable from the reasoned tasting form once it has been severed from the situated work. It is an odd feature that the procedurally situated tasting form does most of the work, but the analytically reasoned tasting form receives most of the credit.

Part of the practice of the analytic tasting form is to reduce sensory experience to "signed objects," that is, actual embodied sensations are made over into a collection of signs and numerations that become available for the assigned interpretations of the coffee industry. The interpretations assigned to those signs come to prevail over the tastes: they replace the tastes and become the tastes. As Garfinkel (1977) explains, "Signed objects are objects whose entire specifications are found and demonstrated by treating them as a collection of marks, indicators, signs, and symbols the sense and reference of which only the analyst is privileged to know, and then assigns to them their interpreted significance. The reader need not leave the page in order to find, formulate, and decide any issues of adequacy." The truth of the situation requires that the taster put some emphasis on the taste of the coffee when deciding issues of adequacy. The analytic tasting form may lead the coffee professional to consult the *Sensory Lexicon* for establishing the sense and reference of the signed registrations of taste features, instead of turning to the reflexive and embodied tasting that is the focus of the procedurally situated tasting form. As Garfinkel (1996, 11) characterized the use of cartographic maps, "the phenomena of the procedural journey are lost with the same technical methods that are used to describe them"; that is, it is the comprehensiveness of the sensory protocol that causes the essential phenomenon that is the focus of a sensory protocol to end up missing. In the case of tasting schedules, just what is it that is lost? The flavor is lost.

Given the gap between the analytic tasting form and the procedurally situated tasting form (they are the same sheet of paper), there is much work left for the "Overall" category to handle. Professional coffee tasters are engaged in a continuing reconsideration of this category of "Overall." Some explain it is an assessment needed for taking into consideration how everything works together, but is that different than the assessment recorded under "Balance"? The Cup of Excellence program explains that "Overall" is a catch-all category for handling "preferred characteristics not fully reflected in the individual scores." Several head tasters warn tasters that the score given there must be consistent with their other evaluations, but if that is so then why even have the category; indeed, some critics of the category suggest that it is a duplication of what has already been assessed. Still others complain it is too vulnerable to being a "subjective" rating. SCI (in a mass email dated March 23, 2020) criticizes, "Subjective attributes, like overall, don't need to be measured," but that belies the point that the cupping form consists of measuring subjective assessments. Nevertheless, "Overall" remains on most forms for the reason that it is handy for tasters who wish to reconcile a total score with a coffee that did not really seem that bad or that good. Hence its survival depends upon its practical benefits more than any objective facility it offers. The value it provides is not given on behalf of the analytically reasoned tasting form but on behalf of the procedurally situated tasting form, and the category "Overall" may be where the procedurally situated form makes an appearance on the analytically reasoned form.

Perullo (2012, 22) warns us that always, "The aesthetics of taste is marginalized because this sense cannot be understood exclusively through formulations and theories." Perhaps it is the function of the "Overall" category to provide a location for the aesthetics of taste to influence the scoring. Formulations and assessments that are oriented toward numerical values tend to overlook some aesthetic dimensions, but these subtle aspects still need to find some way to appear in the tasters' metrological reductions, i.e., into their numerations. We learned that much tasting is performed on behalf of particular clients and is not done in the abstract; accordingly, the situated form often prevails over the abstractions of the reasoned form. Exporters try to taste using the imagination of the importers. How precise can one's numerations for that be? Numbers always appear to be precise, but the history that underlies their production vanishes.

Enrico Meschini explains that the basic quality of the taste can be reached by numeration and that later one can look for the particular notes. This especially holds for how buyers and importers routinely use the formal sensory assessments. Part of Meschini's idea here is that the numeration gives one more information than not having it. The buyer who simply reads verbal descriptions cannot know for certain whether the coffee under consideration is worth further investigation. Even if a score does not explain why the coffee is good or bad, it will indicate whether it is good or bad; thus, numeration can serve as a sort of yellow highlighting pen. Meschini insists upon a score of 81 as the minimum score a coffee needs for him to acquire it for investigation. He knows well that two coffees of "81" are usually different; and that is why after a coffee purveyor receives a candidate coffee, the tasters in the lab need to taste the precise notes. The precision comes from the tasting, but the quantitative sensory analysis has a contributory role to play, although it is often the case that the qualitative assessment is decisive.

When coffee purveyors work this way, a coffee's total score may be less important than the score for one or more particular categories of taste. This is especially true of purveyors who design blends. These coffee designers seek to learn which coffees have the best performance in one or more particular characteristics, such as body, acidity, or aftertaste. As one official at an international cupping explained, "We do not have just one winner, we have one winner for each one of the characteristics." This deals well with the issue that there are many ways to be a good coffee. To this end, there may be a practical benefit to the fragmentation of the taste. As another senior taster told me, "Cupping is obviously not a perfect science. But it is a useful one."

Using Science

Where is the science amid these practices? "Science" exists as an ideal and exists in actuality. Both incarnations reveal human society at its best, but science must be kept de-mystified. There should be no room in it for making it a mythology. Is the tasting schedule a path to science? Formal protocols are needed, but their victories come at a price. Perfection is unattainable, and every rational tool that humans develop carries benefits and costs. Let us consider the benefits of scientific sensory analysis in the context of some actual tasting in a coffee purveyor's lab.

Arcaffè is an Italian roaster of specialty espresso blends for higher-end bars and cafés in Italy and some other countries, including Greece and Israel. Located in Livorno, they prepare their own artisan blends for various price levels. One year they designed a specialty blend of 85% Arabica and 15% Robusta (Italian specialty coffee purveyors must include some Robusta for the sake of the *crema* and the mouthfeel that Robusta provides, and which all Italian drinkers expect). One morning Arcaffè received a telephone call from a dependable and faithful client who expressed dissatisfaction with the latest shipment of the bar's usual blend: they found it too bitter. Arcaffè did not doubt this trusted client and sent one of their tasters to the bar. He returned to Arcaffè's lab with a full bag of the shipped coffee, and their tasters prepared to examine it.

Italian blends are prepared with three to nine different coffees, so if a blend turns out to be "bitter" it can require the detective work of a Sherlock Holmes to determine which of some half dozen beans is the offending one, and just what kind of "bitter" it is contributing. Sometimes each of the component beans must be tasted. I have been asked more than once, "Is 'bitter' something that is objective?" Most professional tasters will reply affirmatively; however, there are many kinds of bitter, and not every case of bitter can be said to be objective. As we have already reviewed, some bitterness is due to molds that developed during the fermentation, the drying, or the transport. Other bitters are due to inherent characteristics of the bean. And still another bitter is caused by over-roasting. For this reason, initially one is faced with a hermeneutic task of determining just what a client *means* when describing a coffee as "bitter," and frequently drinkers are unable to specify this. Additionally, there is the hedonistic response a drinker may have to this bitter. There are pleasant bitters and unpleasant bitters, and as soon as we enter the world of "pleasant," the subjective, hedonistic predilections of the drinker become central. Some professional tasters suggest that most bitters are objectively bad, but I have met Indian exporters who swear that many Turkish buyers prefer coffees that have bitter taints due to molds (I have not met these Turks myself); and I know many American coffee drinkers who sincerely enjoy the bitter that is regularly produced by over-roasting, and even come to depend on it. Some of them operate under the delusion that the "stronger" (i.e., over-roasted bitter) the coffee is, the more caffeine it provides. It can be concluded that some bitters are more objective than others, and there is an imaginary component to all knowledge. In any event, the sensory analysis for Arcaffè's tasters commenced with their determining the nature of the particular "bitter" that was causing the problem.

Accordingly, Arcaffè's tasters' first task was to cup the coffee in order to confirm the complaint and evaluate the bitterness. They did so, and found both the smell in the bag and the color of the beans to be fine, but when they tasted it with the assistance of the standard form designed by their lab, they located a bitterness they associated with roasting. They rated the bitterness 3.5 (scale of 7) and the coffee itself 74, which was too low for its price level. Their protocol for numerating their assessment told them they had a problem. They first surmised that perhaps it was over-roasted because ten days prior to its roasting they complained to their roasters that they were roasting the blends too lightly; they suspected their roaster over-compensated by roasting the beans too darkly. This is a common problem in the coffee industry, one that I have observed at other roasting facilities and also at international competitions: the tasters complain to the roasters that the level of roast is too light or too dark, and the roasters respond by making the opposite error. When it comes to roasting, perfection is elusive; and when perfection does occur, it is as much due to luck as to planning and programming.

To obtain a more precise reading of the roast level, they assessed this specialty blend's roast using a colorimeter (it rated 158), which informed them that it had been given the roast they had intended. This is a decent illustration of how a scientific procedure can aid tasters in their investigation by confirming with an objective measurement what their visual examination had been assessing. The measurement allowed them to rule out one line of inquiry. Some roasting facilities and labs routinely keep records of the colorimetric scores for every coffee they roast, and the keeping of systematic records is another significant part of scientific praxis. Having determined that the client's complaint about its bitterness was valid but also discovering that it had received the correct roast, they grew puzzled. They tasted all of their retained samples of that particular blend that they had roasted during previous weeks, and discovered no problem with any of them, nor did they find a problem with the batches that were roasted following the shipment of the offending bag. Then they tasted the coffee from another bag of that same batch of coffee, which they still possessed, and discovered that it too was bitter. While admitting that this was a genuine problem, rather than expressing frustration, the head taster Enrico Meschini said to me, "This is very interesting!" I was reminded of the joy Sherlock Holmes often expressed at the outset of an especially baffling investigation: "The game is afoot!"

Instead of proceeding to sample each of the component beans, Enrico walked out of the lab to the roasting room to interview the roaster about what might have occurred. The roaster reported that this was the last batch they roasted on the previous Friday. Since they did not have enough hours to let the fresh batch air before packaging, and since letting it sit out over an entire weekend would cause some staling, they packaged it prematurely. It was inside the bag, after its sealing, that the problem developed. During our review of the many ways that coffee can be ruined, we mentioned packaging (see chapter 5). Before leaving the lab for the day, the tasters took the coffee out of the offending five-kilo bag and let it air for a day, with the idea that the bitterness, caused by premature packaging capturing some volatile chemical, might evaporate.

That was indeed what happened. When they tasted the blend the next afternoon, the bitterness had disappeared. Their rating for bitterness rose two points to 5.5, the aftertaste increased half of a point to 4.5, and the total score of the blend increased from 74 to 79.5 (with 80 being their target rating for this price level). Finally, in order to confirm their finding, they used another objective procedure of blindly re-tasting the originally shipped coffee straight from the bag alongside the beans that had just aired for a day, and their diagnosis was confirmed. This latter exercise is a procedure that can also be labeled scientific. "Science" is not any kind of magic; it consists of practical activities, activities that vary considerably in nature and scope; and in every case, they require the supervision by the skilled judgment of experts. The blind tasting here remedied the common phenomenological problem of projecting the meaning (such as "Now it is no longer bitter") onto something and then taking it for granted that the thing possesses that projected meaning-in-itself, separate from our participation. By putting one's pre-judgment out of action, one can obtain a less "subjective" perception of the phenomenon; the success of an objective reading will always rest in part upon the openness that can be sustained when investigating a phenomenon that one does not know.

In this example of professional tasting, we are able to witness five dissimilar aspects of being objective. Using instruments that produce *measurements* (the colorimeter), using a *standard form* for making numerical sensory assessments, using blind tasting as a mechanism to *put out of action any bias* in the outlook they may bring to the cup, and *retaining organized records* of their measurements and analyses compose four of these practices. The fifth aspect that went into their practice of objectivity was the cooperation between the two tasters in the lab; this was an essential component because their *collaboration* served to sharpen each other's focus of attention upon the central gustatory sensations and criticize any judgments made during the course of their inquiry, a sort of dialectical editing of their collaborative thinking. Here is revealed once again the important contribution of intersubjectivity to objective inquiry. I have witnessed this kind of collaboration in the labs of Sandalj, Lavazza, Quarta Caffè, and Arcaffè in Italy; in Três Corações, Dunkin' Donuts, and Comexim in Brazil; in Cascade Estates and Boot Coffee in the USA; in Coffee Day, Gill Coffee, Allana Coffee, and Tata Coffee in India; in Academia Barista Pro and Ben's Coffee in El Salvador; in BKI Coffee in Denmark; in Alma Café in Colombia; and in informal labs in a dozen coffee-producing countries. Most serious professional coffee tasting is undertaken as a collaborative project of experts. As Franco Schillani of Trieste explained to me, "Tasting must take place with at least two people." What is most revealing in the present case is the demonstration that objective, scientific inquiry is not something that consists of a single factor, hypostatized as "science" with a proto-mythical scent. Science does not happen by itself; it consists of different practices employed together and monitored by the collaborative judgments of an intersubjective cohort of experts. The idea that no human hands ever touch science is a fictional portrait. While the method and the protocols have importance themselves, when one places one's faith in science, one is placing one's faith in the experts who know how to use the method and protocol and how to collaborate in that use.

The higher the quality that a coffee is, the more delicate it is and the greater the risks are of contamination. Better coffees require cupping more frequently to monitor the many risks to which it is subject. A coffee of medium quality is not affected as much by minor problems. This difference in care increases the labor costs for these coffees, which entails raising the price. It may have to be raised so high with respect to the price of a medium-quality coffee (and especially with respect to the price levels of the price coffees sold by Arcaffè's competitors) that their client bars would be unwilling to purchase it. What matters most to a bar is making a profit, and when it is unlikely customers will be capable of perceiving the difference in quality between the medium- and higher-quality coffees—or perceive it to a degree that would justify the loss in profit (coffees at an Italian bar are provided at a standard price)—then the higher-quality coffees will suffer. Hence, the capacity of ordinary drinkers to taste flavors has considerable influence on the quality of the coffees that will be made available to them: why sacrifice profit when few drinkers will be able to discern difference in quality?

After the problem was resolved, Meschini reflected upon how much more effort specialty espressos require compared to ordinary espressos. He explained, "I produce these kinds of coffee not for profit, but only because I am passionate about coffee. The price I am able to receive does not justify the labor that is required." Meschini is not alone. Throughout the specialty coffee industry, one encounters these occasions when the "art" of coffee purveying provides its own motives. Larger roasters cannot afford such expensive hobbies. As Franco Schillani stated accurately, "Coffee is serious business." And frequently business will trump flavor.

Calibrating Tasters

We have already discussed calibration briefly in other chapters, but the central role it presently plays in contemporary sensory analysis justifies our making a deeper investigation. Schillani once said to me, "All the good cuppers speak the same language," and he suggested that successful coffee tasting depended upon this. Schillani's statement not only implicates a local cohort of tasters who work together face-to-face, but covers agreement in practices across the profession. Of course, it is easier to commend this than it is to accomplish it; however, more than being surprised by differences in coffee tasters' assessments, I have been surprised by how much agreement there is (and also by how much tolerance there is for disagreement, when that occurs). The success of professional tasting is dependent upon achieving calibration among tasters.

Calibration refers not merely to opinions but to a *shared direct experience* of something tangible that is located and perceived with a common focus. Calibration is more than an alignment of what people think is good or bad; it is an alignment regarding identification of the object that people are aiming at in the first place. Calibration is a shared intersubjectivity, not regarding ideas but regarding tastes. Its focus is the palate, though linguistic calibration is also required. These two calibrations (of the palate and of the language) are related, in that the principal function of the language is to direct the tasters' sensory attention to the transcendental object, the taste. It would seem senseless to try to coordinate taste descriptors and opinions before locating *a thing in common* to which the tasters' descriptors and opinions are being directed, although I have witnessed plenty of discussion of taste descriptors before the target was clearly located and identified by everyone. This is curious and requires investigation.

Intersubjective coordination is not easy to accomplish. For example, what is "fruity" to one taster may be "acidic" to another. Whatever the descriptor, some open-endedness is built into it in order to account for idiosyncrasies of understandings; the point is not to get definitions correct as much as it is to locate something common in the coffee; *until that thing is located it is fruitless to argue about nomenclature.* At the same time, one does not want to be introducing new terms every time one tastes, so there is a need for some standardization of terms. Before the terms can be coordinated and concerted, the transcendental object needs to be shared, and this task requires extraordinary intersubjective communication. Language serves the role of assistant and offers a facility to parties for directing other tasters to some identical thing. Taste descriptors are accounts, and these accounts are used to clarify the objective intelligibility of what the tasters are experiencing. They are used to coordinate the tasters' approach to an identified thing. That is, taste descriptors are used as interactive tools for achieving intersubjective correspondence. Because the descriptors play this active role in organizing the interaction, they are not only ideal representations that can be derived straightforwardly from a dictionary of terms. That their initial function is to direct tasters to an identical transcendental object so that it can be shared, suggests again that the adequate model is not taste $\rightarrow$ taste descriptor but taste $\longleftrightarrow$ taste descriptor.

Calibration regarding tasters' orientations to the identical object is difficult to accomplish when there are a dozen tasters, but the burden of calibration in the industry is greater than that: the accounts of the gustatory phenomena must be aligned with industry-wide international standards, and this sort of intersubjective adequacy is problematic. Even if one grants that it is impossible, it must be admitted it is a necessary impossibility, if the worldwide coffee industry is going to function rationally. Take "bitterness," for example. Mann (2015, 36) reports one taster's advice: " 'You have to make sure that everybody is talking about *exactly* the same thing, because obviously there are many types of bitterness. There is bitterness related to caffeine, the bitterness of cocoa, initial bitterness, and aftertaste bitterness, what have you.' " And this does not address whether bitterness is desired or not, which varies by national gastronomic cultures, between communities, and among persons. Still, a mention of the descriptor "bitter" at once directs tasters to search for it, and what they discover will be used to specify which bitterness is involved. It would help if the taster introducing the account specified further in language which bitterness was meant, as that could narrow the search, but in every instance there will be some reflexivity between the descriptor and its target, and each will inform the other.

"A calibrated cupping panel" is a phrase repeated frequently throughout the coffee world and is the heart of both professional tasting and sensory science. Because it consists of a coordination of intersubjective relations, it is a social phenomenon. Since social interaction is fraught with confusions and miscommunications, it is not easily achieved, and throughout the coffee industry mentions of "calibration" can be cavalier. Proper calibration does happen; otherwise, tasters would be unable to use a common language. However, across the coffee industry "calibration" is used as a gloss for an activity whose specificity is not always defined adequately or carefully researched. By "gloss" is meant that the notion "calibration" possesses an abiding vagueness and is used in an "essentially vague" (Garfinkel 1967) manner. Despite this, it serves as the center of gravity for their professionalism, and for their science.

The practical work of calibrating consists of orienting oneself toward an *emerging conformity*. Penalties for safe scores police any drift in the cuppers' scoring and reinforce the conformity. This is consistent with the warning of Sunil Pinto (the taster from Kushalnagar, India) that calibration can make a taster stop taking risks. In order to be certified as a professional specialty coffee taster, one needs to demonstrate a capacity to evaluate coffees that does not deviate far from the mean scoring of the group of tasters with whom one is tasting. Novice tasters seeking professional certification must pass an examination that confirms they are properly calibrated. To establish a basis for making this judgment objectively, the professional coffee tasting industry requires some reliable standard to which the world's tasters can be calibrated, an equivalent for the meter rule. As we have noted, the taste of coffee is more alive than the meter rule, and its character keeps changing as it ages, according to how it is roasted (including the air pressure and humidity at the time of roasting), the water used, changes during transport, etc. The examining board cannot roast the beans at a central location and then ship them to the various sites where the examinations for certification take place because the taste of beans will be changed by the staling that will occur during the shipping of the roasted beans. The beans must be roasted locally; therefore, the precise taste characteristics of each coffee cannot be confirmed or fully defined prior to the tasting at the site where tasters' calibration is being tested. Professional tasters have responded to this difficulty by utilizing as the mean for evaluating the decisions of the tasters the very mean that is developed at the site of the tasting. That is, the cohort of tasters establish their own mean, at that time and at that place.

This situated, locally created norm is what becomes the equivalent of the meter rule and becomes the basis upon which the calibration of the tasters is measured. The consequence is that there is a possibility for a different norm to be established at hundreds of testing sites. Tasters who satisfy the demands of calibration this way will receive formal certification. Calibration like this reveals clearly the social foundations of objective knowledge. One administrator of a calibration examination explained to the applicant tasters, "If you want to be highly skilled, you should be no more than 1 to 1.5 points off of the group average." Certification is a much sought-for qualification, not only for people whose work requires that certification, but for people throughout the world who want to enjoy fuller participation in the social identity of the international coffee industry. For this reason, there is a widespread commitment to calibrate one's tasting praxis to the "norm," wherever one can find it.

Calibration is the instrument for creating a working society of tasters, a means for all the tasters to get on the same page. The most common form of calibration occurs prior to any official scoring a panel of tasters will undertake. At the more important international competitions, an entire day will be devoted to calibrating the tasters. The hope is that during this context where the assessments do not count officially in the competition, they will be able to work out a local system that makes clear just what meanings their terms, descriptors, and numerations have in the local situation. During calibration, tasters may learn that they are being too harsh in penalizing cups for lack of uniformity or for taints, or too liberal in awarding scores in one or another category. The calibration does not end after the single day of activity but continues throughout all the days of judging coffees. For example, if one has learned on the calibration day that one is being too harsh about taints, then during the actual cupping when one *does* encounter an "off" coffee, one may be reluctant to punish it to the full extent it should be punished. If so, one may discover that one has become too lax in penalizing taints, so one readjusts one's practice in order to come again into alignment with the group. Discussion of scoring among tasters is needed after each flight of judging throughout the competition. The guidelines stipulate, "Discussion of the scores will help to calibrate cuppers, eventually leading to a common language throughout the specialty industry. . . . What is important is that you have adequate discussion."

The most elaborate calibrations occur during the qualification or renewal for calibration certification, when novice or renewing tasters are examined for being properly calibrated; this certification is required for being a professional taster. Coffee Quality Institute (CQI 2013) describes the structure: "The Q Calibration Exam consists of three cupping flights, (three tables with 6 samples each) of coffees with distinct attributes. All Q Graders [Quality Graders] must be in calibration and pass two of the three flights in order to renew their licenses and continue as Licensed Q Graders. Upon passing, the Q Grader license will remain valid for another 36 months, starting on the day of successful completion of calibration." Note that the industry recognizes well that a natural drift occurs in scoring coffees and in the use of taste descriptors, the sort of drift that happens with any natural language or social practice. For that reason, CQI mandates that a recertification examination be taken every 36 months. This demonstrates that the industry recognizes that the problems with calibration are enduring ones, although the confidence displayed by some coffee professionals that they have solved these problems in a conclusive way includes wishful thinking alongside the confident rhetoric.

During each flight of cupping, the tasters are scored for several matters:

(1) The total score of each taster is assessed by awarding 10 points per coffee for remaining within 2 points (plus or minus) of the average score, 8 points for remaining within four points, and 6 points for remaining within 6 points;

(2) Avoid safe scoring, which is any highly conservative scoring that places one's scores within a narrow range that is less than 20% of the range of scoring of the other cuppers. This is an ingenious measure designed to compel the cupper to take serious note of actual taste features and not score in a way that is too conformist;

(3) Each flight of coffees (consisting of six kinds of coffees) includes a repeated sample, and the taster must rate duplicated samples within two points of each other;

(4) Some coffees include a defect that is added deliberately to the cup (e.g., fermented fish oil or quakers); simply the fact that they bear a defect must be identified, not the particular defect they possess. Sometimes the defective coffee is obvious, but usually in one of the three flights the defect will be subtle.

Finally, CQI (2013) stipulates, "The cupper needs to identify at least one of the two coffees identified by the group as the Best and Worst on the cupping table." Here again, best and worst are defined by the cupping scores that are achieved locally and are not determined by the governing board prior to the tasting. As we have discussed, this is necessary; however, it possibly fails to accomplish one of the goals of the calibration, which is to bring the tasters into conformity with an international standard that exists beyond a local cohort of tasters.

While the process of calibration always results in better aligning the local tasters to each other, albeit sometimes at the expense of originality, how well that conforms with some industry standard is left mostly unaddressed, despite the references to "a common language throughout the industry." The cuppers must be "standardized" so coffees can be effectively analyzed and so discoveries about the tastes can be communicated in an intersubjectively adequate way, but the sense and reference of the taste descriptors *need* to remain less than fully determined in order to be sufficiently adaptable to the local needs of the coffee on each occasion of their use. This adaptability assists tasters in being productive regarding the practical tasks of tasting and communicating flavors, and in most of the cuppings I have observed, this has been achieved successfully. Conformity with broader, international standards, especially a single standard valid for all, is more problematic. The calibrations here are not universal and pertain to a finite province of meaning. Another feature of this process is that it often happens that during the calibration exam, most of the tasters who seek certification are not yet professionals (that is their reason for taking the exam). This means that the average judgment of novice tasters becomes the basis for being certified as a professional. This is not a flaw but a real-world contingency.

Professional tasters who operate outside of the CQI certification process still must keep their cupping calibrated. We discussed how importers and roasters receive samples of winning coffees in order to cup them in their labs and calibrate their own palates to continually emerging worldwide standards. In addition, in chapter 7 we observed that exporters regularly make visits to their clients in importing countries (and vice versa) in order to maintain the objective sense and reference of the assessment tools they use in purveying coffees. During these visitations, importers and exporters instruct each other about the tastes of their coffees, what they are really seeking, and how they use key taste descriptors, in a continuing collaboration that is oriented to building a dependable, predictable, and objective system for selling and purchasing coffee.

A Few Tenacious Problems

Lily Kubota, writing in *The Specialty Coffee Chronicle* (2016, 513), observes that rote scores tell us little about what a coffee tastes like:

> Our industry needs more scientific ways to research and understand coffee flavor. The SCA cupping protocol is a valuable tool to understand and evaluate overall coffee quality, but it is not well suited for the kind of scientific research we seek to do in coffee. For example, two coffees might both earn 86 points but taste very different from each other. In order to understand the influences of particular flavors in coffee, there must be a better tool for quantifying what those flavors actually are.

Recently the Sustainable Coffee Institute (SCI) has tackled the problem directly by designing the aforementioned cupping form that provides more places for descriptive assessments. In a report dated March 13, 2020, SCI called attention to the difficulty of being able to describe the differences between two coffees that have the same score. In an email dated September 15, 2020, announcing their new tasting form, SCI wrote, "A score doesn't fully describe aftertaste. . . . I don't know whether you gave it a low score because it was a bad flavor or aftertaste or if it was because of a shorter duration." Accordingly, SCI has included indicating the duration of aftertaste on their form. A similar confusion sometimes occurs with "balance": how does one understand a high score for something that is locatable midway between two extremes and is inherently opposed to being too much of anything? Balance as a taste experience may be too complicated for the scoring mechanism to handle. A coffee might be strong at two extremes and still be balanced; or it could be weak at two poles but still balanced and receive a similar score. If one gives a bad score, which sort of "bad" would one be able to deduce? There is a similar problem with identifying uniformity, in that many forms provide only for scoring *whether* there is uniformity without any having to specify just what the lack of uniformity is composed of or how serious it is.

Any taster who is cupping also copes with confusions that are artifacts of the scoring. Some scores (such as those for flavor) are based on the pleasantness of the taste and other ones (like sweetness or acidity) on the basis of the intensity. Lingle (2001, 35) instructs us, "Cuppers should not rank acidity based on their own personal preference of like and dislike," whereas he explains that "flavor" does receive a preference rating. Lingle's directions, however, conflict with the instructions of some other tasters. Davide Giacalone et al. (2016) report that assessors in sensory descriptive analysis, as opposed to scientific sensory analysis, do not rate the level of intensity but rather provide a "subjective appraisal of the individual attributes." For example, a high score in "acidity" would indicate how well the sourness of the coffee fits within the context of that particular coffee, regardless of absolute intensity. Confusions like these make it difficult to fully understand meaning of quantitative scorings and present challenges to standardization.

Sometimes one must rate a quality of flavor that one has not been able to define well. Suppose that one is handling a coffee that is known for its "licorice" flavor and is asked to judge whether it is any good. If one is unsure what "licorice" in coffee is supposed to taste like, how should the taster proceed? One may be tracking something that is still only a trace. How can anyone rate what they have yet to identify clearly, though it is easy to mark a line on a scale? Those markings that were not more exacting than an exercise of pin-the-tail-on-the-donkey will count just as much as those for categories of taste one clearly understands. When one is tracking a trace, if I am able to use that trace to locate a taste that I then can appreciate, and subsequently define well, I may be so pleased with my accomplishment that I will raise its score.

"Rich" is a common and occasionally accurate descriptor, despite its being a vague one (not found on most professional forms). The SOPPEXCCA cooperative's tasting lab in Jinotega, Nicaragua, made careful evaluations of several of their recently processed coffees. After the coffee that the tasters preferred was given its proper quantitative and qualitative assessments ("citric acidity, sweet, backed up with a bit of dark chocolate"), the head taster stepped back, gestured to the coffee, and pronounced it "very rich," in a sort of concluding global assessment. It had been given an 82.5 score on the SCA form, but the "very rich" seemed to be the more definitive evaluation. Its utility lies not in any definite sense that it carries around inside its wording, but in what it provokes a drinker who hears it to discover in what he or she is drinking.

It is not the taste descriptor itself that matters but what people *do* with the taste descriptor. It does not pay to be too literal-minded with taste descriptors since they will always open up to what the coffee in front of one is presenting. Perullo (2016, 80) contends, "Language is not a cage in which I force the experience of drinking according to a consolidated scheme, but the continuous unfolding of the relationships I make, a carpet along which my feet walk." To assess the correctness of a taste descriptor accurately one cannot confine oneself to examining the word or sign by itself, as if it always carries its definitive sense before any tasting; rather, one must look to the local work that the word enables within the social activities of any given occasion. One must witness *the word's work* inside the course of its usage, wherein it finds its definite sense and reference. Generally, sensory scientists are lacking in linguistic and sociolinguistic expertise, so they fail to track just what a taste descriptor becomes in the hands of skilled practitioners who use the descriptor to accomplish their work. By ignoring this local work that tasters do *with* the taste descriptors, sensory scientists may miss the phenomenon of tasting.

Just what is "rich"? It can be some combination of texture and a good bitterness, but it may not have a precise flavor; yet by using the descriptor, a taster may be able to find it, and even appreciate and rate it. The coffee I am drinking now is "rich." It has a "hazelnut" creaminess that is worth a rating of seven on an eight-point scale. But I need to decide whether to allocate that score to "body," to "flavor," or to both of them. The "rich" can even make a reappearance in "aftertaste," and I can accomplish all that while the descriptor "hazelnut" retains a necessary vagueness, necessary because it is needed to provide sufficient room for its sense and reference to grow, so I can learn from the coffee and discover what I need to know.

When they are divorced from descriptions of taste, the numerical assessments for "body" or "texture" do not mean much. Since the numbers have lost the phenomenon, they have little to report beyond the fact that the coffee's body may or may not be worth making a deeper examination. A mildly pleasing but still not well understood or well defined texture of a coffee presents a problem about how it should be scored. Should its positive qualities, however mild, be allocated to "body" (a.k.a. "mouthfeel") or to "aftertaste"? It can happen that a taster will allocate it to both categories. When this happens, a relatively unimpressively flavored coffee with some body can gain a misleadingly high score; that is, the mechanics of the scoring sheet can produce an artifact. A doubled score like that can raise it above another coffee that possessed an excellent "flavor" but whose excellence was expressed in a single category. For the purpose of further illustration, let us say that a taster has given the mildly pleasing texture of a coffee a score of 5.5 (on an 8-point scale), and this 5.5 has been allocated both to "body" *and* to "aftertaste," resulting in 11 points; by comparison, a coffee that possessed a flavor that was mostly pleasing but an unremarkable body (say 3.0) might have been allocated a 6 score for "flavor," resulting in 9 points. Despite the fact that the flavor of the second coffee might have outweighed the importance of the mildly pleasing texture of the first coffee, this way of scoring has elevated the first coffee above what it merited, and the fairness of the tasting forms' representations of the coffee has diminished. Calibration can minimize some of these problems because it introduces a conservative scoring that leads the coffees to be awarded scores that fall within a narrow range, so the differences produced by the problem of "doubling" are not always large. By this time, the tasters are doing as much bookkeeping as they are tasting.

In a related problem, the bitterness, roundness, aroma, etc. of a coffee are each available for being awarded an equal number of points, but these categories are not always equivalent in importance. It depends on the coffee, and coffees do not present excellence in identical ways. Can the same schedule be used with equal adequacy for every coffee? The tasting form can sometimes "level off" the features that are most important for a particular coffee. A given tasting schedule can fit some coffees better than it fits others. One feature, say roundness, can be so fabulous that its value trumps the cumulative value of several other categories; however, most forms are not built to handle such a situation. Or, I could be willing to sell the store for the "cherry" taste of one coffee, but I cannot award it more than the maximum number of points available for it under the category of "flavor." Alternatively, I can "game" the form. Gaming like this may even be objective if it is justified by my tasting experience, but that is not the objective that is meant by most scientific sensory analysts. Perullo (2016, 10) reminds us that in tasting, wisdom is "a sensitivity that wants to mold itself in accordance with things." Moreover, any practical adjustments with the form in the interest of wisdom can cause a taster to become more occupied with bookkeeping than with tasting, or what Perullo describes as "the frenetic activity of gathering information and data." Perullo is not incorrect, but he seems reluctant to "give unto Caesar" his due regarding the practical needs of communicating in society.

Increasingly in the world of tasters, iPads are relied on to make tabulation more efficient, but this also results in more limited discussion of descriptors, since it keeps the tasters' eyes fixed downwards on their iPads and tabulations, instead of toward their coffee, or toward each other during the discussion sessions. This makes it more difficult to achieve calibration. Even during the day that is devoted especially to calibration, it is unusual that there is sufficient discussion to settle the meaning of most descriptors or coordinate a common method of valuation. Since the calibration day occurs at the start of events when most tasters are a little nervous about their performance and their presentation of self during such an august professional setting, the organizers respond by being protective of their tasters and do not push the tasters to resolve any differences that may arise in their conversation regarding the understanding, definitions, or perspectives about the features they are evaluating. Arguments that might poison the camaraderie may not be worth the increased adequacy of understanding. Instead, very much like the tasters themselves (both lay and professional), the organizers hide behind the quantitative methodology and offer minimal mediation, content to allow the numerated assessments to be voiced without much specification. In this way, the abundant intersubjective resources available during any international tasting are not fully utilized or comprehended. If creating international standards is really an aim, this could be a convenient moment for sorting out some regional preferences, such as differences that are evident among tasters from Central America, East Asia, the Middle East, Europe, and the USA. A standardized understanding is not achievable by fiat; rather, professional tasters must display their knowledge and their practices if the understandings are to be coordinated well. However, whenever there is public display, there is risk.

A final problem is invisible in the literature about tasting coffee. It is peculiar that as empirical as professional tasters wish to be, I never observed a single coffee taster assessing the psychoactive effect of a coffee, or making a passing reference. This is so despite the undeniable truth that it was the psychoactive properties of coffee, not its taste, that first impressed the Sufis, and caused both the Sultan of Cairo and Pope Clement VIII to overrule the objections of their lieutenants during the 16th century. Caffeine has made coffee the global commodity it is. As Pollen (2020) reminds us, "A key point about this beverage is that it changes consciousness." It is the elephant in the room. How can tasters overlook it and claim to be objective? Clearly, their inspections are channeled along particular passageways. Of course, tasters spit out the sips they take; otherwise, they would never sleep at night (something I learned after my first cupping), but there is some caffeinating effect regardless. Is all caffeination the same? It varies by roast level, but does every bean afford the same quantity and quality? A discussion of caffeine would be pertinent to consumers' interests. I am certain that marketers would take good advantage of it.

Resistance

While the temperament of coffee purveyors varies considerably from nation to nation, many coffee purveyors are natural rebels, or at least were so during their youth before finding employment in the coffee business. This has bequeathed to them a degree of originality, and one of the signs of professional tasters is their capacity to pay special attention to those tastes that resist systematization. In addition to such a temperament, the hermeneutics of coffee tasting itself demands a continuing ability to transcend the limits of one's understandings of taste. Part of what professional tasters love about their work is this continual call to track the taste of a coffee that keeps evading their efforts to define it. It helps to make tasting coffee fascinating.

One finding of this research is that the word "professional" in the label "professional taster" refers to there being some resistance to the alienation that can be a consequence of being subordinated to a system, and this resistance is an abiding demand of their profession. That is, professional tasters have a capacity to resist being trapped by their own rigid preferences or the educated routines of sensory analysis. Our desire for knowledge sometimes demands that our understanding be released from schematizations and predecisions. The good news is that most tasters respect and actively cultivate an originality that enables them to continually break through the limits of their understanding about a taste. Such vigilance for becoming trapped by one's own expertise is another characteristic of wisdom. Coffee tasters cannot afford to be ideologues or to describe flavors while being imprisoned inside of their own propaganda. Nicola Perullo (2016, 127) refines this summation: "Gustatory wisdom fights codes when it is *appropriate* to fight them, when the conditions of experience require it."

At any time, a coffee's taste can outstrip the capabilities of a tasting form, and no matter how careful the methodology for assessing taste may be, at some point it will "give out" (Wittgenstein 1972, 84); that is, it will run up against the limits of its capabilities, as the complexities of the real world overwhelm it. Recall "that crazy table" from Boquete, Panama, when the Gesha coffees made their appearance. Thomson Owen of Sweet Maria's has commented, "This sort of cup character . . . is even more hard to quantify" (Koehler 2017, 177). A taster commented, "The first four coffees were very interesting and very very very full of flavors, and I had to go back and forth, and back and forth, because I found they were all very nice, all very intense, all very fruity, all very floral. It is just a matter of where you put your notes and where you didn't." If it is a matter of where one put one's notes, minor contingencies of using the tasting schedule may be responsible for producing a winning coffee. No tasting session is without its moments of confusion, which range from flickers of self-doubt to an aporia, i.e., undecidability. There is so much that can be going on inside a cup of good coffee! Sometimes I spend many days trying to understand some new coffee I have roasted at home. There may be something recognizable, but I am unable to pin it down; while it is not nothing, it may be more than one thing. I envy professional tasters who come up with a fitting descriptor every time.

Coffee tasters are decent phenomenologists. The reason is that not only must they organize their understanding of the flavor of the cups, which involves stabilizing the meaning of the descriptors to a point that they can be communicated and objectivated across the industry, but since there is always more taste in the cup that they have still to identify, they must operate with their descriptors without allowing them to obscure their perception or attunement to discovering what this "more" is. This thinking-beyond while thinking-with the ways they have organized and routinized their understanding requires them to be naturally occurring phenomenologists as their day's work. The habits of thinking that one must continuously transcend are those same habits of thinking that compose professional expertise and lead experts to knowledge about taste; this makes it difficult to see beyond one's routine practices. It is not bad to make a meaning determinate; it is useful because one can then communicate and share it with others, develop it together, alter it, and eventually objectivate it so that everyone can continue to make further contributions. However, retaining the openness of every descriptor, of every notion, is the other side of this effort. Once a taste descriptor is made determinate, its sense may be placed in a lockbox. Developing its meaning should be an ongoing project, and one is always able to learn more. One may have a general idea and then specify it. In Husserl's terms, a descriptor can commence its life as relatively empty and become fulfilled gradually. It progressively becomes more determined, which is part of the social project facing tasters, but it originates in "the *pre*-determinate and the *pre*-expressed" (Bruzina 1970, 157) coherence of the taste that one experienced before the taste was "dressed" by our theories and protocols.

Hesitations, the aporias of tasting coffee, are not unhealthy things, and one should not be in a great hurry to convert them into certainties (as much as we prefer them), for the reason that undecidability assists us, even demands of us, that we *open* our senses and our experience, that we *learn* from and be summoned by the coffee itself. Such summoning can conflict with the dominating spirit of scientific sensory analysis. I too want the best of both worlds. The situation is described comprehensively by Derrida (1992, 250):

> For a [judge's] decision to be just and responsible, it must, in its proper moment, be both regulated and without regulation, it must preserve the law and also destroy or suspend it enough to have to reinvent it in each case. . . . Each case is other, each decision is different and requires an absolutely unique interpretation, which no existing, coded rule can or ought to guarantee absolutely.

For this reason, tasters are always revisiting the form. The tasting form must be prevented from overpowering the assessment, so tasters look for ways to subvert the form, to use it against itself. A tasting form is a *yang* that tasters learn to use in a *yin* way. A form influences the mind and assists the taster to *keep probing* the details of what they are experiencing, but the experience must be allowed to prevail over the lockstep of the form's categories. Truth exceeds correctness, or as William Earle (1955, 131) has put it, "Judgment is not true because it follows rules."

Intersubjectivity

Tasters say that while one can develop a reliable rating system for assessing defects that is straightforward and mechanical, the same cannot be achieved for the positive characteristics. I would rephrase the account to say that it can be done, but it is not accomplished nearly as easily. Its success depends upon cultivating one's subjective acumen and transcending the shackles of the objective formulations that, while needed for social order, can obstruct one's clear seeing, which is the foundation for all knowledge. "Subjective acumen" is misunderstood when one imagines only an individual at work. Robert Barker (2017, 285) has suggested that the real work of tasting is collaborative. Subjectivity is not to be restricted to the intellect of an individual taster—that is simply a prejudice of our individualist culture; rather, it refers to the effective intersubjective collaboration of tasters. As Marcio Hazan of Santos explained to me, "Did you notice how important it was to discuss together, and not just taste alone? Other people can change my mind about the coffee." Collaborative tasting is where the preeminent tasting takes place.

Of course, communal practices can be as misleading as our personal thinking. The tasters for Coffee Day, a chain of gourmet cafés in South India, tend to rate their coffees in the 4-5-6 range (on a 10-point scale) and rarely 7-8-9. Is the standard lower because of the quality of their coffee or by an internalized sense that the coffees from India are inferior? The "body" of one their coffees that I sampled in their lab was surely 7.5 (perhaps 8), but their tasters were reluctant to rate it that high. They somehow had calibrated themselves to a low norm. How do such norms get settled? What would happen if this coffee landed on a table of international judges at a specialty coffee competition? Would these judges, being more accustomed to awarding scores in the 7-8-9 range, make it more likely that the coffee could make it out of the 4-5-6 range for its "body"? Calibration is not a foolproof solution. Nor is intersubjectivity a magic bullet: there are many ways to be mistaken. However, for criticism of one's narrow-mindedness and for being repeatedly jarred into opening up one's perspective, intersubjective relations are much required.

Our analysis here has taken a more interactional approach to coffee tasting than most commentators. Hopefully, this is the contribution that a sociologist can make to the study of these issues. Wiggens (2004, 36) has argued that an interactional approach to tasting is necessary for "understanding the ways in which people's constructions of taste preferences perform actions." An abiding question for professional coffee tasters is what about a given coffee is most important to communicate, but this is not a question that can be resolved by an individual acting alone because communication already invokes social being. There is so much going on inside a cup of coffee that to appreciate it adequately one needs to marshal all of the resources and diverse perspectives one has available. In the end, professional tasters are a collective, with a mission to which they have dedicated their lives. As with Illy Coffee, it is a mission that requires both art and science, both of which depend upon intersubjectivity to protect them from their worst transgressions.

Chapter 10

Tasting for Excellence

A: It was my favorite on the table; it was not over-fermented but presented very sweet tropical fruits.

B: It got too funky for me.

C: Too much process.

Setting the Scene

Cup of Excellence is an international program run by the Alliance for Coffee Excellence (ACE, headquartered in Portland, Oregon), whose mission is to raise the quality of the coffees from a dozen countries in Latin America and Africa. They have had a significant impact upon producing countries, introducing them to the world of specialty coffees, teaching them about desired flavors they can produce, increasing the price levels for their lots of specialty coffee, and socializing them to the taste considerations that consumers of specialty coffees in Europe and North America use when they purchase coffee. They have influenced the culture of coffee in producing countries, expanded the awareness of *cafeteros* (coffee purveyors) about taste, and transformed their agricultural orientation from a preoccupation with quantity to a concern for quality.

In the countries in which it operates, ACE runs annual or biennial coffee competitions that selects the best specialty coffees that each country produces, publicizing the country's coffees in the global market. Winning coffees gain premium prices, which provide funds for local growers, most of whom reinvest their gains in coffee production. They reinvest the funds partly out of a sense of patriotism, knowing that their coffee represents the nation and not only their farm. A previous Cup of Excellence winner in Nicaragua told me that he had used his first-place profits to purchase a dryer for his *finca*, which reduced his dependence on local processors and brokers, increasing his share of the selling price.

The Cup of Excellence competition operates in three stages. First is a Preselection stage that relies on national judges, who devote a full week to carefully assessing each of the submitted samples of coffees for the purpose of removing coffees that would have no chance of becoming a specialty coffee. These national judges are selected by means of a national examination and competition that takes place in the weeks prior to the Preselection tasting, so the most qualified coffee tasters of each country become judges. After the Preselection week, an interval of several weeks is scheduled in which the providers of the coffees chosen to compete in the Cup of Excellence can prepare full lots of their coffees (not only samples), sufficient for them to sell at auction should they become Cups of Excellence. When these lots are ready, they are given a code number for blind tasting and brought to the site of the competition, where a second week of cupping, the National Selection tasting, takes place. During this second stage, the judges, who are the same national panel, reside together in the same hotel. They devote the entire week to scrutinizing these qualifying coffees for the purpose of narrowing them down to the 40 best, which are submitted to an international panel the succeeding week (stage three). Two or three of the national judges join 16 to 20 international judges, and this international tasting panel ranks the top 10 coffees, as well as selecting 25 "International" winners who will receive the title "Cup of Excellence," and also four or five "National" winners.

During the Preselection stage, the tasting is oriented to defects and flaws in the submitted samples that can disqualify coffees from becoming a Cup of Excellence. In the year I observed, 210 samples were submitted, and the national panel was tasked with narrowing them down to 126 coffees that would advance to the National Selection. They use the official Cup of Excellence form, which provides for a maximum score of 100 points. A score of 82 and below is considered ordinary, a score of 86 or above is considered very good, i.e., a "Cup of Excellence" (although this gateway can be lowered to 85 or 84, depending on the year and the country), and 90 and above is considered excellent and is denominated a "Presidential Cup." During the Preselection stage the orientation of the tasters is largely toward the negative ("–") features of the coffees. This is a practical task, and deciding which coffees merit exclusion is more essential than discovering or describing all the positive features of the better coffees. The first day of the week is devoted to calibrating the judges, so that all the tasters can be applying similar standards, and during the initial days there was a broad spread in the scoring. Judges were in agreement regarding which were the worst coffees, and most were in agreement regarding the best coffees; the largest spreads in the scoring were those coffees that sat on the cusp of qualification and elimination. This work of narrowing 210 samples to 126 was fairly straightforward.

Stage two is the National Selection, and the judges' work is still mostly practical: they are tasked with reducing these 126 qualifying coffees to 40. Not only does this require more careful sensory analyses, the judges are also concerned about not sending any sub-quality coffees to the international panel that will perform the judging during the Final Selection week, since they might reflect badly on the country. The tasters are no longer looking only for defects and poor coffees, but they are still more oriented toward identifying coffees that are not-excellent than they are oriented to locating the finer flavored coffees, those that are likely to become Cup of Excellence winners. They pay special attention to the 84–85–86 range of the evaluation, wherein lies the line that divides those coffees that will proceed to the elite judging and those that will become the also-rans. That is, at stage two the tasters are still not looking so much for the positive features ("+") as they are preoccupied with identifying coffees that are "*not* +" because they are primarily tasked with eliminating coffees with scores less than 86. They are not yet concerned with sorting out in any precise order the coffees that score in the 86 to 90+ range. The tasters of the National Selection round also monitor the consistency of the coffees: is the coffee acting the same each time it is roasted and brewed? Consistency is a foundational concern for supplying coffee to markets. The judging in the National Selection process is conservative, the scoring is better calibrated than during the Preselection, and there are few 90+ scores.

The week of the Final Selection is devoted to choosing the Cups of Excellence. In the year I observed, a mostly new panel of judges from 12 countries joined three Nicaraguan national judges in examining the 40 qualifying coffees to determine which coffees would become "Cups of Excellence," which ones would be designated "Presidential Cups," and how the top 10 coffees would be ranked. At this point the judges' attention was focused sharply upon the most positive, truly outstanding taste features of the coffees; that is, during this third stage they were oriented to "+", which calls for a more exacting regime of tasting. After two rounds of tasting, during which they gradually demoted less excellent coffees and were afforded ample opportunity to assess the consistencies of all the coffees, the very best coffees were allowed to advance to the final rounds of tasting during the final two days of the judging, where the coffees faced fierce competition and thoroughgoing sensory analysis. At this point judges became more willing to award higher scores, for a number of reasons: (1) these coffees had received confirmation of their excellence, so there was less risk in giving higher scores; (2) coffees that are able to reach or exceed a score of 90 will earn premium prices at the auction that follows a national competition (the sponsoring agency receives much of its income from a percentage of these sales at auction); and (3) Nicaragua's repetition will benefit by its coffees being judged 90+ by an accredited international panel. In the Final Round, six out of the ten top-rated coffees had their scores raised from the previous rounds: whereas none of them achieved a 90 rating during Round One of the final two days of tastings, and only one of them (the eventual Cup of Excellence winner) received a 90+ in Round Two, five coffees received a 90+ from the international panel during the Final Round:

Round One	Round Two	Final Round
87.63	88.81	90.10
88.33	87.09	89.00
88.33	89.20	88.86
89.22	91.11	91.48
86.20	89.05	88.48
86.47	89.05	89.40
88.56	89.25	90.69
88.13	89.02	90.21
87.87	89.31	88.88
x	88.48	90.17

An enthusiasm for higher scores during the final rounds occurs at most international tasting competitions. This concluding phase could almost be considered a fourth stage, since the tasters also advance from simply describing the coffees to generating a collection of detailed and accurate taste descriptors that will help in selling the winning beans at auction. The judges I observed devoted more of their attention to precise identification and delineation of flavor descriptors, and this became a practical task that accompanied their numerical scoring. In this way, each of the three stages presented the tasters with its own practical tasks that affected the kind of sensory assessments they performed, as these moved from "−" to "*not +*" to "+". During the final three rounds, the tone of the competition changed, as the presence of national media and not a few anxious growers who arrived at the site a day before the awards ceremony increased the intensity with which the tasters worked. Everyone (organizers, roasters, brewers, auditors, tasters) were noticeably happy and relieved that a very intense series of tasks had been completed satisfactorily and that they had done their job well.

Summary of the Scoring

As described, the judges for the week of Preselection and the week of the National Selection three weeks later were accomplished Nicaraguan tasters who had to qualify on the basis of an examination and selection process. Except for two judges, they were the same people both weeks. The international judges for the Finals included three of these national judges, who were joined by 18 international judges. The national Preselection's 16 judges used 42 different flavor descriptors (here a flavor descriptor is a descriptor that can or could be located on the WCA/SCA flavor wheel) for evaluating 81 of the sampled coffees that I observed during the Preselection process. The National Selection's 16 Nicaraguan judges used 53 different flavor descriptors for evaluating 157 samples. And the COE Finals' 21 international judges used 86 flavor descriptors for evaluating 106 presentations of 40 coffees. This means that the international judges employed a wider selection of flavor descriptors. The reasons for this, while unclear, probably have to do with their experience with a wider range of coffees and familiarity with flavors that are characteristic of the cuisine and diets of differing cultures (Japanese, Scandinavians, USA, etc.) as opposed to a panel composed of people from a single country.

There were some descriptors that the national panel relied on that were used less frequently by the international panel. For instance, 63% of the cups at the national level were described as "sweet," while only 48% of the cups at the international tasting were described as "sweet," and Nicaraguans used the descriptor "caramel" more frequently than did international judges. Chocolate, which originated where the Mayans lived in Central America and southern Mexico, and is still a daily staple for Nicaraguans, was used for 35% of the cups at the national tasting, while only for 19% of the cups at the international tasting. At the national tasting 37% of the cups were described as citric, while only 7% of the cups at the international tasting used "citrus," although more specified terms, such as "orange" (16%) and "lemon" (10%) were also employed. "Frutas rojas" (red fruits) is a term that is commonly employed throughout Latin America and was used for 6% of the cups at the national tasting but never used at the international tastings, although occasionally a few specified red berries (raspberry, blackberry, etc.) were employed. The descriptor "cherry" was used for 20% of the cups by the international panel and for only 1% of the cups by the national panel.

Some descriptors reflect actual flavors that are sensed directly, whereas other descriptors have passed through a process of institutionalization and gained iconic status. "Frutas rojas," "caramelo" (caramel), and "citrico" seem to be used by Nicaraguans in iconic ways (i.e., in a standardized manner that reflects a settled praxis of professional tasting that has become routine and during which the meanings have become generalized). "Orange" when used by a North American is usually more of a direct flavor sensation and straightforward description; by contrast, tasters from India use the descriptor "orange" in an iconic manner that essentially substitutes for the idea of "good flavor." It is possible that "peach" in Japan has a similar iconic usage. Every descriptor is both a response to immanent sensory experience and affected by social institutions (including institutionalized semantic references). "Sweet" is richly polymorphic and can signify different things in different circumstances; rarely does it mean that the coffee is actually sugary in taste, although the sensation it describes may affect the same area of the tongue that sugar influences. In some situations, "sweet" can mean that the coffee is not bitter.

"Peaches" was used for 19% of the cups by the international panel but for only 1% of the cups by the national panel. "Grape" was used for 13% of the cups by the international panel and never by the national panel, and "jasmine" was used for 21% of the cups by the international panel and for only 6% of the cups by the national panel. Flavor descriptors like "cherry," "peach," "grape," and "jasmine," as well as "maracuya" (passionfruit) and "panela" (a cake of crude granular sugar cane), are all characteristic of geographic regimes and the diets that correspond to them, so tasters are describing coffees in ways familiar to their daily experience. Nicaraguans use flavors unique to their region, such as "passionfruit"; Dutch tasters were alone in using "blackberry" without hesitation. Hawaiian-based tasters have used "macadamia," even when others may not grasp what it indicates. Indian tasters refer to their rich collection of spices; Washington state tasters refer to apples (Red Delicious, Granny Smith, Gala), etc. The international jurists referred to 21% of the cups with the descriptor "liquor" or similar descriptors ("winey," "Champagne," etc.), while Nicaraguan national jurists used it for only 6% of the cups ("vino tinto") at the National Selection tastings. Use of references that are familiar is natural; however, the professional aim is that the tastes derive from the coffee in an objective way.

During the tasters' discussions, many key tasting references were used in about the same ratios by all three panels of judges, and these include references to body, balance, clean cup, mouthfeel, and acidity. From this we can conclude that the tasters in all the panels possessed similar expertise, knew their jobs well, and were capable of producing calibrated results. What was surprising about these several categories of coffee taste was how during their post-tasting debriefings the judges made few verbal references to body, balance, aftertaste, or fragrance/aroma: references for these categories made by all three of the week-long panels covering the 344 coffee evaluations that I observed ranged from 0 cup references to a maximum of 13% of the cups. By far, the majority of references during the evaluative discussions that followed each flight of tasting were to the single category of "flavor." This was so even though flavor receives only 8 points of the total score, while body, balance, and aftertaste each receive 8 points as well. This means that the scoring is weighted quantitatively in a manner that is not reflected by what seems to be the focal interest of tasters during their post-tasting deliberations about the coffees: tasters are preoccupied with the category of flavor, but the form is less so.

The form, while designed to produce numerical results, is not strictly "objective" in itself or by itself, since it is conceived by designers who make many well-considered decisions that reflect their own objectives and professional training. Tasting schedules vary from country to country, from institute to institute, and from coffee purveyor to coffee purveyor; further, these forms are amended continuously. While the evolution of the forms is slow, consideration of reasonable ways to amend the tasting forms is an abiding concern of professional tasters, who operate collaboratively about such matters. This reveals that alongside the form, there is always an intersubjective footing for the objectivity provided by a tasting protocol.

On most forms the coffees are evaluated on the basis of 100 points, and this is so even though many of the forms do not afford scoring that actually adds up to 100 points. Even those that do add up to 100 have undergone an arbitrary design process directed to producing that 100 figure as an artifact of the form. The Cup of Excellence form uses eight categories that receive eight points each, for a total of 64 points, to which 36 points are added arbitrarily to make 100 (the final score can be reduced by penalties for defects). The Espresso Cupping Form (ECF), which is used by the Specialty

Coffee Association in Europe for certifying espressos as "specialty" coffees, evaluates 11 categories each of which can earn seven points, for a total of 77 points, to which 23 points are added to make the 100 points. One naturally wants to ask, why is "100" so critical to the evaluation? The answer is complicated. Part of it may have to do with a digital fetish for the number 100. In addition, the objectivity of an evaluation depends upon its ability to be communicated successfully across sectors and nations, so that an "80" score can be made to mean roughly the same thing everywhere. By using a basis of 100 points, tasting forms provide for a degree of standardization; however, in actuality, the scores generated on that basis are only partly comparable, and significant discrepancies among the scores get hidden from view, even while the evaluations remain oriented to 100 points. How can a score of "80" mean the identical thing when a cup rating produced by one form commences with 23 points and a cup using another form starts with 36 points? Even so, the social value of an "80" or "90," or "86," in the resulting score remains more or less identical around the world, and given this fact, it is possible that tasters likely do some adjusting of the score (using the erasure ends of their pencils or leaning heavily on the "Overall" category) in the interest of clearer communication.

Cupping forms bear other features that can affect the objectivity of the meanings of the scores. The standard SCA form offers a selection of between 6 and 10 for each category (presumably coffees unable to earn a score of 6 would never make it as far as SCA's cupping tables), and in practice much of the scoring dwells closer to 8. The Espresso Cupping Form affords a wider range and moves at half-point intervals from 1 (very bad) to 7 (very good). As a professional taster who is responsible for certifying espressos in Italy as possessing "specialty" grade, Dr. Enrico Meschini, described it, "The defect of our system is that our scores tend to be concentrated between 4 and 5.5," so the scores run slightly lower than those based on a ten-point scale. In other words, the ECF will systematically produce lower scores than either the SCA or COE forms. For instance, a "fair" coffee will receive 5 points × 7 categories + 23 = 58 points on the ECF, while on the SCA Robusta Fine Coffee Form (which does total to 100) a fair cup may receive 7 points × 10 = 70 points. The COE form offers tasters 1 to 8 scoring, but in the view of Meschini it is less likely that the judges who use that form will ever go below midrange scoring than will judges who use the ECF because the printed options of "0–4–6–8" on the COE form bear different affordances than do the options 1–1.5–2–2.5–3–3.5–4–4.5–5–5.5–6–6.5–7 on the ECF. This reveals the importance of the local contingencies of signed objects (cf. Garfinkel and

Weider 1992, 187 and 198) for every scientific practice. Meschini's point is that the objectivity of scoring is affected by the contingencies of the form that is used, and he worries that the ECF options attract scores that result in total scores that are slightly lower. Of course, it is not a surprise that a score is partly an artifact of the protocol used. What is important is what the score is able to communicate across the industry. All these conditions contingent to the protocol being used make it sensible to conclude that a resulting score is in part dependent upon local processes, despite the apparent objectivity and tidy organization of scores that are oriented to an imaginary 100 points.

Further Observations about the Nature of Scoring

The objectivity of scoring is related to the score having the same meaning for people located in different sectors of the industry and different countries. Objectivity is linked to communicability. Geoff Watts (2013) highlights an aspect of tasting protocols: "One of the goals of cupping is to capture its essential character on paper so that you can talk about it, so that you can communicate about it, which is critical for understanding it. If we don't understand it, it is impossible to control it." Despite this, I have noted that a coffee that receives a 70 score in India can receive a 70 score in the USA, even when they use different protocols. And it is possible that a coffee that receives an 86 score in Colombia will receive close to an 86 score in Italy (though it would earn such a score by means of a different schedule and receiving positive ratings for different parameters). Numerical scores can provide an adequate place to commence a discussion.

There exist differences in national preferences regarding flavors, such as a Korean and Colombian preference for washed coffees and antipathy for naturally processed coffees. The priority that a national coffee culture may give to the other aspects of taste can vary, such as mouthfeel (an interest that predominates among Italian tasters) and aftertaste (a priority for Chinese tasters). One exporter tells me that although quakers (undeveloped beans that never reached maturity, which can lend a papery or cardboard taste to a coffee) will reduce the score of even a good coffee, he is able to sell to Turks all the lots of good coffee with quakers that he has available; he suggested that there was something about that papery-ness that Turks like. Some coffees that contain metal salts or some bitterness or roughness can be tasty for some (one might say, "interesting") and not for others, so long as those tastes are in small doses. The strategy of an exporter is to provide each client from each country with coffee they can use and will accept. An experienced exporter will be familiar with the idiosyncrasies of the taste characteristics of each of the coffees he is exporting and know which are likely to be problems for each country.

World Coffee Research has argued that the task of identifying a flavor and the intensity of a flavor can be strictly objective, and that the subjective component can be limited to the question of whether or not the flavor is liked or disliked. This is a limited understanding of subjectivity. Further, the scoring afforded by most cupping protocols embeds a taster's preferences (self-consciously or not) in much of the numerical evaluation. It may be possible that "body," for instance, could be evaluated only by its heaviness alone, but in practice a heavily bodied coffee that is pleasant will receive higher points for body than a heavily bodied coffee that is unpleasant. In the same manner, a coffee with light body can be good or bad. When one is evaluating the quality of a coffee, factors such as pleasantness are important, which renders the sensation of heaviness on the tongue alone an insufficient basis for scoring. There can be variations among tasters, but what is most important is that each taster works in a consistent way.

Each category of sensory analysis presents its unique range of difficulties. At cuppings around the world, tasters have taken me aside and suggested that the cupping form not only records the analysis, it directs the analysis, and most of them find that this direction helps them to stay organized in their work; at some point, they also comment that the form can confine the experience, and not a few tasters have confessed to me that sometimes there is a need to subvert the form. For instance, since the category "Overall" appears last on the form and not first, it is positioned well for adjusting the preceding scoring. This implies that one has not already adjusted the scores of other categories to resolve such problems. What they do regarding this is not necessarily not being objective and may even contribute to making the forms successful.

This leads us to another question about methodology in sensory analysis. Many tasters advise, "All the categories have to work together." However, the scoring is done by individual categories. Is it essential to strictly separate the ratings for each of the individual categories? If so, just how can the form assess any synergy? Does adding up the scores of what has been individuated capture the synergies? Is the category of "Overall" sufficient for achieving this?

Our topic is *just how* sensory scientists work with the cupping form. A form offers multiple benefits; principal among them is that it provides a routine for rigorously scrutinizing more aspects of taste than a taster would be able to recall. It collects and memorializes the evaluations of the several categories and enables those evaluations to be communicated clearly to other parties. Importantly, it makes possible the comparisons that are so critical for the work of the coffee industry. Above all, a cupping form focuses the mind of the taster. Professional tasters, even those skeptical about the objectivity of the results, prefer to work with a form in hand because it helps them to keep their inquiries organized. There are even some ritual aspects to its use, which contribute to the social solidarity of professional tasters. Most tasters will admit that the total score that their protocol produces is not always appropriate for a coffee they have tasted. Numeration assists thinking, focusing it, but it does not replace thinking. Cuppers at the COE told me things like, "This should have been an 85–86 coffee, but it didn't get there." On such occasions, the methodologically produced objectivity of the protocol is permitted to prevail over intuition regarding the taste of what was in the cup. Permitting an unbiased evaluation to supersede what one is thinking that a coffee will become is an example of being professional. Yet there are also cases where the professional taster senses that the scoring has come out badly wrong, and this will cause the taster to get out the eraser and adjust the ratings of several of the categories. On occasion, it can be the eraser that guarantees a protocol its science by bringing the natural objectivity and the methodologically produced objectivity into better alignment.

Certain specific scores possess a unique value in the industry. Coffees over 90 points receive much attention and higher prices. Accordingly, a "90" has an iconic value that is additional to the sense of 90 as a numerical evaluation. Something similar is true for "86" if that is the minimum score required to be designated a Cup of Excellence. A coffee producer from Matagalpa, Nicaragua, took me to his home to show me his coffees, and he introduced each of his green coffees to me by the numerical rating each received at competitions: "This harvest received an 85." His comment reveals that the numerical score is an important identifying aspect of a coffee. What I really wanted to know from this producer was what the tastes were like, but that clearly had little priority for him, and he was unable to tell me. The "85" derived an iconic sense also, by being so close to the magic "86" that would have qualified it for the Cup of Excellence denomination. In such ways, a coffee's identity is heavily invested in customary social practice, and these numbers escort international coffees, even though what the numbers mean becomes less clear the further they travel; however, an importer will use the numbers to decide which coffees they will sample or purchase. While large orders are normally placed only following careful cupping of a sample, the scores are what prompt importers to request exporters to ship samples of their coffee to them via DHL. Such scores offer some indication to a buyer about where to begin a search, which is preferable to commencing at random.

When samples of highly rated coffees are received by importers, little of the evaluation beyond the numerical score is passed along. An importing coffee firm will re-cup it from scratch, usually using a tasting form its own lab has been developed to suit their specific requirements, which can differ in important ways from the forms used at a national or international competition. Some larger coffee purveyors in Denmark and India expressed a sober skepticism of tasting schedules that are exclusively numerative, and they use more qualitative forms that better fit their specific requirements. On the other hand, some exporters have revealed to me that they prefer sending to potential buyers only the numerical evaluation without transmitting any of the flavor descriptors.

The three panels of judges at the Cup of Excellence occasionally made references to a coffee being "a good cup" whose goodness could not be denied even when they were unable to specify it. Occasionally, when the head judge or his translator/assistant became frustrated with the absence of a description, they would shout "Comentario!" (Comments!), or "There must be a reason you scored it so highly" or "You guys are a little quiet! I'm a bit worried about you!" in order to elicit more commentary. When a well-rated coffee elicited zero descriptors, the judges would be asked "What was so positive?" about the coffee. When one coffee earning a low rating received only the descriptor "café," a second judge shouted out, "Un café sin comentario" (A coffee without commentary). On one occasion the jurors in unison responded to their own silence by shouting out "Comentario!" to the head judge. It is not easy to accurately describe the tastes that a complicated cup of coffee possesses, and one can recognize that it is good coffee before one can identify the flavors precisely or describe what the coffee is doing in one's mouth.

The Nicaraguan national jurists never used "structure" to describe a coffee, but references to structure ("Nice structure," "Good structure," "Unstructured," etc.) were applied by international judges to 7% of the coffees. "Structure" is an evaluation preliminary to further specification and refers to a coffee that possesses a complex array of flavors and taste characteristics that interact with each other yet do so in a stable way throughout the drinking. As we discussed in chapter 8, one might think of it as being similar to "balance," only more complicated. Balance was mentioned for 13% of the cups in the National Selection and 11% of the cups in the International Finals, even though only three times in three weeks of tastings did any taster ever specify the aspects that were being balanced (e.g., "acidity and body"). Nearly all tasting forms include a numeration field for balance, so it is always being scored—but just what is being scored? It can be acidity and body in one case, sweetness and mouthfeel in another, and "citrus" and sweetness in yet another cup. The tasting form itself might be responsible for these omissions since it promotes swift passage to numeration without requiring much specification.

As I have observed, aftertaste can earn for a cup as many points as flavor can; however, aftertaste was rarely mentioned by tasters during their discussions (0% during both the Preselection week and the National Selection week, and for only 2% of the coffees during the Finals). Some lay drinkers hardly pay attention to this aspect of taste; however, it is the aim of the SCA to better educate drinkers about aftertaste, under the policy that the more that drinkers know about coffee quality the more likely it is they will be willing to pay higher prices. Consider how the category of aftertaste can gain objectivity. Objectivity is related to the reproducibility of that sensory experience, and for that to happen there must be some precision about what is being evaluated. Aftertaste bears characteristics of strength, duration, and quality, and it can be bitter or clean. "It just lingers and lingers" can be an asset when the flavor is pleasant but a liability if the flavor is astringent. The secret to evaluating the aftertastes of 300 coffees is to have a routine way to assess it, and the key to this is to calibrate the tasting practices of the judges. In fact, calibration operates at the heart of the protocols for achieving objectivity in tasting. For each of the three weeks of the Cup of Excellence competition, the first day was devoted strictly to calibrating the tasters. The calibration is considered so critical for the success of the science of cupping that when two of the judges for the Preselection were unable to attend the calibration day due to prior commitments, they were excluded from the entire week of judging, and the Cup of Excellence proceeded with Preselection with 16 instead of the 18 cuppers they had planned.

Calibration Again

None of the evaluations performed during the calibration tasting sessions count toward the contest; instead, the coffees sampled are chosen for their ability to present tasters with tasting puzzles so that they make observable an array of the different practices they must use when they evaluate coffees, and so that tasters are able to witness how well their scores align with the assessments of others. Tasters are not prohibited from offering conspicuous and variant assessments; however, they can learn whether any of their assessments are eccentric and reposition them in the direction of the consensus view. Judges who are uncertain about what numbers to give a coffee that possesses certain features can be socialized to a normative assessment, which contributes to the reproducibility and communicability of the scoring. The head judge explained that an 80% correspondence is considered ideal, while a correspondence of less than 65% is a problem. National tasters with low rates of correspondence were not selected to participate during the international stage of the judging; however, by the end of two weeks of tasting together, an 85 score for one taster was an 85 score for any of the other tasters.

Much calibration proceeds in a reflexive manner: one experiences an aftertaste, assesses it, provides a score, and later looks with some eagerness to see what the other tasters have done, which is displayed on a chalkboard, feltboard, or LCD computer screen, and thereby one learns whether one's evaluations were reasonable. During the collaborative debriefing session, the range of scoring (the judges themselves are not identified, only their scores) and the discussion that accompanies the presentation of their scoring teach the judges what the scores mean and which aspects of an attribute typically raise a score and which aspects lower a score, especially relating to the particular coffees under examination. This helps the tasters to get on the same page before the official judging begins.

During the calibration day for the week of National Selection, the head judge gave the panel a high scoring coffee to evaluate. The tasters gave the coffee eight evaluations at 87–89, seven at 90–92, and one at 93–94, for a mean total score of 89.66. Unknown to the cuppers, this same cup was offered in the very next flight of eight coffees, and it received eight evaluations at 87–89 and eight at 90–92, demonstrating that while the calibration was already high, the tasters became more calibrated during the exercise. Equally notable is that the mean score for the coffee during its second flight was 89.5, which was only a fraction of a point in variance with the first time they tasted it. This indicates that the judges knew what they were judging and were able to reproduce their assessments when tasting blindly, possibly because they were applying the same criteria, which is where a panel of tasters want to be. When one judge was asked about the reason for a one-point demotion, the reply was "I thought it was a little different, a little less delicate, it was stronger." This is reliable, professional tasting. A similar phenomenon occurred during the calibration for the international tasters. A coffee that received an average score of 88.24 received an 87.67 during a subsequent flight of tasting. Another that received an 88.24 received an 87.29 when it was re-cupped, which again reveals that the judges' scoring was not arbitrary.

Consistency Again

The tasks of identifying and tracking the taste of a coffee and describing what its flavors are doing is not an easy one. Frequently, the main features of a coffee are obvious, but many times discerning a flavor is like discerning a figure in the foliage. Not infrequently, one has the sensory awareness of a certain something but is unable to say just what that something is. Also, not all coffees present their taste profiles in the same manner: some coffees remain consistent, while other coffees offer a shifting field of flavors and sensory effects, and as soon as a taster thinks they have it in hand, the field can shift once again. Even coffees that sit still can present identifying flavors that are too subtle or too difficult to bring to a sharp resolution.

One taster described a stable coffee as "Transparent, consistently sweet, consistently clear." What is this "consistency" of which tasters often speak? There is the consistency of a single cup of coffee that presents the same flavor from hot to cold and provides that flavor or flavors clearly so that they can be easily recognized and studied. What that coffee has is transparent, and there are no defects (quakers, rotten beans, phenols, etc.) to interfere with taste detection; moreover, the different aspects of its flavors do not get in the way of each other, with the predominance shifting among them. Another taster remarked, "The flavor was unstable." Unstable flavors can still be good, even interesting, but they are more difficult for tasters to identify.

Another kind of consistency, discussed in chapter 8, is that occurring between one and another cup of the same coffee. At the Cup of Excellence, it was not unusual for a coffee to present a differing flavor on a table where other judges were working: "The cups on tables one and three were better than they were on table two," or "Table one and table two were better than table three." At one point, the head judge announced, "This was supposed to be an 86 coffee, but on some of the tables it did better than that." This coffee had earned a mean score of 87.81, and the spread of scores was considerable (five rating levels out of eight). Differences in consistency can result in a variance of the scoring and can throw the scoring out of calibration. What makes the situation challenging is that for any given coffee, it is not always certain which differences derive from the tasters at the different tables and which derive from the coffee itself. An objectivist might blame the coffee, and a subjectivist might blame the tasters.

Among the causes for inconsistencies are quakers that have been unevenly distributed, a grind that is not uniform (some cups receiving finer grounds), a defective bean, differences in maturation, a fortuitous fermentation, etc. A Nicaraguan taster complained, "It was different on different sides of the table," and an international taster commented, "Our table was inconsistent by cups, and then there were even differences as I went from table to table. It was really hard to deal with." Only the head judge is entitled to taste the coffees on other tables before scoring, but many tasters taste the other tables after they have turned in their scoring sheets. When a coffee is the same in all cups and on all tables, it gains additional respect. To say "This was the same on all tables" is a compliment. Once it is known that there are differences, tasters feel freer in their responses, since it becomes less likely that any variation of a judgment will be criticized.

A third kind of consistency is from flight of tasting to flight of tasting: a coffee that is re-roasted and re-cupped (perhaps to try to get it to act more consistently) may or may not present itself in the same way. Most skilled tasters are able to recognize the same coffee when it reappears; nevertheless, they must be able to set aside any expectations they have and taste in an empirical way. In the words of the head judge about a coffee whose rating had changed, "We're judging the coffee in front of us, not on what happened before. So *we* are consistent, but the coffees are changing." Coffees that change from cup to cup, table to table, and flight to flight present tasters with a difficult task since they become more difficult to describe, and tasters may re-cup them in an attempt to tame the variation: "Not consistent enough, so we'll try it again." I have never seen a coffee re-roasted more than twice, and there is no desire to re-cup any coffees that do not seem likely to achieve a specialty grading. As one taster said when there was a large spread of scoring that occurred entirely on the low side of the possible scores, "Bye-bye!"

Consistency is generally a good thing. It is good because it makes identification and description easier and because it is more reliable for coffee buyers who can be more certain that they will receive the taste in the bean that motivated their purchase. For this reason, good coffees that are consistent can receive slightly higher scores than do inconsistent coffees that are better tasting. Not wanting to penalize an excellent coffee for its being inconsistent, tasters may choose to try the coffee again to see if it might become more consistent after another roast. Coffees that present consistent flavor profiles upon re-roasting sometimes receive additional credit for this consistency, which transgresses the rule that only the coffee in front of one is being judged. A coffee that is consistent can be evaluated fairly and accurately since tasters can locate clearly what they are describing. On the other hand, a highly consistent coffee can be boring, or as the tasters will say, "Polite," "Normal," "No tiene nada" (It doesn't have anything).

When a taster says "It doesn't have anything," what is it for which she was searching? What is missing? What is it to "have" something? It is this worldly *thing* that tasters are tracking; and the *work* of searching-and-finding this worldly thing is what we are investigating, and the source of objectivity. Few coffees, even consistent ones, remain identical throughout the time they are being consumed. A coffee starts out hot and cools gradually, and as it cools flavors can change. Evolution of flavors across the changes in temperature is a coffee's "profile." A coffee can get better or worse. "For me, it went flat" might be said of a coffee that excited a taster but "never developed." It might be said, "I wished this coffee stayed as good as it was when it was hot. It lost a lot." Typical assessments are "It became worse with the falling temperature" or "It was good when hot, but as it cooled it lost its sweetness and became papery." Or it could have been "Bitter when hot, but sweet when cold." A taster described a favorable coffee's profile in this way: "This coffee presented an interesting temperature change: when cold, the fruits changed and it developed some melon." Another said, "It came back strong after a weak middle." A taster is not investigating a single sensory phenomenon, but something dynamic.

Intersubjective Collaboration, and Discovery

Flavors that evolve can be complicated, and the work of tasting can become intricate. Always, there is more going on inside a cup of coffee than any settled description of its taste has identified. For this reason, coffee tasters are always probing, looking more deeply into what the coffee is doing than what they have identified already. In this task, flavor descriptors both assist and impede the taster's sensory perception, and tasters offer the advice not to think too much when tasting the coffee. Still one must think, if only to avoid becoming trapped by one's thinking, perhaps made habitual to the point of prejudice. This presents a double-bind that inhabits tasting: one requires a systematic methodology to advance one's investigation, but one cannot allow a methodology or protocol to blind one to that "what more" that the coffee possesses and is still to be discovered. A cupping form should assist such discovery.

Descriptions of flavor profiles can be simple, or they can be detailed. One taster commented, "Orange blossoms when hot, but a lot went away, and it became woody." And another specified, "Raspberry when hot, but it didn't last." One might offer an assessment like, "The floral changed to herbal," while another taster might even specify which flower and which herb. When confronted with an inconsistent coffee, it can happen that an antagonism of flavors occurs when the coffee is hot, leaving the taster uncertain just how to describe it; however, as a coffee cools its taste can become more stable and permit the taster to make a determinate identification of what the coffee contains. "It had to cool down before I could see what was happening." However, tasters know they need to be cautious because indeterminate flavors can be as important as determinate ones, and may be what is most enjoyable about a certain coffee. When this is the case, tasters can be left perplexed. A phenomenological observation is that being perplexed may or may not mean that one has failed to assess the coffee, and knowing the taste of a coffee in a definitive way can be accurate or it can be a case of the taster investing in an unexamined habit. The horizon of understanding is complicated, and it is not always the best policy to come to swift conclusions. On many occasions, a coffee or coffees will so scramble the thinking of a taster that the taster will sit down for a while in order to clear his or her head before returning to the cupping table for another effort to sort matters out.

Some of the details of flavor profiles can become obscured by the contingencies of a cupping form. A few tasting categories feature scales that can be raised or lowered, with arrows placed by the taster to indicate whether the reevaluated scores are improving or growing worse ("Every single one of my arrows goes down"), and so they are able to capture the dynamic character of a coffee's taste. What is it to numerate a taste zero-to-eight without using taste descriptors to describe it? Descriptors expand the sapience of one's tasting, and they are helpful both for the taster's on-site inquiry into a coffee, and for communicating to buyers, marketers, and consumers what is attractive about a coffee. This may be the reason that the judges discuss flavor descriptors more than other aspects of the form.

Flavor descriptors afford tasters a way to think collaboratively about an identifying taste, and these discussions can consist of sequences where one description builds upon the previous one: "lemon" provokes a second "lemon," and "buttery" provokes a second "buttery," as here:

A Super transparent, clean, well-balanced.

B Orange, honeysweet.

C *Limoncello.*

A description like "Floral with citrus" is quite general, but the particular flower and/or citrus fruit can be contributed by a succeeding commenter. The tasters instruct each other:

A   A lemon and honey combination, like a tea that stayed sweet the entire time.

B   Like green tea.

C   A smooth, rich coffee with lemon tea.

A   Complex variety, silky.

B   Solid, but not very articulate.

C   More articulate as it cooled.

Tasters working cooperatively sometimes seem like bees hovering around a flower in bloom.

Frequently taste descriptors and numerical evaluations are proffered together, especially when the descriptors are intended to justify giving a high or low score. This round-robin of description matched its coffee almost perfectly, even though its metaphoric spread is expansive:

A   I gave it a 95. A good coffee. At first, it was 89, but it matured upon cooling, offering a delicate tamarind acidity.

B   Notes of jasmine and tamarind.

C   Like grape or blackberry.

D   *Vinoso* [wine-like].

E   *Vinoso.*

F   *Vinoso.*

G   Rich, apricot.

H   Very clean with some notes of mature fruits and vanilla.

I   Red wine.

J   Raspberries with a bit of liqueur.

K   Cherry.

L   Pineapple cake.

M   Pineapple juice.

Another complete description of one coffee that became one of the top ten Cup of Excellence selections, a coffee that was characterized by being especially clean with an enduring aftertaste but in no way bold, included the descriptors, "Jasmine, sweet, lemon-lime, green apple, black tea. Pink lemonade, grape musk, nectarine, almond, Juicyfruit, complex, lingers, bright, super-clean, silky, transparent. Great lingering aftertaste." Here one can appreciate just how much can be going inside one cup of coffee, and taste descriptors can serve as a roadmap through the confusion. They organize and memorialize what one has found, and they communicate avenues of inquiry to other tasters that merit further specification. A taster's methodology with any protocol succeeds when it assists the taster to reach the limits of what the taster can find, that is, when it carries the taster to where the tastes under scrutiny exceed what has been captured and institutionalized by the taster's practice. At this point, a taster may discover something new.

How does a descriptor direct a taster to the tastes of a coffee? When a colleague suggests *maracuya* (passionfruit), for instance, that inquiry can motivate one's tasting for a time, as if the notion of passionfruit were riding on one's tongue. It is impossible to search for all flavors at once, and giving priority to searching for one can occlude others, which is why collaboration is important in sensory analysis, even though in strict competitions collaboration is forbidden; however, in other situations the collaboration can be robust. It should not be a matter simply of smelling and tasting for flavors that one likes; one should keep oneself open to new aspects that one might be able to discover. A cardinal skill of tasting is to remain open to what is unique and unfamiliar in each cup. One must think while not permitting the thinking to get in one's way.

Judges not only identify and describe the flavors of each cup, they also score them. A high quality that dissipates after a short time can be compared with a high quality that endures, but how should it be compared with a medium quality that lingers? Which is preferable, fruity or chocolate flavors? Acidity can be good, but its duration also matters. A taster must reduce a variety of qualities to a single numerical score, and these assessments require judgment. While such judgments are personal matters, the task for the industry is to develop professional tasters who work in similar predictable ways. Accordingly, calibration is central to the objective values of sensory science. A taster who can communicate across the spectrum of personnel of the coffee industry is more useful than a genius taster whose skills are too idiosyncratic to be understood abroad. Consequently, the task of a "professional" is not only to dive deeply into what a coffee offers but to communicate that to others. Some tasters are better at communicating than tasting, and all tasters have something more to learn from other tasters, which every taster recognizes.

At one point during the cupping discussions that follow each flight of tasting, the head judge made the remark, "The more that you share about the flavor experience, the more we can learn." This is because there is so much going on inside each cup that no one person is able to grasp all of it, no matter how comprehensive their sensory assessment may be. Most thinking in the world is a public activity, and it is natural to test one's fresh insights by consulting one's associates. In that way mistakes can be identified and even fresher ideas can emerge. Generally, the dialectics of intersubjective relations work to clear up the understanding of the tastes and to further the growth of knowledge. Tasters who cup together usually discover more taste properties of the coffee than people who taste alone; however, this fact is subverted by the need to score without being influenced by the opinions of others. Official cupping is performed in near silence, and for most of the time not a word was spoken, with only a few exceptions.

Tasters occasionally offered brief, unsolicited comments after they completed their tasting and were sitting down adding up their scores or making corrections on their tasting sheets. Most commonly, these comments were made to compatriots who were also judges (Dutch conversing with Dutch, Japanese with Japanese, Americans with Americans, and Nicaraguans with Nicaraguans), and the remarks were related to shared commercial interests in their home countries. During the fragrance evaluations there was occasional head-nodding or head-shaking. Even a brief smile or a mild nod can reveal a fellow judge's assessment, as can the intensity with which a judge cups a given cup, the speed with which the level of liquid drops in some of the sample cups of coffee, and a variety of gestures, finger-pointings, and energy flows that are readable. It is impossible for a cupping to be entirely blind, and cuppers whose expertise is legend are tracked by the other cuppers, even those working at other tables. When an insight into flavor is original, it is natural as well as productive to have the insight evaluated by others (since receiving confirmation of one's notions is a naturally occurring component of how knowledge is produced), but it violates the protocol and it was rare that any taster revealed a descriptor or comment. The most common source of conversation during cupping was collaboration regarding cups that possessed flaws that might require disqualification.

It is during each post-tasting discussion period that the intersubjective work of producing objective meaning commences in earnest. The tasters think together. They are called upon, usually by volunteering, to offer a brief public summary of their sensory assessments. Here they orient their words to what their fellows are likely to understand, appreciate, or accept, and this causes a degree of self-censorship, and they withhold their riskier (and more foolish) assessments and provide the portions that they think are more likely to be considered reasonable. Frequently, they employ discourse strategies that help to decenter themselves from the scoring, like reading off their copy of the scoring sheet as if they were simply reporting objectively about what has been written down on the page they are holding ("It says . . ." or "I have . . ." or "According to my commentary . . ."). Reading it just as it was written removes the taster from being in a position of advocacy, so that they can retain at least the appearance of being objective. Even when they are not reading, they will preface their comment with a bit of downgrading, like "It has a woody taste, *a little bit*," "It was too astringent, at least *for me*," and "*For me*, it was a good coffee." That is, never mind whether the description is accurate for the coffee, no one can contest the fact that what is reported describes the opinion of the taster accurately. Such discourse strategies serve to reduce the likelihood that one will receive criticism.

Attending to what others think and being concerned about one's reputation is a natural part of life anywhere in the world and a cause for people to act responsibly. Accordingly, a preoccupation about scoring too high or too low can infect one's scoring and what one reports about one's scoring. All tasters want to be accepted as professionals, although the criteria for that are not always clear; oddly, the more professional and experienced a taster is, the more willing the taster will be to give high or low scores when they think it is warranted. Sometimes a taster offers low scores in order to present themselves as conservative and a person who is not easily swayed. The time devoted to calibration is intended to overcome some of these anxieties. Fears and concerns about being accepted or about getting oneself into trouble are an abiding concern for most people in every situation, and these concerns motivate a large percentage of mundane social interaction. A result of this is that frequently the tasters do not comment enough to enable the collective to develop a corporate assessment in a dialectical manner, which is the wellspring of truth. Faced with the silence of their tasters, the response of the head judge and the assistant was to keep encouraging the judges to speak up.

Intersubjective alignment, especially as fostered by the calibration process, helps ensure the objectivity of sensory evaluations. During the post-session discussions, tasters are able to hear how each of the other tasters are using the flavor descriptors, and they are able to identify ways they may have been misusing them or ways that the significance of the descriptors should be extended. Some descriptors are vaguer than others, and it is during the debriefing sessions that a group of tasters has the opportunity to come to some collective agreement about how to use the descriptors, so that after some time they are able to employ them in analogous ways. Here too, intersubjective work aligns the tasters' understanding and serves the interest of objectivity.

Tasters also pick up useful terminology, especially terminology that is uniquely apt for the coffees being examined. Usage of some descriptors can come in bunches, as if each new term inaugurates a mini-fashion. During the discussion about one flight of coffees, the descriptor "astringent" was introduced for the first time, and it was then applied during the next several flights of tastings. *Serendipitous* instruments of social interaction are essential to all interaction. All local work, which includes scientific work, takes place amid one set of local contingencies or another: there is no situation without local contingencies. When a coffee is determined to be "juicy" or "very spicy," just as soon as the descriptor is introduced, the domain of flavor that they gloss is recollected and then the description may be applied to succeeding coffees until its use gradually abates. Dave Eggers (2018, 81) describes one of the first coffee tasting experiences of the San Francisco–born Yemeni Mokhtar Aklanshali: "Was it toasty? He wrote *toasty*. Was it fruity? He'd heard the word *fruity* a lot that day so he wrote *fruity*. Nearby, someone said they tasted chocolate notes, and Mokhtar said he did, too."

This leaves open the question whether both the first coffees and the later ones really were juicy and spicy, etc., or whether it was simply an instance of projecting an interpretation at one moment and not another. After heavy usage of a term subsides, do the coffees really lack those flavors, or were they simply located outside of that window of usage? The hard truth is that both can occur together, and perhaps necessarily so—it may possess such a flavor *and* its identification is subject to the way a practice of projecting taste descriptors develops. Objective descriptions do not develop by themselves; someone must think of them, and thinking always works by projecting a possible understanding upon what phenomenon is to be understood. It is a necessary condition of knowing. Here again, it is impossible to know for certain where the *sapere* (knowledge) stops and the *sapore* (flavor) begins.

When "delicate" was used to describe cup number 7 (of 10 cups) on the final day of the International Finals, it was picked up and employed to describe cup number 8. It was not used for cup number 9, but it was applied again to cup number 10, which was described as "a bit highly delicate." Does this mean that none of cups 1 through 6 were delicate, or only that no one happened to be thinking about delicacy at that time? "Delicate" will mean what it comes to mean during the discussion of the judges. That is to say, the tasters will witness its use, and thereby learn how to use it; in this way, understanding the meaning of some descriptors is a reflexive process. The question of what "delicate" means is further complicated by what "highly delicate" could mean. It seems peculiar that one can have a high level of something whose nature it is to be subtle. The addition of "a bit" to "highly" is a marvel, producing a description that will need to be interpreted by everyone. When a phrase is indeterminate, and many are, it can collect whatever sense the group fashions for it inside the local situation. As the term is reused, it has the opportunity to acquire a more determinate and stable meaning, which can be institutionalized and become objective. The critical thing is for everyone to come to understand the term in the same way, i.e., to achieve intersubjective adequacy, which is the work of calibration.

Three Kinds of Taste Descriptors

The most stable descriptors are *straightforward descriptors* whose sense is evident, though there will always be local social conventions of use that complicate their sense. Such descriptors can be metaphors, such as "a basket of flowers." In addition, there are *iconic descriptors*, such as "orange" in India, "peachy" in Japan, and "red fruits" in Central America, etc. These are descriptors whose name glosses highly standardized and generalized familiar taste experiences, that have a broad range of application, and whose specificity of reference is developed in the situation of use and not from a dictionary definition. Finally, there are *reflexive descriptors*, descriptors that gain their definiteness of sense and reference from how they organize the meaningfulness of some tasting; they have more recent origins than straightforward or iconic descriptors and are more dependent upon the local work of the parties who are interacting with each other.

Here are a few such assessments of straightforward descriptors:

A Cardboard, cardboard, cardboard.

B Dry, cereal, bitter.

A Guava.

B Chocolate.

C Mandarin.

A Sweet caramel.

B A lot of vanilla.

C Mocha.

D Malt.

Although it can be challenging to work out just how chocolate fits in with guava and mandarin, the meaning of each of these flavor descriptors is not problematic. The tasters are attempting to delineate the region of sensory experience within which each coffee is operating. Their work is collaborative, and the dialectics that takes place among these differing descriptors is productive of new insights. In the last series of descriptors above, that each taster is using a different term to describe roughly the same region of flavor makes it more convincing that each taster is judging originally, rather than simply copying the previous descriptor.

We discussed iconic descriptors when we observed that a score of 86 has a meaning beyond its location on the 100-point scale. Because a score of 86 means that the coffee qualifies as being a specialty coffee, the term "86" implies more than its location on a numerical scale. And we also observed that the descriptor "85" for a coffee that barely failed to make the cut also possesses an iconic sense, as does "90," which is where the elite coffees commence. A country or place of origin of a coffee can be made an iconic descriptor by means of standardized usage. When a customer walks into a café and asks a barista, "I like Sumatrans, do you have any?" there may be some idea of a specific taste in the customer's mind. Some place-origins like Sumatra, or Kenya ("I like coffees from Kenya"), or Jamaica sell a great deal of coffee, so marketers use these iconic identifiers for describing their coffees, even though the flavors that are communicated this way can be inconsistent. What Indonesian coffee may mean to one person, for example, may not be what it means to another. Yes, generally Sumatran coffees are strong and heavy-bodied, but not all. The use of origins as iconic descriptors has become fashionable in North America, less so in Europe because they generally use blends where the barista or manager does not always know what is in the blend the bar has purchased.

To an extent, the use of origins as iconic descriptors is patterned after the use of *terroir* to describe wines; however, *terroirs* are smaller zones than countries are. In recent years there has been an increasing use of the regions or districts where coffee is grown for describing coffees. Having observed a sudden popularity for "Huila" coffees from the Huila province of Colombia, I went to Huila to try to pin down its flavor. I discovered that there were four kinds of tastes that typical Huila coffees have, depending upon which side of the mountain they are grown, at what elevation, and what sort of winds they receive (humid or dry, depending upon the side of the mountain). Moreover, most growers were not very familiar with the flavors of their coffees, except for a few younger processors who had been influenced by Illy Coffee's advisers or some US specialty buyers. Most of the growers that I met would be unable to identify a Huila coffee on a table of Colombian coffees, and yet "Huila coffee" has earned a brand reputation. Happily, the specialty coffee industry is beginning to market coffees by the specific farms where they grow, where it is possible one will find a well-defined, reliable taste.

Several years ago, I visited the grower who won a Cup of Excellence I attended in El Salvador. When I visited his farm in the high Chalatenango region of El Salvador, he admitted to me that he did not know what his coffee tasted like. I asked, "If I presented you with three cups containing the three varieties of coffee that you grow on your own farm, would you be able to pick your winning coffee out from them?" He replied that he did not think he could do so. Prior to the COE competition, he had sold 4 quintals (of a harvest of 23 quintals) to an exporter, but he had no idea to which country that exporter was sending them. This is typical for many smaller farmers and is part of the reason why so little of the value of coffee reaches the farmer. He must pay a commission to the taster (who lives in town and serves a number of *fincas*), who he relies upon for advice about what he is growing. This taster probably also receives a small commission from the exporter (in the range of 0.2–0.5%), which further squeezes the margin.

Varietal types, hybrids, and coffees that have adapted to local conditions can be described in an iconic way, and there were some comments such as "It's like a Pacamara," "It has a Gesha taste," and "It has a little of the profile of a Kenyan coffee—some lemon citrus." In these instances, the iconic descriptors are intended to suggest the taste of the coffees; however, such descriptions are not as informative as providing the specific flavors that the taster is perceiving. A few tasters and many roasters like to play guessing games about the origin. Sometimes these iconic descriptors can successfully capture and communicate sensory qualities, but over time the more successful iconic descriptors become so distorted by market forces that the intelligibility of iconic descriptors becomes diminished. Both the national and international tasters at the Nicaraguan Cup of Excellence almost always restricted their descriptions to specific flavors or taste qualities. Another reason for this is that flavor expectations that ensue from applying an origin as an ideal type can interfere with the direct and unbiased detection of sensory properties.

Occasionally tasters will combine straightforward descriptors with iconic descriptors, such as "This is a perfect type of Nicaraguan coffee . . . with caramel and citric notes." Such a description helps tasters to define Nicaraguan coffees in an iconic way. Here is a situation where the Nicaraguan taster is well poised to teach the international tasters what kinds of flavors best identify a Nicaraguan coffee, and occasionally the Nicaraguan tasters really nailed one of their own coffees. Of course, Nicaraguans have extensive experience with their coffees and know well the tastes that are in a cup. At the same time, international judges have experience with a wider range of flavors, and as we have seen, use a larger set of flavor descriptors effectively, which affords the national tasters an opportunity to learn from the international tasters. At the Cup of Excellence, the educating operated in both directions.

Reflexive descriptors are descriptors whose sense and reference are derived from the intersubjective work of using the descriptors and develop by applying them to the coffees under examination. Their sense emerges from a local situation, where their meanings derive their clarity. In these tastings, the term "bold" (as in "bold acidity") developed a sense over the course of its use, during which the tasters could observe the way to use it appropriately. The sense of "bold" is hardly straightforward. It can be related more to the weight of the coffee in the mouth than to a flavor, and its use was usually restricted to aroma, body, or mouthfeel. Witnessing any use of a descriptor, a taster can adopt it; that is its reflexivity: its use is not well understood until its use is witnessed, and then one can appropriate it. Interestingly, tasters can use these reflexive descriptors even before they are sure of just what is their proper sense; in fact, that is how they sometimes learn what these descriptors mean. Their proper use emerges from the intersubjective dialogue and interaction of the tasters as they collaborate in using the descriptor to engage with the coffee. One learns the meaning not by asking for a definition, but by observing what it does and how it helps tasters to understand a coffee.

Disqualifying Coffees

Another activity in which cooperative or intersubjective interaction plays a decisive role is deciding when a coffee needs to be disqualified for having serious defects, such as phenols, which come from beans that have rotted or spoiled. A single very bad bean can spoil a roast, and tasting it can so affect one's tongue that it becomes difficult to taste subsequent coffees clearly. Coffees with mild taints or only a few quakers merely have their scores reduced and are not disqualified; however, coffees on the borderline between mild and serious defects require some collaboration among the tasters to decide what must be done about them. Tasters are reluctant to disqualify coffees that are very good yet contain a few spoiled beans, so the situation can become complicated. While the tasters do not make the final decision—that is left to the head judge—it is impossible for the head judge to taste all of the cups in the cupping room, so the other tasters will advise the head judge; he or she will come over and taste a suspected cup and make a decision, usually after some brief conversation with the tasters who first identified the cup. Typically, a taster will not call the head judge over on their own but first will consult a partner or two at the table, and together they will decide whether the defect is serious enough to bring it to the attention of the head judge. Most of the very few conversations that took place during the cupping were about suspicious cups.

Once a coffee is disqualified, that is the end of its life at the competition, no matter how much work the producer may have invested into growing and processing it. Tasters are able to detect that a coffee clearly received a good deal of attention at processing time, and they have genuine respect for producers' efforts, so they are reluctant to disqualify such coffees. Their assessment of the work put into processing, as opposed to a coffee that was treated in a casual way, may affect their decision about disqualification; however, they also need to penalize defective processing and protect their tongues from continually tasting a sour or phenolic cup. A truly foul cup receives no breaks. Suspected cups that do not get disqualified can acquire a stigma, and this may lower their numerical evaluation (in addition to penalty reductions for taints or quakers). When this happens, a structure of prejudice can develop in the thinking of the tasters, as suspicions get projected onto the coffee. Here is where the professionalism of a cupper can show itself. After spending 3 to 5 minutes discussing a possible disqualification and rejecting the idea, is a taster able to cup that coffee clearly and with a fresh mind? The fresh and open mind that the taster needs to bring to each cup is an important component of sensory analysis.

The head judge commented about one disqualified coffee, "A very nice coffee, but defects spoiled it on two tables," to which a Nicaraguan taster nodded and added, "Yes, it was a good coffee, but it had phenols." Another coffee that was suspected was not disqualified because after collaboration the tasters decided it was not a defect in the coffee but simply the coffee's own flavor that was responsible; it received an 85.91, and perhaps it would have passed the 86 threshold had it not been subjected to that collaborative attention. How does one decide just when a coffee is defective or is simply bad coffee, and when do flaws get blamed on a coffee's "inherent" qualities and not attributed to a bad bean or a processing flaw; that is, how do tasters pull apart what is inherent from what is "outside"? Is this a subjective or an objective practice? In such a case, is there any difference? Distinguishing a bad coffee from a defective coffee is another seeing-the-animal-in-the-foliage kind of phenomenon. One coffee contained an underlying taste that was appreciated to the extent that despite its having quakers, it was not disqualified: "It was sweet, with good acidity, a lot of its problems were quakers." Another taster liked very much a coffee that was disqualified and remarked, "If it was me buying the coffee, I'd still buy the coffee." A poor-tasting coffee that presented one phenolic cup out of the 20 cups was not disqualified because it was not going to succeed (and thus be passed to the next round) anyway; the head judge told me, "It wasn't going to score high, so I didn't kick it out." These decisions can become intricate and dependent upon intersubjective assessment.

With the increasing popularity of natural processes, the worldwide coffee industry has been confronted with the task of deciding how to think about them and how to evaluate them. Comparing a naturally processed coffee with a washed coffee can be a challenge. For this reason, at most competitions the organizers will try to have the naturals tasted all together during one or two flights of tasting and save the washed coffees for tasting during other flights. The world's professional tasters are not in accord about the value of these natural coffees, and the organizers of competitions—who must respect every judge—have their hands full contending with the problem of arguments that sometimes break out. One result is that a head judge may treat both contending sides with equanimity, but it is possible such a strategy can be offensive to both sides, each of which is certain about the values that must be applied. Another strategy is to avoid much conversation about the issue; however, international panels present a unique and valuable opportunity for the worldwide coffee industry to attempt to sort out such matters. In the long run, any differences in perspectives might enrich everyone's knowledge about the coffees.

Those who are critical of naturals have some backing from mainstream producers who will not purchase natural coffees because they are too risky: one can never be certain of what flavors will arrive, and it requires more intricate work to figure how to roast these beans; even if the roasting goes well, there is no guarantee that the same flavor will be available the next time one orders the green beans. Many of the coffees that were eliminated at the cuppings because of defects were naturally processed coffees. During the National Selection week, a flight containing all naturally processed coffees was arranged, and four out of the ten coffees were disqualified. As the head judge stated, "The problem with these processes is getting a consistent result, and there were some tables that were much worse than others." Flaws get blamed not on the coffees but on the processing, and judges frequently comment about the processing ("A good job" or "The process was not done well"). How do the judges recognize, from the taste that is in their mouths, what derives from the bean and what derives from the processing? Even when it goes well for the coffee, and its taste is excellent and consistent, some judges are reluctant to score a natural coffee highly: "A good process, but for me it seems dangerous." How do they detect such danger before it has manifested, and how do they incorporate that into their scoring? There is not full agreement regarding these dangers, so how can a taster evaluate the processing of these coffees in an objective way? When one judge proclaimed, "It was my favorite on the table; it was not over-fermented but presented very sweet tropical fruits," two other judges responded, "It got too funky for me" and "Too much process." While nearly all judges are oriented to the processing of coffee, they hold varying ideas about what a good process is. One judge may focus on processing for the quality of exotic flavors, and another may examine the processing of a coffee for whether it successfully resulted in a clean and consistent cup.

One coffee received a wide spread in its scoring (from 79 to 90+):

A Pineapple, so bright!

B Bright, my favorite.

C My favorite too.

D A dangerous coffee.

E Too astringent—I thought it was really awful. I didn't want to taste it again.

C Can I buy this coffee?

In an attempt to remain neutral, which is his responsibility, the head judge observed, "This is what we call a controversial coffee." When a naturally processed coffee maintained some consistency, it did well with these tasters; however, when it was inconsistent on the tables, complicating its sensory analysis, it did not do well. One owner of a specialty café expressed a dislike for naturally processed coffees. When I asked him why, he explained, "You can't guess what it is." Some drinkers prefer consistency, and others enjoy unpredictability. Each one is best.

Roasting Level

Tasters around the world have told me that one must taste only what is in the cup and evaluate a coffee based on what one's tongue and mouth detect. How do the complex considerations of processing influence this kind of analysis? A similar problem can occur with the level of roast. As we have discussed, judges sometimes praise a coffee that does not have a good taste, blaming the roasting for any shortcomings. If they are judging only what is in their mouths, how can they upgrade a score based upon how they think a coffee will perform at a more optimal roast?

Roasting is a headache during most competitions. This is because each coffee bears flavors that will optimally expresses themselves at a given roast level. Some coffees taste better roasted lightly, and other coffees perform better at darker roasts. A purveyor who specializes in selling specialty beans to home roasters, Burman Coffee Traders, offers advice about how each of their coffees perform at every roast level, and it is the task of most roasters to examine each green coffee they receive to discover the correct roast level for that coffee. At competitions, it is convenient to roast all of the samples at the same level, or by weight/density since denser, high-grown beans require different roasts than do less dense low-grown beans. A dark roast can burn a low-grown bean, and a light roast may not convert all of a high-grown bean's carbohydrates to sugars. The organizers do not have the time to determine the correct roast level for 210 lots of beans, and they may consider it more objective to give every bean the same roast. But when judging excellence in coffee is it more objective to roast the coffees similarly or at each coffee's optimum level? For these reasons roasting becomes an issue for the judging, and comments like "It was roasted too darkly," and "It was a good coffee but a little over-roasted" are common.

"The roast level is very dark—too high!" "You got some of the bitter from the dark roast when it cooled, but you could still see how good it could be. It was supposed to be 86–87, but we need to re-roast it to be sure." Is it alright not to penalize a coffee for being too bitter because of the roasting, or should one always judge only what is in the mouth? Which is the more objective practice? Also, when should a coffee be sent back for roasting at a different level? One cannot keep re-roasting many dozens of coffees. As the head judge summarized, "If we feel strongly as a group, we have some opportunity to re-roast." During a Best of Panama competition, there was an issue regarding the excellence of a coffee that was somehow detected even though its excellence did not appear in the cup. After some discussion, the head judge sent the coffee back to the roasting room with the instruction to roast it lighter. It came back at the end of the cupping day with a roast that was too light, and so presented a different set of troubles for the tasters.

The head judge said, "Our goal is to find a roast that offers transparency, that will allow us to get a clear look at the coffee, so that we can find the coffee and not the roast." Here both the subjectivity and objectivity are addressed, and the two may not be separable. Getting a clear look at the coffee is one aim ("There were some things in this coffee that we couldn't see clearly because the smokiness obscured them"), and developing aspects of the flavor that were suggested is another. "You could see the potential in this coffee, but it didn't follow through. The thing you could see in this coffee never developed." How does one "see" what is not there?

Objectivity and Strategic Scoring

A Korean taster who disliked naturally processed coffees rated a coffee that received a mean score of 90.75 as being "79 and below." She was asked to explain herself during the post-tasting debriefing, and she said, "I don't understand why we have this kind of coffee—it is over-fermented." Was the 79 score her objective assessment, or was it a score deliberately designed to lower the rating and so a case of strategic scoring? After this happened with several coffees, she came to realize that her low 79 scores were being eliminated from the calculation for being such extreme outliers, so instead she gave a natural processed coffee a score at the low end of the middle range so it would be certain that her low score would be counted in the average. Everyone was surprised by the sudden change in her evaluation, until they realized that her opinion had not changed and that she was only being strategic with her scoring. At another international coffee competition I attended, there were three Korean judges who shared a similar dislike of naturals, and their low scores were substantial enough to lower a natural coffee from first place to sixth place. I conversed with the grower after the competition, and he was deeply wounded. Although I agreed that his coffee was the best one, I suggested that every taster is entitled to his or her preferences. How does objective scoring fit into a situation like that?

Even naturals that have good results can have their score lowered because of perceived dangers, another instance of tasters rating what is not there. Once during the National Selection week, the head judge was reluctant to hand over a highly dangerous, wild coffee to the international judges, so he gave this coffee (which had received a mean score of 87.53) a score of 80. In doing so, he displayed a practical orientation to the future of the coffee in the dynamics of the competition. On this occasion, his strategy had no effect, and he allowed the coffee to pass through to the next stage. A capacity to abandon one's prejudice like this is the equanimity that one who is acting professionally needs to have. Tasters are not only judging each coffee, they are also continuously collaborating in producing a successful competition. The head judge stated for another coffee, "Every now and again you might want to give a coffee a second chance and consider whether it is good enough to move on to Round 2. But you have to be careful when doing this, since you don't want to do that too many times. If I wanted to push it through, I would have given it an 87, but not this time." This illustrates how scoring can be strategic.

Does strategic scoring compromise the objectivity of the numerating? It affects the methodologically based objectivity produced by the protocol, but it may retain faith with the more original objectivity that rests in the cup. To which of these two objectivities should science give priority? This question leads us to ask, "What is science?" Recognizing what exists, and scoring in a manner that respects what exists, is surely science. Science occurs in the world too, so it always operates amidst local contingencies. One can try to limit the influence of those contingencies, but ruling them out of existence by fiat is being ideological, not being scientific.

Objectivity and Local Contingencies

While examining the work of coffee tasters, we have noted the influence local contingencies have upon the professional analyses. Many of these contingencies are viewed as obstacles to objective practice, yet they are unavoidable—the entire world is made up of local contingencies. It is what people do with those contingencies that is decisive. Such contingencies include what one ate for lunch prior to cupping, the interruption of one's thinking as one stoops to pick up a dropped pencil, or embarrassment after dropping a tasting spoon. One excellent coffee (a score of 87.10) suffered from having a position alongside a superior coffee (91.38). Had it been alongside cup number 4 that contained an 84 coffee, its scoring might have been higher. Similarly, a coffee with a light body can suffer from being tasted directly following a heavily bodied coffee, and a "soft" coffee can suffer from being tasted following a dynamic coffee.

Judges develop numerous tiny strategies for navigating their way through this maze of local contingencies. For instance, one way to counteract being influenced by a preceding cup is to taste the cups on a table in both directions, one time moving from cup number one to cup number ten and the next time from cup number ten to cup number one. This can raise additional problems, such as bumping into other tasters as they are moving counter-clockwise while one is moving clockwise, and so cause one to receive criticism for "always being in the way." Social troubles like that are another local contingency, and local contingencies do affect the science. Is tasting in both directions as a solution to being influenced by adjacent cups a subjective practice or an objective one? It is a decent illustration of a subjective practice that is employed on behalf of achieving objectivity. We need to avoid thinking dualistically.

Another local contingency is the particular sense and reference that manages to emerge from the use of a reflexive descriptor over the itinerary of its being used. Its sense has a local historicity, which has given a precise signification to a description that at the outset may have been indeterminate; and this signification can be made available for use by anyone. Further, that locally derived significance may be the result of a serendipitously occurring event. For example, during a debriefing session, while one is considering making an objection to a descriptor proposed by a taster, a second taster quickly confirmed the correctness of that first taster's descriptor. In such a case, one will usually demur from contesting it, since it may appear obnoxious to object to a descriptor that has received confirmation. Without a disconfirmation, that locally established sense can become the publicly accepted assessment of that descriptor, valid for all, and eventually even for oneself. Once it is adopted by everyone, it earns for itself a measure of objectivity. The social interaction is one of the abiding contingencies.

Still another contingency is the social presentation of one's "self" among a collectivity of tasters. If one wishes to present oneself as a prudent and discriminating taster, one might resist giving a coffee that deserves a 90 such a high score, and in that way the objectivity of one's scoring can be damaged. There were a number of moments during the sensory evaluations when the head judge seemed to fear that something like this was happening, and he would intervene and suggest to the judges to be careful about what may be going on. For instance, he once announced, "Pay close attention to the coffees that are 89 and may be deserving of 90. Don't hold back." I would call continuous scrutiny of the ongoing praxis of tasting like this an instance of self-understanding: one not only pays attention to the coffee but simultaneously and continuously assesses the subjective processes by which that understanding is being generated. Radical self-understanding like this is subjective acumen, but it too works in service of the objectivity of the sensory analysis. Close and self-reflective attention to the process of constructing knowledge amounts to a subjective skill that is essential for achieving objective results. In all these many ways objectivity is a contingent production.

The head judge monitored the tasting practices of the judges toward cups that possessed sensory qualities that were salient enough to make the coffee recognizable as one that was evaluated previously. It is poor tasting practice to recycle an evaluation that one has already used for a coffee during a previous assessment; rather, one needs to remain open to the "what more" there is in the cup still to be identified and described. Those coffees that rated 86 and above and so made it to the succeeding round should be tasted freshly, as if for the first time. The assistant to the director of Nicaraguan Specialty

Coffees cautioned the judges, "Limpia su mente!" ("Clear your minds)," and the head judge publicly offered this guideline: "Score them as you have been doing, because we won't know how the 86+ coffees will behave." The advice here is to throw out what one has previously assessed and taste the coffee in a fresh way. Is this a subjective practice or an objective practice? Does it make sense to sustain such a dualism?

The local contingencies of dealing with the demands of the form are so intricate that its technical work can distract one from tasting the flavors adequately. One experienced elder judge who had attended the tryouts for being selected as a national judge became so frustrated with the numerical protocols distracting him from his focus upon tasting the flavors that he became resistant to the requirements to an extent that he was unable to qualify, even though his skill and expertise were widely acknowledged throughout Nicaragua. In the world of coffee, this would not be the first time that the need for standardization trumped tasting.

The capacity to remember which cups contained which flavors is also a critical skill. It is like the game of "Concentration" where one must match what has been hidden behind a square (revealed for a moment and then re-hidden) with another square having the same content. In cupping, some tasters have better ability to recall which cups contained which tastes than others do. Some judges record their judgments after assessing each cup of coffee, while others are able to cup an entire table and then record their assessments. Here again, recording one's assessments on the cupping form requires a good deal of bodily fiddling around, which can be distracting. When judges take a seat to work on their forms after tasting the coffees—adding numbers, checking for inconsistencies, erasing and repairing errors—some will need to get up and go back do more cupping in order to be able to recall clearly what their assessments were. During the post-tasting discussions, some tasters speak directly from recollection, while others need to read their notations from their page as if reconstructing a picture from an archaeological record. Tasters who had little to say may have had difficulty recalling exactly which coffee it was that possessed which specific feature they had noticed. Memory is an important skill in tasting.

Inevitably, a taster develops a personal system for using the form that works for them, but any system of numerating and recording descriptors can be influenced by local contingencies that develop serendipitously, and the "noise" of contingencies can reduce the precision of taste descriptors—a situation can take the best idea and twist it until it is unrecognizable. "Noise" here includes naturally occurring social influences such as copying others (thoughtfully or mindlessly), adopting what has been accepted and ratified by a local cohort, pandering to what one has heard others say, fears about getting into trouble, using validated, routine, or even hack terminology, and so forth. All these factors can distract clear thinking, but they are part of the way that any local situation organizes itself. They are not anathema to science, since adopting accepted terms can reflect a community's informed experience; one does not always have to be original to be wise. The taste descriptors one uses face the natural possibility of being inscribed by others inside a local practice that does things with them one had not intended. One's own ideas are distracted by the itinerary traveled by the terms one uses, by means of the signifying uses to which they are put by others; yet amid all of this, an objectivity can be established. But it is not established by itself; it is established because of the local work parties do to concert their activities so that there is intersubjective adequacy. Intersubjective adequacy and objectivity are practices. Amidst the semiotic movement within an intersubjective space, they are made to work successfully, and descriptors invented by tasters come to lead the tasters.

Conclusion

Objective knowledge indicates knowledge that can be understood in more or less the same way across a group of recipients of that knowledge, and it entails that all parties are able to know what a descriptor or account means without much diversity in interpretation. This knowledge is necessarily accompanied by the preparation, education, training, and socialization of the parties who receive the knowledge. At the same time, knowledge that has been objectified undergoes a process of standardization, possibly even simplification, the necessary price to be paid for some adequacy of meaning on the intersubjective level. A degree of restructuring may be needed in order to conform with widely accepted policies, routines, and social expectations. All of this requires extensive organization as well as discipline, and it does not take place without the participation of the parties who produce objective knowledge by paying close attention to the itinerary of interpretations and local meanings that the knowledge fosters.

The categories and ratings on the "objective" forms collect their significance from how they are being used and understood by the recipients. This is subjective praxis that operates in the service of accomplishing objective knowledge. In more technical language, there is a reflexivity of meaning to which all objective knowledge is subjected and is never able to escape. It is the way things happen in life. Scientific sensory analysts must sustain some vigilance of the itinerary that objective knowledge travels, and for that a practice of continuing self-scrutiny and self-understanding of the intersubjective forces that are in play is required.

Just when, and by means of what activities, does intersubjective knowledge turn into objective knowledge? Take all of the flavor notes that were written on the cupping forms by all the tasters; amassed together they are a collection of subjective sensory assessments. Compare such a collection with the discussions among the tasters about the flavor notes during the debriefings. Which of the two is the more objective? The latter is more objective because during the discussion the most idiosyncratic of the assessments usually do not get voiced, and so they fail to survive the dialectics of discussion. Some assessments get ratified and enhanced, and others are contested and fail to be expanded. This critical back and forth, this listening and attending to what is heard, in the end results in the production of knowledge that is more broadly acceptable. "Universal" may be too bold of a claim for such knowledge, but "objective" is apt. When it is done with care and concentration, it is competent sensory assessment.

Chapter 11

Importers, Roasters, Myths, and Marketers

> A French roast, an Italian roast, and a Viennese roast are all the same thing.
>
> —Benoit Gravel, El Salvador

During our discussion of the practices of exporters, we took the opportunity to describe a few of the tasting practices of importers and roasters because tasting is an exercise in communication and importers needed to be included. Here we take a deeper dive into the practices of importers and roasters and review strategies they use for selling coffee. Once the coffee has arrived at the harbor of an importing nation, it is a short step to the market and to home kitchens. Tasting plays an essential role in these final steps of the journey along the chain of coffee production.

Importers

The strategies of importers vary a good deal. Each importer searches for a niche or is attempting to maintain one, and the kind of tasting they do is dictated by what the niche requires. It is not simply a matter of providing good coffee; it is how they can process and produce *on a repeatable basis* the best coffee they can offer their niche. Many purveyors maintain an excellent business by offering coffees at the lowest possible cost, and price levels sell more coffee than flavor does. Even the better trademarks sell the majority of their coffee during special sales. Other purveyors, such as Starbucks, sell an identity and an ambience that includes simulating a sense of belonging to a community. Other firms market stories for their coffees or emphasize politically progressive motives (social justice, environmentalism, etc.). A few firms center their sales on a coffee's flavor, but some tasting is necessary for all these marketing strategies.

Just as exporters search for clients to match the coffees that have arrived in their labs, trying to fit the coffees to the various national preferences for "normal" coffee (see chapter 1), importers look for coffees they can purvey successfully to the market niche they have established. Quality may not be a problem because coffee traders have the ability to find buyers for any quality they receive, and in order to determine this, they will taste the coffees for defects (in the case of low-cost coffees), general flavor characteristics (medium-priced coffees), or particular flavor characteristics (specialty coffees). Some importers will pay a premium for high-quality grading results, usually as assessed by one of the major international tasting protocols (SCA, CQI, SCI), but other importers have little or no interest in quality coffees; in fact, according to the Indian exporter and taster Sunil Pinto, if you send some importers a superior-quality coffee, "they will think you messed up." A few importers will give negative evaluations to coffees for which some specialty purveyors would be willing to pay a premium.

Even with "price" coffees, importers need to discover ways to roast and blend beans that will minimize unpalatable tastes and contribute something noteworthy that might redeem an unrefined coffee, and so tasting is required. In the case of medium-priced and specialty coffees, once a desirable flavor is identified, say a "papaya" taste, one must discover a roasting profile that will best highlight the selected flavor feature; this requires considerable experimentation, and ongoing tasting is required after each roasting profile for monitoring their success. Once a taste has been adopted and has provided an identity for a firm's coffee, they must keep reproducing that taste on a reliable basis. Achieving "that same flavor" while crops and purchasing strategies keep varying is challenging, and it is tasting that guides their decisions about purchasing and processing. Coffee purveyors are assisted in some degree by the fact that consumers do not always pay close attention to the flavors (see chapter 12).

In the world of coffee, it is not simply a matter of "price" coffees versus "quality" coffees, since many purveyors occupy a location between the two, and most find a formula that takes both into consideration. Many of the largest importers address themselves to the basic features of taste, characteristics that fall under the categories of "body," "sweet," or aftertaste, and their tasting quest is quite general, with one eye always kept on the price. Pellini, a major firm in northern Italy, visits Brazil once a year to prepare their annual blend from the current crop. They start by cupping coffee from many different localities, usually concentrating on Minas Gerais, Cerrado, and Mogiana. Their tasters will experiment with different percentages for a blend; for example, it might be 50% Mogiana, 30% Cerrado, and 20% Minas. They will taste it alongside the previous year's product, and try slightly altering the percentages in order to maintain the target taste. Enrico Meschini of Piantagione Coffee in Livorno, explained, "We are never sure to get the same flavor next year. In fact, we are *sure* we will not get the same flavor. So we make adjustments with the percentages, usually up to about 5% fluctuation."

At the Pellini factory in Verona, for example, their tasting tab reports that they work on about two blends per month. When trying to improve a blend made up of 20% of each of five coffees, for example, they might balance a strategy for enhancing flavor by using some good fresh crop they have purchased with a strategy for increasing the profit margin by including an inexpensive bean or by satisfying their need to use up some quantities of green coffees they still have on hand. Each blend will be submitted to some 20 tasters, some of whom work for their firm and others who are consultants. To avoid complaints by their client coffee bars, their blends tend to be conservative in their design. Each year Nespresso faces a dizzying task of reproducing dozens of labeled flavors and retains a troop of tasters to maintain "that same taste" year to year for dozens of varieties of capsules, work so secret that they were unwilling to grant entrance to their Swiss facility. One can only imagine the sourcing, the percentages that must compose their many blends, the roasting strategies they use for manipulating the coffees to their desired end, etc., but it is for certain they have clearly identified their target tastes. Stabilizing the flavor of a blend and maintaining that identity requires constant tasting.

It is possible to change the way a coffee tastes by changing the roasting profile, and Luigi Odello even claims that "the science of roasting can completely alter the origin." Rob Hoos (2015, 62) elaborates, "By controlling the overall speed of the roast and thus the overall roast time, you are able to scale the length of the reactions you will need in order to achieve certain flavors." By using more time to reach the same color of roast (by lengthening or shortening the development time) one can enhance desired taste characteristics. Using many beans affords a number of strategies: one can use one bean to provide the body, another to offer some acidity, one or two more to contribute unique flavor notes that will make the blend less quotidian, and even another bean to tone down and render milder some stronger, perhaps bitter, beans that were procured at a good price. For example, one might purchase an inexpensive Brazilian Robusta for use as a base and for its body, an inexpensive Indian Monsooned Malabar for its smoothness to tone the Robusta down, and a smaller quantity of more expensive Colombian Arabica for its acidity.

"Good enough" may be the ultimate objective of most importers, but others are interested in purveying exceptional coffees that are the product of a passionate and committed firm that pursues imagination as well as profits. One Italian specialty roaster described their approach: "The work we do concentrates on the aftertaste. On what remains in the mouth. That for us is a reason for research, because when you finish your cup, that taste still persists." In larger firms, the tasters and baristas possess the passion, while marketers and owners are fixated on profit strategies. Buyers, including those who work for the most successful and largest importing firms, often do not explain to exporters or growers what flavors they seek, they just sample the coffee, like it or not, and purchase it or not. Pricing seems to be a stronger motivator than flavor. Discussing Mexico, Dr. Manuel Diaz explains that there has been little growth in the attention paid to flavor by growers and marketers, while the baristas have become the most dynamic player in the purveying of coffee there, putting fresh pressure upon management to develop quality. Expensive coffees are difficult to purvey at a good profit because the standard parsimony of most coffee drinkers limits the market advantage that exceptional-tasting coffee can achieve. The number of smaller firms who are dedicated to quality coffee is surprising, given how costly a business model it is, but in many cases as soon as such a firm is successful, it will be sold to a multinational corporation that has less commitment to flavor; or the specialty purveyors themselves may begin to pay more attention to strategies for maximizing profits. It can be said, without being a socialist, that again and again capitalism damages the tastes of quality coffees.

The first task of the importer is to avoid purchasing coffees that have defects, unless the damage can be reduced and the coffee is very inexpensive. Coffees that bear unique taste features that are the reason for their being purchased will frequently include a description of the taste characteristics in the written contract. When a container of coffee is shipped to an importer's port, a sample will be extracted from the container, using a sort of giant claw that probes the lot at random and pulls out a sample. This will be tasted by an agent on site or at the importer's tasting lab not only for defects (either in the crop or acquired in route) but for compliance regarding the particular taste features agreed upon by the buyer and seller, and matched against the saved pre-shipment sample, all before the coffee will receive permission to be unloaded from the ship. Here there is a considerable problem with communicating about the taste clearly. As discussed earlier, many importers are paranoid that exporters are trying to trick them, and many exporters are skeptical about imagined problems raised by the importers, viewing them to be strategies for renegotiating a lower price after shipment. These problems are endemic, and importers and exporters are mutually distrusting while being mutually dependent.

When Lavazza of Torino determines that a shipment they received is "irregular, with two cups having an earthy taste," what does this "earthy" mean? Is it an "earthy" unique to Lavazza's tasting lab, or is it an objective description? And if it is objective, how do the tasters who work in the lab of Michele Mastruontono at Lavazza locate it, and why is it difficult to communicate it to other professionals? When an exporter's tasters taste, they must not consider their own "earthy," they must imagine Lavazza's tasters' "earthy," which perhaps has its own historicity about which the exporter may know little. The exporter's tasters will cup them alongside a pre-shipment sample as well, but the two samples may taste identical, presenting the exporters with a quandary. All cognition involves an amalgam of what is there and what being projected upon what is there and makes what is there intelligible; therefore, it can be difficult to determine what is real. Objectivity does not arrive with a label on it. However, since a good deal of money is at stake, they will need to locate an objectively existing "earthy." The entire process is made more difficult by the reality that many of the tasting notes sought by an importer never get communicated to the exporters, as part of a strategy for avoiding higher selling prices. An exporter may be aware of a few minor taints (which are less than defects) that they have allowed to slip into the shipment, but they may not mention them for fear of raising more suspicion than is warranted. Accordingly, communication about tastes may not be excellent at any point.

Although communicating with consumers is a stated goal of the Introduction to Cupping class that CQI offers to tasters, roasters, and baristas, only a small number of the taste descriptors used by competition judges is transmitted to potential buyers. If there are 20 tasters at work developing taste descriptors and collaborating about which ones are accurate and pertinent, but only a few descriptors reach potential importers, what is the purpose of all that work identifying and discussing flavors? Having observed how information is transmitted along the chain of production, I would propose as an answer that the principal function of taste descriptors is not to transmit taste descriptors from producers to importers but to sharpen the professional tasters' attentiveness to the flavors of the coffees that are immediately in front of them, so that their sensory assessment becomes more exacting. Moreover, the tasting notes that get transmitted are based on when the coffee was first cupped. Changes in transport, roasting, the local discourse, etc. can render descriptors obsolete. Despite the attention that third-wave coffee purveyors pay to flavor when tracking the traceability of a coffee, the stability of those tastes is not assured. The context of international judges who taste at a given roast level, the context of the tasting performed in an importer's lab (guided by parochial interests of that firm), and the context of a consumer drinking the coffee at home (using various methods of preparation) are so diverse that it would be surprising if many taste descriptors did manage to remain intact. The few words that survive transmission along the chain of production and are placed on a package by a firm's marketers afford too few clues to help the consumer figure out what a coffee tastes like. This is not to say that those descriptors cannot sell coffee ("robust and full bodied"), but the tasting at each stage occurs mostly in a local world, and communicating the sensory experience is difficult.

Roasters

Since roasters and importers operate hand-in-glove, it is difficult to discuss them separately. There is continuous communication about tastes among a firm's tasters. The initial roasting takes places in tandem with sampling. A very light roast will reveal defects best, while also preserving all suggestions of the possible diverse flavors that a coffee could offer. Frequently a medium roast and a dark roast will be made as well, in order to learn other features of the taste. A fast roast will make it easier to assess the acidity, and a slow roast serves well for checking the body potential. A purchase will be made on the basis of these sample roasts, although the roasting accomplished by a firm's giant commercial roaster will differ from that of a sample roaster.

The main idea of roasting is to caramelize all the carbohydrates in the center of the bean without burning the surface. This is not easy to accomplish, since each crop of coffee possesses a different density. One wants to rescue the sugars by caramelizing everything, roasting slowly enough not to turn the surface into charcoal but still giving the heat an opportunity to reach deep inside the cellular structure of the bean. Dense beans possess superior flavor and complexity but can be difficult to roast completely. The most valuable acids get produced at temperatures between 128°F and 180°F, but the volume of beans one is roasting and the ambient humidity at the time will influence the temperature required. The roaster needs to tailor the intensity and duration of the heat to what the cellular structure of the bean is able to handle, and this entails experimentation and continual adjustment, and guesswork is never entirely dispensed with. One is roasting the chemical compounds inside the beans, and the objective is to get the bean to absorb as much heat as it can without burning. Temperatures that are too low ("baking" the beans) will be insufficient for promoting chemical reactions; light roasts can create too many variations in the flavors, while a deep roast will destroy the complexity and the aroma. The challenge is to turn any complexity a bean possesses into something highly desirable.

Pressure from moisture building up inside the bean before the moisture escapes will increase the rate and quantity of the chemical reactions (Hoos 2015, 57). After the coffee bean pops ("cracks"), a different kind of chemical transformation occurs. The time to first crack is measured and monitored, and the period between the initial color change of the bean and first crack is known as "the Maillard reaction," which at first involves a non-enzymatic browning. One can proceed to this first crack slowly or quickly, and generally the slower the progression the more complex the flavors will be. The period between the first crack and the conclusion of the roast is called "the development time." In addition to proceeding swiftly or slowly to first crack, and possibly altering the temperature after first crack, one can introduce plateaus or dips to help prevent burning the exterior of the beans. Some roasters move to first crack quickly with high heat and then shut off the heat during most of the development time, monitoring the internal temperature all the while; others build up slowly to prevent burning and to reach deep inside the bean safely. A roasting "profile" can include all of these combinations.

If one has a bean with faults, such as astringent flavors or earthy odors, one can roast it darkly to burn them up, including defects that derive from molds; many roasters roast their coffee so darkly it will develop a bitter flavor from the roasting. Customers who are able to apply their preferred routine of milk, sugar, or flavorings to these darkly roasted coffees, even before they sip it to judge its characteristics, will not notice; lighter roasts can produce so many unique flavor characteristics that they confound a customer's routine, which is a reason why some consumers prefer dark roasts. "International" flavored creamers have boosted dark roasts.

Roasting lightly achieves a more complex taste and preserves more of the caffeine; but if one roasts too lightly, the coffee will taste sour. It is generally accepted that consumers will tolerate bitterness more than they will tolerate sourness (Saragosa 2015). The result is that much coffee is over-roasted, and that over-roasting will dull the liveliness of coffees (Hoos 2015, 46). In brief, the taste of a coffee will commence with a vegetal flavor, proceed to sourness, and then develop acidic flavors; further roasting will reduce the acidity but increase the sweetness as the interior caramelizes. Even further roasting will make the coffee slightly bitter, and still further roasting will make a coffee fully bitter. Hoos (2015, 53) explains, "Early on, you start with more 'enzymatic flavor tones' residual from the terroir of the coffee and the balance of chemical compounds in the plant." As the beans caramelize, sugar browning will cover up these enzymatic flavors, so one may be forced to choose between enzymatic coffees and caramelized coffees. Fortunately, one does not have to choose the same coffee every day. Many purveyors try to combine both benefits by blending two different roasts together; sometimes it works (they may call it a "balanced" coffee), and sometimes not. By lengthening or shortening the development time (the time after first crack), taking more time to reach the same color, one can cause different flavors to manifest. It is a creative activity, which is why roasters generally love their work. Hoos (2015, 30) writes, "You could intentionally give a coffee a tea-like structure, or a caramel-like mouthfeel, or give it a heavy, buttery body all by manipulating the length that the Maillard [the time to first crack] is permitted to generate melanoidins." One teaches oneself to adjust the heat supply to what each bean can handle. Beans too light in weight cannot be pushed to a dark roast, while beans with a dense cellular structure respond well to a deep roast.

Roasters will tell you, "We cup at all degrees of roast to find out where the bean wants to be." They may say, "I think I prefer this. But first I'll roast it darker and taste the result." The initial roastings by the importer and by the roaster rely on a sample roasting machine, often a small Probat roaster. That produces a result that is not equivalent to what larger commercial roasters produce, since in their lab they experiment with only small batches of beans, while production is always with large batches. Manuel Diaz once joked, "Sample roasting tells you everything but the truth." The problem is "scaling up" the roasting to match the volume that one's firm requires. This requires careful cupping after the first scaled-up roast to insure one has duplicated what the sample roaster achieved. A roaster in Coeur d'Alene, Idaho, explained that each "drum-to-bean ratio has a sweet spot that needs to be found" (Starr and Nielson 2006, 25).

The complexity of these tasks makes the procedure suitable for computerization, so that the many small decisions can be repeated with precision.

The problem is that the perfect roast on one day may not be the perfect roast on a subsequent day. In some climates, the humidity or external temperature can experience drastic changes; accordingly, the digitized rendering, while a sound place to begin, is not decisive, and the roaster must still attend to every event during the roasting. There are sensors to aid them, sensors for color, sensors for gases being expelled, etc., but as Manuel Diaz also suggests, "Never trust sensors." Most roasters trust their eyes that gauge the color and their nose that smells the developing scent each step of the way. It might be said that science provides vital assistance but that art makes the final determinations. The powder of the ground roasted bean will be matched to the corresponding color test number (CTN), but the roasters always calibrate the CTN with their tongues. Leonardo Lelli, an artisan in Bologna, says that during roasting, he pays attention to each tiny change from one second to the next (Robson 2020): "I hear the cracks, and I watch the color, and I smell the aromas, and only when it all feels right, I take out and cool the coffee." Following this, the result will be tasted.

Chad Norris of Victrola Coffee Tasters summarizes the situation (Starr and Nielson 2006, 25): "I'm not so sure that digital roast profiling is the end all and be all. There are certain variables that happen on a daily basis depending on where you roast. You need to know the science that's going on, but you also need the human hand behind it. . . . We would like more manual control, if possible." And James Freeman of Emeryville (San Francisco's East Bay) phrases the predicament that roasters face in a concise way (Starr and Nielson 2006, 26): "I'm opposed to automation, but I'm *for* information." This perspective is refreshingly non-doctrinaire, but it is contradictory to the more firmly held positions of J. M. Juran (1988), who claims, "You can't have quality if you can't measure it," and Michael Bloomberg (2013, 41) who asserts, "If you can't measure it, you can't manage it." The skepticism of coffee purveyors mirrors that of the astronomers studied by Hoeppe (2014, 247), who reports "many researchers' lack of trust in the promises of the automatization." Some coffee purveyors have suggested to me that rule one is that no rules apply, and they subscribe to the belief that one must always taste the result. Benoit Gravel, a coffee purveyor in El Salvador who plants, harvests, processes, blends, roasts, and serves his own coffee in his own cafés, proposes, "Coffee is not mathematics—you cannot blend a super body with a super acidic coffee and get $1 + 1 = 2$. It's not deductive, you just have to make it and try it. One of the desirable traits can disappear. You never know." In the coffee industry, there is a clash of cultures between those who claim to know and those who believe one can never know for certain, and this epistemological divide does not show any sign of being resolved. Those who profit from being able to control knowledge, even from an ability to sell it (courses, computer programs, certifications, etc.), act more confidently about what they know. The further one is located from the practical tasks of purveying coffee, the more likely it is one will claim to know. As noted, hands-on practices of purveying coffee foster humility.

Communicating the Roast Level

Roasters communicate about their coffees' tastes with their colleagues, importers, and tasting consultants, and they also communicate with consumers about the roast, but even such an elementary matter—one easily measured by an Agtron colorimeter—is steeped in confusing communication. Recently, I was given a bag of "100% Kona" coffee. Apart from my skepticism about the "100%," I checked the bag to see if it indicated the level of roast, hoping at least that it was not a dark roast. The bag stated the roast level was "medium," but there are many mediums in the world; in fact, "medium" roasts are a global fantasy. What in Hawaii is labeled "medium" will be labeled "dark" in Scandinavia and "light" in southern Italy. This is because the meaning of each gloss is indexical, derived from the conventions in play at the time and place that the gloss is applied. Denmark labels "medium" what they roast lightly, and Seattle labels "medium" what they roast darkly. Perhaps customers prefer purchasing roasts labeled "medium." I have visited coffee purveyors who sell "medium" and "dark" bags of coffee that bear beans having the same roast. In Montreal, I complained to a smaller roaster-vendor about how dark a "medium" roast was at the firm's café, and the barista confessed to me that he lacked enough medium roast to fill the pound bags that had been already labeled "medium," so he filled them with a "French Roast." In another café that served gourmet coffee, I was pleased to find that they were offering both a "dark" roast and a "light" roast, so I ordered the "light," only to find it dark. When I quizzed them about it, they told me that they did not have enough of their Colombian light to brew, so they mixed in some dark roast. I now pay no attention to labels. Somehow, I knew before opening the bag of 100% Kona coffee that despite the stated roast, its level would be dark.

Dark roasts are labeled "medium" all over the USA. Some packages will read "Dark/Medium," which given the situation is perhaps the most apt gloss of all. This way the purveyor can cover most bases, and customers may project the roast they are searching for onto what they read. Purveyors label their roast "Viennese Roast," "French Roast," and "Italian Roast." I have confounded many baristas by asking them to explain the difference to me, and their explanations vary, although the main idea is that there is only a shade of difference among them, increasing toward dark in the order listed. I think more than conveying information about the roast level, the international place name motivates adding the gloss to a label. It is news from nowhere. Or as Benoit Gravel phrased it well, "A French roast, an Italian roast, and a Viennese roast are all the same thing." Given the differences that arise naturally from local custom and the essential indexicality of these glosses, many coffee purveyors would be unable to attach these labels consistently to a collection of dark roasts that sit in the bean trays of a cupping table.

Marketers

Similar obfuscation occurs with other taste descriptors, like "well balanced" (discussed in detail in chapter 8) and "full bodied." Of course, a firm's professional tasters understand just what they are describing, but the marketers have their own ideas, and since advertising, including package design, sells more coffee than flavor does, the professional tasters are frequently overruled. Many if not most packages claim that the coffee is "well blended" or has "good body," but these are empty signifiers and indicate little more than the fact that the coffee one is considering for purchase is a product of commodified capitalism, and so will be mostly tasteless. Few consumers could explain any "balance" in what they are drinking, even if the package did offer them a clue.

In Italy, there is a fondness for the descriptor "intenso," roughly translated as "bold," and some firms will give each variety they purvey a rating for it. What are they rating? What does it mean to say "Illy Intenso"? What is it that is intense—the taste, the level of roast, the amount of caffeine? Here we run into one of the ironies of the coffee trade: many consumers like darkly roasted, bitter coffees because they believe they provide more caffeine, when in fact some of the caffeine goes up with the smoke during the roasting, so the intensity of the bitterness and the intensity of the caffeine are separate phenomena. Lavazza Modo Mio's high-quality "¡Tierra!" capsule states "*Intensità 7.*" When I puzzled over what such a "7" (it is so specific) could define, I went to discover their website, which stated a different numeration for the *Intensità* of their "¡Tierra!" capsule. Another Italian firm, 101Caffè, produces a 16-page booklet for the capsules they purvey and give each capsule its own *Intensità* rating. Their brochure offers the explanation, "Intensity refers to the whole of the perceived aroma and fragrances that are released from the coffee in the cup." Do they mean "aroma"? I noted that the few "monorigine" (single-origin) coffees they offer had been given low intensity ratings, so perhaps it is not aroma; since these coffees had lighter roasts, perhaps the "intensity" refers to how much the coffee has been burned.

"Bold" is a popular descriptor, but its meaning is shrouded in indeterminacy. Here is a discussion between two lay coffee drinkers being interviewed by one of my students in Oregon:

A   It's definitely bold.

B   It's a very bold coffee.

A   I definitely agree with the boldness . . .

A   It was really sour, bitter, too strong. But bold.

INTERVIEWER: What do you mean by "bold"?

A   *He* was the one that said "bold." How is bold?

Here the first taster offers the taste descriptor "bold." Possibly his immanent preoccupation was with getting through the exercise without appearing dumb, but he did closely attend to the coffee before offering his descriptor, a descriptor with which Taster B agreed. Taster B's agreement leads Taster A to double down on his account. But when the interviewer asks the tasters to explain to her just what this descriptor means, Taster A pretends that he was not the one who proposed the descriptor. His gambit makes it evident that he lacked a clear understanding of the meaning of his descriptor. Probably Taster B also did not have a clear understanding about what was intended by the account he was confirming, so when the two tasters consolidated their affirmation of the descriptor, they were validating an account that lacked specific content; and yet this is a normal way that people speak intelligibly.

THE FETISHIZATION OF ORIGINS

"Single origin" coffees have become very popular in the USA, partly due to an increasing interest in identifying tastes with geographic locations, patterned after the wine industry's trope of "terroir." There is no reason why a single-origin coffee should taste better than a coffee that has been blended, so the demand for single-origin is partly a fetish, though it is one in which I am a participant, and I happily face the challenges of learning which regions offer which flavors.

Defining the identity of a coffee is an exercise in reifying experience, i.e., essentialism. Unfortunately, identities are transitory. Tasters sometimes defer describing the flavors and instead participate in a guessing contest of "What is this coffee's origin?" Instead of deriving the tastes from what is in the cup, they go straight from the cup to an ideal type (say, "Sumatran," or "Kenyan") and then download their descriptions of the flavor in the cup from a preconceived list of characteristics derived from the ideal type. This renders sensory analysis too abstract and general, and instead of being responsive to the world, a demand is made that the world conform to preconceived categories. Taste profiles that are affiliated to origins are elusive and variable, in the way Henri Bergson (1910, 130–131) describes the fleeting nature of our simplest sensations:

> I still give the same name to the sensation experienced [before], and I speak as if only my taste had changed, whilst the scent and the flavor have remained the same. Thus, I again solidify the sensation; and when its changeableness becomes so obvious that I cannot help recognizing it, I abstract this changeableness to give it a name of its own and solidify it in the shape of a *taste*. But in reality there are neither identical sensations nor multiple tastes: for sensations and tastes seem to me to be objects as soon as I isolate and name them, while in the human soul there are only *processes*.

As soon as one prepares the perfect coffee, one discovers one is unable to reproduce it. As soon as one thinks one knows a coffee, it will change, and we must continually stretch the ideal type we have developed for it to contain all of its flavors underneath that banner. As consumers become more aware of the range of coffee flavors, and, encouraged by the specialty coffee industry, take up the challenge to learn the tastes of single origins, they may be confounded at every turn. Overwhelmed by the industry's canonical descriptions of origin flavors and by the analytical sensory regimes of scientific sensory analysts, lay drinkers learn how to talk appropriately but can be orphaned from their own tongues and noses.

In order to develop a roster of single origins that is comparable to terroirs, the coffee industry needs to define geographic regions ("geographic indications"), identify the characteristic tastes, link the two in unambiguous ways, and develop the sustainability of the footprints over several harvests. This requires a tasting language sophisticated enough to capture the flavor differences of coffees unique to different origins (Lingle 2001, 2). Defining flavor variables that refuse to stay put can make the establishment of a stable relationship between taste and place difficult. Equally, defining the proper boundaries of a "place" can pose a challenge. A researcher in Colombia used more than a thousand variables that referred to soil samples, temperatures, solar radiation, etc. to locate geographic clusters. The researcher reported, "On the technical side, it was very heavy work." However, in an era of climate change, what stable relations between terroir and taste can be sustained? Even with a "paroxysm of analytical recognition" (Perullo 2012, 112; English tr. 2016, 81), it will be problematic to sustain a stable relationship, rendering a return to "the so-called taste of origin" unlikely (Perullo 2012, 24; English tr. 2016, 9). The ontological predilections of contemporary culture lead us to consider "terroir" to be a fixed space that bears all of its properties inherently, without our participation being necessary, but reificatory thinking like this leads to mythologies, and the actual situation is more dynamic. Better than asking, "What is this terroir?" is the question "What is this terroir continuously becoming, here and now?" (Perullo 2018a, 98). The inventor of the aroma wheel, Prof. Ann Noble, holds that "terroir does not exist" (Perullo 2018a, 97), and it can be argued correctly that " 'origin' is always part of a flow" (Perullo 2018a, 107).

Naturally, as much as they are motivated by science, these labelers of origins and terroirs are marketers, and any way to sell some coffee is good enough. But marketers of origins tend to cannibalize themselves, and few single origins are able to endure the marketplace unscathed. Let us review some case studies. My venture to Huila, Colombia, was instructive. I was impressed by how quickly the coffee from Huila established itself as a popular single origin, but after purchasing several nice tasting bags of Huila coffee, I was unable to nail down an identifying taste. When I was in Colombia, I made a visit to the Huila District, in the far south of the country in the mountainous headwaters of the Amazon River. Huila produces 10,000 bags of coffee annually. The northern section of Huila has coffees that possess good body, while the southern section has coffees with good acidity and some fruitiness, often described as "red fruits" (*frutas rojas*). When I was there, they explained to me that the district actually produces four different identifiable kinds of coffee, each with its own flavor profile. The variations result from differences in elevation and on which side of the mountain they grow. Having discovered there are four separate identities, I became curious how it had won a reputation as a single-origin coffee. Of course, nearly all Colombian coffee is good, except perhaps for the coffee labeled as "Gorge" coffee that was sold at a northern Oregon truck stop and bore the description "Unmistakably Colombian Flavor." If Huila had four varieties, and Colombia has a couple dozen geographically identified coffees (each of them featuring multiple flavor profiles), how is it possible that the flavor that one is meant to associate with "Colombia" could be stable? Rather, a hollow single-origin "Colombia" is being used to sell coffee.

Georg Simmel (1978, 112) describes how an ideal type can collect an infinite series of notions under its unity, although "Ultimate comprehension is transferred to infinity, since every point in one series refers to the others in the series for its understanding." One must keep readjusting the synthesis of tastes one has developed to sustain the identity of a single origin that has become one's habit, and predictability is possible only within a broad range. The first coffee given an origin identity was "Mocca," which was not a place where coffee was grown but a port from where coffee was shipped, the principal port of Yemen a short distance across the Red Sea from Ethiopia, where coffee was born. All coffee that was gathered at the Port of Mocca (Mocha, Mokka, Makka) and shipped from there was named "Mocca." Anthony Capella (2009, 86) describes the fiction of this single origin in his novel, *The Various Flavors of Coffee*:

> "Some merchants swear that moccas have a faint chocolate taste. Some even adulterate other beans with cocoa powder to replicate it. What do you think?"
>
> I searched my memory. "Some have a note of chocolate, certainly. But not the very finest—those seem to me to have an extraordinary fragrant quality, more in the range of honeysuckle or vanilla."
>
> "My feelings exactly. Which would tell us what?"
>
> "That mocca is not one coffee but several."

The same can be said for "Java." Similarly, during the first half of the 20th century, coffees in Brazil were named for railway lines that brought them to market in Brazil's port of Santos: Mogiana, Alta Paulista, Noroeste. Each railroad line had its own taste, based upon the crops that were collected at the many stops along the route. The individual characteristics of the separate regions along each route were amalgamated into one identity, an autochthonously blended coffee, yet merchants would buy and sell the coffee with these monikers affixed, as if they defined something that was more than transitory.

Why is it difficult to answer the question, "What does 'Kona' taste like?" It is because after this Hawaiian coffee became popular, a clever purveyor of coffee sold thousands of tons of cheap Indonesian beans as "Kona," largely destroying the identity of that single origin's flavor. In response, the State of Hawaii has made it illegal to sell any coffee labeled "Kona" that contains less than 15% Kona beans. Fifteen percent? I'm not sure how many professional tasters could catch the trace of a flavor that was only 15% of a blend. If as Simmel suggests, the comprehension of the range of meanings that can be collected under an ideal type "is transferred to infinity," how much greater is the infinity that can occur when 85% of the remaining flavors keep varying across the flavor spectrum? Good luck. And at the price, I will pass.

Tales of single-origins do not stop there. My favorite coffee is a genuine Jamaican Blue Mountain, fed to me for two years by one of my graduate students who had a Fulbright research grant near the main Blue Mountain processing facility, and who regularly shipped me the genuine article, smuggled out by workers with whom he used to get stoned. My problem was purchasing the coffee once his research ended, since 10 times more coffee is sold as Blue Mountain than is grown. Coffee growers in both Puerto Rico and Santo Domingo sell product under that origin label, but more "Blue Mountain" coffee grown in Guatemala is sold than that grown in any other country, including Jamaica. Occasionally, I am convinced by some astronomical pricing to purchase some, always to be disappointed. I now pass on this origin, too.

Luigi Odello describes the situation soundly:

> When we speak of mono-origins, we need to be very attentive and not over-generalize. You'll find books that describe it like "This origin is this," "That origin is that." As soon as any origin becomes popular everyone will get into the act and use the name, such as Santo Domingo has done with Jamaican Blue Mountain, in order to make money. And now you don't know whether what you have is a Santo Domingo or a Jamaican. In this way, the flavor characteristics of the origin become confused. *It is always better to stick with the descriptive adjectives for the flavor.*

A recent craze in the world of coffee is the Gesha coffee developed in Boquete, Panama. No sooner did it win widespread popularity that it was simulated all over the world. Unless one buys it directly from a known Panamanian grower, one cannot know what one is purchasing, and even in the Boquete region alone the flavor profiles vary considerably from one year to the next and by the *finca* that is growing it. My favorite clone was a bag of "Geisha" I purchased in the Lima, Peru airport, which featured an attractive line drawing of a Japanese geisha lady on the package, even though Japan has nothing to do with this.

During the months I was visiting professor at Sun Yat-Sen University in Guangzhou, China, I struggled to find quality coffee. At last I found a few boutique cafés that featured an impressive coffee menu that included "Colombia Supremo," "Brazilian Santos," "Ethiopian Yirgacheffe," "Indonesian Sumatran," and even my beloved "Jamaican Blue Mountain," whose plausibility was enhanced by the fact that they were charging $2 more per cup for it. I tried it, and it tasted like ordinary coffee to me. Perhaps the invented single-origin "Brazilian Santos" should have been a giveaway, since few beans from Brazil do not at some point on their journey pass through Santos. I managed to meet the wholesaler on his fortnightly visit to one of the cafés, and I invited him to lunch. I asked him, "All of the cafés you service feature coffees from Jamaica, Columbia, Brazil, Ethiopia, etc. From where do you get all of those coffees, and how do you taste them for quality and legitimacy?" He replied, "All the coffee we sell are from Indonesia, regardless of what it says. The beans just get graded differently." Perhaps they get away with it because the cafés grind the coffees freshly just prior to serving, which is what kept me returning to these cafés even after I learned the truth about them.

Indonesian coffees are said to be "earthy," but much of their identity derives from the fact that they are always given a dark roast, mostly to burn off the many defects they often bear. This "identity" sometimes makes it to the package descriptions, which describe the coffee as "dark." It has even found success with this roast-derived identity, but it is hardly the identity of a "single origin." Nespresso, whose Indonesian capsule is also a dark roast, has managed to maintain the identifying taste of its "Mysore Nuggets" for many years now. It commenced as a legitimate approximation of the peanut husk flavor that we have mentioned, but now that Mysore's coffees are receiving better processing, this characteristic flavor has waned, and the real Mysore coffee has evolved past the frozen-in-time Nespresso simulation. Which is more faithful to the "true" origin? Would Nespresso's customers consider a real, contemporary Mysore coffee to be inauthentic? Are there true origins, and if so, what is their actual nature?

The Story on the Packaging

Packaging bears information that could offer clues to the taste of the coffee inside, although most of the time the effort fails. Three clear, simple taste descriptors would be sufficient, along with an accurate statement about the roast level and an indication of the countries of origin, but except for the costlier specialty coffees, this information is usually not included. I once asked the owner of a medium-sized purveyor of specialty coffees in Los Angeles why information about the flavor is not included routinely on the package, and he replied that taste descriptors do not sell that much coffee. "Then what sells coffee?" I asked him, and he replied, "A compelling story about the farm and family that produced the coffee." After he explained this to me, I began to take note of the elaborate tales that appear on many coffee packages. A good deal of this is well motivated: often a small roaster will visit the source farm that grows the coffee they have been purchasing and be genuinely moved by the lifestyle, the labor, the family's tradition of growing coffee, their affiliation with the land, etc., and develop a romantic description of the coffee's producers. Many of these purveyors return home inspired and are admirably motivated to make that "directly traded" coffee into the best taste possible, for their customers and for the family of growers they have come to adopt. There is much that is healthy about this, and it serves both sides. But the problem is that as soon as any marketing strategy becomes successful, it is copied by everyone, and before long one cannot discern the simulation from the genuine article. Now many packages are designed to look like they are directly traded when they are not; ironically, those who operate in a genuine way may have inferior writing skills.

There is some mythologizing involved in everyone's thinking, and these stories easily become enchantments for buyers of coffee. Here are two such stories that accompanied coffees:

> Currently, Finca Camelias is managed by the fifth generation of the Benavente family, providing work and helping people from the village Panibaj and its environs. As is tradition, the coffee is handcrafted working in wet processing and combining modern production practices in the field of coffee, with the priority of friendly, efficient and productive ecological management that guarantees coffee quality.

Family tradition, assistance to an indigenous community, concern for the environment, and a blend of the art and science of coffee production make a just-so story for the telling, all of which is put to use in the marketing. In an era where food is anonymous, a personal touch brings coffee production closer to the consumer, if only in the imagination. The myth of traceability is respected, since it evokes artisan craft and a connectivity between grower and consumer.

A consumer may like the idea of assisting a cooperative venture run by Nicaraguan women or supporting a strictly shade-grown coffee plantation in India. Despite the highly commendable sentiments, each feature of these stories becomes a meme, and before long anyone who has never traveled can market their coffee successfully by using these memes. Packages crop up with memes like "100% indigenous coffee," "micro-lot," "organic," "single origin," "direct trade," "sustainable," "socially responsible," "roasted in small batches," "small lot coffee," etc., all of which possess merit, if only they were true. With the increasing importance of traceability, purveyors may provide geographic specifications and even a tracing number, although such elaborate technology is more readily available to a large farm than it is to a poor cooperative. The label can look like this: "*Facenda Apucama Francis*: A cerrado de Minas (Brazil), 'Mundo Novo' varietal, altitude 1260 meters, naturally processed. 'Delicate flavor.'" The name of their varietal, the elevation, processing type, and the farm name are probably little help to most purchasers, but the point is not to convey useful data but to display the form of being a coffee purveyor who takes traceability seriously. Such an ad on a package is mostly a claim to be authentic. The improbable mixture of idioms ("A" cerrado "de"; "Brazil" instead of "Brasil" alongside the use of meters instead of feet) is devised not to communicate information but to simulate authenticity, for which some coffee buyers are willing to pay. The point is to feel connected with an origin and to be convinced that it is not anonymous food, both of which are responses to the alienation felt by many postmodern consumers, more than it is a serious commitment to a local community in Brazil or transmitting information about the coffee's taste. With all the memes, tropes, and cultural mythology that are provided as explanations for the coffee, perhaps it is better not to read labels and to just taste the package's contents. Somehow, most of the brilliant tasting and hard work of sensory assessment at many stages along the chain of production get reduced to a pitifully thin result, a situation that presents obstacles for the possibility of tracing flavors to their source.

Tracing Traceability

Purveyors of specialty coffees promote mindfulness in tasting coffees, as well as virtues that stem from tracking the coffees we drink "from seed to cup."

This idea can provide a vehicle for coffee drinkers to become more aware of flavors that can be associated with origins, whether countries, terroirs, or farms, and it helps to combat the alienation that proceeds from consuming anonymous food. Likewise, the coffee boards of producing countries commend to growers trying to understand the flavors of the coffees they grow. Communicating about taste is a route to both better coffee and higher profits. "Traceability" has become a catchword in the modern coffee industry, and it holds the promise of improving the tastes of coffees by getting producers and drinkers alike to really understand the tastes of the coffees they hold in their hands. In order to accomplish this, this attunement to taste must pass through and travel along the chain of coffee production (see the diagram in chapter 2). Just how are objective tastes communicated from grower to exporter, or from importer to barista? The coffee industry is part of the global economy; in fact, it nearly invented the global economy. Accordingly, it is an eager participant in the standardization and system building that is required for the international trading of commodities.

Myths play a vital function in our social lives and do considerable good. They carry a sort of truth, though none are entirely true. When one adopts a positivist version of objectivity and thinks everything one establishes must be so just the way one thinks it, then myths can impede thinking. Simmel (1978, 67) observed, "Our mind has a remarkable ability to think of its contents as being independent of the act of thinking." Ignorance stems from what one knows, not from what one does not know. As long as one recognizes that the myths one invokes are only tropes intended to assist understanding and not command it, they can play a useful heuristic role.

At the intersection of any two adjacent occupants on the production chain (e.g., growers/brokers; importers/exporters; baristas/consumers), there exists a unique problem of communicating about taste, and a new opportunity for meanings to become confused. As former SCA Director Ric Rhinehart (2020, 20) put it, "The broad market often stumbles over the more nuanced concepts of quality and specific attributes." People across the world's coffee industry struggle to communicate successfully about taste. Initially, I assumed that there was a universally adopted system for describing tastes, but during years of inquiry I learned that there is too little communication about taste "from ripening to roast" taking place for me to be able to accept the traceability of taste as more than mythology. Despite the many calls for a common language, it is a tower of Babel. As Nicola Perullo of the University of Gastronomic Sciences in Italy has suggested, the notion of a taste of the origin is an ideological simplification.

Most brokers I have met in Europe and Latin America do not worry much about taste as they instinctively keep their eyes fixed upon their computer screens' price lists. Those few brokers who search for a specific taste generally choose to keep that taste hidden from the farmers from whom they purchase their coffee, in fear that if their sources knew what tastes they were seeking, the prices for them would rise. Most Colombian growers of specialty coffees I queried did not know, and could not say, what flavors their principal clients are seeking. Most growers and consumers know little about the tastes of their own coffees, which are part of their daily lives. This situation rendered moot much of my planned research into the communication of tastes "from growers to consumers," which motivated this monograph, and I surrendered any strong notion of tracing the understanding of taste from the beginning to the end of the chain of production. This often happens with sociological research—it is a discovering enterprise, and we do not always discover what we expected to find. If it were otherwise, our research would not be worthy of trusting. Instead, a narrower study has been made of how the flavors discovered by professionals *can* be communicated, especially in the middle range of the chain of production, where the exporters and importers meet, although I have studied all positions on the chain.

Growers

In chapter 10, we described the owner of the farm who won a Cup of Excellence in Latin America and who admitted that he had no idea what his coffee tasted like, and the story among growers in India is similar. A Mysore District grower confessed while serving us tea, "I never drink coffee. We drink tea." He could be growing turnips. In Coorg, a traditional coffee district in India, another grower sells some of his crop, including his best Arabica, to a specialty roaster. It is a coffee that features an earthy, nutty flavor that receives good reviews, but he himself has never tasted it.

National coffee boards, international industry groups, and importers need to spend time with growers. At every international competition, the organizers should sit down with producers of the 10 winning coffees of a competition and have them taste all of the winning coffees, including their own, while professional tasters carefully describe to them their unique features, so that the owners can locate those tastes with their own tongues. If this was done, it would be a short step for owners to become motivated to grow better coffees; indeed, many of the younger growers (the children and grandchildren of the proprietors) have begun to do this.

Consumers

A similar ignorance operates in the palates of many consumers across the world. The morning coffee of choice in India is Nescafé, served proudly, or a thick syrup of coffee and chicory diluted with boiled and sweetened milk. In Brazil, the best coffees are shipped to New York, Italy, and Japan, and most Brazilians know only the leftovers of the harvest, which is served out of kettle-drum steel urns where they grow stale. In El Salvador, where the popular Pacamara coffee was developed, or Panama, where the full potential of the Gesha was ascertained, there are few places where ordinary people can go to drink these coffees. There is little advantage for a drinker of coffee to live in a coffee-producing country.

Italy boasts of its coffee sophistication, but it is difficult to find. Consumers there report what consumers report everywhere: "I have coffee just to have a break." Italy takes its espresso for granted as the world's standard, so few purveyors there explore how they could improve the taste. It was difficult to find good coffee in China, beyond some international chains. The most "indigenous" coffee they serve is Vietnamese coffee prepared with a metal filter that requires 15 minutes for the coffee to drip through, by which time the coffee is cool. At a few gourmet bars in China, counterfeit coffees are served that are never what is claimed, but few clients notice.

Coffee sensibilities in the USA were destroyed decades ago by the percolator and by the habit of using milk and sugar inherited from the Dutch and English tradition of tea drinking. A typical perspective of the American coffee drinkers I interviewed was "I like it, but I'm used to the burnt taste of the darkly roasted coffee I buy at Costco." Few consumers were able to communicate the tastes they prefer. If these consumers ever met the growers face-to-face, what could the two of them possibly discuss?

How does one accurately ascertain *just what* is occurring to a consumer's palate when they find some desirable taste in a coffee? Surveys reduce a complex matter to a serendipitous selection of bubbles on a form. Coffee researchers are eager to learn what consumers really think, but their research designs are inadequate: methods that elicit consumers' taste preferences on forms secure numerical results but do not reveal much about the tasters' actual thinking. Lay tasters are offered no opportunity to dialogue with researchers, and no basis for genuine communication is laid. Questions consumers may pose are routinely dismissed, and there is more interaction between the bubble-forms and the machines that tabulate them than between researchers and the lay drinkers. Worst of all, the survey methodology *imposes* a value system upon the consumer, who has no power to influence that system, rendering the results unreliable.

When consumers are ignorant about the tastes of the coffee they drink, it can be a benefit for some coffee purveyors who may be able to find ways to sell them lousy coffee at a good profit. Encouraging the use of flavorings not only permits them to sell coffee with undetected defects, it creates an additional stream of revenue for the flavorings. Still more profitable is to purchase and roast super-cheap beans that are less dense and have inferior cellular development, which will permit the purveyor to add flavorings during the processing, such as vanillin, hazelnut, etc., which the empty spaces between the cell walls of the beans are able to absorb.

The *Certified Specialty Coffee* handbook from Italy (Meschini and Milani n.d.) wisely suggests on its first page that an aim of the specialty coffee industry is "breaking strong habits." An American-born Indian roaster in Delhi laments, "There's still some education to be done," a sentiment that is echoed around the world. But James Hoffman, a London roaster (and 2007 World Barista Champion), is skeptical about "educating the consumer." An accomplished barista, Hoffman has undoubtedly made a comprehensive appraisal of what consumers can learn. His skepticism is shared by Tracy Ging, who studied consumers of specialty coffees for the SCA, and discovered that consumers "reacted strongly against the concept of education." That study rated even sophisticated drinkers as "slightly knowledgeable," having difficulty describing the coffees they themselves prefer. The bottom line of the study was that one should not come between a coffee drinker and their first cup of coffee in the morning, education or not. It is a perfect storm—not only is much of what consumers know misinformation, they do not wish to be educated. A seriously complicating factor is that the very notion of "educating" drinkers is probably elitist, and lacks the respect owed to people who are entitled to their lives, especially early in the morning.

This situation renders any study of communication from growers to consumers problematic for the reason that neither of them are tasting very much. Despite the popularity of the rhetoric of "traceability," it remains an idea that is more theoretical than actual, but this does not mean that it can never become actual.

Purveyors

Professional roasters and café owners work on the front lines of communicating coffee's flavors, and this is where fulfilling the promise of traceability is most likely to occur. Roasters know their coffees well, and most professional coffee purveyors recognize they can always learn more themselves, so they are naturally decent teachers. Moreover, there is no shortage of enthusiasm for talking about their product. *Everyone* who works in the coffee industry is enthusiastic about their work no matter what role they play, an enthusiasm that is not equaled in every profession.

At larger firms, tasters and marketers are often unable to agree about how to describe their product, and the descriptions that result confuse buyers more than educate them. Using flowery adjectives can alienate consumers, making them skeptical, and some precise descriptions provide more than clients are able to absorb. A description like "dried papaya with a tamarind finish" might nail a flavor perfectly but be too much information, especially when "with earthy notes resembling cinnamon" is appended to it, as if every taster on the staff needed to weigh in with their opinion. Enthusiastic tasters must keep the capabilities of their clients in mind when developing descriptors, instead of orienting their description to the opinion of their fellow tasters. Other descriptions are anodynes, like "balanced character, round, and harmonious," which is too general to communicate much and encourages dull thinking. Many descriptors on labels are nonsense syllables, and they are treated as such by consumers. Too many of the world's coffees are "sweet, with notes of chocolate." When we asked our consumers whether they could locate this "sweet," several suggested to us that coffee is bitter, not sweet. If there were more points of contact between purveyors and consumers, and places where they could listen to each other, a common language might develop. The language between purveyors and consumers does not have to be the same language as that between exporters and importers, or the one used by international tasters, but whoever is involved in communicating must listen as well as speak.

Cafés are perfect places where this can happen, but many servers (not to be confused with baristas) know little beyond a local routine. When you ask the server at your espresso bar if they can tell you where the coffee comes from, the likely response will be the name of their distributor. Or they may inspect the bag, perhaps for the first time, which frequently fails to list a country of origin. Since the tastes of the world's crops necessarily vary from year to year, if a purveyor can reach its target profile by using a Brazilian coffee one year and a Guatemalan the next, what difference does the origin make, so why provide it? Given annual changes, they would need to continually be reprinting their packaging. Even better, try asking a server to clarify what is a "medium body." Few are able to explain "body" well, and more training is required, especially in medium-sized chains, if servers are to become educators. More strategies for addressing less sophisticated clients are needed. Communication is a two-way street, and the capacity of those who are listening varies widely, so servers need to pay attention to their customer's thinking if tastes are going to be traceable as far as the consumer.

Exporters and Importers

The best exporters do not evaluate coffee for what they themselves like; instead, they work with the imagination of their clients, and this orientation operates all the way through the coffee chain. Many smaller exporters do not try to describe the flavors of their crops for fear of saying something that might deter an inquirer from making a purchase. Using numbers obtained from a sensory assessment is safer because it communicates less; however, one taster for an importer told me that the taste assessments of his form and by most exporters are so different that he does not rely on the scores that accompany the coffees. When sampling coffees that come to his firm, "I just taste it straight, I'm not influenced by scores." Importers know what flavors they are seeking, so many exporters prefer to just let them find them; besides, there remains the problem of communicating the tastes adequately. Calling a coffee "nutty" in India is usually an insult, but it can be a compliment in the USA, so asking for a nutty coffee can confuse some Indian purveyors and produced an unhappy result. As mentioned, the more serious problem is that many importers disguise the flavor profiles of the coffees they seek. The result is that there can be a break in the traceability of the coffee's taste, right at the node of importer and exporter where the communication about taste should be at its optimum.

Tasters

Riding to the rescue are the coffee tasters. As we have learned, determining the influences of processing, selecting, roasting, blending, and preparation is difficult because there are so many factors that work together, but professional tasters are up to the task. If an origin does not have a single identifying flavor, what consequence does this have for traceability? If one is able to trace no more than a subset of many factors, tracing flavor will have limited utility. This accords with the way Perullo (2018d) describes the problem of defining wines: "There exist so many different styles and projects to make wine, and just as many variables—dependent on conscious choices as well as uncontrollable factors—that it is impossible to include them all in a definitive and final piece of regulation." Regulation and predictability may be a goal, but it is never to be achieved.

Tasters describe flavors accurately, then they attempt the difficult task of adequately communicating the described flavor across the industry and finally to the consumer. The two tasks, taste description and communication, are joined at the hip, despite the wishes of positivist science. At lower levels, much tasting involves "scoring" samples, during which tasters look for defects or for compliance with the consistent flavor of a firm's brand. At the higher end is descriptive cupping. Both kinds of tasting can use numerating protocols, or not. Most specialty coffee tasters are committed to the idea of traceability, and it is a notion that stimulates passion and increases the commitment of people in the coffee industry. However, if what I have discovered is true, the ontology of traceability is flawed, despite the human relationships that specialty coffee purveyors have established and which do operate, to everyone's benefit.

The fostering of genuine and intimate communication between producers and purveyors should always be encouraged and celebrated. One of the principal benefits of traceability is that purveyors of coffee from importing nations are teaching growers and processors from exporting nations how to cup their coffees and which of their coffees possess the most outstanding flavors, flavors that can earn them higher prices. They are teaching these growers to taste and by so doing to improve their standard of living. The result is a win-win situation; however, what is the empirical reality operating? It is that a purveyor of coffee in the importing country establishes personal relations with a grower or processor of the exporting country, and they do business together, often supported by face-to-face meetings that are capable of producing two-way interpersonal education and respect, making both sides more committed to each other, and to coffee. The notion of an identical understanding of the flavor of some coffee, an understanding that passes through each stage of the chain of production, is an idealization of the social reality, which in actuality consists of narrower, more occasioned relations.

The specialty coffee industry itself is engaged in deconstructing the notion of the "chain" of production and replacing it with the more nuanced idea of a "systems map," which acknowledges that there are diverse, complex, and unique commercial relations that include people who were excluded in the "chain" (e.g., NGOs, research institutions, financial services, government regulation agencies, etc.). While the notion of a "systems map" is an improvement, there is still at work the suggestion of a totalization (Sartre 1976, 45–47) that is accepted to be a conceptually integrated, organized global community, when in reality there are only shifting and occasional relations developed by parties who make efforts to establish trading interactions. The designers of the systems map acknowledge this, "recognizing that the interactions of the parts are not static, but dynamic and fluid . . . while recognizing previously invisible actors and telling multiple stories" (Specialty Coffee Association 2020). Not every "actor" of the map knows every other, nor do they need to. The idea of a personal connection between the drinker and the grower is somewhat mitigated by the systems map compared with the chain, but the map is a more mature depiction of the operative commercial relations since it produces more interfaces or "nodes" among actors in the coffee industry, thus appropriately expanding the complexity of the model. While education regarding taste sometimes extends to institutions larger than the exporter or importer, and conceptual integration is encouraged and attempted, there remains an aspect of the coffee systems map that preserves the mythic outlook of the explanatory framework of the chain of production. This serves to organize and motivate the many varied participants in global coffee production and creates a sense of belonging to a whole, even if the whole is a continually shifting collection of interconnectedly dependent parts. It is a postmodern mythology, in that the new model speaks not of "a system" but of "systems" plural, rendering it more responsive to the actual occasioned social relations that compose the map.

I am not arguing here against the utility of the notion of traceability, I am only commending a clearer understanding of what it really is. In fact, the relationships that "traceability" fosters bear considerable promise for the industry. There is nothing wrong with dreams, but I am suggesting that the myth of traceability should not be overly reified or turned into a messianism. It is certain that messianism sells coffee too, perhaps more quickly than taste does; but the two are not mutually exclusive: consumers *can* be socialized by means of the notion of traceability to pay more attention to tastes. Perhaps this is where the myth of traceability can make its principal contribution. Its function, like myths everywhere, is to offer a vision that motivates actors and inspires actions. And there is nothing wrong with making money in the process, especially when consumers can be taught to taste their coffee.

Chapter 12

Some Discovered Practices of Lay Coffee Drinkers[1]

> Creating the right ambience may be the only way to help people appreciate coffee. Sometimes giving less information is better—just let them discover what they want from that cup.
>
> —Angelo Segoni, Lecce, Italy

Taste and Ethnomethodological Study of Local Orderlinesses

What is the experience of ordinary coffee drinkers as they drink their coffee? Research into taste as a sense requires being attentive to analytic, conceptual work and to embodied multi-sensorial engagement. Identifying and describing flavors is grounded in local contingencies of a social activity; in this chapter we examine features of the organization of the local orderliness of coffee tasting by lay drinkers and of their talk about the coffees they are tasting. Contrary to recent literature on sense-deciphering that emphasizes culture, public codes (Cerulo 2018), and status ambitions (Ott 2018), since tasting coffee is a locally occasioned activity, here we respect the local occasions and unravel the order of the talking and drinking that inhabits them.

This avenue of investigation was motivated by the global coffee industry's interest in how lay drinkers experience their coffee, since coffee purveyors envision charging higher prices for better-tasting coffee as a possible solution

---

1. Chapter 12 was written by Giolo Fele and Kenneth Liberman; a version of this chapter appeared in *Symbolic Interaction*, vol. 44 (2021).

to the global price crisis in coffee. Coffee purveyors believe that only by charging more for a cup of coffee can sufficient funds be generated to prevent making coffee growing unprofitable, which is leading to the failure of many of the world's family-owned plantations, especially in the face of increasing expenses caused by climate change. The situation has stirred interest in discovering what lay coffee drinkers usually taste when they drink their coffee, with the idea that if consumers can better appreciate the flavors of what they are drinking some may be willing to pay more for the better coffees.

When the Specialty Coffee Association began undertaking research into the experience of ordinary coffee drinkers they encountered a problem: many drinkers they interviewed did not share the coffee industry's interest in taste. Not only did they seem not to taste much, they were uninterested in learning to taste (Ging 2012). We thought ethnomethodological research strategies and studying audio and video recordings of ordinary drinkers' practices of might give us access to the real-world experience of coffee drinkers and thereby assist coffee purveyors.

The literature on how lay coffee drinkers make sense of tastes when they are asked to do so suggests a recurring phenomenon: "Our field experiment showed that, by and large, naïve coffee consumers were not able to detect quality differences in a blind test between two samples widely different in intrinsic quality (as defined from an industry perspective)" (Giacalone et al. 2016, 2468). Lay drinkers are represented as unable to detect the quality of a coffee, and their capacity to recognize a good taste is unreliable. This is particularly true when lay drinkers taste blindly, without reference to the brand, the price, or the label (Samoggia and Riedel 2018). When they are left alone—that is, when they have to identify independently the value and worth of a product—the literature suggests that lay drinkers are poor assessors and do not match the standards provided by industry assessments. Typically, lay drinkers make casual tries based upon personal individual preferences: "Overall, our findings suggest that people are not able to point out high and low-quality coffees: their perception of coffee quality mostly looks like a random process" (Giacalone et al. 2016; see also Ott 2018). Lay drinkers struggle to identify and describe just what was pleasing or special about their preferred tastes (Ging 2012).

While lay drinkers have been considered in this negative light, in terms of what they are not doing, we were interested to learn what lay drinkers *are* doing when they actually drink coffee. However, each time we attempted to capture the lived experience of a coffee drinker searching for taste, we found that our coffee drinkers were submerged in imminent social demands of the occasion, demands that eclipsed their interest in taste.

Just because taste is our research interest does not entail that it is necessarily the interest of ordinary coffee drinkers. We discovered that drinking coffee is not always for the purpose of experiencing the taste and that many consumers do not pay close attention to the flavors in their coffee. Some drinkers are more concerned with having their newspaper at hand when the coffee arrives, or in using a favorite ceramic cup instead of a paper cup, or in other mundane concerns. We could not easily identify the tasting practices of lay drinkers because they themselves were not orienting to the tastes. In most cases, the sociality of the occasion—conversing with friends, enjoying the ambience of a bar or café and how it can offer a pause in routine, or interacting with us competently during our research—was given priority over the flavors.

Many ordinary coffee drinkers have little to offer about taste because they are not tasting anything in particular. A typical response was "They all tasted similar to me; it was difficult to distinguish flavors"—a comment that was applied to coffees that ranged from $3 to $25 per pound. Our test subjects wrote comments like "No particular taste descriptors" or "some coffee notes." One drinker volunteered that it is difficult "getting your head around trying to find the flavor." Having our subjects re-taste coffee made it harder for them to distinguish tastes. This left us with the impossible task of trying to elicit from them what for the most part was never there.

This offered a new twist to ethnomethodology's unique adequacy principle, whereby researchers are required to suspend the employment of a research methodology until they have located the methods that the parties themselves are using to organize the local orderliness. We were prepared to adapt to the local tasting practices of coffee drinkers, but such tasting practices were sparse. While we are interested in the tastes of coffee, the lay drinkers were oriented to organizing the local orderliness of their affairs. What is worse, but fascinating to us as ethnomethodological researchers, their local concerns kept getting in the way of our studying the work of their noticing flavors. Talk always accompanied their drinking, guided it, and diverted it even when it assisted it. As Vannini et al. (2012, 16) observe, "Understanding most of our sensations, and thus our senses, depends heavily on the language that we use." Language was a distracting component of their experience when these drinkers were tasting coffee.

This required us to change our focus, in keeping with the phenomenological insistence upon remaining faithful to the phenomenon itself, a tenet that underlies the unique adequacy principle. At first reluctant to impose our ethnomethodology upon the work of our lay drinkers, we discovered that the real danger was imposing our interest in taste upon people who were up to other things. Losing one's focal topic in this way can be disorienting, but it can also signal the start of an exercise in original discovery. As Heath and Luff (2018, 467) suggest, quasi-naturalistic experiments are primarily exploratory. In our case, we were first seeking what experience lay drinkers have with the taste of coffee and, second, what methods we might discover that would be adequate for examining their practices of drinking coffee. Taking our guidance from the actual practices of the participants, we began to pay attention to the local demands of the social interaction to which our drinkers themselves were oriented. These adventitious local matters that kept diverting our coffee drinkers made it difficult for us to ignore them. In our quasi-naturalistic sessions of coffee drinking, the social context of the occasion was more important to the drinkers than the coffee was. In fact, we came to question whether it was sound to consider coffee drinking apart from its occasioned social context. Purging a situation of what is really there is not a sound path to objectivity, even when what is there is disparaged as being "subjective." The rigor of imposing a pre-established vision of what is "objective" upon a scene is a rigor that is less compelling to us than the rigor of studying what is really there.

There is no distortion-free methodology, and in our study, our very presence created a unique situation. Surely, coffee drinkers are always directed by the context of their drinking; but "context" is too vague a notion, so we were interested to specify *just what* social contexts were active. We identified both microsocial and macrosocial practices. The microsocial practices emerged in and as the local occasion of the coffee drinking, and the macrosocial practices impinged upon the situation from time to time as the parties searched for vocabulary that had its origin in one or another status regime of coffee consumption. Since the latter "taste" was too removed from the taste that was happening on their tongues, we focused our inquiry on the microsocial practices, which include the clustering of taste descriptors, using taste descriptors in a serendipitous fashion, and adopting discursive formats, which then led us to investigate the serendipitous nature of emerging social structures. People's *in vivo* practices do not always conform to the expectations of formal analytic social theorists, and social interaction can be *less* deliberate, *less* plan-full, and *less* concept-centered than most social scientists assume that it is.

The Research Setting

We organized several sessions with lay coffee drinkers in San Diego (USA) and Trento (Italy), with volunteers collected from cafés, students, librarians, and retirees. None had specific training in sensorial analysis, but all had knowledge of the coffee as a beverage in their everyday routine; we tried to enlist people who claimed to be passionate about their coffee drinking. During 2019, we involved a total of 74 lay drinkers who worked in 15 different groups. The meetings were video- and/or audio-recorded. The sessions were held in coffee houses and on university premises and lasted between 45 and 90 minutes. Participants were told only that we were interested in knowing how consumers describe the taste of coffees and that it was not a marketing initiative.

After an initial round of introductions, oriented to familiarizing the participants with the setting and each other, we provided coffees that had different flavor characteristics. We simply asked them to describe the coffees they were tasting; however, following the advice of the sommelier Émile Peynaud (1987, 116), who explains that tasting features can be made more concrete by presenting at least two cups of wine, we offered a routine where the drinkers tasted three different coffees. During the tasting of the first cup, we received a few particular taste descriptors, but as soon as the second coffee was tasted, the parties spontaneously found their way to comparing the coffees, and a local method of comparing likes and dislikes was adopted.

Originally, we had developed a primitive tasting schedule that we believed would help the drinkers focus upon the task of tasting, but we abandoned that when it kept getting in the way of their tasting. After each cup, each participant was asked to speak about the coffee, without much direction. We asked them to retain some coffee in the serving cup because we had them taste the coffee again after it cooled, or with sugar or cream. The coffees were served blindly. We informed the participants that at the end of the drinking we would reveal what coffee they drank and read them the description that the producer placed on their packaging.

The coffee drinking was not embedded in a truly naturally occurring activity but was the special topic of the gathering. The participants had their experience mostly silently, engaging with the coffee, sipping it, drinking it rather than spitting it out; only after having had a personal experience with each coffee were they asked to talk about the coffee they had just tasted. Their remarks were specific to the coffees and not about what they generally like or dislike. In this way, the participants reported about their sensations of actual close tasting. Some of them alternated their talking with their tasting, when it was necessary to refresh their experience in order to better specify, understand, and clarify their assessments.

The setting was an "ethnographic" (Mann 2015) or a "quasi-naturalistic" experiment (Heath and Luff 2018). While we sought occasions of naturally occurring drinking in everyday contexts (see Mann 2015, 2018), this was not feasible since most coffee drinking is private. Neither was the setting of our research like any laboratory experiment for sensorial analysis, where participants are asked to produce their assessments of food or beverages while sitting in isolated booths, with no interaction among the participants, in controlled laboratory conditions (neutral lights, soft color of the walls, restricted interaction with food, etc.), and directed to comply with evaluation sheets that reduce taste experiences to fragmented entities. In our sessions, the participants were gathered in comfortable places, sitting around a table in a café or on campus, and invited to taste and name what they sensed, to share that knowledge, and to engage in discovering more regarding the taste. The audio and video recordings were then transcribed and analyzed. Through this approach, it was possible to explore in detail their particular practices of tasting and how they organized the task at hand.

Three Ethnomethods Used in Searching for Taste

What do lay coffee drinkers say when they are asked to describe what they are tasting? How do they approach their drinking? We identified three methods that participants routinely employed for making sense of the taste: *clustering*, *objectivating*, and *calibrating*.

Clustering

Coffee descriptors trend in ensembles. The task of defining taste is often approached by lay drinkers through a series of descriptors, not just one. The work of discovering taste involves the mobilization of several descriptors that cluster together. That is, the work of finding the right taste descriptor usually produces a series of descriptors that work together as a group.

When a descriptor is used by a participant, that descriptor can be appropriated by other participants, in a sort of echo. Clustering is usually a joint accomplishment of a group, and is a conspicuous example of the fact that consensual findings are grounded in the local contingencies of the interaction, contingencies that are often serendipitous, as in this transcript from chapter 8:

    Allen: Fruit pie.

    Barbara: Maybe peach. I got a peach cobbler.

    Sherrie: Yes, or apricot.

Allen describes the taste with a general metaphor. Barbara specifies what *kind* of fruit it is and also specifies the kind of pie. Finally, Sherrie offers her agreement, contributing a descriptor that belongs to the domain of fruit, thereby remaining within the same semantic spectrum.

In another tasting, which we presented in chapter 8, Silvio was the first to provide an account of a mouthfeel that was evident but for which he could not think of a descriptor, except that it was "a tingling, something." Luca shadows Silvio by mentioning that he found a sensation "similar to spicy" and later by specifying that it tingles a bit. Luca tracked the suggestion that Silvio provided, confirming the existence of that specific tongue sensation. After that, Silvio referred the sensation experienced by Luca to what he experienced before, "it is *that* tingling that I was speaking about," so the tingling enjoyed a sort of bandwagon effect. Luca adopts "tingling" as a way to respecify his first observation ("similar to spicy"), in this way confirming the account provided by Silvio. Silvio was then finally able to objectivate (see "Objectivating" below) his first tentative and hesitant sensation by affixing a deictic "that" to the tingling, an objectivation that is a discursive move that strengthens Silvio's commitment to his descriptor.

In the next transcript, "floral" is proposed tentatively, but it suffices for making it a public gloss that can facilitate the collaborative work of the parties:

    Alice: Do you think it's floral, or—?

    Sami: "Floral." I'll have to try it again.

    Cherise: Maybe there is a slight floral finish.

    Sami: Oh, "a slight floral finish."

"Floral" is repeated to sustain its public witnessing and to encourage its interrogation by the parties, and Cherise offers a candidate account, along with some downgrading; Sami repeats that too, neither confirming nor disconfirming it but sustaining its life as a witnessable gloss that parties can use in their local work of producing social order. "Floral" has a future in this conversation, but what "floral" will come to mean remains to be established. Although indeterminate, the descriptor guides the lay drinkers' inquiry, and the sense and reference it collects may later become affiliated to Cherise's account. In this way, a group moves tendentiously and collectively to an objective ending, and they also teach each other how to speak properly for the occasion. In fact, speaking properly competes with tasting for the drinkers' attention! Here they are teaching each other to speak intelligently about coffee.

The phenomenon of *clustering* the descriptors occurs commonly, regardless of the level of expertise of the coffee drinker. The adopted descriptors seem beholden to the local contingencies of the talk as much as they are the product of careful or deliberate sensory analysis. They compose some of the "random" of which Giacalone et al. (2016) spoke.

Objectivating

Organizing the orderliness of local affairs routinely involves "the congregational work of producing social facts" (Garfinkel 2002, 245), and objectivation plays a paramount role in this congregational work. As employed by Husserl, Schutz, Gurwitsch, Berger and Luckmann, and Garfinkel, "objectivation" refers to an activity more than to the result of that activity. Aron Gurwitsch (1966, 139) explains, "The objectivating function belongs to an act." While objectivation (*Objektivierung*) shares a semantic field with objectification (*Versachlichung*) and reification (*Verdinglichung*), these terms evoke increasing degrees of devitalization, and objectivating is the generative social practice with which the life of all three commences. "The process by which the externalized products of human activity attain the character of objectivity is objectivation" (Berger and Luckmann 1966, 34).

Objectification and reification never entirely absolve themselves of the reality that their exteriority remains "bound to consciousness" (Figal 2010, 112), even though reified social facts "in their concreteness" (Garfinkel 2002, 65) come to be accepted as existing "in their own right" (Garfinkel 2002, 117). While important distinctions of these three closely aligned terms become leveled off in English, usually to "objectification," these distinctions are key to understanding social life. Berger and Luckmann (1966, 89) write, "Reification can be described as an extreme step in the process of objectivation, whereby the objectivated world loses its comprehensibility as a human enterprise and becomes fixated as a non-human, non-humanizable, inert facticity."

Edmund Husserl (1970b, 314) explains that the purpose of objectivating is to convert "essentially subjective and occasional expressions" into expressions that can be understood without directing one's attention to the circumstances of the utterance. That is, in much mundane social interaction, possibilities and tentative suggestions are progressively developed into objective findings, always in the service of clear communication. The objectivated corpus, "the intersubjectively identical thing," facilitates the task of "subjects 'understanding one another' " (Husserl 1982, 363). Alfred Schutz (1967, 134) elaborates that a purpose of objectivating notions is to establish an "already constituted meaning-context" that can be given equally to all. In this way, an intersubjective infrastructure is gradually built. Schutz (1967, 37) specifies, "What we call the world of subjective meaning is, therefore, abstracted in the social sphere from the constituting process." Objectivating is a method parties use to convert a confirmed account into a social fact that parties can orient to as being external to their own activities: "Objectivation is the work of turning our thinking or activities into objects that are publicly available for people to use for organizing the local orderlinesses of their affairs" (Liberman 2018).

Garfinkel (1952, 114) describes his inquiries as studies of how people "go about the business of constructing, testing, maintaining, altering, validating, questioning, and defining an order together." This vision of our intersubjective life is applied to the mundane work of sensorial practices by Lorenza Mondada (2019, 51), who criticizes both the neurocognitive sciences and generic social theorizing about status markers for missing what is most vital for rigorous social inquiry into the practices of sensing, namely, "an account focusing on activities in which people actually perceive, sense, and experience the world, make relevant the sensory features of these experiences for others, and share them intersubjectively, by collectively and jointly producing and coordinating them, and by publicly expressing, displaying, and witnessing them." Here we are undertaking this sort of inquiry.

In one panel of coffee drinkers, the first person to offer a candidate account, Walt, proposed the cup as being "bitter"; a second drinker, Lara, confirmed the account by adding "extremely bitter," and just as rapidly a third drinker, Mohammed, objectivated the account by speaking of "the strong bitterness." The objectivation moment abides in that "the" (line 10).

This was followed by "very bitter," "then got bitter," and a chorus that followed afterword:

1	WALT:	I can start, so I guess before I had it with sugar I thought it was kind of bitter and
2		maybe a little watery.
3		. . .
4	LARA:	I thought it was also extremely bitter and very compact. So I kind of felt like it was a
5		kind of brick, of a ( ) of stone that I was
6		throwing down and then afterwards it left like a really numb and oily film in my throat.
7		So, also with sugar I didn't really appreciate
8		the taste or the feeling in my mouth too much.
9	HOST:	Ok ok ok.
10	MOHAMMED:	I also felt the strong bitterness.
11	CHERISE:	I also had the feeling in the beginning that it was very bitter, but maybe that is also
12		because usually I drink it with milk . . .
13	JULIA:	I think that often an espresso that I don't really like, the first sensation is kind of
14		sensation is kind of vinegarish, then got bitter . . .

Having objectivated "bitter" as a competent term, "bitter" became the happening descriptor for the rest of the afternoon, and the descriptor was applied to many subsequent coffees.

A consequence of objectivating is that what is objectivated gains a life of its own (Liberman 2013, 87), one that can outstrip the intentions of its authors. Consider the following:

1	ALICE:	I don't know, I think I almost want to say I like that one better.
2	DONNA:	You like 32 better?
3	ALICE:	I think I do!
4	PAULA:	I like 32 the best.
5	ALICE:	Yahh. Yahh.

6	DONNA:	And you think it is the ˆfloralˆ?
7		...
8	ALICE:	This one is really good, I can't put my finger on what it is, but—I didn't taste ˆfloralˆ. To me it's not souurr.
9	DONNA:	Like nutty cocoa, like that's kind of what I'm thinking.
10	ALICE:	Yahhh. That's, there's something about that.
11		I mean this is—I can't put my finger on it. this is—I can't put my finger on it.
12		...
13	ALICE:	I'm still trying to figure out what it was I tasted.
14		...
15	ALICE:	I just know I liked it better. I don't know why!

Most drinkers do not present a candidate account (e.g., a taste descriptor) in a conclusive way but propose their candidate accounts tentatively. In line 1 of the transcript, Alice proposes an assessment that displays uncertainty and falls short of being a definitive assertion. Her assessment is probed by Donna, who by not disagreeing gives Alice the confidence to make her assertion stronger, although it is still downgraded ("I think," line 3). Paula then offers a confirmation of Alice's account, with which Alice agrees more strongly (5). Donna offers a query about the particular flavor that may be responsible for her positive assessment, yet it seems that Donna herself is not entirely sure just what the descriptor "floral" can mean. The accent given this term indicates to the parties that "floral" possesses a future as *a public gloss*, as well as being a probe for what it might mean. Interestingly, it is made a social object *before* its meaning is settled. Husserl (1982, 355) tells us that phenomena are "objectivatable clearly or obscurely"; that is, objectivated notions do not need to become clear and distinct before people can begin to engage with them. Husserl (1982, 356) suggests that verbal objectivations can be "perhaps quite obscure." The critical thing for an objectivation is that it provides a focal point for parties to collect, progressively refine, and make consistent and efficacious an understanding-in-common.

However, Alice (line 8) dismisses "floral" as an appropriate descriptor, while retaining a prosodic contour that intimates it is still working as a public gloss. She offers a second descriptor ("souurr"), downgraded by its negative formatting, which is another practical technique that our drinkers use for trying to stay out of trouble (since not having a given flavor may be less subject to opprobrium than a positive claim that it possesses one). Here imagined social consequences of what a drinker has to say intrude on a candid exploration of accurate taste descriptors.

Donna, who remains more oriented than Alice or Paula to finding taste descriptors, offers a taste account (line 9), but as with most first formulations of descriptors, she downgrades it ("kind of," and affixing an "I'm thinking," rather than making an objective assertion). Her account is confirmed by Alice, but Alice still struggles with finding a precise taste descriptor, and despite sincere and concentrated effort that extends through five minutes of drinking, she is unable to describe the flavor (13). After further discussion, Alice concludes only that "I just know I liked it better. I don't know why!" This is a comment typical among lay coffee drinkers. The favored coffee 32 was the gourmet blend of the hosting café and not the Yuban (a commercial American brand), nor the Starbucks.

Once a taste descriptor is asserted, even if it is tenuous and downgraded, it becomes a public gloss available for use in the interaction. Once that gloss is objectivated, that object has an itinerary of its own, independent of the speaker who proposed it. "They are Durkheim's social facts" (Garfinkel 2002, 269). It is commonplace that a speaker who introduces the account will be held responsible for whatever the objectivated account may collect over the subsequent course of talking. For this reason, that speaker will pay close attention to the future of the descriptor since she/he may need to be an authority for what it collects during the ensuing discussion. In this way, the course of events largely rests outside of the hands of the individual speaker. We consider these investigations to be specifications of the sociality that produces objectivities.

Calibrating

Drinkers must align their thinking in order to employ taste descriptors in a common fashion. "Calibrating" is the term adopted by the professional tasting industry to describe parties' work to maintain an adequacy of intersubjective understanding sufficient for allowing reasonable communication when assessing flavors. The term serves to describe the mundane intersubjective phenomenon whereby parties gravitate toward an "interchangeability of standpoints" (Schutz 1971, 11–13), whereby they come to see matters "with the same typicality." Calibrating fortifies a "reciprocity of perspectives," making it possible to take for granted that any differences in perspectives are irrelevant for the purposes at hand. Schutz (1971, 12) explains that "such knowledge is conceived to be objective and anonymous, i.e., detached from and independent of the situation." Calibrating is an intersubjective tool used for constructing objectivity.

Lawless and Heymann (2010) describe the process this way: "Calibration refers to the training of a descriptive panel so that their frame of reference for the scale is internalized according to a reference standard." Before the process can engender internalization, according to Berger and Luckmann (1966, 61) there must first be externalization, secondly objectivation, and only "as the third moment" internalization, which Berger and Luckmann define as the process "by which the objectivated social world is retrojected into consciousness in the course of socialization." The aim of externalization is to facilitate the parties' witnessing the tools they will use for ordering the occasion, and they have opportunities to correct or adjust understandings. The key to understanding calibrating is not what is internalized but what is externalized, since parties must first objectivate taste assessments and teach consociates how to use them. What is more, sociality being what it is, the process of calibrating is never completed.

Calibration operates in service of practical objectivity. No one considers it reasonable for all tasters to achieve an identical evaluation, but persons who operate at the extremes (giving evaluations much higher or much lower than the mean) make it difficult for a collection of people, or an industry, to operate together in an orderly and predictable way. In calibrating, people become more reasonable about their thinking, which in practice means that they operate in conformity with standards. Importantly, calibrating requires that people listen as well as speak.

Among our lay drinkers there were not yet any standards and there was no one to assure the participants there was a right answer, so the participants kept adapting their evaluations to each other, in an effort to remain on the same page. In this next transcript, a portion of which was examined briefly in chapter 9, Helena, Margrit, and Mohammed attempt to calibrate their understanding of the taste descriptor "oily":

1	HELENA:	I felt the second one was very watery and
2		bitter and burnt and smoked, that's definitely something I felt and that I really like. I was
3		wondering, some people described coffee as *oily*. I think you were using it for the first
4		one.

5	MARGRIT:	Yeah.
6	HELENA:	But I don't understand what that means.
7	MARGRIT:	It's kind of like the feeling that it leaves in my mouth, so I described it first as compact
8		and *oily*, because it kind of stays, the flavor
9		and everything stays in my mouth for a long
10		time. Kind of like ( ).
11	HELENA:	Yeah, ok. So the first one would be more *oily*
12		than the third one?
13	MARGRIT:	The first? Yeah, I described the first one as compact and *oily*.
14	MOHAMMED:	Do you mean the *smoothness*?
15	MARGRIT:	Not *smooth*, it's more like a kind of film that it leaves . . .
16	MOHAMMED:	OK.
17	HELENA:	With the first one?
18	MARGRIT:	With the first, right exactly.
19	HELENA:	Yeah, yeah. ( ) But then—
20	MOHAMMED:	It's like the frozen *yogurt* you eat, and it fills your mouth? No?
21	MARGRIT:	Yeah yeah. Like, yeah. For me it's very hard to distinguish pure taste from the way it feels
22		in my mouth . . .

Helena was enumerating a list of possible characterizations for the second coffee that was served very watery and bitter, and burnt and smoked (line 1), and then raised the possibility of *oily* (3), based upon a taste characterization made in a previous tasting flight by Margrit. Helena says that she did not understand the meaning of that "oily" (6), which prevented the "oily" from becoming a shared characterization, hindering confirmation of Margrit's account.

What Helena said served as an invitation to Margrit to clarify the term, and Margrit offered a description (lines 7–10) aimed at specifying the mouthfeel sensation of that coffee: "It's kind of like the feeling that it leaves in my mouth, so I described it first as compact and *oily*, because it kind of stays, the flavor and everything stays in my mouth for a long time."

Once the term has been described, Helena can assess the appropriateness of the term as a characterization for the coffee. It is not just an understanding of the term as if it was an item in a dictionary; the parties must taste and witness for themselves whether and how that term can characterize the experience of their tasting. They use the term to find the taste in the cup. To calibrate her tasting with others', Helena explores which coffee could be characterized as being *oily* (11): "Yeah, ok. So the first one would be more *oily* than the third one?" Margrit (13) then confirms that that characterization is appropriate for describing that coffee.

Calibrating is the how participants monitor the appropriateness of a term, a measurement or description regarding its semantic content and regarding *how* that account can be used and applied. Coffee drinkers employ a descriptor not only to learn what it means but to learn how to use it: it is a social exercise that applies what has been objectivated to an actually experienced and experienceable world, and parties learn how their experiences can be meaningfully shared.

Following the exchange between Helena and Margrit, Mohammed asks for more clarification (14), offering a term ("smoothness") in order to learn whether that could be similar to "oily": "Do you mean the smoothness?" Calibrating is a way that accounts of a sensation are made mutually comprehensible. The request for specification by Mohammed causes Margrit to provide another description of the sensation (15) connected to the feeling of the particular perceptions in the mouth, specifying the meaning of "oily."

In Mohammed's reply (20), "It's like the frozen yogurt you eat, and it fills your mouth? No?" he solicits confirmation of his understanding of the explanation offered by Margrit, based on his own experience, and he tries to make explicit what kind of sensations are in play. It is his best attempt at describing his experience of what he is tasting, and not only a matter of using words. The situation is that at last he is in touch with a taste sensation; that is, whether or not the taste descriptor is apt, it has succeeded in leading Mohammed to a transcendental object. As always, the social context impinges upon his searching and understanding: he wants to get his understanding confirmed without exposing his ignorance, and any move from sensation into discourse will render his insights vulnerable to sophistries.

Calibrating is an opportunity for the participants to compare their evaluations of their experiences, to adjust their assessments, and to practice the same standards. It can be an occasion to discover, and make more explicit, discrepancies or divergences in their experiences. It is a process by which parties achieve intersubjective adequacy, and this achievement is always a local effort. Calibrating is an essential part of the sociality of the occasion.

Calibrating appears to fit inside our model right after objectivation has been performed and the parties are struggling to get on the same page (and to discover that page). It takes place—again, cooperatively—continuously thereafter, without relief. While calibrating occurs in an incipient way during the clustering and objectivating phases, its most intensive operation occurs during the stages that immediately follow the production of a publicly objectivated account, since over time people become less out-of-synchrony with each other. After people have shared and coordinated their understandings of an objectivated account, an adequacy of intersubjective communication is achieved. Calibrating is how people remain inside the social loop as a competent participant. There is scope for individuality, but the trend is toward cooperation, if not conformity. By studying calibration among our coffee drinkers, we can learn about the ways that calibration operates more broadly in society.

The Serendipitous Origins of Order

We want to topicalize an aspect of our data that has been there all along without our having paid it special attention. We suspect it has a hidden presence in everyone's data. It is related to how the local contingencies of social interaction kept getting in the way of our research. It especially relates to the first two of our three categories of practices (clustering and objectivating) of the talking about taste. Topicalizing this aspect helps specify what Garfinkel (1952, 114) referred to in his doctoral dissertation as the "odd communion" of constructing and defining an order together: the "oddness" of this communion is in part derived from *the serendipitous nature* of the many contingencies that steer the objectivating practices used by parties in mundane situations.

This topic is also affiliated with what Harvey Sacks has referred to as the interaction machine, about which Christian Meyer (2018, 275) writes, "It is mainly the machine itself that produces interactional sequences (Sacks 1992, 240) and less the drivers who fuel it with their interactions. In other words, interaction acquires, once set up, a self-perpetuating dynamic." We accept that the workings of this "machine" is what has motivated most of the interests and investigations of both Sacks and Schegloff. What is impressive about this interaction machine is the serendipitous nature of the routines that establish it.

During one of the lay drinking sessions in San Diego, a single tentative mention of "cherry" by a drinker guided the succeeding half-hour of tasting: suddenly everywhere there appeared coffees presenting a cherry taste, where before there was not one. "Cherry" had its origin as a serendipitous account, and the confirmation it gained was likely gratuitous; nevertheless, as soon as it was objectivated and became a social fact for the parties, the parties forgot that the descriptor was their own concerted production. This sort of amnesia accompanies the production of any social fact, and objectivation is often succeeded by a disengagement from what is objectivated. "Cherry" (or earlier, "bitter") became a fact independent of the local situation, even as its production emerged from contingent features of the interaction.

The unplanned dominance of serendipitous structures occurred not only with drinkers' accounts, it occurred with what ethnomethods came to be adopted by a group for their sensory assessment. When a first drinker began to compare a second coffee with a first coffee as soon as that second coffee arrived, announcing that she "liked more" the second coffee ("I personally liked the second one more than the first one"), from that point forward, the group ceased to offer taste descriptors, since the social pattern had serendipitously shifted to *an ethnomethod of comparing coffees*: "I liked the third the most, but I liked the first more than the second." The parties effected this change in the local organization of their tasting even though no deliberate decisions had been taken or approved, or even discussed. The shift was autochthonous.

The comparison method developed as an unexpected consequence of our changing the structure of our tasting sessions. A similar unexpected consequence took place during some test runs with panels of University of Trento students when the drinkers were asked to rate each coffee for a few taste characteristics (sweetness, roundness, aroma) on a 10-point scale. Instead of our form escorting the drinkers to specify taste characteristics, as we had hoped, an *ethnomethod of numerating* each aspect—*without* discussing any flavor attributes—developed serendipitously, and the lay drinkers' talk about taste consisted of numerating without discussing what their numbers meant. In fact, the drinkers used the numbers as a convenient but serendipitous device to shield themselves from having to commit publicly to any particular taste descriptor, reducing their exposure to criticism. They became numerators, as we referred to them. In his studies of beer tastings, Wright (2014, 177 and 227) discusses how numerating facilitates and simplifies the coordination of a party of tasters: "Numbers have a significant agency in translating and making mobile different sensory accounts to enable and simplify processes of standardization through comparison, ranking and filtering." The clearness of a simple organizational ethnomethod can give parties a way to interact in an orderly and predictable way; no matter which methodological device we tried to employ to make their actual taste experiences more observable, our drinkers found a shortcut that reduced their exposure. That is, our test students' ethnomethod of numerating was exercised as an interactional strategy that helped them to organize a clear local orderliness that minimized interactional risks. This ethnomethod of numeration can be found at work among expert professional coffee tasters too, which they use similarly for keeping their social interaction orderly and reducing social risks.

Here they were assessing sweetness, and Lara's assessment is arbitrary. She asks what the ratings were for sweetness for the previous two coffees. Lucia replies,

> LUCIA: The first was 5.
>
> GINA: And the second?
>
> LUCIA: The second 9.
>
> LARA: A 7!
>
> GINA: OK. The velvet texture . . . ?

Here the numbers direct the drinkers' assessment as much as the taste does; the ethnomethod of numerating here obscures the phenomenon, but the drinkers swiftly move on to the next aspect to be assessed (texture) without ever discussing any details of the sweetness.

That parties readily conform to a pattern is not surprising. What is surprising is that each and every new ethnomethod *diverted* them from their task of describing tastes and that the pattern with which they conform developed *accidentally*: much of the time it is nothing more inevitable than a card drawn from a deck. Certain descriptors are used, confirmed, and objectivated, and then the parties are stuck with them. By "stuck" is meant that once a routine of use commences serendipitously, any effort to change the objectivated descriptors or redirect a local routine that uses them will require elaborate, confusing, or even incoherent interactional work. Collective processes of making sense may have less to do with the content of the sense and more with the contingencies of the local social interaction, and structural features of the public discourse that are accidental can be adopted simply because of the contribution they make to keeping the interaction clearly organized. If this is the case, some incoherence is unsurprising.

Frederic Bartlett (1958, 185) describes this "incoherence" well when he writes, "When I look into my collection of recorded discussions . . . I come constantly upon instances of how people start developing an argument sequence, perhaps rather tentatively, and reach a stage at which it is very much easier to go on than to go back. A little beyond this there comes a stage when, if they do make an effort to go back, they become hesitant, ineffective, and very often incoherent." Bartlett keenly calls this stage "the point of no return," by which he means that not long after a serendipitous flow—including one not fully comprehended—is set into motion, the interaction machine does not afford parties easy opportunities for repairs (Schegloff 1997) or redirection, except subversively. The point of no return is inhabited by parties who are busy circumspectively looking for that next "next" (Liberman 2018, 9) that they will be required to perform, in conformity with the emerging structures of the talk as they best understand them.

Continuing past "the point of no return" happens whether or not the accounts as objectivated are correct; that is, whether the objectivated account may lead parties down a wrong track seems not to matter much, and the contingent dynamics of the local interaction have as much—or more—to do with the result than does the topic that motivated the parties to come together (in our case, finding the taste of the coffee), which was part of the fascination for Sacks and Schegloff and a founding object of wonder for ethnomethodology and conversation analysis.

Much social psychological research proceeds under the notion that people mostly knowingly think, plan, and strategize about organizing a local orderliness. And like all sociologists' analyses, ethnomethodology occasionally assumes that people know what they are doing more than they really do, i.e., that words, concepts, and formal analytic thinking drive interaction even when they do not, and that social interaction is mostly based on individual consciousness and what people work out on their own. Too many assumptions of voluntarism, rationally based decision-making, and plan-filled action proceed intact in ethnomethodology even while Harold Garfinkel espoused a stirring critique of "formal analytic theorizing" and its practices, drawing upon the nondualism of Merleau-Ponty (1962, 1968), Heidegger (1996), and Derrida (1989). People's *in vivo* practices do not always conform to the expectations of analytic social theorists, and social interaction has been exposed as *less* deliberate, *less* planned, and *less* concept-centered than even Garfinkel recognized. Much social structure is serendipitous.

Garfinkel (2002, 190–191 and 245–248) did argue that local orderliness was "autochthonous," and here we offer specifications of details that can populate these autochthonous orders. The "autochthonous nature of local affairs" means that it is impossible to predict which ethnomethods people will adopt for providing orderliness, for the reason that the people themselves do not "know" them until they come upon them and use them in the local occasion. This is another reason why the unique adequacy principle holds that the field method required for grasping a local situation is unique to each occasion, and therefore can only be discovered, not known in advance. Here, we identify and describe features of everyday social interaction that operate across many social settings. These features are tenacious and possess an intransigence.

Interestingly, an ethnomethod adopted by lay drinkers can be disrupted by their encountering a real taste, as was the case with the "ferrous" taste identified in a coffee, which was discussed in chapter 8. At any time a real taste can disrupt their activity, causing them to pull themselves away from the work of organizing the local orderliness and return to the task of better identifying, describing, and communicating the taste. Still, this taste will be subjected to the contingencies of the local course of interaction, which includes their ways of talking. Their activity is pedagogical—not simply in the sense that the parties teach each other how to taste and how to describe tastes but in the sense that they also teach each other *how to survive in the interaction* by picking up terms and protocols and then using them for navigating safely through a developing order of practices. This sets up an asymmetry in our data: we are interested in how they learn to taste, while they are interested in surviving the conversation. In brief, these lay drinkers are taken up with the talk of the occasion as much as the taste; and in our studies, it often seems that drinkers become so happy about coming upon a local orderliness that will render their participation less risky that we are unable to get them back on track to pay close attention to the flavors of coffee they are drinking, and to describe these flavors. Problems like these plague most research into tasting, whether or not the researchers are aware of them.

Our priority, like Mondada (2019), was not to study talk about tasting but to study tasting; yet, since the parties here were themselves preoccupied with their talk and were less interested in taste than we expected, we ended up studying their social practices of interaction. Our investigation recalls the problem of "Shils's Complaint" to a team of sociologists who were researching juries, where Shils complained (Garfinkel 2002, 96–97) that he was able to use Bales's method for analyzing the working of small groups to discover what makes of jurors a small group, but he could not use them to learn what makes jurors *jurors*. We justified studying their coffee drinking this way by the fact that that was their priority and by the recognition that sensing taste never operates in pure isolation, apart from some sociality.

As random and serendipitous as is the adoption of taste descriptors by lay drinkers, on occasion drinkers were able to use them to discover flavors, and to discover taste itself. The flavors that some of the drinkers found were not necessarily definitive of the coffee, but they were sufficient for engaging them in further pursuit of flavor. Discursive practices, both microsocial and macrosocial, were never absent, but from time to time a transcendental taste in the coffee they were drinking broke through the interactional activity and grabbed their attention, as with "ferrous" and the oral haptics of "oily." How did this happen?

The first step was for a drinker to appreciate *that* there was a taste to coffee. Surprisingly for us, many of our drinkers, including those reporting they had a daily coffee habit, experienced some wonder upon discovering the diversity of flavors that a cup of coffee can present, and they expressed pleasure about this unexpected discovery; moreover, this motivated some of our participants to offer us profuse thanks at the conclusion of our session for having invited them to participate. It seemed that many of our lay drinkers were unaware that a coffee can possess a flavor that identifies it uniquely, so they were happy to learn that coffee can have this variety, and that they can go search for it. They were learning about tastes. One person who came to our session with the understanding that specialty coffees needed to be bitter, as a positive feature, was surprised and pleased to discover that a coffee could also present a bitter taste that was undesirable. The recognition that there was both a "good" bitter and a "bad" bitter enhanced her understanding of gourmet coffees and led her to pay closer attention to the bitterness of coffees.

Once this first step has been taken, some drinkers were able to cultivate an ability to *find tastes*. Drinkers may begin to get in touch with their sense of taste and initiate explorations of their own. These explorations were not cognitive exercises but sensual tours motivated by immediate bodily experiences. As Vannini et al. (2012, 14–15) have described, "Both structuralism and symbolic anthropology tend to overemphasize cognitive and abstract meaning at the expense of the carnality and the practical value of bodily experience." Although it happened infrequently, the carnal effect of a prominent taste can break through the locally developed methods. More important than a catalog of salient tastes was the way that such carnal experience provoked the drinkers' curiosity about flavors and caused them to search for them. On occasion, they were transformed from passive recipients of taste into being active seekers.

This experiencing involves more than "fixing exclusively, as a static and defenseless object" (Perullo 2018a, 28) a flavor, "which would mean to betray" that flavor. Betray in what sense? By ignoring the "knots and weaves" of the drinkers' own taste experiences, "the laces and connections that are intertwined and make up the whole" (Perullo 2018a, 49). Another remarkable development can occasionally happen: instead of reducing their sensory experience to a name, the drinkers began to appreciate that names, the descriptors they use, work as metaphors for something that *is still ongoing* and yet to be fully understood. Even if the taste descriptors developed serendipitously or were adopted from some drinkers' notion of what taste-as-distinction (Wright 2014, 33) calls for, they can lead the drinkers into the tangle of weaves that a coffee's flavor presents, and thereby aid their exploration. But taste descriptors can also obscure further inquiries, and drinkers learn that taste descriptors do not capture everything there is to experience—that is, they learn that there is always more to the taste than they have noticed. It is then that they learn to look for that "more" in a "continuous exploration of experience" (Perullo 2016, 44). In sensory experience, "Discovery is preferred over judgment" (Perullo 2018, 57).

Let us take up again the oral haptics of the drinking of Helena, Margrit, and Mohammed, and their discovery that texture/mouthfeel is a part of taste. Overlooked by most American drinkers, Italian espresso drinking is primarily tactile. Here, the parties pay close attention to this aspect of experiencing coffee. After some discussion and re-tasting, including the calibrating surrounding "smooth," the sense of touch offered by the coffee is made into a noticeable. In the transcript about the "oily" taste, Mohammed speaks from the actuality of his tasting experience when he discusses how "it fills your mouth" and is "like the frozen yogurt" (page 384, line 20), and in this way he expands the sapience of his sensory experience.

The list of aspects that makes for "a good cup" of coffee is extensive and involves not only taste and smell but also what is visual (e.g., the steam that rises out of a fresh cup of coffee, a spectacle that has been given iconic form in the world of coffee purveying). Vannini et al. (2012, 5) emphasize that taste should not be made an isolated essence: "The taste, the smell, the tactile feel of coffee in the morning—no one sensation is distinct from the others—blend into a total sensual experience in which the whole is greater than the sum of its parts." It is the multi-sensuality of sensory experience that makes it difficult to describe, possibly because description often betrays it; nevertheless, description is required for communication.

Any discovery of an experience of taste as sense by our lay drinkers still must reckon with organizing some objective sense for what they have been doing, so another step in a pedagogy for exploring what one is drinking is that drinkers learn to apply taste descriptors to their experience. This can involve an unfamiliar, sometimes unwelcome, ability to use taste descriptors in a manner that reintroduces some of the alienation created by a regime of taste descriptors. They become lay linguists, engage in semiotic adventures, and their talk comes to prevail over the immanent multi-sensory experience. Using taste descriptors in a way that fosters discovery while minimizing abstractions requires considerable hermeneutic skill, and it is not uncommon for descriptors to guide and assist even while they obscure and alienate.

Describing flavors directs the tongue's explorations, but there is at work more than a nominalist determinism. The taste descriptors guide drinkers to their experience and lead them *through* their experience, which reflexively transforms those words so that the descriptors gain significance and pertinence as words-in-use. Taste descriptors are employed not just for describing tastes but for finding tastes. We can call this "the social construction of reality" if we like, but the gloss is too general to offer much service. When we examine the specific details that compose such "construction," it appears that *reality* too—here pleasurable or unpleasurable flavors—has a role to play. The impetus provided by discursive practices can prompt lay drinkers to commence exploring and discovering flavors, exploration that can develop into an enduring interest, permanently transforming the way drinkers experience coffee and causing them to cultivate what Vannini et al. (2012, 20) call "the intentionality of sensory perception."

By cultivating their sensory attention, coffee drinkers can learn to keep themselves open for a taste that calls for a bodily response. Vannini et al. (2012, 28) describe this as "somatic work," which is not something strictly cognitive but embodied engagement. Vannini et al. (2012, 55) speak of "performing wine," which involves not the passive accounting of features but active participation. This somatic work *can* take place, but some social interaction composes its context and influences it; one way or another, some talk accompanies tasting. Thinking is occasioned, and serendipitously developed local ethnomethods become a part of every occasion. When people undertake sensorial experiences, there will always be local social demands that divert and shape the parties' attention to tastes. Sense never operates alone, apart from some sociality. The senses, the social, and the intentionality of consciousness are always mixed together.

Why Do Good People Prefer Bad Coffee?

Whatever routine people have found, they are never eager to have it disrupted, especially with regard to their coffee drinking, which they may consider to be a ritual that falls inside their personal domain. Coffee drinkers do not want advice to arrive just before they drink their coffee. As James Hoffman complained to the 2011 SCA Symposium, "They're simply not interested." No one is interested in advice about how to drink the coffee they have been drinking every morning for 20 years. Gabriel Marcel once said there is a human tendency to become stuck in one's habits and received ideas, to the point that persons are not always "available" to respond to anything novel (Bakewell 2016, 86). Ging (2012) reports that coffee consumers they contacted were unwilling to learn anything that differed from what they already knew (or thought they knew; Ging reports that much of the lay drinkers' knowledge was incorrect). In every country we studied, our work depended upon affiliating with local experts—producers, processors, exporters, etc.—and at some point, no matter what the country (Mexico, Italy, Brazil, Denmark, India, El Salvador, etc.), these informants confessed, during a moment of intimacy, that the people of their country were incapable of distinguishing good coffee from bad coffee. In India it was the 47% chicory they preferred; in the UK it was the copious sugar and cream they use; in Italy it was how badly they scorch their beans. We have already enumerated the list.

The most important surprise of these investigations of lay coffee drinkers is how little attention most lay drinkers actually pay to the flavors in their cups. Even when the coffee is not overwhelmed by sugar and cream and can be tasted, there is little interest in paying attention to taste. Yet drinkers love their coffee anyway. They love its warmth, the caffeine, and the company; however, for most lay drinkers taste is an afterthought. After a century of cheap coffee across the world, drinkers do not demand much. Even coffee drinkers who claim to be passionate about their coffee recognize little about the taste, such as the research subject in San Diego who claimed much expertise and preferred the Folgers. Ott (2018, 121) describes a customer who had berated the coffee at his hotel and who announced at a specialty café, "I need a good strong cup of coffee, uh, a large, dark, French roast, please." The barista knew that his café did not ever sell that kind of coffee, but he replied, "Okay, we can do that." When asked why, he explained that he assumed the customer would not be able to tell the difference.

After tasting three coffees and spending an hour discussing them, one test subject in Italy confessed, "The taste I'm looking for in a café or bar is also influenced by the fact that I've never noticed it." Respect truth wherever one finds it. A test subject in San Diego explained, "In the morning, during the coffee part of the breakfast I don't really taste the coffee." For nearly half of our taste subjects, the complicated flavors one can find in coffee seemed to come as a complete surprise, so instead of asking them to describe flavors, we asked 20 drinkers in San Diego, "What part of the mouth does it work on?" No one could come up with a reply. In Mysore, India, there is a characteristic peanut taste in their washed coffees that is due to using too many immature beans, the result of trying to cut harvesting expenses. A taster from Hawaii, Andrew Hertzel, has described it with perfect accuracy as "peanut shell," meaning the husk that surrounds the nut. However, if one drinks it frequently, it becomes part of what one expects, and one can even come to miss it when it is not there, despite how flat it is. Sunil Pinto once mused that as India improves its processing and the under-ripe beans are removed from the lots, the Mysore coffee is losing its characteristic peanut taste, and according to Sunil, "The result is that people are missing the 'nuttiness.'" What one is accustomed to expect can provide its own satisfaction whenever that expectation is fulfilled, even if the taste is no better than ordinary.

During the sampling of coffees that we gave to students at the University of Trento, we offered three cups from Lavazza's Modo Mio brand of capsules. In one flight of coffees, Cup 1 was Lavazza's *Intensamente*, which has 50% Robusta. Cup 2 was *Deliziosamente*, with 100% Arabica. Unknown to the students, Cup 3 was the same as Cup 1. The *vellutato* ("velvety," i.e., texture) of Cup 1 was rated 10 by four students working cooperatively, and the velvet of the identical Cup 3 was rated a 1. The serendipitous dynamics of the local interaction or the sequencing of the coffees steered them to such a contradictory position, revealing that the actual taste was probably not the principal focus of their attention. This sort of contradiction happened frequently. In a second flight of three cups, Cup 1 was *Appassionamente*, whose body was rated as 8. Again, the same coffee was presented as Cup 3, where the body was assessed as 3.

American tasters were much the same. Blindly tasting, a group of lay tasters preferred Folgers, which sold at $3.14/pound, over an Ethiopian medium roast from an award-winning roaster that sold for $25/pound. One test subject who was enthusiastic about participating in our tasting, declaring "I *love* coffee," was among those who preferred the Folgers. Of course, they are entitled to their opinion, and there can be no question that they are the best authority regarding what they like. But what sort of authority is it?

Favorite brands are important, and households have turned their favorite brand into family traditions that can extend across two or three generations. One lay drinker informed us, "In our family we've always thought that Yuban was the best." When a friend was making some Yuban in a Mr. Coffee machine, I (KL) offered her some extraordinary Gesha beans from Panama, thinking to educate her. Her reply was, "Let me just drink my coffee first, and then I'll try yours." Another friend was willing to try some of my costly specialty coffee, but after drinking a half-cup of it, he tossed it out and made himself a cup of Folgers that was more suitable for his much preferred artificial creamer/sweetener. Most coffee purveyors tell similar stories. Still another friend from Bogotá reported to me that her Colombian friend in the USA asked her to bring some Colombian coffee with her when she visited. When my friend asked what kind, the answer was "The very plainest brand, the Sello Rojo." Colombia has many diverse and wonderful coffees, but Sello Rojo is not one of them; however, it was probably the coffee she had become accustomed to while growing up. There is much more to drinking coffee than taste, and a sociologist should not ignore such things (Simmel 1997).

Teaching Taste

There is a final question regarding how the lived somatic work of experiencing flavors can be encouraged and made to thrive, and even inspire the millions of people who drink coffee daily. Since moments of genuine tasting are fleeting, the challenge for the coffee industry is to discover where those moments reside and how they can be extended. One goal of coffee research is to gain access to the judgment of lay drinkers, to their thinking about coffee and to how they have organized the understandings they have about coffee, which like all knowledge can be idiosyncratic. In specialty cafés, baristas are charged with the task of teaching customers how to discover flavors, and they sometimes "guide customers in interpreting their own sensory experiences" (Ott 2018, 67). This is not an easy task because it requires training lay drinkers to make contact with their sensory experiences (Ott 2018, 6), getting them to tune in to slowly evolving transformations of the coffee in the cup as they are drinking it, noticing changes as the coffee cools, and most difficult of all, getting them to describe them. Some customers do not understand what all the fuss is about, yet one must always treat one's clients and friends with courtesy. Perullo (2018c, 23) writes, "Exercising taste is a continuous education in diplomacy, the diplomacy of convivial relations." Ott (2018, 91) reports one barista's advice: "It's important not to be aggressive educationally," and he warns against "over-explaining" how to taste.

The delicacy of disrupting long-held habits suggests that a subtle approach to teaching lay drinkers how to notice tastes would be best. One barista reported that latte art is a great way to begin a casual conversation and will afford plenty of opportunities to introduce ideas about tastes. Ott (2018, 93) describes the strategy of one barista who cunningly provokes questioning by customers by providing little information in his menus: "I'm very into small menus. I want people to ask me questions, you know, and make it hard for people. At [my coffee bar] it's a very streamlined, small menu. It has espresso and alternate espresso and everyone goes, 'What's alternate espresso?' And then 'I will tell you what it is.' So, that's like the start, right there, making people ask questions about it." This places the initiative for the learning in the hands of the customer, and this more active role can make them more willing to discuss flavors. Angelo Segoni of Quarta Caffè in Lecce (Puglia) suggests that being modest in one's efforts to offer instruction is the best strategy, since detailed pedagogies or lectures only alienate the drinker further from embodied engagement. So Segoni advocates conversations, occasioned by questions initiated by the drinker. At most only *one* aspect of drinking coffee should be raised. Segoni suggests, "Creating the right ambience may be the only way to help people appreciate something, since it involves not only what is in the cup but the entire experience. Sometimes giving less information is better—just let them discover what they want from that cup."

Identifying, recognizing, analyzing, and naming coffee flavors are grounded in the serendipitous contingencies of locally organized social activity, and they sometimes *disappear* there. Discovering what drinkers are tasting without these local organizational affairs may not be feasible, no matter how much we would like to study only taste. At the site of drinking, no such "without" exists, possibly not ever, except in some abstract theorizing about tasting developed by social scientists or coffee professionals. If the parties are more preoccupied with the sociality of the occasion than with the taste of what they are drinking, this is another discovery.

Part IV

Science and Its Labors

Wonder rather than doubt is the root of all knowledge.

—Abraham Heschel

Chapter 13

Science and Objective Practices

not as land looks like on a map
but as sea bord seen by men sailing

—Ezra Pound, Canto LIX (1950, 324)

Science (from *scientia*, Latin for "technical knowing") has become a major participant in coffee purveying. Every coffee purveyor speaks of it, but the quantity of their invocations of science exceeds competent applications of science. However, scientific strategies have contributed more tightly organized coffee-related inquiries into breeding, processing, roasting, and brewing, which are helping coffee purveyors improve the taste of coffees. Today preferred phrasings of coffee purveyors run something like "Brewing for peak flavor requires a scientific precision" (Danielle Sacks 2014). Q- and R-Grading Instructor Dr. Manuel Diaz speaks frequently of "science-based standards." A young farmer in Colombia told me with much conviction, "If they are processing in an unscientific way, the flavors will change."

What is this ubiquitous term "scientific"? When people speak its name, are they thinking the same thing? The name may remain the same, but how many varieties of practice can be collected under its heading? I asked the young Colombian farmer what science was; he replied that it is being careful not to dry the cherries in mud, and when one is washing the beans to always use clear water. Perhaps former US President Donald Trump described it for many: "it's called science, and, all of a sudden, something is better" (Swan 2020). Science is many things to many people. When people speak of science, they are often simultaneously engaged in formulating what it is. As a word, it possesses a material being, but its immaterial being—its meaning—can vary considerably between the person who utters it and the person who hears it, so some coordination of this meaning is required (even if this requirement is inconspicuous) whenever its name is spoken; it is like when everyone applauds "democracy" while entertaining different ideas about it as they applaud. It is even possible for a word to be spoken and for all heads to nod without people being clear about what is meant, even for themselves.

Hegel (1969, 590) describes science as "the systematic employment of the understanding," and he emphasizes that its main aim is to establish "regulative unity." Once a unity is established, it can be used as an aid for collecting and organizing knowledge, so that knowledge can accumulate and be retrieved handily when needed. Regulative unities afford parties an appropriate technology for organizing the orderliness of the local communication and the affairs of investigators and researchers who must work together. Eventually, this confers a moral force upon the developing unity, which contributes to keeping the unity's regime in place, at least until the succeeding scientific "revolution." This is why Hegel refers to the regulative unity as a "merely regulative unity." Regulations carry with them their own charisma that proceeds from their capacity to provide order for social affairs, an order that has value independently of any truth value that the regulations may or may not have.

Science is embarrassed and occasionally offended by its indebtedness to the local contingencies of social interaction. "It is the aim of science to so objectify experience that it no longer contains any historical element. The scientific experiment does this by its methodical procedure. The historico-critical method, moreover, does the same thing in the human sciences. Both methods are concerned to guarantee, through the objectivity of their approach, that these basic experiences can be repeated by anyone" (Gadamer, 1975, 311). Being able to be repeated by anyone and needing participants to work on the same page are essential to science.

Always, there are several separate but related notions of objectivity at work. There is an objectivity that is produced in the intersubjective life of a community so that something can be understood as the same by everyone. This is a natural objectivity that we fashion in everyday life, one that is based upon the confirmability, reconfirmability, and hence repeatability of some thinking. We will call this first objectivity *Objectivity A*. It is first because coordinating communicability is necessary before making arguments and assertions and compiling theories, and indeed arguments are frequently motivated by the contributions they are able to make to organizing the communication. In fact, formal assertions began their life on the streets of Babylon and other Akkadian, Aramite, Elamite, and other Mesopotamian towns (humanity's first urban civilizations), and later Greek municipalities (Bar-Hillel 1964), as *a means for coordinating communicability* during public disputes that were resolved by civil judges; hence, the arguments in these local disputes needed to adopt formal, standard ways that fostered clear communication among parties. This was the initial context in which public objectivity took form. Once a common set of standards for thinking was adopted, the participants needed to attune their arguments to those standards. Both law and logic emerged from this social situation, and so the kinds of objectivity that law and logic provide occurred subsequent to this immediate and practical need for social order in the prehistorical arenas of public discourse and public thought.

There is a second objectivity that lives a life that is more independent of the social contingencies, "in itself" as it were, and it is imagined to have its being in an essence whose nature was fixed before and separately from the collaborative efforts of the parties who were able to define it. It too carries the demand that it remain the same and be repeatable, and this requirement for repeatability can abolish its history and occlude whatever was unique and singular about a situation. In many circumstances this second objectivity, which we will call *Objectivity B*, relies on the metrological (reason that possesses metrics) techniques of mathematized sciences. Types of this second objectivity used by coffee purveyors include separation by size or weight, measuring the time from first crack to second crack (to help the roaster subtly tweak the caramelization to bring out the best flavor), editing the beans by photometrics (removing defects—black and dark beans are easy to identify, but light green beans are harder to eliminate), measurements of density, levels of viscosity, the amount of dissolved solids in brewing techniques, etc. Numerical measurements (e.g., "78 kg per hectoliter") assist coffee purveyors in manipulating the flavors of a coffee. An importer receiving an objective account along with a shipment of green beans will read the numbers, taste the coffees, and reflexively provide a schema of interpretation that makes the numerations intelligible. Much comparison is required, and any instance of Objectivity B must be transformed into a practical objectivity if it is going to be efficacious. This entails that this practical objectivity will necessarily bear a "subjective" component: in the world of coffee, the measurements themselves are gradually converted into ideal types that carry idealizations of their gustatory influences, and this ideal-typical system always remains a work in progress, for oneself and for the industry.

It often happens that during the scientific work of Objectivity B the local contingencies will disappear, and then thinkers can be carried far from the actual matters that motivated their inquiry. This makes evident to us yet a third species of objectivity, *Objectivity C*: bringing the investigations closer to *the object*, making contact with the object, and sustaining that contact throughout one's investigation. When the Madison, Wisconsin, purveyor of green specialty coffees John Burman contends that comprehensive sensory evaluation is a matter of perception and practice, he is speaking principally of Objectivity C. No matter what practice of Objectivity B is in play, Objectivity C cannot be missing, since the capacity to maintain an attentive contact with the taste is the skill that enables tasters to keep their heads clear for what the next cup is offering them, a skill that is paramount for accurate sensory assessment.

Merleau-Ponty (1968, 14–15) contrasts Objectivity B and Objectivity C: "The true is the *objective*, is what I have succeeded in determining by measurement, or more generally by the *operations* that are authorized by the variables or by the entities I have defined relative to an order of facts. Such determinations owe nothing to our *contact* with the things: they express an effort of approximation that would have no meaning with regard to the lived experience." In fact, Objectivity C requires considerable discipline and a capacity to sharply attune one's senses to the object that founds this objectivity. "The object X is not something given all at once" (Bruzina 1970, 69); rather, our intentional awareness brings it progressively to light, in "a process in which objects are brought to the point at which they stand as fully given" (Bruzina 1970, 46).

This emphasis on immediate contact with the object of inquiry reveals the affinity that Objectivity C shares with Edmund Husserl's first methodological principle of *Evidenz* (evidence; see chapter 3), which is the direct witnessing of things themselves in their mode of self-givenness. Only evidence that comes from direct and immanent experience can properly be made the basis for truth. Husserl (1969b, 12) states, "Evidence is, in an extremely broad sense, an 'experiencing' of something that is, and is this; it is precisely a mental seeing of something itself," and only this direct witnessing can serve as a reliable grounding for judgments. We can carry out predicative analyses, develop protocols, construct models, etc., but all of them must be based upon direct, immanent evidence or "immediate grounding" (Husserl 1982, 338). Husserl explains, "The primal source of all legitimacy lies in immediate evidence and, more narrowly delimited, in originary evidence, or in the originary givenness motivating it." This "originarily presentive consciousness . . . is the ultimate legitimating source of all rational assertions." Its evidence *is limited to* what is actually presented and seized upon in immediate seeing (Husserl

1982, 37), without anything being brought in from the outside to interpret it. This latter includes methodologically derived objectivities: only what is *actually* presented to our experience by the object, with nothing added to it, is admitted as foundational. This the meaning of Objectivity C.

Elizabeth Ströker (1997, 204) emphasizes that this is not any miraculous capacity for gaining absolute truth, since our immanent experience of something can be mistaken; but it is the starting point for any truth. Accordingly, if it is mistaken, it must be proven to be mistaken in light of better evidence that is obtained by further direct and immanent experience. This is a methodology for analyzing reality. Husserl (1982, 339) proposes, "All predicative and conceptual rational cognizing leads back to *evidence*. Properly understood, only originary evidence is the source of legitimation '*originaliter*.'" Mediated evidence that emerges from predicative, formal analytic, or methodologically driven reflection is not original but derived. This direct evidence of Objectivity C is the proper basis for judgments.

We should appreciate that this list of objectivities (A, B, and C) is not necessarily exhaustive, but all three of them are ubiquitous. Also, they are not mutually exclusive, and it is not extraordinary for them to operate together.

In their public communications, most coffee purveyors give priority to Objectivity B: "A tool that we need is an objective, repeatable, measurable system for looking at what are the actual flavors and aromas present in a given sample of coffee" (Neuschwander 2019). Similarly, Giacanole et al. (2016) propose three methodological principles that they hold to be critical for reliable coffee tasting: using a larger pool of assessors, guaranteeing the anonymity of the coffee, and clearly specifying the particular sensory properties rather than making holistic judgments. As far as best practices go, they are correct about all three; however, there is a danger of becoming too sanguine about resolving all of the fundamental problems, including the ironies and contradictions, that professional tasters face regularly, for the reason that these principles only reduce the problems and do not remove them altogether. Adding the word "scientific" to "sensory analysis" does not seal the deal; tangible benefits come only with practical action, which invariably ensnares us once again inside our own contradictions. It is true that the coffee industry needs more science, but it needs science not as rhetoric but as effective practices.

The contradictions require that we not work alone but continually solicit the critical judgments of our peers, and sharing data across an expansive cohort of researchers is perhaps the most vital component of the scientific method. Its importance stems from the way it allows knowledge to be built up objectively (here, our Objectivity A), be compared with similar kinds of knowledge, and be subject to the criticism of other knowledgeable persons. This keeps returning researchers to the precincts of social interaction, and to the local historicity of their affairs, matters that advocates of Objectivity B sometimes prefer to ignore.

Science has to do with following reason, respecting acknowledged "facts," avoiding inconsistencies, and applying considerable equanimity toward whatever one's inquiries are disclosing and toward each conclusion one reaches. Restraint is part of the intellectual discipline of any scientist. Knowing that beliefs can introduce bias, scientists are congenitally slow to form beliefs, and they are quick to abandon them. They delay making commitments, keeping themselves "from being persuaded" (Figal 2010, 343), not as a caution that will limit the criticism of their peers but as a sound strategy for ascertaining reliable knowledge. Rather than trying to avoid contradictions, sensory scientists should search for them. A signal practice of a professional taster is to pay particular attention to any tastes that are capable of resisting systematization. This capacity owes much to a skill described by Earle (1955, 40) as being the "act of the subject freeing itself of its immediate existence in the world of experiencing, so as to stand back and look at or cognize what it had." To this end, protocols for coffee tasting can be ways of transcending one's limited perspectives. This is an aspect of Objectivity B, but here its distance from the object can place it into conflict with Objectivity C. It is no simple question how we can employ both of these objectivities in the same investigation. Yet we do.

What exactly do we mean when people say, "We need to follow the science?" Most are in agreement with this assertion, but what does it mean? And does it mean the same thing to each person? How many kinds of "science" are there, and how do we delimit science? Science consists of *different practices*; it is not just one thing. Further, genuine science procures much of its noble reputation by following practices that are exceedingly mundane. Lingle (2001, 29) offers an illustration: "It is extremely important to use the same equipment each time so that the results between cuppings done on different days are comparable." Science is not magic; it consists of the employment of a wide ensemble of practices. Götz Hoeppe (2012, 1149) discovered something similar during his study of astronomers at La Silla Observatory in Chile: "Practices at the observatory are inevitably specific to local arrangements of instrumentation and modes of usage, but they are generally directed at producing data of trans-local epistemic use." While science dreams of universals, its work is always local.

Control

Science as we know it developed during the Enlightenment in the era of colonialism, when various projects of controlling affairs from the top down were at their peak. As Luigi Odello has explained, the professional work of coffee purveyors includes controlling and rendering stable an objective taste that can be commercialized. Science has a predisposition toward fixing things in their places, which renders the things more predictable and more susceptible to being controlled. The ubiquitous preference among coffee purveyors for "consistency" is part of this project. There is no reason why a coffee that is inconsistent from cup to cup or from harvest to harvest cannot have excellent taste. Perullo (2016, 63; my translation) advises that when we drink, we remain flexible enough to notice and appreciate "the tangle of locomotive lines that we explore without being able to control anything." The problem is that surprise and unpredictability make a coffee wild and difficult to control. The interest to tame and stabilize the identities of tastes and coffees has motivated scientific sensory analysis to attempt a universal reification of tastes, which can then be better controlled. "Above all, however, with objectivity we cultivate the illusion of control over the things of the world, and this reassures us." (Perullo 2016, 19). As Merleau-Ponty (1968, 18) observes, scientific praxis operates as though "what is is not that upon which we have openness, but only that upon which we can operate." If necessary, scientists prefer to operate with manageable derivatives (Merleau-Ponty 1968, 150) instead of the actual things because actual things are more difficult to dominate.

Are the certainties of the object so fragile that they cannot withstand more exposure to the light of inquiry? What is the best way for scientists to handle "the uncontrolled diversity of the fact" (Heidegger 1967, 211)? Is the solution "to be even more analytical, have more training, and categorize and regulate the products further, i.e., professionals must learn more scientific techniques in order to more perfectly control the influences that could possibly disturb their evaluations" (Hennion and Teil 2004b, 529)? Justifiable concerns lead scientists to seek more control over their data, so they tighten the horizon of their search to produce ever-better-defined objects for the purposes of their inquiries. So transformed, these user-designed objects obscure and belie the narrowing of perspective that has contributed to their manufactured clarity.

The insistence upon retaining control motivates the Western scientific spirit, a spirit that perhaps is embodied most strongly in engineers. Being in control, or believing one is in control, can provide existential reassurance in a chaotic universe, but it also brings a hidden bias of its own that less original second- and third-tier scientists are unable to surmount, and the result is that they are content to settle into their objectifications.

Scientists dream of discovering straightforward causal principles that will assist their projects of control. But worldly events are rarely straightforward; more commonly, they are complex, overdetermined, and contradictory. There are many facets to coffee production, each of which exerts influence upon taste: genetics, soil, climate, harvesting, processing, fermentation, selection, storage, blending, roasting, packaging, and brewing—in short, everything that we have reviewed in parts II and III. Dedicated coffee professionals have made progress, but they have not mastered fully a single one of these steps. Roasting, for example, bears too many contingencies to enable the finest scientific approach to build a straightforward model, although some aspects have been determined: "Development time is not simply one set of chemical reactions occurring: rather, it is a multi-dimensional interaction between many separate chemical reactions that are not only happening on their own, but also interplaying with one another" (Hoos 2015, 37). Lingle (2001, 5) tells us that coffee has more than 400 organic and inorganic chemical compounds, while Hoos (2015, 22) claims there are over 600 volatile organic compounds in a roasted bean. Which person is it who can claim to be in control of each one of these? Even if one knows how to handle one organic compound, by doing so one may countermand the benefits of another—and there are hundreds of them. As Hoos (2015, 48) summarizes, "It is really difficult to wrap all of that information up into a nice, neat little ball to tell someone what the adjusting of the development time of a coffee will do to the overall flavor." Another purveyor of specialty coffee speaks similarly: "Flavor is so complex to understand because the bean is composed of thousands of different chemical components. Fortunately, there are more than five hundred volatile components in coffee. And these five hundred components do not exist simply one at a time; rather, they interact with each other in the form of various synergies." This is a sensory analyst who appreciates the limitations of science even as he uses its methods and protocols.

An illustration from geography will help to illuminate the problem. Hydrologists may invest resources in developing the most accurate ocean-level measuring systems they can devise, and with these tools they can produce lengthy printouts of levels and locations for a variety of variables. But rarely does the world function under the auspices a single or even several indicators. Complex forces like sea rise or the taste of a coffee are the result of numerous factors, each of which interacts with each other. An obvious factor in sea rise is that the ocean is not only rising, the land may also be subsiding; therefore, no matter how elegant are the metrological techniques in which hydrologists have great confidence, their models may simplify the picture to the point of being unreliable. For example, the rising ocean and the subsidence of the Mississippi River Delta create an interdependent system, and so the Army Corps of Engineers constructed a levee for New Orleans that they predicted, using calculations based on models for sea rise they had constructed, would last for a hundred years, but the levee broke after the first hurricane. The Army Corps of Engineers is an iconic version of the spirit of dominating science. There is always more taking place than a scientific model can account for, a situation that has caused Lingle (2001, 5) to concede that "the difficulty in establishing the nature of coffee's unique and popular flavor has both intrigued and frustrated flavor chemists for a long time."

Most measurements operate remotely from experience. The very practices that make metrological analysis "more objective" in the sense of Objectivity B render it inept at connecting the measurements to lived experience, i.e., Objectivity C. Chemical acidity (pH) is not the same as sensed acidity because it is *how* the sour interacts with other flavors present (sweet, bitter, salt, umami), i.e., "sour taste modulation," that produces our gustatory experience. Speaking of perfumes, Morana Alaç (2017, 148) comments, "The link between molecular properties and odor quality is still contested territory." Metrological techniques can offer information, but the experience of the taster will need to determine what to do with the information. To explain the taste of a blend of coffees by trying to link flavors to chemical analyses is like trying to explain "the artistic form" by deriving it "from the chemical nature of the colors" (Simmel 1959, 350). Science has spent more than a century steeped in its dreams of operating causalities for the sake of gaining control over things. Steven Shapin (2011, 38) describes this project: "From the nineteenth century, it was thought possible in principle to *replace* the language of qualities, and even the language of descriptive predicates, with that of constituents. We would eventually be able to align the vocabulary of tastes with the specific chemical constituents that caused those tastes." We still await such capacity to control tastes. While postmodern thinkers have developed skepticism regarding the likelihood of identifying causalities to an extent that would provide technicians with total control, some coffee purveyors continue to pursue these dreams.

Despite the Trieste scientist who assured me that "Genetics is *everything*," the genetics of a coffee plant do not determine everything—the same bean as in Ethiopia can be denser in Central America (they grow at different elevations and in different soils), which affects the roasting profile necessary, which in turn affects the flavor. Terroir, if there is such a thing when stripped of its mythopoetics, cannot determine everything either because the climate (winds, sunshine, the timing of rains) keeps changing every year. Fermentation is a heaving pile of live worms, impossible to control with much precision, even if one were able to reliably determine certain causal relationships. Of course, there is no harm to experimental research; discoveries are always welcome. But we can leave our dreams of straightforward causal relations behind. Such research has the "goal of conquering nature through obedience [to the applied method], the new attitude of attacking and forcing nature's secrets from it" (Gadamer 1975, 313).

The self-discipline of scientists is revealed in the advice of senior taster Manuel Diaz: "When you do science, you need to follow your method." It is true that methods need to be routinized if they are to result in standardized application; however, they should not be so routinized that we blindly imitate ourselves. Science requires us to be more than brilliant "technicians of method" (Husserl 1970a, 56), and it will not suffice to substitute a sound method for paying close attention. In other words, Objectivity C demands something beyond what is necessary for achieving Objectivity B. Alfred Schutz (1970b, 130) writes, "Methodology can never establish what topic is relevant to us, nor can rules of operation supply the focus of our motivational interest." While there can be at work a "naive faith in method and in the objectivity that can be attained through it" (Gadamer 1975, 322), naive faith has no place in science.

Dividing and Counting

Scientific practice conforms with what Popper (1972, 178) has called "the rationality principle," which involves making "an idealized reconstruction of the problem situation, to make the action rationally understandable." This is to hold that scientific analysis must engage in a reduction of naturally occurring phenomena, since those phenomena are so complicated that some simplification of the issues is required in order to be made "understandable."

Scientific praxis proceeds by dividing the naturally occurring world into a finite number of segments so that what each one contains can be counted. Science divides things into parts and then studies how each part behaves. Its techniques involve isolating features that can be measured, but these features can distort the picture of the natural existence of what is being examined.

This division, and accompanying metrological strategies (Garfinkel 2002, 269–272), characterize the initial steps of any science, steps that were first described by Descartes (1983, 11) in his second rule of methods: "To divide each of the difficulties I would examine it into as many parts as possible and as was required in order to better resolve them." Heidegger (1991, 56) suggests that a succeeding step is to establish "a cognition that secures natural processes as calculable stuff." In this way, the world is made over into the static order of objective facts: "Physiological-physical inquiry breaks up and reinterprets [nature]" (Heidegger 1967, 210). The aim of gaining *secure* knowledge is paramount, an aim that prescribes that the natural world be reinterpreted as representedness and Objectivity B, by the end of which the natural processes can end up missing-in-action. Ironically, the more secure the knowledge is, the less that is known. Schutz (1971, 130) comments,

> The natural scientist, in unquestioned tradition, accepts the inherited idealizations and unclarified suppositions as technics without becoming conscious of the shift which the originally living meaning of the aim to get knowledge of the world itself has experienced. In the process of mathematization of the natural sciences, says Husserl, we measure the life-world for a well-fitting garment of ideas. This cloak of ideas has the effect that we take a method to be true being.

Emmanuel Levinas (1998) takes a similarly skeptical view of the practice of dividing and counting: "When science penetrates this human world, it pulverizes it into atoms the better to mathematize it, suffocates it to better eternize it."

When this praxis analyzes something that exists dynamically and as a whole, the analysts numerate individuated aspects of that dynamic behavior. To facilitate this numeration, they divide what exists as a whole into parts that can be measured, counted, and evaluated. For example, a forest biologist will analyze a decaying log by dividing its lifespan of decay into nine stages, partly arbitrarily and partly by observing stages that have enough integrity to be categorized separately, and then at each stage the biologist will measure the size and weight of a sample of the material, and identify and count the insects, fungi, etc. that are inhabiting the decaying log. At the conclusion of this process, it still remains for a *whole* to be reconstructed on the basis of these analyzed parts if the scientific study is going to make some sense, but what is produced is necessarily an artifact of the scientific praxis and is not equivalent to the dynamic whole that was the original phenomenon or what is actually or naturally objective. In the case of coffee, taste is divided into five, six, eight, or ten categories, and each of those categories are evaluated numerically. At the end of the sensory analysis, these numbers will be added up, and the *total score* will become part of the coffee's identity, and the basis for its being bought and sold.

It bears recollection that Objectivity C is the natural objectivity of the coffee that sits in the cup and that bears a taste that is the source of what is to be known. This differs from the methodologically produced objectivity, Objectivity B, which can be a numerical result of a scientifically based protocol and is intended to be an adequate *representation* of what is in the cup. In order to be rigorous about one's method of investigation, a researcher needs to be careful not to conflate these two objectivities. Each of them has validity and fruitful uses, but of different kinds; they are not identical. Sensory science especially should be vigilant about preventing Objectivity B from eclipsing the Objectivity C altogether, since the latter works in service of the former and is the goose that lays the golden eggs. A rigorous and scientific method needs to keep these objectivities distinct and active.

Most tasting protocols require individuating aspects of taste that naturally work together as an ensemble, rating them separately, and providing a summary score that almost always requires some interpretative work in order to be able to correspond with the real objectivity of a taste that has made its presence. Taste category by taste category, numerations are distributed, and then the scores of the categories are added together. But what has happened to the unity? If the acidity is influencing the sweetness, how does separating them out for individual numerations contribute to our understanding the unity? Does the category "balance" provide for that? Or must one postpone assessment of synergies until one reaches the "overall" category, that category that some sensory analysts argue is the least objective of all? Could it be that the "overall" category is what rescues the real objectivity of the coffee from oblivion?

Knowing by means of Objectivity B reckons everything as something calculable, and if it is not calculable, it does not get reckoned. Yet, as Simmel (1997, 132) has explained, what we want from food and drink is aesthetic satisfaction, which operates in a different realm. When we limit our inspection by reducing our experience to "sense-data," it reduces a drinker's active participation to that of a passive recipient, treating "the mind as the passive spectator recording external stimuli" (Vannini et al. 2012, 43), when tasting is necessarily *an activity*. Smells and flavors become merely "information" that we use for the purposes of management and control, and the connections that smells and flavors have with our memory and experience are made inconsequential, possibly even dismissed as being too subjective. This is a distortion. The actual situation is that we constantly project interests, possibilities, objections, and enthusiasms, and what we sense conforms to these interests and curiosities. "The taste, the pleasure, the effect are not exogenous variables, or automatic attributes, of the objects. They are the reflexive result of bodily practices, collected and orchestrated" (Hennion and Teil 2004b, 523). Gurwitsch (1964: 148) puts the matter concisely: "Wholes cannot be reduced to elements."

Our interests, our pleasures, our memories, etc. are all part of why we drink coffee, and they provide the context in which its taste is located and experienced. Gurwitsch (1964, 130) observes, "The datum has its phenomenal identity only *within* the contexture." In our search for reliable, fixed data, we distort its sense and reference and instead transport that "data" to a context that we have constructed for our own purposes. We can and should do so, since there are benefits and even new discoveries that working this way can provide us, but we should not for a minute think that we ourselves do not sustain a "subjective bias" when we do so. Perullo (2016, 57) asks whether we ignore existing non-measurable qualities simply because we cannot measure them. What is objectivity here? "Phenomenology affirms that truth depends on its object" (Levinas 1998, 6), and this is what grounds its objectivity, which is Objectivity C: truth is grounded in the real relations between humans and objects. We are always implicated. The notion of truth in the absence of humans is nonsensical, and the discipline of phenomenology is "to discover the sense in which an object is reached and, consequently, the sense in which it is posited as existing" (Levinas 1998, 64). Phenomenology studies what is actual.

The individuation of taste elements, a technique necessary for numeration, should not be allowed to distort our own cognition of the real objectivity of the taste in a cup any longer than it takes to derive an insight based on a course of rigorous, methodical assessment. Breaking up a naturally occurring phenomenon into sections or individual units in order to measure them can provide numbers than ensure ready comparability; however, breaking a phenomenon down like that may disguise its natural flow and cause scientists to lose the phenomenon, the experience the tastes had for the people whose assessments were the basis for the numerical data. Not only can the original sense vanish, it may not be recoverable, since it can disappear beneath the weight of the numbers that offer a reassuring veneer of objectivity. The irony is that since the natural sense of how the taste cohered for a taster has disappeared altogether and is no longer recoverable, it is never missed. That is why Perullo (2018, 267) offers the suggestion that we open up to "the continuity of processes" *before* our drink "is analyzed and dissected into discrete parts."

The Colombian sensory scientist Rodrigo Alarcón explained to me, "The numerical assessments are clues, indications of possibilities, not some sort of compulsory law-giver that assures that this coffee has to be the best one, or that this coffee will be very good for everyone in the world. But it offers *some relevant issues about flavors that can be tasted*; it can offer some good suggestions, but it cannot make anything compulsory" (emphasis mine). All three of our objectivities have constructive roles to play. Dr. Enrico Meschini of Italy, who considers numeration to be more objective than verbal description, nevertheless understands that if the numbers are to be scientific they must be kept meaningful: "I understand well that the number is not the absolute solution—it's important to understand well how I came to read a '6' instead of a '5.'" This is also why one professional taster who was feverishly adding his numerations on his SCA scoring sheet looked up at me and confessed, "I have more faith in the Notes section." His sentiment has been endorsed by the Sustainable Coffee Institute, which has explained that one of the motives for their redesigning the professional cupping form was to provide more room for notes, additional lines that accompany each category of taste being assessed. Clearly there are many in the coffee industry, scientists included, who are working earnestly to find reliable ways of better connecting Objectivity B with Objectivity C.

Alarcón has devoted much time to considering the nature of numerating tastes. He observes that sensory assessment works not with cardinal numbers but with ordinal numbers; that is, the numbers do not represent absolute quantities—they arise from comparisons (more and less, better and worse). The number "2" is not necessarily twice the value of "1." Alarcón specifies, "You are not measuring things, you are measuring differences," and he suggests that this limits the kind of mathematical operations that one can apply to the numerical data one has generated. There is no sense in computing average deviations, for instance, because part of the content of the numbers is metaphorical. In much of science, the data is reduced to numeric representation, and when that result is severed from the *in vivo* reality that it was intended to represent, calculations can lead to nonsense. If the numeration is used to assist retaining contact with the taste, then it has benefit. As Alarcón reminds us, "Coffee is a living thing."

It is not a matter of downgrading the importance of quantitative research strategies, it is a matter of learning how to use them without losing the phenomenon. The challenge for scientific sensory analysis is to keep the mathematical statistics and not lose the coffee. This is a most critical question, but it is only one instance of the much larger historical task of how humanity can use rationalization in ways that serve the imagination instead of limit it. We have reached a truly universal problem, for it applies to all domains of modern human existence. We want to use all the scientific tools, but we do not want to use them in a way that they cast spells upon us.

Objectivity A: Rendering the Work Communicable

We have been ignoring the initial objectivity, Objectivity A. The first function of using a tasting schedule is to facilitate common, intersubjective understanding of taste descriptors so that they will mean the same thing to all of the personnel who work in each sector of the chain of coffee production. Mutual understanding is needed to accomplish things, and so we need to describe how they concert their understandings (see chapter 12). When one must share one's understanding of a taste, objectivity becomes the crucial tool. Making tastes objective is part of the local work of coffee purveyors, and it is work for which there is no time-out. Further, Objectivity B is dependent upon the practices whereby Objectivity A is established and made operative. As Wright (2014, 99) informs us, the beer aroma wheel was developed for the purpose of facilitating communication with customers. Professional tasting requires cultivating the ability to classify subjective sense experience in a manner that can be rendered communicable by means of their objective (Objectivity A) representations. But we should never forget that these objective representations are locally constructed artifacts and that what is original is the experience of tastes, which is the primordial object of scientific investigation.

Creating a local orderliness (Objectivity A) reduces the ambiguity of the situation and makes it less likely that parties will get into trouble, or look stupid before their peers by making a mistake, or be hampered by the insecurities that haunt people when they work together. The importance of these matters is confirmed by the fact that Objectivity B and Objectivity C will usually yield to Objectivity A, a situation that unavoidably keeps introducing a quantum of chaos into the focused labors of Objectivity B and Objectivity C.

Sticking with standard practices and ideologized notions can assist communication with others. Numeration plays a similar role: a system that involves numerating offers participants direct and immediate ways to share an activity. The intention of numeration may be scientific, whether that of Objectivity B or Objectivity C, but an additional benefit of numeration is to offer a method for *coordinating the local interaction* in an orderly manner. That is, a vital point about numerating is its shareability, in addition to any achievements it can make in the realm of Objectivity B. In this regard, ideology and numeration serve the same purpose of facilitating social solidarity and communication. Numeration provides tasters with a clear agenda. In more simple terms, it offers a solution to a practical problem that every person faces in any situation: "What am I supposed to be doing?" The physical presence of a sheet and a pencil can offer a taster a life-raft; it gives him or her something to do. It provides an orderliness for collaborative work. It allows participants to share an activity that makes some objective sense in the sense that what a matter means for one taster is more or less what it means for another taster. This is more difficult to institute (and institutions are needed) than it sounds, and it requires constant supervision and monitoring by every one of the participants.

The reduction of experience to rules or what Adorno (1973, 153) calls "order-creating invariance" assists in producing social order, whether it be traffic flow (Liberman 2019) or the rules of pairing wine with food: it establishes grounds and structures for communicating. For this reason, protocols are comfortable (Perullo 2016, 134). Intersubjective comprehensibility may have priority over validity, and "linguistic *conventions* of signification have priority over significative *intentions*" (Zahavi 2001, 172). This latter finding is perhaps the most significant discovery of the field of conversation analysis, where maintaining the system that is providing for the local orderliness is the primary task to which conversing parties are oriented.

One reason why scientific analysis prevails in coffee tasting is that it simplifies complex affairs to a point where one can operate and communicate more clearly with other actors about those affairs. This is to say that its success is not always because the reductions of the objectivist paradigm are more correct. Requirements for clarity of meaning, social structure and social order, certainty, etc. have been decisive for buttressing the durability of scientific reductions and are partly responsible for their prevalence over more rigorously detailed examinations of the lived world. The cost is that the object one is investigating is restricted in a way that can compromise the research (Merleau-Ponty 1968, 24). According to Heidegger and his students, the orderliness of scientific praxis can lead its practitioners to favor apodictic certainty over truth. *Apophansis* "only studies the pure forms of the significations" (Levinas 1998, 8) and not the meanings; consequently, it operates in the realm of correctness and not that of truth.

The objectivity afforded by the *Flavor Wheel*, the *Lexicon*, tasting schedules, etc. helps parties to coordinate understandings. The process is similar to how formal logic is used by philosophers who debate and explore issues in epistemology, metaphysics, etc., as described in my monograph, *Dialectical Practice in Tibetan Philosophical Culture* (Liberman 2004). Among Tibetan philosopher-monks, the strict, formal logic they adhere to in their public debates, which have a history of 900 years and a heritage in India before that, was exercised not only for the purpose of proving their assertions and discovering truths but also for providing a local orderliness that permits debaters to coordinate their thinking. The important discovery of the monograph was that there were occasions where truth interests would be set aside for the sake of preserving the orderliness of the debaters' dialectics. That is, they used logic as *a local organizational device*. In coffee tasting scientific practices are sometimes used in a similar way.

Abandoning Naturally Occurring Phenomena

Natural tasting in everyday settings differs from routinized protocols for tasting. It is assumed that the latter technique is more reliable, more objective, and more scientific, but does it approximate how coffee drinkers taste, and if not, how might that limit its utility? Metrological studies of taste are more remote still. We have discussed the example of losing the lived experience of acidity in the process of reducing the perceived acidity to a pH measurement; however, pH is a straightforward measure to make, while human perception is not. Real experience is more complicated research than making measurements; Merleau-Ponty (1962, 324) observes, "The real lends itself to unending exploration; it is inexhaustible." The straightforward character of most reduced data is given priority not because the information is more reliable but because it is easier to obtain. This is fine, so long as the users of the data are able to recall that the data is a reduced version of reality and not necessarily more reliable because it is objective (in the sense of Objectivity B).

The greatest danger is to keep the scope of awareness so narrow that one fails to notice the scope is narrow. Figal (2010, 110) warns, "As 'objectification,' the theoretical attitude toward human life amounts to a 'devitalization,' which conceals originary inner experience." In order to measure phenomena, science must first objectify them, which requires stalling their natural flow and redefining them as if the more static version was their true state. One cannot lift something out from the environment in which it occurs naturally, isolate it, and still possess the identical thing. Objectifications like that are artifacts of a scientific praxis that renders tasting a third-person phenomenon. This is justified by suggesting that tasting as a first-person phenomenon is too "subjective." But tasting *is* a first-person phenomenon. Science labors to turn dynamic processes into stable things; however, an experience as it occurs naturally is never a state but always a *durée*, a flow that is lived through. The flavor of a cup of coffee changes as it sits there, as it cools, as our palate discovers its properties, and even while our tasting faculty grows more numb after each cup. We should leave behind "the illusion of the absolute view from above" (Merleau-Ponty 1968, 27), or, as we have been saying, we can carry out some reckoning from this remote location so long as we keep re-grounding ourselves in Objectivity C. In short, successful cupping requires both being close *and* being "above." Because "controlling from a distance seems to be one of the main bases of objective knowledge" (Perullo 2016, 30), we administer a top-down inquiry, even as the coffee keeps reasserting itself from the bottom up.

How this alternation proceeds has much to do with the practices of the sensory analysts and their chosen protocol. Sensory scientists sometimes defer making contact with the flavor to a later stage, and instead they give priority to their collaborative project of developing a model and its algorithms. It is the methodology and not the taste that pilots their inquiries, i.e., the analytic gaze lords over the coffee from on high and administers a top-down policy of understanding, rather than their inquiry leading the methods from the bottom up. When analyzing this way, it is not impossible to become lost inside one's methods. An interest in promising innovations in modeling, either models developed by oneself or by others, often receives more of the researchers' attention than what they study. In the social sciences, researchers may never have personal contact with the people they study, since the researchers are able to download all of their data from the internet without leaving their offices. Sometimes they are entirely unfamiliar with the actual circumstances in which the data was collected, nor have they had an opportunity to evaluate any of the contingent details that might have influenced the research subjects' responses. The numbers generated are accepted as opaque "facts." They are opaque because the researchers have lost contact with what they mean. Contemporary social scientists know a great deal about using three-dimensional modeling. An expert panel of the American Sociological Association's Quantitative Methods Section that I attended (a colleague of mine was a member of the panel) devoted the entire two hours of their session to sharing their admiration for the shapes of their three-dimensional models without ever once discussing the people they were modeling or any of the possible social policy implications of the results of their studies. It was as if these social scientists were suspended in air, without grounding in the actual people that were the source of the data or in the looks of the world for the vision of their subjects. Nor did they display interest in the future consequences of their research. They occupied an untethered and unpopulated space (although many of them study "populations") somewhere between the people who generated their data and the effects that their findings might have upon them. Another colleague once explained that professionals do not develop concerns about the uses of their research because that is not their job and such concerns might impair their objectivity. Instead, their occupation is to keep refining their models; this is what is recognized as real science.

In some scientific sensory analysis, it can even happen that the taste itself is rendered absent from the scene by the reduction of tastes to their numerical representations, which somehow gain a status of being more objective than taste itself. In reducing tastes to numbers, a "licorice" flavor can be converted to a number on a 1-to-10-point scale. What number should be given to a pleasing taste of licorice that is very mild, compared with a strong and more evident licorice taste that is not as pleasant (perhaps for the reason that it is too strong)? If the former is given a 6.5 and the latter a 4, what is one to make of that, even if the protocol has been submitted to a hundred tasters, and what assurances are there that all of the respondents have applied the same criteria? What is a person who lives halfway across the world to make of the meaning of such a "4"? Merely converting experience to numbers and then comparing numbers is insufficient for qualifying as sensory analysis. Numbers must mean something that can be identified. It is an objective accounting, but nothing licorice-like may survive the transoceanic conveyance of the data; nevertheless, the accountant who monitors the tasters' tasting schedules works assiduously and with competence to produce an aggregate score of all the judges' ratings, an average that is often taken to a second decimal point—"4.26"—since the more decimal points there are the more objectivity may be ascribed to it. We should always be careful to ask about which objectivity we are speaking about. Here is meant both Objectivity A and Objectivity B, while Objectivity C has been set aside. The numerical result will be treated as if it was the correct culmination of everyone's concerns, as if one now possessed some adequately defined *thing*, when in fact one possess a metrological artifact. Here we encounter one more irony: at the very moment that matters appear the most objective and precise, they lose all relation to the flavor. Garfinkel (2002) describes this situation: "Mathematical statistics has a monopoly on adequate demonstration of objectivity and in specifying and managing contingencies of designed enterprises. . . . But with these descriptions the phenomenon so described is lost."

An insistence to quantify lived experience can help us to keep track of events and offers precision that can lead to discoveries, although at the same time it can distract us from the ongoing focused attention that is required to be capable of following up the "licorice" until we learn just what it is. This latter is *object*-ivity, a mode of Objectivity C whose core consists of finding *it* and cultivating "a thinking that engages in, and lingers with, what is worth questioning" (Heidegger 1991, 9). What is worth questioning should be guiding the choices we make when developing a research design, and this would be an occasion when the inquiry leads the methods. When we adopt a protocol straightforwardly, occasionally we become lazy and permit ourselves to ignore this question and apply by rote the priorities of the formal method: if the method requires a number to the second decimal point, we produce one. By our compliance procedure, we can turn away from the ultimate target for which we developed the procedures, until we reach a point where that target may disappear from the scene entirely or be reintroduced in narrative form only during the final moments of writing our report. Overpowering the flavor with the very best protocol can be a biased way to work, yet we defend ourselves by suggesting that maintaining our contact with the strange licorice flavor would be too subjective to be dependable. All of our scientific tasks and procedures should be developed for the purpose of making our close attentiveness to the flavor something more *object*-ive. This "objective" also professes to be more reliable, as well as suitable for sharing with others.

Charts, three-dimensional models, and high scores produce saliencies that in themselves are without meaning, but scientists can pick up any of these saliencies, the artifacts of our method, and go searching for what they mean. In this way, Objectivity B contributes a great deal, but its contributions depend upon what unexpected connectivities researchers will discover that they might never have thought to consider had their methodology not produced those saliencies. In this way, Objectivity B has genuine efficacy, but that is because of the practical work that researchers do with its findings and not because they are inherently truer than the products of the other two objectivities we have been considering.

When *smell* and *taste* become submerged underneath our calculations that are clear, distinct, remote, and visual, their most vital nature is overlooked and only the results of our metrological manipulations survive. A limbic system that is stirred by aromas is not at all rational, yet aromas are able to change the mood of a person. Heidegger (1967, 211) tells us, "The comprehension of things as a mere manifold of sensory givens is the presupposition for the mathematical-physical definition of bodies," but can these mathematized renderings of sensation address how aromas change the mood of a person? What is the sense of requiring that we always defer to the "thick veil" (Heidegger 1967, 110) of rationalist protocols? We can learn how to use them productively, yes, but why do we need to surrender the rest of the tasting experience to them? At some point in the tasting, our rational project must take a back seat.

Garfinkel's investigations of cartography can offer us direction here. He (1996, 6) writes,

> *Documentary* maps are found as principal possessions of map libraries. They are objects of extensive scholarship. The way-finding journeys they describe are cartographers' pride of profession and technical stock in trade. *Procedural* maps present cartography with an incommensurably alternate research experience. I speak of that experience as incommensurably alternate in that with procedural maps the analyst must collect descriptive specifics of *following the map*, jobs that must be done *in situ* just in an actual case of a journey.

In his masterwork *The Cantos*, Ezra Pound (1950, 324) offers the same insight in poetic form:

> not as land looks like on a map
> but as sea bord seen by men sailing

With Garfinkel and Pound, Objectivity C is alive and well.

It is fine and even necessary to develop formal-rational representations for the purpose of retaining insights, for accumulating analyses, and for communicating them across a cohort of fellow scientists; humanity has always achieved its technological progress by means of communication and cooperation. But it is not necessary to sever our representations from the world, *replacing* the world with our models. The trouble this can lead to was made evident for us by the crash of Asiana Airlines Flight 214 at San Francisco International Airport (SFO) in 2013, whose pilots arriving from Asia relied exclusively upon the automatic pilot features of the plane's guidance system, even when they could see that their descent was too rapid, a problem that investigators named "automation addiction." Of course, we want the benefits of every new technology, but we need to preserve the dominance of thinking reason.

Our formal-rational representations should be used to offer assistance for probing our immanent experience. A *procedural* sensory assessment necessarily examines local details and registers these discoveries in a *documentary* record. That documentary version is essential for communicating clearly and for becoming a durable account that can serve as a basis for cooperation and collective reflection. Accounts are oriented to the task of organizing social affairs—the coming auction, an anticipated grading by a government agency, the head roaster's known priorities; however, after these *in situ* procedural activities are completed, the documentary version may have the final word. Since it will be what survives, the formal document can claim all the victories; however, the document that results conceals its history. Being deprived of its context, it will be given a kind of being that exists only in European ontology: a thing in itself. This is an independent existence that is projected upon an object of our engagement, which is thought to possess a static essence that is believed to found its being independently of our participation. Of course, this is a constructed artifact that is dependent upon everything that has brought it into being, including the ideas we have projected. This reification of being is an imposition of the European imagination and an ontological distortion. Transmitting the documentary record of a course of sensory analysis along the chain of coffee production is not necessarily to be tracking a coffee's taste because the taste is no longer a tangible part of the document. If there is taste, it must be revivified by each occupant of the chain, using the documentary record as the basis. Coffee purveyors regularly accomplish just this, using the document to direct their tasting, to find their way back *to the procedural tasting* in and as its flow, and then they use what they find to reflexively make sense of the document: the document and the lived procedure are a pair, so there is no justification for making the documentary record into an independent objectivity. That record is clearly legible, yet without the procedural tasting it renders us "illiterate regarding any contact with the crust of the world" (Perullo 2016, 52).

Martin Heidegger gives priority to the live circumspective finding-of-one's-place in a situation (*Befindlichkeit*, sometimes translated as "attunement," the keen attentiveness that we have been arguing is the source for Objectivity C in tasting coffee). Heidegger (1996, 128) writes, "There is not the slightest justification for minimizing the 'evidence' of attunement by measuring it against the apodictic certainty of the theoretical cognition of something merely objectively present." Apodictic certainty is the certainty that is gained by formal analytic reasoning (Objectivity B), and here Heidegger sets it against "the evidence of attunement," which would be our immanent experience with the coffee we are drinking (Objectivity C), which is something that precedes the formal analysis. What Heidegger wishes to avoid is the substitution of Objectivity B for Objectivity C by replacing experience in the course of procedural tasting with methodologically produced, analytic "facts." Theoretical cognition works productively with the scientific artifacts, i.e., the facts that are the products of our analytic stance. While they can contribute to our understanding, it would be a critical error to allow them to occlude immanent experience altogether or cause us to lose our direct access to that experience.

We should interrogate here especially the meaning of Heidegger's phrase "something merely objectively present," which is a critical phrasing. Why does Heidegger say "merely" here? It is because there is so much to the world, to our world, so many networks of relations underlying even the most mundane experience, that they render very thin what we can establish analytically about a disembodied object. Our analytically objective rendering would be like a taxidermist's eagle compared to an eagle that flies; that is, it is an objectivist *reduction* that levels off the being of the thing, reducing it to only what can be captured and preserved within the gridlines of our analytic forms. Science requires that the actual world, which by its nature is dynamic and evolving, be reformulated as a static version of itself, the better to tame its wildness, to make measurements, and be available for our control (so far as we are able, which usually is not as far as we think). Taxidermy replaces being, and "such formalizations level down the phenomenon to the extent that the true phenomenal content gets lost" (Heidegger 1996, 82). "Phenomenal" here is a reference to what is real for our lived experience and not what is imagined, no matter how educated the theorizing is. Heidegger's message for us is that what matters most to positivist science may miss, despite its energetic efforts, what is most important to our experience. Our lives are not simply engaged with objects; rather, we are engaged with our *projects*, and our agency is a necessary and very real part of what must be examined: it is what we *do* with our objects that matters, not what the objects can be said to mean "in themselves," because in themselves objects do not mean anything. To appreciate this, one only needs to undertake the most cursory research with how ordinary drinkers experience their coffee: flavors do not exist in themselves, they exist as a project for their tasting.

Heidegger criticizes the "direct seeing" of empirical science because such seeing, even with its abundant confidence, or perhaps because of it, is in truth already compromised by what it is looking for. "Theoretical looking at the world has always flattened it down to the uniformity of what is purely objectively present, although, of course, a new abundance of what can be discovered in pure determination lies within that uniformity" (Heidegger 1996, 130). Heidegger's advice is to stop commandeering phenomena by applying directly and straightforwardly our conceptual-theoretical grids, not because he is opposed to science (he acknowledges the value of its interrogations) but because those theoretical grids can obscure vital matters that are also important for science and that always accompany whatever is being made objectively available (Objectivity B). Importantly, Heidegger reminds us that these theoretical grids of scientific praxis can provide us with "a new abundance" of discoveries, which lead us along paths that we may never have chosen without their direction. Many of the most significant victories of objective science are not the direct result of the metrological methodologies used but the contribution of the scientists' imagination in the face of considering objectified representations that are the products of their methodology, and which scientists display for each other (Objectivity A). That does not entail that these theoretical grids capture the entire story, perhaps not even what is most important to know. Just as Illy Coffee needs both art and science, we require both imagination and reason. Perullo (2016, 18) suggests, "There is too rigid of a separation inserted between reason and imagination." This conforms with the seminal insight of Abraham Heschel that is embedded in the walkway to the entrance of the University of Oregon Library: "Wonder rather than doubt is the root of all knowledge."

In a nutshell, the aim not only of the present research but of human science generally is to ascertain how we can have the best of these two worlds—the considerable discoveries of formal analysis *and* the rich insights that originate in our lived experience. This is a perennial question for that thinking being called *Homo sapiens,* the question that will not go away.

The notion that the route to objective knowledge rests upon our ability to eliminate lived experience is like volunteering to be blind. It is not science but scientism, the simulacrum of scientific-like activities. Why, if even physicists are insistent upon the fact that the role of the observer can never be omitted, does popular culture insist upon a mythology of the objective that is committed to the ignorant notion that the best route to objectivity involves removing subjectivity from the research protocol? Being subjective does not disqualify the possibility that it can be made objective. Everything is subjective, and anything can be made objective; but we must be clear about just what objectivity is. We seek to better integrate analytic and experiential knowledge without damaging or limiting our understanding by any of the deleterious effects of the prejudices of "subjectivity," which must also include the prejudices of science. We easily overlook our own prejudices, and we are distracted by each and every received method that is applied by rote without reflexive critical analysis, and we use them to pre-structure our understanding. The sociologist of knowledge Karl Mannheim (1952, 40) laments that the categories of scientific analysis can "distort the authenticity of direct experience." There are no easy paths here, and we are always in our own way. The scientific theme is guaranteed only when we develop our knowledge in terms of the things themselves (Objectivity C). For this, listening and paying attention are better suited than dominating.

Rigorous scientific analysis has led society past many ignorant prejudices, and it is certain that it has more work to do. We have acquired much useful information about the natural world, but it has been largely confined inside the grid of our theoretical interpretations of being, according to which a naturally flowing river is reduced to a numerical representation of the cubic-inches-per-second of flow, a measurement that has contributed successfully to the erection of the hydroelectric plants (Heidegger 1977, 16) like the one that powers the computer I am using now. Yet we do not know how long this present historical moment, with its reductionist perspectives, will endure, and it remains a contingent sociohistorical event. Since Hegel, social scientists of every stripe have recognized and described the fundamental dialectical nature of history, which endlessly undoes and remakes the life-world of every era.

Science too is a series of endless revisions-without-end. This is why humility is a more appropriate attitude than confidence. Nevertheless, objectivist inquiry in our analytic era is so widespread that few scholars or coffee professionals have the originality or courage to challenge an objectivist paradigm that has so narrowed down its analyses that the most essential phenomena of everyday human experience are lost, and then forgotten, much in the way that people have become perfectly satisfied with drinking coffee that is inferior to the freshly roasted coffee that people were drinking a century ago. It is possible, even likely, for any one of our studies to lose the world, but it can help to constantly recall Heidegger's advice, which I repeat: "There is not the slightest justification for minimizing the 'evidence' of attunement by measuring it against the apodictic certainty of the theoretical cognition of something merely objectively present." Certainty is a wonderful thing, but not at the price of losing the world.

Presuppositions of Science

The particular ways people regularly make sense of what they taste and their habits of feeling flavors influence the tastes they sense. Much tasting is self-fulfilling prophesy. Experience is always infected by the thoughts we project about how things will be. From an epistemological perspective every experience, including every thought, is grasped according to the pre-structures of our habitual ways of understanding; not infrequently, we may be unable to fulfill the sense we have projected. When the US Supreme Court discovers that a reasonable and favored legal argument cannot be made to work for resolving a case, they must return to the beginning and re-examine their presuppositions. That is why failure, even confusion, can lead to fresh knowledge. There is no experience that does not commence its life without presuppositions busy at work.

It is a goal of science to operate without presuppositions; however, the best we can accomplish is to maintain continuous suspicion about our presuppositions, try to identify them, and expose them to ourselves and to each other. It is a misapprehension to think that one can remove bias entirely—that is a dream that lives in never-never land. Some scientists consider themselves superior to philosophers, and philosophers return the favor: "The practice of deliberate and careful procedure is not enough for philosophy" (Figal 2010, 39). Why is careful procedure insufficient? Because philosophy's commitment to think without presuppositions is more informed, more comprehensive, and less myopic than that of the natural sciences. While scientists aim at presuppositionless investigation, they do not usually attain more than partial success, largely because they are so heavily invested in the active application of their methods of investigating that they do not have much time left over to devote to self-reflection, and so they "do not attain to the presuppositionlessness of philosophy" (Figal 2010, 39).

Unlike what happens in much scientific praxis, philosophers "have refused the right to install themselves in absolute knowledge" (Merleau-Ponty 1963, 5), and they pay closer attention to the processes by which knowledge becomes what it is. Merleau-Ponty describes this with great beauty: "What makes a philosopher is the movement which leads back without ceasing from knowledge to ignorance, from ignorance to knowledge, and a kind of rest in this movement." Much of the time, scientists shun ignorance altogether, while many professional tasters appreciate living inside the "rest in this movement" and are less afraid to address ignorance about knowledge such as what a taster may believe has been acquired: they know there is always more going on in the cup. With this approach, they are able keep learning, so sometimes professional tasters perform better than sensory scientists. It is an odd situation: the scientists are in pursuit of certainties, whereas the professional tasters are pursuing coffee. More significant is that the best tasters are able to locate and abide inside that "rest" Merleau-Ponty identifies, the "rest in this movement" that has abandoned any obsession to establish certitudes, in favor of a suspension of belief substantial enough to permit the taste to reveal itself without being constantly submerged by what we already know, or think we know, at the hands of our expertise and our projects that produce and preserve the unity of that knowledge, a unity that is essential for Objectivity A, the objectivity that enables clear communication with others. Science is never entirely free of its projects, at least to the extent that philosophy can be. The more one is able to inquire without being dominated by one's presuppositions, keeping only the slightest possible grip upon them, the more one can learn.

Biases operate mostly unseen. Since they frame what is known, it is as difficult to make them evident as it is for the eye to see itself. "Methodological criteria then are nothing but concealed ways of stipulating and defining subject matters" (Earle 1955, 92). Daston and Galison (2007, 369) observe, "Once internalized by a scientific collective, these various ways of seeing were lodged deeper than evidence; they defined what evidence was." Science circumscribes the objectness of things, constricting our relation with them, and by so doing it confines the thing within our predefinition of the object, which can conceal the very way that the thing shows itself from itself. Heidegger (1967, 102) comments, "Method is not one piece of equipment of science among others but the primary component out of which is first determined what can become an object and how it becomes an object." This means that the objectivity of a flavor results from the method; all of the ingenious and elaborate strategies of researchers are "performed within a framework of sense that has already been achieved" (Zahavi 2001, 54). Heidegger (1967, 180) concludes, "There is no presuppositionless science, because the essence of science consists in such presupposing, in such pre-judgments about the object."

The tasting schedule used by professional tasters is not strictly neutral. It presents in advance what objects can be discovered. The form directs the taster regarding what to search for. What the taster finds is located *with* the aid of the form, since the taster uses the categories of the schedule to locate tastes that further clarify what the categories themselves mean. "Taste . . . was handed over to codes that are already known" (Perullo 2016, 80) so that "the otherness of the matter paradoxically almost disappears" (Perullo 2016, 81). This "otherness" is what can best disrupt our presuppositions, and so it is essential to science, and it is counterproductive to make it disappear. It is essential because by its disruption it forces us to return to the things themselves, to the beginnings for a fresh accounting, as in our Supreme Court example. While there is comfort in taming what is other, such domination can confine our world to what we already know, when it is the higher aim of science to learn what we do not know.

Being an expert can impede understanding an experience because it is a locus that may proceed to closure too swiftly (Perullo 2018a, 53) when its real business is exposure. This may be a reason why most senior professional tasters pooh-pooh their expertise and solicit and respect opinions of younger tasters. Heidegger (1982, 114) says, "No matter how logically rigorous concepts may be, if they are blind then they are worthless." Even the best science consists of "cognitive position-takings" (Husserl 1982, 59) and "continuously co-accepted" positings that may be nothing more than unexamined received notions that are habitually accepted beforehand (Husserl 1982, 61). A framework of sense can be already established *prior* to the so-called "empirical" inquiry. Husserl does not exempt sciences from his proscription against presuppositions, and includes "all sciences relating to this natural world no matter how firmly they stand there for me, no matter how much I admire them" (1982, 61). Husserl is not denying them their value or importance, nor is he even a skeptic, far from it; his concern is only to reveal the ways they have pre-structured their understanding and to expose the unrecognized biases that are at work.

The "continuously co-accepted," hidden presuppositions about which Husserl speaks include every contingency of the tasks that scientists carry out as they work in concert with each other (and scientists always work in concert with each other: without the continuous criticism and collaboration of colleagues, it would no longer be science). Sense-making is a collective, social process that often is less the result of logic and more the result of contingencies that arise *sui generis* in the local situation (see chapter 12), including the many accidents that flow from how the situation has happened to get structured, a structure that then is adopted by all the parties present, who witness and then copy the emerging structure. Universal findings are rooted in local circumstances. While science dreams of universals, its work is always local.

In sum, I am proposing that the superimposition of meaning is deleterious and works to the detriment of objectivity, yet superimposition is ubiquitous since it is the very structure of understanding. Efforts to escape this dilemma (especially when such escapes are routinized under the illusion of having found guarantees for objectivity, secured by routine practices) can make matters worse. What we need is objectivity, and not a metaphysics of objectivity.

Subjectivity

There is only one remedy for reducing the damage that our presuppositions inflict, and that is to be vigilantly self-reflective. This is a subjective talent, and so objectivity requires subjectivity for distinguishing, by means of reason and intuition, what really is objective and what is nothing more than the artifact of a presupposed method. That is to say, objectivity is produced by subjectivity (Goodstein 2017, 346). In addition to the subjective activity that produces a method, it is the additional responsibility of subjectivity to expose the hidden assumptions of our conceptual constructions. Subjectivity is indispensable; without it, we would be condemned to always believe our own presuppositions. Preventing the local contexts of theory, language, social obligations, etc. from intervening too greatly in our assessments is a much-needed practice, one that is critical for objective assessment. Any restraint of these contextual influences would be the achievement of an active subjectivity.

This necessity for subjectivity does not mean that cognition cannot follow "logical" procedures. According to Husserl (1973, 17), an act of judgment that violates the principles and rules of formal logic cannot result in truth; however, Husserl specifies that these principles and rules are "the merely negative conditions of the possibility of truth," and he insists that there also exist positive conditions for truth:

> But on the other hand, even if it satisfies the requirements of these laws, it does not thereby attain its goal: truth. Accordingly, this insight compels us to ask the question of what must be added over and above these formal conditions of the possibility of truth if an activity of cognition is to reach its goal. These supplementary characteristics of intuitability lie on the subjective side and concern the *subjective characteristics of intuitability, of self-evidence* and the *subjective characteristics of its attainment*.

Husserl observes that many judgments that appear to conform to formal principles and that "pass themselves off as yielding knowledge later prove to be illusory," which therefore demands that we undertake continuous critique of their truth value, a critique that is informed by the subjective conditions of the attainment of evidence.

A perfect illustration is that of the professional taster who has rated carefully a coffee sample according to the various criteria of a tasting form and used its grids to reach a numerical summary that the taster at once recognizes misses the mark. At this point the professional taster employs that great instrument of truth-telling, the eraser end of the pencil, and works backward from the total to find a more accurate way to represent the coffee. More simply put, one needs to submit any protocol of formal analysis to a thinking that is broader in scope and more attuned to the experience than simple mechanical compliance with a formal procedure. Formal procedures are necessary but insufficient. Both the congress of reason and the counsel of experience are needed. Formal protocols contribute to the accuracy and scope of sensory analysis, but they are imperfect. While perfection is unattainable, many gross errors can be corrected by a self-reflective awareness that remains active and attentive. This why insisting upon the banishment of all subjective activity is an ideological folly, a practice of "scientific thinking" that has fallen out of the boat. Both more intelligence and additional courage are required.

In spite of this situation, many coffee purveyors have constituted themselves into a cheering section for banishing subjectivity, which reveals that they are working with a flawed and unsophisticated epistemology.

Maya Zuniga (2017) has endorsed a negative view of subjectivity: "Sensory science strives to reduce that subjectivity . . . what it amounts to is proper training, and that is really what is critical for those objective and accurate measurements." It is nothing so easy as that. As Elizabeth Bakewell (2016, 41) has written, "If I treated all these as purely 'subjective' elements to be stripped away in order to be 'objective' about my coffee, I would find there was nothing left of my cup of coffee as a phenomenon—that is, as it appears in the experience of me, the coffee-drinker."

One cannot banish subjectivity without banishing as well the objectivity that it is capable of producing, since the objectivity of objects relies on subjectivity:

> The new manner in which being proffers itself consists not only in the fact that being now comes to light as objectness. Rather, what is new is that this coming-to-light manifests a decisiveness with which being is determined within the realm of the subjectivity of Reason, and only there. . . . That is, the Objectivity of Objects is completely based in subjectivity. (Heidegger 1991, 80)

A companion to this subjective praxis of producing objectivity is the employment of quantitative strategies of representation. Heidegger emphasizes that the subjectivity of Reason unleashes the "total reckoning up of everything as something calculable." Accordingly, it is the intention of sensory science to replace sense experience with sense-data; however, a reliance upon "sense-data" is grounded in a theory of sense-data and "involves us in all sorts of categories which could not themselves be the data of any sense" (Earle 1955, 91). It is not as simple as a matter of sense-data leading directly to fact: sense-data → fact. This is a scientific just-so story. Rather, the epistemological situation is that consciousness and phenomenon are mutually transformative: consciousness ⟷ thing. Further, the sense-data are never quite so clear in the first place but require being organized by consciousness before finding their way to intelligibility. Carefully monitored intersubjective activity and deliberation play a central role here. Subjectivity cannot be removed since it is present from the beginning. "We must, therefore, be subjective, since there is subjectivity in the situation" (Merleau-Ponty 1973, 9). And this is not even to mention that properly speaking, "The physical thing does not have any odor, color, taste in itself" (Earle 1955, 115). We are the ones with noses, eyes, and tongues. "Subjectivity is not a weakness of the self to be corrected or controlled, like bad eyesight or a florid imagination. It *is* the self" (Daston and Galison 2007, 374). Our understanding is very much needed for making sense of affairs. William James (1890, 488) spoke of sense-data as a "blooming, buzzing confusion," and they need us to provide them structure. The perpetual question we face is how to prevent the usable knowledge that we thereby attain from being guided to excesses by our stereotypes. This problem is tenacious, but the solution cannot be to deny the reality of the situation or invent a box in which all journeys may be kept (Patchen 1967, 287), but to employ a vigilant self-understanding. This too requires subjective capabilities.

For example, consider Ric Rhinehart, acting as head taster, advising his judges that when tasting naturally processed coffees, they need to be careful not to become too severe in punishing the coffees for lack of uniformity. This is subjectivity working properly on behalf of objectivity, and this is how objectivity is achieved. Instead of imagining the scientific task to be some "insane Cartesian project" (Clastres 1989, 191) in which all uniformities would be treated the same, we need to be cognizant of the entire situation and direct our subjectivity to the task of creating reliable, objective knowledge. The physicist Heisenberg, renowned for acknowledging the role subjectivity plays in all objective scientific inquiry, developed what is known as "the uncertainty principle." In coffee purveying there exist as many uncertainties as certainties, and each of these uncertainties poses financial risks. How is it that a naturally processed coffee that tastes better than a washed version of the same crop will sometimes receive a lower score? If the taste is scored strictly on quality it could never be the case that a presumed bacterial change that was serendipitous to the bean would be penalized (e.g., a downgrading in flavor from 9 to 8) because, in the words of a professional taster, it was too "risky" to commend so highly to the buyer for whom he was working. This is an objective assessment in that something that existed was identified there, but a judgment-call on behalf of his client's investment was a subjective adjustment. There should be no talk of reducing such subjectivity; rather, it is learning how to best employ subjectivity that should be the topic under discussion by purveyors of coffee.

Subject-Object Dualism

Some professional tasters follow an obsolete epistemology in their attempts to address the subjective and the objective aspects of taste. By keeping these two strictly separated, they misunderstand and abuse their essentially interdependent character, or in Simmel's (1978, 67) words, "the mutual dependence of subject and object." Earle (1955, 33) also summarizes the problem: "It is as useless to look for a pure subject without any object as to look for an object which is not the object for a subject." Neither can be separated from the other, since originally a thing is "a simple perception of content which does not distinguish between subject and object and is not yet divided between them" (Simmel 1978, 67). The perceived world is beneath, or prior to, any antinomy of subject and object, which is a dualism that infects human cognition in nearly every society. Dualism is an artifact of the intellect, not a primordial phenomenon: "It is naïve to stop at the subject-object correlation conceived in the anthropological mundane manner . . . to do this is to be blind precisely to the great problem of this paradox" (Husserl 1970a, 262).

The solidification, or reification, that arises from treating our inventions as existing independently of ourselves and able to stand alone as transcendental signifieds misleads us into believing our fictions. Our dualistic thinking makes their invented independence seem concrete and "enables us to give them fixed names in spite of their instability" (Bergson 1910, 23). Behold: the taste descriptors of the *Lexicon*. Even the most cursory usage of the *Lexicon* quickly reveals that the descriptors act not individually but as an ensemble, as a system of differentiations that allow them to carve out of tasting the many flavors of coffees. Together the descriptors point the taster toward regions of taste. When one tastes a coffee under the direction of these descriptors, one finds what they might be specifying, and this finding reflexively defines what these descriptors really mean. In this way they are "developingly objective," and these objectivations, achieved by the parties (not by the *Lexicon*'s definitions, though with the help of them) direct the parties to what they can mean. In this work, the subject and the object are mutually determinative, but in reality neither the "subjective" nor the "objective" is separable from the other, not empirically nor ontologically. And yet keeping them strictly separate appears to be one of the principal tasks of modern sensory science.

Transforming tastes into external objects that stand over against us and exist in themselves independently has the unfortunate consequence of robbing taste of its depth and its many ineffable promises. Appreciating and respecting the ineffable should not be a violation of the scientific method. Merleau-Ponty (1968, 101–102) describes the situation with care:

> Things offer themselves only to someone who wishes not to have them but to see them, not to hold them as with forceps, or to immobilize them as under the objective of a microscope, but to let

> them be and to witness their continued being—to someone who therefore limits himself to giving them the hollow, the free space they ask for in return, the resonance they require, who follows their own movement . . . a question consonant with the porous being from which it obtains not an *answer*, but a confirmation of its astonishment.

The ambition of science and philosophy alike is to ground our knowledge in basic certainties and then build up knowledge from those grounds. "Any statement . . . must have somewhere an ultimate basis, a supreme authority, which provides legitimacy to other members of the series without needing legitimation itself. This is the scheme into which our empirical knowledge has to be integrated" (Simmel 1978, 109). This works well in mathematics, which always begins with axioms whose truth is presumed at the start. However, in real life, seeking grounds leads to a problem of infinite regress because as soon as we have located a grounding for our knowledge, that grounding too will need its own grounds, and the certainty that we so confidently think we have firmly established proves to be more elusive than we imagined.

Phenomenology's Rigor

Phenomenology offers a different kind of rigor than that of positive science. It is a rigor that not only examines the things of the world but simultaneously examines *itself* as it is examining those things. Accordingly, the analytic gaze is oriented in two directions at once: one gaze is outward and the other is inward. A positive science that only gazes outwardly in a straightforward way is naive, no matter how clever it is, and it is vulnerable to self-delusions that may never get revealed. In Husserl's terminology consciousness needs to "purify" itself of its addictions to the pre-structures of its understanding by constantly making evident the latent presuppositions that are always at work behind the scene organizing the intelligibility of what we are investigating. Husserl's entire project was designed to expose (to oneself) our presuppositions, of which we were mostly unaware until we began to apply phenomenological self-criticism, or what Husserl (1969a, 153) calls "radical self-understanding."

A second aspect to phenomenology's rigor is the obligation an empirical inquiry has to never abandon the endogenous coherence of the matters with which one's investigations are engaged. "To the things themselves" has been phenomenology's rallying cry since Husserl and his student Heidegger. In the case of coffee tasting, here the "thing" is the original coherence of the flavor of the tasting. Since the coherence emerges out of lived experience, it necessarily depends on the flow of affairs, or what Perullo (46) has referred to as "the context, the process and the whole tangle." The natural flow of our real life can be overwhelming at times, and so positive science proposes to tame it by dividing it up and re-identifying it outside of its natural context, in order to make it more susceptible to rational control and manipulation. These latter are alright as supplements to the endogenous coherence, but not as a substitute for them. Garfinkel (2007, 41–42) commends this work of scientists, so long as the world that is remade for serving analytic purposes is not mistaken for the actual world: "Formal methods provide for the practical observability and practical objectivity of a science's particular objects." Science can make all the brilliant analytic moves it wishes, so long as it does not forget that it is what is making them and that the results are artifacts of an applied method, and not the world in itself.

An illustration of an intelligent way to apply scientific sensory analysis is the method used by the *Caffè Speciali Certificati* certification for specialty espresso coffees in Europe. These analysts employ a strict, consistent protocol and invest most of their faith in numerated assessments, but they made a conscious decision *not* to establish a minimum score for qualification. Although they express some dissatisfaction that they do not use a minimum level for qualification, they have learned that it occasionally happens that their "objective" evaluation fails to capture adequately the coherence of the taste of an espresso that should qualify except that on the basis of the numeration alone it did not. They retain their policy because its worth keeps proving itself by allowing certification of espressos that merit certification. They utilize all of the available science and technology, but in the end they submit the information to a higher intellectual faculty, and they make the final decision themselves. It conforms with the explanation of one of Götz Hoeppe's astronomers: "You always need to use your knowledge to verify what you are doing" (Hoeppe 2014, 246). This is the right way to use science to the maximum benefit; one's mind needs to be kept turned on to the very end, without any coasting on the laurels of an approved methodology. Humanity is coming to a more sophisticated appreciation of the inadequacies of adopted methods of analysis in the natural and social sciences, but some lament this decline of positivism and hearken for everything to be defined clearly in advance.

Objectivity Revisited

In a lecture, Luigi Odello posed the question that motivates these investigations: "What is the center of the objectivity of sensorial analysis?" Just which objectivity are we thinking of? Does Odello's question mean "Is there an objective flavor that stands independently of the taster?" (Objectivity B) or "Is there a flavor that anyone else will also taste?" (Objectivity A). When something in the taste grabs us, is that an objective taste; when it calls us to shift our attention to a more proximate position, it is surely Objectivity C. We know that not everyone may notice it or be influenced by it to the same degree, since taste does not exist independently of the taster; therefore, to make it more available to others, to communicate it, we engage in objectivation, an activity that is collaborative, which returns us to the tasks of Objectivity A. An aim of Objectivity A, the objectivity that establishes common understanding, is to guide another to Objectivity C, to a direct encounter of a flavor itself in all its specificity. Only when we speak loosely of "objectivity" can it be something straightforward, as if it is a methodology that resides on some shelf and could be reached for anytime and put into service when needed. Perhaps regrettably, life is not that simple, so the "center" of objectivity in sensory analysis is multi-faceted.

Interestingly, the European Union Court of Justice issued a decision that the non-independence of tastes renders tastes ineligible for copyright protection. In order to be protected by copyright, the court explained, the taste of a food product must be capable of being classified as a "work"—which requires first "an original intellectual creation," and second an "expression" of that creation. And that work must be expressed in a manner that makes it identifiable with sufficient precision and objectivity. Regarding this last requirement, the court found that "the taste of a food product cannot be identified with precision and objectivity." The Court wrote,

> Unlike, for example, a literary, pictorial, cinematographic or musical work, which is a precise and objective expression, the taste of a food product will be identified essentially on the basis of taste sensations and experiences, which are subjective and variable. They depend on, amongst other things, factors particular to the person tasting the product concerned, such as age, food preferences and consumption habits, as well as on the environment or context in which the product is consumed.

This may be why some seek electronic instruments that can match the human tongue, and perhaps one day replace it. One can be sure that as soon as they are able to better define tastes in such an objective way (Objectivity B), they will return to the Court of Justice and again try to copyright tastes so that a profit can be made.

How can we produce more than a paper objectivity? We sometimes act as if by doing things in a standardized and consistent way, we become objective, but standardization and objectivity are not identical. There is objectivity in the cup, but it is not the objectivity-in-itself (Objectivity B) that some tasters want it to be, since it is always captured and interpreted by active subjectivity and intersubjectivity. Our task here has been to identify and describe the outlines of these objectivities, and to clarify them without distorting them, and we have discovered that there are many objectivities that needed to be described. The solution lies not in the direction of formulating better verbal accounts (theoretical or methodological) but in the direction of the circulation of the tastes that are in the cup. It would be convenient if a solution lay simply in some further formalization of a protocol for tasting; however, every professional taster I have come to know is astutely aware that any tasting protocol can become a trap; the problems are dense and obstinate. We want all of the good protocols we can get, but we do not ever want to lose sight of their truth, in spite of our hopes and dreams.

Chapter 14

A Scientific Critique of Scientific Practices

> How we can break the spell of our own fore-meanings?
> —Hans-Georg Gadamer (1975, 217)

A problem science faces, even as we praise it, is that scientists need to devote more time to studying the nature of thinking. They have adopted certain procedures and gained considerable competence with them, but they sometimes confine themselves to the narrow scope of their chosen routines, so they risk missing what lies outside that scope. At the heart of scientific praxis is conceiving ways to submit an idea to experimental testing. Carefully designed situations are devised for testing hypotheses, which are drawn formally and clearly so that all of the scientists collaborating can understand them in similar ways, and this leads to knowledge about which one can be reasonably certain. Problems can arise from how we interpret data, and especially regarding reckoning what that data actually represents. There are occasions when the situation that researchers set up for testing a hypothesis is so remote from any actual real-world situation that as much as those who interpret the data desire to extrapolate from the situation of the experiment to the world in the way it is lived, it would be a distortion to do so. Moreover, while hypotheses are an important part of scientific life, to require that every thought, idea, or experience be converted to a hypothesis before it can be taken seriously would exclude much knowledge; it would so severely narrow down our purview that it might impair opportunities to broaden our knowledge. If thinking becomes scientific by being operationalized in a controlled experiment, that is fine; we should cultivate and pursue as many shrewd and soundly designed experiments as we can. However, we should not ignore insights that are derived from our experience of situations that are not controlled, since uncontrolled situations vastly outnumber controlled ones. Of course, it is inevitable that uncontrolled events will have their way.

The Latin *scientia* is a knowing that is more technical and less related to wisdom than is *sapere*, which also means "to know" (and "to taste"). "Scientia" traveled via French to English, where it became "science," and it grew more technical and implies some systematic, formal organization of one's thinking. It is good to be organized, especially about one's thinking, but any organization whatsoever will introduce *its own* structural demands that will necessarily affect the objectivity of any understanding it leads to. Immanent structural demands necessary for maintaining the organization of one's own thinking are applied, and there are demands that proceed from the need to foster clear communication among collaborating scientists. These local organizational demands are the most immediate tasks we confront, and they present themselves without relief; further, any cohort of scientists is as subject to social influences as any other grouping of persons, even when they intend to keep these influences to a minimum. Gadamer (1975, 362) makes the observation that "Faced with the socially motivated tendency toward uniformity with which language forces understanding into particular schematic forms which hem us in, our desire for knowledge seeks to release itself from these schematizations and predecisions." Organization and "release" are the dual aspects of *sapere*, knowledge as insight and wisdom, whereas *scire* confines itself more strictly to the organizational side of thought; however, both this organization that establishes the "uniformity" of our knowledge and the release that Gadamer commends are essential for serious scientific reflection.

One method for accomplishing this release is dialectics, whether it is Socratic, Hegelian, or even Tibetan dialectics, and dialectics has a pedigree that is older than that of science. Dialectics is intended to keep disrupting the hegemony of any naively accepted structure of understanding. As Herbert Marcuse (1964, 141) has suggested, "Dialectical logic attains its truth if it has freed itself from the deceptive objectivity which conceals the factors behind the facts." A reliance on systematic organization, especially when it is done by some rote rehearsing of procedures instead of being employed mindfully, can impede knowledge at the same time that it assists it. Genuine knowledge, science included, demands that we sustain mindfulness and radical self-understanding in order to keep renewing and revivifying the structures that we use for organizing our thinking. We can and should develop a science that is centered on experimentation, but we must also acknowledge that science, in its broadest and original sense, as "knowing," involves *sapere* as well as *scire*.

Because some practices of "knowing" are less straightforward than experimental inquiry, they may produce a knowledge about which one is less certain, and this can cause researchers to feel some unease. But an obsession with being certain, and with always needing to possess the confidence certainty offers us, can itself become an impediment to knowledge, and especially an impediment to that openness that often leads us to discover what we do not already know, which is something that plays a vital role in any science. Certainty must have been one of those sirens that cast spells upon Ulysses as he was roped to the mast of his ship. Of course, the more money that the coffee industry invests in methods and protocols, the more certainty it expects. Capitalism almost always weighs in on the side of certainty, and it has done so in the field of tasting coffee. Considered from the perspective of the evolution of *Homo sapiens*, such certainty has the capacity to restrict knowing. The challenge that the coffee industry faces, that all of humanity faces, is to learn how to use experimental science in a way that enhances our understanding without suffocating it.

Heidegger (1994, 102) argues that truth is a characteristic of beings themselves and not a matter of the assertions we make about them. This is to say that truth exceeds correctness, since correctness, or the determinations of assertions, presupposes "the openness of beings by which they become capable of being ob-jects. . . . Accordingly, correctness cannot constitute the original essence of truth if it itself is dependent on something more original" (Heidegger 1994, 82). Logic is necessary of course, but truth exceeds logistics. According to Heidegger (1994, 19), "Openness is the ground and the soil and the arena of all correctness. Thus, as long as truth is conceived as correctness, and correctness itself passes unquestioned, [the correctness] remains groundless." There can be no question of surrendering our witnessing of the world to our routine protocols, although we very much depend upon those protocols for organizing successful social collaborations about our inquiries.

Truth does not lie in objects we can fix and use for the purposes of our analytic routines; it lies across the fuller horizon of our experience, the open "texture" that we witness, out of which the objects reveal their nature as they evolve. By fixing things firmly, one can be certain without attaining truth; in modern times, this has become standard practice. Close oneself off from the texture, from the horizon of experience as it is actually lived, and one is likely to become imprisoned in a myopia that limits what any science will be able to accomplish.

Faced with the uncertainties of coffee production in a time of climate change and unpredictability in the coffee market, purveyors of coffee have increasingly turned to science for effective solutions. The larger the coffee purveyor and the more money at stake, the more compelling becomes the certainty that it is believed science will provide. Science can better assist the coffee industry in some domains than in others. The difficulty is that science too—real science (the science without the quotation marks)—always operates with some uncertainty. Scientific models rarely predict exactly how matters will turn out; rather, they offer a range of probabilities based upon the assumptions made, assumptions that must be limited in order to enable scientists to make measurements and calculations. In the best of circumstances, this range of probabilities is sufficient for getting to the moon and back or designing a vaccine that works. Sometimes the precision achieved is heroic, but it is never 100%. Models are based on prudent assessment of a reduced field of circumstances that are reformulations of natural situations. In complex research, such as wind forecasts or election predictions, models often fall short.

Anthony Fauci, the Director of the US National Institute of Allergy and Infectious Diseases during the coronavirus outbreak, summarized the challenge eloquently: "I've looked at all the models. I've spent a lot of time on the models. They don't tell you anything. You can't really rely upon models." Here is a genuine scientist, whose self-certainty is tempered by humility in the face of the unknown. A real scientist sounds like this. The tastes of many coffees constitute another domain of unknowns, and so scientific sensory analysis should cultivate a Fauci-like humility. The problem in the coffee industry is that the more certain scientists sound, the more money they can collect (in consulting fees, product sales, or research grants), and scientists who are the boldest often prove compelling to large purveyors of coffee who seek guarantees for the success of their production and marketing strategies. The result is that frequently the first scientists in the door are marketers of "science" rather than real scientists, and science is forced to defer to the popular version of scientific practice known as scientism.

Popper (1972, 185) defines "scientism" as "the slavish imitation of the method and language of science." Industry groups teach classes on "the science of roasting," but it can be a challenge to distinguish genuine scientific methods from simulations of scientific narration. What is it that makes roasting a science? Is it a science? *What* is science? Why do people everywhere like to call things "science," and how many different things can stand as suitable referents for the label? To what are we committing ourselves when we say that we will "follow the science"? This "science" is as elusive as "objectivity." John Cleese remarked, "the great problem [with understanding the Covid pandemic] is that . . . the people who say we must follow the science haven't noticed that the science changes about every forty-eight hours." Of course the science changes. Everything changes, so why should science be any different? The idea it is different requires that operating scientifically means making the world over into static entities, no longer vulnerable to change and transformation.

The *Coffee Tasters' Flavor Wheel* and *The Sensory Lexicon*

The Specialty Coffee Association (SCA) and World Coffee Research (WCR) have collaborated in a number of productive projects that involve sustainability research, seed and hybrid testing, coffee processing, brewing, and professional coffee tasting in efforts to apply science to urgent needs of the worldwide coffee industry. At one of SCA's meetings, while introducing two new tools for assessing taste, Hanna Neuschwander (2019) said, "Sensory descriptive analysis is a process where trained professional tasters who are trained and calibrated on a particular methodology use a tool called the World Coffee Research *Sensory Lexicon* . . . and they can take a coffee sample and determine what flavors are present in it and what are the intensity levels. . . . It works because they taste the samples with reference materials for those flavors and aromas." The tool of the *Sensory Lexicon*, distributed freely by WCR, provides a common and authoritative language for tasters, and is an effort to tame the wildness of sensory description.

Food consumer researchers Davide Giacanole et al. (2019, 464) address this need for customary professional coffee tasters to operate in a more scientific manner:

> Generally speaking, expert cupping is more anchored in the product grading tradition than it is in proper sensory science. Indeed, in spite of their widespread application, from a scientific point of view current cupping procedures can be criticized on several grounds. Firstly, while sensory science methods rely on a larger pool of assessors to ensure robustness in the results, the coffee branch mostly relies on few expert tasters with years of experience. Oftentimes, only one or two tasters are responsible for the quality grading of a large number of coffee samples, sometimes amounting to more than 200 cups per day. Furthermore, the tasting is often not blind, meaning that the expert cuppers will typically have information about the coffee variety, supplier,

etc. Finally, until recently [i.e., with the *Sensory Lexicon*] there was no consensus regarding the sensory vocabulary or the use of particular scales, which still vary quite substantially depending on the country of origin of the coffee, and even on the individual company performing the cupping.

Consensus is a means by which objectivity is established, but consensus can come at a cost: the language may be rendered less responsive to the situation, and pre-established notions can eclipse the naturally occurring coherence of what is being tasted, forcing it into norms that when substituted for scene-specific sensory descriptors can close down our own gustatory interrogation. Top-down impositions of language can suppress further empirical bottom-up inspection. We are gifted the certainty we have long been seeking, but at the cost of some originality and contact with immanent experience. The purpose of language should be to disclose things, not imprison us "within a linguistically schematized habitat" (Gadamer 1975, 402).

As any linguist will tell you, people will not remain confined within linguistic lock-boxes for long and are very good at liberating themselves from language schemata. Here again there exists that tension between structure and creativity, between order and entropy, that operates in all human affairs. The same words that guide an inquiry can become a prison:

> I may believe that the flavor pleases me when a slight effort of attention would prove the contrary. In short, the word with well-defined outlines, the rough and ready word, which stores up the stable, common, and consequently impersonal element in the impressions of mankind, overwhelms or at least covers over the delicate and fugitive impressions of our individual consciousness. To maintain the struggle on equal terms, the latter ought to express themselves in precise words; but these words, as soon as they were formed, would turn against the sensation which gave birth to them, and, invented to show that the sensation is unstable, they would impose on it their own stability. (Bergson 1910, 131)

Too often sensory science studies operate with a naive epistemology, thinking that taste is a simple response-to-stimulus procedure. As Husserl lectured in 1920 (2001, 606), "Perceptual consciousness is not an empty box into which a perceptual object shows up unannounced and ready-made; rather, *the perceptual object* is immanently constituted in it by an exceedingly subtle sense-giving structure of perception" (my emphasis). It is this sense-giving, making meaningful activity that must be investigated thoroughly. Consciousness is not only sense-giving, work that includes the projection of ways of interpretation (methodological and theoretical) and the constitution and maintenance of various unities of identity (of flavor descriptors, of origins, of terroirs, etc.); significantly, this consciousness is also capable of being conscious of its acts of self-giving, and so it can provide itself with abundant opportunities to see more originally and to occasionally avoid becoming locked inside its pre-judged prejudices. This inner perceiving is a self-perceiving, and such radical self-understanding needs to play an active role in all scientific activity.

Using taste descriptors requires a comprehensive understanding about how language works. As we have learned, descriptors mean what they do because of the sign-system that the signs create together. But that system *keeps transforming* itself, and this necessary instability renders objectivity difficult, unless we stab the tastes in the heart. The creativity of language does not cease with providing fixed significations for the signs that inhabit a sign-system; it rests in *the constant interplay among the signs* within a system, so that the system itself is continuously transforming the meanings of each of the component signs even as the system is being transformed. "The dictionary is not a language, and the rules do not form a rigid, closed system but are rather combined anew with every expression" (Figal 2010, 192).

Every language, every local dialect (including the local dialects of scientists), also bears what Figal (2010, 212) calls an "openness of texture," a flexibility that is necessary for being responsive to what is addressing us. Endlessly innovative and self-transforming, a system for signifying adapts to the world even as the ways it organizes our understanding transform that world. In response to the world, the system and its components keep adjusting. Its semiotic resources are used by parties in their task of revealing and describing flavors, and they employ every potential that the ever-developing sign-system offers. Each taste descriptor is woven into the fabric of significances that has been instituted by the system (Figal 2010, 224). Signs are not "vehicles for a signification which allegedly belongs to them" (Merleau-Ponty 1964, 43); rather, signs belong to a signifying system, which provides signs with the local resources they possess.

A professional taster who was teaching me how to use his tasting schedule explained, "It's a fairly simple form in terms of its structure, but not nearly so simple in its implementation." That is because a tasting schedule does not work by itself (such an assumption would be scientism), but *is made to work* by the things that a taster does with the form. The situation is mediated by the form, by the taste descriptors, the *Flavor Wheel*, the *Lexicon*, and the protocol, which present a taster with a texture of meanings that comes to life only within a situation in which the taster has a hand. In making a tasting schedule work, the professional taster exploits the emerging possibilities that the situation affords. All these tools for sensory analysis carry risks of limiting us to "a linguistically schematized habitat," but tools are necessary, and they are justified when they are used to bring us closer to the object. It is unsurprising that the *Sensory Lexicon* and the *Coffee Tasters' Flavor Wheel* accomplish *both* of these at once, i.e., to both provoke the probing and limit it. Nearly every occasion that involves formal analytic reason or language introduces both of these together: the alienation introduced by reason *and* the liberating force of reason are wedded to each other.

Scientists working with SCA and WCR sometimes display insufficient humility when making claims about the tools they have designed, and this renders it less likely that the contradictions that necessarily inhabit the use of any formal analytic procedure will be identified or reduced. I have used the *Lexicon* and the *Flavor Wheel* as tools in my classes, and they have proven to be productive for teaching students to extend and refine their gustatory awareness. The inner circle of the tasting wheel has been especially helpful for teaching students to attune their attention to the tastes of coffees. Used in a judicious way, these tools are scientific; but when claims made about them are too extreme, we have departed science and entered the realm of scientism. The designers of the *Lexicon* write (WCR 2016),

> When the World Coffee Research Sensory Lexicon is used properly by trained sensory professionals, the same coffee evaluated by two different people—no matter where they are, what their prior taste experiences is, what culture they originate from, or any other difference among them—will achieve the same intensity score for each attribute. An evaluator in Texas will get "blueberry, flavor: 4" just the same as one in Bangalore.

Not a chance. Even if both sensory analysts choose "4," what their two "4"s might mean is likely to differ. The designers of the *Lexicon* are attempting to apply that "mechanical objectivity" described by Daston and Galison (2010, 115–190) by nailing the flavor of "blueberry" to a can of Oregon blueberries; however, such mechanistic strategies were debunked by scientists a century ago. Besides, as a resident of Oregon I can report that I usually reference blueberries that do not come in a tin, and I would prefer to continue to do so.

It is always nice to be presented with a comprehensive glossary of taste descriptors, but if we accept the use of taste descriptors as the *Lexicon* has it, we will condemn ourselves to a nominalist version of their use, and even worse, we will miss how taste descriptors can be made to work in precise ways to help coffee drinkers to discover tastes. It is not a question of disparaging these tools. It is a matter of learning how to use them in a more epistemologically appropriate way. Many, if not most, of my informants praise them. Angelo Segoni of Italy thinks, "The tasting wheel helps to unify the language," and so facilitates communication, which is an essential ingredient of any science. The Brazilian master cupper Marcio Hazan endorses the *Lexicon*'s idea that one can identify the presence of a flavor before making a hedonistic assessment: "Every cupper would say it is 'woody,' but they might disagree about whether it is good or bad." And even the critic Nicola Perullo (2016, 25), much like myself, admits their utility: "There is no intention to doubt the importance of these models in absolute terms: the outcome of complex processes, of brilliant minds, such mythographies have all the legitimacy of life conquered and built step-by-step and with difficulty, at least in our cultures and society." But we should not let ourselves become blind to the reality that none of these achievements are ultimate—that is why they keep changing. Here again there appears the critical tension between a justifiable need of the industry to standardize its assessments and the scientific demand to remain attentive to the singularity that each specialty coffee offers, an aspect that needs to be included in every sensory evaluation.

The *Lexicon* and *Flavor Wheel* present a false ontology when they present tastes as static entities that exist in themselves and ignore taste as a contingent nexus where a taster meets an emerging flavor. In the history of humanity no one has successfully been able to control meanings completely. The *Lexicon* hopes to change that. The *Flavor Wheel* offers the benefit of intimating that there is an abundance of complexity to flavors, wheels within wheels. Shapin (2012, 178) has described tasting wheels as intersubjectivity engines: "The point is not taste objectivity; it is taste intersubjectivity. The Aroma Wheel is a homespun intersubjectivity engine." The notion of confining the complexity of the tastes of coffee to 104 chosen descriptors (or 110; it keeps changing), while useful as a heuristic tool, is unconvincing, nor is there really any need for the *Lexicon* to suggest that it is complete. It is every bit as useful without making universal claims. Codifications are formulated for the purpose of facilitating communication among parties, but codes do not endure forever because their inadequacies are congenital. They are updated continuously as part of the practical, mundane work of organizing social interaction, and every solution is temporary. Prof. Edgar

Chambers of Kansas State University is partly critical of the very flavor wheel he helped design: "Flavor is multidimensional," and the standard wheel does not adequately reflect that complexity (Gupta 2016). Chambers now offers a three-dimensional tree-shaped model, which can suggest and preserve more of the interconnections among the flavors. Such updates are welcome, but they will never be ultimate. Hence the production of a definitive lexicon that boasts of its universal applicability is unreasonable: there must be enough room left for the world to keep growing. Again, Ted Lingle (2001, 3) has it right when he writes, "The basic difficulty in coffee flavor terminology is inherent in our language." The solution cannot be to learn to be more rigid in our employment of taste descriptors.

Scientism dreams in absolutes, while science does not. The most careful lexicographic labors will be arbitrary, so they could never be ultimate. Other than by means of an arbitrary process, how else could a flavor called "isovaleric acid" come to be one of the flavors? No doubt, there is a local historicity to the inclusion of such an idiosyncrasy, and this reveals the contingent character of scientists' decisions. *Descriptors are conventions*, not God-given truths: they are neither eternal nor independently existing. Take, for example, a "rhubarb" flavor: should it be placed along with the bitter tastes, the alcohols, or the spices? A decision must be made. Is the decision that is taken always right? Just because one's expert colleagues agree does not make it a truth. Where "rhubarb" is placed on a flavor wheel will cause it to acquire (and lose) meaningful associations, each of which will have some utility. To that extent, a decision is always right, since associations are always gained; but associations are also lost, making adjustments and repairs fellow travelers of any codification. "There is nothing fully observable, no inspection of the thing that would be without gaps and that would be total" (Merleau-Ponty 1968, 77). A practical problem here should be considered: what possible communicative benefit does "isovaleric acid" or "rhubarb" offer? It becomes necessary for us to take into consideration also the person who is reading the terms, since what they are capable of understanding participates in establishing the sense and reference of the description. This is another reason why descriptors do not stand alone in their pre-defined truths. One must consider the social and communicative context of the decisions and avoid imagining non-existent absolute meanings. Much careful work went into the composition of the *Flavor Wheel*, but every composition relies on moments of bricolage, and it would be a retrospective illusion to deny the role that local contingencies and intersubjective deliberations played in the composition of the 110 descriptors.

Why is the *Flavor Wheel* so compelling, even for the many tasters who never use it? The widespread adoption of the *Flavor Wheel* owes as much to its graphics as to its science. For its considerable beauty, it is posted on the wall of nearly every tasting lab in world. They sit there "like peacocks" (Perullo 2016, 45), admired as a celebration of coffee tasting, but I have never observed a single taster who consulted it during the course of their work. Perhaps this is because any canonical coffee *Flavor Wheel* and accompanying *Lexicon* restrict the natural developingly objective life of taste descriptors and stifle some of the creative aspects of taste description.

In India, coffee tasters are more cognizant of the realities of relativism and the importance of the openness of experience than tasters are in Europe and the US. The director of the Indian Coffee Board once explained to me, "I don't know what his terms mean, and vice-versa." Indians are unlikely to submit to the *diktat* of a *Lexicon*. Why should an Indian taster adopt a lexicon that is foreign to Indian culinary culture? How can one correlate the way an American will describe taste with what an Indian will find salient, when one is a vegetarian and the other was raised on hamburgers? Taste descriptors should be allowed to differ. Throughout history, whenever a European has made a claim of universal pertinence, it was likely that a colonial outlook was in play. While this aspect is beyond the scope of this study, social scientists have long observed that many scientists are prone to speak in a colonialist timbre, even as they are engaged in administering charitable aid to their colonial clients.

The *Sensory Lexicon* claims universality; however, in the real, empirical world, there exist only particulars. The unities of identity that we invent to assist us in our task of identifying and examining flavors are our invented conventions. A phenolic taint or an excessive fermentation might be called "*rio*" by Italians and disliked by them, while it can pass unnoticed by Japanese, and possibly be appreciated in the Middle East. Or if it is identified by a Japanese taster, it may be given a different label, such as "green." When Chinese, Koreans, and Japanese can taste a greater variety of salty flavors than Europeans, how far does the universality of the meaning of "salty" reach? Naturally processed coffees receive disparate sensory assessments. Sweet Maria's rated an El Salvadoran coffee highly and described it as tasting "like red wine," while most of the tasters for the El Salvador Cup of Excellence rejected it as "fermented."

The first flavor wheel to be developed was for beer, completed around 1970, so these instruments are quite recent. The wine aroma wheel was developed during the mid-1980s, invented at UC Davis by Ann Noble.

Since then, flavor wheels for many products have been produced, and while they can be used to sensitize consumers to the range of possible flavors, their ambition to be made canonical is excessive. They have something to contribute, so long as they do not replace the consumers' own capacity to sense. One needs to learn to use them while preserving the originality of one's own sensory experience.

In proposing a fundamental invariance to the meaning of 110 taste descriptors, the *Lexicon* transforms tastes, which are naturally indefinite, into things that are clear and distinct as long as one considers them in the abstract, remote from actual coffee drinking. Such a "happily ever after" solution may have enough plausibility to convince us, but as soon as the coffee arrives, the application of these descriptors and the clarity of their sense and relevance become complicated, in the way that Piora cheese exceeds the capacity of the cheese tasting wheel. Descriptors adopted from the chart may bear some invariance earned by having been adjudicated by a team of sensory analysts and incorporated into the *Lexicon*, but the invariance they have (say "fruity," for instance) is still an invariance that somehow keeps changing from cupping to cupping, even in my kitchen. If such a statement appears less than logical, that is because tasting operates beyond the limits of logic, and in the end no amount of logistics can tame what tastes are capable of doing. As Wittgenstein (1972, 84) observes wisely, "Reasons will soon give out." Part of the focus of our research has been to track the local historicity of such invariance.

The effort to define descriptors from the top down is fraught with the quest to make knowledge certain. But that is not always an accomplishment. "Empirical" research, in sociology at least, properly takes place from the bottom up, although categorial organization always plays some role in organizing the data into unities (e.g., "coding data"), which can become a source for molesting data. It can be more important to remain faithful to the thing itself, in the way it shows itself from itself, than to remain faithful to any pre-existing formal analytic lexicon. If the fit is forced, it is not the tastes that should change but the lexicon. The victory of the *Flavor Wheel* lies in giving us *better* access to the phenomenon, not perfect access; therefore, it makes little sense to use it to use it in a way that causes us to *lose* access. While the need for standardization across the globe is genuine, and we require objective categories to help us direct others to *just what* we have found, if they are going to succeed, categories always require some local work by the people who use them. Since what the *Flavor Wheel* offers is a two-dimensional account of a three-dimensional phenomenon, its shortcomings must be mitigated by the ways we use it. The categories by themselves do not reach as far as the actual "just what." Cognition of this "just what" is achieved by the mostly invisible work that people do *with* the categories. In that respect, the *Flavor Wheel* is a social organizational object, and its utility rests in how local parties use it for organizing the intersubjective intelligibility of their tasting.

The use of vocabularies "substantially depending on the country of origin of the coffee" is nothing out of the ordinary, nor are there reasonable grounds for criticizing it. Must the colonized speak only the language of the colonizers? Across the great wide world, languages differ; this is a fact of life. Not a single linguist believes it is reasonable to recommend that everyone on earth speak the same language (or think the same thoughts, or have the same gustatory experiences). People require systems of thought and analysis that fit local needs, and such a situation is not a bit inferior to a situation that sustains a standardized and international homogeneity; in fact, diversity is the wealth of humanity. It increases the likelihood that people will have creative insights and make discoveries, discoveries that can then be shared with other traditions. These recommendations of sensory scientists are well intended, but they need to be better informed by linguistics and social science: languages evolve. To criticize the professional coffee tasting industry for having "no consensus regarding the sensory vocabulary" is to misapprehend the nature of language, especially given regional differences of food culture and gustatory orientations. No one would want a language that is incapable of evolving, at least until we reach a point where we know everything, a promise that is delusory. Words and their meanings will function in the indexical ways that they do whether or not we want them to; however, this is not a license for misusing descriptors. Everything is provisional. The project of turning taste descriptors into fixed essences, whose significance by definition can never change, is more than an epistemological misunderstanding, it is tortured metaphysics.

The coffee industry seems determined to hold fast to its mission: "Without a precise and efficient way of measuring coffee cup quality, [we] will be limited by the variability and unreliability associated with current sensory methods that were designed for coffee grading" (WCR 2013). An important question is whether it is even possible for us to remedy variability and unreliability. They certainly cannot be willed away. The world *is* variable, and we would not want to live a world that is not (imagine, for instance, remaining stuck for the rest of our lives with our grandparents' Yuban coffee). We should work assiduously to reduce unreliability, but is removing it altogether a reasonable possibility? Suggesting, even in narrated bravado, that we will be able to do so is to participate in mythological thinking, which is scientism and not science. We very much require the latter, but so far as we are able we should do without the former.

The scientists working with WCR say that they seek "a common reliable system . . . using descriptive analyses, an industry sensory expert panel, an anchor sensory lab, robust statistical designs and integrated laboratory methods." We are interested to inquire, just what is it that makes careful sensory analysis "robust"? It cannot mean weeding out the "inexact" descriptors, since every description will remain partly inexact, and even an inexact descriptor can be used as an effective tool for probative tasting. It is the inexactness of poems that enables a poem to lead a reader to truths, and the truth the reader finds is partly his or her own achievement. This is the significance of the observation of Merleau-Ponty (1973, 84) that "the meaning of a word is not behind it but in front." Further, "A significative intention is never total, never final, never adequate" (Bruzina 1970, 113); and the more we insist on the correctness of our preferred framework of analysis, the less we are likely to succeed: "Insistence on the possibility of knowledge that is directed and aimed really only forecloses experience" (Figal 2010, 7). Sensory science canonizes its methods to a degree that can render it incapable of adequately appreciating new contents and new experiences, leaving a field of petrification that enables it only to rehearse what it already knows.

The sites of tasting are far from being anything foreclosed: "The theoretical and practical challenges involved in shaping our collective existence can never be definitively resolved because the future remains fundamentally—necessarily—open" (Goodstein 2017, 346). Figal (2010, 173) concurs: "Instead of taking the open as a 'measure,' the human being now takes his measure from his own 'intentions and planning.' In doing so, he 'misses' himself all the more fundamentally." The *Lexicon* is desirable when used as a weak version of itself, which entails that it preserves a modesty that proceeds from recognizing that there is much we do not know. The achievement of the *Flavor Wheel* and the *Lexicon* is greater than its designers imagine, because of the work the tools facilitate, and this work would be better appreciated if the scientism were surrendered. Instead, they assert the *insistence* common to scientism, which requires that scientific sensory analysts swagger as they claim universality for contingent truths they have come upon correctly. Perhaps the less one is confident, the more swagger is needed, and some variety of "a universe completely determined in itself" (Gurwitsch 2009, 487) is invoked in the hope of girding one's knowledge more securely. Real scientists never swagger.

The investigators who compiled the *Lexicon* commence with reductionist procedures, which, after receiving confirmation by their fellow analysts, generate a self-confidence that is not scientific. It is true that the chaos presented by an interesting cup of coffee can be overwhelming and that there is a need to tame that chaos if one is going to be able to control it ("You need a system"), but equally important, *more* important even, is not to lose the local site of the tastes. What a truly professional taster seeks most is the real that is *not* imported by the analysis. Rodrigo Alarcón of Colombia composes our problem well:

> Regarding the protocol of SCA, it is the beginning of an effort to standardize the qualifications for specialty coffee, but regarding the plurality of the reality that we face, there is not only one truth in the world, particularly in this coffee world. I can say that it [the SCA form and protocol] is just a little dress for a very big world. It is too tiny, too small of a purview for measuring, for weighing, the huge amount of possibilities in terms of coffee. Of course, it is a very good platform, a very good beginning of this effort to standardize and rank coffees coming from different worlds. But the instrument is too small compared with the greatness of the different kinds of flavor that can exist. That is why Colombians have issues with the SCA platform.

The *Lexicon*'s scientists are well aware that subjectivity is part of the experience, but they understate its importance and have created a narrative that suggests that "subjectivity can be brought in later." Such an absurd acknowledgment of subjectivity may spring from a premonition that they might be criticized if they were to ignore subjectivity altogether; accordingly, they developed a place to put it. However, this is nothing more than an artifact produced by their skills at narration and not any sort of rigorous science. The artifacts of our methods seem to possess their own self-existence, but there is always something more to a flavor for which we have cultivated a unity of sense than what we have constructed. Instead of closing off our inquiries and our experiences, we need to develop analytic strategies that keep ourselves always ready to discover what we need to learn most—what we do not yet know.

Dramaturgy and Narrations

Part of the work of professional sensory analysts involves building accounts for the tastes they are sensing so that their colleagues can consider them, use them to inspect the coffee further, and possibly amend how they summarize a coffee's taste. Naturally, as soon as language intervenes, poetics and even some sophistics commence. Scientific sensory analysts are no different, since they must use language too, except that they select an idiom that better services scientific aspirations, an idiom that includes its own narrative style and theatrics. Scientific sensory analysis can read as if it were an acting out a scientistic version of sensory analysis, and dramaturgical trappings are everywhere evident, such as the clean white coats that Nestlé's coffee tasters dress up in for their group photo in their Swiss lab, which is used in Nespresso's advertising and on Nestlé's web page. Why would people who are tasting coffee wear white coats? Must coffee tasting labs look sterile in order to more securely keep all sources of bias at bay? As Norman Mailer (1969, 26) once remarked of NASA scientists, their dress is "white as toothpaste." Most real coffee tasters use brown, coffee-colored aprons, which are a result of years of experience tasting coffee, but these technicians are intent upon distinguishing themselves as scientists, and so white is their chosen color scheme. It is as much theater as science. The narratives they use express certainty and confidence, such as "Specialty coffee certification has armed itself with strict procedures, elaborated and followed with the purpose of achieving a secure and demonstrable standard of quality" (my translation); however, the inclusion of "secure" is self-praise before it is an accomplishment.

Sensory scientists employ a technical rhetoric; there is much of talk about scientific rigor, less specification. Their method for determining cup quality is able to "stand the rigors needed in scientific research" (WCR 2013). Professional tasters like to utter the word "protocol." They do not call for objectivity in their tasting but for being "perfectly objective" without specifying which kind of objectivity they mean. "Perfectly" is an invocation to the science gods and may be an admission that being perfectly objective is unlikely (the attainable objective is to be imperfectly objective). The preference of "scientific" sensory analysts (the adjective "scientific" is stressed) is for a dry, metronomic speech that maintains a level prosodic contour that belies "a technological narcissism" (Mailer 1970, 64). What Mailer (1969, 27) wrote about NASA's Houston scientists holds for many scientific sensory scientists: "Information flow was programmed.... There was no way to suggest any philosophical meandering. They always talk in code. It happened to be technical code." It comprises a sub-dialect: "I'll walk you through it," "inter-individual variation," and the ubiquitous use of capitalized acronyms (TDS—total dissolved solids; PE—percentage of extraction, BT—brewing temperature), which are forms of shorthand required for having one's prose recognized as being a scientific narrative. However, the more confident the tone of the writing is, the more it merits mistrust.

Heidegger (1984, 106) calls attention to the dramaturgical rigor of formal analyses, observing that logic "creates the semblance that this formal argumentation is the most rigorous." The structure of a narrative of strict law-governedness, a narrative that diminishes the importance of contingent details that are always upsetting the apple-cart, is a literary obligation that every scientist learns to execute. It is important to note that this metronomic comportment of the discourse is recognizable on its face, in the speaking rhythms of some tasters. "It is a way of being as well as a way of knowing" (Daston and Galison 2010, 4). Adorno (1973, 300) describes the style similarly: "A positivist scientific bustle . . . breaks men of the habit of experiencing the real objectivity to which they are subjected." Sensory scientists project a self-assuredness that has become an object of longing for others in the coffee industry. Those who are skeptical keep silent and complain only afterwards, while sycophants become enthusiastic.

The dramaturgy is not limited to costumes and discourse but include elegant models that, while intended to encode relevant data, in reality provide little information. One such model is that of the spider graph, which plots six taste characteristics about a central point, with lines drawn from point to point until the model resembles the web of a spider. This one, used at a conference of Brazilian coffee purveyors in Guarujá, Brazil, is typical:

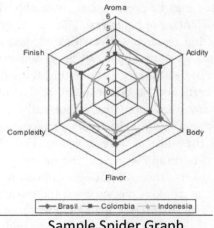

Sample Spider Graph

Although spider graphs are not universally admired by professional tasters, it is their scientific appearance that has led to their being adopted by coffee firms, some of which place a copy of the spider graph in the file for each of the coffees they purvey, thinking to adorn their records with scientific garments. Odello displays a spider graph for many coffees whose taste characteristics he describes to his students. Spider graphs are models that can be made to substitute for the real thing. They are so striking that one hardly misses the fact that few tastes have survived the analytic reduction and that few of the subjective components that generated the numerations have survived the representation. The above spider graph was used to illustrate how well-balanced the typical Brazilian coffee can be, with the balance supposedly revealed by the symmetry of this spider graph (few spider graphs are this symmetrical). Removed this far from the complex actions of tastes, these pictorial representations of six glosses for characteristics could not be capable of capturing anything so dynamic as "balance." I agree with the opinion of Manuel Diaz: "Basically, spider graphs are useless." How can a "4" in acidity be equated with a "4" in aroma? While the numbers look to be the model of objectivity, apart from obfuscating the real objectivity, they accomplish little beyond some scientistic adornment.

Another example of the theatrics of scientific modeling is the saddle-shaped graph. "Saddle shape response curves are notoriously hard to interpret" (Cotter 2020). The task is difficult because it consists of interpreting graphs, treated as the pride of their profession, rather than deciphering tastes; nevertheless, the graphs are introduced as though they can replace actual activities. They may be presented as more objective; however, actual activities have the advantage of being real. Like spider graphs, saddle graphs are generated by having research subjects tick off descriptors from a list of pre-selected qualities, some of which can be so unfamiliar to the subjects that their selection can be arbitrary. Despite this, the saddle graph translates indecisiveness into certainty. No doubt, many of the subjects' choices were sincere, but how many were authentic? Importantly, the research methodology does not provide a way for the reader or researcher to discern which selections made by the subjects were arbitrary. This affords the scientific reporter the freedom to fill in the gaps in the meaning that the choices had for the lay coffee drinkers. This will not be a difficult task, since little of the lived experience of the drinkers has survived the research design to permit the drinkers to speak for themselves, giving the writer of the scientific report license to speak on their behalf. There will be no argument.

The Predicative Framework

The online advertisement for Luigi Odello's excellent book *Espresso Italian Tasting* (2001) speaks of "The tasting card and the method to use for correct sensory evaluation," which expresses the confidence that is characteristic of scientific sensory analysis. Scientific practice maintains a strong foundationalism that aims to ground claims to certainty in "correct" judgments, but Hegel (1969, 38) expresses skepticism about such a project when he suggests these formulas "concern only the correctness of the knowledge of facts, not truth itself." Heidegger too tells us that we can have everything perfectly correct and still lose the truth (1994, 23); he clarifies that while correctness and truth are both problems, they are not identical (Heidegger 1984, 4).

Heidegger (1971a, 111) criticizes some investigative practices for "forcing everything under its dominion from the start, even before it can survey it." Sensory analysts can become lost inside the predicative frameworks that are used to structure experimental designs. In most sensory experiments, the coffee descriptors are pre-selected by the researcher (test designs that facilitate computation of the results are preferred), and test subjects may not be able to recognize all the pre-selected categories they must rate by choosing a corresponding bubble for filling. Limited to those categories and to those bubbles, they fill in a page's worth of bubbles, and in this act their selections are converted into clear and definitive responses, which then are available for unambiguous use in subsequent calculations. In this way, the test drinkers' own free exploration is distracted and stifled, while an ideology of precision and correctness is maintained. This contravenes the warning Heidegger (1982, 160) gives when he advises us to "not shut ourselves off from the phenomena by a framework of concepts." Merleau-Ponty (1968, 24) comments, "One can remain within the objectivist ontology only by restricting the 'object' one gives oneself in a way that compromises the research. Here the objectivist ideology is directly contrary to the development of knowledge."

Standard, approved, and "correct" taste descriptors (there can be so much approval surrounding the activity that we feel reassured) function as categorial helpmates. This is Garfinkel's term (1993a) for one way of biasing our inquiry, and he suggests that any truly empirical inquiry must address directly the specific phenomenal details of what one perceives "without the benefit of categorial helpmates." When one constantly imports categories into one's sensory analyses, then one's tasting cannot be empirical, especially when the categories are those imposed by other people. All that is left is what Garfinkel (1993b, 16) describes as "inventions on top of inventions, until finally you're engaged in very educated data," which are then paraded as facts. Garfinkel's student Howard Schwartz (2002, 8) suggests, "The notion of 'fact' is really a gloss for a series of technical constraints on the procedures for describing phenomena."

Sensory scientists use specious data like this to reinterpret the object as "not the object of my subjective experience" but as "the physical thing of the natural sciences" (Schutz 1970a, 20), a status that garlands its objectivity by describing the object's identifying characteristics "in logico-mathematical terms." In the words of Eugene Gendlin (1967, 261), formal analytic research strategies operate from a view that gives "all power to axiomatic concepts and none to givenness." The actual taste experience is ignored or appears in the scientific account as though the scientist has been gazing at lived experience through the wrong end of a pair of binoculars, something that is considerably less than attunement to the phenomenon. Sensory scientists sometimes diminish the scope of non-metrological research by calling it "infrahuman research" (Wise et al. 2000), which is an oddly demeaning term for what is primordial, before any methodological reductions. In this way, the methodologically reduced object is treated as what is primordial, when in fact our immanent perception was prior to it and is the basis for any methodologically reduced object. As Merleau-Ponty (1964, 25) explains, "Perception is a nascent *logos*; it teaches us, outside all dogmatism, the true conditions of objectivity itself."

It must be emphasized that we can continue to work with predicative, formal analytic structures, taking full advantage of all the calculations, saliencies, and discoveries they offer, but our awareness must continuously monitor and judge the adequacy of their use. We should "follow the science" wherever it leads, and with equanimity, but this does not require us to become blind to what is, even after we have rendered sensory experience in predicative terms. Sensory analysis requires more than taking a method off the shelf and applying it straightforwardly, ever assured that we have netted truth; we must think.

Too many of the judgments of science have been arranged in advance, with barely a keyhole's worth of sight made available to the actual world for influencing our investigation, not enough to risk disruption of the ways we have pre-structured our understanding. The important point is that the truth or falsity of sensory assessment is not *fully* knowable by the correctness of the judgment as measured and calculated by an accepted method, nor by a more pragmatic strategy that involves calibration of tasting by a cohort of professional tasters, but only by retreating to a more primitive and primordial reckoning of the fundamental relations between the taster who experiences a taste and the coffee. The latter is the most difficult, which is why it is sometimes set aside. This may sound like a heresy, but its truth should be obvious. Something is to be gained and lost by every method of inquiry. Perullo (2018a, 57) promotes retrieving what is lost: discovery.

Examining the reductionism of physics, Heidegger (1967, 210) compares light waves with what the eye sees, and he asks, "What more truly is, that crude chair with the tobacco pipe depicted in the painting by Van Gogh, or the waves that respond to the colors used in the painting?" Similarly, we can ask ourselves whether the paintings of Cezanne are objective or subjective. The truth of Cezanne's art is located in the precision of the representation of an experience and cannot be reduced to any mechanical fidelity. The important fidelity is the one we have to the experience. Take, for instance, Cezanne's series of paintings of the Montagne Sainte-Victoire, no two of which are identical. Although the mountain and its details are identical, each painting is extraordinarily unique: Cezanne is faithful to the truth of his experience on each of the occasions (morning, sunset; summer, winter; joy, loneliness). He is faithful to the real objectivity of the situation by not ruling out of bounds the subjectivity that is active; this was the accomplishment of the objectivity of the Impressionists. Cezanne is objective by being subjective and achieves scrupulous accuracy. Identifying and describing real objectivity is not easy, but it is real. Instead of subsuming the actual experiences of drinking coffee under a methodological materialism, so that during the process of research the subjects are made to feel inadequate, we need to access in an accurate way just what these subjects are witnessing, even when their experience falls outside of the limits of our research priorities.

Certainty Addictions

Bertrand Russell (1975, 28) sums up our problem well when he writes, "In the modern world, the stupid are cocksure while the intelligent are full of doubt." Heidegger (1967, 65) suggests that modern science has "a passion for authoritative knowledge," and there is a search for "an indubitable and universally binding certainty" (118). Above all, chaos must be subdued, and for it "the tranquil kingdom of laws" (Hegel 1977, 96) substituted. Accordingly, some of science is oriented to developing strategies for making the knowledge they acquire authoritative. As we know well, the purview of law is narrower than that of morality; however, it is more authoritative. Schwartz (2002) observes, " 'Science' . . . usually involves sharpening up a rather 'fuzzy' picture as to 'what's really going on out there.'" People wish to routinize their inquiries in order to institute a methodology that will lead them to sure, objective knowledge. The trappings of authority can be secured, but that may be all that is accomplished.

There is a tendency, an obsession even, to try to secure understanding, but "the love of clarity is a distraction" (Earle 1955, 138). Investigating the historical roots of this obsession for certainty is beyond the scope of this study, but the habit is well entrenched in European civilization. When considering the origins of the modern quest for certainty, Heidegger (1967, 99) suggests that "the essential historical-metaphysical basis for the priority of *certainty*, which first made the acceptance and metaphysical development of the mathematical possible, [was] Christianity and the *certainty of salvation*." Rather than trying to fix understanding, we would do better to follow Hegel's lead (1977, 28–32): truth is the whole movement of thought knowing itself. We can be reasonably certain about any finite province of meaning or what Heidegger calls "a clearing-in-the-woods," but what is beyond the clearing—that which Hegel (1977, 341) describes as "this nothingness of everything that lies beyond sense-certainty"—remains undiscovered. This is why humility is called for more than confidence is. A rational spirit certain of itself and self-authenticating is no ally. The tastes of an interesting cup of coffee demand humility, provoke it even. Instead, some sensory scientists, who are never to be found naked, will invoke their categorial helpmates. They would get vertigo without them, but the best coffee tasters prefer vertigo. Without some vertigo, one should become suspicious about the tasting.

Certainties require confirmation by one's colleagues. I used to tell my students that just because another person agrees with you does not make something true, and I joked that it takes three people in agreement to establish a certainty. Every scientific accomplishment requires some social legitimation, and of course tasters in every context must keep aligning their palates with each other. As we learned in chapters 8 and 9, a collective calibrated palate is essential for objectivity. Every cohort of tasters, whether an international panel or a small café, must calibrate the practices of their tasters. Brian Ott (2018, 69 and 72) reports, "The barista's sensory capacity is bound in a way of tasting that is standardized across employees," and "Specialty coffee bars seek to align the palates of their employees to produce a consistent product." This social confirmation must be maintained if the tasters are to keep operating in the realm of certainty within that "clearing."

This is why Coffee Quality Institute requires the continuing recertification of its officially recognized tasters. Taste descriptors that are developed for local use and that may come into vogue must have their usage standardized if they are to be intelligible. While their protocols are based on reason, that reason is attuned to local circumstances, and power relations can influence the situation. Starbucks, Nestlé, etc. issue their rules and methods from the top down, and everyone is expected to fall in line, producing "the order and the authority of a sure knowledge, precisely, a knowledge sure of itself, determined and determining" (Derrida 2009, 278). It is a knowledge that seeks to retain "mastery of its object" (Derrida 2009, 280). We emphasize that the establishment of a routinized system of recognized and official guarantees for correct and objective reason is insufficient for the establishment of truth. In fact, the term "establishment" itself works counter to openness and can offer a warrant for passing truth by.

Epistemological Delusions

In addition to ontological problems relating to the nature of entities and their essences, scientism inflicts itself with an unsophisticated epistemology that causes considerable damage. Understanding is subtler than the simplistic reductive models of scientism. Memory, imagination, and anticipation are constituent aspects of knowing, and so should not be banished from tasting research. Simply because they are difficult to quantify does not entail that they do not exist. Even if we set aside memory and imagination, it is still impossible to remove all prejudice, since every notion requires some pre-understanding that is projected on experience; this is because projection is how understanding organizes itself. As much as one may regret it, the pre-judgments of prejudice are the only game there is. With his usual eloquence, Hegel (1969, 37) summarizes, "Spirit is enmeshed in the bonds of its categories."[1] The best we can accomplish is to sustain continuous self-analyses that keep exposing our categories as they surface, revealing how we constantly infect our inquiry. Those who have found relief by taking "proper" measures that remove such bias are those whose prejudices may be the most obstinate.

When we examine the structures of thinking, we discover that the projection of sense drives our understanding. If some offer an objection that

---

1. For Hegel, "spirit" is the societal "mind" or consciousness that is occupied with knowing.

that is the very kind of problem that science is attempting to remedy, it must be repeated that it is not remediable. This is the fundamental contradiction of human sapience. It is not that providing rational grounds is bad; in fact, it is indispensable, although its utility may lie more in the direction of laying the grounds for a communicative competence that facilitates collaborative thinking than it does in laying the grounds for truth. Reasons are tidy, but tastes are messy, so what are sensory scientists to do? They can choose scientism, but if their rational praxis pretends that their methods existed before the tastes did, with every notion being well defined before any experience has commenced, and perceived tastes are compelled to be dependent on pre-definitions of their being, then the sensory analysts will be guilty of believing their own propaganda.

Mistaking our objectivated unities for the original objects is an epistemological error that everyone opposes, yet few are capable of shaking the practice. There are indeed objects, but the objects that *we* have produced with our thinking, including all of the hard-won precipitates of scientific methodologies, are not *those* objects. Our error lies in thinking that what one has in hand is a solution certain to guarantee the correctitude of one's data. The problem is not with our protocol, the problem is our naive and totalistic faith in it. Because we believe our propaganda, self-critical analyses will wither, and our confidence will become the enemy of knowledge. The drive toward order can institute a regime that closes off thinking and confines it within a self-made prison. The greatest danger is to hold fast to a tight epistemic practice that narrows the scope of awareness to the extent that one never notices that the scope has been narrowed.

In chapter 11, we cited Simmel (1978, 67): "Our mind has a remarkable ability to think of its contents as being independent of the act of thinking." Berger and Luckmann (1966, 89) offer an extended reflection upon this stubborn problem:

> Reification implies that humans are capable of forgetting their own authorship of the human world, and further, that the dialectic between humans, the producers, and their products is lost to consciousness. The reified world is, by definition, a dehumanized world. It is experienced by humans as a strange facticity, an *opus alienum* over which they have no control rather than as the *opus proprium* of their own productive activity.
>
> It will be clear from our previous discussion of objectivation that, as soon as an objective social world is established,

the possibility of reification is never far away. The objectivity of the social world means that it confronts humans as something outside of themselves. The decisive question is whether one still retains the awareness that, however objectivated, the social world was made by humans, and therefore can be remade by them. In other words, reification can be described as an extreme step in the process of objectivation, whereby the objectivated world loses its comprehensibility as a human enterprise and becomes fixated as a non-human, non-humanizable, inert facticity.

The narrative of objective science is law-governedness. It is the essence of law-governedness to provide its own foundation, but that is an impossible dream that infects our thinking and causes us to abandon humility for false confidence. While there is a need for being empirical and for trying to ground our thinking, what will ground those grounds? Possibly we will be able to find further grounds that can ground those grounds, but what will ground those grounds? We quickly find our way to an endless regress and necessarily come face to face with a groundlessness just where we assumed we could gain firm footing. If logic proceeds according to rules, how can that logic justify those very rules from which it receives its own justification?

Simmel (1978, 109–110) too asks what is the criterion of criteria:

> The truth of any statement can be known only on the basis of criteria that are completely certain and general. Such criteria . . . may be legitimated by higher-level criteria, in such a fashion that hierarchical series of cognition is constructed, the validity of each one depending on the preceding one. However, if this series is not to be suspended in air it must have somewhere an ultimate basis . . . yet we shall never know what this absolute knowledge is. Its real content can never be established with the same certainty . . . because the attempt to find an antecedent for what appeared to be the ultimate principle is endless.

Groundlessness is part of our real existential situation, and it must be faced instead of masked. If humanity is to survive, our methods of knowing need to evolve in accord with the way things are, and we need to learn how to think without being continuously entrapped by structures invented by our own habits of thinking and analysis, which are convincing simply because they have educated pedigrees and we believe that they are founded upon rock-hard grounds whose hardness appears only because we have not investigated thoroughly enough. Simmel (1978, 123) has pointed out, "Dogmatism may base the certainty of knowledge upon some criterion as upon a rock, but what supports the rock?" If life is not clear and well defined the way we prefer, then we may need to choose fidelity to truth over fidelity to method.

Numeration

Sometimes when scientific investigation runs into an intractable doubt, instead of celebrating the insights that contradictions engender, researchers take refuge in metrological strategies, using metrics to find again a path to certainty. Not unlike the Count on Sesame Street, they look for things that can be counted. And still, when used skillfully by expert tasters, strategies of numeration can make contributions to sensory analysis, so long as they retain the phenomenon.

In both lay and professional tasting it is not unusual that some numeration will be put into service, and occasionally interfere, with the tasters' task of developing appropriate taste descriptors. Numbers are easier to share than concepts are. In fact, they are so convenient for arbitrating differences that they are adopted, though their adoption can promote some curtailment of articulating, considering, exchanging, and assessing the descriptive details of tasters' differing perceptions. Let us consider this illustration of two highly competent senior tasters in Italy who examine in a collaborative way a sample of coffee. At lines 5 through 8, they use numbers instead of employing descriptors. They have been working together for so many years, tasting many coffees each day, that their numbers mean more to them than they mean to us.[2]

Sensory Analysis of a Decaffeinated Coffee

1	A	It's a bit fruity, a light winey taste. [made available as a public account]
2	B	Yes.
3	B	[Sips again, spits it out] To me it is a bit bitter.
4	A	Yes that cup, but this other one isn't bitter, you saw.

---

2. Translation is by Giolo Fele and myself.

5	A	[Sips again] Four and a half.
6	B	[Nods "maybe"]
7	A	Four, three and a half [looks to B].
8	B	The first one maybe three and a half.
9	A	Yes, the first one.
10	A	The acidity is good, no? Four and a half. [Both write on their scoring sheets.]
11	A	It has an almond taste.
12	B	Maybe vanilla. [They write down both almond and vanilla.]
13	B	[Sips again, spits] A bit of sweetness.
14	A	It is a little sweet, more or less. [Writes "a little sweetness."]
15		But it has poor body.
16	B	Oh, four.
17	A	That would be a gift.
18	B	[Sips again, spits.] Four, or three and a half, yes.

In line 7 especially, they are reckoning the bitterness together, although it is difficult to determine whether they are orienting to the intensity or to the quality of the bitterness; nevertheless, the way that they use their numerating allows them to check and repair each other's errors in what seems to be an effective manner. The gaze that A gives to B at line 7 is an essential part of the collaboration, and I could fill a book with photos of this look that were evident in my video recordings, looks that reveal an openness to the future of a collaboratively developing summary account of a coffee's taste that has been proposed. The look is tied directly to the need for social confirmation to ratify the correctness of an account. Collaborative work with numbers occurs again in lines 16 to 18 with respect to the coffee's body. Numeration is an important recourse for their collaborative assessment and has priority over verbal description. Here they are tasting a sample in order to decide whether to recommend purchase. If their firm does make the purchase, they will use the green beans from this sample, roast them again, and compare the taste with the shipment of coffee when the shipment arrives by boat, in order to determine whether they have received the identical coffee they purchased. In that event, this record, including both the numerations and the taste descriptors, will become the basis for that decision. How months later they are able to reconstruct specifics from the generality of their numerations presents an interesting hermeneutic question. Here we can conclude both that numeration can be used successfully in collaborative sensory evaluations and also that a focus upon numeration may distract the tasters from focusing upon developing more precise taste descriptors.

During another tasting in Italy, a professional taster reported on the assessment of a panel of lay tasters who were baristas and coffee bar managers: "The acidity had a mean of 5, and the bitterness had a mean of 4, so the acidity is greater than the bitterness." The project of comparing acidity and bitterness this way is similar to comparing apples and oranges. Surely numbers can be compared, but can acidity and bitterness be compared adequately by means of a simple practice of numerating? Do not the particular acidity and the particular bitterness play essential roles and require more specification? Further, there is no attention paid to how the two interact: do they influence each other in the same way, or to the same degree? Moreover, some of the drinkers whose evaluations were factored into the average score displayed an imperfect understanding of just what "acidity" and "bitterness" mean in coffee, so speaking of "more" (it was not made explicit more of exactly what) in the context of a one-point difference is to elaborate upon what may be a fiction; yet it is a fiction that promoted much discussion among the tasters, and so it contributed something. Interestingly, the coffee's characteristics seemed to be made more real *because* there were numbers affixed to them. Since the numerations were close for the two categories of taste (acidity and bitterness), can one assert the coffee is a balanced one? An assertion of "balance" made on the basis of these two scores would seem to be quite abstract; however, an abstract result could motivate the tasters to re-taste the coffee and assess the balance in a way that is more attentive than they previously had managed to do. Once again, we are able to learn that the efficacy of numeration depends upon how tasters *use* the numbers in real situations. There is no magic to the meaning of scores when scores are separated from the situation and then reified. In both of these illustrations, it is not a matter of whether numeration is suitable or not, generally speaking; it is a matter of *how* the numerating is used within the specific contingencies of each local situation. Husserl (1970a, 46) writes, "Mathematical natural science . . . becomes a sort of *technique*; that is, it becomes a mere art of achieving, through a calculating technique according to technical rules, results the genuine sense of whose truth can be attained only by concretely intuitive thinking actually directed at the subject matter itself. . . . The *original* thinking that genuinely gives meaning to this technical process and truth to the correct results is [incorrectly] excluded."

It is possible that people in the coffee industry, laboring under the burdens of a false ontology and an unsophisticated epistemology, and feeling vulnerable to criticism directed to how objective their sensory assessments really are, turn more quickly to quantitative strategies than do people in other fields of scientific research. Numeration is beneficial, but deference to numeration, by which one is willing to overrule one's own experience without always knowing why—i.e., simply believing in the primacy of metrological analyses over experiential insight—is a form of voluntary ignorance. In chapter 7 we described how the Brazilian exporter Marcio Hazan had a personal habit of handling and smelling fresh green beans that were unrelated to the coffees he was examining, a habit in which he persisted all day long, every day. At the end of a day, he can invent a brand-new blend of coffees, based only on the smell and feel of the green beans with which he had been playing. Further, there is no metrological tool that Marcio is unwilling to consult if it could aid him in his work; however, he places only limited faith in numeration. His son, the third generation of the Hazan family to work in coffee purveying, describes his father's practice of tasting coffee:

> All of the big coffee enterprises want to use numbers and develop mathematical formulae for making the blends. They want to use computers and make their blends with numbers, and get a good result. But my father has no confidence that it can really work that way. The big companies try to do it that way, but it's not the way that blending really works. My father imagines the blends more than he thinks about them analytically, and he finds a way of mixing the blend that will produce a successful result. There are too many variables, each crop is slightly different, and you have to taste. My father loves the work, and he is good at it.

We can gain additional insight by examining the utility of metrological analysis in other scientific fields. My skepticism about some metrological strategies employed by scientists is a consequence of their fundamental ontology and epistemology being wrong, which causes them not to get things right. While I appreciate that they need to simplify their inquiries in order to gain some control over their parameters, the things themselves possess a complexity that must be respected. More importantly, things are never static—*they flow*. We attempt to name tastes to help us create a unity of reference for them, but they are less stable than are our identifications. Bergson (1910, 131) writes, "Sensations and tastes seem to me to be objects as soon as I isolate and name them, and in the human soul there are only processes." Much of what sensory science gets wrong can be attributed to the taxidermic strategies they use, which result from the metrological practices that are commonly employed across much European thinking.

Let us review the issue from the perspective of paleo-archaeology, where the disciplinary energies are trained upon the task of ordering the evolution of hominids. Tattersall and Schwartz (2000, 139) describe the situation:

> One of the colleagues Alan Walker invited to participate in the analysis of the Nariokotome skeleton was Joan Richtsmeier, who had been in the forefront in the application of sophisticated mathematical analyses to the study of cranial shape. Walker's idea in taking this analytical route was to reconstruct the growth trajectory of the *Homo erectus* skull and face, from the young Nariokotome individual to the adult. . . . As much as we appreciate the high-tech aspects of this kind of analysis, as skeptics at heart we are a bit wary of placing huge amounts of faith in fancy morphometric studies (i.e., using measurements to try to capture shape). Having worked together on diverse projects for over 25 years, we have found little occasion to resort to the use of calipers. Not, of course, that we think no one should measure anything. But it's been our experience that, until you sort out the nature of the morphologies, it's hard to know what to measure and why you should measure it. In keeping with this thought, we also feel that measurements alone do not definitively provide the data upon which you should delineate species. . . . To use measurements, you have to begin with an assumption, which then you can quantify accordingly.

This is intelligent science: they prioritize understanding why they are measuring and knowing what to measure before commencing to measure.

Every time a new jaw or finger-bone is discovered, years are spent weighing whether or not it represents a new species. The notion of "species" itself is imprecise. Just where does *Homo sapiens sapiens* begin, and how would we recognize when it has evolved into a subsequent species? Louis Leakey's granddaughter has argued that during the last half-century *Homo sapiens* has already given way to a new species of hominid, a result of a quantum leap in the quantity of thoughts that the average human entertains each hour. The point of evolutionary theory is that species are not inherent essences, but transitory moments in the course of a continuing evolution. Long before *Homo sapiens sapiens* streamed out of Africa 80,000–120,000 years ago, *Homo neanderthalis* left Africa and arrived in Europe, and survived there for 400,000 years or more. Similarly, when *Homo erectus* left Africa they migrated to eastern Asia. Somehow (we have been unable to determine exactly how) *Homo sapiens* contributed to the extinction of both *Homo neanderthalis* and *Homo erectus*, but their identities as a separate species were not so absolute that their genes could not mix with those of *Homo sapiens*, giving today's Europeans their light skin and hairiness and Chinese a number of their identifying genetic traits. There are really only genes, which possess an extraordinary ability to change and recombine. Any transitory stabilization of genetic complexes can be cognized as a separate species; however, this may be little more than a lack of perspective, a project of our reckoning up a conceptual unity for an enduring complex. A new species of hominid is discovered every few years. If they possess a unity, it is because we manufacture an identity for them, just in the way we manufacture unities for the flavor profiles of single origin coffees. Species, races, and flavors are concepts that we devise for ordering our knowledge about what endures; they exist, but they do not exist in themselves with stable essences that do not change, in the way we imagine they do. The basic nature of species is to be transitory.

Genes are interconnectedly dependent, with those connections reforming themselves continuously into partially novel complexes; importantly, their associations with other genes are transformed over time, rendering the notion of "race" nothing more than the reified product of a flawed intellectual outlook. Vegetative landraces are similar. How many *Homo erectus* genes or features are necessary before the remains of an ancient hominid is no longer *Homo sapiens*? Whatever the answer is, that answer will be a social convention, a short-lived best conclusion of scientists working collaboratively in as careful a way as they can. Measurements can be made, but as Tattersall and Schwartz explain, they are not decisive. Reificatory practices, often gaining propulsion by the metrological techniques that are employed and relied upon, do not always serve analysts well. Mistaking the objectivity of quantitative measures for reality makes for a weak science, although some evolutionary theorists can convince themselves that at each node of evolutionary theory they finally have matters right. The better theorists do not reify their theories. Both the humans and the scientific theories they invent are evolutionary phenomena. One would think that scholars of evolution would be the last ones in line to engage in reificatory practices; however, reification is how humans do much of their thinking, a cultural or perhaps species-level predisposition that has led us to nearly every benefit and every blunder civilization has made since the Sumerians. Perhaps it is time for us to evolve some more. Our task as rational beings, as *Homo sapiens sapiens* (the duplicate "*sapiens*" in our official name is a duplication we may one day be able to live up to) is to learn to study life without reifying it.

Producing numbers with which one can undertake brilliant calculations does not give anyone a license to forget what the numbers represent. "To take orientation from measurability is misleading if, in doing so, one disregards the everyday contexts in which it stands" (Figal 2010, 139). Nor is it adequate to reconstruct from whatever numerical end-product presents itself a just-so story that can return our life to us. Rather, every step of the way one should keep track of what our metrological reductions mean. One can make all the relevant measures of tastes, but one still needs to maintain contact with the tastes. One cannot simply convert these tastes into numbers and then abandon what they represent. Numbers can be used to assist this work, but they cannot replace it. Like advisers to a government, numeration has considerable counsel to contribute, but locating, making contact with, and describing what is the most identifying aspect of a coffee, i.e., what is really working at the heart of the cup, is the professional task at hand.

The practical demands of most tasting protocols compel coffee tasters to provide numbers, but they are not usually compelled to specify the details of just how what they are examining earned their numbers. Even in the most professional settings, expert tasters participate in round-the-rally debriefing sessions that follow their tasting and that consist mostly of offering up numbers. For the most part the numbers are left to speak for themselves. The situation is tolerated in part because a taster (and this is true for both lay and professional tasters) can safely hide behind a number, reduce personal exposure, and say nothing that would commit the taster to any public assertion that would leave the taster open to criticism. In the case of lay drinkers, it has been fascinating for me to note how they are able to numerate taste categories (e.g., balance, roundness) before they have understood what the categories mean. Conversations between roasters at a firm and the roasters' assistants usually get down to finer details. Since they work together daily as a collective, there is less need for protecting the public presentation of self, and they can be more frank about expressing their judgments. Here is where mathematical statistics can contribute to their understanding (as in our example), especially since in those contexts it is less likely that their numerating will lose contact with the phenomenon.

Each marking and sign on a scoring form is always and originally paired with an actual experience that they gloss. Measurements are a vital part of the tasks at hand and can be made a fruitful practice; when used as aids for reflection, they are helpful, but when substituted for reflection, the practice can interfere with tasting. Whenever an aspect is rendered as a sign, when the sign gets severed from its paired lived experience, intractable hermeneutic problems arise. These problems increase whenever the methodology misleads investigators into thinking that their work is finished *before* they have established close contact with the taste. Skill in numeration can work like sophistry, even as the glibness of the rhetoric conceals a dearth of experience. Numerated scoring can become an example of what Hegel described when he wrote that the bare result can be a corpse that has left behind the tendency that guided it. Scores are opaque, and what they leave behind can be more substantial than what they carry forward. Hegel (1977, 3) criticizes metrological practice: "Instead of getting involved in the real issue, this kind of activity is always beyond it; instead of tarrying with it and losing itself in it, this kind of knowing is forever grasping at something new; it remains essentially preoccupied with itself instead of being preoccupied with the real issue and surrendering to it." The reader should kindly appreciate that I am not arguing against quantitative sensory assessment. Even in strictly qualitative assessment the same problems occur; and there is always a price set for a coffee, so numeration is in no case avoidable. But even there, as several of my informants have told me, one has to taste for oneself to be able to know the right pricing levels.

Senior coffee tasters in Brazil, Colombia, and India have explained to me policies like "Our way of tasting in India is not with numbers." Gill Coffee Traders in Bylakuppe, India, use a form that has only four categories—aroma, body, acidity, and flavor—which are rated on a five-point scale, with nearly all of the scores being 2 and 3 with only an occasional 4. Interestingly, there is never an aggregated total. This is quite radical: they would not presume to reduce the phenomenon to a numerical total. My own conclusion is that the question "Are metrological strategies more reliable than qualitative tasting?" is not the right question. The right question is "Have my methods, whatever they are, aided me in making contact with the taste and exploring it adequately?"

Radical Self-Understanding

Like all practices of thinking, formal reasoning can be routinized to the point of numbing one's insight with oversimplification; in the worst cases, theories acquire ideological commitments. To avoid restricting one's thinking to rehearsals of previous reifications (one's own or those of others), a radical self-understanding needs to become an enduring part of one's practice of thinking. Radical self-understanding is an aspect of negative dialectics, where one identifes and anticipates the folds and hollows of one's reflections, to which one's thinking may be channeled. Pulling the rug out from under one's habits of thinking can provide fresh looks at the world and reduce the bias that one has unknowingly made part of the foundation of one's cognizing. A method that is straightforward is not necessarily adequate for self-reflective tasks like these.

Husserl wrote, "The sciences are lacking in philosophical spirit." What did he have in mind? An established procedure "must always and again get clear about its essence" (Figal 2010, 30), and the work of radical self-understanding should not cease. This "getting clear" is tasked with revealing the details of any logistics that takes itself for granted, exposing to reexamination the routine ways that ideas have been synthesized in one's thinking. In Hegelian terms (1969, 761), if scientific thought is only a thinking that clings to the determinations one has already made or received, without examining the understanding that is doing the determining, one "finds all its thoughts without exception are of no avail" (Hegel 1969, 763). That is why Hegel says that "the Notion" needs itself for an object. Reflexive vigilance of this kind is absent in some scientific practice.

Husserl (1970, 56) writes of the mathematized natural sciences: "The developed method, the progressive fulfillment of the task, is, as method, an art which is handed down; but its true meaning is not necessarily handed down with it." That is why the scientist must continually "inquire back into the original meaning of all the meaning-structures and methods." Taking a protocol for granted is inadequate: one must know what one is doing. Assertive judgments are aids to inquiry, but any comprehensive philosophical method sometimes needs to undermine assertive judgments (Perullo 2012, 175), continuously exposing to itself its own ideological structuring. Such reflexive understanding of understanding is the inerrant route to any radically presuppositionless inquiry, and so is the right path to objectivity, although it requires much more than straightforward interrogation, and the discipline involved can never let up.

What is science? Its rigor often uses metrological skills, but those skills and methods do not exhaust the responsibilities of science. Science requires not only careful methods but continuous contact with the object being studied and attentiveness to how one is organizing one's experience of it, along with attentiveness to just how that organizing has been influencing what is discovered. There are already many trillions of lines of code, and still science must face up to greater responsibilities. To be worthy of the high status science receives, reflexive and dialectical surveillance are required along with metrological skills; science needs "constantly to maintain a questioning of the origin, grounds and limits of our conceptual, theoretical or normative apparatus" (Derrida 1992, 248). When one is preoccupied exclusively with the demands of a protocol, or when one acts as if success is merely a matter of doing things right, one can entrap oneself inside a self-deluding myopia. When important things are being overlooked (even worse, overlooked systematically, even as this systemic character is what keeps reassuring us that we are doing things right), can we consider it genuine science? A scientific method that blindly follows its routines without continuous radical self-examination is not science but scientism.

It is not an insurmountable challenge for scientists to use their methodology while engaging in perpetual self-examination. Each movement of thinking should *know itself* as it unfolds, even as it is engaging with its object. It needs to know itself in order to keep itself open to every aspect that a transcendent object may present. Only this will lead to genuine objectivity. A scientific method with radical self-understanding does not gaze only at the object under scrutiny; it sustains a second inquiry that examines reflexively the structuring one is administering as one's understanding develops. Surely, thinking needs to categorize, to abstract, to build unities of meaning with which it can operate and explore. The problem does not lie with these activities. It is when thinking fails to simultaneously sustain an enduring and radical self-understanding that it quits its full potential, and yields to an ignorance of its own devising.

Hegel (1977, 333) is making the same point when he writes,

> When, therefore, Reason speaks of something *other* than itself, it speaks in fact only of itself; so doing, it does not go out of itself. . . . Since in confronting the content, pure insight at first knows it only as a *content* and not yet as its own self, it does not recognize itself in it. Complete insight is therefore attained when the content, which to begin with was objective to it, is recognized as its own. Its result, however, will thus be neither the re-establishment of the errors it struggles against, nor merely its original Notion, but an insight which recognizes the absolute negation of itself to be its own actual existence.

With Hegel's aid, and ever since Hegel, humanity has gradually made its way to a more sophisticated appreciation of the ironies and inadequacies of the methods of reasoning we adopt and develop. Many of these methods have gained their influential positions by how they serve humans in the practice of coordinating their thinking and their social interaction as much as they have contributed to the ascertainment of truth. Some lament the progress in negative dialectics as decline and hearken for everything to be clear and well-defined "again." But life was never that clear, and if humanity is to survive, our methods of knowing need to evolve in accord with just the way things are: our minds are always in our way.

The real aim of objective inquiry is to undertake "a comprehensive examination of the prejudices that hold the human mind captive and lead it away from the true knowledge of things, thus carrying out a methodical self-purification of the mind that is more a discipline than a method" (Gadamer 1975, 313). Both metrological and hermeneutic strategies agree that such an effort is needed; what divides them is that positivist scientists are readier to adopt a method that is so routinized it forgets to see what it is examining. That is a path for lazy scientists; genuine inquiry, on the other hand, will include a dialectical discipline of radical self-understanding. Perullo (2016; 113; translations mine) endorses the analytic gaze, but he also warns that the formal analysis "must not prevail over a direct listening that is free of prejudice, balanced, and open." Fortunately, most professional coffee tasters are unwilling to don any scientistic straitjacket. They are tenacious in resisting the alienation produced by subordination to a system, and this resistance is a demand of their profession. Much of the time professional tasters cultivate an originality that enables them to continually break through the limits of their understanding. Originality like this is what identifies genuine expertise, and it is worth celebrating.

Assessing a flavor requires some opening-up for it to be identified. Citing Gadamer, Figal (2010, 7) endorses a radical proposal: "Experience cannot culminate in knowledge; experience culminates only 'in that openness to experience that is freed up by experience.'" Openness to experience is the touchstone of any coffee taster's practice, lay or professional. Robert Barker (2017, 298) advises, "Approach each coffee with an open mind." Openness in coffee tasting suggests that one should maintain no more than a "light" hold of one's descriptors, because it is likely that despite one's best efforts one has missed something essential. The common advice to "cup with flexibility" is a guardrail of professional coffee tasting, and despite the disparagement of coffee tasters by scientific sensory analysts, I have doubts that the latter are capable of cupping with the same degree of flexibility.

Being able to have the mind clear for the next cup is not a formal analytic skill; openness like that is a life skill. Getting one's thinking cluttered up with a previous descriptor or by some fresh demands of the tasting form can confound any analysis. Of course, this does not negate the contributions predicative analysis can make; scientific sensory analysis is useful, but it is one among many tools that are available to tasters. William Earle (1955, 93) has offered this advice, which can benefit all who engage in sensory analysis: "Impatience or anxiety before the inexhaustible and infinite leads to nothing but closure within some particular facet of the real, some particular method of investigation. For us, reality is and must always be open; and the preservation of this open infinity is important for preserving the authentic bits of knowledge we can acquire."

Appendix

Sample Tasting Schedules

© E. Meschini & P. Milani   rev. 35, 17feb21

Espresso cupping form

date		time		test code		cupper		

sample description

blend					single origin		Rob	Arab
producing country				pr./state		producing area		
description			criv.	process		crop	producer	
estate						lot/microlot		
cult. var. & approx %								
ICO marks/lot number					sample ref.		prep. on	
trader				trader ref.		exp. brand		
certifications					int. ref.			
other						colorimeter	old	new
roasted on		by		with		storage method	given on	
g in	g out	t (brewing)		filter dim.		roasting curve		

Cream

Colour

	1	2	3	4	5	6	6,5	7	7,5	8	8,5	9	9,5	10	
	no		++ light/++dark		+ light/+ dark		suff.	red-yellowish		brown-reddish			striped		,

brown / uniform

Aspect/Persistency

	1	2	3	4	5	6	6,5	7	7,5	8	8,5	9	9,5	10	
	very poor		poor		insufficient		suff.	quite compact		compact/long-lasting			very compact/longlasting		,

good / almost uniform

Roasted

fair / not uniform

Aroma

	1	2	3	4	5	6	6,5	7	7,5	8	8,5	9	9,5	10	
	very defective		defective		insuff.		suff.	perceivable		complex and intense			outstanding		,
Unpleasant perceptions						Pleasant perceptions									

dark/light / uneven

Bitterness (quality)

	1	2	3	4	5	6	6,5	7	7,5	8	8,5	9	9,5	10	
	very bad		bad		insufficient		suff.	pleasant		very pleasant			outstanding		,

very dark/very light / highly uneven

Acidity (quality)

	1	2	3	4	5	6	6,5	7	7,5	8	8,5	9	9,5	10	
	very aggressive		aggressive		insufficient		absent	perceivable		pleasant		very pleasant	outstanding		,

burnt/raw / very bad

Flavour

	1	2	3	4	5	6	6,5	7	7,5	8	8,5	9	9,5	10	
	very bad		bad		insuff.		suff.	perceivable		complex and intense			outstanding		,
Unpleasant perceptions						Pleasant perceptions									

Colour / Homogeneity

Sweetness

	1	2	3	4	5	6	6,5	7	7,5	8	8,5	9	9,5	10	
	absent		barely perceivable		insufficient		suff.	perceivable		remarkable			outstanding		,

Body (quality)

	1	2	3	4	5	6	6,5	7	7,5	8	8,5	9	9,5	10	
	very dry		dry		insufficient		suff.	smooth		round		velvety	outstanding		,

Aftertaste

	1	2	3	4	5	6	6,5	7	7,5	8	8,5	9	9,5	10	
	very unpleasant		unpleasant		insuff.		suff.	perceivable		complex and intense			outstanding		,
Unpleasant perceptions						Pleasant perceptions									

Overall balance (quality)

	1	2	3	4	5	6	6,5	7	7,5	8	8,5	9	9,5	10	
	absent		very poor		poor		insuff.	suff.		good		balanced	outstanding		,

remarks

	astringency	1	2	3	4	5	6	7	8	9	10	**partial assessment**	
	defects	1	2	3	4	5	6	7	8	9	10		,
		1	2	3	4	5	6	7	8	9	10	penalties	-

personal evaluation

espresso final assessment

from	to		from	to	
70	75	barely adequate	85,5	90	excellent
75,5	80	good	90,5	100	outstanding
80,5	85	remarkable			

comments

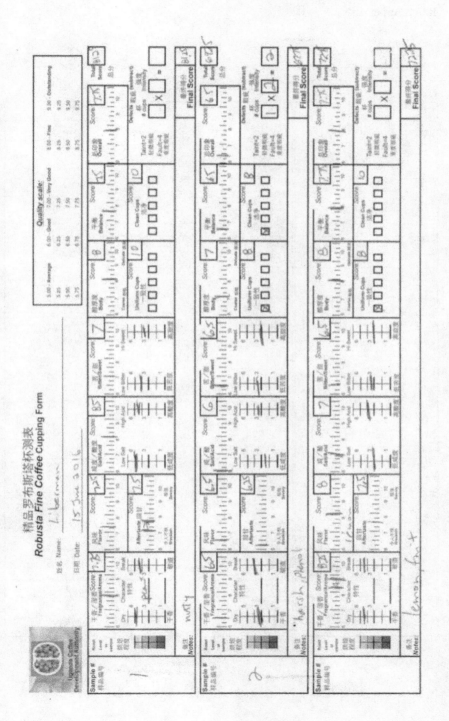

Appendix

NAME:
TABLE:
DATE:

Sustainable Coffee INSTITUTE CUPPING FORM

SAMPLE #	SAMPLE #	SAMPLE #
ROAST LEVEL: DARK / STANDARD / LIGHT — FERMENT LEVEL: HIGH / MED / LOW / NONE	ROAST LEVEL: DARK / STANDARD / LIGHT — FERMENT LEVEL: HIGH / MED / LOW / NONE	ROAST LEVEL: DARK / STANDARD / LIGHT — FERMENT LEVEL: HIGH / MED / LOW / NONE
NOTES:	NOTES:	NOTES:
FRAGRANCE 6–10 LOW/HIGH — INTENSITY	FRAGRANCE 6–10 LOW/HIGH — INTENSITY	FRAGRANCE 6–10 LOW/HIGH — INTENSITY
NOTES:	NOTES:	NOTES:
AROMA 6–10 LOW/HIGH — INTENSITY	AROMA 6–10 LOW/HIGH — INTENSITY	AROMA 6–10 LOW/HIGH — INTENSITY
NOTES:	NOTES:	NOTES:
FLAVOR 6–10 LOW/HIGH — INTENSITY	FLAVOR 6–10 LOW/HIGH — INTENSITY	FLAVOR 6–10 LOW/HIGH — INTENSITY
NOTES:	NOTES:	NOTES:
ACIDITY 6–10 FLAT/BRIGHT — INTENSITY	ACIDITY 6–10 FLAT/BRIGHT — INTENSITY	ACIDITY 6–10 FLAT/BRIGHT — INTENSITY
NOTES:	NOTES:	NOTES:
BODY 6–10 THIN/THICK — THICKNESS	BODY 6–10 THIN/THICK — THICKNESS	BODY 6–10 LIGHT/HEAVY — THICKNESS
NOTES:	NOTES:	NOTES:
SWEETNESS 6–10 LOW/HIGH — INTENSITY	SWEETNESS 6–10 LOW/HIGH — INTENSITY	SWEETNESS 6–10 LOW/HIGH — INTENSITY
NOTES:	NOTES:	NOTES:
AFTERTASTE 6–10 SHORT/LONG — DURATION	AFTERTASTE 6–10 SHORT/LONG — DURATION	AFTERTASTE 6–10 SHORT/LONG — DURATION
NOTES:	NOTES:	NOTES:
FRESH CROP 6–10 NONE/INTENSE — WOODY	FRESH CROP 6–10 NONE/INTENSE — WOODY	FRESH CROP 6–10 NONE/INTENSE — WOODY
NOTES:	NOTES:	NOTES:
OFF FLAVOR (-2, -1, 0, 1, 2)	OFF FLAVOR (-2, -1, 0, 1, 2)	OFF FLAVOR (-2, -1, 0, 1, 2)
NOTES:	NOTES:	NOTES:
UNIFORMITY (-2, -1, 0, 1, 2)	UNIFORMITY (-2, -1, 0, 1, 2)	UNIFORMITY (-2, -1, 0, 1, 2)
NOTES:	NOTES:	NOTES:
NOTES: — TOTAL SCORE	NOTES: — TOTAL SCORE	NOTES: — TOTAL SCORE

F00145 20-01-2015

Test af råkaffe

Dato: _____ Ref. fra lev.:_____

Kvalitet: _____

Vareprøve: ☐   Afskibningsprøve: ☐   Andet: ☐

Smagere:			
Råbønne: 1(bad) 5 (good)			
Ristning: 1(uneven) 5 (fine)			
Syrlighed: G (good) F (fair) S (slight) N (none)			
Krop: F (full) GB (good) FB (fair) SB (slight)			
Aroma: SP(special) GF(good) N(nice) FF(fair) SF(slight)			

Renhed (beskrivelse):			

Offtaste	Fermented			Foul			Chemical		
	Fruity			Earthy			Oldish		
	Winey			Mouldy			Harsh		
	Sour			Mysty			Others		
Robusta	Neutral								
	Fairly Neutral								
	Moderate robusta taste								
	Normal robusta taste								
	Strong robusta taste								

Afvist: ☐   Godkendt: ☐   Andet: ☐

Bemærkninger:_____

Anvendelse: _____

Bibliography

Adorno, Theodor. 1973. *Negative Dialectics.* New York: Seabury Press.
———. 1974. *Minima Moralia.* London: Verso.
———. 1982. *Against Epistemology: A Metacritique: Studies in Husserl and the Phenomenological Antinomies.* Cambridge, MA: MIT Press.
———. 2000. *Introduction to Sociology.* Stanford, CA: Stanford University Press.
———. 2008. *Lectures on Negative Dialectics.* Cambridge: Polity Press.
AFP. 2016. "Togo's chocolate surge a sweet deal for farmers." *IOL,* May 14, 2016, www.iol.co.za/business-report/international/togos-chocolate-surge-a-sweet-deal-for-farmers-2021293.
Alaç, Morana. 2017. "We Like to Talk About Smell: A Worldly Take on Language, Sensory Experience, and the Internet." *Semiotica* 215: 143–192.
Alcala, Stephanie. 2019. "A Search from Within: Investigating the Genetic Composition of Panamanian Geisha." *25 Magazine* (SCA), no. 9.
Artusi, Nicolás. 2014. *Café: de etiopia a Starbucks.* Buenos Aires: Planeta.
Associated Press. 2018. "Hasbro trademarks Play-doh's scent: sweet, slightly musky." *CBC,* May 18, 2018, www.cbc.ca/news/business/hasbro-play-doh-scent-trademark-1.4669857.
Azienda Riunite Caffè. 2013. *Il caffè: classificazione, assaggio, tostatura.* Milano: ARC.
Bakewell, Elizabeth. 2016. *At the Existentialist Café.* New York: Other Press.
Bar-Hillel, Yeshoshua. 1954. "Indexical Expressions." *Mind* 63: 359–379.
———. 1964. "Bgidat halogicanum" [Logician's Treason]. *Iyyun* 14: 120–125.
Barker, Robert. 2017. "Craft of Cupping." In *The Book of Roast,* 283–295. Portland, OR: Roast Magazine.
Bartlett, Frederic. 1958. *Thinking: An Experimental and Social Study.* London: Allen and Unwin.
Bengali, Shashank. 2014. "A Coffee Culture Begins to Stir." *Los Angeles Times,* December 9, 2014.
Berger, Peter L., and Thomas Luckmann. 1966. *The Social Construction of Reality.* New York: Doubleday.
Bergson, Henri. 1910. *Time and Free Will.* London: George Allen & Unwin.

Bjelic, Dusan. 2019. "'Hearability' Versus 'Hearership': Comparing Garfinkel's and Schegloff's Accounts of the Summoning Phone." *Human Studies* 42: 695–716.
Bloomberg, Michael. 2013. Interview, *The Economist* [November 9 Podcast].
Boyle, Richard. 2014. "A History of Ceylon Coffee." *Sri Lankan Airlines Magazine (Serendip)*, January 2014.
Brando, Carlos H. J. 2013. "The Use of Water in Processing." SCA News, July 8, 2013.
Bruzina, Ronald. 1970. *Logos and Eidos: The Concept in Phenomenology*. The Hague: Mouton.
Capella, Anthony. 2009. *The Various Flavors of Coffee*. New York: Bantam Books.
Carbone, Mauro. 2004. *The Thinking of the Sensible*. Evanston, IL: Northwestern University Press.
Cerulo, Karen. 2018. "Scents and Sensibility: Olfaction, Sense-Making, and Meaning Attribution." *American Sociological Review* 83 (2): 361–389.
Chaturved, Satyarat. 2012. "GM Crops." *Hindu*, August 24, 2012.
Cho, Nicholas. 2011. "I Want Coffee, Not *Coffee*." *Specialty Coffee Chronicle*, no. 4.
Clastres, Pierre. 1989. *Society Against the State*. New York: Zone Books.
Coffee Quality Institute (CQI). 2013. "Cupping Skills Class Q4." Portland: CQI.
Collins, Randy, and Michael Makowsky. 1972. *The Discovery of Society*. New York: Random House.
Cotter, Andrew F. 2020. "Investigating Consumer Preferences for Black Coffee." Specialty Coffee Expo Season Podcast, May 15, 2020. sca.coffee/sca-news/video/expo-2020/investigating-consumer-preferences-for-black-coffee.
Croijmans, Ilja. 2020. "The Vocabulary of Flavor." *25 Magazine* (SCA), no. 12.
Dahl, Göran. 1994. "Documentary Meaning—Understanding or Critique?" *Philosophy and Social Criticism* 20 (1/2): 103–121.
Daston, Lorraine, and Peter Galison. 2007. *Objectivity*. New York: Zone Books.
Derrida, Jacques. 1978. "Force and Signification." In *Writing and Difference*, 3–30. Chicago: University of Chicago Press.
———. 1982. *Margins of Philosophy*. Chicago: University of Chicago Press.
———. 1989. *Edmund Husserl's "Origin of Geometry."* Lincoln: University of Nebraska Press.
———. 1992. "Force of Law." In *Deconstruction and the Possibility of Justice*. Oxfordshire: Routledge, 3–67.
———. 2009. *The Beast and the Sovereign, vol. I*. Chicago: University of Chicago Press.
Descartes, René. 1983. *Discourse on the Method for Conducting One's Reason Well*. Indianapolis: Hacket.
Dewey, John. 2002. *Human Nature and Conduct*. Amherst, NY: Prometheus.
Dougherty, Deirdre M. 2008. "A Sense of Taste with a Sense of Place: Coffee Identities Across the United States and El Salvador." MA thesis, Georgetown University.
Dunn, Elizabeth G. 2019. "The Hidden Struggle to Save the Coffee Industry from Disaster." *Medium*, November 28, 2019, medium.com/s/thenewnew/the-fight-to-save-coffee-c80e4e17cd81.

Earle, William, 1955. *Objectivity*. Chicago: Quadrangle Books.
Eggers, Dave. 2018. *The Monk of Mokha*. New York: Alfred A. Knopf.
Eliot, T. S. 1963. "The Love Song of J. Alfred Prufrock." In *Collected Poems 1909–1962*. New York: Harcourt, Brace & World.
Emerson, Ralph Waldo. 1907. "Self Reliance." In *Essays*. New York: Charles E. Merrill. Project Gutenberg, www.gutenberg.org/files/16643/16643-h/16643-h.htm#SELF-RELIANCE.
Euromonitor International. 2019. "Coffee in Azerbaijan." *Euromonitor International*, November, 2019. www.euromonitor.com/coffee-in-azerbaijan/report.
Fele, Giolo, and Kenneth Liberman. 2021. "Some Discovered Practices of Lay Coffee Drinkers." *Symbolic Interaction* 44 (1): 40–62.
Figal, Günter. 2010. *Objectivity*. Albany: State University of New York Press.
Gadamer, Hans-Georg. 1975. *Truth and Method*. New York: The Seabury Press.
Garfinkel, Harold. 1952. "The Perception of the Other: A Study in Social Order." PhD diss., Harvard University.
———. 1956. "Some Sociological Concepts and Methods for Psychiatrists." *Psychiatric Research Reports*, 6: 181–198.
———. 1966. Lecture for Sociology 148. University of California, Los Angeles, May 12, 1966.
———. 1967. *Studies in Ethnomethodology*. Englewood Cliffs, NJ: Prentice-Hall.
———. 1977. Lectures for Sociology 248. University of California, Los Angeles, April 18, 1977, and May 11, 1977.
———. 1993a. "Ethnomethodological Misreading of Aron Gurwitsch on the Phenomenal Field," (edited by C. Eisenmann and M. Lynch), originally a lecture from Sociology 271, UCLA April 26, 1993.
———. 1993b. "The List of Perspicuous Settings." Unpublished manuscript.
———. 1996. "Notes Comparing Two Analytic Formats of Occasion Maps of Way Finding Journeys: 'Documentary' and 'Essentially Procedural.'" Lecture, September 24, 1996.
———. 2002. *Ethnomethodology's Program*. Lanham, MD: Rowman & Littlefield.
———. 2007. "The Lebenswelt Origins of the Sciences." *Human Studies* 30: 9–56.
Garfinkel, Harold, and Kenneth Liberman. 2007. "Introduction: The Lebenswelt Origins of the Sciences." *Human Studies* 30: 3–7.
Garfinkel, Harold, Michael Lynch, and Eric Livingston. 1981. "The Work of a Discovering Science Construed with Materials from the Optically Discovered Pulsar." *Philosophy of the Social Sciences* 11: 131–158.
Garfinkel, Harold, and Harvey Sacks. 1970. "On Formal Structures of Practical Actions." In *Theoretical Sociology*, edited by John C. McKinney and Edward Tiryakian, 337–366. New York: Appleton-Century-Crofts.
Garfinkel, Harold, and D. Lawrence Weider. 1992. "Two Incommensurable, Asymmetrically Alternate Technologies of Social Analysis." In *Text in Context*, edited by Graham Watson and Robert M. Seiler, 175–206. Newbury Park, CA: Sage.

Gendlin, Eugene. 1967. "Analysis." In *What Is a Thing?* by Martin Heidegger, 245–296. Chicago: Henry Regnery.

Gherardi, Silvia. 2009. "Practice? It's a Matter of Taste!" *Management Learning*, 40 (5): 535–550.

Giacalone, Davide, Toke Reinholt Fosgaard, Ida Steen, and Mortin Münchow. 2016. "Quality Does Not Sell Itself." *British Food Journal* 118 (10): 2462–2474.

Giacalone, Davide, Tina Kreuzfeldt Degn, Ni Yang, Chujiao Liu, Ian Fisk, & Mortin Münchow. 2019. "Common Roasting Defects in Coffee: Aroma Composition, Sensory Characterization, and Consumer Perception." *Food Quality & Preference* 71: 463–474.

Ging, Tracy. 2012. *People Who Drink Specialty Coffee*. Anaheim, CA: Specialty Coffee Association.

Goffman, Erving. 1959. *The Presentation of Self in Everyday Life*. New York: Doubleday.

Goodstein, Elizabeth S. 2017. *Georg Simmel and the Disciplinary Imaginary*. Stanford, CA: Stanford University Press.

Greene, David. 2020. "Funny Guy John Cleese Riffs on 'Why There Is No Hope' in His New Show." *NPR*, July 31, 2020, npr.org/2020/07/31/897615446/funny-guy-john-cleese-riffs-on-why-there-is-no-hope-in-his-new-show.

Gupta, Sujata. 2016. "One Man's Quest to Reinvent the Wheel—the Flavor Wheel, That Is." *NPR*, December 30, 2016, npr.org/sections/thesalt/2016/12/30/506144786.

Gurwitsch, Aron. 1964. *Field of Consciousness*. Pittsburgh: Duquesne University Press.

———. 1966. *Studies in Phenomenology and Psychology*. Evanston, IL: Northwestern University Press.

———. 2009. "Review of Maurice Merleau-Ponty, *Phénoménologie de la Perception*." In *The Collected Works of Aron Gurwitsch (1901–1973) Volume I. Constitutive Phenomenology in Historical Perspective*, 487–490. Dordrecht: Springer.

Halevy, Alon. 2011. *The Infinite Emotions of Coffee*. Mountain View, CA: Macchiatone Communications.

Heath, Christian, and Paul Luff. 2018. "The Naturalistic Experiment: Video and Organizational Interaction." *Organizational Research Methods* 21 (2): 466–488.

Hegel, G. W. F. 1969. *Science of Logic*. Atlantic Highlands, NJ: Humanities Press.

———. 1977. *Phenomenology of Spirit*. Translated by A. V. Miller. Oxford: Oxford University Press.

Heidegger, Martin. 1967. *What Is a Thing?* Chicago: Henry Regnery Company.

———. 1971a. *Poetry, Language, Thought*. New York: Harper & Row.

———. 1971b. *On the Way to Language*. New York: Harper & Row.

———. 1977. *The Question Concerning Technology*. New York: Harper & Row.

———. 1982. *The Basic Problems of Phenomenology*. Bloomington: Indiana University Press.

———. 1984. *The Metaphysical Foundations of Logic*. Bloomington: Indiana University Press.

———. 1991. *The Principle of Reason*. Bloomington: Indiana University Press.

———. 1994. *Basic Questions of Philosophy*. Bloomington: Indiana University Press.
———. 1996. *Being and Time*. New York: Harper & Row.
Hennion, Antoine. 2004. "Pragmatics of Taste." In *The Blackwell Companion to the Sociology of Culture*, edited by M. Jacobs and N. Hanrahan, 131–144. Oxford: Blackwell.
Hennion, Antoine, and Geneviève Teil. 2004a. "Discovering Quality or Performing Taste? A Sociology of the Amateur." In *Qualities of Food*, edited by Mark Harvey, Andrew McMeekin, and Alan Warde, 19–37. Manchester: Manchester University Press.
Hennion, Antoine, and Geneviève Teil. 2004b. "L'attività riflessiva dell'amatore: un approccio pragmatico al gusto." *Rassegna italiana di sociologia* 4: 519–542.
Hill, Maria. 2014. "The Cost of a Cup of Coffee." *SCA News*, September 15, 2014.
Hoeppe, Götz. 2012. "Astronomers at the Observatory." *Anthropological Quarterly* 85 (4): 1141–1160.
———. 2014. "Working Data Together: The Accountability and Reflexivity of Digital Astronomical Practice." *Social Studies of Science*, 44 (2): 243–270.
Hoos, Rob. 2015. *Modulating the Flavor Profile of Coffee*. Portland, Oregon: Rob Hoos Coffee.
Hopkins, Burt. 2010. *The Philosophy of Husserl*. Montreal: McGill-Queen's University Press.
Horkheimer, Max, and Theodor Adorno. 1972. *Dialectics of Enlightenment*. New York: Herder and Herder.
Houtman, Jasper. 2016. *The Coffee Visionary*. Petaluma, CA: Roundtree Press.
Husserl, Edmund. 1969a. *Formal and Transcendental Logic*. The Hague: Martinus Nijhoff.
———. 1969b. *Cartesian Meditations*. Translated by Dorion Cairns. The Hague: Martinus Nijhoff.
———. 1970a. "The Origin of Geometry." In *The Crisis of the European Sciences and Transcendental Phenomenology*, 353–378. Evanston, IL: Northwestern University Press.
———. 1970b. *Logical Investigations*. Translated by J. N. Findlay. London: Routledge.
———. 1973. *Experience and Judgment: Investigations in a Genealogy of Logic*. Edited by Ludwig Landgrebe. Evanston, IL: Northwestern University Press.
———. 1982. *Ideas Pertaining to a Pure Phenomenology and to a Phenomenological Philosophy*. The Hague: Martinus Nijhoff.
———. 1999. *The Idea of Phenomenology*. Dordrecht: Kluwer.
———. 2001. *Analyses Concerning Passive and Active Syntheses: Lectures on Transcendental Logic*. Dordrecht: Kluwer.
International Comunicaffe. 2020. "Brazil Exported 40 Million Bags of All Forms of Coffee (-3.6%) in CY 2019/20, Says Cecafé." July 14, 2020, www.comunicaffe.com/brazil-exported-40-million-bags-of-all-forms-of-coffee-3-6-in-cy-2019-20-says-cecafe/.

Jackson, Roger R. 2006. "Deconstructive and Foundationalist Tendencies in Indian and Tibetan Buddhism." In *Buddhisms and Deconstructions*, edited by Jin Y. Park, 89–108. Lanham, MD: Rowman & Littlefield.

Jaffe, Daniel. 2014. *Brewing Justice: Fair Trade Coffee, Sustainability, and Survival.* Oakland: University of California Press.

James, William. 1890. *Principles of Psychology*. New York: Dover Publications.

Juran, Joseph M. 1988. *Quality Control Handbook*. New York: McGraw-Hill.

Koehler, Jeff. 2017. *Where the Wild Coffee Grows*. New York: Bloomsbury.

Kramer, Matt. 2008. "The Notion of Terroir." In *Wine and Philosophy*, edited by Fritz Allhoff, 225–234. Oxford: Blackwell.

Kubota, Lily. 2016. "Coffee Taster's Flavor Wheel Revised for the First Time in Over 20 Years." *Specialty Coffee Chronicle*, January 19, 2016.

Lawless, Harry T., and Hildegarde Heymann. 2010. *Sensory Evaluation of Food*. Dordrecht: Springer.

Levinas, Emmanuel. 1979. *Totality and Infinity*. The Hague: Martinus Nijhoff.

———. 1981. *Otherwise than Being, or Beyond Essence*. The Hague: Martinus Nijhoff.

———. 1998. *Discovering Existence with Husserl*. Evanston, IL: Northwestern University Press.

Liberman, Kenneth. 1980. "Ambiguity and Gratuitous Concurrence in Intercultural Communication." *Human Studies* 3 (1): 65–86.

———. 1985. *Understanding Interaction in Central Australia: An Ethnomethodology of Australian Aboriginal People*. London: Routledge.

———. 1999. "The Social Praxis of Communicating Meanings." *Text* 19 (1): 57–72.

———. 2004. *Dialectical Practice in Tibetan Philosophical Culture: An Ethnomethodological Inquiry into Formal Reasoning*. Lanham, MD: Rowman & Littlefield. (Paper edition 2007.)

———. 2007. *Husserl's Criticism of Reason*. Lanham, MD: Lexington Books.

———. 2012. "Semantic Drift in Conversations." *Human Studies* 35 (2): 263–277.

———. 2013. *More Studies in Ethnomethodology*. Albany: State University of New York Press.

———. 2018. "Objectivation Practices." *Social Interaction. Video-Based Studies of Human Sociality* 1 (2). tidsskrift.dk/socialinteraction/article/view/110037/159343.

———. 2019. "A Study at 30th Street." *Language & Communication* 65: 92–104.

———. 2020. *Filosofia ed etnometodologia*. Milano: Mimesis.

Lingis, Alphonso. 1985. *Libido*. Bloomington: Indiana University Press.

Lingle, Ted. 2001. *The Coffee Cupper's Handbook*. Long Beach, CA: Specialty Coffee Association.

Livingston, Eric. 1986. *The Ethnomethodological Foundations of Mathematics*. London: Routledge.

———. 2008. *Ethnographies of Reason*. Aldershot, UK: Ashgate.

Lynch, Michael. 1985. *Scientific Practice and Ordinary Action*. Cambridge: Cambridge University Press.

Mailer, Norman. 1969. "Of a Fire on the Moon, Part I." *Life Magazine*, August 29, 1969.
———. 1970. "Of a Fire on the Moon, Part III," *Life Magazine*, January 9, 1970.
Mann, Anna. 2015. "Tasting in Mundane Practices: Ethnographic Interventions in Social Science Theory." PhD diss., University of Amsterdam.
———. 2018. "Ordering Tasting in a Restaurant: Experiencing, Socializing, and Processing Food." *Senses and Society* 13 (2): 135–146.
Mannheim, Karl. 1952. "On the Interpretation of *Weltanschauung*." In *Essays in the Sociology of Knowledge*, 33–83. London: Routledge.
Marcuse, Herbert. 1964. *One-Dimensional Man*. Boston: Beacon Press.
McKenna, Maryn. 2020. "Coffee Rust Is Going to Ruin Your Morning." *Atlantic*, September 2020.
Mead, George Herbert. 1934. *Mind, Self, and Society*. Chicago: University of Chicago Press.
Meister, Erin. 2017. *New York City Coffee*. Charleston, SC: American Palate.
Merleau-Ponty, Maurice. 1962. *Phenomenology of Perception*. London: Routledge and Kegan Paul.
———. 1963. *In Praise of Philosophy*. Evanston, IL: Northwestern University Press.
———. 1964. *The Primacy of Perception*. Evanston, IL: Northwestern University Press.
———. 1968. *The Visible and the Invisible*. Evanston, IL: Northwestern University Press.
———. 1973. *Consciousness and the Acquisition of Language*. Evanston, IL: Northwestern University Press.
Meschini, Enrico, and Paolo Milani. n.d. *Caffè Speciali Certificati*. Livorno: Associazione Caffè Speciali Certificati.
Meyer, Christian. 2010. "Self, Sequence, and the Senses." PhD diss., Universität Bielefeld.
———. 2018. *Culture, Practice, and the Body*. Stuttgart: J.B. Metzler.
Mondada, Lorenza. 2019. "Contemporary Issues in Conversation Analysis." *Journal of Pragmatics* 145: 47–62.
Neuschwander, Hanna. 2019. "#54 | Re:co Podcast—Hanna Neuschwander on Unlocking Coffee's Flavor Code (S5, Ep. 1)." Specialty Coffee Association, June 3, 2019, sca.coffee/sca-news/podcast/54/reco-podcast-hanna-neuschwander-on-unlocking-coffees-flavor-code-s5-ep-1.
Nietzsche, Friedrich. 1994. *On the Genealogy of Morality*. Edited by Keith Ansell-Pearson, translated by Carol Diethe. Cambridge: Cambridge University Press.
Novak, Michael. 1970. *The Experience of Nothingness*. London: Routledge.
Odello, Luigi. 2001. *Espresso Italiano Tasting*. Brescia: Centro Studi Assaggiatori Società Cooperativa.
———. 2003. *Espresso Italiano Specialist*. Brescia: Centro Studi Assaggiatori Società Cooperativa.
———. 2007. *Analisi Sensoriali*. Brescia: Centro Studi Assaggiatori Società Cooperativa.
———. 2008. "Editoriale." *L'assaggio* 24: 5–6.
O'Connor, Brian. 2004. *Adorno's Negative Dialectic: Philosophy and the Possibility of Critical Rationality*. Cambridge, MA: MIT Press.

Ott, Brian. 2018. *Sense Work: Inequality and the Labor of Connoisseurship.* PhD thesis, University of Oregon.
Patchen, Kenneth. 1967. *Collected Poems.* New York: New Directions.
Paz, Octavio. 1956. *The Bow and the Lyre.* New York: McGraw-Hill.
Pendergrast, Mark. 2010. *Uncommon Grounds.* New York: Basic Books.
Perullo, Nicola. 2012. *Il gusto come esperienza.* Milano: Mimesis. (English translation: *Taste as Experience.* New York: Columbia University Press, 2016.)
———. 2016. *Epistenologia: il vino e la creatività del tatto.* Milano: Mimesis. (English translation: *Epistenology: Wine as Experience, Part One—Wine and the Creativity of Touch.* New York: Columbia University Press, 2021.)
———. 2018a. *Epistenologia: il gusto non è un senso ma un compito.* Milano: Mimesis. (English translation: *Epistenology: Wine as Experience, Part Two—Taste as a Task.* New York: Columbia University Press, 2021.)
———. 2018b. "Haptic Taste as a Task." *The Monist* 101: 261–276.
———. 2018c. "Pollenzo Manifesto." Bra: Università di Scienze Gastronomiche di Pollenzo.
———. 2018d. "On Taste." In *Taste,* edited by Andrea Pavoni et al. London: University of Westminster Press.
Peynaud, Émile. 1987. *The Taste of Wine.* New York: Wiley.
Pollen, Michael. 2020. *Caffeine.* Newark, NJ: Audible Original.
Popper, Karl. 1972. *Objective Knowledge.* Oxford: Oxford University Press.
Pound, Ezra. 1950. *The Cantos of Ezra Pound.* New York: Harcourt, Brace & World.
Quiñones-Ruiz, Xiomara. 2020. "The Diverging Understandings of Quality by Coffee Chain Actors-Insights from Colombian Producers and Austrian Roasters." *Sustainability* 12 (July): 6137.
Rhinehart, Ric. 2020. Interview. *Specialty Coffee Chronicle.* Specialty Coffee Association.
Ritzer, George. 1993. *The McDonaldization of Society.* Thousand Oaks, CA: Pine Forge Press.
Robson, David. 2020. "How the World Came to Run on Coffee." BBC, September 17, 2019. Video, 22:59. www.bbc.com/reel/video/p07nkgsb/how-the-world-came-to-run-on-coffee.
Roden, Claudia. 1994. *Coffee: A Connoisseur's Companion.* NY: Random House.
Russell, Bertrand. 1975. *Mortals and Others,* vol. 2. London: Routledge.
Rorty, Richard. 1987. "Science as Solidarity." In *The Rhetoric of the Human Sciences,* edited by J. S. Nelson, A. Megill, and D. N. McCloskey, 38–52. Madison: University of Wisconsin Press.
Sage Emma. 2016. "Shade-Grown Coffee." *Specialty Coffee Chronicle,* Fall 2016.
Sacks, Danielle. 2014. "Brewing the Perfect Cup." *Fast Company,* September 2014, 88–91, 104.
Sacks, Harvey. 1992. *Lectures on Conversation.* Oxford: Basil Blackwell.
Sallis, John. 2018. "The Play of Translation." *International Yearbook for Hermeneutics,* 1–14. Tübingen: Mohr Siebeck.

Samoggia, Antonella, and Bettina Riedel. 2018. "Coffee Consumption and Purchasing Behavior Review: Insights for Further Research." *Appetite* 129: 70–81.
Saragosa, Manuela. 2015. "Coffee: Do Italians Do It Better?" BBC News, August 13, 2015, www.bbc.com/news/business-33527053.
Sartre, Jean-Paul. 1976. *Critique of Dialectical Reason*. London: NLB.
———. 2007. *Existentialism Is a Humanism*. Edited by John Kulka. New Haven: Yale University Press.
Scalabrin, Simone, L. Toniutti, G. Di Gaspero, D. Scaglione, G. Magris, M. Vidotto, S. Pinosio, et al. 2020. "A Single Polyploidization Event at the Origin of the Tetraploid Genome of *Coffea arabica* Is Responsible for the Extremely Low Genetic Variation in Wild and Cultivated Germplasm." *Scientific Reports* 10: 4642.
Schegloff, Emmanuel. 1997. "Third Turn Repair." In *Towards a Social Science of Language 2*, edited by G. Guy, C. Feagin, D. Schiffrin, and J. Baugh, 31–40. Amsterdam: John Benjamins.
Schillani, Franco. 1999. *La valutazione del caffè*. Trieste: Pacorini.
Schutz, Alfred. 1967. *The Phenomenology of the Social World*. Evanston, IL: Northwestern University Press.
———. 1970a. "Phenomenology and the Foundations of the Social Sciences." In *Collected Papers, vol. III*, 40–50. The Hague: Martinus Nijhoff.
———. 1970b. *Reflections on the Problem of Relevance*. New Haven: Yale University Press.
———. 1971. *Collected Papers, vol. I: The Problem of Social Reality*. The Hague: Martinus Nijhoff.
Schwartz, Howard. 2002. "Data: Who Needs It?" *Ethnographic Studies* 7: 7–32.
Sedgewick, Augustine. 2020. *Coffeeland: One Man's Dark Empire*. London: Penguin.
Shapin, Steven. 2011. "Changing Tastes: How Things Tasted in the Early Modern Period and How They Taste Now." Hans Rausing Lecture, Uppsala University, October 7, 2011. www.idehist.uu.se/office-for-history-of-science/hans-rausing-lectures/hans-rausing-lecture-2011/.
———. 2012. "The sciences of subjectivity." *Social Studies of Science* 42: 170–184.
Shibru, Admasu, Bayetta Bellachew, Tesfaye Shimbar, Endale Taye, and Taye Kuta. 2008. "Report." Addis Ababa: Ethiopian Institute of Agricultural Research.
Simmel, Georg. 1958. "Anfang einer unvollendeten Selbstdarstellung." In *Buch des Dankes an Georg Simmel*, edited by K. Gassen and M. Landmann, 9–10. Berlin: Duncker & Humblot.
———. 1959. "How Is Society Possible?" In *Essays on Sociology, Philosophy, and Aesthetics*, edited by Kurt Wolff, 337–356. New York: Harper & Row.
———. 1978. *The Philosophy of Money*. London: Routledge.
———. 1997. "Sociology of the Meal." In *Simmel on Culture*, edited by David Frisby and Macuradi Featherstone, 130–137. London: Sage.
———. 2013. *Filosofía del paisaje*. Madrid: Casimiro.
Snyder, Gary. 1980. *The Real Work*. New York: New Directions.

Specialty Coffee Association. 2020. "The Coffee Systems Map." sca.coffee/coffee-systems-map#CoffeeSystemsMap.
Starr, Joel, and Joan Nielson. 2006. "Roast Profiling," *Tea and Coffee Journal*, July 2006, 24–27.
Ströker, Elizabeth. 1997. "Evidence." In *Encyclopedia of Phenomenology*, edited by Lester Embree and Elizabeth A. Behnke, 202–204. Dordrecht: Kluwer.
Suchman, Lucy. 1987. *Plans and Situated Action*. Cambridge: Cambridge University Press.
Swan, Jonathan. 2020. "Donald Trump Interview Transcript with Jonathan Swan of Axios on HBO." Rev.com, August 3, 2020, www.rev.com/blog/transcripts/donald-trump-interview-transcript-with-axios-on-hbo.
Sweeney, Kevin W. 2008. "Is There Coffee or Blackberry in My Wine?" In *Wine and Philosophy*, edited by Fritz Allhoff, 205–218. Oxford: Blackwell.
Tattersall, Ian, and Jeffrey Schwartz. 2000. *Extinct Humans*. New York: Westview Press.
Tay, Karla. 2019. "Guatemala: Coffee Annual." USDA Foreign Agricultural Service, May 15, 2019, www.fas.usda.gov/data/guatemala-coffee-annual-4.
Thompson, Evan. 2007. *Mind in Life*. Cambridge, MA: Belknap Press.
Thorn, Jon. 2006. *The Coffee Companion*. Philadelphia: Running Press.
Tucker, Catherine. 2011. *Coffee Culture: Local Experiences, Global Connections*. London: Routledge.
Turner, Spencer. 2010. "Cupping Revisited." *Roast Magazine*, March/April 2010.
———. 2018. "Universal Truths of Coffee Scoring." *Roast Magazine*, July/August 2018.
Vannini, Phillip, Dennis Waskul, and Simon Gottschalk. 2012. *The Senses in Self, Society, and Culture*. London: Routledge.
Watts, Geoff. 2013. "11. Geoff Watts—'Creating Extraordinary Coffee: A Story and a Recipe' | WCLF 2013." World Coffee Leaders Forum, posted September 24, 2014. Video, 47:32. www.youtube.com/watch?v=QsdP3tKUl0Q.
Weber, Max. 1958. *The Protestant Ethic and the Spirit of Capitalism*. New York: Charles Scribner's Sons.
Wechselberger, Johanna, and Tobias Hierl. 2009. *The Ultimate Coffee Book*. Vienna: Braumüller.
Weissman, Michaele. 2008. *God in a Cup*. Hoboken, NJ: John Wiley & Sons.
Wiggins, Sally. 2004 "Talking about Taste: Using a Discursive Psychological Approach to Examine Challenges to Food Evaluations." *Appetite* 43: 29–38.
Wise, Paul M., Mats J. Olsson, and William S. Cain. 2000. "Quantification of Odor Quality." *Chemical Sciences* 25 (4): 429–443.
Wittgenstein, Ludwig. 1972. *Philosophical Investigations*. Oxford: Blackwell.
———. 1978. *Remarks on Colour*. Berkeley: University of California Press.
World Coffee Research (WCR). 2013. "Coffee Cup Quality." February 14, 2013, worldcoffeeresearch.org/coffee-cup-quality/2/14/13 (link obsolete).
———. 2016. *Sensory Lexicon*. College Station, Texas: World Coffee Research.

Wright, Steven Timothy. 2014. "Accounting for Taste: Conversation, Categorisation and Certification in the Sensory Assessment of Craft Brewing." PhD thesis, Lancaster University.
Zahavi, Dan. 2001. *Husserl and Transcendental Intersubjectivity*. Athens: Ohio University Press.
———. 2014. *Self and Other: Exploring Subjectivity, Empathy, and Shame*. Oxford: Oxford University Press.
Zuniga, Maya. 2017. "SCA Lectures Podcast #9: Building a Sensory Program." Specialty Coffee Association, November 17, 2017, scanews.coffee/2017/11/27/sca-lectures-podcast-9-building-sensory-program.

Authors Index

Adorno, Theodor, 2, 79–80, 87–92, 94, 117, 221, 248, 416, 455
Alaç, Morena, 200, 204, 273, 409
Alacala, Stephanie, 20
Artusi, Nicolás, 254
Azienda Riunite Caffè, 22, 23, 181, 234, 271

Bakewell, Elizabeth, 1, 85, 96, 394, 431
Bar-Hillel, Yehoshua, 199, 403
Barker, Robert 252, 259, 303, 474
Bartlett, Frederic, 389
Bengali, Shashank, 31
Benjamin, Walter, 2
Berger, Peter and Thomas Luckmann, 15, 82, 378, 379, 383, 462
Bergson, Henri, 200, 355, 433, 444, 467
Bloomberg, Michael, 351
Boyle, Richard, 29
Brando, Carlos, 174
Bruzina, Ronald, 95, 123, 152, 153, 155, 202, 210, 301, 404, 452

Capella, Anthony, 357
Carbone, Mauro, 139
Cerulo, Karen, 371
Chaturved, Satyarat, 72
Cho, Nicholas, 120
Clastres, Pierre, 432
Collins, Randall and Makowsky, Michael, 49

Cotter, Andrew, 456
Croijmans, Ilja, 272

Dahl, Göran, 107
Daston, Lorraine and Peter Galison, 14, 65–71, 201, 254, 256, 427, 432, 446, 455
Derrida, Jacques, 215, 238, 246, 255, 270, 302, 389, 461, 473
Descartes, Rene, 415
Dewey, John, 160
Dougherty, 169, 250
Dunn, Eliabeth, 51, 163

Earle, William, 12, 75, 106, 113, 129, 150, 152, 160, 244, 249, 255, 280, 302, 406, 427, 431, 433 456, 475
Eggers, Dave, 327
Eliot, T. S., 139
Emerson, Ralph Waldo, 255

Figal, Günter, 14, 65, 74, 79, 94, 114, 115, 116, 121, 122, 125, 126, 149, 153, 154, 204–205, 207, 215, 229, 378, 406, 417, 426, 427, 445, 452, 470, 472, 474

Gadamer, Hans-Georg, 14, 106, 156, 403, 410, 439, 440, 444, 474
Garfinkel, Harold, 2, 7, 8, 14, 68, 70, 78, 82, 83, 84, 106, 107, 114, 116,

Garfinkel, Harold *(continued)*
119, 121, 126, 199, 200, 208, 229, 238, 243, 245, 246, 254, 262, 263, 275, 276, 282, 283, 291, 378, 382, 386, 389, 380, 411, 420, 321, 435, 457–458
Garfinkel, Harold and Harvey Sacks, 191
Garfinkel, Harold and Kenneth Liberman, 224
Garfinkel, Harold and Larry Weider, 313
Gendlin, Eugene, 115, 458
Gherardi, Silvia, 199, 273
Giaccalone, Davide, et al., 12, 296, 372, 405, 443
Ging, Tracy, 365, 372, 394
Goffman, Erving, 11
Goodstein, Elizabeth, 36, 70, 95, 429, 452
Gupta, Sujata, 448
Gurwitsch, Aron, 85, 93, 96, 126, 251, 281, 378, 413, 452

Halevy, Alon, 22, 24, 27, 29, 38, 45, 53
Heath, Christian and Paul Luff, 374, 376
Hegel, G. W. F., 13, 66, 93, 111, 115, 139, 402, 457, 459, 460, 461, 471, 472, 473
Heidegger, Martin, 13, 14, 15, 67, 75, 76, 78, 79, 82, 86, 96, 97, 109, 112, 115, 125, 126, 157, 161, 197, 248, 262, 267, 268, 389, 407, 411, 416, 420, 421, 423, 424, 425, 427–428, 431, 441, 455, 457, 459, 460
Hennion, Antoine and Geneviève Teil, 84, 117–118, 122, 139, 140, 161, 162, 239, 407, 413
Hill, Maria, 52
Hoeppe, Götz, 7, 70, 351, 406, 435
Hoos, Rob, 345, 349, 350, 408
Hopkins, Burt, 80

Horkheimer, Max and Theodor Adorno, 276
Houtman, Jasper, 218
Husserl, Edmund, 1, 8, 14, 15, 66, 74, 75, 77, 79, 80, 84, 87, 88, 96, 114, 121, 122, 123, 149, 153, 208, 254, 256, 257, 379, 404, 405, 410, 428, 429, 433, 434, 444, 466, 472

Jaffe, Daniel, 30, 31, 33, 52, 54, 55, 56, 57, 61, 62, 163
James, William, 70, 432
Juan, Joseph, 351

Koehler, Jeff, 26, 30, 31, 35, 236, 301
Kramer, Matt, 159
Kubota, Lily, 295

Lawless and Heymann, 383
Levinas, Emmanuel, 86, 158, 194, 279, 411, 413, 417
Liberman, Kenneth, 77, 82, 87, 100, 121, 125, 194, 232
Lingle, Ted, 100–101, 130, 133, 137, 139, 143, 144, 146, 154, 164, 180, 199, 212, 228, 234, 251, 270, 273, 296, 356, 406, 408, 409, 448
Lingis, Alphonso, 76
Livingston, Eric, 7, 282
Lynch, Michael, 7, 263

Mannheim, Karl, 105–107, 425
Marcuse, Herbert, 440
Mailer, Norman, 66, 454
Mann, Ann, 11, 291, 376
McKenna, Maryn, 31, 47
Mead, George H., 77
Meister, Erin, 30
Merleau-Ponty, Maurice, 76, 82, 101, 109, 125, 139, 153, 389, 404, 407, 416, 417, 418, 427, 431, 433–434, 445, 448, 452, 457, 458

Meschini, Enrico and Paolo Milani, 365
Mondada, Lorenza, 118, 379, 390
Meyer, Christian, 386

Neuschwander, Hanna, 405, 443
Nietzsche, Friedrich, 14, 80, 215
Novak, Michael, 69

O'Connor, Brian, 92
Odello, Luigi, 11, 12, 83, 249, 258
Ott, Brian, 83, 137, 243, 256, 262, 273, 278, 371, 372, 394, 396, 460

Patchen, Kenneth, 432
Paz, Octavio, 67
Pendergast, Mark, 21, 25–31, 32, 34, 35, 38–43, 53, 56, 60, 61, 110, 111, 169, 174, 179, 190, 241
Perullo, Nicola, 6–7, 15, 40, 45, 66, 70, 93, 105, 112, 117, 138, 139, 140, 145, 148, 149, 156–161, 237–239, 242, 249, 250, 252, 253, 260, 263, 279, 284, 297, 298, 300, 356, 367, 391–392, 396, 407, 413, 414, 416, 418, 423, 424, 428, 435, 447, 449, 459, 472, 474
Peynaud, Émile, 375
Pollen, Michael, 300
Popper, Karl, 73, 74, 77, 109, 410, 442
Pound, Ezra, 421

Quiñones-Ruiz, 51, 57, 58

Ritzer, George, 36
Robson, David, 351
Roden, Claudia, 21, 25, 26, 27, 30, 31, 37, 42, 45, 134, 187
Rorty, Richard, 80
Russell, Bertrand, 459

Sacks, Danielle, 401
Sacks, Harvey, 386

Sage, Emma, 140
Sallis, John, 214
Samoggia and Riedel, 372
Saragosa, Manuela, 350
Sartre, Jean-Paul, 368
Scalabrin, et al., 20
Sedgewick, 53, 181
Schegloff, Emmanuel, 389
Schutz, Alfred, 5, 68, 77, 85, 126, 199, 200, 225, 378, 382–383, 410, 411, 458
Schwartz, Howard, 458, 460
Shapin, Steven, 81, 83, 86, 205, 211, 249, 407, 447
Simmel, Georg, 2, 36, 70, 80, 84, 95, 112, 119, 280, 357, 362, 396, 409, 412, 433, 434, 462, 463, 464
Snyder, Gary, 157
Starr, Joel and Joan Nielson, 350, 351
Ströker, Elizabeth, 84, 405
Suchman, Lucy, 7
Swan, Jonathan, 401
Sweeny, Kevin, 158

Tattersal Ian and Jeffrey Schwartz, 468
Tay, Karla, 163
Thompson, Evan, 79
Thorn, Jon, 19, 20, 21, 25, 26, 30, 37, 40, 44, 52, 58, 134, 168, 180
Tucker, Catherine, 24, 30, 31, 36, 37, 39, 40, 44, 47, 52, 54, 56, 57, 174
Turner, Spencer, 132, 171

Vannini, Phillip, Dennis Waskula, and Simon Gottschalk, 111, 119, 149, 160, 206, 276, 373, 391, 392, 393, 412

Weber, Max, 66
Wechselberger, Johanna and Tobias Hierl, 20, 24, 25, 36, 180
Weissman, 20, 24, 40, 41, 58, 60, 62, 129–131, 164, 173, 174, 236, 263, |265

Wiggins, Sally, 230, 303
Wise, Paul, et al., 458
Wittgenstein, Ludwig, 89, 199, 217, 267, 301, 450
Wright, Steven 230, 249, 250, 255, 278, 387, 392, 415

World Coffee Research (WCR), 201, 203, 451–452, 454

Zahavi, Dan, 76, 77, 78, 80, 83, 95, 94, 107, 127, 144, 154, 216, 257, 416, 428
Zuniga, Maya, 72, 431

Subject Index

(including oral comments by professional tasters)

accounts, 77, 82, 85, 210, 216, 219, 228, 256, 276, 282, 290–291, 341, 354, 377–378, 381, 382, 384–387, 389, 403, 422, 450, 453, 464–465
Alarcón, Rodrigo, 184, 261, 279, 414, 453
Alliance for Coffee Excellence (ACE), 172, 265, 305
Alma Café, 213
Arcaffè, 285–286, 289

"balance," 147, 215, 231–235, 269, 296, 317, 396
Balzac, Honore de, 31
baristas, 48, 50, 83, 143, 217, 218, 256, 278, 366
Baskerville, Arnold, 78, 157, 177, 181
bitterness, 135, 180, 270, 285–286, 291
blending, 179–190
Boot, Willem, 3, 11, 57, 148, 161, 179, 236, 265
Brazil, 33, 179, 236, 278, 357
Burman Coffee Traders, 268, 269, 336, 404

caffeine, 20, 59, 270, 286, 299, 300, 353
calibration, 78, 151, 217, 225, 266, 276, 289–295, 307, 317–318, 382–386

chain of coffee production, 47–62, 134, 135, 149, 225, 279, 362, 368
Choi, San, 234
clean cup, 147, 166
Coffee Day (India), 303
Coffee Quality Institute (CQI), 145, 272, 277, 293, 461f.
coherency, 124, 126, 245–246, 252, 275, 281, 301, 435
communication, 11, 47, 49–50, 74, 99, 102, 144–145, 149, 151, 152, 153, 159, 172–173, 191f., 212, 213–214, 218, 226, 242, 251, 268, 278, 312, 313, 325, 402–403, 415–416, 447, 462
Colombia, 22, 23, 40, 57, 108, 163, 172, 191, 213, 219, 245, 278, 313, 330, 356–357, 396, 401
Conary, Scott, 136, 245
consistency, 8, 42, 50, 72–73, 84, 98–99, 104, 147, 160, 187, 215, 223, 237, 245, 256, 263, 271–273, 283, 307–308, 314, 319–322, 334, 368, 381, 407, 435, 460
consumers, 6, 268, 344, 348, 364–365, 371–397
contact with the taste, 7, 75, 79, 93–94, 99, 114–115, 121–122, 125, 138, 204,

contact with the taste *(continued)* 210, 229, 250, 253, 404, 446, 451, 470, 471
Cup of Excellence, 8, 108, 172, 212, 213, 242, 245, 283, 305ff.

defects, 147, 150, 164, 175ff.
dialectics, 14, 87, 89, 123, 217, 440, 472
Diaz, Manuel, 3, 19, 63, 91, 156, 202, 220, 250, 259, 278, 279, 346, 350, 351, 401, 410, 456
direct-trade, 57, 60, 164, 360, 361, 368
dualism, 65, 121, 253, 432–433
Duque, Jaime, 136
dynamic nature of coffee, 21, 129–140, 155, 157, 161, 183, 195, 197, 222, 231, 234, 245, 265, 269, 321, 322, 418, 456

effective presence, 202, 204, 250
El Salvador, 10, 22, 43, 54, 62, 158, 163, 189, 184, 210
empirical, 6, 88, 94, 103, 123, 140, 249, 251, 299, 444, 457
England, 30–31, 37
epistemology, 12, 65, 86–88
essentialism, 81, 139, 335, 422, 451, 468
Ethiopia, 24, 25, 34, 35, 57, 148, 163, 174, 213, 236
ethnomethodology, 6, 7, 15, 82, 107, 114, 116–120, 125, 199–200, 228, 243, 261, 267, 277, 371–374, 385–389
exporters, 27, 29, 48, 164, 168, 175, 177, 179, 183, 185–189, 191–195, 248, 251, 271, 314, 344, 397, 457

Fair-trade, 52, 54, 55, 66
Fedele, Vince, 164, 169, 260
Fele, Giolo, 12, 13, 138, 160, 212
fermentation, 59, 105, 108, 133, 134, 165, 173–174, 194–195, 271

Flavor Wheel, 158, 209–210, 417, 443, 446–452
flavorings, 58–59
France, 31, 38

Gill Coffee Traders, 166, 471
Ging, Tracy, 365
Giuliano, Peter, 48, 51, 237
Gravel, Benoit, 351, 353

Hazan, Marcio, 22, 97, 179, 184, 260, 274, 303, 447, 467
Heath, Christian, 203
hermeneutics of tasting, 153, 157, 160, 165, 198, 210, 221, 229, 244, 258, 268, 277, 300, 324
Hertzel, Andrew, 395
Hill, James, 53
Hoffman, James, 365, 394
Howell, George, 263
humility, 10, 150, 260–261, 263, 276, 279, 425, 442, 460

Illy Coffee, 11, 32, 54, 57, 130, 172, 178, 303, 424
importers, 188, 192–194, 343
indexical meaning, 23, 199, 203, 208, 209, 267, 328, 352
India, 31–32, 163, 169, 186, 213, 262, 278, 449
instructed action, 221–227, 257, 262, 273–277, 378, 384, 390
Intelligentsia Coffee, 59, 164, 172
intersubjectivity, 9, 23, 70, 76–86, 118, 124, 127, 152, 212, 214, 216, 220, 223, 225, 228, 247, 257, 273, 288, 290, 302–303, 326–327, 382–383, 447
ironies, 8–10, 13, 14, 70, 88, 153, 157, 193, 250, 281, 291, 301, 315, 393, 420, 446, 473

Subject Index | 501

Italy, 27–29, 34, 40, 99, 110, 186, 219, 260, 285

Kant, 67
Kenjige, Pradeep, 99

Lamastus, Wilford, 62, 236
Lavazza Coffee, 212, 233, 347, 353
Lexicon of flavors, 199, 201–203, 219, 283, 417, 433, 443–444, 446–447, 450, 453
local details, 2, 8, 116, 194, 261ff., 264, 338

Macbeth, Doug, 214, 230, 277
Martinelli, Lorenzo, 99, 247
Mastruontono, Michele, 347
measurement, 70, 72, 84, 99, 287, 351, 404, 468, 470
Menon, Sunalini, 133, 207, 234, 231
Meschini, Enrico, 23, 104, 234, 248, 284, 287, 289, 312–313, 345, 414
methodologically provided objectivities, 36, 79, 89, 90, 123, 315, 405, 412
metrological practices, 84–85, 184, 244, 284, 403, 409, 464ff.
mimesis, 221, 276

Nespresso, 4, 185, 345, 359, 454
naturally processed coffee, 108–109
Nicaragua, 202, 209, 213, 297, 306
Noble, Ann, 356, 450
normal coffee, 24ff.
numeration, 9–10, 72, 159, 183, 220, 257, 259, 278–279, 286, 315, 416, 464

objectivation, 82, 151, 216, 225, 228
objectivity, 1, 2–6, 8–9, 50, 65–92, 97–98, 121, 122, 125, 143, 148, 149, 150, 156, 182, 187, 201, 216, 220, 226, 242, 252, 256, 262, 277, 278, 288, 321, 328, 339, 341, 402–406, 415, 419–420, 423, 429, 436–437, 458, 373
Odello, Luigi, 11, 12, 208, 227, 244, 248, 250, 263, 345, 358, 407, 436
openness, 79, 94, 125, 150, 152, 156, 182, 204, 252, 263, 301, 441, 479–475
Owen, Thomson, 301

packaging labels, 221, 231, 241, 353, 359–360
Panama, 163, 235
participation, 112, 160, 161–162, 205, 393
Peet, Alfred, 41, 218, 222
Pellini Coffee, 191, 344, 345
Peterson, Rachel, 62
phenomenology, 15, 94–95, 114, 119, 124, 206, 211, 262, 266, 301, 413, 434ff.
Pinto, Sunil, 170–171, 186, 291, 344, 395
processing, 169–175
protocols, 79, 87, 97, 98, 99, 124–126, 150f., 153, 161, 176, 243–247, 249, 258–260, 437, 441, 454

Rasmussen, Casper, 49, 272
reason, 70, 88, 89, 264, 446, 450, 462, 473
reflexive nature of understanding, 100, 106, 140, 149, 155, 177, 207–210, 282, 291, 328, 331–332, 341, 445
Rhinehart, Ric, 236, 362, 432
reification, 114–115, 130, 158, 217, 255, 356, 422, 433, 469–470
riddle of subjective objectivity, 5, 8–9, 11–12
río (and riado) taste, 27, 110, 111, 188, 189, 214, 216, 225
roasters, 28, 46, 58, 176, 286, 336, 348–352, 366, 470

Schillani, Franco, 2, 11, 24, 97, 184, 241, 247, 252, 260, 288, 289
science, 8, 11, 66, 68, 80, 87, 94, 96, 97, 99, 125–126, 173, 242, 256, 285–287, 351, 401–406, 410, 418, 419, 440f., 448, 439ff., 468–469, 472–473
scientism, 425, 442, 445, 446–447, 452, 461
Segoni, Angelo, 135, 371, 397, 447
self-understanding, 50, 87, 88, 95, 126, 255, 339, 429, 434, 440, 445, 471
semantic drift, 203, 208, 227, 270, 293, 294, 297
semiotics, 10, 96, 226, 230, 249, 270, 445
sensory science, 8, 96, 112, 115, 149, 202, 342, 407, 412, 415, 444, 457ff.
serendipity principle, 82, 109, 158, 181, 193–194, 219, 220, 276, 327, 339, 340, 373–374, 386–393, 395, 397
Silver, Nate, 71
singularity, 152, 159, 245, 279–280, 447
situated knowledge, 71, 102, 105, 119, 158, 199, 200, 262, 267, 280
Songer, Paul, 212
Sorenson, Duane, 236
Specialty Coffee Association (SCA), 48, 49, 58, 108, 164, 242, 260, 270, 271, 272, 295, 369, 443
spider graphs, 455–456

Spindler, Susie, 172, 195
standardization, 139, 145, 148, 152, 156, 159, 166, 208, 218, 243, 245
Starbucks, 44, 54, 57, 60, 243, 248, 252
Sustainable Coffee Institute, 243, 271, 283, 295, 414
Sweet Maria's Coffee, 301, 449
sweetness, 146–147

taste descriptors, 10, 92, 100, 199, 200, 202–204, 207, 217, 230, 265–271, 273, 297, 322–324, 328–332
tasting schedules, 198, 203, 210, 277–285, 298, 302, 311, 445, 477–481
texture, 144, 235, 298, 388, 392, 395
Torta, Luca, 155, 231, 233
traceability, 49, 170, 360–369
traces, 148–149, 153, 196, 267, 296, 358
transcendent object, 121, 122, 124, 152
triangulation, 113
Turks, 25–27, 260

Vietnam, 32–33

Watts, Geoff, 54, 61, 96, 136, 146, 163, 164, 172, 243, 258, 263, 313
"what more," 9, 301, 321, 339, 427
wisdom (in tasting), 157, 298–300, 440
World Coffee Research (WCR), 53, 201, 239, 314, 443, 446

www.ingramcontent.com/pod-product-compliance
Lightning Source LLC
Chambersburg PA
CBHW021811250825
31486CB00014B/85